CODE OF FEDERAL
REGULATIONS

I0036530

Title 11
Federal Elections

Revised as of January 1, 2018

Containing a codification of documents
of general applicability and future effect

As of January 1, 2018

With Ancillaries

Published by the Office of the Federal Register
National Archives and Records Administration
as a Special Edition of the Federal Register

Table of Contents

Cite this Code: CFR

To cite the regulations in this volume use title, part and section number. Thus, 11 CFR 1.1 *refers to title 11, part 1, section 1.*

Explanation

The Code of Federal Regulations is a codification of the general and permanent rules published in the Federal Register by the Executive departments and agencies of the Federal Government. The Code is divided into 50 titles which represent broad areas subject to Federal regulation. Each title is divided into chapters which usually bear the name of the issuing agency. Each chapter is further subdivided into parts covering specific regulatory areas.

Each volume of the Code is revised at least once each calendar year and issued on a quarterly basis approximately as follows:

Title 1 through Title 16..as of January 1
Title 17 through Title 27 ....as of April 1
Title 28 through Title 41 ....as of July 1
Title 42 through Title 50..as of October 1

The appropriate revision date is printed on the cover of each volume.

LEGAL STATUS

The contents of the Federal Register are required to be judicially noticed (44 U.S.C. 1507). The Code of Federal Regulations is prima facie evidence of the text of the original documents (44 U.S.C. 1510).

HOW TO USE THE CODE OF FEDERAL REGULATIONS

The Code of Federal Regulations is kept up to date by the individual issues of the Federal Register. These two publications must be used together to determine the latest version of any given rule.

To determine whether a Code volume has been amended since its revision date (in this case, January 1, 2018), consult the "List of CFR Sections Affected (LSA)," which is issued monthly, and the "Cumulative List of Parts Affected," which appears in the Reader Aids section of the daily Federal Register. These two lists will identify the Federal Register page number of the latest amendment of any given rule.

EFFECTIVE AND EXPIRATION DATES

Each volume of the Code contains amendments published in the Federal Register since the last revision of that volume of the Code. Source citations for the regulations are referred to by volume number and page number of the Federal Register and date of publication. Publication dates and effective dates are usually not the same and care must be exercised by the user in determining the actual effective date. In instances where the effective date is beyond the cut-off date for the Code a note has been inserted to reflect the future effective date. In those instances where a regulation published in the Federal Register states a date certain for expiration, an appropriate note will be inserted following the text.

OMB CONTROL NUMBERS

The Paperwork Reduction Act of 1980 (Pub. L. 96–511) requires Federal agencies to display an OMB control number with their information collection request.

Many agencies have begun publishing numerous OMB control numbers as amendments to existing regulations in the CFR. These OMB numbers are placed as close as possible to the applicable recordkeeping or reporting requirements.

PAST PROVISIONS OF THE CODE

Provisions of the Code that are no longer in force and effect as of the revision date stated on the cover of each volume are not carried. Code users may find the text of provisions in effect on any given date in the past by using the appropriate List of CFR Sections Affected (LSA). For the convenience of the reader, a "List of CFR Sections Affected" is published at the end of each CFR volume. For changes to the Code prior to the LSA listings at the end of the volume, consult previous annual editions of the LSA. For changes to the Code prior to 2001, consult the List of CFR Sections Affected compilations, published for 1949-1963, 1964-1972, 1973-1985, and 1986-2000.

"[RESERVED]" TERMINOLOGY

The term "[Reserved]" is used as a place holder within the Code of Federal Regulations. An agency may add regulatory information at a "[Reserved]" location at any time. Occasionally "[Reserved]" is used editorially to indicate that a portion of the CFR was left vacant and not accidentally dropped due to a printing or computer error.

INCORPORATION BY REFERENCE

What is incorporation by reference? Incorporation by reference was established by statute and allows Federal agencies to meet the requirement to publish regulations in the Federal Register by referring to materials already published elsewhere. For an incorporation to be valid, the Director of the Federal Register must approve it. The legal effect of incorporation by reference is that the material is treated as if it were published in full in the Federal Register (5 U.S.C. 552(a)). This material, like any other properly issued regulation, has the force of law.

What is a proper incorporation by reference? The Director of the Federal Register will approve an incorporation by reference only when the requirements of 1 CFR part 51 are met. Some of the elements on which approval is based are:

(a) The incorporation will substantially reduce the volume of material published in the Federal Register.

(b) The matter incorporated is in fact available to the extent necessary to afford fairness and uniformity in the administrative process.

(c) The incorporating document is drafted and submitted for publication in accordance with 1 CFR part 51.

What if the material incorporated by reference cannot be found? If you have any problem locating or obtaining a copy of material listed as an approved incorporation by reference, please contact the agency that issued the regulation containing that incorporation. If, after contacting the agency, you find the material is not available, please notify the Director of the Federal Register, National Archives and Records Administration, 8601 Adelphi Road, College Park, MD 20740-6001, or call 202-741-6010.

CFR INDEXES AND TABULAR GUIDES

A subject index to the Code of Federal Regulations is contained in a separate volume, revised annually as of January 1, entitled CFR INDEX AND FINDING AIDS. This volume contains the Parallel Table of Authorities and Rules. A list of CFR titles, chapters, subchapters, and parts and an alphabetical list of agencies publishing in the CFR are also included in this volume.

An index to the text of "Title 3—The President" is carried within that volume.

The Federal Register Index is issued monthly in cumulative form. This index is based on a consolidation of the "Contents" entries in the daily Federal Register.

A List of CFR Sections Affected (LSA) is published monthly, keyed to the revision dates of the 50 CFR titles.

REPUBLICATION OF MATERIAL

There are no restrictions on the republication of material appearing in the Code of Federal Regulations.

INQUIRIES

For a legal interpretation or explanation of any regulation in this volume, contact the issuing agency. The issuing agency's name appears at the top of odd-numbered pages.

For inquiries concerning CFR reference assistance, call 202-741-6000 or write to the Director, Office of the Federal Register, National Archives and Records Administration, 8601 Adelphi Road, College Park, MD 20740-6001 or e-mail *fedreg.info@nara.gov.*

SALES

The Government Publishing Office (GPO) processes all sales and distribution of the CFR. For payment by credit card, call toll-free, 866-512-1800, or DC area, 202-512-1800, M-F 8 a.m. to 4 p.m. e.s.t. or fax your order to 202-512-2104, 24 hours a day. For payment by check, write to: US Government Publishing Office – New Orders, P.O. Box 979050, St. Louis, MO 63197-9000.

ELECTRONIC SERVICES

The full text of the Code of Federal Regulations, the LSA (List of CFR Sections Affected), The United States Government Manual, the Federal Register, Public Laws, Public Papers of the Presidents of the United States, Compilation of Presidential Documents and the Privacy Act Compilation are available in electronic format via *www.ofr.gov.* For more information, contact the GPO Customer Contact Center, U.S. Government Publishing Office. Phone 202-512-1800, or 866-512-1800 (toll-free). E-mail, *ContactCenter@gpo.gov.*

The Office of the Federal Register also offers a free service on the National Archives and Records Administration's (NARA) World Wide Web site for public law numbers, Federal Register finding aids, and related information. Connect to NARA's web site at *www.archives.gov/federal-register.*

The e-CFR is a regularly updated, unofficial editorial compilation of CFR material and Federal Register amendments, produced by the Office of the Federal Register and the Government Publishing Office. It is available at *www.ecfr.gov.*

OLIVER A. POTTS,
Director,
Office of the Federal Register
January 1, 2018

THIS TITLE

Title 11—FEDERAL ELECTIONS is composed of one volume. This volume contains Chapter I—Federal Election Commission and Chapter II—Election Assistance Commission. The contents of this volume represent all current regulations codified under this title of the CFR as of January 1, 2018.

Indexes to regulations for "parts 1–7," "parts 100–116," "parts 200–201," "parts 9001–9007 and 9012," "part 9008," and "parts 9031–9039," appear in the Finding Aids section of this volume.

A Redesignation table appears in the Finding Aids section of this volume.

For this volume, Michele Bugenhagen was Chief Editor. The Code of Federal Regulations publication is under the direction of John Hyrum Martinez, assisted by Stephen J. Frattini.

Title 11—Federal Elections

1

CHAPTER I—FEDERAL ELECTION COMMISSION

PART 1—PRIVACY ACT

AUTHORITY: 5 U.S.C. 552a.

SOURCE: 41 FR 43064, Sept. 29, 1976, unless otherwise noted.

§ 1.1 Purpose and scope.

(a) The purpose of this part is to set forth rules informing the public as to what information is maintained by the Federal Election Commission about identifiable individuals and to inform those individuals how they may gain access to and correct or amend information about themselves.

(b) The regulations in this part carry out the requirements of the Privacy Act of 1974 (Pub. L. 93–579) and in particular 5 U.S.C. 552a as added by that Act.

(c) The regulations in this part apply only to records disclosed or requested under the Privacy Act of 1974, and not to requests for information made pursuant to 5 U.S.C. 552, the Freedom of Information Act, or requests for reports and statements filed with the Federal Election Commission which are public records and available for inspection and copying pursuant to 52 U.S.C. 30109(a)(4)(C) and 30111(a)(4)

[41 FR 43064, Sept. 29, 1976, as amended at 45 FR 21209, Apr. 1, 1980; 79 FR 77843, Dec. 29, 2014]

§ 1.2 Definitions.

As defined in the Privacy Act of 1974 and for the purposes of this part, unless otherwise required by the context, the following terms shall have these meanings:

Act means the Federal Election Campaign Act of 1971, as amended and chapters 95 and 96 of the Internal Revenue Code of 1954.

Commission means the Federal Election Commission, its Commissioners and employees. Until March 5, 2018, the Commission is located at 999 E Street NW, Washington, DC 20463. Beginning on March 5, 2018, the Commission will be located at 1050 First Street NE, Washington, DC 20463. The Commission's internet website address (*www.fec.gov*) remains unchanged.

Commissioner means an individual appointed to the Federal Election Commission pursuant to 52 U.S.C. 30106(a).

Individual means a citizen of the United States or an alien lawfully admitted for permanent residence.

Maintain includes maintain, collect, use or disseminate.

Record means any item, collection, or grouping of information about an individual that is maintained by an agency, including but not limited to his or her education, financial transactions, medical history, and criminal or employment history and that contains his or her name, or the identifying number, symbol or other identifying particular assigned to the individual, such as finger or voice print or a photograph.

Routine use means the use of such record for a purpose compatible with the purpose for which the information was collected.

Systems of Records means a group of any records under the control of the Federal Election Commission from which information is retrieved by the name of the individual or by some identifying number, symbol, or other identifying particular assigned to the individual.

[41 FR 43064, Sept. 29, 1976, as amended at 75 FR 30, Jan. 4, 2010; 79 FR 77843, Dec. 29, 2014; 82 FR 60852, Dec. 26, 2017]

§ 1.3 Procedures for requests pertaining to individual records in a record system.

(a) Any individual may request the Commission to inform him or her whether a particular record system named by the individual contains a record pertaining to him or her. The request may be made in person or in writing at the location and to the person specified in the notice describing that record system.

(b) An individual who believes that the Commission maintains records pertaining to him or her but who cannot determine which record system contains those records, may request assistance by mail or in person from the Commission's Chief Privacy Officer during the hours of 9 a.m. to 5:30 p.m. at the street address identified in the definition of "Commission" in § 1.2.

(c) Requests under paragraphs (a) or (b) of this section shall be acknowledged by the Commission within 15 days from the date of receipt of the request. If the Commission is unable to locate the information requested under paragraphs (a) or (b) of this section, it shall so notify the individual within 15 days after receipt of the request. Such acknowledgement may request additional information to assist the Commission in locating the record or it may advise the individual that no record or document exists about that individual.

[41 FR 43064, Sept. 29, 1976, as amended at 50 FR 50778, Dec. 12, 1985; 75 FR 31, Jan. 4, 2010; 82 FR 60852, Dec. 26, 2017]

§ 1.4 Times, places, and requirements for identification of individuals making requests.

(a) After being informed by the Commission that a record system contains a record pertaining to him or her, an individual may request the Commission to disclose that record in the manner described in this section. Each request for the disclosure of a record or a copy of it shall be made at the Federal Election Commission at the street address identified in the definition of "Commission" in § 1.2, and to the system manager identified in the notice describing the systems of records, either in writing or in person. Requests may be made by specifically authorized agents or by parents or guardians of individuals.

(b) Each individual requesting the disclosure of a record or copy of a record shall furnish the following information with his or her request:

(1) The name of the record system containing the record;

(2) Proof as described in paragraph (c) of this section that he or she is the individual to whom the requested record relates;

(3) Any other information required by the notice describing the record system.

(c) Proof of identity as required by paragraph (b)(2) of this section shall be provided as described in paragraphs (c)(1) and (2) of this section. Requests made by an agent, parent, or guardian, shall be in accordance with the procedures described in § 1.10.

(1) Requests made in writing shall include a statement, signed by the individual and either notarized or witnessed by two persons (including witnesses' addresses). If the individual appears before a notary, he or she shall submit adequate proof of identification in the form of a drivers license, birth certificate, passport or other identification acceptable to the notary. If the statement is witnessed, it shall include a sentence above the witnesses' signatures that they personally know the individual or that the individual has submitted proof of his or her identification to their satisfaction. In any case in which, because of the extreme sensitivity of the record sought to be seen or copied, the Commission determines that the identification is not adequate, it may request the individual to submit additional proof of identification.

(2) If the request is made in person, the requestor shall submit proof of identification similar to that described in paragraph (c)(1) of this section, acceptable to the Commission. The individual may have a person of his or her own choosing accompany him or her when the record is disclosed.

[41 FR 43064, Sept. 29, 1976, as amended at 50 FR 50778, Dec. 12, 1985; 82 FR 60852, Dec. 26, 2017]

§1.5 Disclosure of requested information to individuals.

(a) Upon submission of proof of identification as required by §1.4, the Commission shall allow the individual to see and/or obtain a copy of the requested record or shall send a copy of the record to the individual by registered mail. If the individual requests to see the record, the Commission may make the record available either at the location where the record is maintained or at a place more suitable to the requestor, if possible. The record shall be made available as soon as possible but in no event later than 15 days after proof of identification.

(b) The Commission must furnish each record requested by an individual under this part in a form intelligible to that individual.

(c) If the Commission denies access to a record to an individual, he or she shall be advised of the reason for the denial and advised of the right to judicial review.

(d) Upon request, an individual will be provided access to the accounting of disclosures from his or her record under the same procedures as provided above and in §1.4.

§1.6 Special procedure: Medical records. [Reserved]

§1.7 Request for correction or amendment to record.

(a) Any individual who has reviewed a record pertaining to him or her that was furnished under this part, may request the Commission to correct or amend all or any part of that record.

(b) Each individual requesting a correction or amendment shall send the request to the Commission through the person who furnished the record.

(c) Each request for a correction or amendment of a record shall contain the following information:

(1) The name of the individual requesting the correction or amendment;

(2) The name of the system of records in which the record sought to be amended is maintained;

(3) The location of the system of records from which the individual record was obtained;

(4) A copy of the record sought to be amended or corrected or a sufficiently detailed description of that record;

(5) A statement of the material in the record that the individual desires to correct or amend;

(6) A statement of the basis for the requested correction or amendment including any material that the individual can furnish to substantiate the reasons for the correction or amendment sought.

§1.8 Agency review of request for correction or amendment of record.

(a) The Commission shall, not later than ten (10) days (excluding Saturdays, Sundays and legal holidays) after the receipt of the request for a correction or amendment of a record under §1.7, acknowledge receipt of the request and inform the individual whether information is required before the correction or amendment can be considered.

(b) If no additional information is required, within ten (10) days from receipt of the request, the Commission shall either make the requested correction or amendment or notify the individual of its refusal to do so, including in the notification the reasons for the refusal, and the appeal procedures provided in §1.9.

(c) The Commission shall make each requested correction or amendment to a record if that correction or amendment will tend to negate inaccurate, irrelevant, untimely, or incomplete matter in the record.

(d) The Commission shall inform prior recipients of any amendment or correction or notation of dispute of such individual's record if an accounting of the disclosure was made. The individual may request a list of prior recipients if an accounting of the disclosure was made.

§1.9 Appeal of initial adverse agency determination on amendment or correction.

(a) Any individual whose request for a correction or amendment has been denied in whole or in part, may appeal that decision to the Commissioners no later than one hundred eighty (180) days after the adverse decision is rendered.

(b) The appeal shall be in writing and shall contain the following information:

(1) The name of the individual making the appeal;

(2) Identification of the record sought to be amended;

(3) The record system in which that record is contained;

(4) A short statement describing the amendment sought; and

(5) The name and location of the agency official who initially denied the correction or amendment.

(c) Not later than thirty (30) days (excluding Saturdays, Sundays and legal holidays) after the date on which the Commission receives the appeal, the Commissioners shall complete their review of the appeal and make a final decision thereon. However, for good cause shown, the Commissioners may extend that thirty (30) day period. If the Commissioners extend the period, the individual requesting the review shall be promptly notified of the extension and the anticipated date of a decision.

(d) After review of an appeal, the Commission shall send a written notice to the requestor containing the following information:

(1) The decision and, if the denial is upheld, the reasons for the decision;

(2) The right of the requestor to institute a civil action in a Federal District Court for judicial review of the decision; and

(3) The right of the requestor to file with the Commission a concise statement setting forth the reasons for his or her disagreement with the Commission denial of the correction or amendment. The Commission shall make this statement available to any person to whom the record is later disclosed, together with a brief statement, if appropriate, of the Commission's reasons for denying the requested correction or amendment. The Commission shall also send a copy of the statement to prior recipients of the individual's record if an accounting of the disclosures was made.

§ 1.10 Disclosure of record to person other than the individual to whom it pertains.

(a) Any individual who desires to have a record covered by this part disclosed to or mailed to another person may designate such person and authorize such person to act as his or her agent for that specific purpose. The authorization shall be in writing, signed by the individual and notarized or witnessed as provided in § 1.4(c).

(b) The parent of any minor individual or the legal guardian of any individual who has been declared by a court of competent jurisdiction to be incompetent, due to physical or mental incapacity or age, may act on behalf of that individual in any matter covered by this part. A parent or guardian who desires to act on behalf of such an individual shall present suitable evidence of parentage or guardianship, by birth certificate, certified copy of a court order, or similar documents, and proof of the individual's identity in a form that complies with § 1.4(c) of this part.

(c) An individual to whom a record is to be disclosed in person, pursuant to this part may have a person of his or her own choosing accompany him or her when the record is disclosed.

§ 1.11 Fees.

(a) The Commission shall not charge an individual for the costs of making a search for a record or the costs of reviewing the record. When the Commission makes a copy of a record as a necessary part of the process of disclosing the record to an individual, the Commission shall not charge the individual for the cost of making that copy.

(b) If an individual requests the Commission to furnish a copy of the record, the Commission shall charge the individual for the costs of making the copy. The fee that the Commission has established for making a copy is ten cents ($.10) per page.

§ 1.12 Penalties.

Any person who makes a false statement in connection with any request for a record, or an amendment or correction thereto, under this part, is subject to the penalties prescribed in 18 U.S.C. 494 and 495.

§ 1.13 General exemptions. [Reserved]

§ 1.14 Specific exemptions.

(a) No individual, under the provisions of these regulations, shall be entitled to access to materials compiled in its systems of records identified as FEC audits and investigations (FEC 2) or FEC compliance actions (FEC 3). These exempted systems relate to the Commission's power to exercise exclusive civil jurisdiction over the enforcement of the Act under 52 U.S.C. 30107(a)(6) and (e); and to defend itself in actions filed against it under 52 U.S.C. 30107(a)(6). Further the Commission has a duty to investigate violations of the Act under 52 U.S.C. 30109(a)(2); to conduct audits and investigations pursuant to 52 U.S.C. 30111(b), 26 U.S.C. 9007 and 9038; and to refer apparent violations of the Act to the Attorney General or other law enforcement authorities under 52 U.S.C. 30109(a)(5) and 30107(a)(9). Information contained in FEC systems 2 and 3 contain the working papers of the Commission staff and form the basis for either civil and/or criminal proceedings pursuant to the exercise of the powers and duties of the Commission. These materials must be protected until such time as they are subject to public access under the provision of 52 U.S.C. 30109(a)(4)(B) or 5 U.S.C. 552, or other relevant statutes.

(b)(1) Pursuant to 5 U.S.C. 552a(j)(2), records contained in FEC 12, Office of Inspector General Investigative Files, are exempt from the provisions of 5 U.S.C. 552a, except subsections (b), (c)(1) and (2), (e)(4) (A) through (F), (e) (6), (7), (9), (10), and (11) and (f), and the corresponding provisions of 11 CFR part 1, to the extent this system of records relates in any way to the enforcement of criminal laws.

(2) Pursuant to 5 U.S.C. 552a(k)(2), FEC 12, Office of Inspector General Investigative Files, is exempt from 552a (c)(3), (d), (e)(1), (e)(4)(G), (H), and (I), and (f), and the corresponding provisions of 11 CFR part 1, to the extent the system of records consists of investigatory material compiled for law enforcement purposes, except for material that falls within the exemption included in paragraph (b)(1) of this section.

(c) The provisions of paragraph (a) of this section shall not apply to the extent that application of the subsection would deny any individual any right, privilege or benefit to which he or she would otherwise be entitled to receive.

[41 FR 43064, Sept. 29, 1976, as amended at 45 FR 21209, Apr. 1, 1980; 60 FR 4073, Jan. 20, 1995; 75 FR 31, Jan. 4, 2010; 79 FR 77843, Dec. 29, 2014]

PART 2—SUNSHINE REGULATIONS; MEETINGS

AUTHORITY: 5 U.S.C. 552b.

SOURCE: 50 FR 39972, Oct. 1, 1985, unless otherwise noted.

§ 2.1 Scope.

These regulations are promulgated pursuant to the directive of 5 U.S.C. 552b(g) which was added by section 3(a) of Public Law 94–409, the Government in the Sunshine Act, and specifically implement section 3 of that Act.

§ 2.2 Definitions.

(a) *Commission. Commission* means the Federal Election Commission.

(b) *Commissioner* or *Member. Commissioner* or *Member* means an individual appointed to the Federal Election Commission pursuant to 52 U.S.C. 30106(a), but does not include a proxy or other designated representative of a Commissioner.

(c) *Person. Person* means an individual, including employees of the Commission, partnership, corporation, association, or public or private organization, other than an agency of the United States Government.

(d) *Meeting.* (1) *Meeting* means the deliberation of at least four voting members of the Commission in collegia where such deliberations determine or result in the joint conduct or disposition of official Commission business. For the purpose of this section, *joint conduct* does not include, for example, situations where the requisite number of members is physically present in one place but not conducting agency business as a body (e.g., at a meeting at which one member is giving a speech while a number of other members are present in the audience). A deliberation conducted through telephone or similar communications equipment by means of which all persons participating can hear each other will be considered a *meeting* under this section.

(2) The term *meeting* does not include the process of notation voting by circulated memorandum for the purpose of expediting consideration of routine matters. It also does not include deliberations to schedule a meeting, to take action to open or close a meeting, or to release or withhold information, or to change the subject matter of a meeting under 11 CFR 2.5, 2.6 and 2.7.

[50 FR 39972, Oct. 1, 1985, as amended at 50 FR 50778, Dec. 12, 1985; 65 FR 9206, Feb. 24, 2000; 79 FR 77844, Dec. 29, 2014; 82 FR 60852, Dec. 26, 2017]

§ 2.3 General rules.

(a) Commissioners shall not jointly conduct, determine or dispose of Commission business other than in accordance with this part.

(b) Except as provided in 11 CFR 2.4, every portion of every Commission meeting shall be open to public observation.

(c) No additional right to participate in Commission meetings is granted to any person by this part. A meeting is not part of the formal or informal record of decision of the matters discussed therein except as otherwise required by law. Statements of views or expressions of opinions made by Commissioners or FEC employees at meetings are not intended to represent final determinations or beliefs.

(d) Members of the public attending open Commission meetings may use small electronic sound recorders to record the meeting, but the use of other electronic recording equipment and cameras requires advance notice to and coordination with the Commission's Press Officer.

§ 2.4 Exempted meetings.

(a) *Meetings required by statute to be closed.* Meetings concerning matters specifically exempted from disclosure by statutes which require public withholding in such a manner as to leave no discretion for the Commission on the issue, or which establish particular types of matters to be withheld, shall be closed to public observation in accordance with the procedures of 11 CFR 2.5.

(1) As required by 52 U.S.C. 30109(a)(12), all Commission meetings, or portions of meetings, pertaining to any notification or investigation that a violation of the Act has occurred, shall be closed to the public.

(2) For the purpose of this section, *any notification or investigation that a violation of the Act has occurred* includes, but is not limited to, determinations pursuant to 52 U.S.C. 30109, the issuance of subpoenas, discussion of referrals to the Department of Justice, or consideration of any other matter related to the Commission's enforcement activity, as set forth in 11 CFR part 111.

(b) *Meetings closed by Commission determination.* Except as provided in 11 CFR 2.4(c), the requirement of open meetings will not apply where the Commission finds, in accordance with 11 CFR 2.5, that an open meeting or the release of information is likely to result in the disclosure of:

(1) Matters that relate solely to the Commission's internal personnel decisions, or internal rules and practices;

(i) This provision includes, but is not limited to, matters relating to Commission policies on working conditions, or materials prepared predominantly for internal use, the disclosure of which would risk circumvention of Commission regulations; but

(ii) This provision does not include discussions or materials regarding employees' dealings with the public, such as personnel manuals or Commission directives setting forth job functions or procedures;

(2) Financial or commercial information obtained from any person which is privileged or confidential;

(3) Matters which involve the consideration of a proceeding of a formal nature by the Commission against a specific person or the formal censure of any person;

(4) Information of a personal nature where disclosure would constitute a clearly unwarranted invasion of personal privacy;

(5) Investigatory records compiled for law enforcement purposes, or information which if written would be contained in such records, but only to the extent that the production of such records or information would:

(i) Interfere with enforcement proceedings,

(ii) Deprive a person of a right to a fair trial or an impartial adjudication,

(iii) Constitute an unwarranted invasion of personal privacy,

(iv) Disclose the identity of a confidential source,

(v) Disclose investigative techniques and procedures, or

(vi) Endanger the life or physical safety of law enforcement personnel;

(6) Information the premature disclosure of which would be likely to have a considerable adverse effect on the implementation of a proposed Commission action, as long as the Commission has not already disclosed the content or nature of its proposed action, or is not required by law to disclose it prior to final action; or

(7) Matters that specifically concern the Commission's participation in a civil action or proceeding, or an arbitration, or involving a determination on the record after opportunity for a hearing.

(c) Nothwithstanding the applicability of any exemptions set forth in 11 CFR 2.4(b), the Commission may determine that the public interest requires a meeting to be open.

[50 FR 39972, Oct. 1, 1985, as amended at 75 FR 31, Jan. 4, 2010; 79 FR 77844, Dec. 29, 2014]

§ 2.5 Procedures for closing meetings.

(a) *General.* No meeting or portion of a meeting may be closed to the public observation under this section unless a majority of the Commissioners votes to take such action. The closing of one portion of a meeting shall not justify closing any other portion of a meeting.

(b) *Certification.* Each time the Commission votes to close a meeting, the General Counsel shall publicly certify that, in his or her opinion, each item on the agenda may properly be closed to public observation. The certification shall state each relevant exemption provision. The original copy of the certification shall be attached to, and preserved with, the statement required by 11 CFR 2.5(d).

(c) *Voting procedures.* (1) No meeting need be held to consider closing a meeting. The Commission may vote to close a meeting or any portion thereof by using its notation vote procedures.

(i) A separate vote shall be taken with respect to each item on an agenda proposed to be closed in whole or in part pursuant to 11 CFR 2.4, or with respect to any information proposed to be withheld under 11 CFR 2.4.

(ii) A single vote may be taken with respect to a particular matter to be discussed in a series of closed meetings, or with respect to any information concerning such series of meetings, so long as each meeting in the series is scheduled to be held no more than 30 days after the initial meeting.

(iii) This section shall not affect the Commission's practice of setting dates for closed meetings more than 30 days in advance of such meetings.

(2) The Commission Secretary shall record the vote of each Commissioner participating in the vote. No proxies, written or otherwise, shall be counted.

(3)(i) A Commissioner may object to a recommendation to close the discussion of a particular matter or may assert a claim of exemption for a matter scheduled to be discussed in an open meeting. Such objection or assertion will be discussed by the Commission at the next scheduled closed meeting, to determine whether the matter in question should be discussed in a closed meeting.

(ii) An *objection for the record only* will not cause the objection to be placed on any agenda.

(d) *Public statement of vote.* (1) If the Commission votes to close a meeting, or any portion thereof, under this section, it shall make publicly available within 24 hours a written statement of the vote. The written statement shall contain:

(i) A citation to the provision(s) of 11 CFR 2.4 under which the meeting was closed to public observation and an explanation of why the specific discussion comes within the cited exemption(s);

(ii) The vote of each Commissioner participating in the vote;

(iii) A list of the names of all persons expected to attend the closed meeting and their affiliation. For purposes of this section, affiliation means title or position, and name of employer, and in the case of a representative, the name of the person represented. In the case of Commission employees, the statement will reflect, through the use of titles rather than individual names, that the Commissioners, specified division heads and their staff will attend; and

(iv) The signature of the Commission Secretary.

(2) The original copy of the statement shall be maintained by the Commission Secretary. A copy shall be posted on a public bulletin board located in the Commission's Public Records Office.

(e) *Public request to close a meeting.* A person whose interests may be directly affected by a portion of a meeting may request that the Commission close that portion to the public for any of the reasons referred to in 11 CFR 2.4. The following procedures shall apply to such requests:

(1) The request must be made in writing and shall be directed to the Chairman of the Commission.

(2) The request shall identify the provisions of 11 CFR 2.4 under which the requestor seeks to close all or a portion of the meeting.

(3) A recorded vote to close the meeting or a portion thereof shall be taken.

(4) Requests made under this section shall become part of the official record of the underlying matter and shall be disclosed in accordance with 11 CFR 2.6 on completion of the matter.

(5) If the Commission decides to approve a request to close, the Commission will then follow the procedures for closing a meeting set forth in 11 CFR 2.5 (a) through (d).

[50 FR 39972, Oct. 1, 1985, as amended at 65 FR 9206, Feb. 24, 2000]

§ 2.6 Transcripts and recordings.

(a) The Commission Secretary shall maintain a complete transcript or electronic recording adequate to record fully the proceedings of each meeting, or portion of a meeting, closed to public observation. An electronic recording of a meeting shall be coded, or other records shall be kept in a manner adequate to identify each speaker.

(b)(1) In the case of any meeting closed pursuant to 11 CFR 2.4(b), as the last item of business, the Commission will determine which, if any, portions of the electronic recording or transcript and which if any, items of information withheld under 11 CFR 2.5 contain information which should be withheld pursuant to 11 CFR 2.4.

(2) Portions of transcripts or recordings determined to be outside the scope of any exemptions under 11 CFR 2.6(b)(1) shall be promptly made available to the public through the Commission's Public Records Office at a cost sufficient to cover the Commission's actual cost of duplication or transcription. Requests for such copies shall be made and processed in accordance with the provisions of 11 CFR part 5.

(3) Portions of transcripts or electronic recordings not made available immediately pursuant to 11 CFR 2.6(b)(1), and portions of transcripts or recordings withheld pursuant to 11 CFR 2.4(a), will be made available on request when the relevant exemptions no longer apply. Such materials shall be requested and processed under the provisions of 11 CFR 2.6(b)(2).

(c) A complete verbatim copy of the transcript or a complete electronic recording of each meeting, or portion of a meeting, closed to the public, shall be maintained by the Commission Secretary in confidential files of the Commission, for a minimum of two years subsequent to such meeting, or a minimum of one year after the conclusion of any agency proceeding with respect to which the meeting, or portion of the meeting, was held, whichever occurs later.

[50 FR 39972, Oct. 1, 1985, as amended at 75 FR 31, Jan. 4, 2010]

§2.7 Announcement of meetings and schedule changes.

(a)(1) In the case of each meeting, the Commission shall publicly announce and shall submit such announcement for publication in the FEDERAL REGISTER at least seven days prior to the day on which the meeting is to be called to order. The Commission Secretary shall also forward a copy of such announcement for posting in the Commission's Public Records Office.

(2) Announcements made under this section shall contain the following information:

(i) The date of the meeting;

(ii) The place of the meeting;

(iii) The subject matter of the meeting;

(iv) Whether the meeting is to be open or closed to the public; and

(v) The name and telephone number of the official designated by the agency to respond to requests for information about the meeting.

(b) The public announcement and submission for publication shall be made when required by 11 CFR 2.7(a) in the case of every Commission meeting unless a majority of the Commissioners decide by recorded vote that Commission business requires that the meeting be called at an earlier date, in which case the Commission shall make at the earliest practicable time, the announcement required by this section and a concurrent submission for publication of that announcement in the FEDERAL REGISTER.

(c) The time or place of a meeting may be changed following the public announcement required by 11 CFR 2.7 (a) or (b) only if the Commission announces the change at the earliest practicable time.

(d) The subject matter of a meeting, or the determination of the Commission to open or close a meeting, or portions of a meeting, to the public may be changed following the public announcement required by 11 CFR 2.7 (a) or (b) only if:

(1) A majority of the entire membership of the Commission determines by recorded vote that Commission business so requires and that no earlier announcement of the change was possible; and

(2) The Commission publicly announces the change and the vote of each member upon the change at the earliest practicable time. Immediately following this announcement, the Commission shall submit for publication in the FEDERAL REGISTER a notice containing the information required by 11 CFR 2.7(a)(2), including a description of any change from the earlier published notice.

§2.8 Annual report.

The Commission shall report annually to Congress regarding its compliance with the requirements of the Government in the Sunshine Act and of this part, including:

(a) A tabulation of the total number of Commission meetings open to the public;

(b) The total number of such meetings closed to the public;

(c) The reasons for closing such meetings; and

(d) A description of any litigation brought against the Commission under the Sunshine Act, including any costs assessed against the Commission in such litigation (whether or not paid by the Commission).

PART 4—PUBLIC RECORDS AND THE FREEDOM OF INFORMATION ACT

AUTHORITY: 5 U.S.C. 552, as amended.

SOURCE: 44 FR 33368, June 8, 1979, unless otherwise noted.

§4.1 Definitions.

As used in this part:

(a) *Commission* means the Federal Election Commission, established by the Federal Election Campaign Act of 1971, as amended.

(b) *Commissioner* means an individual appointed to the Federal Election Commission pursuant to 52 U.S.C. 30106(a).

13

(c) *Request* means to seek the release of records under 5 U.S.C. 552.

(d) *Requestor* is any person who submits a request to the Commission.

(e) *Act* means the Federal Election Campaign Act of 1971, as amended by the Federal Election Campaign Act Amendments of 1974, 1976, and 1979, and unless specifically excluded, includes chapters 95 and 96 of the Internal Revenue Code of 1954 relating to public financing of Federal elections.

(f) *Public Disclosure and Media Relations Division* of the Commission is that division which is responsible for, among other things, the processing of requests for public access to records which are submitted to the Commission pursuant to 52 U.S.C. 30108(d), 30109(a)(4)(B)(ii), and 30111(a).

(g) *Direct costs* means those expenditures which the Commission actually incurs in searching for and duplicating (and, in the case of commercial use requestors, reviewing) documents to respond to a FOIA request. Direct costs include the salary of the employee performing the work (the basic rate of pay for the employee plus 16 percent of that rate to cover benefits) and the cost of operating duplicating equipment. Direct costs do not include overhead expenses such as the cost of space and heating or lighting the facility in which the records are stored.

(h) *Search* means all time spent reviewing, manually or by automated means, Commission records for the purpose of locating those records that are responsive to a FOIA request, including page-by-page or line-by-line identification of material within documents. Search time does not include review of material in order to determine whether the material is exempt from disclosure.

(i) *Review* means the process of examining a document located in response to a commercial use request to determine whether any portion of the document located is exempt from disclosure. Review also refers to processing any document for disclosure, *i.e.*, doing all that is necessary to excise exempt portions of the document and otherwise prepare the document for release. Review does not include time spent by the Commission resolving general legal or policy issues regarding the application of exemptions.

(j) *Duplication* means the process of making a copy of a document necessary to respond to a FOIA request. Examples of the form such copies can take include, but are not limited to, paper copy, microform, audio-visual materials, or machine readable documentation (e.g., magnetic tape or disk).

(k) *Commercial use* means a purpose that furthers the commercial, trade, or profit interests of the requestor or the person on whose behalf the request is made. The Commission's determination as to whether documents are being requested for a commercial use will be based on the purpose for which the documents are being requested. Where the Commission has reasonable cause to doubt the use for which the requestor claims to have made the request or where that use is not clear from the request itself, the Commission will seek additional clarification before assigning the request to a specific category.

(l) *Educational institution* means a preschool, a public or private elementary or secondary school, an institution of graduate higher education, an institution of undergraduate higher education, an institution of professional education, and an institution of vocational education, which operates a program or programs of scholarly research.

(m) *Non-commercial scientific institution* means an organization that is not operated on a commercial basis, as that term is defined in paragraph (k) of this section, and which is operated solely for the purpose of conducting scientific research the results of which are not intended to promote any particular product or industry.

(n) *Representative of the news media* means a person actively gathering news for an entity that is organized and operated to publish or broadcast news to the public. The term news means information that is about current events or that would be of current interest to the public. Examples of news media entities include, but are not limited to, television or radio stations broadcasting to the public at large, and publishers of periodicals (but only in those instances when they can qualify as disseminators of news, as defined in this paragraph) who make their products available for purchase or subscription by the general public. A freelance journalist may be regarded as working for a news organization and therefore considered a representative of the news media if that person can demonstrate a solid basis for expecting publication by that news organization, even though that person is not actually employed by that organization. The best means by which a freelance journalist can demonstrate a solid basis for expecting publication by a news organization is by having a publication contract with that news organization. When no such contract is present, the Commission will look to the freelance journalist's past publication record in making this determination.

(o) *Record* and any other term used in this part in reference to information includes any information that would be a Commission record subject to the requirements of this part when maintained by the Commission in any format, including an electronic format.

[44 FR 33368, June 8, 1979, as amended at 45 FR 31291, May 13, 1980; 52 FR 39212, Oct. 21, 1987; 65 FR 9206, Feb. 24, 2000; 79 FR 77844, Dec. 29, 2014; 81 FR 92439, Dec. 23, 2016]

§4.2 Policy on disclosure of records.

(a) The Commission will make the fullest possible disclosure of records to the public, consistent with the rights of individuals to privacy, the rights of persons contracting with the Commission with respect to trade secret and commercial or financial information entitled to confidential treatment, and the need for the Commission to promote free internal policy deliberations and to pursue its official activities without undue disruption.

(b) All Commission records shall be available to the public unless they are specifically exempt under this part.

(c) To carry out this policy, the Commission shall designate a Freedom of Information Act Officer.

§4.3 Scope.

The regulations in this part implement the provisions of the Freedom of Information Act, 5 U.S.C. 552, with re-spect to the availability of records for inspection and copying.

[44 FR 33368, June 8, 1979, as amended at 45 FR 31291, May 13, 1980]

§4.4 Availability of records.

(a) In accordance with 5 U.S.C. 552(a)(2), the Commission shall make the following materials available for public inspection and copying:

(1) Statements of policy and interpretation which have been adopted by the Commission;

(2) Administrative staff manuals and instructions to staff that affect a member of the public;

(3) Opinions of Commissioners rendered in enforcement cases, General Counsel's Reports and non-exempt 52 U.S.C. 30109 investigatory materials shall be placed on the public record of the Agency no later than 30 days from the date on which all respondents are notified that the Commission has voted to close such an enforcement file;

(4) Copies of all records, regardless of form or format, which have been released to any person under this paragraph (a) and which, because of the nature of their subject matter, the agency determines have become or are likely to become the subject of subsequent requests for substantially the same records; and

(5) A general index of the records referred to in paragraph (a)(4) of this section.

(b) In accordance with 5 U.S.C. 552(a)(3), the Commission shall make available, upon proper request, all non-exempt Agency records, or portions of records, not previously made public pursuant to 5 U.S.C. 552(a)(1) and (a)(2).

(c) The Commission shall maintain and make available current indexes and supplements providing identifying information regarding any matter issued, adopted or promulgated after April 15, 1975 as required by 5 U.S.C. 552(a)(2)(C) and (E).These indexes and supplements shall be published and made available on at least a quarterly basis for public distribution unless the Commission determines by Notice in the FEDERAL REGISTER that publication would be unnecessary, impracticable, or not feasible due to budgetary considerations. Nevertheless, copies of any index or supplement shall be made available upon request at a cost not to exceed the direct cost of duplication.

(d) The Freedom of Information Act and the provisions of this part apply only to existing records; they do not require the creation of new records.

(e) If documents or files contain both disclosable and nondisclosable information, the nondisclosable information will be deleted and the disclosable information released unless the disclosable portions cannot be reasonably segregated from the other portions in a manner which will allow meaningful information to be disclosed.

(f) All records created in the process of implementing provisions of 5 U.S.C. 552 will be maintained by the Commission in accordance with the authority granted by General Records Schedule 14, approved by the National Archives and Records Service of the General Services Administration.

(g) The Commission encourages the public to explore the information available on the Commission's World Wide Web site, located at *http:// www.fec.gov.* The site includes a Commission publication, *Availability of FEC Information,* which provides a detailed listing of the types of documents available from the FEC, including those available under FOIA, and directions on how to locate and obtain them.

[44 FR 33368, June 8, 1979, as amended at 45 FR 31291, May 13, 1980; 65 FR 9206, Feb. 24, 2000; 79 FR 77844, Dec. 29, 2014]

§ 4.5 Categories of exemptions.

(a) No requests under 5 U.S.C. 552 shall be denied release unless the record contains, or its disclosure would reveal, matters that are:

(1) Specifically authorized under criteria established by an executive order to be kept secret in the interest of national defense or foreign policy and are in fact properly classified pursuant to such Executive order;

(2) Related solely to the internal personnel rules and practices of the Commission;

(3) Specifically exempted from disclosure by statute, provided that such statute (A) requires that the matters be withheld from the public in such a manner as to leave no discretion on the issue, or (B) establishes particular criteria for withholding or refers to particular types of matters to be withheld;

(4) Trade secrets and commercial or financial information obtained from a person which are privileged or confidential. Such information includes confidential business information which concerns or relates to the trade secrets, processes, operations, style of work, or apparatus, or to the production, sales, shipments, purchases, transfers, identification of customers, inventories, or amount of source of income, profits, losses, or expenditures of any person, firm, partnership, corporation, or other organization, if the disclosure is likely to have the effect of either impairing the Commission's ability to obtain such information as is necessary to perform its statutory functions, or causing substantial harm to the competitive position of the person, firm, partnership, corporation, or other organization from which the information was obtained, unless the Commission is required by law to disclose such information. These procedures shall be used for submitting business information in confidence:

(i) A request for confidential treatment shall be addressed to the Chief FOIA Officer, Federal Election Commission, at the street address identified in the definition of "Commission" in § 1.2, and shall indicate clearly on the envelope that it is a request for confidential treatment.

(ii) With each submission of, or offer to submit, business information which a submitter desires to be treated as confidential under paragraph (a)(4) of this section, the submitter shall provide the following, which may be disclosed to the public: (A) A written description of the nature of the subject information, and a justification for the request for its confidential treatment, and (B) a certification in writing under oath that substantially identical information is not available to the public.

(iii) Approval or denial of requests shall be made only by the Chief FOIA Officer or his or her designees. A denial shall be in writing, shall specify the reason therefore, and shall advise the submitter of the right to appeal to the Commission.

(iv) For good cause shown, the Commission may grant an appeal from a denial by the Chief FOIA Officer or his or her designee if the appeal is filed within fifteen (15) days after receipt of the denial. An appeal shall be addressed to the Chief FOIA Officer, Federal Election Commission, at the street address identified in the definition of "Commission" in §1.2 and shall clearly indicate that it is a confidential submission appeal. An appeal will be decided within twenty (20) days after its receipt (excluding Saturdays, Sundays and legal holidays) unless an extension, stated in writing with the reasons therefore, has been provided the person making the appeal.

(v) Any business information submitted in confidence and determined to be entitled to confidential treatment shall be maintained in confidence by the Commission and not disclosed except as required by law. In the event that any business information submitted to the Commission is not entitled to confidential treatment, the submitter will be permitted to withdraw the tender unless it is the subject of a request under the Freedom of Information Act or of judicial discovery proceedings.

(vi) Since enforcement actions under 52 U.S.C. 30109 are confidential by statute, the procedures outlined in §4.5(a)(4) (i) thru (v) are not applicable.

(5) Inter-agency or intra-agency memoranda or letters which would not be available by law to a party in litigation with the Commission.

(6) Personnel and medical files and similar files, the disclosure of which would constitute a clearly unwarranted invasion of personal privacy.

(7) Records or information compiled for law enforcement purposes, but only to the extent that the production of such law enforcement records or information:

(i) Could reasonably be expected to interfere with enforcement proceedings;

(ii) Would deprive a person of a right to a fair trial or an impartial adjudication;

(iii) Could reasonably be expected to constitute an unwarranted invasion of personal privacy;

(iv) Could reasonably be expected to disclose the identity of a confidential source, including a State, local, or foreign agency or authority or any private institution which furnished information on a confidential basis, and, in the case of a record or information compiled by a criminal law enforcement authority in the course of a criminal investigation, or by an agency conducting a lawful national security intelligence investigation, information furnished by a confidential source;

(v) Would disclose techniques and procedures for law enforcement investigations or prosecutions, or would disclose guidelines for law enforcement investigations or prosecutions if such disclosure could reasonably be expected to risk circumvention of the law; or

(vi) Could reasonably be expected to endanger the life or physical safety of any individual.

(b) Whenever a request is made which involves access to records described in 11 CFR 4.5(a)(7); and

(1) The investigation or proceeding involves a possible violation of criminal law; and

(2) There is reason to believe that—

(i) The subject of the investigation or proceeding is not aware of its pendency; and

(ii) Disclosure of the existence of the records could reasonably be expected to interfere with enforcement proceedings;

The agency may, during only such time as that circumstance continues, treat the records as not subject to the requirements of the Freedom of Information Act.

(c) Any reasonably segregable portion of a record shall be provided to any person requesting such record after deletion of the portions which are exempt. The amount of information deleted shall be indicated on the released portion of the record, unless including that indication would harm an interest protected by an exemption in paragraph (a) of this section under which the deletion is made. If technically feasible, the amount of the information deleted shall be indicated at the place in the record where such deletion is made.

(d) If a requested record is one of another government agency or deals with subject matter to which a government agency other than the Commission has exclusive or primary responsibility, the request for such a record shall be promptly referred by the Commission to that agency for disposition or guidance as to disposition.

(e) Nothing in this part authorizes withholding of information or limiting the availability of records to the public, except as specifically provided in this part; nor is this part authority to withhold information from Congress.

[44 FR 33368, June 8, 1979, as amended at 50 FR 50778, Dec. 12, 1985; 52 FR 23638, June 24, 1987; 52 FR 39212, Oct. 21, 1987; 65 FR 9206, Feb. 24, 2000; 75 FR 31, Jan. 4, 2010; 79 FR 77844, Dec. 29, 2014; 82 FR 60852, Dec. 26, 2017]

§ 4.6 Discretionary release of exempt records.

The Commission may, in its discretion, release requested records despite the applicability of the exemptions in § 4.5(a), if it determines that it is in the public interest and that the rights of third parties would not be prejudiced.

§ 4.7 Requests for records.

(a) [Reserved]

(b)(1) Requests for copies of records pursuant to the Freedom of Information Act shall be addressed to Chief FOIA Officer, Federal Election Commission, at the street address identified in the definition of "Commission" in § 1.2. The request shall reasonably describe the records sought with sufficient specificity with respect to names, dates, and subject matter, to permit the records to be located. A requester will be promptly advised if the records cannot be located on the basis of the description given and that further identifying information must be provided before the request can be satisfied.

(2) Requests for Commission records and copies thereof shall specify the preferred form or format (including electronic formats) of the response. The Commission shall accommodate requesters as to form or format if the record is readily available in that form or format. When requesters do not specify the form or format of the response, the Commission shall respond in the form or format in which the document is most accessible to the Commission.

(c) The Commission shall determine within twenty working days after receipt of a request, or twenty working days after an appeal is granted, whether to comply with such request, unless in unusual circumstances the time is extended or subject to § 4.9(f)(3), which governs advance payments. In the event the time is extended, the requestor shall be notified of the reasons for the extension and the date on which a determination is expected to be made, but in no case shall the extended time exceed ten working days. An extension may be made if it is—

(1) Necessary to locate records or transfer them from physically separate facilities; or

(2) Necessary to search for, collect, and appropriately examine a large quantity of separate and distinct records which are the subject of a single request; or

(3) Necessary for consultation with another agency which has a substantial interest in the determination of the request, or with two or more components of the Commission which have a substantial subject matter interest therein.

(d) If the Commission determines that an extension of time greater than ten working days is necessary to respond to a request satisfying the "unusual circumstances" specified in paragraph (c) of this section, the Commission shall so notify the requester and give the requester an opportunity to limit the scope of the request so that it may be processed within the time limit prescribed in paragraph (c) of this section, or arrange with the Commission an alternative time frame for processing the request or a modified request.

(e) The Commission may aggregate and process as a single request requests by the same requester, or a group of requesters acting in concert, if the Commission reasonably believes that the requests actually constitute a single request that would otherwise satisfy the unusual circumstances specified in paragraph (c) of this section, and the requests involve clearly related matters.

(f) The Commission uses a multi-track system to process requests under the Freedom of Information Act that is based on the amount of work and/or time involved in processing requests. Requests for records are processed in the order they are received within each track. Upon receipt of a request for records, the Commission shall determine which track is appropriate for the request. The Commission may contact requesters whose requests do not appear to qualify for the fastest tracks and provide such requesters the opportunity to limit their requests so as to qualify for a faster track. Requesters who believe that their requests qualify for the fastest tracks and who wish to be notified if the Commission disagrees may so indicate in the request and, where appropriate and feasible, shall also be given an opportunity to limit their requests.

(g) The Commission shall consider requests for the expedited processing of requests in cases where the requester demonstrates a compelling need for such processing.

(1) The term compelling need means:

(i) That a failure to obtain requested records on an expedited basis could reasonably be expected to pose an imminent threat to the life or physical safety of an individual; or

(ii) With respect to a request made by a person primarily engaged in disseminating information, urgency to inform the public concerning actual or alleged Federal government activity.

(2) Requesters for expedited processing must include in their requests a statement setting forth the basis for the claim that a "compelling need" exists for the requested information, certified by the requester to be true and correct to the best of his or her knowledge and belief.

(3) The Commission shall determine whether to grant a request for expedited processing and notify the requester of such determination within ten days of receipt of the request. Denials of requests for expedited processing may be appealed as set forth in §4.8. The Commission shall expeditiously determine any such appeal. As soon as practicable, the Commission shall process the documents responsive to a request for which expedited processing is granted.

(h) Any person denied access to records by the Commission shall be notified immediately giving reasons therefore, and notified of the right of such person to appeal such adverse determination to the Commission.

(i) The date of receipt of a request under this part shall be the date on which the FOIA Officer actually receives the request.

[44 FR 33368, June 8, 1979, as amended at 45 FR 31292, May 13, 1980; 50 FR 50778, Dec. 12, 1985; 52 FR 39213, Oct. 21, 1987; 65 FR 9206, Feb. 24, 2000; 75 FR 31, Jan. 4, 2010; 82 FR 60853, Dec. 26, 2017]

§4.8 Appeal of denial.

(a) Any person who has been notified pursuant to §4.7(h) of this part that his/her request for inspection of a record or for a copy has been denied, or who has received no response within twenty working days (or within such extended period as is permitted under §4.7(c) of this part) after the request has been received by the Commission, may appeal the adverse determination or the failure to respond by requesting the Commission to direct that the record be made available.

(b) The appeal request shall be in writing, shall clearly and prominently state on the envelope or other cover and at the top of the first page "FOIA Appeal", and shall identify the record in the form in which it was originally requested.

(c) The appeal request should be delivered or addressed to the Chief FOIA Officer, Federal Election Commission, at the street address identified in the definition of "Commission" in §1.2.

(d) The requestor may state facts and cite legal or other authorities as he/she deems appropriate in support of the appeal request.

(e) For good cause shown, the Commission may disclose a record which is subject to one of the exemptions listed in §4.5 of this part.

(f) The Commission will make a determination with respect to any appeal within twenty days (excluding Saturdays, Sundays and legal holidays) after receipt of the appeal (or within such extended period as is permitted under §4.7(c) of this part). If on appeal, the denial of the request for a record or a copy is in whole or in part upheld, the Commission shall advise the requestor of the denial and shall notify him/her of the provisions for judicial review of that determination as set forth in 5 U.S.C. 552(a)(4).

(g) Because of the risk of misunderstanding inherent in oral communications, the Commission will not entertain any appeal from an alleged denial or failure to comply with an oral request. Any person who has orally requested a copy of a record that he/she believes to have been improperly denied should resubmit the request in writing as set forth in § 4.7.

[44 FR 33368, June 8, 1979, as amended at 50 FR 50778, Dec. 12, 1985; 75 FR 31, Jan. 4, 2010; 79 FR 16663, Mar. 26, 2014; 81 FR 34863, June 1, 2016; 82 FR 60853, Dec. 26, 2017]

§ 4.9 Fees.

(a) *Exceptions to fee charges*—(1) *General.* Except for a commercial use requester, the Commission will not charge a fee to any requester for the first two hours of search time and the first 100 pages of duplication in response to any FOIA request.

(2) *Free computer search time.* For purposes of this paragraph, the term *search time* is based on the concept of a manual search. To apply this to a search conducted by a computer, the Commission will provide the equivalent dollar value of two hours of professional staff time, calculated according to paragraph (c)(4) of this section, in computer search time. Computer search time is determined by adding the cost of the computer connect time actually used for the search, calculated at the rate of $25.00 per hour, to the cost of the operator's salary for the time spent conducting the computer search, calculated at the professional staff time rate set forth at paragraph (c)(4) of this section.

(3) *Definition of pages.* For purposes of this paragraph, the word *pages* refers to paper copies of a standard agency size which will normally be 8½″ × 11″ or 8½″ × 14″. Thus, while a requester would not be entitled to 100 free computer disks, for example, a requester would be entitled to 100 free pages of a computer printout.

(4) *Minimum charge.* The Commission will not charge a fee to any requester when the allowable direct cost of that FOIA request is equal to or less than the Commission's cost of routinely collecting and processing a FOIA request fee.

(b) *Fee reduction or waiver*—(1) The Commission will consider requests for the reduction or waiver of any fees assessed pursuant to paragraph (c)(1) of this section if it determines, either as a result of its own motion or in response to a written submission by the requester, that disclosure of the information is in the public interest because it is likely to contribute significantly to public understanding of the operations or activities of the government and that disclosure of the information is not primarily in the commercial interest of the requester.

(2) A request for a reduction or waiver of fees shall be made in writing by the FOIA requestor; shall accompany the relevant FOIA request so as to be considered timely; and shall include a specific explanation as to why the fee for that FOIA request should be reduced or waived, applying the standard stated in paragraph (b)(1) of this section to the facts of that particular request. In addition, the explanation shall include: the requester's (and user's, if the requester and the user are different persons or entities) identity, qualifications and expertise in the subject area, and ability and intention to disseminate the information to the public; and a discussion of any commercial or personal benefit that the requestor (and user, if the requestor and user are different persons or entities) expects as a result of disclosure, including whether the information disclosed would be resold in any form at a fee above actual cost.

(c) *Fees to be charged.* (1) The FOIA services provided by the Commission in response to a FOIA request for which the requestor will be charged will depend upon the category of the requestor. The categories of FOIA requestors are as follows:

(i) *Commercial use requestors.* A requestor of documents for commercial use will be assessed reasonable standard charges for the full allowable direct costs of searching for, reviewing for release and duplicating the records sought, according to the Commission's schedule of fees for those services as set forth at paragraph (c)(4) of this section. A commercial use requestor is not entitled to two hours of free search time nor 100 free pages of duplication of documents.

(ii) *Educational and non-commercial scientific institution requestors.* The Commission will provide documents to requestors in this category for the cost of duplication of the records provided by the Commission in response to the request, according to the Commission's schedule of fees as set forth at paragraph (c)(4) of this section, excluding charges for the first 100 pages of duplication. Requestors in this category will not be charged for search time. To be eligible for inclusion in this category, requestors must show that the request is being made as authorized by and under the auspices of a qualifying institution and that the records are not sought for a commercial use, but are sought in furtherance of scholarly (if the request is from an educational institution) or scientific (if the request is from a non-commercial scientific institution) research.

(iii) *Requestors who are representatives of the news media.* The Commission will provide documents to requestors in this category for the cost of duplication of the records provided by the Commission in response to the request, according to the Commission's schedule of fees as set forth at paragraph (c)(4) of this section, excluding charges for the first 100 pages of duplication. Requestors in this category will not be charged for search time. To be eligible for inclusion in this category, the requestor must meet the criteria listed at 11 CFR 4.1(n) and his or her request must not be made for a commercial use. A request for records supporting the news dissemination function of the requestor shall not be considered to be a request that is for a commercial use.

(iv) *All other requestors.* The Commission will charge requestors who do not fit into any of the categories listed in paragraph (c)(1)(i), (ii) or (iii) of this section the full direct costs of searching for and duplicating records in response to the request, according to the Commission's schedule of fees as set forth at paragraph (c)(4) of this section, excluding charges for the first two hours of search time and the first 100 pages of duplication. Requests from persons for records about themselves will continue to be treated under the fee provisions of the Privacy Act of 1974, which permit fees only for duplication.

(2) The Commission may assess fees for the full allowable direct costs of searching for documents in response to a request even if the Commission fails to locate any documents which are responsive to that request and, in the case of commercial use requestors, of reviewing documents located in response to a request which the Commission determines are exempt from disclosure.

(3) If the Commission estimates that search or duplication charges are likely to exceed $25.00, it will notify the requestor of the estimated amount of the fee unless the requestor has indicated in advance a willingness to pay a fee as high as that estimated by the Commission. Through this notification, the Commission will offer the requestor the opportunity to confer with Commission staff to reformulate the original request in order to meet the requestor's needs at a lower cost.

(4) The following is the schedule of the Commission's standard fees. The cost of staff time will be added to all of the following fees, generally at the *Professional* rate listed below, except for the cost of *Photocopying from photocopying machines* which has been calculated to include staff time.

PHOTOCOPYING

Photocopying from photocopying machines— $.07 per page
Photocopying from microfilm reader-printer—$.15 per page
Paper copies from microfilm-paper print machine—$.05 per frame page

REELS OF MICROFILM

Daily film (partial or complete roll)—$2.85 per roll
Other film (partial or complete roll)—$5.00 per roll

PUBLICATIONS: (NEW OR NOT FROM AVAILABLE STOCKS)

Cost of photocopying document—$.07 per page
Cost of binding document—$.30 per inch

PUBLICATIONS: (AVAILABLE STOCK)

If available from stock on hand, cost is based on previously calculated cost as stated in the publication (based on actual cost per copy, including reproduction and binding). Commission publications for which fees will be charged include, but are not limited to, the following: Advisory Opinion Index, Report on Financial Activity, Financial Control and Compliance Manual, MUR Index, and Guideline for Presentation in Good Order.

COMPUTER TAPES

Cost to process the request at the rate of $25.00 per hour connect time plus the cost of the computer tape ($25.00) and professional staff time (see Staff Time).

COMPUTER INDEXES (INCLUDING NAME SEARCHES)

Cost to process the request at the rate of $25.00 per hour connect time plus the cost of professional staff time (see Staff Time).

STAFF TIME

Clerical: $4.50 per each half hour (agency average of staff below a GS–11) for each request.
Professional: $12.40 per each half hour (agency average of staff at GS–11 and above) for each request.

OTHER CHARGES

Certification of a Document: $7.35 per quarter hour.
Transcripts of Commission meetings not previously transcribed: $7.50 per half hour (equivalent of a GS–11 executive secretary).
The Commission will not charge a fee for ordinary packaging and mailing of records requested. When a request for special mailing or delivery services is received the Commission will package the records requested. The requestor will make all arrangements for pick-up and delivery of the requested materials. The requestor shall pay all costs associated with special mailing or delivery services directly to the courier or mail service.

(5) Upon receipt of any request for the production of computer tape or microfilm, the Commission will advise the requestor of the identity of the private contractor who will perform the duplication services. If fees are charged for the production of computer tape or microfilm, they shall be made payable to that private contractor and shall be forwarded to the Commission.

(d) *Interest charges.* FOIA requestors should pay fees within 30 days following the day on which the invoice for that request was sent to the requestor. If the invoice is unpaid on the 31st day following the day on which the invoice was sent, the Commission will begin assessing interest charges, which will accrue from the date the invoice was mailed. Interest will be charged at a rate that is equal to the average investment rate for the Treasury tax and loan accounts for the 12-month period ending on September 30 of each year, rounded to the nearest whole percentage point, pursuant to 31 U.S.C. 3717. The accrual of interest will be stayed by the Commission's receipt of the fee, even if the fee has not yet been processed.

(e) *Aggregating requests.* A requestor may not file multiple requests, each seeking portions of a document or documents, in order to avoid payment of fees. When the Commission reasonably believes that a FOIA requestor or group of requestors acting in concert is attempting to break a request down into a series of requests for the purpose of evading the assessment of fees, the Commission will aggregate any such requests and charge the appropriate fees. In making this determination, the Commission will consider the time period in which the requests have occurred, the relationship of the requestors, and the subject matter of the requests.

(f) *Advance payments.* The Commission will require a requestor to make an advance payment, *i.e.,* a payment before work is commenced or continued on a request, when:

(1) The Commission estimates or determines that allowable charges that a requestor may be required to pay are likely to exceed $250. In such a case, the Commission will notify the requestor of the likely cost and, where the requestor has a history of prompt payment of FOIA fees, obtain satisfactory assurance of full payment, or in the case of a requestor with no FOIA fee payment history, the Commission will require an advance payment of an amount up to the full estimated charges; or

(2) A requestor has previously failed to pay a fee in a timely fashion (*i.e.,* within 30 days of the date of the billing). In such a case, the Commission

may require that the requestor pay the full amount owed plus any applicable interest or demonstrate that the fee has been paid and make an advance payment of the full amount of the estimated fee before the Commission begins to process a new request or a pending request from that requestor.

(3) If the provisions of paragraph (f) (1) or (2) of this section apply, the administrative time limits prescribed in 11 CFR 4.7(c) will begin only after the Commission has received the payments or the requestor has made acceptable arrangements to make the payments required by paragraph (f) (1) or (2) of this section.

[52 FR 39213, Oct. 21, 1987, as amended at 75 FR 31, Jan. 4, 2010]

PART 5—ACCESS TO PUBLIC DISCLOSURE AND MEDIA RELATIONS DIVISION DOCUMENTS

Sec.
5.1 Definitions.
5.2 Policy on disclosure of records.
5.3 Scope.
5.4 Availability of records.
5.5 Request for records.
5.6 Fees.

AUTHORITY: 52 U.S.C. 30108(d), 30109(a)(4)(B)(ii), 30111(a); 31 U.S.C. 9701.

SOURCE: 45 FR 31293, May 13, 1980, unless otherwise noted.

§5.1 Definitions.

(a) *Commission* means the Federal Election Commission established by the Federal Election Campaign Act of 1971, as amended.

(b) *Commissioner* means an individual appointed to the Federal Election Commission pursuant to 52 U.S.C. 30109 6(a).

(c) *Request* means to seek access to Commission materials subject to the provisions of the Federal Election Campaign Act of 1971, as amended.

(d) *Requestor* is any person who submits a request to the Commission.

(e) *Act* means the Federal Election Campaign Act, as amended by the Federal Election Campaign Act Amendments of 1974, 1976, and 1979, and unless specifically excluded, includes chapters 95 and 96 of the Internal Revenue Code of 1954 relating to public financing of Federal elections.

(f) *Public Disclosure and Media Relations Division* of the Commission is that division which is responsible for, among other things, the processing of requests for public access to records which are submitted to the Commission pursuant to 52 U.S.C. 30109(a)(4)(B)(ii) and 30111(a).

[45 FR 31293, May 13, 1980, as amended at 65 FR 9207, Feb. 24, 2000; 79 FR 77844, Dec. 29, 2014; 81 FR 94240, Dec. 23, 2016]

§5.2 Policy on disclosure of records.

(a) The Commission will make the fullest possible disclosure of records to the public, consistent with the rights of individuals to privacy, the rights of persons contracting with the Commission with respect to trade secrets and commercial or financial information entitled to confidential treatment, and the need for the Commission to promote free internal policy deliberations and to pursue its official activities without undue disruption.

(b) Nothing herein shall be deemed to restrict the public availability of Commission records falling outside provisions of the Act, or to restrict such public access to Commission records as is available pursuant to the Freedom of Information Act and the rules set forth as part 4 of this chapter.

§5.3 Scope.

(a) The regulations in this part implement the provisions of 52 U.S.C. 30108(d), 30109(a)(4)(B)(ii), and 30111(a).

(b) Public access to such Commission records as are subject to the collateral provisions of the Freedom of Information Act and are not included in the material subject to disclosure under this part (described in 11 CFR 5.4(a)) shall be governed by the rules set forth as part 4 of this chapter.

[45 FR 31293, May 13, 1980, as amended at 79 FR 77844, Dec. 29, 2014]

§5.4 Availability of records.

(a) In accordance with 52 U.S.C. 30111(a), the Commission shall make the following material available for public inspection and copying through the Commission's Public Disclosure and Media Relations Division:

(1) Reports of receipts and expenditures, designations of campaign depositories, statements of organization, candidate designations of campaign committees and the indices compiled from the filings therein.

(2) Requests for advisory opinions, written comments submitted in connection therewith, and responses issued by the Commission.

(3) With respect to enforcement matters, any conciliation agreement entered into between the Commission and any respondent.

(4) Opinions of Commissioners rendered in enforcement cases and General Counsel's Reports and non-exempt 52 U.S.C. 30109 investigatory materials shall be placed on the public record of the Agency no later than 30 days from the date on which all respondents are notified that the Commission has voted to close such an enforcement file.

(5) Letter requests for guidance and responses thereto.

(6) The minutes of Commission meetings.

(7) Material routinely prepared for public distribution, e.g. campaign guidelines, FEC Record, press releases, speeches, notices to candidates and committees.

(8) Audit reports (if discussed in open session).

(9) Agendas for Commission meetings.

(b) The provisions of this part apply only to existing records; nothing herein shall be construed as requiring the creation of new records.

(c) In order to ensure the integrity of the Commission records subject to the Act and the maximum availability of such records to the public, nothing herein shall be construed as permitting the physical removal of any Commission records from the public facilities maintained by the Public Disclosure and Media Relations Division other than copies of such records obtained in accordance with the provisions of this part.

(d) Release of records under this section is subject to the provisions of 5 U.S.C. 552a.

[45 FR 31293, May 13, 1980, as amended at 65 FR 9207, Feb. 24, 2000; 79 FR 77844, Dec. 29, 2014; 81 FR 94240, Dec. 23, 2016]

§ 5.5   Request for records.

(a) A request to inspect or copy those public records described in 11 CFR 5.4(a) may be made in person or by mail. The Public Disclosure and Media Relations Division is open Monday through Friday between the hours of 9 a.m. and 5 p.m. and is located at the Federal Election Commission at the street address identified in the definition of "Commission" in § 1.2.

(b) Each request shall describe the records sought with sufficient specificity with respect to names, dates and subject matter to permit the records to be located with a reasonable amount of effort. A requester will be promptly advised if the requested records cannot be located on the basis of the description given and that further identifying information must be provided before the request can be satisfied.

(c) Requests for copies of records not available through the Public Disclosure and Media Relations Division shall be addressed to the Chief FOIA Officer, Federal Election Commission, at the street address identified in the definition of "Commission" in § 1.2. Requests for Commission records not described in 11 CFR 5.4(a) shall be treated as requests made pursuant to the Freedom of Information Act (5 U.S.C. 552) and shall be governed by 11 CFR part 4. In the event that the Public Disclosure and Media Relations Division receives a written request for access to materials not described in 11 CFR 5.4(a), it shall promptly forward such request to the Commission FOIA Officer for processing in accordance with the provisions of part 4 of this chapter.

[45 FR 31293, May 13, 1980, as amended at 50 FR 50778, Dec. 12, 1985; 75 FR 31, Jan. 4, 2010; 81 FR 94240, Dec. 23, 2016; 82 FR 60853, Dec. 26, 2017]

§ 5.6   Fees.

(a)(1) Fees will be charged for copies of records which are furnished to a requester under this part and for the staff time spent in locating and reproducing such records. The fees to be levied for services rendered under this part shall not exceed the Commission's direct cost of processing requests for those records computed on the basis of the actual number of copies produced and the staff time expended in fulfilling the particular request, in accordance with the following schedule of standard fees:

Photocopying from microfilm reader-printer—$.15 per page
Photocopying from photocopying machines—$.05 per page
Paper copies from microfilm—Paper Print Machine—$.05 per frame/page

REELS OF MICROFILM

Daily film (partial or complete roll)—$2.85 per roll
Other film (partial or complete roll)—$5.00 per roll

PUBLICATIONS: (NEW OR NOT FROM STOCKS AVAILABLE)

Cost of photocopying (reproducing) document—$.05 per page
Cost of binding document—$.30 per inch
Plus cost of staff research time after first ½ hour (see Research Time)

PUBLICATIONS: (AVAILABLE STOCK)

If available from stock on hand, cost is based on previously calculated cost as stated in the publication (based on actual cost per copy, including reproduction and binding).

COMPUTER TAPES:

Cost ($.0006 per Computer Resource Unit Utilized—CRU) to process the request plus the cost of the computer tape ($25) and professional staff time (see Research Time). The cost varies based upon request.

COMPUTER INDEXES:

No charge for 20 or fewer requests for computer indexes, except for a name search as described below.
C Index—Committee Index of Disclosure Documents—No charge for requests of 20 or fewer committee ID numbers. Requests for more than 20 ID numbers will cost $.05 for each ID number requested.
E Index (Parts 1–4)—Candidate Index of Supporting Documents—No charge for requests of 20 or fewer candidate ID numbers. Requests for more than 20 ID numbers will cost $.10 for each ID number requested.
D Index—Committee Index or Candidates Supported/Opposed—No charge for requests of 20 or fewer committee ID numbers. Requests for more than 20 ID numbers will cost $.30 for each committee ID number requested.
E Index (Complete)—Candidate Index of Supporting Documents—No charge for requests of 20 or fewer committee ID numbers. Requests for more than 20 ID numbers will cost $2.00 for each candidate ID number requested.

G Index—Selected List of Receipts and Expenditures—No charge for requests of 20 or fewer committee ID numbers. Requests for more than 20 ID numbers will cost $2.00 for each ID number requested.
Other computer index requests for more than 20 ID numbers will cost $.0006 per CRU (Computer Resource Unit) utilized.
Name Search—A computer search of an entire individual contributor file for contributions made by a particular individual or individuals will cost $.0006 per CRU (Computer Resource Unit) utilized.

RESEARCH TIME/PHOTOCOPYING TIME

Clerical: First ½ hour is free; remaining time costs $4.50 per each half hour (agency average of staff below a GS–11) for each request.
Professional: First ½ hour is free; remaining time costs $12.40 per each half hour (agency average of staff at GS–11 and above) for each request.

OTHER CHARGES

Certification of a Document: $7.35 per quarter hour.
Transcripts of Commission meetings not previously transcribed: $7.50 per half hour (equivalent of a GS–11 executive secretary).

(2) Upon receipt of any request for the production of computer tape or microfilm, the Commission will advise the requester of the identity of the private contractor who will perform the duplication services. The fee for the production of computer tape or microfilm shall be made payable to that private contractor and shall be fowarded to the Commission.

(b) Commission publications for which fees will be charged under 11 CFR 5.6(a) include, but are not limited to, the following:

Advisory Opinion Index
Report on Financial Activity
Financial Control and Compliance Manual
MUR Index
Guideline for Presentation in Good Order
Office Account Index

(c) In the event the anticipated fees for all pending requests from the same requester exceed $25.00, records will not be searched, nor copies furnished, until the requester pays, or makes acceptable arrangements to pay, the total amount due.

Similarly, if the records requested require the production of microfilm or of computer tapes, the Commission will not instruct its contractor to duplicate the records until the requester has submitted payment as directed or has made acceptable arrangements to pay the total amount due. If any fee is not precisely ascertainable, an estimate will be made by the Commission and the requester will be required to forward the fee so estimated. In the event any advance payment differs from the actual fee, an appropriate adjustment will be made at the time the copies are made available by the Commission.

(d) The Commission may reduce or waive payments of fees hereunder if it determines that such waiver or reduction is in the public interest because the furnishing of the requested information to the particular requester involved can be considered as primarily benefiting the general public as opposed to primarily benefiting the person or organization requesting the information.

[49 FR 30460, July 31, 1984, as amended at 52 FR 39214, Oct. 21, 1987]

PART 6—ENFORCEMENT OF NON-DISCRIMINATION ON THE BASIS OF HANDICAP IN PROGRAMS OR ACTIVITIES CONDUCTED BY THE FEDERAL ELECTION COMMISSION

AUTHORITY: 29 U.S.C. 794.

SOURCE: 49 FR 33211, Aug. 22, 1984, unless otherwise noted.

§ 6.101   Purpose.

The purpose of this part is to effectuate section 119 of the Rehabilitation, Comprehensive Services, and Developmental Disabilities Amendments of 1978, which amended section 504 of the Rehabilitation Act of 1973 to prohibit discrimination on the basis of handicap in programs or activities conducted by Executive agencies or the United States Postal Service.

§ 6.102   Application.

This part applies to all programs or activities conducted by the Commission.

§ 6.103   Definitions.

For purposes of this part, the term—

(a) *Auxiliary aids* means services, including attendant services, or devices that enable handicapped persons, including those with impaired sensory, manual, or speaking skills to have an equal opportunity to participate in, and enjoy the benefits of, programs or activities conducted by the Commission. For example, auxiliary aids useful for persons with impaired vision include readers, Brailled materials, audio recordings, and other similar services and devices. Auxiliary aids useful for persons with impaired hearing include telephone handset amplifiers, telephones compatible with hearing aids, telecommunication devices for deaf persons (TDD's), interpreters, notetakers, written materials, and other similar services and devices. Although auxiliary aids are explicitly required only by 11 CFR 6.160(a)(1), they may also be used to meet other requirements of this part.

(b) *Commission* means the Federal Election Commission.

(c) *Complete complaint* means a written statement that contains the complainant's name and address and describes the Commission's actions in sufficient detail to inform the Commission of the nature and date of the alleged violation of section 504. It shall be signed by the complainant or by someone authorized to do so on his or her behalf. Complaints filed on behalf of classes or third parties shall describe or identify (by name, if possible) the alleged victims of discrimination.

(d) *Facility* means all or any portion of buildings, structures, equipment, roads, walks, parking lots, rolling stock or other conveyances, or other real or personal property whether owned, leased or used on some other basis by the Commission.

(e) *Handicapped person* means any person who has a physical or mental impairment that substantially limits one or more major life activities, has a record of such an impairment, or is regarded as having such an impairment. As used in this definition, the phrase:

(1) *Physical or mental impairment* includes—

(i) Any physiological disorder or condition, cosmetic disfigurement, or anatomical loss affecting one or more of the following body systems: Neurological; musculoskeletal; special sense organs; respiratory, including speech organs; cardiovascular; reproductive; digestive; genitourinary; hemic and lymphatic; skin; and endocrine; or

(ii) Any mental or psychological disorder, such as mental retardation, organic brain syndrome, emotional or mental illness, and specific learning disabilities. The term *physical or mental impairment* includes, but is not limited to, such diseases and conditions as orthopedic, visual, speech, and hearing impairments, cerebral palsy, epilepsy, muscular dystrophy, multiple sclerosis, cancer, heart disease, diabetes, mental retardation, emotional illness, drug addiction, and alcoholism.

(2) *Major life activities* includes functions such as caring for one's self, performing manual tasks, walking, seeing, hearing, speaking, breathing, learning, and working.

(3) *Has a record of such an impairment* means has a history of, or has been misclassified as having, a mental or physical impairment that substantially limits one or more major life activities.

(4) *Is regarded as having an impairment* means—

(i) Has a physical or mental impairment that does not substantially limit major life activities but is treated by the Commission as constituting such a limitation;

(ii) Has a physical or mental impairment that substantially limits major life activities only as a result of the attitudes of others toward such impairment; or

(iii) Has none of the impairments defined in 11 CFR 6.103(e)(1) but is treated by the agency as having such an impairment.

(f) *Qualified handicapped person* means—

(1) With respect to any Commission program or activity under which a person is required to perform services or to achieve a level of accomplishment, a handicapped person who, with reasonable accommodation, meets the essential eligibility requirements and who can achieve the purpose of the program or activity; and

(2) With respect to any other program or activity, a handicapped person who meets the essential eligibility requirements for participation in, or receipt of benefits from, that program or activity.

(g) *Section 504* means section 504 of the Rehabilitation Act of 1973 (Pub. L. 93–112, 87 Stat. 394 (29 U.S.C. 794)), as amended by the Rehabilitation Act Amendments of 1974 (Pub. L. 93–516, 88 Stat. 1617), and the Rehabilitation, Comprehensive Services, and Developmental Disabilities Act of 1978 (Pub. L. 95–602, 92 Stat. 2955). As used in this part, section 504 applies only to programs or activities conducted by the Commission and not to any federally assisted programs or activities that it administers.

[49 FR 33211, Aug. 22, 1984, as amended at 50 FR 50778, Dec. 12, 1985; 82 FR 60853, Dec. 26, 2017]

§§ 6.104–6.109 [Reserved]

§ 6.110 Evaluation.

(a) Within one year of the effective date of this part, the Commission will conduct, with the assistance of interested persons, including handicapped persons and organizations representing handicapped persons, and evaluation of its compliance with section 504. This evaluation will include a determination of whether the Commission's policies and practices, and the effects thereof, meet the requirements of this part and whether modification of any such policies or practices is required to comply with section 504. If modification of any policy or practice is found to be required as a result of this evaluation, the Commission will proceed to make the necessary modifications.

(b) For at least three years following completion of the evaluation required under paragraph (a), the Commission will maintain on file and make available for public inspection:

(1) A list of the interested persons consulted;

(2) A description of areas examined and any problems identified; and

(3) A description of any modifications made.

§ 6.111 Notice.

The Commission will make available to employees, applicants, participants, beneficiaries, and other interested persons information regarding the provisions of this part and its applicability to the programs or activities conducted by the Commission. The Commission will make such information available to them in a manner it finds necessary to effectively apprise such persons of the protections against discrimination assured them by section 504 and the provisions of this part.

§§ 6.112–6.129 [Reserved]

§ 6.130 General prohibitions against discrimination.

(a) No qualified handicapped person shall, on the basis of handicap, be excluded from participation in, be denied the benefits of, or otherwise be subjected to discrimination under any program or activity conducted by the Commission.

(b)(1) The Commission, in providing any aid, benefit, or service, may not, directly or through contractual, licensing, or other arrangements, on the basis of handicap—

(i) Deny a qualified handicapped person the opportunity to participate in or benefit from the aid, benefit, or service;

(ii) Afford a qualified handicapped person an opportunity to participate in or benefit from the aid, benefit, or service that is not equal to that afforded others;

(iii) Provide a qualified handicapped person with an aid, benefit, or service that is not as effective in affording equal opportunity to obtain the same result, to gain the same benefit, or to reach the same level of achievement as that provided to others;

(iv) Provide different or separate aids, benefits, or services to handicapped persons or to any class of handicapped persons than is provided to others unless such action is necessary to provide qualified handicapped persons with aids, benefits, or services that are as effective as those provided to others;

(v) Aid or perpetuate discrimination against a qualified handicapped person by providing significant assistance to an agency, organization, or person that discriminates on the basis of handicap in providing any aid, benefit, or service to beneficiaries of the recipient's program, except that this paragraph does not apply to candidates or conventions receiving public financing under title 26, United States Code;

(vi) Deny a qualified handicapped person the opportunity to participate as a member of planning or advisory boards; or

(vii) Otherwise limit a qualified handicapped person in the enjoyment of any right, privilege, advantage, or opportunity enjoyed by others receiving the aid, benefit, or service.

(2) The Commission may not deny a qualified handicapped person the opportunity to participate in programs or activities that are not separate or different, despite the existence of permissibly separate or different programs or activities.

(3) The Commission may not, directly or through contractual or other arrangements, utilize criteria or methods of administration the purpose or effect of which would—

(i) Subject qualified handicapped persons to discrimination on the basis of handicap;

(ii) Defeat or substantially impair accomplishment of the objectives of a program or activity with respect to handicapped persons; or

(iii) Perpetuate the discrimination of another agency.

(4) The Commission may not, in determining the site or location of a facility, make selections the purpose or effect of which would—

(i) Exclude handicapped persons from, deny them the benefits of, or otherwise subject them to discrimination under any program or activity conducted by the Commission; or

(ii) Defeat or substantially impair the accomplishment of the objectives of a program or activity with respect to handicapped persons.

(5) The Commission, in the selection of procurement contractors, may not use criteria that subject qualified handicapped persons to discrimination on the basis of handicap.

(6) The Commission may not administer a certification program in a manner that subjects qualified handicapped persons to discrimination on the basis of handicap, nor may the Commission establish requirements for the programs or activities of certified entities that subject qualified handicapped persons to discrimination on the basis of handicap. However, the programs or activities of entities that are certified by the Commission are not, themselves, covered by this part.

(c) The exclusion of nonhandicapped persons from the benefits of a program limited by Federal statute or Executive order to handicapped persons or the exclusion of a specific class of handicapped persons from a program limited by Federal statute or Executive Order to a different class of handicapped persons is not prohibited by this part.

(d) The Commission will administer programs and activities in the most integrated setting appropriate to the needs of qualified handicapped persons.

§§ 6.131–6.139 [Reserved]

§ 6.140 Employment.

No qualified handicapped person shall, on the basis of handicap, be subjected to discrimination in employment under any program or activity conducted by the Commission. The definitions, requirements, and procedures of section 501 of the Rehabilitation Act of 1973 (29 U.S.C. 791), as established in 29 CFR part 1613, shall apply

to employment in federally conducted programs or activities.

§§ 6.141–6.148 [Reserved]

§ 6.149 Program accessibility: Discrimination prohibited.

Except as otherwise provided in 11 CFR 6.150 and 11 CFR 6.151, no qualified handicapped person shall be denied the benefits of, be excluded from participation in, or otherwise be subjected to discrimination under any program or activity conducted by the Commission because its facilities are inaccessible to or unusable by handicapped persons.

§ 6.150 Program accessibility; Existing facilities.

(a) *General.* The Commission will operate each program or activity so that the program or activity, when viewed in its entirety, is readily accessible to and usable by handicapped persons. This paragraph does not—

(1) Necessarily require the Commission to make each of its existing facilities accessible to and usable by handicapped persons;

(2) Require the Commission to take any action that it can demonstrate would result in a fundamental alteration in the nature of a program or activity or in undue financial and administrative burdens. The Commission has the burden of proving that compliance with 11 CFR 6.150(a) would result in such alterations or burdens. The decision that compliance would result in such alteration or burdens must be made by the Commission after considering all agency resources available for use in the funding and operation of the conducted program or activity, and must be accompanied by a written statement of the reasons for reaching that conclusion. If an action would result in such an alteration or such burdens, the Commission will take any other action that would not result in such an alteration or such a burden but would nevertheless ensure that handicapped persons receive the benefits and services of the program or activity.

(b) *Methods.* The Commission may comply with the requirements of this section through such means as redesign of equipment, reassignment of services to accessible buildings, assignment of aides to beneficiaries, home visits, delivery of services at alternate accessible sites, alteration of existing facilities and construction of new facilities, use of accessible rolling stock, or any other methods that result in making its programs or activities readily accessible to and usable by handicapped persons. The Commission is not required to make structural changes in existing facilities where other methods are effective in achieving compliance with this section. The Commission, in making alterations to existing buildings, will meet accessibility requirements to the extent compelled by the Architectural Barriers Act of 1968, as amended (42 U.S.C. 4151–4157) and any regulations implementing it. In choosing among available methods for meeting the requirements of this section, the Commission will give priority to those methods that offer programs and activities to qualified handicapped persons in the most integrated setting appropriate.

(c) *Time period for compliance.* The Commission will comply with the obligations established under this section within sixty days of the effective date of this part except that where structural changes in facilities are undertaken, such changes will be made within three years of the effective date of this part, but in any event as expeditiously as possible.

(d) *Transition plan.* In the event that structural changes to facilities will be undertaken to achieve program accessibility, the Commission will develop, within six months of the effective date of this part, a transition plan setting forth the steps necessary to complete such changes. The plan will be developed with the assistance of interested persons, including handicapped persons and organizations representing handicapped persons. A copy of the transition plan will be made available for public inspection. The plan will, at a minimum—

(1) Identify physical obstacles in the Commission's facilities that limit the accessibility of its programs or activities to handicapped persons;

(2) Describe in detail the methods that will be used to make the facilities accessible;

(3) Specify the schedule for taking the steps necessary to achieve compliance with this section and, if the time period of the transition plan is longer than one year, identify steps that will be taken during each year of the transition period;

(4) Indicate the official responsible for implementation of the plan; and

(5) Identify the persons or groups with whose assistance the plan was prepared.

§ 6.151 Program accessibility: New construction and alterations.

Each building or part of a building that is constucted or altered by, on behalf of, or for the use of the Commission shall be designed, constructed, or altered so as to be readily accessible to and usable by handicapped persons. The definitions, requirements, and standards of the Architectural Barriers Act, 42 U.S.C. 4151–4157, as established in 41 CFR 101–19.600 to 101–19.607, apply to buildings covered by this section.

§§ 6.152–6.159 [Reserved]

§ 6.160 Communications.

(a) The Commission will take appropriate steps to ensure effective communication with applicants, participants, personnel of other Federal entities, and members of the public.

(1) The Commission will furnish appropriate auxiliary aids where necessary to afford a handicapped person an equal opportunity to participate in, and enjoy the benefits of, a program or activity conducted by the Commission.

(i) In determination what type of auxiliary aid is necessary, the Commission will give primary consideration to the requests of the handicapped person.

(ii) The Commission need not provide individually prescribed devices, readers for personal use or study, or other devices of a personal nature.

(2) Where the Commission communicates with applicants and beneficiaries by telephone, telecommunications devices for deaf persons (TDD's), or equally effective telecommunication systems will be used.

(b) The Commission will ensure that interested persons, including persons with impaired vision or hearing, can obtain information as to the existence and location of accessible services, activities, and facilities.

(c) The Commission will provide signage at a primary entrance to each of its inaccessible facilities, directing users to a location at which they can obtain information about accessible facilities. The international symbol for accessibility shall be used at each primary entrance of an accessible facility.

(d) The Commission will take appropriate steps to provide handicapped persons with information regarding their section 504 rights under the Commission's programs of activities.

(e) This section does not require the Commission to take any action that it can demonstrate would result in a fundamental alteration in the nature of a program or activity or in undue financial and administrative burdens. The Commission has the burden of proving that compliance with this section would result in such alterations or burdens. The decision that compliance would result in such alteration or burdens must be made by the Commission after considering all agency resources available for use in the funding and operation of the conducted program or activity, and must be accompanied by a written statement of the reasons for reaching that conclusion. If an action required to comply with this section would result in such an alteration or such burdens, the Commission will take any other action that would not result in such an alteration or such a burden but would nevertheless ensure that, to the maximum extent possible, handicapped persons receive the benefits and services of the program or activity.

§§ 6.161–6.169 [Reserved]

§ 6.170 Compliance procedures.

(a) Except as provided in paragraph (b) of this section, this section applies to all allegations of discrimination on the basis of handicap in programs or activities conducted by the Commission.

(b) The Commission will process complaints alleging violations of section 504 with respect to employment according to the procedures established in 29 CFR part 1613 pursuant to section 501

of the Rehabilitation Act of 1973 (29 U.S.C. 791).

(c) Responsibility for implementation and operation of this section shall be vested in the Rehabilitation Act Officer.

(d)(1)(i) Any person who believes that he or she or any specific class of persons of which he or she is a member has been subjected to discrimination prohibited by this part may file a complaint with the Rehabilitation Act Officer.

(ii) Any person who believes that a denial of his or her services will result or has resulted in discrimination prohibited by this part may file a complaint with the Rehabilitatin Act Officer.

(2) All complete complaints must be filed within 180 days of the alleged act of discrimination. The Commission may extend this time period for good cause.

(3) Complaints filed under this part shall be addressed to the Rehabilitation Act Officer, Federal Election Commission, at the street address identified in the definition of "Commission" in § 1.2.

(e) The Commission will notify the Architectural and Transportation Barriers Compliance Board upon receipt of any complaint alleging that a building or facility that is subject to the Architectural Barriers Act of 1968, as amended (42 U.S.C. 4151–4157), or section 502 of the Rehabilitation Act of 1973, as amended (29 U.S.C. 792), are not readily accessible and usable to handicapped persons.

(f)(1) The Commission will accept and investigate a complete complaint that is filed in accordance with paragraph (d) of this section and over which it has jurisdiction. The Rehabilitation Act Officer will notify the complainant and the respondent of receipt and acceptance of the complaint.

(2) If the Rehabilitation Act Officer receives a complaint that is not complete (See 11 CFR 6.101(c)), he or she will notify the complainant within 30 days of receipt of the incomplete complaint, that additional information is needed. If the complainant fails to complete the complaint within 30 days

31

of receipt of this notice, the Rehabilitation Act Officer will dismiss the complaint without prejudice.

(3) If the Rehabilitation Act Officer receives a complaint over which the Commission does not have jurisdiction, the Commission will promptly notify the complainant and will make reasonable efforts to refer the complaint to the appropriate governmental entity.

(g) Within 180 days of receipt of a complete complaint for which it has jurisdiction, the Commission will notify the complainant of the results of the investigation in a letter containing—

(1) Findings of fact and conclusions of law;

(2) A description or a remedy for each violation found; and

(3) A notice of the right to appeal.

(h) Appeals of the findings of fact and conclusions of law or remedies must be filed by the complainant within 90 days of receipt from the Commission of the letter required by § 6.170(g). The Commission may extend this time for good cause.

(i) Timely appeals to the Commission shall be addressed to the Rehabilitation Act Officer, Federal Election Commission, at the street address identified in the definition of "Commission" in § 1.2.

(j) The Commission will notify the complainant of the results of the appeal within 60 days of the receipt of the request. If the Commission determines that it needs additional information from the complainant, it shall have 60 days from the date it receives the additional information to make its determination on the appeal.

(k) The Commission may extend the time limits in paragraphs (g) and (j) of this section for good cause.

(l) The Commission may delegate its authority for conducting complaint investigations to other Federal agencies, except that the authority for making the final determination may not be delegated.

[49 FR 33211, Aug. 22, 1984, as amended at 50 FR 50778, Dec. 12, 1985; 82 FR 60853, Dec. 26, 2017]

§§ 6.171–6.999   [Reserved]

PART 7—STANDARDS OF CONDUCT

Sec.
7.1   Scope.
7.2   Definitions.
7.3   Interpretation and guidance.
7.4   Reporting suspected violations.
7.5   Corrective action.
7.6   Outside employment and activities by Commissioners.
7.7   Prohibition against making complaints and investigations public.
7.8   Ex parte communications in enforcement actions.

AUTHORITY: 52 U.S.C. 30106, 30107, and 30111; 5 U.S.C. 7321 et seq. and app. 3.

SOURCE: 76 FR 70330, Nov. 14, 2011, unless otherwise noted.

§ 7.1   Scope.

(a) The regulations in this part apply to members and employees of the Federal Election Commission ("Commission").

(b) In addition, members and employees of the Commission are subject to the following regulations:

(1) 5 CFR part 735 (Employee Responsibilities and Conduct);

(2) 5 CFR part 2634 (Executive Branch Financial Disclosure, Qualified Trusts, and Certificates of Divestiture);

(3) 5 CFR part 2635 (Standards of Ethical Conduct for Employees of the Executive Branch); and

(4) 5 CFR part 4701 (Supplemental Standards of Ethical Conduct for Employees of the Federal Election Commission).

§ 7.2   Definitions.

As used in this part:

(a) *Commission* means the Federal Election Commission.

(b) *Commissioner* means a member of the Federal Election Commission, in accordance with 52 U.S.C. 30106.

(c) *Designated Agency Ethics Official* means the employee designated by the Commission to administer the provisions of the Ethics in Government Act of 1978 (5 U.S.C. appendix), as amended, and includes a designee of the Designated Agency Ethics Official. The General Counsel serves as the Commission's Designated Agency Ethics Official.

(d) *Employee* means an employee of the Federal Election Commission and includes a special Government employee as defined in 18 U.S.C. 202(a).

(e) *Ex parte communication* means any written or oral communication by any person outside the agency to any Commissioner or any member of any Commissioner's staff, but not to any other Commission employee, that imparts information or argument regarding prospective Commission action or potential action concerning any pending enforcement matter.

(f) *Inspector General* means the individual appointed by the Commission to administer the provisions of the Inspector General Act of 1978, as amended (5 U.S.C. appendix), and includes any designee of the Inspector General.

[76 FR 70330, Nov. 14, 2011, as amended at 79 FR 77844, Dec. 29, 2014; 82 FR 60853, Dec. 26, 2017]

§7.3 Interpretation and guidance.

(a) A Commissioner or employee seeking advice and guidance on matters covered by this part or 5 CFR parts 735, 2634, 2635, 2640, or 4701 may consult with the Designated Agency Ethics Official. The Designated Agency Ethics Official should be consulted before undertaking any action that might violate this part or 5 CFR parts 735, 2635, 2640, or 4701 governing the conduct of Commissioners or employees.

(b) The Designated Agency Ethics Official, a Commissioner, or an employee may request an opinion from the Director of the Office of Government Ethics regarding an interpretation of 5 CFR parts 2634, 2635, or 2640.

§7.4 Reporting suspected violations.

Commissioners and employees shall disclose immediately any suspected violation of a statute or of a rule set forth in this part or of a rule set forth in 5 CFR parts 735, 2634, 2635, 2640, or 4701 to the Designated Agency Ethics Official, the Office of Inspector General, or other appropriate law enforcement authorities.

§7.5 Corrective action.

A violation of this part or 5 CFR parts 735, 2634, 2635, 2640, or 4701 by an employee may be cause for appropriate corrective, disciplinary, or adverse action in addition to any penalty prescribed by law.

§7.6 Outside employment and activities by Commissioners.

No member of the Commission may devote a substantial portion of his or her time to any other business, vocation, or employment. Any individual who is engaging substantially in any other business, vocation, or employment at the time such individual begins to serve as a member of the Commission will appropriately limit such activity no later than 90 days after beginning to serve as such a member.

§7.7 Prohibition against making complaints and investigations public.

(a) Commission employees are subject to criminal penalties if they discuss or otherwise make public any matters pertaining to a complaint or investigation under 52 U.S.C. 30109, without the written permission of the person complained against or being investigated. Such communications are prohibited by 52 U.S.C. 30109(a)(12)(A).

(b) Section 30109(a)(12)(B) of Title 52 of the United States Code provides as follows: "Any member or employee of the Commission, or any other person, who violates the provisions of [52 U.S.C. 30109(a)(12)(A)] shall be fined not more than $2,000. Any such member, employee, or other person who knowingly and willfully violates the provisions of [52 U.S.C. 30109(a)(12)(A)] shall be fined not more than $5,000."

[79 FR 77844, Dec. 29, 2014]

§7.8 Ex parte communications in enforcement actions.

In order to avoid the possibility of prejudice, real or apparent, to the public interest in enforcement actions pending before the Commission pursuant to 52 U.S.C. 30109:

(a) Except to the extent required for the disposition of enforcement matters as required by law (as, for example, during the normal course of an investigation or a conciliation effort), no Commissioner or member of any Commissioner's staff shall make or entertain any *ex parte* communications.

(b) The prohibition of this section shall apply from the time a complaint is filed with the Commission pursuant to 52 U.S.C. 30109(a)(1) or from the time that the Commission determines on the basis of information ascertained in the normal course of its supervisory responsibilities that it has reason to believe that a violation has occurred or may occur pursuant to 52 U.S.C. 30109(a)(2), and such prohibition shall remain in force until the Commission has concluded all action with respect to the enforcement matter in question.

(c) Any written communication prohibited by paragraph (a) of this section shall be delivered to the General Counsel, who shall place the communication in the case file.

(d) A Commissioner or member of any Commissioner's staff involved in handling enforcement actions who receives an offer to make an oral communication or any communication concerning any enforcement action pending before the Commission as described in paragraph (a) of this section, shall decline to listen to such communication. If unsuccessful in preventing the communication, the Commissioner or employee shall advise the person making the communication that he or she will not consider the communication and shall prepare a statement setting forth the substance and circumstances of the communication. Within 48 hours of receipt of the communication, the Commissioner or any member of any Commissioner's staff shall prepare a statement setting forth the substance and circumstances of the communication and shall deliver the statement to the General Counsel for placing in the file in the manner set forth in paragraph (c) of this section.

(e) Additional rules governing *ex parte* communications made in connection with Commission enforcement actions are found at 11 CFR 111.22. Rules governing *ex parte* communications made in connection with public funding, Commission audits, litigation, rulemakings, and advisory opinions are found at 11 CFR part 201.

[76 FR 70330, Nov. 14, 2011 , as amended at 79 FR 77844, Dec. 29, 2014]

PART 8—COLLECTION OF ADMINISTRATIVE DEBTS

AUTHORITY: 31 U.S.C. 3701, 3711, and 3716–3720A, as amended; 52 U.S.C. 30101 *et seq.*; 31 CFR parts 285 and 900–904.

SOURCE: 75 FR 19875, Apr. 16, 2010, unless otherwise noted.

§ 8.1 Purpose and scope.

This part prescribes standards and procedures under which the Commission will collect and dispose of certain debts owed to the United States, as described in 11 CFR 8.2. The regulations in this part implement the Debt Collection Improvement Act of 1996, 31 U.S.C. 3701, 3711, and 3716–3720A, as amended; and the Federal Claims Collection Standards, 31 CFR parts 900–904. The activities covered include: the collection of claims of any amount; compromising claims; suspending or terminating the collection of claims; referring debts to the U.S. Department of the Treasury for collection action; and referring debts under this part 8 of more than $100,000 (exclusive of any interest and charges) to the Department of Justice for litigation.

§ 8.2 Debts that are covered.

(a) The procedures covered by this part apply to debts that are either owed by current and former Commission employees, or arise from the provision of goods or services by contractors or vendors doing business with the Commission.

(b) The procedures covered by this part do not apply to any of the following debts:

(1) Debts that are covered by 11 CFR 111.51, regarding debts arising from compliance matters, administrative fines, alternative dispute resolution, repayments, and court judgments arising under the statutes specified in 11 CFR 111.51(a).

(2) Debts involving criminal actions of fraud, the presentation of a false claim, or misrepresentation on the part of the debtor or any other person having an interest in the claim.

(3) Debts based in whole or in part on conduct in violation of the antitrust laws.

(4) Debts under the Internal Revenue Code of 1986.

(5) Debts between the Commission and another Federal agency. The Commission will attempt to resolve interagency claims by negotiation in accordance with Executive Order 12146, 3 CFR pp. 409–12 (1980 Comp.).

(6) Debts that have become subject to salary offset under 5 U.S.C. 5514.

§ 8.3 Administrative collection of claims.

(a) The Commission shall act to collect all claims or debts. These collection activities will be undertaken promptly and follow up action will be taken as appropriate in accordance with 31 CFR 901.1.

(b) The Commission may take any and all appropriate collection actions authorized and required by the Debt Collection Act of 1982, as amended by the Debt Collection Improvement Act of 1996, 31 U.S.C. 3701 *et seq.* The U.S. Department of the Treasury regulations at 31 CFR 285.2, 285.4, 285.7 and 285.11, and the Federal Claims Collection Standards issued jointly by the Department of Justice and the U.S. Department of the Treasury at 31 CFR parts 900–904 also apply. The Commission has adopted these regulations by cross-reference.

(c) The Commission will refer to the Dept. of Treasury all debt that has been delinquent for more than 180 days, and may refer to the Dept. of Treasury any debt that has been delinquent for 180 days or less. On behalf of the Commission, the U.S. Department of the Treasury will attempt to collect the debt, in accordance with the statutory and regulatory requirements and authorities applicable to the debt and action. This may include referral to another debt collection center, a private collection contractor, or the Department of Justice for litigation. *See* 31 CFR 285.12 (Transfer of debts to Treasury for collection). This requirement does not apply to any debt that:

(1) Is in litigation or foreclosure;

(2) Will be disposed of under an approved asset sale program;

(3) Has been referred to a private collection contractor for a period of time acceptable to the U.S. Department of the Treasury; or

(4) Will be collected under internal offset procedures within three years after the debt first became delinquent.

(d) The U.S. Department of the Treasury is authorized to charge a fee for services rendered regarding referred or transferred debts. The Commission will add the fee to the debt as an administrative cost, in accordance with 11 CFR 8.5.

§ 8.4 Bankruptcy claims.

When the Commission learns that a bankruptcy petition has been filed by a debtor, before proceeding with further collection action, the Commission will take any necessary action in accordance with the provision of 31 CFR 901.2(h).

§ 8.5 Interest, penalties, and administrative costs.

(a) The Commission shall assess interest, penalties, and administrative costs on debts owed to the United States Government in accordance with 31 U.S.C. 3717 and 31 CFR 901.9.

(b) The Commission shall waive collection of interest and administrative costs on a debt or any portion of the debt that is paid in full within thirty days after the date on which the interest begins to accrue.

(c) The Commission may waive collection of interest, penalties, and administrative costs if it:

(1) Determines that collection is against equity and good conscience or not in the best interest of the United States, including when an administrative offset or installment agreement is in effect; or

(2) Determines that waiver is appropriate under the criteria for compromise of debts set forth at 31 CFR 902.2(a).

(d) The Commission is authorized to impose interest and related charges on debts not subject to 31 U.S.C. 3717, in accordance with common law.

SUBCHAPTER A—GENERAL

PART 100—SCOPE AND DEFINITIONS (52 U.S.C. 30101)

Subpart A—General Definitions

Subpart B—Definition of Contribution (52 U.S.C. 30101(8))

Subpart C—Exceptions to Contributions

Subpart D—Definition of Expenditure (52 U.S.C. 30101(9))

Subpart E—Exceptions to Expenditures

AUTHORITY: 52 U.S.C. 30101, 30104, 30111(a)(8), and 30114(c).

SOURCE: 45 FR 15094, Mar. 7, 1980, unless otherwise noted.

Subpart A—General Definitions

§ 100.1 Scope.

This subchapter is issued by the Federal Election Commission to implement the Federal Election Campaign Act of 1971, as amended, 52 U.S.C. 30101 et seq.

[79 FR 16663, Mar. 26, 2014, as amended at 79 FR 77844, Dec. 29, 2014]

§ 100.2 Election (52 U.S.C. 30101(1)).

(a) *Election* means the process by which individuals, whether opposed or unopposed, seek nomination for election, or election, to Federal office. The specific types of elections, as set forth at 11 CFR 100.2 (b), (c), (d), (e) and (f) are included in this definition.

(b) *General election.* A general election is an election which meets either of the following conditions:

(1) An election held in even numbered years on the Tuesday following the first Monday in November is a general election.

(2) An election which is held to fill a vacancy in a Federal office (*i.e.*, a special election) and which is intended to result in the final selection of a single individual to the office at stake is a general election. See 11 CFR 100.2(f).

(c) *Primary election.* A primary election is an election which meets one of the following conditions:

(1) An election which is held prior to a general election, as a direct result of which candidates are nominated, in accordance with applicable State law, for election to Federal office in a subsequent election is a primary election.

(2) An election which is held for the expression of a preference for the nomination of persons for election to the office of President of the United States is a primary election.

(3) An election which is held to elect delegates to a national nominating convention is a primary election.

(4) With respect to individuals seeking federal office as independent candidates, or without nomination by a major party (as defined in 26 U.S.C. 9002(6)), the primary election is considered to occur on one of the following dates, at the choice of the candidate:

(i) The day prescribed by applicable State law as the last day to qualify for a position on the general election ballot may be designated as the primary election for such candidate.

(ii) The date of the last major party primary election, caucus, or convention in that State may be designated as the primary election for such candidate.

(iii) In the case of non-major parties, the date of the nomination by that party may be designated as the primary election for such candidate.

(5) With respect to any major party candidate (as defined at 26 U.S.C. 9002(6)) who is unopposed for nomination within his or her own party, and who is certified to appear as that party's nominee in the general election for the office sought, the primary election is considered to have occurred on the date on which the primary election was held by the candidate's party in that State.

(d) *Runoff election. Runoff election* means the election which meets either of the following conditions:

(1) The election held after a primary election, and prescribed by applicable State law as the means for deciding which candidate(s) should be certified as a nominee for the Federal office sought, is a runoff election.

(2) The election held after a general election and prescribed by applicable State law as the means for deciding which candidate should be certified as an officeholder elect, is a runoff election.

(e) *Caucus or Convention.* A caucus or convention of a political party is an election if the caucus or convention has the authority to select a nominee for federal office on behalf of that party.

(f) *Special election. Special election* means an election which is held to fill a vacancy in a Federal office. A special election may be a primary, general, or runoff election, as defined at 11 CFR 100.2 (b), (c) and (d).

§ 100.3 Candidate (52 U.S.C. 30101(2)).

(a) *Definition. Candidate* means an individual who seeks nomination for election, or election, to federal office. An individual becomes a candidate for Federal office whenever any of the following events occur:

(1) The individual has received contributions aggregating in excess of $5,000 or made expenditures aggregating in excess of $5,000.

(2) The individual has given his or her consent to another person to receive contributions or make expenditures on behalf of that individual and such person has received contributions aggregating in excess of $5,000 or made expenditures aggregating in excess of $5,000.

(3) After written notification by the Commission that any other person has received contributions aggregating in excess of $5,000 or made expenditures aggregating in excess of $5,000 on the individual's behalf, the individual fails to disavow such activity by letter to the Commission within 30 days of receipt of the notification.

(4) The aggregate of contributions received under 11 CFR 100.3(a) (1), (2), and (3), in any combination thereof, ex-

ceeds $5,000, or the aggregate of expenditures made under 11 CFR 100.3(a) (1), (2), and (3), in any combination thereof, exceeds $5,000.

(b) *Election cycle.* For purposes of determining whether an individual is a candidate under this section, contributions or expenditures shall be aggregated on an election cycle basis. An election cycle shall begin on the first day following the date of the previous general election for the office or seat which the candidate seeks, unless contributions or expenditures are designated for another election cycle. For an individual who receives contributions or makes expenditures designated for another election cycle, the election cycle shall begin at the time such individual, or any other person acting on the individual's behalf, first receives contributions or makes expenditures in connection with the designated election. The election cycle shall end on the date on which the general election for the office or seat that the individual seeks is held.

§ 100.4 Federal office (52 U.S.C. 30101(3)).

Federal office means the office of President or Vice President of the United States, Senator or Representative in, or Delegate or Resident Commissioner to, the Congress of the United States.

§ 100.5 Political committee (52 U.S.C. 30101(4), (5), and (6)).

Political committee means any group meeting one of the following conditions:

(a) Except as provided in 11 CFR 100.5 (b), (c) and (d), any committee, club, association, or other group of persons which receives contributions aggregating in excess of $1,000 or which makes expenditures aggregating in excess of $1,000 during a calendar year is a political committee.

(b) Any separate segregated fund established under 52 U.S.C. 30118(b)(2)(C) is a political committee.

(c) Any local committee of a political party is a political committee if: it receives contributions aggregating in excess of $5,000 during a calendar year; it makes payments exempted from the definition of contribution, under 11

CFR 100.80, 100.87, and 100.89 and expenditure, under 11 CFR 100.140, 100.147, and 100.149, which payments aggregate in excess of $5,000 during a calendar year; or it makes contributions aggregating in excess of $1,000 or makes expenditures aggregating in excess of $1,000 during a calendar year.

(d) An individual's principal campaign committee or authorized committee(s) becomes a political committee(s) when that individual becomes a candidate pursuant to 11 CFR 100.3.

(e) The following are examples of political committees:

(1) *Principal campaign committee. Principal campaign committee* means a political committee designated and authorized by a candidate pursuant to 11 CFR 101.1 and 102.1.

(2) *Single candidate committee. Single candidate committee* means a political committee other than a principal campaign committee which makes or receives contributions or makes expenditures on behalf of only one candidate.

(3) *Multi-candidate committee. Multi-candidate committee* means a political committee which (i) has been registered with the Commission or Secretary of the Senate for at least 6 months; (ii) has received contributions for Federal elections from more than 50 persons; and (iii) (except for any State political party organization) has made contributions to 5 or more Federal candidates.

(4) *Party committee. Party committee* means a political committee which represents a political party and is part of the official party structure at the national, State, or local level.

(5) *Delegate committee.* A delegate committee is a group of persons that receives contributions or makes expenditures for the sole purpose of influencing the selection of one or more delegates to a national nominating convention. The term *delegate committee* includes a group of delegates, a group of individuals seeking selection as delegates and a group of individuals supporting delegates. A delegate committee that qualifies as a political committee under 11 CFR 100.5 must register with the Commission pursuant to 11 CFR part 102 and report its receipts and disbursements in accordance with 11 CFR part 104. (See definition of *delegate* at 11 CFR 110.14(b)(1).)

(6) *Leadership PAC. Leadership PAC* means a political committee that is directly or indirectly established, financed, maintained or controlled by a candidate for Federal office or an individual holding Federal office but which is not an authorized committee of the candidate or individual and which is not affiliated with an authorized committee of the candidate or individual, except that leadership PAC does not include a political committee of a political party.

(7) *Lobbyist/Registrant PAC. See* 11 CFR 104.22(a)(3).

(f) A political committee is either an authorized committee or an unauthorized committee.

(1) *Authorized committee. An authorized committee* means the principal campaign committee or any other political committee authorized by a candidate under 11 CFR 102.13 to receive contributions or make expenditures on behalf of such candidate, or which has not been disavowed pursuant to 11 CFR 100.3(a)(3).

(2) *Unauthorized committee. An unauthorized committee* is a political committee which has not been authorized in writing by a candidate to solicit or receive contributions or make expenditures on behalf of such candidate, or which has been disavowed pursuant to 11 CFR 100.3(a)(3).

(g) *Affiliated committee.* (1) All authorized committees of the same candidate for the same election to Federal office are affiliated.

(2) All committees (including a separate segregated fund, *see* 11 CFR part 114) established, financed, maintained or controlled by the same corporation, labor organization, person, or group of persons, including any parent, subsidiary, branch, division, department, or local unit thereof, are affiliated. *Local unit* may include, in appropriate cases, a franchisee, licensee, or State or regional association.

(3) Affiliated committees sharing a single contribution limitation under paragraph (g)(2) of this section include all of the committees established, financed, maintained or controlled by—

(i) A single corporation and/or its subsidiaries;

(ii) A single national or international union and/or its local unions or other subordinate organizations;

(iii) An organization of national or international unions and/or all its State and local central bodies;

(iv) A membership organization, (other than political party committees, *see* 11 CFR 110.3(b)) including trade or professional associations, *see* 11 CFR 114.8(a), and/or related State and local entities of that organization or group; or

(v) The same person or group of persons.

(4)(i) The Commission may examine the relationship between organizations that sponsor committees, between the committees themselves, or between one sponsoring organization and a committee established by another organization to determine whether committees are affiliated.

(ii) In determining whether committees not described in paragraphs (g)(3) (i)–(iv) of this section are affiliated, the Commission will consider the circumstantial factors described in paragraphs (g)(4)(ii) (A) through (J) of this section. The Commission will examine these factors in the context of the overall relationship between committees or sponsoring organizations to determine whether the presence of any factor or factors is evidence of one committee or organization having been established, financed, maintained or controlled by another committee or sponsoring organization. Such factors include, but are not limited to:

(A) Whether a sponsoring organization owns controlling interest in the voting stock or securities of the sponsoring organization of another committee;

(B) Whether a sponsoring organization or committee has the authority or ability to direct or participate in the governance of another sponsoring organization or committee through provisions of constitutions, bylaws, contracts, or other rules, or through formal or informal practices or procedures;

(C) Whether a sponsoring organization or committee has the authority or ability to hire, appoint, demote or otherwise control the officers, or other decisionmaking employees or members of another sponsoring organization or committee;

(D) Whether a sponsoring organization or committee has a common or overlapping membership with another sponsoring organization or committee which indicates a formal or ongoing relationship between the sponsoring organizations or committees;

(E) Whether a sponsoring organization or committee has common or overlapping officers or employees with another sponsoring organization or committee which indicates a formal or ongoing relationship between the sponsoring organizations or committees;

(F) Whether a sponsoring organization or committee has any members, officers or employees who were members, officers or employees of another sponsoring organization or committee which indicates a formal or ongoing relationship between the sponsoring organizations or committees, or which indicates the creation of a successor entity;

(G) Whether a sponsoring organization or committee provides funds or goods in a significant amount or on an ongoing basis to another sponsoring organization or committee, such as through direct or indirect payments for administrative, fundraising, or other costs, but not including the transfer to a committee of its allocated share of proceeds jointly raised pursuant to 11 CFR 102.17;

(H) Whether a sponsoring organization or committee causes or arranges for funds in a significant amount or on an ongoing basis to be provided to another sponsoring organization or committee, but not including the transfer to a committee of its allocated share of proceeds jointly raised pursuant to 11 CFR 102.17;

(I) Whether a sponsoring organization or committee or its agent had an active or significant role in the formation of another sponsoring organization or committee; and

(J) Whether the sponsoring organizations or committees have similar patterns of contributions or contributors which indicates a formal or ongoing relationship between the sponsoring organizations or committees.

(5) Notwithstanding paragraphs (g)(2) through (g)(4) of this section, no authorized committee shall be deemed affiliated with any entity that is not an authorized committee.

[45 FR 15094, Mar. 7, 1980, as amended at 45 FR 34867, May 23, 1980; 52 FR 35534, Sept. 22, 1987; 54 FR 34109, Aug. 17, 1989; 54 FR 48580, Nov. 24, 1989; 61 FR 3549, Feb. 1, 1996; 67 FR 78679, Dec. 26, 2002; 68 FR 67018, Dec. 1, 2003; 74 FR 7302, Feb. 17, 2009; 79 FR 77844, Dec. 29, 2014]

§ 100.6 Connected organization (52 U.S.C. 30101(7)).

(a) *Connected organization* means any organization which is not a political committee but which directly or indirectly establishes, administers, or financially supports a political committee. A connected organization may be a corporation (including a corporation without capital stock), a labor organization, a membership organization, a cooperative or a trade association.

(b) For purposes of 11 CFR 100.6, organizations which are members of the entity (such as corporate members of a trade association) which establishes, administers, or financially supports a political committee are not organizations which directly or indirectly establish, administer or financially support that political committee.

(c) For purposes of 11 CFR 100.6, the term *financially supports* does not include contributions to the political committee, but does include the payment of establishment, administration and solicitation costs of such committee.

§§ 100.7–100.8 [Reserved]

§ 100.9 Commission (52 U.S.C. 30101(10)).

Commission means the Federal Election Commission.

[45 FR 15094, Mar. 7, 1980, as amended at 50 FR 50778, Dec. 12, 1985; 82 FR 60853, Dec. 26, 2017]

§ 100.10 Person (52 U.S.C. 30101(11)).

Person means an individual, partnership, committee, association, corporation, labor organization, and any other organization, or group of persons, but does not include the Federal govern-ment or any authority of the Federal government.

§ 100.11 State (52 U.S.C. 30101(12)).

State means each State of the United States, the District of Columbia, the Commonwealth of Puerto Rico, and any territory or possession of the United States.

§ 100.12 Identification (52 U.S.C. 30101(13)).

Identification means, in the case of an individual, his or her full name, including: First name, middle name or initial, if available, and last name; mailing address; occupation; and the name of his or her employer; and, in the case of any other person, the person's full name and address.

§ 100.13 National committee (52 U.S.C. 30101(14)).

National committee means the organization which, by virtue of the bylaws of a political party, is responsible for the day-to-day operation of the political party at the national level, as determined by the Commission.

§ 100.14 State Committee, subordinate committee, district, or local committee (52 U.S.C. 30101(15)).

(a) *State committee* means the organization that by virtue of the bylaws of a political party or the operation of State law is part of the official party structure and is responsible for the day-to-day operation of the political party at the State level, including an entity that is directly or indirectly established, financed, maintained, or controlled by that organization, as determined by the Commission.

(b) *District or local committee* means any organization that by virtue of the bylaws of a political party or the operation of State law is part of the official party structure, and is responsible for the day-to-day operation of the political party at the level of city, county, neighborhood, ward, district, precinct, or any other subdivision of a State.

(c) *Subordinate committee of a State, district, or local committee* means any organization that at the level of city, county, neighborhood, ward, district, precinct, or any other subdivision of a State or any organization under the control or direction of the State committee, and is directly or indirectly established, financed, maintained, or controlled by the State, district, or local committee.

[67 FR 49110, July 29, 2002]

§ 100.15 Political party (52 U.S.C. 30101(16)).

Political party means an association, committee, or organization which nominates or selects a candidate for election to any Federal office, whose name appears on an election ballot as the candidate of the association, committee, or organization.

§ 100.16 Independent expenditure (52 U.S.C. 30101(17)).

(a) The term *independent expenditure* means an expenditure by a person for a communication expressly advocating the election or defeat of a clearly identified candidate that is not made in cooperation, consultation, or concert with, or at the request or suggestion of, a candidate, a candidate's authorized committee, or their agents, or a political party committee or its agents. A communication is "made in cooperation, consultation, or concert with, or at the request or suggestion of, a candidate, a candidate's authorized committee, or their agents, or a political party committee or its agents" if it is a coordinated communication under 11 CFR 109.21 or a party coordinated communication under 11 CFR 109.37.

(b) No expenditure by an authorized committee of a candidate on behalf of that candidate shall qualify as an independent expenditure.

(c) No expenditure shall be considered independent if the person making the expenditure allows a candidate, a candidate's authorized committee, or their agents, or a political party committee or its agents to become materially involved in decisions regarding the communication as described in 11 CFR 109.21(d)(2), or shares financial responsibility for the costs of production or dissemination with any such person.

[68 FR 451, Jan. 3, 2003]

§ 100.17 Clearly identified (52 U.S.C. 30101(18)).

The term *clearly identified* means the candidate's name, nickname, photograph, or drawing appears, or the identity of the candidate is otherwise apparent through an unambiguous reference such as "the President," "your Congressman," or "the incumbent," or through an unambiguous reference to his or her status as a candidate such as "the Democratic presidential nominee" or "the Republican candidate for Senate in the State of Georgia."

[60 FR 35304, July 6, 1995]

§ 100.18 Act (52 U.S.C. 30101(19)).

Act means the Federal Election Campaign Act of 1971, as amended, 52 U.S.C. 30101 *et. seq.*

[79 FR 77845, Dec. 29, 2014]

§ 100.19 File, filed, or filing (52 U.S.C. 30104(a)).

With respect to documents required to be filed under 11 CFR parts 101, 102, 104, 105, 107, 108, and 109, and any modifications or amendments thereto, the terms *file, filed,* and *filing* mean one of the actions set forth in paragraphs (a) through (f) of this section. For purposes of this section, document means any report, statement, notice, or designation required by the Act to be filed with the Commission or the Secretary of the Senate.

(a) *Where to deliver reports.* Except for documents electronically filed under paragraph (c) of this section, a document is timely filed upon delivery to the Federal Election Commission, at the street address identified in the definition of "Commission" in §1.2; or the Secretary of the United States Senate, Office of Public Records, 119 D Street NE., Washington, DC 20510 as required by 11 CFR part 105, by the close of business on the prescribed filing date.

(b) *Timely filed.* (1) A document, other than those addressed in paragraphs (c) through (f) of this section, is timely filed if:

(i) Deposited:

(A) As registered or certified mail in an established U.S. Post Office;

(B) As Priority Mail or Express Mail, with a delivery confirmation, in an established U.S. Post Office; or

(C) With an overnight delivery service and scheduled to be delivered the next business day after the date of deposit and recorded in the overnight delivery service's on-line tracking system; and

(ii) The postmark on the document must be dated no later than 11:59 p.m. Eastern Standard/Daylight Time on the filing date, except that pre-election reports must have a postmark dated no later than 11:59 p.m. Eastern Standard/Daylight Time on the fifteenth day before the date of the election.

(2) Documents, other than those addressed in paragraphs (c) through (f) of this section, sent by first class mail or by any means other than those listed in paragraph (b)(1)(i) of this section must be received by the close of business on the prescribed filing date to be timely filed.

(3) As used in this paragraph (b) of this section and in 11 CFR 104.5,

(i) Overnight delivery service means a private delivery service business of established reliability that offers an overnight (*i.e.*, next business day) delivery option.

(ii) Postmark means a U.S. Postal Service postmark or the verifiable date of deposit with an overnight delivery service.

(c) *Electronically filed reports.* For electronic filing purposes, a document is timely filed when it is received and validated by the Federal Election Commission by 11:59 p.m. Eastern Standard/Daylight Time on the filing date.

(d) *48-hour and 24-hour reports of independent expenditures*—(1) *48-hour reports of independent expenditures.* A 48-hour report of independent expenditures under 11 CFR 104.4(b) or 109.10(c) is timely filed when it is received by the Commission by 11:59 p.m. Eastern Standard/Daylight Time on the second day following the date on which independent expenditures aggregate $10,000 or more in accordance with 11 CFR 104.4(f), any time during the calendar year up to and including the 20th day before an election.

(2) *24-hour reports of independent expenditures.* A 24-hour report of independent expenditures under 11 CFR 104.4(c) or 109.10(d) is timely filed when it is received by the Commission by 11:59 p.m. Eastern Standard/Daylight Time on the day following the date on which independent expenditures aggregate $1,000 or more, in accordance with 11 CFR 104.4(f), during the period less than 20 days but more than 24 hours before an election.

(3) *Permissible means of filing.* In addition to other permissible means of filing, a 24-hour report or 48-hour report of independent expenditures may be filed using a facsimile machine or by electronic mail if the reporting entity is not required to file electronically in accordance with 11 CFR 104.18. Political committees, regardless of whether they are required to file electronically under 11 CFR 104.18, may file 24-hour reports using the Commission's website's on-line program.

(e) *48-hour statements of last-minute contributions.* In addition to other permissible means of filing, authorized committees that are not required to file electronically may file 48-hour notifications of contributions using facsimile machines. All authorized committees that file with the Commission, including electronic reporting entities, may use the Commission's website's on-line program to file 48-hour notifications of contributions. *See* 11 CFR 104.5(f).

(f) *24-hour statements of electioneering communications.* A 24-hour statement of electioneering communications under 11 CFR 104.20 is timely filed when it is received by the Commission by 11:59 p.m. Eastern Standard/Daylight Time on the day following the disclosure date. (*See* 11 CFR 104.20(a)(1) and (b)). In addition to other permissible means of filing, a 24-hour statement of electioneering communications may be filed using a facsimile machine or by electronic mail if the reporting entity is not required to file electronically in accordance with 11 CFR 104.18.

[67 FR 12839, Mar. 20, 2002, as amended at 68 FR 416, Jan. 3, 2003; 68 FR 3995, Jan. 27, 2003; 70 FR 13091, Mar. 18, 2005; 73 FR 79601, Dec. 30, 2008; 82 FR 60853, Dec. 26, 2017]

§ 100.20 Occupation (52 U.S.C. 30101(13)).

Occupation means the principal job title or position of an individual and whether or not self-employed.

§ 100.21 Employer (52 U.S.C. 30101(13)).

Employer means the organization or person by whom an individual is employed, and not the name of his or her supervisor.

§ 100.22 Expressly advocating (52 U.S.C. 30101(17)).

Expressly advocating means any communication that—(a) Uses phrases such as "vote for the President," "re-elect your Congressman," "support the Democratic nominee," "cast your ballot for the Republican challenger for U.S. Senate in Georgia," "Smith for Congress," "Bill McKay in '94," "vote Pro-Life" or "vote Pro-Choice" accompanied by a listing of clearly identified candidates described as Pro-Life or Pro-Choice, "vote against Old Hickory," "defeat" accompanied by a picture of one or more candidate(s), "reject the incumbent," or communications of campaign slogan(s) or individual word(s), which in context can have no other reasonable meaning than to urge the election or defeat of one or more clearly identified candidate(s), such as posters, bumper stickers, advertisements, etc. which say "Nixon's the One," "Carter '76," "Reagan/Bush" or "Mondale!"; or

(b) When taken as a whole and with limited reference to external events, such as the proximity to the election, could only be interpreted by a reasonable person as containing advocacy of the election or defeat of one or more clearly identified candidate(s) because—

(1) The electoral portion of the communication is unmistakable, unambiguous, and suggestive of only one meaning; and

(2) Reasonable minds could not differ as to whether it encourages actions to elect or defeat one or more clearly identified candidate(s) or encourages some other kind of action.

[60 FR 35304, July 6, 1995]

§ 100.23 [Reserved]

§ 100.24 Federal election activity (52 U.S.C. 30101(20)).

(a) As used in this section, and in part 300 of this chapter,

(1) *In connection with an election in which a candidate for Federal office appears on the ballot* means:

(i) The period of time beginning on the date of the earliest filing deadline for access to the primary election ballot for Federal candidates as determined by State law, or in those States that do not conduct primaries, on January 1 of each even-numbered year and ending on the date of the general election, up to and including the date of any general runoff.

(ii) The period beginning on the date on which the date of a special election in which a candidate for Federal office appears on the ballot is set and ending on the date of the special election.

(2) *Voter registration activity.*

(i) Voter registration activity means:

(A) Encouraging or urging potential voters to register to vote, whether by mail (including direct mail), e-mail, in person, by telephone (including pre-recorded telephone calls, phone banks and messaging such as SMS and MMS), or by any other means;

(B) Preparing and distributing information about registration and voting;

(C) Distributing voter registration forms or instructions to potential voters;

(D) Answering questions about how to complete or file a voter registration form, or assisting potential voters in completing or filing such forms;

(E) Submitting or delivering a completed voter registration form on behalf of a potential voter;

(F) Offering or arranging to transport, or actually transporting potential voters to a board of elections or county clerk's office for them to fill out voter registration forms; or

(G) Any other activity that assists potential voters to register to vote.

(ii) Activity is not voter registration activity solely because it includes a brief exhortation to register to vote, so long as the exhortation is incidental to a communication, activity, or event. Examples of brief exhortations incidental to a communication, activity, or event include:

(A) A mailer praises the public service record of mayoral candidate X and/or discusses his campaign platform.

The mailer concludes by reminding recipients, "Don't forget to register to vote for X by October 1st."

(B) A phone call for a State party fundraiser gives listeners information about the event, solicits donations, and concludes by reminding listeners, "Don't forget to register to vote."

(3) *Get-out-the-vote activity.*

(i) Get-out-the-vote activity means:

(A) Encouraging or urging potential voters to vote, whether by mail (including direct mail), e-mail, in person, by telephone (including pre-recorded telephone calls, phone banks and messaging such as SMS and MMS), or by any other means;

(B) Informing potential voters, whether by mail (including direct mail), e-mail, in person, by telephone (including pre-recorded telephone calls, phone banks and messaging such as SMS and MMS), or by any other means, about:

(*1*) Times when polling places are open;

(*2*) The location of particular polling places; or

(*3*) Early voting or voting by absentee ballot;

(C) Offering or arranging to transport, or actually transporting, potential voters to the polls; or

(D) Any other activity that assists potential voters to vote.

(ii) Activity is not get-out-the-vote activity solely because it includes a brief exhortation to vote, so long as the exhortation is incidental to a communication, activity, or event. Examples of brief exhortations incidental to a communication, activity, or event include:

(A) A mailer praises the public service record of mayoral candidate X and/or discusses his campaign platform. The mailer concludes by reminding recipients, "Vote for X on November 4th."

(B) A phone call for a State party fundraiser gives listeners information about the event, solicits donations, and concludes by reminding listeners, "Don't forget to vote on November 4th."

(4) *Voter identification* means acquiring information about potential voters, including, but not limited to, obtaining voter lists and creating or enhancing voter lists by verifying or adding information about the voters' likelihood of voting in an upcoming election or their likelihood of voting for specific candidates. The date a voter list is acquired shall govern whether a State, district, or local party committee has obtained a voter list within the meaning of this section.

(b) As used in part 300 of this chapter, *Federal election activity* means any of the activities described in paragraphs (b)(1) through (b)(4) of this section.

(1) Voter registration activity during the period that begins on the date that is 120 calendar days before the date that a regularly scheduled Federal election is held and ends on the date of the election. For purposes of voter registration activity, the term "election" does not include any special election.

(2) The following activities conducted in connection with an election in which one or more candidates for Federal office appears on the ballot (regardless of whether one or more candidates for State or local office also appears on the ballot):

(i) Voter identification.

(ii) Generic campaign activity, as defined in 11 CFR 100.25.

(iii) Get-out-the-vote activity.

(3) A public communication that refers to a clearly identified candidate for Federal office, regardless of whether a candidate for State or local election is also mentioned or identified, and that promotes or supports, or attacks or opposes any candidate for Federal office. This paragraph applies whether or not the communication expressly advocates a vote for or against a Federal candidate.

(4) Services provided during any month by an employee of a State, district, or local committee of a political party who spends more than 25 percent of that individual's compensated time during that month on activities in connection with a Federal election.

(c) *Exceptions. Federal election activity* does not include any amount expended or disbursed by a State, district, or local committee of a political party for any of the following activities:

(1) A public communication that refers solely to one or more clearly identified candidates for State or local office and that does not promote or support, or attack or oppose a clearly identified candidate for Federal office; provided, however, that such a public communication shall be considered a Federal election activity if it constitutes voter registration activity, generic campaign activity, get-out-the-vote activity, or voter identification.

(2) A contribution to a candidate for State or local office, provided the contribution is not designated to pay for voter registration activity, voter identification, generic campaign activity, get-out-the-vote activity, a public communication, or employee services as set forth in paragraphs (a)(1) through (4) of this section.

(3) The costs of a State, district, or local political convention, meeting or conference.

(4) The costs of grassroots campaign materials, including buttons, bumper stickers, handbills, brochures, posters, and yard signs, that name or depict only candidates for State or local office.

(5) Voter identification activity that is conducted solely in connection with a non-Federal election held on a date on which no Federal election is held, and which is not used in a subsequent election in which a Federal candidate appears on the ballot.

(6) Get-out-the-vote activity that is conducted solely in connection with a non-Federal election held on a date on which no Federal election is held, provided that any communications made as part of such activity refer exclusively to:

(i) Non-Federal candidates participating in the non-Federal election, if the non-Federal candidates are not also Federal candidates;

(ii) Ballot referenda or initiatives scheduled for the date of the non-Federal election; or

(iii) The date, polling hours, and locations of the non-Federal election.

(7) *De minimis* costs associated with the following:

(i) On the Web site of a party committee or an association of State or local candidates, posting a hyperlink to a state or local election board's web page containing information on voting or registering to vote;

(ii) On the Web site of a party committee or an association of State or local candidates, enabling visitors to download a voter registration form or absentee ballot application;

(iii) On the Web site of a party committee or an association of State or local candidates, posting information about voting dates and/or polling locations and hours of operation; or

(iv) Placing voter registration forms or absentee ballot applications obtained from the board of elections at the office of a party committee or an association of State or local candidates.

[67 FR 49110, July 29, 2002, as amended at 71 FR 8932, Feb. 22, 2006; 71 FR 14360, Mar. 22, 2006; 75 FR 55267, Sept. 10, 2010]

§ 100.25 Generic campaign activity (52 U.S.C. 30101(21)).

Generic campaign activity means a public communication that promotes or opposes a political party and does not promote or oppose a clearly identified Federal candidate or a non-Federal candidate.

[67 FR 49110, July 29, 2002]

§ 100.26 Public communication (52 U.S.C. 30101(22)).

Public communication means a communication by means of any broadcast, cable, or satellite communication, newspaper, magazine, outdoor advertising facility, mass mailing, or telephone bank to the general public, or any other form of general public political advertising. The term *general public political advertising* shall not include communications over the Internet, except for communications placed for a fee on another person's Web site.

[71 FR 18612, Apr. 12, 2006]

§ 100.27 Mass mailing (52 U.S.C. 30101(23)).

Mass mailing means a mailing by United States mail or facsimile of more than 500 pieces of mail matter of an identical or substantially similar nature within any 30-day period. A mass mailing does not include electronic mail or Internet communications. For purposes of this section, *substantially similar* includes communications that include substantially the same template or language, but vary in non-material respects such as communications customized by the recipient's name, occupation, or geographic location.

[67 FR 49110, July 29, 2002]

§100.28 Telephone bank (52 U.S.C. 30101(24)).

Telephone bank means more than 500 telephone calls of an identical or substantially similar nature within any 30-day period. A telephone bank does not include electronic mail or Internet communications transmitted over telephone lines. For purposes of this section, *substantially similar* includes communications that include substantially the same template or language, but vary in non-material respects such as communications customized by the recipient's name, occupation, or geographic location.

[67 FR 49110, July 29, 2002]

§100.29 Electioneering communication (52 U.S.C. 30104(f)(3)).

(a) *Electioneering communication* means any broadcast, cable, or satellite communication that:

(1) Refers to a clearly identified candidate for Federal office;

(2) Is publicly distributed within 60 days before a general election for the office sought by the candidate; or within 30 days before a primary or preference election, or a convention or caucus of a political party that has authority to nominate a candidate, for the office sought by the candidate, and the candidate referenced is seeking the nomination of that political party; and

(3) Is targeted to the relevant electorate, in the case of a candidate for Senate or the House of Representatives.

(b) For purposes of this section—(1) *Broadcast, cable, or satellite communication* means a communication that is publicly distributed by a television station, radio station, cable television system, or satellite system.

(2) *Refers to a clearly identified candidate* means that the candidate's name, nickname, photograph, or drawing appears, or the identity of the candidate is otherwise apparent through an unambiguous reference such as "the President," "your Congressman," or "the incumbent," or through an unambiguous reference to his or her status as a candidate such as "the Democratic presidential nominee" or "the Republican candidate for Senate in the State of Georgia."

(3)(i) *Publicly distributed* means aired, broadcast, cablecast or otherwise disseminated through the facilities of a television station, radio station, cable television system, or satellite system.

(ii) In the case of a candidate for nomination for President or Vice President, *publicly distributed* means the requirements of paragraph (b)(3)(i) of this section are met and the communication:

(A) Can be received by 50,000 or more persons in a State where a primary election, as defined in 11 CFR 9032.7, is being held within 30 days; or

(B) Can be received by 50,000 or more persons anywhere in the United States within the period between 30 days before the first day of the national nominating convention and the conclusion of the convention.

(4) *A special election* or a *runoff election* is a primary election if held to nominate a candidate. A *special election* or a *runoff election* is a general election if held to elect a candidate.

(5) *Targeted to the relevant electorate* means the communication can be received by 50,000 or more persons—

(i) In the district the candidate seeks to represent, in the case of a candidate for Representative in or Delegate or Resident Commissioner to, the Congress; or

(ii) In the State the candidate seeks to represent, in the case of a candidate for Senator.

(6)(i) Information on the number of persons in a Congressional district or State that can receive a communication publicly distributed by a television station, radio station, a cable television system, or satellite system, shall be available on the Federal Communications Commission's Web site, *http://www.fcc.gov.* A link to that site is available on the Federal Election Commission's Web site, *http://www.fec.gov*. If the Federal Communications Commission's Web site indicates that a communication cannot be received by 50,000 or more persons in the specified Congressional district or State, then such information shall be a complete defense against any charge that such communication constitutes an electioneering communication, so long as such information is posted on the Federal Communications Commission's Web site on or before the date the communication is publicly distributed.

(ii) If the Federal Communications Commission's Web site does not indicate whether a communication can be received by 50,000 or more persons in the specified Congressional district or State, it shall be a complete defense against any charge that a communication reached 50,000 or more persons when the maker of a communication:

(A) Reasonably relies on written documentation obtained from the broadcast station, radio station, cable system, or satellite system that states that the communication cannot be received by 50,000 or more persons in the specified Congressional district (for U.S. House of Representatives candidates) or State (for U.S. Senate candidates or presidential primary candidates);

(B) Does not publicly distribute the communication on a broadcast station, radio station, or cable system, located in any Metropolitan Area in the specified Congressional district (for U.S. House of Representatives candidates) or State (for U.S. Senate candidates or presidential primary candidates); or

(C) Reasonably believes that the communication cannot be received by 50,000 or more persons in the specified Congressional district (for U.S. House of Representatives candidates) or State (for U.S. Senate candidates or presidential primary candidates).

(7)(i) *Can be received by 50,000 or more persons* means—

(A) In the case of a communication transmitted by an FM radio broadcast station or network, where the Congressional district or State lies entirely within the station's or network's protected or primary service contour, that

the population of the Congressional district or State is 50,000 or more; or

(B) In the case of a communication transmitted by an FM radio broadcast station or network, where a portion of the Congressional district or State lies outside of the protected or primary service contour, that the population of the part of the Congressional district or State lying within the station's or network's protected or primary service contour is 50,000 or more; or

(C) In the case of a communication transmitted by an AM radio broadcast station or network, where the Congressional district or State lies entirely within the station's or network's most outward service area, that the population of the Congressional district or State is 50,000 or more; or

(D) In the case of a communication transmitted by an AM radio broadcast station or network, where a portion of the Congressional district or State lies outside of the station's or network's most outward service area, that the population of the part of the Congressional district or State lying within the station's or network's most outward service area is 50,000 or more; or

(E) In the case of a communication appearing on a television broadcast station or network, where the Congressional district or State lies entirely within the station's or network's Grade B broadcast contour, that the population of the Congressional district or State is 50,000 or more; or

(F) In the case of a communication appearing on a television broadcast station or network, where a portion of the Congressional district or State lies outside of the Grade B broadcast contour—

(*1*) That the population of the part of the Congressional district or State lying within the station's or network's Grade B broadcast contour is 50,000 or more; or

(*2*) That the population of the part of the Congressional district or State lying within the station's or network's broadcast contour, when combined with the viewership of that television station or network by cable and satellite subscribers within the Congressional district or State lying outside the broadcast contour, is 50,000 or more; or

(G) In the case of a communication appearing exclusively on a cable or satellite television system, but not on a broadcast station or network, that the viewership of the cable system or satellite system lying within a Congressional district or State is 50,000 or more; or

(H) In the case of a communication appearing on a cable television network, that the total cable and satellite viewership within a Congressional district or State is 50,000 or more.

(ii) Cable or satellite television viewership is determined by multiplying the number of subscribers within a Congressional district or State, or a part thereof, as appropriate, by the current national average household size, as determined by the Bureau of the Census.

(iii) A determination that a communication can be received by 50,000 or more persons based on the application of the formula at paragraph (b)(7)(i)(G) or (H) of this section shall create a rebuttable presumption that may be overcome by demonstrating that—

(A) One or more cable or satellite systems did not carry the network on which the communication was publicly distributed at the time the communication was publicly distributed; and

(B) Applying the formula to the remaining cable and satellite systems results in a determination that the cable network or systems upon which the communication was publicly distributed could not be received by 50,000 persons or more.

(c) The following communications are exempt from the definition of *electioneering communication*. Any communication that:

(1) Is publicly disseminated through a means of communication other than a broadcast, cable, or satellite television or radio station. For example, electioneering communication does not include communications appearing in print media, including a newspaper or magazine, handbill, brochure, bumper sticker, yard sign, poster, billboard, and other written materials, including mailings; communications over the Internet, including electronic mail; or telephone communications;

(2) Appears in a news story, commentary, or editorial distributed through the facilities of any broadcast, cable, or satellite television or radio station, unless such facilities are owned or controlled by any political party, political committee, or candidate. A news story distributed through a broadcast, cable, or satellite television or radio station owned or controlled by any political party, political committee, or candidate is nevertheless exempt if the news story meets the requirements described in 11 CFR 100.132(a) and (b);

(3) Constitutes an expenditure or independent expenditure provided that the expenditure or independent expenditure is required to be reported under the Act or Commission regulations;

(4) Constitutes a candidate debate or forum conducted pursuant to 11 CFR 110.13, or that solely promotes such a debate or forum and is made by or on behalf of the person sponsoring the debate or forum; or

(5) Is paid for by a candidate for State or local office in connection with an election to State or local office, provided that the communication does not promote, support, attack or oppose any Federal candidate. *See* 11 CFR 300.71 for communications paid for by a candidate for State or local office that promotes, supports, attacks or opposes a Federal candidate.

[67 FR 65210, 65217, Oct. 23, 2002, as amended at 70 FR 75717, Dec. 21, 2005; 79 FR 16663, Mar. 26, 2014]

§§ 100.30–100.32 [Reserved]

§ 100.33 Personal funds.

Personal funds of a candidate means the sum of all of the following:

(a) *Assets.* Amounts derived from any asset that, under applicable State law, at the time the individual became a candidate, the candidate had legal right of access to or control over, and with respect to which the candidate had—

(1) Legal and rightful title; or

(2) An equitable interest;

(b) *Income.* Income received during the current election cycle, of the candidate, including:

(1) A salary and other earned income that the candidate earns from bona fide employment;

(2) Income from the candidate's stocks or other investments including interest, dividends, or proceeds from the sale or liquidation of such stocks or investments;

(3) Bequests to the candidate;

(4) Income from trusts established before the beginning of the election cycle;

(5) Income from trusts established by bequest after the beginning of the election cycle of which the candidate is the beneficiary;

(6) Gifts of a personal nature that had been customarily received by the candidate prior to the beginning of the election cycle; and

(7) Proceeds from lotteries and similar legal games of chance; and

(c) *Jointly owned assets.* Amounts derived from a portion of assets that are owned jointly by the candidate and the candidate's spouse as follows:

(1) The portion of assets that is equal to the candidate's share of the asset under the instrument of conveyance or ownership; provided, however,

(2) If no specific share is indicated by an instrument of conveyance or ownership, the value of one-half of the property.

[73 FR 79601, Dec. 30, 2008]

§§ 100.34–100.50 [Reserved]

Subpart B—Definition of Contribution (52 U.S.C. 30101(8))

SOURCE: 67 FR 50585, Aug. 5, 2002, unless otherwise noted.

§ 100.51 Scope.

(a) The term *contribution* includes the payments, services, or other things of value described in this subpart.

(b) For the purpose of this subpart, a contribution or payment made by an individual shall not be attributed to any other individual, unless otherwise specified by that other individual in accordance with 11 CFR 110.1(k).

§ 100.52 Gift, subscription, loan, advance or deposit of money.

(a) A gift, subscription, loan (except for a loan made in accordance with 11 CFR 100.82 and 100.83), advance, or deposit of money or anything of value made by any person for the purpose of influencing any election for Federal office is a contribution.

(b) For purposes of this section, the term *loan* includes a guarantee, endorsement, and any other form of security.

(1) A loan that exceeds the contribution limitations of 52 U.S.C. 30116 and 11 CFR part 110 shall be unlawful whether or not it is repaid.

(2) A loan is a contribution at the time it is made and is a contribution to the extent that it remains unpaid. The aggregate amount loaned to a candidate or committee by a contributor, when added to other contributions from that individual to that candidate or committee, shall not exceed the contribution limitations set forth at 11 CFR part 110. A loan, to the extent it is repaid, is no longer a contribution.

(3) Except as provided in paragraph (b)(4) of this section, a loan is a contribution by each endorser or guarantor. Each endorser or guarantor shall be deemed to have contributed that portion of the total amount of the loan for which he or she agreed to be liable in a written agreement. Any reduction in the unpaid balance of the loan shall reduce proportionately the amount endorsed or guaranteed by each endorser or guarantor in such written agreement. In the event that such agreement does not stipulate the portion of the loan for which each endorser or guarantor is liable, the loan shall be considered a loan by each endorser or guarantor in the same proportion to the unpaid balance that each endorser or guarantor bears to the total number of endorsers or guarantors.

(4) A candidate may obtain a loan on which his or her spouse's signature is required when jointly owned assets are used as collateral or security for the loan. The spouse shall not be considered a contributor to the candidate's campaign if the value of the candidate's share of the property used as collateral equals or exceeds the amount of the loan that is used for the candidate's campaign.

(5) If a political committee makes a loan to any person, such loan shall be subject to the limitations of 11 CFR part 110. Repayment of the principal amount of such loan to such political

committee shall not be a contribution by the debtor to the lender committee. Such repayment shall be made with funds that are subject to the prohibitions of 11 CFR 110.20 and part 114. The payment of interest to such committee by the debtor shall be a contribution only to the extent that the interest paid exceeds a commercially reasonable rate prevailing at the time the loan is made. All payments of interest shall be made from funds subject to the prohibitions of 11 CFR 110.20 and part 114.

(c) For purposes of this section, the term *money* includes currency of the United States or of any foreign nation, checks, money orders, or any other negotiable instruments payable on demand.

(d)(1) For purposes of this section, the term *anything of value* includes all in-kind contributions. Unless specifically exempted under 11 CFR part 100, subpart C, the provision of any goods or services without charge or at a charge that is less than the usual and normal charge for such goods or services is a contribution. Examples of such goods or services include, but are not limited to: Securities, facilities, equipment, supplies, personnel, advertising services, membership lists, and mailing lists. If goods or services are provided at less than the usual and normal charge, the amount of the in-kind contribution is the difference between the usual and normal charge for the goods or services at the time of the contribution and the amount charged the political committee.

(2) For purposes of paragraph (d)(1) of this section, *usual and normal charge for goods* means the price of those goods in the market from which they ordinarily would have been purchased at the time of the contribution; and usual and normal charge for any services, other than those provided by an unpaid volunteer, means the hourly or piecework charge for the services at a commercially reasonable rate prevailing at the time the services were rendered.

[67 FR 50585, Aug. 5, 2002, as amended at 67 FR 78680, Dec. 26, 2002; 79 FR 16663, Mar. 26, 2014; 79 FR 77845, Dec. 29, 2014]

§100.53 Attendance at a fundraiser or political event.

The entire amount paid to attend a fundraiser or other political event and the entire amount paid as the purchase price for a fundraising item sold by a political committee is a contribution.

§100.54 Compensation for personal services.

The payment by any person of compensation for the personal services of another person if those services are rendered without charge to a political committee for any purpose, except for legal and accounting services provided under 11 CFR 100.85 and 100.86, is a contribution. No compensation is considered paid to any employee under any of the following conditions:

(a) *Paid on an hourly or salaried basis.* If an employee is paid on an hourly or salaried basis and is expected to work a particular number of hours per period, no contribution results if the employee engages in political activity during what would otherwise be a regular work period, provided that the taken or released time is made up or completed by the employee within a reasonable time.

(b) *Paid on commission or piecework basis.* No contribution results where an employee engages in political activity during what would otherwise be normal working hours if the employee is paid on a commission or piecework basis, or is paid only for work actually performed and the employee's time is considered his or her own to use as he or she sees fit.

(c) *Vacation or earned leave time.* No contribution results where the time used by the employee to engage in political activity is bona fide, although compensable, vacation time or other earned leave time.

[67 FR 50585, Aug. 5, 2002, as amended at 81 FR 34863, June 1, 2016]

§100.55 Extension of credit.

The extension of credit by any person is a contribution unless the credit is extended in the ordinary course of the person's business and the terms are substantially similar to extensions of credit to nonpolitical debtors that are of similar risk and size of obligation. If a creditor fails to make a commercially reasonable attempt to collect the debt, a contribution will result. (See 11 CFR 116.3 and 116.4.) If a debt owed by a political committee is forgiven or settled for less than the amount owed, a contribution results unless such debt is settled in accordance with the standards set forth at 11 CFR 116.3 and 116.4.

§ 100.56　Office building or facility for national party committees.

A gift, subscription, loan, advance, or deposit of money or anything of value to a national party committee for the purchase or construction of an office building or facility is a contribution.

§ 100.57　[Reserved]

Subpart C—Exceptions to Contributions

Source: 67 FR 50585, Aug. 5, 2002, unless otherwise noted.

§ 100.71　Scope.

(a) The term *contribution* does not include payments, services or other things of value described in this subpart.

(b) For the purpose of this subpart, a contribution or payment made by an individual shall not be attributed to any other individual, unless otherwise specified by that other individual in accordance with 11 CFR 110.1(k).

§ 100.72　Testing the waters.

(a) *General exemption.* Funds received solely for the purpose of determining whether an individual should become a candidate are not contributions. Examples of activities permissible under this exemption if they are conducted to determine whether an individual should become a candidate include, but are not limited to, conducting a poll, telephone calls, and travel. Only funds permissible under the Act may be used for such activities. The individual shall keep records of all such funds received. See 11 CFR 101.3. If the individual subsequently becomes a candidate, the funds received are contributions subject to the reporting requirements of the Act. Such contributions must be reported with the first report filed by

the principal campaign committee of the candidate, regardless of the date the funds were received.

(b) *Exemption not applicable to individuals who have decided to become candidates.* This exemption does not apply to funds received for activities indicating that an individual has decided to become a candidate for a particular office or for activities relevant to conducting a campaign. Examples of activities that indicate that an individual has decided to become a candidate include, but are not limited to:

(1) The individual uses general public political advertising to publicize his or her intention to campaign for Federal office.

(2) The individual raises funds in excess of what could reasonably be expected to be used for exploratory activities or undertakes activities designed to amass campaign funds that would be spent after he or she becomes a candidate.

(3) The individual makes or authorizes written or oral statements that refer to him or her as a candidate for a particular office.

(4) The individual conducts activities in close proximity to the election or over a protracted period of time.

(5) The individual has taken action to qualify for the ballot under State law.

§ 100.73　News story, commentary, or editorial by the media.

Any cost incurred in covering or carrying a news story, commentary, or editorial by any broadcasting station (including a cable television operator, programmer or producer), Web site, newspaper, magazine, or other periodical publication, including any Internet or electronic publication, is not a contribution unless the facility is owned or controlled by any political party, political committee, or candidate, in which case the costs for a news story:

(a) That represents a *bona fide* news account communicated in a publication of general circulation or on a licensed broadcasting facility; and

(b) That is part of a general pattern of campaign-related news accounts that give reasonably equal coverage to all opposing candidates in the circulation or listening area, is not a contribution.

[67 FR 50585, Aug. 5, 2002, as amended at 71 FR 18613, Apr. 12, 2006]

§100.74 Uncompensated services by volunteers.

The value of services provided without compensation by any individual who volunteers on behalf of a candidate or political committee is not a contribution.

§100.75 Use of a volunteer's real or personal property.

No contribution results where an individual, in the course of volunteering personal services on his or her residential premises to any candidate or to any political committee of a political party, provides the use of his or her real or personal property to such candidate for candidate-related activity or to such political committee of a political party for party-related activity. For the purposes of this section, an individual's residential premises, shall include a recreation room in a residential complex where the individual volunteering services resides, provided that the room is available for use without regard to political affiliation. A nominal fee paid by such individual for the use of such room is not a contribution.

§100.76 Use of church or community room.

No contribution results where an individual, in the course of volunteering personal services to any candidate or political committee of a political party, obtains the use of a church or community room and provides such room to any candidate for candidate-related activity or to any political committee of a political party for party-related activity, provided that the room is used on a regular basis by members of the community for non-commercial purposes and the room is available for use by members of the community without regard to political affiliation. A nominal fee paid by such individual for the use of such room is not a contribution.

§100.77 Invitations, food, and beverages.

The cost of invitations, food and beverages is not a contribution where such items are voluntarily provided by an individual volunteering personal services on the individual's residential premises or in a church or community room as specified at 11 CFR 100.75 and 100.76 to a candidate for candidate-related activity or to any political committee of a political party for party-related activity, to the extent that: The aggregate value of such invitations, food and beverages provided by the individual on behalf of the candidate does not exceed $1,000 with respect to any single election; and on behalf of all political committees of each political party does not exceed $2,000 in any calendar year.

[69 FR 68238, Nov. 24, 2004]

§100.78 Sale of food or beverages by vendor.

The sale of any food or beverage by a vendor (whether incorporated or not) for use in a candidate's campaign, or for use by a political committee of a political party, at a charge less than the normal or comparable commercial rate, is not a contribution, provided that the charge is at least equal to the cost of such food or beverage to the vendor, to the extent that: The aggregate value of such discount given by the vendor on behalf of any single candidate does not exceed $1,000 with respect to any single election; and on behalf of all political committees of each political party does not exceed $2,000 in a calendar year.

§100.79 Unreimbursed payment for transportation and subsistence expenses.

(a) *Transportation expenses.* Any unreimbursed payment for transportation expenses incurred by any individual on behalf of any candidate or any political committee of a political party is not a contribution to the extent that:

(1) The aggregate value of the payments made by such individual on behalf of a candidate does not exceed $1,000 with respect to a single election; and

(2) The aggregate value of the payments made by such individual on behalf of all political committees of each political party does not exceed $2,000 in a calendar year.

(b) *Subsistence expenses.* Any unreimbursed payment from a volunteer's personal funds for usual and normal subsistence expenses incidental to volunteer activity is not a contribution.

§ 100.80 **Slate cards and sample ballots.**

The payment by a State or local committee of a political party of the costs of preparation, display, or mailing or other distribution incurred by such committee with respect to a printed slate card, sample ballot, palm card, or other printed listing(s) of three or more candidates for any public office for which an election is held in the State in which the committee is organized is not a contribution. The payment of the portion of such costs allocable to Federal candidates must be made from funds subject to the limitations and prohibitions of the Act. If made by a political committee, such payments shall be reported by that committee as disbursements, but need not be allocated in committee reports to specific candidates. This exemption shall not apply to costs incurred by such a committee with respect to the preparation and display of listings made on broadcasting stations, or in newspapers, magazines, and similar types of general public political advertising such as billboards. *But see* 11 CFR 100.24, 104.17(a) and part 300, subpart B for exempt activities that also constitute Federal election activity.

§ 100.81 **Payments by corporations and labor organizations.**

Any payment made or obligation incurred by a corporation or a labor organization is not a contribution, if under the provisions of 11 CFR part 114 such payment or obligation would not constitute an expenditure by the corporation or labor organization.

§ 100.82 **Bank loans.**

(a) *General provisions.* A loan of money to a political committee or a candidate by a State bank, a federally chartered depository institution (including a national bank) or a depository institution whose deposits and accounts are insured by the Federal Deposit Insurance Corporation or the National Credit Union Administration is not a contribution by the lending institution if such loan is made in accordance with applicable banking laws and regulations and is made in the ordinary course of business. A loan will be deemed to be made in the ordinary course of business if it:

(1) Bears the usual and customary interest rate of the lending institution for the category of loan involved;

(2) Is made on a basis that assures repayment;

(3) Is evidenced by a written instrument; and

(4) Is subject to a due date or amortization schedule.

(b) *Reporting.* Such loans shall be reported by the political committee in accordance with 11 CFR 104.3(a) and (d).

(c) *Endorsers and guarantors.* Each endorser or guarantor shall be deemed to have contributed that portion of the total amount of the loan for which he or she agreed to be liable in a written agreement, except that, in the event of a signature by the candidate's spouse, the provisions of 11 CFR 100.52(b)(4) shall apply. Any reduction in the unpaid balance of the loan shall reduce proportionately the amount endorsed or guaranteed by each endorser or guarantor in such written agreement. In the event that such agreement does not stipulate the portion of the loan for which each endorser or guarantor is liable, the loan shall be considered a contribution by each endorser or guarantor in the same proportion to the unpaid balance that each endorser or guarantor bears to the total number of endorsers or guarantors.

(d) *Overdrafts.* For purposes of this section, an overdraft made on a checking or savings account of a political committee shall be considered a contribution by the bank or institution unless:

(1) The overdraft is made on an account that is subject to automatic overdraft protection;

(2) The overdraft is subject to a definite interest rate that is usual and customary; and

(3) There is a definite repayment schedule.

(e) *Made on a basis that assures repayment.* A loan, including a line of credit, shall be considered made on a basis that assures repayment if it is obtained using either of the sources of repayment described in paragraphs (e)(1) or (2) of this section, or a combination of paragraphs (e)(1) and (2) of this section:

(1)(i) The lending institution making the loan has perfected a security interest in collateral owned by the candidate or political committee receiving the loan, the fair market value of the collateral is equal to or greater than the loan amount and any senior liens as determined on the date of the loan, and the candidate or political committee provides documentation to show that the lending institution has a perfected security interest in the collateral. Sources of collateral include, but are not limited to, ownership in real estate, personal property, goods, negotiable instruments, certificates of deposit, chattel papers, stocks, accounts receivable and cash on deposit.

(ii) Amounts guaranteed by secondary sources of repayment, such as guarantors and cosigners, shall not exceed the contribution limits of 11 CFR part 110 or contravene the prohibitions of 11 CFR 110.4, 110.20, part 114 and part 115; or

(2) The lending institution making the loan has obtained a written agreement whereby the candidate or political committee receiving the loan has pledged future receipts, such as public financing payments under 11 CFR part 9001 through part 9012, or part 9031 through part 9039, contributions, or interest income, provided that:

(i) The amount of the loan or loans obtained on the basis of such funds does not exceed the amount of pledged funds;

(ii) Loan amounts are based on a reasonable expectation of the receipt of pledged funds. To that end, the candidate or political committee must furnish the lending institution documentation, *i.e.*, cash flow charts or other financial plans, that reasonably establish that such future funds will be available;

(iii) A separate depository account is established at the lending institution or the lender obtains an assignment from the candidate or political committee to access funds in a committee account at another depository institution that meets the requirements of 11 CFR 103.2, and the committee has notified the other institution of this assignment;

(iv) The loan agreement requires the deposit of the public financing payments, contributions and interest income pledged as collateral into the separate depository account for the purpose of retiring the debt according to the repayment requirements of the loan agreement; and

(v) In the case of public financing payments, the borrower authorizes the Secretary of the Treasury to directly deposit the payments into the depository account for the purpose of retiring the debt.

(3) If the requirements set forth in this paragraph are not met, the Commission will consider the totality of the circumstances on a case-by-case basis in determining whether a loan was made on a basis that assures repayment.

(f) This section shall not apply to loans described in 11 CFR 100.83.

[67 FR 50585, Aug. 5, 2002, as amended at 67 FR 78680, Dec. 26, 2002; 79 FR 16663, Mar. 26, 2014]

§ 100.83 **Brokerage loans and lines of credit to candidates.**

(a) *General provisions.* Any loan of money derived from an advance on a candidate's brokerage account, credit card, home equity line of credit, or other line of credit available to the candidate, including an overdraft made on a personal checking or savings account of a candidate, provided that:

(1) Such loan is made in accordance with applicable law and under commercially reasonable terms; and

(2) The person making such loan makes loans derived from an advance on a candidate's brokerage account, credit card, home equity line of credit, or other line of credit in the normal course of the person's business.

(b) *Endorsers and guarantors.* Each endorser, guarantor, or co-signer shall be deemed to have contributed that portion of the total amount of the loan derived from an advance on a candidate's brokerage account, credit card, home equity line of credit, or other line of credit available to the candidate, for which he or she agreed to be liable in a written agreement, including a loan used for the candidate's routine living expenses. Any reduction in the unpaid balance of the loan, advance, or line of credit shall reduce proportionately the amount endorsed or guaranteed by each endorser or guarantor in such written agreement. In the event that such agreement does not stipulate the portion of the loan, advance, or line of credit for which each endorser, guarantor, or co-signer is liable, the loan shall be considered a contribution by each endorser or guarantor in the same proportion to the unpaid balance that each endorser, guarantor, or co-signer bears to the total number of endorsers or guarantors. However, if the spouse of the candidate is the endorser, guarantor, or co-signer, the spouse shall not be deemed to make a contribution if:

(1) For a secured loan, the value of the candidate's share of the property used as collateral equals or exceeds the amount of the loan that is used for the candidate's campaign; or

(2) For an unsecured loan, the amount of the loan used for in connection with the candidate's campaign does not exceed one-half of the available credit extended by the unsecured loan.

(c) *Routine living expenses.* (1) A loan derived from an advance on a candidate's brokerage account, credit card, home equity line of credit, or other line of credit available to the candidate, that is used by the candidate solely for routine living expenses, as described in 11 CFR 100.153, does not need to be reported under 11 CFR part 104 provided that the loan, advance, or line of credit is repaid exclusively from the personal funds of the candidate or payments that would have been made irrespective of the candidacy pursuant to 11 CFR 113.1(g)(6).

(2) Any repayment, in part or in whole, of the loan, advance, or line of credit described in paragraph (c)(1) of this section by the candidate's authorized committee constitutes the personal use of campaign funds and is prohibited by 11 CFR 113.2.

(3) Any repayment or forgiveness, in part or in whole, of the loan, advance, or line of credit described in paragraph (c)(1) of this section by a third party (other than a third party whose payments are permissible under 11 CFR 113.1(g)(6)) or the lending institution is a contribution, subject to the limitations and prohibitions of 11 CFR parts 110 and 114, and shall be reported under 11 CFR part 104.

(4) Notwithstanding paragraph (c)(1) of this section, the portion of any loan or advance from a candidate's brokerage account, credit card account, home equity line of credit, or other line of credit that is used for the purpose of influencing the candidate's election for Federal office shall be reported under 11 CFR part 104.

(d) *Repayment.* The candidate's authorized committee may repay a loan from the candidate that is derived from an advance on a candidate's brokerage account, credit card, home equity line of credit, or other line of credit available to the candidate, directly to the candidate or the original lender. The amount of the repayment shall not exceed the amount of the principal used for the purpose of influencing the candidate's election for Federal office and interest that has accrued on that principal.

(e) *Reporting.* Loans derived from an advance on a candidate's brokerage account, credit card, home equity line of credit, or other line of credit available to the candidate shall be reported by the candidate's principal campaign committee in accordance with 11 CFR part 104.

§ 100.84 Office building for State, local, or district party committees or organizations.

A donation made to a non-Federal account of a State, local, or district party committee or organization in accordance with 11 CFR 300.35 for the purchase or construction of an office building is not a contribution. A donation includes a gift, subscription, loan, advance, or deposit of money or anything of value.

§100.85 Legal or accounting services to political party committees.

Legal or accounting services rendered to or on behalf of any political committee of a political party are not contributions if the person paying for such services is the regular employer of the individual rendering the services and such services are not attributable to activities that directly further the election of any designated candidate for Federal office. For purposes of this section, a partnership shall be deemed to be the regular employer of a partner. Amounts paid by the regular employer for such services shall be reported by the committee receiving such services in accordance with 11 CFR 104.3(h).

§100.86 Legal or accounting services to other political committees.

Legal or accounting services rendered to or on behalf of an authorized committee of a candidate or any other political committee are not contributions if the person paying for such services is the regular employer of the individual rendering the services and if such services are solely to ensure compliance with the Act or 26 U.S.C. 9001 *et seq.* and 9031 *et seq.* For purposes of this section, a partnership shall be deemed to be the regular employer of a partner. Amounts paid by the regular employer for these services shall be reported by the committee receiving such services in accordance with 11 CFR 104.3(h).

§100.87 Volunteer activity for party committees.

The payment by a state or local committee of a political party of the costs of campaign materials (such as pins, bumper stickers, handbills, brochures, posters, party tabloids or newsletters, and yard signs) used by such committee in connection with volunteer activities on behalf of any nominee(s) of such party is not a contribution, provided that the following conditions are met:

(a) *Exemption not applicable to general public communication or political advertising.* Such payment is not for cost incurred in connection with any broadcasting, newspaper, magazine, bill board, direct mail, or similar type of general public communication or political advertising. For purposes of this paragraph, the term *direct mail* means any mailing(s) by a commercial vendor or any mailing(s) made from commercial lists.

(b) *Allocation.* The portion of the cost of such materials allocable to Federal candidates must be paid from contributions subject to the limitations and prohibitions of the Act. *But see* 11 CFR 100.24, 104.17(a), and part 300, subpart B for exempt activities that also constitute Federal election activity.

(c) *Contributions designated for particular Federal candidates.* Such payment is not made from contributions designated by the donor to be spent on behalf of a particular candidate or candidates for Federal office. For purposes of this paragraph, a contribution shall not be considered a designated contribution if the party committee disbursing the funds makes the final decision regarding which candidate(s) shall receive the benefit of such disbursement.

(d) *Distribution of materials by volunteers.* Such materials are distributed by volunteers and not by commercial or for-profit operations. For the purposes of this paragraph, payments by the party organization for travel and subsistence or customary token payments to volunteers do not remove such individuals from the volunteer category.

(e) *Reporting.* If made by a political committee such payments shall be reported by the political committee as disbursements in accordance with 11 CFR 104.3 but need not be allocated to specific candidates in committee reports.

(f) *State candidates and their campaign committees.* Payments by a State candidate or his or her campaign committee to a State or local political party committee for the State candidate's share of expenses for such campaign materials are not contributions, provided the amount paid by the State candidate or his or her committee does not exceed his or her proportionate share of the expenses.

(g) *Exemption not applicable to campaign materials purchased by national party committees.* Campaign materials purchased by the national committee of a political party and delivered to a

State or local party committee, or materials purchased with funds donated by the national committee to such State or local committee for the purchase of such materials, shall not qualify under this exemption. Rather, the cost of such materials shall be subject to the limitations of 52 U.S.C. 30116(d) and 11 CFR 109.32.

[67 FR 50585, Aug. 5, 2002, as amended at 67 FR 78680, Dec. 26, 2002; 79 FR 77845, Dec. 29, 2014]

§ 100.88 Volunteer activity for candidates.

(a) The payment by a candidate for any public office (including State or local office), or by such candidate's authorized committee, of the costs of that candidate's campaign materials that include information on or any reference to a candidate for Federal office and that are used in connection with volunteer activities (such as pins, bumper stickers, handbills, brochures, posters, and yard signs) is not a contribution to such candidate for Federal office, provided that the payment is not for the use of broadcasting, newspapers, magazines, billboards, direct mail or similar types of general public communication or political advertising.

(b) The payment of the portion of the cost of such materials allocable to Federal candidates shall be made from contributions subject to the limitations and prohibitions of the Act. For purposes of this section, the term *direct mail* means any mailing(s) by commercial vendors or mailing(s) made from lists that were not developed by the candidate. *But see* 11 CFR 100.24, 104.17(a), and part 300, subparts D and E for exempt activities that also constitute Federal election activity.

§ 100.89 Voter registration and get-out-the-vote activities for Presidential candidates.

The payment by a State or local committee of a political party of the costs of voter registration and get-out-the-vote activities conducted by such committee on behalf of the Presidential and Vice Presidential nominee(s) of that party, is not a contribution to such candidate(s) provided that the following conditions are met:

(a) *Exemption not applicable to general public communication or political advertising.* Such payment is not for the costs incurred in connection with any broadcasting, newspaper, magazine, billboard, direct mail, or similar type of general public communication or political advertising. For purposes of this paragraph, the term *direct mail* means any mailing(s) by a commercial vendor or any mailing(s) made from commercial lists.

(b) *Allocation.* The portion of the costs of such activities allocable to Federal candidates is paid from contributions subject to the limitations and prohibitions of the Act. *But see* 11 CFR 100.24, 104.17(a), and part 300, subpart B for exempt activities that also constitute Federal election activity.

(c) *Contributions designated for particular Federal candidates.* Such payment is not made from contributions designated to be spent on behalf of a particular candidate or candidates for Federal office. For purposes of this paragraph, a contribution shall not be considered a designated contribution if the party committee disbursing the funds makes the final decision regarding which candidate(s) shall receive the benefit of such disbursement.

(d) *References to House or Senate candidates.* For purposes of this section, if such activities include references to any candidate(s) for the House or Senate, the costs of such activities that are allocable to that candidate(s) shall be a contribution to such candidate(s) unless the mention of such candidate(s) is merely incidental to the overall activity.

(e) *Phone banks.* For purposes of this section, payment of the costs incurred in the use of phone banks in connection with voter registration and get-out-the-vote activities is not a contribution when such phone banks are operated by volunteer workers. The use of paid professionals to design the phone bank system, develop calling instructions and train supervisors is permissible. The payment of the costs of such professional services is not an expenditure but shall be reported as a disbursement in accordance with 11 CFR 104.3 if made by a political committee.

(f) *Reporting of payments for voter registration and get-out-the-vote activities.* If made by a political committee, such payments for voter registration and get-out-the-vote activities shall be reported by that committee as disbursements in accordance with 11 CFR 104.3, but such payments need not be allocated to specific candidates in committee reports except as provided in 11 CFR paragraph (d) of this section.

(g) *Exemption not applicable to donations by a national committee of a political party to a State or local party committee for voter registration and get-out-the-vote activities.* Payments made from funds donated by a national committee of a political party to a State or local party committee for voter registration and get-out-the-vote activities shall not qualify under this exemption. Rather, such funds shall be subject to the limitations of 52 U.S.C. 30116(d) and 11 CFR 109.32.

[67 FR 50585, Aug. 5, 2002, as amended at 67 FR 78680, Dec. 26, 2002; 69 FR 68238, Nov. 24, 2004; 75 FR 31, Jan. 4, 2010; 79 FR 77845, Dec. 29, 2014]

§100.90 Ballot access fees.

Payments made to any party committee by a candidate or the authorized committee of a candidate as a condition of ballot access are not contributions.

§100.91 Recounts.

A gift, subscription, loan, advance, or deposit of money or anything of value made with respect to a recount of the results of a Federal election, or an election contest concerning a Federal election, is not a contribution except that the prohibitions of 11 CFR 110.20 and part 114 apply.

[67 FR 50585, Aug. 5, 2002, as amended at 67 FR 78680, Dec. 26, 2002]

§100.92 Candidate debates.

Funds provided to defray costs incurred in staging candidate debates in accordance with the provisions of 11 CFR 110.13 and 114.4(f) are not contributions.

§100.93 Travel by aircraft or other means of transportation.

(a) *Scope and definitions.* (1) This section applies to all campaign travelers who use non-commercial travel.

(2) Campaign travelers who use commercial travel, such as a commercial airline flight, charter flight, taxi, or an automobile provided by a rental company, are governed by 11 CFR 100.52(a) and (d), not this section.

(3) For the purposes of this section:

(i) *Campaign traveler* means

(A) Any candidate traveling in connection with an election for Federal office or any individual traveling in connection with an election for Federal office on behalf of a candidate or political committee; or

(B) Any member of the news media traveling with a candidate.

(ii) *Service provider* means the owner of an aircraft or other conveyance, or a person who leases an aircraft or other conveyance from the owner or otherwise obtains a legal right to the use of an aircraft or other conveyance, and who uses the aircraft or other conveyance to provide transportation to a campaign traveler. For a jointly owned or leased aircraft or other conveyance, the service provider is the person who makes the aircraft or other conveyance available to the campaign traveler.

(iii) *Unreimbursed value* means the difference between the value of the transportation service provided, as set forth in this section, and the amount of payment for that transportation service by the political committee or campaign traveler to the service provider within the time limits set forth in this section.

(iv) *Commercial travel* means travel aboard:

(A) An aircraft operated by an air carrier or commercial operator certificated by the Federal Aviation Administration, provided that the flight is required to be conducted under Federal Aviation Administration air carrier safety rules, or, in the case of travel which is abroad, by an air carrier or commercial operator certificated by an appropriate foreign civil aviation authority, provided that the flight is required to be conducted under air carrier safety rules; or

(B) Other means of transportation operated for commercial passenger service.

(v) *Non-commercial travel* means travel aboard any conveyance that is not commercial travel, as defined in paragraph (a)(3)(iv) of this section.

(vi) *Comparable aircraft* means an aircraft of similar make and model as the aircraft that actually makes the trip, with similar amenities as that aircraft.

(b) *General rule.* (1) No contribution is made by a service provider to a candidate or political committee if:

(i) Every candidate's authorized committee or other political committee on behalf of which the travel is conducted pays the service provider, within the required time, for the full value of the transportation, as determined in accordance with paragraphs (c), (d), (e) or (g) of this section, provided to all campaign travelers who are traveling on behalf of that candidate or political committee; or

(ii) Every campaign traveler for whom payment is not made under paragraph (b)(1)(i) of this section pays the service provider for the full value of the transportation provided to that campaign traveler as determined in accordance with paragraphs (c), (d), (e) or (g) of this section. *See* 11 CFR 100.79 and 100.139 for treatment of certain unreimbursed transportation expenses incurred by individuals traveling on behalf of candidates, authorized committees, and political committees of political parties.

(2) Except as provided in 11 CFR 100.79, the unreimbursed value of transportation provided to any campaign traveler, as determined in accordance with paragraphs (c), (d) or (e) of this section, is an in-kind contribution from the service provider to the candidate or political committee on whose behalf, or with whom, the campaign traveler traveled. Contributions are subject to the reporting requirements, limitations and prohibitions of the Act.

(3) When a candidate is accompanied by a member of the news media, or by security personnel provided by any Federal or State government, the news media or government security provider may reimburse the political committee paying for the pro-rata share of the travel by the member of the media or security personnel, or may pay the service provider directly for that prorata share, up to the applicable amount set forth in paragraphs (c)(1), (c)(3), (d), (e), or (g) of this section. A payment made directly to the service provider may be subtracted from the amount for which the political committee is otherwise responsible without any contribution resulting. No contribution results from reimbursement by the media or a government security provider to a political committee in accordance with this paragraph.

(c) *Travel on aircraft.* When a campaign traveler uses aircraft for noncommercial travel, other than a government aircraft described in paragraph (e) of this section or a candidate or family owned aircraft described in paragraph (g) of this section, reimbursement must be provided no later than seven (7) calendar days after the date the flight began at one of the following rates to avoid the receipt of an in-kind contribution:

(1) *Travel by or on behalf of Senate, presidential, or vice-presidential candidates.* A Senate, presidential, or vice-presidential candidate traveling on his own behalf, or any person traveling on behalf of such candidate or the candidate's authorized committee must pay the pro rata share per campaign traveler of the normal and usual charter fare or rental charge for travel on a comparable aircraft of comparable size. The pro rata share shall be calculated by dividing the normal and usual charter fare or rental charge by the number of campaign travelers on the flight that are traveling on behalf of such candidates or their authorized committees, including members of the news media, and security personnel traveling with a candidate. No portion of the normal and usual charter fare or rental charge may be attributed to any campaign travelers that are not traveling on behalf of such candidates or their authorized committees, or any other passengers, except as permitted under paragraph (b)(3) of this section.

(2) *Travel by or on behalf of House candidates and their leadership PACs.* Except as otherwise provided in paragraphs (e) and (g) of this section, a campaign traveler who is a candidate for election for the office of Representative in, or Delegate or Resident Commissioner to, the Congress, or a person traveling on behalf of any such candidate or any authorized committee or leadership PAC of such candidate, is

prohibited from non-commercial travel on behalf of any such candidate or any authorized committee or leadership PAC of such candidate.

(3) *Other campaign travelers.* When a candidate's authorized committee pays for a flight pursuant to paragraph (c)(1) of this section, no payment is required from other campaign travelers on that flight. Otherwise, a campaign traveler not covered by paragraphs (c)(1) or (c)(2) of this section, including persons traveling on behalf of a political party committee, separate segregated fund, nonconnected political committee, or a leadership PAC other than a leadership PAC of a candidate for election for the office of Representative in, or Delegate or Resident Commissioner to, the Congress, must pay the service provider no less than the following for each leg of the trip:

(i) In the case of travel between cities served by regularly scheduled first-class commercial airline service, the lowest unrestricted and non-discounted first-class airfare;

(ii) In the case of travel between a city served by regularly scheduled coach commercial airline service, but not regularly scheduled first-class commercial airline service, and a city served by regularly scheduled coach commercial airline service (with or without first-class commercial airline service), the lowest unrestricted and non-discounted coach airfare; or

(iii) In the case of travel to or from a city not served by regularly scheduled commercial airline service, the normal and usual charter fare or rental charge for a comparable commercial aircraft of sufficient size to accommodate all campaign travelers, and security personnel, if applicable.

(d) *Other means of transportation.* If a campaign traveler uses any means of transportation other than an aircraft, including an automobile, or train, or boat, the campaign traveler, or the political committee on whose behalf the travel is conducted, must pay the service provider within thirty (30) calendar days after the date of receipt of the invoice for such travel, but not later than sixty (60) calendar days after the date the travel began, at the normal and usual fare or rental charge for a comparable commercial conveyance of

sufficient size to accommodate all campaign travelers, including members of the news media traveling with a candidate, and security personnel, if applicable.

(e) *Government conveyances—*(1) *Travel by or on behalf of candidates, their authorized committees, or House candidate Leadership PACs.* If a campaign traveler traveling on behalf of a candidate, an authorized committee, or the leadership PAC of a House candidate uses an aircraft that is provided by the Federal government, or by a State or local government, the campaign traveler, or the political committee on whose behalf the travel is conducted, must pay the government entity, within the time specified by that government entity, *either:*

(i) The pro rata share per campaign traveler of the normal and usual charter fare or rental charge for the flight on a comparable aircraft of sufficient size to accommodate all campaign travelers. The pro rata share shall be calculated by dividing the normal and usual charter fare or rental charge by the number of campaign travelers on the flight that are traveling on behalf of candidates, authorized committees, or House candidate leadership PACs, including members of the news media, and security personnel, if applicable. No portion of the normal and usual charter fare or rental charge may be attributed to any other campaign travelers or any other passengers, except as permitted under paragraph (b)(3) of this section. For purposes of this paragraph, the comparable aircraft need not accommodate any government-required personnel and equipment; or

(ii) The private traveler reimbursement rate, as specified by the governmental entity providing the aircraft, per campaign traveler.

(2) *Other campaign travelers.* When a candidate's authorized committee, or a House candidate's leadership PAC pays for a flight pursuant to paragraph (e)(1) of this section, no payment is required from any other campaign travelers on that flight. Otherwise, a campaign traveler not covered by paragraph (e)(1) of this section, including persons traveling on behalf of a political party committee, separate segregated fund, nonconnected political committee, or a

leadership PAC other than a leadership PAC of a candidate for the office of Representative in, or Delegate or Resident Commissioner to, the Congress, must pay the government entity, within the time specified by that government entity, either:

(i) For travel to or from a military airbase or other location not accessible to the general public, the lowest unrestricted and non-discounted first-class airfare to or from the city with regularly scheduled first-class commercial airline service that is geographically closest to the military airbase or other location actually used; or

(ii) For all other travel, in accordance with paragraph (c)(3) of this section.

(3) If a campaign traveler uses a conveyance, other than an aircraft, that is provided by the Federal government, or by a State or local government, the campaign traveler, or the political committee on whose behalf the travel is conducted, must pay the government entity in accordance with paragraph (d) of this section.

(f) *Date and public availability of payment rate.* For purposes of paragraphs (c), (d), (e), and (g) of this section, the payment rate must be the rate available to the general public for the dates traveled or within seven (7) calendar days thereof. The payment rate must be determined by the time the payment is due under paragraph (c), (d), (e) or (g) of this section.

(g) *Aircraft owned or leased by a candidate or a candidate's immediate family member.* (1) For non-commercial travel by a candidate, or a person traveling on behalf of a candidate, on an aircraft owned or leased by that candidate or an immediate family member of that candidate, the candidate's authorized committee must pay:

(i) In the case of travel on an aircraft that is owned or leased under a shared-ownership or other time-share arrangement, where the travel does not exceed the candidate's or immediate family member's proportional share of the ownership interest in the aircraft, the hourly, mileage, or other applicable rate charged the candidate, immediate family member, or other service provider for the costs of the travel; or

(ii) In the case of travel on an aircraft that is owned or leased under a shared-ownership or other time-share arrangement, where the travel exceeds the candidate's or immediate family member's proportional share of the ownership interest in the aircraft, the rate specified in paragraph (c) of this section (House candidates are prohibited from engaging in such travel); or

(iii) In the case of travel on an aircraft that is not owned or leased under a shared-ownership or other time-share arrangement, the *pro rata* share per campaign traveler of the costs associated with the trip. Associated costs include, but are not limited to, the cost of fuel and crew, and a proportionate share of maintenance costs.

(2) A candidate, or an immediate family member of the candidate, will be considered to own or lease an aircraft under paragraph (g)(1) of this section if the candidate or the immediate family member of the candidate has an ownership interest in an entity that owns the aircraft, provided that the entity is not a corporation with publicly traded shares.

(3) A proportional share of the ownership interest in an aircraft means the amount of use to which the candidate or immediate family member is entitled under an ownership or lease agreement. Prior to each flight, the candidate's committee must obtain a certification from the service provider that the candidate's planned use of the aircraft will not exceed the candidate's or immediate family member's proportional share of use under the ownership or lease agreement. *See* paragraph (j) of this section for related recordkeeping requirements.

(4) For the purposes of this section, an "immediate family member" of a candidate is the father, mother, son, daughter, brother, sister, husband, wife, father-in-law, or mother-in-law of the candidate.

(h) *Preemption.* In all respects, State and local laws are preempted with respect to travel in connection with a Federal election to the extent they purport to supplant the rates or timing requirements of 11 CFR 100.93.

(i) *Reporting.* (1) In accordance with 11 CFR 104.13, a political committee on whose behalf the unreimbursed travel is conducted must report the receipt of an in-kind contribution and the making of an expenditure under paragraph (b)(2) of this section.

(2) When reporting a disbursement for travel services in accordance with this section, a political committee on whose behalf the travel is conducted must report the actual dates of travel for which the disbursement is made in the "purpose of disbursement" field.

(j) *Recordkeeping.* (1) For travel on non-commercial aircraft conducted under paragraphs (c)(1), (c)(3)(iii), (e)(1), or (g) of this section, the political committee on whose behalf the travel is conducted shall maintain documentation of:

(i) The service provider and the size, model, make and tail number (or other unique identifier for military aircraft) of the aircraft used;

(ii) An itinerary showing the departure and arrival cities and the date(s) of departure and arrival, a list of all passengers on such trip, along with a designation of which passengers are and which are not campaign travelers or security personnel; and

(iii)(A) The rate for the comparable charter aircraft available in accordance with paragraphs (c), (e) and (f) of this section, including the airline, charter or air taxi operator, and travel service, if any, offering that fare to the public, and the dates on which the rates are based; or

(B) The private traveler reimbursement rate available in accordance with paragraph (e)(1)(ii) of this section, and the dates on which the rate is based.

(iv) Where the travel is aboard an aircraft owned in part by the candidate or an immediate family member of the candidate, the ownership or lease agreement specifying the amount of use of the aircraft corresponding to the candidate's or an immediate family member's ownership interest in the aircraft, as required by paragraph (g)(1)(i) and (ii) and (g)(3) of this section, and the certification required by paragraph (g)(3) of this section.

(2) For travel on non-commercial aircraft conducted under paragraph (c)(3)(i), (c)(3)(ii), or (e)(2)(i) of this section, the political committee on whose behalf the travel is conducted shall maintain documentation of:

(i) The service provider and the size, model, make and tail number (or other unique identifier for military aircraft) of the aircraft used;

(ii) An itinerary showing the departure and arrival cities and the date(s) of departure and arrival, a list of all passengers on such trip, along with a designation of which passengers are and which are not campaign travelers; and

(iii) The lowest unrestricted non-discounted airfare available in accordance with paragraphs (c)(3), (e)(2)(i), and (f) of this section, including the airline offering that fare, flight number, travel service, if any, providing that fare, and the dates on which the rates are based.

(3) For travel by other conveyances, the political committee on whose behalf the travel is conducted shall maintain documentation of:

(i) The service provider and the size, model and make of the conveyance used;

(ii) An itinerary showing the departure and destination locations and the date(s) of departure and arrival, a list of all passengers on such trip, along with a designation of which passengers are and which are not campaign travelers or security personnel; and

(iii) The commercial fare or rental charge available in accordance with paragraphs (d) and (f) of this section for a comparable commercial conveyance of sufficient size to accommodate all campaign travelers including members of the news media traveling with a candidate, and security personnel, if applicable.

[74 FR 63964, Dec. 7, 2009]

§ 100.94 **Uncompensated Internet activity by individuals that is not a contribution.**

(a) When an individual or a group of individuals, acting independently or in coordination with any candidate, authorized committee, or political party committee, engages in Internet activities for the purpose of influencing a Federal election, neither of the following is a contribution by that individual or group of individuals:

(1) The individual's uncompensated personal services related to such Internet activities;

(2) The individual's use of equipment or services for uncompensated Internet activities, regardless of who owns the equipment and services.

(b) *Internet activities.* For the purposes of this section, the term "Internet activities" includes, but is not limited to: Sending or forwarding electronic messages; providing a hyperlink or other direct access to another person's Web site; blogging; creating, maintaining, or hosting a Web site; paying a nominal fee for the use of another person's Web site; and any other form of communication distributed over the Internet.

(c) *Equipment and services.* For the purposes of this section, the term "equipment and services" includes, but is not limited to: Computers, software, Internet domain names, Internet Service Providers (ISP), and any other technology that is used to provide access to or use of the Internet.

(d) Paragraph (a) of this section also applies to any corporation that is wholly owned by one or more individuals, that engages primarily in Internet activities, and that does not derive a substantial portion of its revenues from sources other than income from its Internet activities.

(e) This section does not exempt from the definition of contribution:

(1) Any payment for a public communication (as defined in 11 CFR 100.26) other than a nominal fee;

(2) Any payment for the purchase or rental of an e-mail address list made at the direction of a political committee; or

(3) Any payment for an e-mail address list that is transferred to a political committee.

[71 FR 18613, Apr. 12, 2006, as amended at 81 FR 94240, Dec. 23, 2016]

Subpart D—Definition of Expenditure (52 U.S.C. 30101(9))

SOURCE: 67 FR 50585, Aug. 5, 2002, unless otherwise noted.

§ 100.110 Scope.

(a) The term *expenditure* includes payments, gifts or other things of value described in this subpart.

(b) For the purpose of this subpart, a payment made by an individual shall not be attributed to any other individual, unless otherwise specified by that other individual. To the extent that a payment made by an individual qualifies as a contribution, the provisions of 11 CFR 110.1(k) shall apply.

§ 100.111 Gift, subscription, loan, advance or deposit of money.

(a) A purchase, payment, distribution, loan (except for a loan made in accordance with 11 CFR 100.113 and 100.114), advance, deposit, or gift of money or anything of value, made by any person for the purpose of influencing any election for Federal office is an expenditure.

(b) For purposes of this section, the term *payment* includes payment of any interest on an obligation and any guarantee or endorsement of a loan by a candidate or a political committee.

(c) For purposes of this section, the term *payment* does not include the repayment by a political committee of the principal of an outstanding obligation that is owed by such committee, except that the repayment shall be reported as disbursements in accordance with 11 CFR 104.3(b).

(d) For purposes of this section, the term *money* includes currency of the United States or of any foreign nation, checks, money orders, or any other negotiable instrument payable on demand.

(e)(1) For purposes of this section, the term *anything of value* includes all in-kind contributions. Unless specifically exempted under 11 CFR part 100, subpart E, the provision of any goods or services without charge or at a charge that is less than the usual and normal charge for the goods or services is an expenditure. Examples of such goods or services include, but are not limited to: Securities, facilities, equipment, supplies, personnel, advertising services, membership lists, and mailing lists. If goods or services are provided at less than the usual and normal charge, the amount of the expenditure is the difference between the usual and normal charge for the goods or services at the time of the expenditure and the amount charged the candidate or political committee.

(2) For the purposes of paragraph (e)(1) of this section, *usual and normal charge for goods* means the price of those goods in the market from which they ordinarily would have been purchased at the time of the expenditure; and usual and normal charge for services, other than those provided by an unpaid volunteer, means the hourly or piecework charge for the services at a commercially reasonable rate prevailing at the time the services were rendered.

§ 100.112 Contracts, promises, and agreements to make expenditures.

A written contract, including a media contract, promise, or agreement to make an expenditure is an expenditure as of the date such contract, promise or obligation is made.

§ 100.113 Independent expenditures.

An independent expenditure that meets the requirements of 11 CFR 104.4 or part 109 is an expenditure, and such independent expenditure is to be reported by the person making the expenditure in accordance with 11 CFR 104.4 and part 109.

§ 100.114 Office building or facility for national party committees.

A payment, distribution, loan, advance, or deposit of money or anything of value made by, or on behalf of, a national party committee for the purchase or construction of an office building or facility is an expenditure.

Subpart E—Exceptions to Expenditures

SOURCE: 67 FR 50585, Aug. 5, 2002, unless otherwise noted.

§ 100.130 Scope.

(a) The term *expenditure* does not include payments, gifts, or other things of value described in this subpart.

(b) For the purpose of this subpart, a payment made by an individual shall not be attributed to any other individual, unless otherwise specified by that other individual. To the extent that a payment made by an individual qualifies as a contribution, the provisions of 11 CFR 110.1(k) shall apply.

§ 100.131 Testing the waters.

(a) *General exemption.* Payments made solely for the purpose of determining whether an individual should become a candidate are not expenditures. Examples of activities permissible under this exemption if they are conducted to determine whether an individual should become a candidate include, but are not limited to, conducting a poll, telephone calls, and travel. Only funds permissible under the Act may be used for such activities. The individual shall keep records of all such payments. *See* 11 CFR 101.3. If the individual subsequently becomes a candidate, the payments made are subject to the reporting requirements of the Act. Such expenditures must be reported with the first report filed by the principal campaign committee of the candidate, regardless of the date the payments were made.

(b) *Exemption not applicable to individuals who have decided to become candidates.* This exemption does not apply to payments made for activities indicating that an individual has decided to become a candidate for a particular office or for activities relevant to conducting a campaign. Examples of activities that indicate that an individual has decided to become a candidate include, but are not limited to:

(1) The individual uses general public political advertising to publicize his or her intention to campaign for Federal office.

(2) The individual raises funds in excess of what could reasonably be expected to be used for exploratory activities or undertakes activities designed to amass campaign funds that would be spent after he or she becomes a candidate.

(3) The individual makes or authorizes written or oral statements that refer to him or her as a candidate for a particular office.

(4) The individual conducts activities in close proximity to the election or over a protracted period of time.

(5) The individual has taken action to qualify for the ballot under State law.

§ 100.132 News story, commentary, or editorial by the media.

Any cost incurred in covering or carrying a news story, commentary, or editorial by any broadcasting station (including a cable television operator, programmer or producer), Web site, newspaper, magazine, or other periodical publication, including any Internet or electronic publication, is not an expenditure unless the facility is owned or controlled by any political party, political committee, or candidate, in which case the cost for a news story:

(a) That represents a *bona fide* news account communicated in a publication of general circulation or on a licensed broadcasting facility; and

(b) That is part of a general pattern of campaign-related news account that give reasonably equal coverage to all opposing candidates in the circulation or listening area, is not an expenditure.

[67 FR 50585, Aug. 5, 2002, as amended at 71 FR 18613, Apr. 12, 2006]

§ 100.133 Voter registration and get-out-the-vote activities.

Any cost incurred for activity designed to encourage individuals to register to vote or to vote is not an expenditure if no effort is or has been made to determine the party or candidate preference of individuals before encouraging them to register to vote or to vote, except that corporations and labor organizations shall engage in such activity in accordance with 11 CFR 114.4 (c) and (d). *See also* 11 CFR 114.3(c)(4).

§ 100.134 Internal communications by corporations, labor organizations, and membership organizations.

(a) *General provision.* Any cost incurred for any communication by a membership organization, including a labor organization, to its members, or any cost incurred for any communication by a corporation to its stockholders or executive or administrative personnel, is not an expenditure, except that the costs directly attributable to such a communication that expressly advocates the election or defeat of a clearly identified candidate (other than a communication primarily devoted to subjects other than the express advocacy of the election or defeat of a clearly identified candidate) shall, if those costs exceed $2,000 per election, be reported to the Commission on FEC

Form 7 in accordance with 11 CFR 104.6.

(b) *Definition of labor organization.* For purposes of this section, *labor organization* means an organization of any kind (any local, national, or international union, or any local or State central body of a federation of unions is each considered a separate labor organization for purposes of this section) or any agency or employee representative committee or plan, in which employees participate and that exists for the purpose, in whole or in part, of dealing with employers concerning grievances, labor disputes, wages, rates of pay, hours of employment, or conditions of work.

(c) *Definition of stockholder.* For purposes of this section, *stockholder* means a person who has a vested beneficial interest in stock, has the power to direct how that stock shall be voted, if it is voting stock, and has the right to receive dividends.

(d) *Definition of executive or administrative personnel.* For purposes of this section, executive or administrative personnel means individuals employed by a corporation who are paid on a salary rather than hourly basis and who have policymaking, managerial, professional, or supervisory responsibilities.

(1) This definition includes—

(i) Individuals who run the corporation's business, such as officers, other executives, and plant, division, and section managers; and

(ii) Individuals following the recognized professions, such as lawyers and engineers.

(2) This definition does not include—

(i) Professionals who are represented by a labor organization;

(ii) Salaried foremen and other salaried lower level supervisors having direct supervision over hourly employees;

(iii) Former or retired personnel who are not stockholders; or

(iv) Individuals who may be paid by the corporation, such as consultants, but who are not employees, within the meaning of 26 CFR 31.3401(c)–(1), of the corporation for the purpose of the collection of, and liability for, employee tax under 26 CFR 31.3402(a)–(1).

(3) Individuals on commission may be considered executive or administrative

personnel if they have policymaking, managerial, professional, or supervisory responsibility and if the individuals are employees, within the meaning of 26 CFR 31.3401(c)–(1), of the corporation for the purpose of the collection of, and liability for, employee tax under 26 CFR 31.3402(a)–(1).

(4) The Fair Labor Standards Act, 29 U.S.C. 201, *et seq.* and the regulations issued pursuant to such Act, 29 CFR part 541, may serve as a guideline in determining whether individuals have policymaking, managerial, professional, or supervisory responsibilities.

(e) *Definition of membership organization.* For purposes of this section membership organization means an unincorporated association, trade association, cooperative, corporation without capital stock, or a local, national, or international labor organization that:

(1) Is composed of members, some or all of whom are vested with the power and authority to operate or administer the organization, pursuant to the organization's articles, bylaws, constitution or other formal organizational documents;

(2) Expressly states the qualifications and requirements for membership in its articles, bylaws, constitution or other formal organizational documents;

(3) Makes its articles, bylaws, constitution or other formal organizational documents available to its members;

(4) Expressly solicits persons to become members;

(5) Expressly acknowledges the acceptance of membership, such as by sending a membership card or including the member's name on a membership newsletter list; and

(6) Is not organized primarily for the purpose of influencing the nomination for election, or election, of any individual for Federal office.

(f) *Definition of members.* For purposes of this section, the term *members* includes all persons who are currently satisfying the requirements for membership in a membership organization, affirmatively accept the membership organization's invitation to become a member, and either:

(1) Have some significant financial attachment to the membership organization, such as a significant investment or ownership stake; or

(2) Pay membership dues at least annually, of a specific amount predetermined by the organization; or

(3) Have a significant organizational attachment to the membership organization that includes: affirmation of membership on at least an annual basis and direct participatory rights in the governance of the organization. For example, such rights could include the right to vote directly or indirectly for at least one individual on the membership organization's highest governing board; the right to vote on policy questions where the highest governing body of the membership organization is obligated to abide by the results; the right to approve the organization's annual budget; or the right to participate directly in similar aspects of the organization's governance.

(g) *Additional considerations in determining membership.* Notwithstanding the requirements of paragraph (f) of this section, the Commission may determine, on a case-by-case basis, that persons who do not precisely meet the requirements of the general rule, but have a relatively enduring and independently significant financial or organizational attachment to the organization, may be considered members for purposes of this section. For example, student members who pay a lower amount of dues while in school, long term dues paying members who qualify for lifetime membership status with little or no dues obligation, and retired members may be considered members of the organization.

(h) *Members of local unions.* Notwithstanding the requirements of paragraph (f) of this section, members of a local union are considered to be members of any national or international union of which the local union is a part and of any federation with which the local, national, or international union is affiliated.

(i) *National federation structures.* In the case of a membership organization that has a national federation structure or has several levels, including, for example, national, state, regional and/or local affiliates, a person who qualifies as a member of any entity within the federation or of any affiliate

67

by meeting the requirements of paragraphs (f)(1), (2), or (3) of this section shall also qualify as a member of all affiliates for purposes of paragraphs (d) through (i) of this section. The factors set forth at 11 CFR 100.5(g)(2), (3) and (4) shall be used to determine whether entities are affiliated for purposes of this paragraph.

(j) *Non-applicability of state law in determining status of membership organizations.* The status of a membership organization, and of members, for purposes of this section, shall be determined pursuant to paragraphs (d) through (i) of this section and not by provisions of state law governing unincorporated associations, trade associations, cooperatives, corporations without capital stock, or labor organizations.

(k) *Definition of election.* For purposes of this section, *election* means two separate processes in a calendar year, to each of which the $2,000 threshold described above applies separately. The first process is comprised of all primary elections for Federal office, whenever and wherever held; the second process is comprised of all general elections for Federal office, whenever and wherever held. The term election shall also include each special election held to fill a vacancy in a Federal office (11 CFR 100.2(f)) or each runoff election (11 CFR 100.2(d)).

(l) *Definition of corporation.* For purposes of this section, *corporation* means any separately incorporated entity, whether or not affiliated.

(m) *Reporting.* When the aggregate costs under this section exceed $2,000 per election, all costs of the communication(s) shall be reported on the filing dates specified in 11 CFR 104.6, and shall include the total amount expended for each candidate supported.

[67 FR 50585, Aug. 5, 2002, as amended at 79 FR 16663, Mar. 26, 2014]

§ 100.135 Use of a volunteer's real or personal property.

No expenditure results where an individual, in the course of volunteering personal services on his or her residential premises to any candidate or political committee of a political party, provides the use of his or her real or personal property to such candidate for candidate-related activity or to such political committee of a political party for party-related activity. For the purposes of this section, an individual's residential premises shall include a recreation room in a residential complex where the individual volunteering services resides, provided that the room is available for use without regard to political affiliation. A nominal fee paid by such individual for the use of such room is not an expenditure.

§ 100.136 Use of a church or a community room.

No expenditure results where an individual, in the course of volunteering personal services to any candidate or political committee of a political party, obtains the use of a church or community room and provides such room to any candidate for candidate-related activity or to any political committee of a political party for party-related activity, provided that the room is used on a regular basis by members of the community for non-commercial purposes and the room is available for use by members of the community without regard to political affiliation. A nominal fee paid by such individual for the use of such room is not an expenditure.

§ 100.137 Invitations, food, and beverages.

The cost of invitations, food, and beverages is not an expenditure where such items are voluntarily provided by an individual in rendering voluntary personal services on the individual's residential premises or in a church or community room as specified at 11 CFR 100.135 and 100.136 to a candidate for candidate-related activity or to a political committee of a political party for party-related activity, to the extent that: The aggregate value of such invitations, food and beverages provided by the individual on behalf of the candidate does not exceed $1,000 with respect to any single election; and on behalf of all political committees of each political party does not exceed $2,000 in any calendar year.

[67 FR 50585, Aug. 5, 2002, as amended at 79 FR 77845, Dec. 29, 2014]

§ 100.138 Sale of food and beverages by vendor.

The sale of any food or beverage by a vendor (whether incorporated or not) for use in a candidate's campaign, or for use by a political committee of a political party, at a charge less than the normal or comparable commercial charge, is not an expenditure, provided that the charge is at least equal to the cost of such food or beverage to the vendor, to the extent that: The aggregate value of such discount given by the vendor on behalf of any single candidate does not exceed $1,000 with respect to any single election; and on behalf of all political committees of each political party does not exceed $2,000 in a calendar year.

§ 100.139 Unreimbursed payment for transportation and subsistence expenses.

(a) *Transportation expenses.* Any unreimbursed payment for transportation expenses incurred by any individual on behalf of any candidate or political committee of a political party is not an expenditure to the extent that:

(1) The aggregate value of the payments made by such individual on behalf of a candidate does not exceed $1,000 with respect to a single election; and

(2) On behalf of all political committees of each political party does not exceed $2,000 in a calendar year.

(b) *Subsistence expenses.* Any unreimbursed payment from a volunteer's personal funds for usual and normal subsistence expenses incident to volunteer activity is not an expenditure.

§ 100.140 Slate cards and sample ballots.

The payment by a State or local committee of a political party of the costs of preparation, display, or mailing or other distribution incurred by such committee with respect to a printed slate card, sample ballot, palm card, or other printed listing(s) of three or more candidates for any public office for which an election is held in the State in which the committee is organized is not an expenditure. The payment of the portion of such costs allocable to Federal candidates must be made from funds subject to the limitations and prohibitions of the Act. If made by a political party committee, such payments shall be reported by that committee as disbursements, but need not be allocated in committee reports to specific candidates. This exemption shall not apply to costs incurred by such a committee with respect to the preparation and display of listings made on broadcasting stations, or in newspapers, magazines, and similar types of general public political advertising such as billboards. *But see* 11 CFR 100.24, 104.17(a), and part 300, subpart B for exempt activities that also constitute Federal election activity.

§ 100.141 Payment by corporations and labor organizations.

Any payment made or obligation incurred by a corporation or labor organization is not an expenditure if under the provisions of 11 CFR part 114 such payment or obligation would not constitute an expenditure by the corporation or labor organization.

§ 100.142 Bank loans.

(a) *General provisions.* Repayment of a loan of money to a candidate or a political committee by a State bank, a federally chartered depository institution (including a national bank) or a depository institution whose deposits and accounts are insured by the Federal Deposit Insurance Corporation or the National Credit Union Administration is not an expenditure by the lending institution if such loan is made in accordance with applicable banking laws and regulations and is made in the ordinary course of business. A loan will be deemed to be made in the ordinary course of business if it:

(1) Bears the usual and customary interest rate of the lending institution for the category of loan involved;

(2) Is made on a basis that assures repayment;

(3) Is evidenced by a written instrument; and

(4) Is subject to a due date or amortization schedule.

(b) *Reporting.* Such loans shall be reported by the political committee in accordance with 11 CFR 104.3(a) and (d).

(c) *Endorsers and guarantors.* Each endorser or guarantor shall be deemed to have contributed that portion of the total amount of the loan for which he or she agreed to be liable in a written agreement, except that, in the event of a signature by the candidate's spouse, the provisions of 11 CFR 100.52(b)(4) shall apply. Any reduction in the unpaid balance of the loan shall reduce proportionately the amount endorsed or guaranteed by each endorser or guarantor in such written agreement. In the event that the loan agreement does not stipulate the portion of the loan for which each endorser or guarantor is liable, the loan shall be considered an expenditure by each endorser or guarantor in the same proportion to the unpaid balance that each endorser or guarantor bears to the total number of endorsers or guarantors.

(d) *Overdrafts.* For the purpose of this section, repayment of an overdraft made on a checking or savings account of a political committee shall be considered an expenditure unless:

(1) The overdraft is made on an account that is subject to automatic overdraft protection; and

(2) The overdraft is subject to a definite interest rate and a definite repayment schedule.

(e) *Made on a basis that assures repayment.* A loan, including a line of credit, shall be considered made on a basis that assures repayment if it is obtained using either of the sources of repayment described in paragraphs (e)(1) or (2) of this section, or a combination of paragraphs (e)(1) or (2) of this section:

(1)(i) The lending institution making the loan has perfected a security interest in collateral owned by the candidate or political committee receiving the loan; the fair market value of the collateral is equal to or greater than the loan amount and any senior liens as determined on the date of the loan; and the candidate or political committee provides documentation to show that the lending institution has a perfected security interest in the collateral. Sources of collateral include, but are not limited to, ownership in real estate, personal property, goods, negotiable instruments, certificates of deposit, chattel papers, stocks, accounts receivable and cash on deposit.

(ii) Amounts guaranteed by secondary sources of repayment, such as guarantors and cosigners, shall not exceed the contribution limits of 11 CFR part 110 or contravene the prohibitions of 11 CFR 110.4, 110.20, part 114 and part 115; or

(2) The lending institution making the loan has obtained a written agreement whereby the candidate or political committee receiving the loan has pledged future receipts, such as public financing payments under 11 CFR part 9001 through part 9012 or part 9031 through 9039, contributions, or interest income, provided that:

(i) The amount of the loan(s) obtained the basis of such funds does not exceed the amount of pledged funds;

(ii) Loan amounts are based on a reasonable expectation of the receipt of pledged funds. To that end, the candidate or political committee must furnish the lending institution documentation, *i.e.,* cash flow charts or other financial plans, that reasonably establish that such future funds will be available;

(iii) A separate depository account is established at the lending institution or the lender obtains an assignment from the candidate or political committee to access funds in a committee account at another depository institution that meets the requirements of 11 CFR 103.2, and the committee has notified the other institution of this assignment;

(iv) The loan agreement requires the deposit of the public financing payments, contributions, interest or other income pledged as collateral into the separate depository account for the purpose of retiring the debt according to the repayment requirements of the loan; and

(v) In the case of public financing payments, the borrower authorizes the Secretary of the Treasury to directly deposit the payments into the depository account for the purpose of retiring the debt.

(3) If the requirements set forth in paragraph (e) of this section are not met, the Commission will consider the totality of circumstances on a case-by-case basis in determining whether a loan was made on a basis that assures repayment.

(f) This section shall not apply to loans described in 11 CFR 100.83 and 100.143.

[67 FR 50585, Aug. 5, 2002, as amended at 67 FR 78680, Dec. 26, 2002]

§100.143 Brokerage loans and lines of credit to candidates.

Repayment of a loan of money derived from an advance on a candidate's brokerage account, credit card, home equity line of credit, or other line of credit available to the candidate, as described in 11 CFR 100.83, is not an expenditure.

§100.144 Office building for State, local, or district party committees or organizations.

A payment, distribution, loan, advance, or deposit of money or anything of value, made by, or on behalf of, a State, local, or district party committee or organization for the purchase or construction of an office building in accordance with 11 CFR 300.35 is not an expenditure.

§100.145 Legal or accounting services to political party committees.

Legal or accounting services rendered to or on behalf of any political committee of a political party are not expenditures if the person paying for such services is the regular employer of the individual rendering the services and such services are not attributable to activities that directly further the election of any designated candidate for Federal office. For purposes of this section, a partnership shall be deemed to be the regular employer of a partner. Amounts paid by the regular employer for such services shall be reported by the committee receiving such services in accordance with 11 CFR 104.3(h).

§100.146 Legal or accounting services to other political committees.

Legal or accounting services rendered to or on behalf of an authorized committee of a candidate or any other political committee are not expenditures if the person paying for such services is the regular employer of the individual rendering such services and if the services are solely to ensure compliance with the Act or 26 U.S.C. 9001 *et*

seq. and 9032 *et seq.* For purposes of this section, a partnership shall be deemed to be the regular employer of a partner. Amounts paid by the regular employer for these services shall be reported by the committee receiving such services in accordance with 11 CFR 104.3(h). Expenditures for these services by a candidate certified to receive Primary Matching Funds under 11 CFR part 9034 do not count against such candidate's expenditure limitations under 11 CFR part 9035 or 11 CFR 110.8. Unless paid for with federal funds received pursuant to 11 CFR part 9005, disbursements for these services by a candidate who is certified to receive payments from the Presidential Election Campaign Fund under 11 CFR part 9005 do not count against that candidate's expenditure limitations under 11 CFR 110.8.

§100.147 Volunteer activity for party committees.

The payment by a state or local committee of a political party of the costs of campaign materials (such as pins, bumper stickers, handbills, brochures, posters, party tabloids or newsletters, and yard signs) used by such committee in connection with volunteer activities on behalf of any nominee(s) of such party is not an expenditure, provided that the following conditions are met:

(a) *Exemption does not apply to general public communications or political advertising.* Such payment is not for costs incurred in connection with any broadcasting, newspaper, magazine, billboard, direct mail, or similar type of general public communication or political advertising. For the purposes of this paragraph, the term *direct mail* means any mailing(s) by a commercial vendor or any mailing(s) made from commercial lists.

(b) *Allocation.* The portion of the cost of such materials allocable to Federal candidates is paid from contributions subject to the limitations and prohibitions of the Act. *But see* 11 CFR part 300 for exempt activities that also constitute Federal election activity.

(c) *Contributions designated for Federal candidates.* Such payment is not made from contributions designated by the donor to be spent on behalf of a particular candidate or candidates for Federal office. For purposes of this paragraph, a contribution shall not be considered a designated contribution if the party committee disbursing the funds makes the final decision regarding which candidate(s) shall receive the benefit of such disbursement.

(d) *Distribution of materials by volunteers.* Such materials are distributed by volunteers and not by commercial or for-profit operations. For the purposes of this paragraph, payments by the party organization for travel and subsistence or customary token payments to volunteers do not remove such individuals from the volunteer category.

(e) *Reporting.* If made by a political party committee, such payments shall be reported by that committee as disbursements, in accordance with 11 CFR 104.3, but need not be allocated to specific candidates in committee reports.

(f) *State candidates and their campaign committees.* Payments by a State candidate or his or her campaign committee to a State or local political party committee for the State candidate's share of expenses for such campaign materials are not expenditures, provided the amount paid by the State candidate or his or her committee does not exceed his or her proportionate share of the expenses.

(g) *Exemption not applicable to campaign materials purchased by national party committees.* Campaign materials purchased by the national committee of a political party and delivered to a State or local party committee, or materials purchased with funds donated by the national committee to such State or local committee for the purchase of such materials, shall not qualify under this exemption. Rather, the cost of such materials shall be subject to the limitations of 52 U.S.C. 30116(d) and 11 CFR 109.32.

[67 FR 50585, Aug. 5, 2002, as amended at 67 FR 78680, Dec. 26, 2002; 79 FR 77845, Dec. 29, 2014]

§ 100.148 Volunteer activity for candidate.

The payment by a candidate for any public office (including State or local office), or by such candidate's authorized committee, of the costs of that candidate's campaign materials that include information on or any reference to a candidate for Federal office and that are used in connection with volunteer activities (such as pins, bumper stickers, handbills, brochures, posters, and yard signs) is not an expenditure on behalf of such candidate for Federal office, provided that the payment is not for the use of broadcasting, newspapers, magazines, billboards, direct mail or similar types of general public communication or political advertising. The payment of the portion of the cost of such materials allocable to Federal candidates shall be made from contributions subject to the limitations and prohibitions of the Act. For purposes of this section, the term direct mail means mailings by commercial vendors or mailings made from lists that were not developed by the candidate. *But see* 11 CFR 100.24, 104.17(a), and part 300, subparts D and E for exempt activities that also constitute Federal election activity.

§ 100.149 Voter registration and get-out-the-vote activities for Presidential candidates.

The payment by a State or local committee of a political party of the costs of voter registration and get-out-the-vote activities conducted by such committee on behalf of the Presidential and Vice Presidential nominee(s) of that party is not an expenditure for the purpose of influencing the election of such candidates provided that the following conditions are met:

(a) *Exemption not applicable to general public communication or political advertising.* Such payment is not for the costs incurred in connection with any broadcasting, newspaper, magazine, billboard, direct mail, or similar type of general public communication or political advertising. For purposes of this paragraph, the term direct mail means any mailing(s) by a commercial vendor or any mailing(s) made from commercial lists.

(b) *Allocation.* The portion of the costs of such activities allocable to Federal candidates is paid from contributions subject to the limitations and prohibitions of the Act. *But see* 11

CFR 100.24, 104.17(a), and part 300, subpart B for exempt activities that also constitute Federal election activity.

(c) *Contributions designated for Federal candidates.* Such payment is not made from contributions designated to be spent on behalf of a particular candidate or candidates for Federal office. For the purposes of this paragraph, a contribution shall not be considered a designated contribution if the party committee disbursing the funds makes the final decision regarding which candidate(s) shall receive the benefit of such disbursement.

(d) *References to House or Senate candidates.* For purposes of this section, if such activities include references to any candidate(s) for the House or Senate, the costs of such activities that are allocable to that candidate(s) shall be an expenditure on behalf of such candidate(s) unless the mention of such candidate(s) is merely incidental to the overall activity.

(e) *Phone banks.* For purposes of this section, payment of the costs incurred in the use of phone banks in connection with voter registration and get-out-the-vote activities is not an expenditure when such phone banks are operated by volunteer workers. The use of paid professionals to design the phone bank system, develop calling instructions and train supervisors is permissible. The payment of the costs of such professional services is not an expenditure but shall be reported as a disbursement in accordance with 11 CFR 104.3 if made by a political committee.

(f) *Reporting of payments for voter registration and get-out-the-vote activities.* If made by a political committee, such payments for voter registration and get-out-the-vote activities shall be reported by that committee as disbursements, in accordance with 11 CFR 104.3 but such payments need not be allocated to specific candidates in committee reports except as provided in paragraph (d) of this section.

(g) *Exemption not applicable to donations by a national committee of a political party to a State or local party committee for voter registration and get-out-the-vote activities.* Payments made from funds donated by a national committee of a political party to a State or local party committee for voter registration

and get-out-the-vote activities shall not qualify under this exemption. Rather, such funds shall be subject to the limitations of 52 U.S.C. 30116(d) and 11 CFR 109.32.

[67 FR 50585, Aug. 5, 2002, as amended at 67 FR 78680, Dec. 26, 2002; 69 FR 68238, Nov. 24, 2004; 79 FR 77845, Dec. 29, 2014]

§ 100.150 Ballot access fees.

Amounts transferred by a party committee to another party committee or payments made to the appropriate State official of fees collected from candidates or their authorized committees as a condition of ballot access are not expenditures.

§ 100.151 Recounts.

A purchase, payment, distribution, loan, advance, or deposit of money or anything of value made with respect to a recount of the results of a Federal election, or an election contest concerning a Federal election, is not an expenditure except that the prohibitions of 11 CFR 110.20 and part 114 apply.

[67 FR 50585, Aug. 5, 2002, as amended at 67 FR 78680, Dec. 26, 2002]

§ 100.152 Fundraising costs for Presidential candidates.

(a) *Costs incurred in connection with the solicitation of contributions.* Any costs incurred by a candidate or his or her authorized committee(s) in connection with the solicitation of contributions are not expenditures if incurred by a candidate who has been certified to receive Presidential Primary Matching Fund Payments, or by a candidate who has been certified to receive general election public financing under 26 U.S.C. 9004 and who is soliciting contributions in accordance with 26 U.S.C. 9003(b)(2) or 9003(c)(2) to the extent that the aggregate of such costs does not exceed 20 percent of the expenditure limitation applicable to the candidate. These costs shall, however, be reported as disbursements pursuant to 11 CFR part 104.

(b) *Definition of in connection with the solicitation of contributions.* For a candidate who has been certified to receive general election public financing under

26 U.S.C. 9004 and who is soliciting contributions in accordance with 26 U.S.C. 9003(b)(2) or 9003(c)(2), *in connection with the solicitation of contributions* means any cost reasonably related to fundraising activity, including the costs of printing and postage, the production of and space or air time for, advertisements used for fundraising, and the costs of meals, beverages, and other costs associated with a fundraising reception or dinner.

(c) *Limitation on costs that may be exempted.* For a candidate who has been certified to receive Presidential Primary Matching Fund Payments, the costs that may be exempted as fundraising expenses under this section shall not exceed 20% of the overall expenditure limitation under 11 CFR 9035.1, and shall equal the total of:

(1) All amounts excluded from the state expenditure limitations for exempt fundraising activities under 11 CFR 110.8(c)(2), plus

(2) An amount of costs that would otherwise be chargeable to the overall expenditure limitation but that are not chargeable to any state expenditure limitation, such as salary and travel expenses. See 11 CFR 106.2.

§ 100.153   Routine living expenses.

Payments by a candidate from his or her personal funds, as defined at 11 CFR 100.33, for the candidate's routine living expenses that would have been incurred without candidacy, including the cost of food and residence, are not expenditures. Payments for such expenses by a member of the candidate's family as defined in 11 CFR 113.1(g)(7), are not expenditures if the payments are made from an account jointly held with the candidate, or if the expenses were paid by the family member before the candidate became a candidate.

[67 FR 50585, Aug. 5, 2002, as amended at 73 FR 79601, Dec. 30, 2008]

§ 100.154   Candidate debates.

Funds used to defray costs incurred in staging candidate debates in accordance with the provisions of 11 CFR 110.13 and 114.4(f) are not expenditures.

§ 100.155   Uncompensated Internet activity by individuals that is not an expenditure.

(a) When an individual or a group of individuals, acting independently or in coordination with any candidate, authorized committee, or political party committee, engages in Internet activities for the purpose of influencing a Federal election, neither of the following is an expenditure by that individual or group of individuals:

(1) The individual's uncompensated personal services related to such Internet activities;

(2) The individual's use of equipment or services for uncompensated Internet activities, regardless of who owns the equipment and services.

(b) *Internet activities.* For the purposes of this section, the term "Internet activities" includes, but is not limited to: Sending or forwarding electronic messages; providing a hyperlink or other direct access to another person's website; blogging; creating, maintaining, or hosting a website; paying a nominal fee for the use of another person's website; and any other form of communication distributed over the Internet.

(c) *Equipment and services.* For the purposes of this section, the term "equipment and services" includes, but is not limited to: Computers, software, Internet domain names, Internet Service Providers (ISP), and any other technology that is used to provide access to or use of the Internet.

(d) Paragraph (a) of this section also applies to any corporation that is wholly owned by one or more individuals, that engages primarily in Internet activities, and that does not derive a substantial portion of its revenues from sources other than income from its Internet activities.

(e) This section does not exempt from the definition of expenditure:

(1) Any payment for a public communication (as defined in 11 CFR 100.26) other than a nominal fee;

(2) Any payment for the purchase or rental of an e-mail address list made at the direction of a political committee; or

(3) Any payment for an e-mail address list that is transferred to a political committee.

[71 FR 18613, Apr. 12, 2006, as amended at 81 FR 94240, Dec. 23, 2016]

PART 101—CANDIDATE STATUS AND DESIGNATIONS (52 U.S.C. 30102(e))

Sec.
101.1 Candidate designations (52 U.S.C. 30102(e)(1)).
101.2 Candidate as agent of authorized committee (52 U.S.C. 30102(e)(2)).
101.3 Funds received or expended prior to becoming a candidate (52 U.S.C. 30102(e)(2)).

AUTHORITY: 52 U.S.C. 30102(e), 30104(a)(11), and 30111(a)(8).

§101.1 Candidate designations (52 U.S.C. 30102(e)(1)).

(a) *Principal Campaign Committee.* Within 15 days after becoming a candidate under 11 CFR 100.3, each candidate, other than a nominee for the office of Vice President, shall designate in writing, a principal campaign committee in accordance with 11 CFR 102.12. A candidate shall designate his or her principal campaign committee by filing a Statement of Candidacy on FEC Form 2, or, if the candidate is not required to file electronically under 11 CFR 104.18, by filing a letter containing the same information (that is, the individual's name and address, party affiliation, and office sought, the District and State in which Federal office is sought, and the name and address of his or her principal campaign committee at the place of filing specified at 11 CFR part 105). Each principal campaign committee shall register, designate a depository, and report in accordance with 11 CFR parts 102, 103, and 104.

(b) *Authorized committees.* A candidate may designate additional political committees in accordance with 11 CFR 102.13 to serve as committees which will be authorized to accept contributions or make expenditures on behalf of the candidate. For each such authorized committee, other than a principal campaign committee, the candidate shall file a written designation with his or her principal campaign committee.

The principal campaign committee shall file such designations at the place of filing specified at 11 CFR part 105.

[45 FR 15103, Mar. 7, 1980, as amended at 45 FR 21209, Apr. 1, 1980; 65 FR 38422, June 21, 2000; 68 FR 3995, Jan. 27, 2003; 73 FR 79601, Dec. 30, 2008]

§101.2 Candidate as agent of authorized committee (52 U.S.C. 30102(e)(2)).

(a) Any candidate who receives a contribution as defined at 11 CFR part 100, subparts B and C obtains any loan, or makes any disbursement, in connection with his or her campaign shall be considered as having received such contribution, obtained such loan or made such disbursement as an agent of his or her authorized committee(s).

(b) When an individual becomes a candidate, any funds received, loans obtained, or disbursements made prior to becoming a candidate in connection with his or her campaign shall be deemed to have been received, obtained or made as an agent of his or her authorized committee(s).

[45 FR 15103, Mar. 7, 1980, as amended at 67 FR 78680, Dec. 26, 2002]

§101.3 Funds received or expended prior to becoming a candidate (52 U.S.C. 30102(e)(2)).

When an individual becomes a candidate, all funds received or payments made in connection with activities conducted under 11 CFR 100.72(a) and 11 CFR 100.131(a) or his or her campaign prior to becoming a candidate shall be considered contributions or expenditures under the Act and shall be reported in accordance with 11 CFR 104.3 in the first report filed by such candidate's principal campaign committee. The individual shall keep records of the name of each contributor, the date of receipt and amount of all contributions received (see 11 CFR 102.9(a)), and all expenditures made (see 11 CFR 102.9(b)) in connection with activities conducted under 11 CFR 100.72 and 11 CFR 100.131 or the individual's campaign prior to becoming a candidate.

[50 FR 9995, Mar. 13, 1985, as amended at 67 FR 78680, Dec. 26, 2002; 75 FR 31, Jan. 4, 2010]

PART 102—REGISTRATION, ORGANIZATION, AND RECORDKEEPING BY POLITICAL COMMITTEES (52 U.S.C. 30103)

Sec.
102.1 Registration of political committees (52 U.S.C. 30103(a)).
102.2 Statement of organization: Forms and committee identification number (52 U.S.C. 30103(b), (c)).
102.3 Termination of registration (52 U.S.C. 30103(d)(1)).
102.4 Administrative termination (52 U.S.C. 30103(d)(2)).
102.5 Organizations financing political activity in connection with Federal and non-Federal elections, other than through transfers and joint fundraisers: Accounts and accounting.
102.6 Transfers of funds; collecting agents.
102.7 Organization of political committees (52 U.S.C. 30102(a)).
102.8 Receipt of contributions (52 U.S.C. 30102(b)).
102.9 Accounting for contributions and expenditures (52 U.S.C. 30102(c)).
102.10 Disbursement by check (52 U.S.C. 30102(h)(1)).
102.11 Petty cash fund (52 U.S.C. 30102(h)(2)).
102.12 Designation of principal campaign committee (52 U.S.C. 30102(e)(1) and (3)).
102.13 Authorization of political committees (52 U.S.C. 30102(e)(1) and (3)).
102.14 Names of political committees (52 U.S.C. 30102(e)(4) and (5)).
102.15 Commingled funds (52 U.S.C. 30102(b)(3)).
102.16 Notice: Solicitation of contributions (52 U.S.C. 30120).
102.17 Joint fundraising by committees other than separate segregated funds.

AUTHORITY: 52 U.S.C. 30102, 30103, 30104(a)(11), 30111(a)(8), and 30120.

SOURCE: 45 FR 15104, Mar. 7, 1980, unless otherwise noted.

§ 102.1 Registration of political committees (52 U.S.C. 30103(a)).

(a) *Principal campaign committees.* Each principal campaign committee shall file a Statement of Organization in accordance with 11 CFR 102.2 no later than 10 days after designation pursuant to 11 CFR 101.1. In addition, each principal campaign committee shall file all designations, statements and reports which are filed with such committee at the place of filing specified at 11 CFR part 105.

(b) *Authorized committees.* Each authorized committee(s) shall file only one Statement of Organization in accordance with 11 CFR 102.2 no later than 10 days after designation pursuant to 11 CFR 101.1. Such Statement(s) shall be filed with the principal campaign committee of the authorizing candidate.

(c) *Separate segregated funds.* Each separate segregated fund established under 52 U.S.C. 30118(b)(2)(C) shall file a Statement of Organization with the Federal Election Commission no later than 10 days after establishment. This requirement shall not apply to a fund established solely for the purpose of financing political activity in connection with State or local elections. Examples of establishment events after which a fund would be required to register include, but are not limited to: A vote by the board of directors or comparable governing body of an organization to create a separate segregated fund to be used wholly or in part for federal elections; selection of initial officers to administer such a fund; or payment of the initial operating expenses of such a fund.

(d) *Other political committees.* All other committees shall file a Statement of Organization no later than 10 days after becoming a political committee within the meaning of 11 CFR 100.5. Such statement(s) shall be filed at the place of filing specified at 11 CFR part 105.

[45 FR 15104, Mar. 7, 1980, as amended at 79 FR 77845, Dec. 29, 2014]

§ 102.2 Statement of organization: Forms and committee identification number (52 U.S.C. 30103(b), (c)).

(a) *Forms.* (1) The Statement of Organization shall be filed in accordance with 11 CFR part 105 on Federal Election Commission Form 1, which may be obtained from the Federal Election Commission. The Statement shall be signed by the treasurer and shall include the following information:

(i) The name, address, and type of committee;

(ii) The name, address, relationship, and type of any connected organization or affiliated committee in accordance with 11 CFR 102.2(b);

(iii) The name, address, and committee position of the custodian of books and accounts of the committee;

(iv) The name and address of the treasurer of the committee;

(v) If the committee is authorized by a candidate, the name, office sought (including State and Congressional district, when applicable) and party affiliation of the candidate; and the address to which communications should be sent;

(vi) A listing of all banks, safe deposit boxes, or other depositories used by the committee;

(vii) The Internet address of the committee's official web site, if such a web site exists. If the committee is required to file electronically under 11 CFR 104.18, its electronic mail address, if such an address exists; and

(viii) If the committee is a principal campaign committee of a candidate for the Senate or the House of Representatives, the principal campaign committee's electronic mail address.

(2) Any change or correction in the information previously filed in the Statement of Organization shall be reported no later than 10 days following the date of the change or correction by filing an amended Statement of Organization or, if the political committee is not required to file electronically under 11 CFR 104.18, by filing a letter noting the change(s). The amendment need list only the name of the political committee and the change or correction.

(3) A committee shall certify to the Commission that it has satisfied the criteria for becoming a multicandidate committee set forth at 11 CFR 100.5(e)(3) by filing FEC Form 1M no later than ten (10) calendar days after qualifying for multicandidate committee status.

(b) For purposes of 11 CFR 102.2(a)(1)(ii), political committees shall disclose the names of any connected organization(s) or affiliated committee(s) in accordance with 11 CFR 102.2(b) (1) and (2).

(1) *Affiliated committee* includes any committee defined in 11 CFR 100.5(g), 110.3(a) or (b), or 110.14(j) or (k).

(i) A principal campaign committee is required to disclose the names and addresses of all other authorized committees that have been authorized by its candidate. Authorized committees

need only disclose the name of their principal campaign committee.

(ii)(A) Political committees established by a single parent corporation, a single national or international union, a single organization or federation of national or international unions, a single national membership organization or trade association, or any other similar group of persons (other than political party organizations) are required to disclose the names and addresses of all political committees established by any subsidiary, or by any State, local, or other subordinate unit of a national or international union or federation thereof, or by any subordinate units of a national membership organization, trade association, or other group of persons (other than political party organizations).

(B) Political committees established by subsidiaries, or by State, local, or other subordinate units are only required to disclose the name and address of each political committee established by their parent or superior body, e.g., parent corporation, national or international union or organization or federation of such unions, or national organization or trade association.

(2) *Connected organization* includes any organization defined at 11 CFR 100.6.

(c) *Committee identification number.* Upon receipt of a Statement of Organization under 11 CFR part 102 by the Commission, an identification number shall be assigned to the committee, receipt shall be acknowledged, and the political committee shall be notified of the number assigned. This identification number shall be entered by the political committee on all subsequent reports or statements filed under the Act, as well as on all communications concerning reports and statements.

[45 FR 15104, Mar. 7, 1980, as amended at 50 FR 50778, Dec. 12, 1985; 54 FR 34109, Aug. 17, 1989; 54 FR 48580, Nov. 24, 1989; 58 FR 42173, Aug. 6, 1993; 65 FR 38422, June 21, 2000; 68 FR 3995, Jan. 27, 2003; 68 FR 64516, Nov. 14, 2003; 68 FR 67018, Dec. 1, 2003; 73 FR 79601, Dec. 30, 2008; 82 FR 60853, Dec. 26, 2017]

§ 102.3 Termination of registration (52 U.S.C. 30103(d)(1)).

(a)(1) A political committee (other than a principal campaign committee) may terminate only upon filing a termination report on the appropriate FEC Form or upon filing a written statement containing the same information at the place of filing specified at 11 CFR part 105. Except as provided in 11 CFR 102.4(c), only a committee which will no longer receive any contributions or make any disbursements that would otherwise qualify it as a political committee may terminate, provided that such committee has no outstanding debts and obligations. In addition to the Notice, the committee shall also provide a final report of receipts and disbursements, which report shall include a statement as to the purpose for which such residual funds will be used, including a statement as to whether such residual funds will be used to defray expenses incurred in connection with an individual's duties as a holder of federal office.

(2) An authorized committee of a qualified Member, as defined at 11 CFR 113.1(f), shall comply with the requirements of 11 CFR 113.2 before any excess funds are converted to such Member's personal use. All other authorized committees shall include in their termination reports a statement signed by the treasurer, stating that no noncash committee assets will be converted to personal use.

(b) Except as provided at 11 CFR 102.4, a principal campaign committee may not terminate until it has met the requirements of 11 CFR 102.3(a) and until all debts of any other authorized committee(s) of the candidate have been extinguished.

[45 FR 15104, Mar. 7, 1980, as amended at 45 FR 21209, Apr. 1, 1980; 56 FR 34126, July 25, 1991]

§ 102.4　Administrative termination (52 U.S.C. 30103(d)(2)).

(a) The Commission, on its own initiative or upon the request of the political committee itself, may administratively terminate a political committee's reporting obligation on the basis of the following factors:

(1) The committee's aggregate reported financial activity in one year is less than $5000;

(2) The committee's reports disclose no receipt of contributions for the previous year;

(3) The committee's last report disclosed minimal expenditures;

(4) The committee's primary purpose for filing its reports has been to disclose outstanding debts and obligations;

(5) The committee has failed to file reports for the previous year;

(6) The committee's last report disclosed that the committee's outstanding debts and obligations do not appear to present a possible violation of the prohibitions and limitations of 11 CFR parts 110 and 114;

(7) The committee's last report disclosed that the Committee does not have substantial outstanding accounts receivable;

(8) The committee's outstanding debts and obligations exceed the total of the committee's reported cash on hand balance.

(b) The Commission shall send a notification to the committee treasurer of its intent to administratively terminate that committee and may request the treasurer to submit information with regard to the factors set forth at 11 CFR 102.4(a). The treasurer shall respond, in writing, within 30 days of receipt of the Commission's notice or request and if the committee objects to such termination, the committee's response shall so state.

(c) The Commission shall administratively terminate a committee if such committee fails to object to the Commission's action under 11 CFR 102.4(b) and the Commission determines that either:

(1) The committee has complied with the debt settlement procedures set forth at 11 CFR part 116.

(2) The Commission has approved the forgiveness of any loan(s) owed the committee which would have otherwise been considered a contribution under the Act in violation of 11 CFR part 110;

(3) It does not appear from evidence available that a contribution in violation of 11 CFR parts 110 and 114 will result.

[45 FR 15104, Mar. 7, 1980, as amended at 60 FR 64273, Dec. 14, 1995]

§ 102.5 Organizations financing political activity in connection with Federal and non-Federal elections, other than through transfers and joint fundraisers: Accounts and accounting.

(a) *Organizations that are political committees under the Act, other than national party committees.* (1) Each organization, including a State, district, or local party committee, that finances political activity in connection with both Federal and non-Federal elections and that qualifies as a political committee under 11 CFR 100.5 shall either:

(i) Establish a separate Federal account in a depository in accordance with 11 CFR part 103. Such account shall be treated as a separate Federal political committee that must comply with the requirements of the Act including the registration and reporting requirements of 11 CFR parts 102 and 104. Only funds subject to the prohibitions and limitations of the Act shall be deposited in such separate Federal account. *See* 11 CFR 103.3. All disbursements, contributions, expenditures, and transfers by the committee in connection with any Federal election shall be made from its Federal account, except as otherwise permitted for State, district and local party committees by 11 CFR part 300 and paragraph (a)(5) of this section. No transfers may be made to such Federal account from any other account(s) maintained by such organization for the purpose of financing activity in connection with non-Federal elections, except as provided by 11 CFR 300.33, 300.34, 106.6(c), 106.6(f), and 106.7(f). Administrative expenses for political committees other than party committees shall be allocated pursuant to 11 CFR 106.6(c) between such Federal account and any other account maintained by such committee for the purpose for financing activity in connection with non-Federal elections. Administrative expenses for State, district, and local party committees are subject to 11 CFR 106.7 and 11 CFR part 300; or

(ii) Establish a political committee that shall receive only contributions subject to the prohibitions and limitations of the Act, regardless of whether such contributions are for use in connection with Federal or non-Federal elections. Such organization shall register as a political committee and comply with the requirements of the Act.

(2) Only contributions meeting any of the conditions set forth in paragraphs (a)(2)(i), (ii), or (iii) of this section may be deposited in a Federal account established under paragraph (a)(1)(i) of this section, see 11 CFR 103.3, or may be received by a political committee established under paragraph (a)(1)(ii) of this section:

(i) Contributions designated for the Federal account;

(ii) Contributions that result from a solicitation which expressly states that the contribution will be used in connection with a Federal election; or

(iii) Contributions from contributors who are informed that all contributions are subject to the prohibitions and limitations of the Act.

(3) State, district, and local party committees that intend to expend Levin funds raised pursuant to 11 CFR 300.31 for activities identified in 11 CFR 300.32(b)(1) must either:

(i) Establish one or more separate Levin accounts pursuant to 11 CFR 300.30(c)(2); or

(ii) Demonstrate through a reasonable accounting method approved by the Commission (including any method embedded in software provided or approved by the Commission) that whenever such organization makes a payment that organization has received sufficient funds subject to the limitations and prohibitions of the Act or the requirements of 11 CFR 300.30(c)(1) or (3) to make such payment. Such organization shall keep records of amounts received or expended under this paragraph and, upon request, shall make such records available for examination by the Commission.

(4) Solicitations by Federal candidates and Federal officeholders for State, district, and local party committees are subject to the restrictions in 11 CFR 300.31(e) and 11 CFR part 300, subpart D.

(5) State, district, and local party committees and organizations may establish one or more separate allocation accounts to be used for activities allocable pursuant to 11 CFR 106.7 and 11 CFR 300.33.

(b) *Organizations that are not political committees under the Act.* (1) Any organization that makes contributions, expenditures, and exempted payments under 11 CFR 100.80, 100.87 and 100.89 and 11 CFR 100.140, 100.147 and 100.149, but that does not qualify as a political committee under 11 CFR 100.5, must keep records of receipts and disbursements and, upon request, must make such records available for examination by the Commission. The organization must demonstrate through a reasonable accounting method that, whenever such an organization makes a contribution or expenditure, or payment, the organization has received sufficient funds subject to the limitations and prohibitions of the Act to make such contribution, expenditure, or payment.

(2) Any State, district, or local party organization that makes payments for certain Federal election activities under 11 CFR 300.32(b) must either:

(i) Establish one or more Levin accounts pursuant to 11 CFR 300.30(b) into which only funds solicited pursuant to 11 CFR 300.31 may be deposited and from which payments must be made pursuant to 11 CFR 300.32 and 300.33. See 11 CFR 300.30(c)(2)(i); or

(ii) Demonstrate through a reasonable accounting method approved by the Commission (including any method embedded in software provided or approved by the Commission) that whenever such organization makes a payment that organization has received sufficient funds subject to the limitations and prohibitions of the Act or the requirements of 11 CFR 300.31 to make such payment. Such organization shall keep records of amounts received or expended under this paragraph and, upon request, shall make such records available for examination by the Commission. See 11 CFR 300.30(c)(2)(ii).

(3) All such party organizations shall keep records of deposits to and disbursements from such Federal and Levin accounts, and upon request, shall make such records available for examination by the Commission.

(c) *National party committees.* Between November 6, 2002, and December 31, 2002, paragraphs (a) and (b) of this section apply to national party committees. After December 31, 2002, national party committees are prohibited from raising and spending non-Federal funds. Therefore, this section does not apply to national party committees after December 31, 2002.

[67 FR 49111, July 29, 2002, as amended at 67 FR 78680, Dec. 26, 2002; 69 FR 68067, Nov. 23, 2004]

§ 102.6 Transfers of funds; collecting agents.

(a) *Transfers of funds; registration and reporting required*—(1) *Who may make transfers under this section.* (i) Transfers of funds may be made without limit on amount between affiliated committees whether or not they are political committees under 11 CFR 100.5.

(ii) Subject to the restrictions set forth at 11 CFR 300.10(a), 300.31 and 300.34(a) and (b), transfers of funds may be made without limit on amount between or among a national party committee, a State party committee and/or any subordinate party committee whether or not they are political committees under 11 CFR 100.5 and whether or not such committees are affiliated.

(iii) Transfers of joint fundraising proceeds may be made without limit on amount between organizations or committees participating in the joint fundraising activity provided that no participating committee or organization governed by 11 CFR 102.17 received more than its allocated share of the funds raised.

(iv) Transfers under paragraphs (a)(1) (i) through (iii) shall be made only from funds which are permissible under the Act. See 11 CFR parts 110, 114 and 115.

(2) *When registration and reporting required.* Except as provided in 11 CFR 102.6(b), organizations or committees making transfers under 11 CFR 102.6(a)(1) shall count such transfers against the reporting thresholds of the Act for determining whether an organization or committee is a political committee under 11 CFR 100.5.

(b) *Fundraising by collecting agents; No reporting required*—(1) *Definition of collecting agent.* A collecting agent is an organization or committee that collects and transmits contributions to one or more separate segregated funds to which the collecting agent is related. A collecting agent may be either:

(i) A committee, whether or not it is a political committee as defined in 11 CFR 100.5, affiliated with the separate segregated fund under 11 CFR 110.3; or

(ii) The connected organization of the separate segregated fund as defined in 11 CFR 100.6; or

(iii) A parent, subsidiary, branch, division, department, or local unit of the connected organization of the separate segregated fund; or

(iv) A local, national or international union collecting contributions on behalf of the separate segregated fund of any federation with which the local, national or international union is affiliated. *See* 11 CFR 114.1(e).

(2) *Collecting agent not required to report.* A collecting agent that is an unregistered organization and that follows the procedures of 11 CFR 102.6(c) is not required to register and report as a political committee under 11 CFR parts 102 and 104, provided that the organization does not engage in other activities such as making contributions or expenditures for the purpose of influencing federal elections.

(3) *Who is not a collecting agent*—(i) *Commercial fundraising firm.* A separate segregated fund or a collecting agent may hire a commercial fundraising firm to assist in fundraising; however, the commercial fundraising firm shall not be considered as a collecting agent for the purpose of this section. Rather, the commercial fundraising firm shall be considered to be the agent of the separate segregated fund or collecting agent.

(ii) *Individuals.* An individual who collects contributions for a separate segregated fund shall not be considered a collecting agent for the purpose of this section. Individuals who collect contributions are subject to the requirements of 11 CFR 102.8 and the provisions of 11 CFR part 110.

(4) *Separate segregated fund may collect contributions.* Nothing in this section shall preclude a separate segregated fund from soliciting and collecting contributions on its own behalf.

(c) *Procedures for collecting agents*—(1) *Separate segregated fund responsible for acts of collecting agent.* The separate segregated fund shall be responsible for ensuring that the recordkeeping, re-

porting and transmittal requirements of this section are met.

(2) *Solicitation for contributions.* A collecting agent may include a solicitation for voluntary contributions to a separate segregated fund in a bill for membership dues or other payments such as conference registration fees or a solicitation for contributions to the collecting agent. The collecting agent may only solicit contributions from those persons permitted to be solicited under 11 CFR part 114. The solicitation for contributions must meet all of the requirements for proper solicitations under 11 CFR 114.5.

(i) The collecting agent may pay any or all of the costs incurred in soliciting and transmitting contributions to the separate segregated fund.

(ii) If the separate segregated fund pays any solicitation or other administrative expense from its own account, which expense could be paid for as an administrative expense by the collecting agent, the collecting agent may reimburse the separate segregated fund no later than 30 calendar days after the expense was paid by the separate segregated fund.

(3) *Checks combining contributions with other payments.* A contributor may write a check that represents both a contribution and payment of dues or other fees. The check must be drawn on the contributor's personal checking account or on a non-repayable corporate drawing account of the individual contributor. Under a payroll deduction plan, an employer may write a check on behalf of its employees to a union or its agent, which check represents a combined payment of voluntary contributions to the union's separate segregated fund and union dues or other employee deductions.

(4) *Transmittal of contributions.* The full amount of each contribution collected by a collecting agent on behalf of a separate segregated fund shall be transmitted to that fund within 10 or 30 days as required by 11 CFR 102.8.

(i) Checks made payable to the separate segregated fund shall be transmitted by the collecting agent directly to the separate segregated fund in accordance with 11 CFR 102.8.

(ii) To transfer all other contributions, a collecting agent shall either:

(A) Establish a transmittal account to be used solely for the deposit and transmittal of funds collected on behalf of the separate segregated fund. Funds deposited into this account are subject to the prohibitions and limitations of the Act. If any expenditure is made from the account, other than a transfer of funds to an affiliated committee, the account shall be considered a depository of the recipient committee and all activity of that account shall be reported; or

(B) Deposit the contributions collected into the collecting agent's treasury account. The collecting agent shall keep separate records of all receipts and deposits that represent contributions to the separate segregated fund and, in the case of cash contributions, the collecting agent shall make separate deposits of such funds; or

(C) Deposit the contributions collected into an account otherwise established solely for State or local election activity. The collecting agent shall keep separate records of all receipts and deposits that represent contributions to the separate segregated fund; or

(D) In the case of cash contributions, transmit the contributions to the separate segregated fund in the form of money orders or cashier's checks.

(5) *Contributor information.* The collecting agent shall comply with the requirements of 11 CFR 102.8 regarding transmittal of contributions and contributor information to the separate segregated fund, except that if contributions of $50 or less are received at a mass collection, a record shall be kept of the date, the total amount collected, and the name of the function at which the collection was made.

(6) *Retention of records.* The collecting agent shall retain all records of contribution deposits and transmittals under this section for a period of three years and shall make these records available to the Commission on request. The separate segregated fund shall keep a record of all transmittals of contributions received from collecting agents under this section, and shall retain these records for a period of three years.

(7) *Reporting of funds received through collecting agents.* A separate segregated fund receiving contributions collected by a collecting agent shall report the full amount of each contribution received as a contribution from the original contributor to the extent required by 11 CFR 104.3(a).

[48 FR 26300, June 7, 1983, as amended at 68 FR 451, Jan. 3, 2003; 69 FR 63920, Nov. 3, 2004]

§ 102.7   Organization of political committees (52 U.S.C. 30102(a)).

(a) Every political committee shall have a treasurer and may designate, on the committee's Statement of Organization, an assistant treasurer who shall assume the duties and responsibilities of the treasurer in the event of a temporary or permanent vacancy in the office or in the event the treasurer is unavailable.

(b) Except as provided in subsection (a), no contribution or expenditure shall be accepted or made by or on behalf of a political committee at a time when there is a vacancy in the office of the treasurer.

(c) No expenditure shall be made for or on behalf of a political committee without the authorization of its treasurer or of an agent authorized orally or in writing by the treasurer.

(d) Any candidate who receives a contribution, as defined at 11 CFR part 100, subparts B and D, obtains any loan or makes any disbursement in connection with his or her campaign, shall be considered as having received the contribution, obtained the loan or made the disbursement as an agent of such authorized committee(s).

[45 FR 15104, Mar. 7, 1980, as amended at 67 FR 78680, Dec. 26, 2002]

§ 102.8   Receipt of contributions (52 U.S.C. 30102(b)).

(a) Every person who receives a contribution for an authorized political committee shall, no later than 10 days after receipt, forward such contribution to the treasurer. If the amount of the contribution is in excess of $50, such person shall also forward to the treasurer the name and address of the contributor and the date of receipt of the contribution. If the amount of the contribution is in excess of $200, such person shall forward the contribution, the identification of the contributor in accordance with 11 CFR 100.12, and the date of receipt of the contribution. Date of receipt shall be the date such person obtains possession of the contribution.

(b)(1) Every person who receives a contribution of $50 or less for a political committee which is not an authorized committee shall forward such contribution to the treasurer of the political committee no later than 30 days after receipt.

(2) Every person who receives a contribution in excess of $50 for a political committee which is not an authorized committee shall, no later than 10 days after receipt of the contribution, forward to the treasurer of the political committee: The contribution; the name and address of the contributor; and the date of receipt of the contribution. If the amount of the contribution is in excess of $200, such person shall forward the contribution, the identification of the contributor in accordance with 11 CFR 100.12, and the date of receipt of the contribution. Date of receipt shall be the date such person obtains possession of the contribution.

(c) The provisions of 11 CFR 102.8 concerning receipt of contributions for political committees shall also apply to earmarked contributions transmitted by an intermediary or conduit.

§ 102.9 Accounting for contributions and expenditures (52 U.S.C. 30102(c)).

The treasurer of a political committee or an agent authorized by the treasurer to receive contributions and make expenditures shall fulfill all recordkeeping duties as set forth at 11 CFR 102.9(a) through (f):

(a) An account shall be kept by any reasonable accounting procedure of all contributions received by or on behalf of the political committee.

(1) For contributions in excess of $50, such account shall include the name and address of the contributor and the date of receipt and amount of such contribution.

(2) For contributions from any person whose contributions aggregate more than $200 during a calendar year, such account shall include the identification of the person, and the date of receipt and amount of such contribution.

(3) For contributions from a political committee, such account shall include the identification of the political committee and the date of receipt and amount of such contribution.

(4) In addition to the account to be kept under paragraph (a)(1) of this section, for contributions in excess of $50, the treasurer of a political committee or an agent authorized by the treasurer shall maintain:

(i) A full-size photocopy of each check or written instrument; or

(ii) A digital image of each check or written instrument. The political committee or other person shall provide the computer equipment and software needed to retrieve and read the digital images, if necessary, at no cost to the Commission.

(b)(1) An account shall be kept of all disbursements made by or on behalf of the political committee. Such account shall consist of a record of:

(i) The name and address of every person to whom any disbursement is made;

(ii) The date, amount, and purpose of the disbursement; and

(iii) If the disbursement is made for a candidate, the name and office (including State and congressional district, if any) sought by that candidate.

(iv) For purposes of 11 CFR 102.9(b)(1), *purpose* has the same meaning given the term at 11 CFR 104.3(b)(3)(i)(A).

(2) In addition to the account to be kept under 11 CFR 102.9(b)(1), a receipt or invoice from the payee or a cancelled check to the payee shall be obtained and kept for each disbursement in excess of $200 by or on behalf of, the committee, except that credit card transactions, shall be documented in accordance with 11 CFR 102.9(b)(2)(ii) and disbursements by share draft or check drawn on a credit union account shall be documented in accordance with 11 CFR 102.9(b)(2)(iii).

(i)(A) For purposes of 11 CFR 102.9(b)(2), *payee* means the person who provides the goods or services to the committee or agent thereof in return for payment, except for an advance of $500 or less for travel and subsistence to an individual who will be the recipient of the goods or services.

(B) For any advance of $500 or less to an individual for travel and subsistence, the expense voucher or other expense account documentation and a cancelled check to the recipient of the advance shall be obtained and kept.

(ii) For any credit card transaction, documentation shall include a monthly billing statement or customer receipt for each transaction and the cancelled check used to pay the credit card account.

(iii) For purposes of 11 CFR 102.9(b)(2), a carbon copy of a share draft or check drawn on a credit union account may be used as a duplicate record of such draft or check provided that the monthly account statement showing that the share draft or check was paid by the credit union is also retained.

(c) The treasurer shall preserve all records and accounts required to be kept under 11 CFR 102.9 for 3 years after the report to which such records and accounts relate is filed.

(d) In performing recordkeeping duties, the treasurer or his or her authorized agent shall use his or her best efforts to obtain, maintain and submit the required information and shall keep a complete record of such efforts. If there is a showing that best efforts have been made, any records of a committee shall be deemed to be in compliance with this Act. With regard to the requirements of 11 CFR 102.9(b)(2) concerning receipts, invoices and cancelled checks, the treasurer will not be deemed to have exercised best efforts to obtain, maintain and submit the records unless he or she has made at least one written effort per transaction to obtain a duplicate copy of the invoice, receipt, or cancelled check.

(e)(1) If the candidate, or his or her authorized committee(s), receives contributions that are designated for use in connection with the general election pursuant to 11 CFR 110.1(b) prior to the date of the primary election, such candidate or such committee(s) shall use an acceptable accounting method to distinguish between contributions received for the primary election and contributions received for the general election. Acceptable accounting methods include, but are not limited to:

(i) The designation of separate accounts for each election, caucus or convention; or

(ii) The establishment of separate books and records for each election.

(2) Regardless of the method used under paragraph (e)(1) of this section, an authorized committee's records must demonstrate that, prior to the primary election, recorded cash on hand was at all times equal to or in excess of the sum of general election contributions received less the sum of general election disbursements made.

(3) If a candidate is not a candidate in the general election, any contributions made for the general election shall be refunded to the contributors, redesignated in accordance with 11 CFR 110.1(b)(5) or 110.2(b)(5), or reattributed in accordance with 11 CFR 110.1(k)(3), as appropriate.

(f) The treasurer shall maintain the documentation required by 11 CFR 110.1(l), concerning designations, redesignations, reattributions and the dates of contributions. If the treasurer does not maintain this documentation, 11 CFR 110.1(l)(5) shall apply.

[45 FR 15104, Mar. 7, 1980, as amended at 52 FR 773, Jan. 9, 1987; 67 FR 69946, Nov. 19, 2002;79 FR 16663, Mar. 26, 2014]

§ 102.10 Disbursement by check (52 U.S.C. 30102 (h)(1)).

All disbursements by a political committee, except for disbursements from the petty cash fund under 11 CFR 102.11, shall be made by check or similar draft drawn on account(s) established at the committee's campaign depository or depositories under 11 CFR part 103.

§ 102.11 Petty cash fund (52 U.S.C. 30102(h)(2)).

A political committee may maintain a petty cash fund out of which it may make expenditures not in excess of $100 to any person per purchase or transaction. If a petty cash fund is maintained, it shall be the duty of the treasurer of the political committee to keep and maintain a written journal of all disbursements. This written journal shall include the name and address of every person to whom any disbursement is made, as well as the date, amount, and purpose of such disbursement. In addition, if any disbursement is made for a candidate, the journal shall include the name of that candidate and the office (including State and Congressional district) sought by such candidate.

§ 102.12 Designation of principal campaign committee (52 U.S.C. 30102(e)(1) and (3)).

(a) Each candidate for Federal office (other than a nominee of a political party to the Office of Vice President) shall designate in writing a political committee to serve as his or her principal campaign committee in accordance with 11 CFR 101.1(a) no later than 15 days after becoming a candidate. Each principal campaign committee shall register, designate a depository and report in accordance with 11 CFR parts 102, 103 and 104.

(b) No political committee may be designated as the principal campaign committee of more than one candidate.

(c)(1) No political committee which supports or has supported more than one candidate may be designated as a principal campaign committee, except that, after nomination, a candidate for the office of President of the United States nominated by a political party may designate the national committee of such political party as his or her principal campaign committee. A national committee which is so designated shall maintain separate books of account with respect to its function as a principal campaign committee.

(2) For purposes of 11 CFR 102.12(c), the term *support* does not include contributions by an authorized committee in amounts aggregating $2,000 or less per election to an authorized committee of any other candidate, except that the national committee of a political party which has been designated as the principal campaign committee of that party's Presidential candidate may contribute to another candidate in accordance with 11 CFR part 110.

[45 FR 15104, Mar. 7, 1980, as amended at 71 FR 54899, Sept. 20, 2006]

§ 102.13 Authorization of political committees (52 U.S.C. 30102(e)(1) and (3)).

(a)(1) Any political committee authorized by a candidate to receive contributions or make expenditures shall be authorized in writing by the candidate. Such authorization must be filed with the principal campaign committee in accordance with 11 CFR 102.1(b).

(2) If an individual fails to disavow activity pursuant to 11 CFR 100.3(a)(3) and is therefore a candidate upon notice by the Commission, he or she shall authorize the committee in writing.

(b) A candidate is not required to authorize a national, State or subordinate State party committee which solicits funds to be expended on the candidate's behalf pursuant to 11 CFR part 109, subpart D.

(c)(1) No political committee which supports or has supported more than one candidate may be designated as an authorized committee, except that two or more candidates may designate a political committee established solely for the purpose of joint fundraising by such candidates as an authorized committee.

(2) For purposes of 11 CFR 102.13(c), the term *support* does not include contributions by an authorized committee in amounts aggregating $2,000 or less per election to an authorized committee of any other candidate, except that the national committee of a political party which has been designated as the principal campaign committee of that party's Presidential candidate may contribute to another candidate in accordance with 11 CFR part 109, subpart D and 11 CFR part 110.

[45 FR 15104, Mar. 7, 1980, as amended at 67 FR 78680, Dec. 26, 2002; 71 FR 54899, Sept. 20, 2006]

§ 102.14 Names of political committees (52 U.S.C. 30102(e)(4) and (5)).

(a) The name of each authorized committee shall include the name of the candidate who authorized such committee. Except as provided in paragraph (b) of this section, no unauthorized committee shall include the name of any candidate in its name. For purposes of this paragraph, "name" includes any name under which a committee conducts activities, such as solicitations or other communications, including a special project name or other designation.

(b)(1) A delegate committee, as defined at 11 CFR 100.5(e)(5), shall include the word *delegate(s)* in its name and may also include in its name the name of the presidential candidate which the delegate committee supports.

(2) A political committee established solely to draft an individual or to encourage him or her to become a candidate may include the name of such individual in the name of the committee provided the committee's name clearly indicates that it is a draft committee.

(3) An unauthorized political committee may include the name of a candidate in the title of a special project name or other communication if the title clearly and unambiguously shows opposition to the named candidate.

(c) The name of a separate segregated fund established pursuant to 11 CFR 102.1(c) shall include the full name of its connected organization. Such fund may also use a clearly recognized abbreviation or acronym by which the connected organization is commonly known. Both the full name and such abbreviation or acronym shall be included on the fund's Statement of Organization, on all reports filed by the fund, and in all notices required by 11 CFR 109.11 and 110.11. The fund may make contributions using its acronym or abbreviated name. A fund established by a corporation which has a number of subsidiaries need not include the name of each subsidiary in its name. Similarly, a separate segregated fund established by a subsidiary need not include in its name the name of its parent or another subsidiary of its parent.

[45 FR 15104, Mar. 7, 1980, as amended at 45 FR 21209, Apr. 1, 1980; 57 FR 31426, July 15, 1992; 59 FR 17269, Apr. 12, 1994; 59 FR 35785, July 13, 1994; 67 FR 78680, Dec. 26, 2002]

§ 102.15　Commingled funds (52 U.S.C. 30102(b)(3)).

All funds of a political committee shall be segregated from, and may not be commingled with, any personal funds of officers, members or associates of that committee, or with the personal funds of any other individual. See also 11 CFR 103.3 and part 114 and 52 U.S.C. 30118.

[45 FR 15104, Mar. 7, 1980, as amended at 79 FR 77846, Dec. 29, 2014]

§ 102.16　Notice: Solicitation of contributions (52 U.S.C. 30120).

Each political committee shall comply with the notice requirements for solicitation of contributions set forth at 11 CFR 110.11.

§ 102.17　Joint fundraising by committees other than separate segregated funds.

(a) *General.* Nothing in this section shall supersede 11 CFR part 300, which prohibits any person from soliciting, receiving, directing, transferring, or spending any non-Federal funds, or from transferring Federal funds for Federal election activities.

(1)(i) Political committees may engage in joint fundraising with other political committees or with unregistered committees or organizations. The participants in a joint fundraising effort under this section shall either establish a separate committee or select a participating committee, to act as fundraising representative for all participants. The fundraising representative shall be a reporting political committee and an authorized committee of each candidate for federal office participating in the joint fundraising activity. If the participants establish a separate committee to act as the fundraising representative, the separate committee shall not be a participant in any other joint fundraising effort, but the separate committee may conduct more than one joint fundraising effort for the participants.

(ii) The participants may hire a commercial fundraising firm or other agent to assist in conducting the joint fundraising activity. In that case, however, the fundraising representative shall still be responsible for ensuring that the recordkeeping and reporting requirements set forth in this section are met.

(2) The procedures in 11 CFR 102.17(c) will govern all joint fundraising activity conducted under this section. The participants in joint fundraising activity may include political party committees (whether or not they are political committees under 11 CFR 100.5), candidate committees, multicandidate committees, and unregistered organizations which do not qualify as collecting agents under 11 CFR 102.6(b).

(3) A fundraising representative conducting joint fundraising under this section is distinguished from an unregistered organization acting as a collecting agent under 11 CFR 102.6(b). If a separate segregated fund or an unregistered organization qualifies and acts as a collecting agent under 11 CFR 102.6(b), the provisions of 11 CFR 102.17 will not apply to that fundraising activity.

(b) *Fundraising representatives*—(1) *Separate fundraising committee as fundraising representative.* Participating committees may establish a separate political committee to act as fundraising representative for all participants. This separate committee shall be a reporting political committee and shall collect contributions, pay fundraising costs from gross proceeds and from funds advanced by participants, and disburse net proceeds to each participant.

(2) *Participating committee as fundraising representative.* All participating committees may select one participant to act as fundraising representative for all participants. The fundraising representative must be a political committee as defined in 11 CFR 100.5. The fundraising representative and any other participating committees may collect contributions; however, all contributions received by other participants shall be forwarded to the fundraising representative as required by 11 CFR 102.8. The fundraising representative shall pay fundraising costs from gross proceeds and from funds advanced by participants and shall disburse net proceeds to each participant.

(3) *Funds advanced for fundraising costs.* (i) Except as provided in 11 CFR 102.17(b) (3)(ii) and (iii), the amount of funds advanced by each participant for fundraising costs shall be in proportion to the allocation formula agreed upon under 11 CFR 102.17 (c)(1).

(ii) A participant may advance more than its proportionate share of the fundraising costs, however, the amount advanced which is in excess of the participant's proportionate share shall not exceed the amount that participant could legally contribute to the remaining participants. *See* 11 CFR 102.12(c)(2) and part 110.

(iii) If all the participants are affiliated under 11 CFR 110.3 or if the participants are all party committees of the same political party, there is no limit on the amount a participant may advance for fundraising costs on behalf of the other participants.

(c) *Joint fundraising procedures.* The requirements of 11 CFR 102.17(c)(1) through (8) shall govern joint fundraising activity conducted under this section.

(1) *Written agreement.* The participants in a joint fundraising activity shall enter into a written agreement, whether or not all participants are political committees under 11 CFR 100.5. The written agreement shall identify the fundraising representative and shall state a formula for the allocation of fundraising proceeds. The formula shall be stated as the amount or percentage of each contribution received to be allocated to each participant. The fundraising representative shall retain the written agreement for a period of three years and shall make it available to the Commission on request.

(2) *Fundraising notice.* In addition to any notice required under 11 CFR 110.11, a joint fundraising notice shall be included with every solicitation for contributions.

(i) This notice shall include the following information:

(A) The names of all committees participating in the joint fundraising activity whether or not such committees are political committees under 11 CFR 100.5; and

(B) The allocation formula to be used for distributing joint fundraising proceeds; and

(C) A statement informing contributors that, notwithstanding the stated allocation formula, they may designate their contributions for a particular participant or participants; and

(D) A statement informing contributors that the allocation formula may change if a contributor makes a contribution which would exceed the amount that contributor may give to any participant.

(ii) In the following situations, the notice shall include the following additional information:

(A) If one or more participants engage in the joint fundraising activity solely to satisfy outstanding debts, a statement informing contributors that the allocation formula may change if a participant receives sufficient funds to pay its outstanding debts; and

(B) If one or more participants can lawfully accept contributions that are prohibited under the Act, a statement informing contributors that contributions from prohibited sources will be distributed only to those participants that can accept them.

(3) *Separate depository account.* (i) The participants or the fundraising representative shall establish a separate depository account to be used solely for the receipt and disbursement of the joint fundraising proceeds. All contributions deposited into the separate depository account must be permissible under the Act. Each political committee shall amend its Statement of Organization to reflect the account as an additional depository. If one or more participants can lawfully accept contributions that are prohibited under the Act, the participants may either establish a second depository account for contributions received from prohibited sources or they may forward such contributions directly to the nonfederal participants.

(ii) The fundraising representative shall deposit all joint fundraising proceeds in the separate depository account within ten days of receipt as required by 11 CFR 103.3. The fundraising representative may delay distribution of the fundraising proceeds to the participants until all contributions are received and all expenses are paid.

(iii) For contribution reporting and limitation purposes, the date of receipt of a contribution by a participating political committee is the date that the contribution is received by the fundraising representative. The fundraising representative shall report contributions in the reporting period in which they are received. Participating political committees shall report joint fundraising proceeds in accordance with 11 CFR 102.17(c)(8) when such funds are received from the fundraising representative.

(4) *Recordkeeping requirements.* (i) The fundraising representative and participating committees shall screen all contributions received to insure that the prohibitions and limitations of 11 CFR parts 110 and 114 are observed. Participating political committees shall make their contributor records available to the fundraising representative to enable the fundraising representative to carry out its duty to screen contributions.

(ii) The fundraising representative shall collect and retain contributor information with regard to gross proceeds as required under 11 CFR 102.8 and shall also forward such information to participating political committees. The fundraising representative shall also keep a record of the total amount of contributions received from prohibited sources, if any, and of all transfers of prohibited contributions to participants that can accept them.

(iii) The fundraising representative shall retain the records required under 11 CFR 102.9 regarding fundraising disbursements for a period of three years. Commercial fundraising firms or agents shall forward such information to the fundraising representative.

(5) *Contribution limitations.* Except to the extent that the contributor has previously contributed to any of the participants, a contributor may make a contribution to the joint fundraising effort which contribution represents the total amount that the contributor could contribute to all of the participants under the applicable limits of 11 CFR 110.1 and 110.2.

(6) *Allocation of gross proceeds.* (i) The fundraising representative shall allocate proceeds according to the formula stated in the fundraising agreement. If distribution according to the allocation formula extinguishes the debts of one or more participants and results in a surplus for those participants or if distribution under the formula results in a violation of the contribution limits of 11 CFR 110.1(a), the fundraising

representative may reallocate the excess funds. Reallocation shall be based upon the remaining participants' proportionate shares under the allocation formula. If reallocation results in a violation of a contributor's limit under 11 CFR 110.1, the fundraising representative shall return to the contributor the amount of the contribution that exceeds the limit.

(ii) Designated contributions which exceed the contributor's limit to the designated participant under 11 CFR part 110 may not be reallocated by the fundraising representative absent the prior written permission of the contributor.

(iii) If any participants can lawfully accept contributions from sources prohibited under the Act, any such contributions that are received are not required to be distributed according to the allocation formula.

(7) *Allocation of expenses and distribution of net proceeds.* (i) If participating committees are not affiliated as defined in 11 CFR 110.3 prior to the joint fundraising activity and are not committees of the same political party;

(A) After gross contributions are allocated among the participants under 11 CFR 102.17(c)(6), the fundraising representative shall calculate each participant's share of expenses based on the percentage of the total receipts each participant had been allocated. If contributions from sources prohibited under the Act have been received and distributed under 11 CFR 102.17(c)(6)(iii), those contributions need not be included in the total receipts for the purpose of allocating expenses under this section. To calculate each participant's net proceeds, the fundraising representative shall subtract the participant's share of expenses from the amount that participant has been allocated from gross proceeds.

(B) A participant may only pay expenses on behalf of another participant subject to the contribution limits of 11 CFR part 110.

(C) The expenses from a series of fundraising events or activities shall be allocated among the participants on a per-event basis regardless of whether the participants change or remain the same throughout the series.

(ii) If participating committees are affiliated as defined in 11 CFR 110.3 prior to the joint fundraising activity or if participants are party committees of the same political party, expenses need not be allocated among those participants. Payment of such expenses by an unregistered committee or organization on behalf of an affiliated political committee may cause the unregistered organization to become a political committee.

(iii) Payment of expenses may be made from gross proceeds by the fundraising representative.

(8) *Reporting of receipts and disbursements—(i) Reporting receipts.* (A) The fundraising representative shall report all funds received in the reporting period in which they are received. The fundraising representative shall report the total amount of contributions received from prohibited sources during the reporting period, if any, as a memo entry. Each Schedule A filed by the fundraising representative under this section shall clearly indicate that the contributions reported on that schedule represent joint fundraising proceeds.

(B) After distribution of net proceeds, each participating political committee shall report its share of net proceeds received as a transfer-in from the fundraising representative. Each participating political committee shall also file a memo Schedule A itemizing its share of gross receipts as contributions from original contributors to the extent required under 11 CFR 104.3(a).

(ii) *Reporting disbursements.* The fundraising representative shall report all disbursements in the reporting period in which they are made.

[48 FR 26301, June 7, 1983, as amended at 56 FR 35909, July 29, 1991; 67 FR 49112, July 29, 2002]

PART 103—CAMPAIGN DEPOSITORIES (52 U.S.C. 30102(h))

AUTHORITY: 52 U.S.C. 30102(h), 30111(a)(8).

SOURCE: 45 FR 15108, Mar. 7, 1980, unless otherwise noted.

§ 103.1 Notification of the commission.

Each committee shall notify the Commission of the campaign depository(ies) it has designated, pursuant to 11 CFR 101.1 and 103.2.

§ 103.2 Depositories (52 U.S.C. 30102(h)(1)).

Each political committee shall designate one or more State banks, federally chartered depository institutions (including a national bank), or depository institutions the depositor accounts of which are insured by the Federal Deposit Insurance Corporation, Federal Savings and Loan Insurance Corporation, or the National Credit Union Administration, as its campaign depository or depositories. One or more depositories may be established in one or more States. Each political committee shall maintain at least one checking account or transaction account at one of its depositories. Additional accounts may be established at each depository.

§ 103.3 Deposit of receipts and disbursements (52 U.S.C. 30102(h)(1)).

(a) All receipts by a political committee shall be deposited in account(s) established pursuant to 11 CFR 103.2, except that any contribution may be, within 10 days of the treasurer's receipt, returned to the contributor without being deposited. The treasurer of the committee shall be responsible for making such deposits. All deposits shall be made within 10 days of the treasurer's receipt. A committee shall make all disbursements by check or similar drafts drawn on an account at its designated campaign depository, except for expenditures of $100 or less made from a petty cash fund maintained pursuant to 11 CFR 102.11. Funds may be transferred from the depository for investment purposes, but shall be returned to the depository before such funds are used to make expenditures.

(b) The treasurer shall be responsible for examining all contributions received for evidence of illegality and for ascertaining whether contributions received, when aggregated with other contributions from the same contributor, exceed the contribution limitations of 11 CFR 110.1 or 110.2.

(1) Contributions that present genuine questions as to whether they were made by corporations, labor organizations, foreign nationals, or Federal contractors may be, within ten days of the treasurer's receipt, either deposited into a campaign depository under 11 CFR 103.3(a) or returned to the contributor. If any such contribution is deposited, the treasurer shall make his or her best efforts to determine the legality of the contribution. The treasurer shall make at least one written or oral request for evidence of the legality of the contribution. Such evidence includes, but is not limited to, a written statement from the contributor explaining why the contribution is legal, or a written statement by the treasurer memorializing an oral communication explaining why the contribution is legal. If the contribution cannot be determined to be legal, the treasurer shall, within thirty days of the treasurer's receipt of the contribution, refund the contribution to the contributor.

(2) If the treasurer in exercising his or her responsibilities under 11 CFR 103.3(b) determined that at the time a contribution was received and deposited, it did not appear to be made by a corporation, labor organization, foreign national or Federal contractor, or made in the name of another, but later discovers that it is illegal based on new evidence not available to the political committee at the time of receipt and deposit, the treasurer shall refund the contribution to the contributor within thirty days of the date on which the illegality is discovered. If the political committee does not have sufficient funds to refund the contribution at the time the illegality is discovered, the political committee shall make the refund from the next funds it receives.

(3) Contributions which on their face exceed the contribution limitations set forth in 11 CFR 110.1 or 110.2, and contributions which do not appear to be excessive on their face, but which exceed the contribution limits set forth in 11 CFR 110.1 or 110.2 when aggregated with other contributions from the same contributor, and contributions which cannot be accepted under

the net debts outstanding provisions of 11 CFR 110.1(b)(3) and 110.2(b)(3) may be either deposited into a campaign depository under 11 CFR 103.3(a) or returned to the contributor. If any such contribution is deposited, the treasurer may request redesignation or reattribution of the contribution by the contributor in accordance with 11 CFR 110.1(b), 110.1(k) or 110.2(b), as appropriate. If a redesignation or reattribution is not obtained, the treasurer shall, within sixty days of the treasurer's receipt of the contribution, refund the contribution to the contributor.

(4) Any contribution which appears to be illegal under 11 CFR 103.3(b) (1) or (3), and which is deposited into a campaign depository shall not be used for any disbursements by the political committee until the contribution has been determined to be legal. The political committee must either establish a separate account in a campaign depository for such contributions or maintain sufficient funds to make all such refunds.

(5) If a contribution which appears to be illegal under 11 CFR 103.3(b) (1) or (3) is deposited in a campaign depository, the treasurer shall make and retain a written record noting the basis for the appearance of illegality. A statement noting that the legality of the contribution is in question shall be included in the report noting the receipt of the contribution. If a contribution is refunded to the contributor because it cannot be determined to be legal, the treasurer shall note the refund on the report covering the reporting period in which the refund is made.

[52 FR 774, Jan. 9, 1987]

§103.4 Vice Presidential candidate campaign depositories.

Any campaign depository designated by the principal campaign committee of a political party's candidate for President shall be the campaign depository for that political party's candidate for the office of Vice President.

PART 104—REPORTS BY POLITICAL COMMITTEES AND OTHER PERSONS (52 U.S.C. 30104)

AUTHORITY: 52 U.S.C. 30101(1), 30101(8), 30101(9), 30102(i), 30104, 30111(a)(8) and (b), 30114, 30116, 36 U.S.C. 510.

SOURCE: 45 FR 15108, Mar. 7, 1980, unless otherwise noted.

§104.1 Scope (52 U.S.C. 30104(a)).

(a) *Who must report.* Each treasurer of a political committee required to register under 11 CFR part 102 shall report in accordance with 11 CFR part 104.

(b) *Who may report.* An individual seeking federal office who has not attained candidate status under 11 CFR 100.3, the committee of such an individual or any other committee may voluntarily register and report in accordance with 11 CFR parts 102 and 104.

An individual shall not become a candidate solely by voluntarily filing a report, nor shall such individual, the individual's committee, nor any other committee be required to file all reports under 11 CFR 104.5, unless the individual becomes a candidate under 11 CFR 100.3 or unless the committee becomes a political committee under 11 CFR 100.5.

§ 104.2 Forms.

(a) Each report filed by a political committee under 11 CFR part 104 shall be filed on the appropriate FEC form as set forth below at 11 CFR 104.2(e).

(b) Forms may be obtained from the Federal Election Commission at the street address identified in the definition of "Commission" in § 1.2.

(c) A committee may reproduce FEC forms for its own use provided they are not reduced in size.

(d) With prior approval of the Commission a committee may use, for reporting purposes, computer produced schedules of itemized receipts and disbursements provided they are reduced to the size of FEC forms. The committee shall submit a sample of the proposed format with its request for approval.

(e) The following forms shall be used by the indicated type of reporting committee:

(1) *Presidential committees.* The authorized committees of a candidate for President or Vice President shall file on FEC Form 3–P.

(2) *Congressional candidate committees.* The authorized committees of a candidate for the Senate or the House of Representatives shall file on FEC Form 3.

(3) *Political Committees Other than Authorized Committees.* Political committees other than authorized committees shall file reports on FEC Form 3–X.

[45 FR 15108, Mar. 7, 1980, as amended at 45 FR 21209, Apr. 1, 1980; 50 FR 50778, Dec. 12, 1985; 82 FR 60853, Dec. 26, 2017]

§ 104.3 Contents of reports (52 U.S.C. 30104(b), 30114).

(a) *Reporting of receipts.* Each report filed under § 104.1 shall disclose the total amount of receipts for the reporting period and for the calendar year (or for the election cycle, in the case of an authorized committee) and shall disclose the information set forth at paragraphs (a)(1) through (a)(4) of this section. The first report filed by a political committee shall also include all amounts received prior to becoming a political committee under § 100.5 of this chapter, even if such amounts were not received during the current reporting period.

(1) *Cash on hand.* The amount of cash on hand at the beginning of the reporting period, including: currency; balance on deposit in banks, savings and loan institutions, and other depository institutions; traveler's checks owned by the committee; certificates of deposit, treasury bills and any other committee investments valued at cost.

(2) *Categories of receipts for all political committees other than authorized committees.* All committees other than authorized committees shall report the total amount of receipts received during the reporting period and, except for itemized and unitemized breakdowns, during the calendar year for each of the following categories:

(i) Contributions from persons other than any committees;

(A) Itemized contributions from persons, other than any committees, including contributions from individuals;

(B) Unitemized contributions from persons, other than any committees, including contributions from individuals;

(C) Total contributions from persons other than any committees, including contributions from individuals;

(ii) Contributions from political party committees, including contributions from party committees which are not political committees under the Act;

(iii) Contributions from political committees, including contributions from committees which are not political committees under the Act but excluding contributions from any party committees;

(iv) Total contributions;

(v) Transfers from affiliated committees or organizations and, where the reporting committee is a political party committee, transfers from other party committees of the same party, regardless of whether such committees are affiliated;

(vi) All loans;

(vii) Offsets to operating expenditures;

(A) Itemized offsets to operating expenditures (such as rebates and refunds);

(B) Unitemized offsets to operating expenditures (such as rebates and refunds);

(C) Total offsets to operating expenditures;

(viii) Other receipts:

(A) Itemized other receipts (such as dividends and interest);

(B) Unitemized other receipts (such as dividends and interest);

(C) The total sum of all other receipts.

(ix) The total sum of all receipts.

(3) *Categories of receipts for authorized committees.* An authorized committee of a candidate for Federal office shall report the total amount of receipts received during the reporting period and, except for itemized and unitemized breakdowns, during the election cycle in each of the following categories:

(i) Contributions from persons other than any committees;

(A) Itemized contributions from persons, other than any committees, including contributions from individuals, but excluding contributions from a candidate to his or her authorized committees;

(B) Unitemized contributions from persons, other than any committees, including contributions from individuals, but excluding contributions from a candidate to his or her authorized committees;

(C) Total contributions from persons other than any committees, including contributions from individuals, but excluding contributions from a candidate to his or her authorized committees;

(ii) Contributions from the candidate, excluding loans which are reported under 11 CFR 104.3(a)(3)(vii));

(iii) Contributions from political party committees, including party committees which are not political committees under the Act, except that expenditures made under 11 CFR part 109, subpart D (52 U.S.C. 30116(d)),by a party committee shall not be reported as contributions by the authorized committee on whose behalf they are made;

(iv) Contributions from committees, including contributions from committees which are not political committees under the Act, but excluding contributions from any party committees;

(v) Total contributions;

(vi) Transfers from other authorized committee(s) of the same candidate, regardless of amount;

(vii) Loans;

(A) All loans to the committee, except loans made, guaranteed, or endorsed by a candidate to his or her authorized committee;

(B) Loans made, guaranteed, or endorsed by a candidate to his or her authorized committee including loans derived from a bank loan to the candidate or from an advance on a candidate's brokerage account, credit card, home equity line of credit, or other lines of credit described in 11 CFR 100.83 and 100.143; and

(C) Total loans;

(viii) For authorized committee(s) of Presidential candidates, federal funds received under chapters 95 and 96 of the Internal Revenue Code of 1954 (Title 26, United States Code);

(ix) Offsets to operating expenditures;

(A) Itemized offsets to operating expenditures (such as refunds and rebates);

(B) Unitemized offsets to operating expenditures (such as refunds and rebates);

(C) Total offsets to operating expenditures;

(x) Other receipts;

(A) Itemized other receipts (such as dividends and interest);

(B) Unitemized other receipts (such as dividends and interest);

(C) Total other receipts;

(xi) Total receipts.

(4) *Itemization of receipts for all political committees including authorized and unauthorized committees.* The identification (as defined at § 100.12 of this chapter) of each contributor and the aggregate year-to-date (or aggregate election-cycle-to-date, in the case of an authorized committee) total for such contributor in each of the following categories shall be reported.

(i) Each person, other than any political committee, who makes a contribution to the reporting political committee during the reporting period, whose contribution or contributions aggregate in excess of $200 per calendar year (or per election cycle in the case of an authorized committee), together with the date of receipt and amount of any such contributions, except that the reporting political committee may elect to report such information for contributors of lesser amount(s) on a separate schedule;

(ii) All committees (including political committees and committees which do not qualify as political committees under the Act) which make contributions to the reporting committee during the reporting period, together with the date of receipt and amount of any such contribution;

(iii) Transfers;

(A) For authorized committees of a candidate for Federal office, each authorized committee which makes a transfer to the reporting committee, together with the date and amount of such transfer;

(B) For committees which are not authorized by a candidate for Federal office, each affiliated committee or organization which makes a transfer to the reporting committee during the reporting period and, where the reporting committee is a political party committee, each transfer of funds to the reporting committee from another party committee regardless of whether such committees are affiliated, together with the date and amount of such transfer;

(iv) Each person who makes a loan to the reporting committee or to the candidate acting as an agent of the committee, during the reporting period, together with the identification of any endorser or guarantor of such loan, the date such loan was made and the amount or value of such loan;

(v) Each person who provides a rebate, refund or other offset to operating expenditures to the reporting political committee in an aggregate amount or value in excess of $200 within the calendar year (or within the election cycle, in the case of an authorized committee), together with the

date and amount of any such receipt; and

(vi) Each person who provides any dividend, interest, or other receipt to the reporting political committee in an aggregate value or amount in excess of $200 within the calendar year (or within the election cycle, in the case of an authorized committee), together with the date and amount of any such receipt.

(b) *Reporting of disbursements.* Each report filed under §104.1 shall disclose the total amount of all disbursements for the reporting period and for the calendar year (or for the election cycle, in the case of an authorized committees) and shall disclose the information set forth at paragraphs (b)(1) through (b)(4) of this section. The first report filed by a political committee shall also include all amounts disbursed prior to becoming a political committee under §100.5 of this chapter, even if such amounts were not disbursed during the current reporting period.

(1) *Categories of disbursements for political committees other than authorized committees.* All political committees other than authorized committees shall report the total amount of disbursements made during the reporting period and, except for itemized and unitemized breakdowns, during the calendar year in each of the following categories:

(i) Operating expenditures;

(A) Itemized operating expenditures;

(B) Unitemized operating expenditures;

(C) Total operating expenditures;

(ii) Transfers to affiliated committees or organizations and, where the reporting committee is a political party committee, transfers to other political party committees regardless of whether they are affiliated;

(iii) Repayment of all loans;

(iv) Offsets;

(A) Itemized offsets to contributions (including contribution refunds);

(B) Unitemized offsets to contributions (including contribution refunds);

(C) Total offsets to contributions;

(v) Contributions made to other political committees;

(vi) Loans made by the reporting committee;

(vii) Independent expenditures made by the reporting committee;

(viii) Expenditures made under 11 CFR part 109, subpart D (52 U.S.C. 30116(d)), See 11 CFR 104.3(a)(3)(iii);

(ix) Other disbursements;

(A) Itemized other disbursements;

(B) Unitemized other disbursements;

(C) Total other disbursements;

(x) Total disbursements.

(2) *Categories of disbursements for authorized committees.* An authorized committee of a candidate for Federal office shall report the total amount of disbursements made during the reporting period and, except for itemized and unitemized breakdowns, during the election cycle in each of the following categories:

(i) Operating expenditures;

(A) Itemized operating expenditures;

(B) Unitemized operating expenditures;

(C) Total operating expenditures;

(ii) Transfers to other committees authorized by the same candidate;

(iii) Repayment of loans;

(A) Repayment of loans made, guaranteed, or endorsed by the candidate to his or her authorized committee including loans derived from a bank loan to the candidate or from an advance on a candidate's brokerage account, credit card, home equity line of credit, or other lines of credit described in 11 CFR 100.83 and 100.143;

(B) Repayment of all other loans;

(C) Total loan repayments;

(iv) For an authorized committee of a candidate for the office of President, disbursements not subject to the limitations of 11 CFR 110.8 (52 U.S.C. 30116(b));

(v) Offsets;

(A) Itemized offsets to contributions (including contribution refunds);

(B) Unitemized offsets to contributions (including contribution refunds);

(C) Total offsets to contributions;

(vi) Other disbursements;

(A) Itemized other disbursements;

(B) Unitemized other disbursements;

(C) Total other disbursements;

(vii) Total disbursements.

(3) *Itemization of disbursements by political committees other than authorized committees.* Each political committee, other than an authorized committee, shall report the full name and address

of each person in each of the following categories, as well as the information required by each category;

(i) Each person to whom an expenditure in an aggregate amount or value in excess of $200 within the calendar year is made by the reporting committee to meet the committee's operating expenses, together with the date, amount, and purpose of such operating expenditure;

(A) As used in 11 CFR 104.3(b)(3), *purpose* means a brief statement or description of why the disbursement was made.

(B) Examples of statements or descriptions which meet the requirements of 11 CFR 104.3(b)(3) include the following: dinner expenses, media, salary, polling, travel, party fees, phone banks, travel expenses, travel expense reimbursement, and catering costs. However, statements or descriptions such as *advance, election day expenses, other expenses, expenses, expense reimbursement, miscellaneous, outside services, get-out-the-vote* and *voter registration* would not meet the requirements of 11 CFR 104.3(b)(3) for reporting the purpose of an expenditure.

(ii) Each affiliated committee to which a transfer is made by the reporting committee during the reporting period and, where the reporting committee is a political party committee, each transfer of funds by the reporting committee to another political party committee, regardless of whether such committees are affiliated, together with the date and amount of such transfer;

(iii) Each person who receives a loan repayment from the reporting committee during the reporting period, together with the date and amount of such loan repayment;

(iv) Each person who receives a contribution refund or other offset to contributions from the reporting committee where such contribution refund was reported under 11 CFR 104.3(b)(1)(iv), together with the date and amount of such refund or offset;

(v) Each political committee which has received a contribution from the reporting committee during the reporting period, together with the date and amount of any such contribution, and, in the case of a contribution to an authorized committee, the candidate's name and office sought (including State and Congressional district, if applicable);

(vi) Each person who has received a loan from the reporting committee during the reporting period, together with the date and amount or value of such loan;

(vii) (A) Each person who receives any disbursement during the reporting period in an aggregate amount or value in excess of $200 within the calendar year in connection with an independent expenditure by the reporting committee, together with the date, amount, and purpose of any such independent expenditure(s);

(B) For each independent expenditure reported, the committee must also provide a statement which indicates whether such independent expenditure is in support of, or in opposition to a particular candidate, as well as the name of the candidate and office sought by such candidate (including State and Congressional district, when applicable), and a certification, under penalty of perjury, as to whether such independent expenditure is made in cooperation, consultation or concert with, or at the request or suggestion of, any candidate or any authorized committee or agent of such committee;

(C) The information required by 11 CFR 104.3(b)(3)(vii) (A) and (B) shall be reported on Schedule E as part of a report covering the reporting period in which the aggregate disbursements for any independent expenditure to any person exceed $200 per calendar year. Schedule E shall also include the total of all such expenditures of $200 or less made during the reporting period.

(viii) Each person who receives any expenditure from the reporting committee during the reporting period in connection with an expenditure under 11 CFR part 109, subpart D (52 U.S.C. 30116(d)),together with the date, amount, and purpose of any such expenditure as well as the name of, and office sought by (including State and Congressional district, when applicable), the candidate on whose behalf the expenditure is made; and

(ix) Each person who has received any disbursement within the reporting period not otherwise disclosed in accordance with 11 CFR 104.3(b)(3) to whom the aggregate amount or value of disbursements made by the reporting committee exceeds $200 within the calendar year, together with the date, amount and purpose of any such disbursement.

(4) *Itemization of disbursements by authorized committees.* Each authorized committee shall report the full name and address of each person in each of the following categories, as well as the information required by each category.

(i) Each person to whom an expenditure in an aggregate amount or value in excess of $200 within the election cycle is made by the reporting authorized committee to meet the authorized committee's operating expenses, together with the date, amount and purpose of each expenditure.

(A) As used in this paragraph, *purpose* means a brief statement or description of why the disbursement was made. Examples of statements or descriptions which meet the requirements of this paragraph include the following: dinner expenses, media, salary, polling, travel, party fees, phone banks, travel expenses, travel expense reimbursement, and catering costs. However, statements or descriptions such as *advance, election day expenses, other expenses, expenses, expense reimbursement, miscellaneous, outside services, get-out-the-vote* and *voter registration* would not meet the requirements of this paragraph for reporting the purpose of an expenditure.

(B) In addition to reporting the purpose described in paragraph (b)(4)(i)(A) of this section, whenever an authorized committee itemizes a disbursement that is partially or entirely a personal use for which reimbursement is required under 11 CFR 113.1(g)(1)(ii)(C) or (D), it shall provide a brief explanation of the activity for which reimbursement is required.

(ii) Each authorized committee of the same candidate to which a transfer is made by the reporting committee during the reporting period, together with the date and amount of such transfer;

(iii) Each person who receives a loan repayment, including a repayment of a loan of money derived from an advance on a candidate's brokerage account, credit card, home equity line of credit, or other lines of credit described in 11 CFR 100.83 and 100.143, from the reporting committee during the reporting period, together with the date and amount of such loan repayment;

(iv) [Reserved]

(v) Each person who receives a contribution refund or other offset to contributions from the reporting committee where such contribution refund was reported under 11 CFR 104.3(b)(2)(v), together with the date and amount of such refund or offset.

(vi) Each person who has received any disbursement(s) not otherwise disclosed under paragraph (b)(4) of this section to whom the aggregate amount or value of such disbursements exceeds $200 within the election cycle, together with the date, amount, and purpose of any such disbursement.

(c) *Summary of contributions and operating expenditures.* Each report filed pursuant to §104.1 shall disclose for both the reporting period and the calendar year (or the election cycle, in the case of the authorized committee):

(1)(i) The total contributions to the reporting committee;

(ii) The total offsets to contributions;

(iii) The net contributions (subtract total offsets from total contributions);

(2)(i) The reporting committee's total operating expenditures;

(ii) The total offsets to operating expenditures;

(iii) The net operating expenditures (subtract total offsets from total operating expenditures).

(d) *Reporting debts and obligations.* Each report filed under 11 CFR 104.1 shall, on Schedule C or D, as appropriate, disclose the amount and nature of outstanding debts and obligations owed by or to the reporting committee. Loans, including a loan of money derived from an advance on a candidate's brokerage account, credit card, home equity line of credit, or other lines of credit described in 11 CFR 100.83, obtained by an individual prior to becoming a candidate for use in connection with that individual's campaign shall be reported as an outstanding loan owed to the lender by the candidate's principal campaign committee, if such loans are outstanding at the time the individual becomes a candidate. Where

such debts and obligations are settled for less than their reported amount or value, each report filed under 11 CFR 104.1 shall contain a statement as to the circumstances and conditions under which such debts or obligations were extinguished and the amount paid. *See* 11 CFR 116.7.

(1) In addition, when a political committee obtains a loan from, or establishes a line of credit at, a lending institution as described in 11 CFR 100.82(a) through (d) and 100.142(a) through (d), it shall disclose in the report covering the period when the loan was obtained, the following information on schedule C-1 or C-P-1:

(i) The date and amount of the loan or line of credit;

(ii) The interest rate and repayment schedule of the loan, or of each draw on the line of credit;

(iii) The types and value of traditional collateral or other sources of repayment that secure the loan or the line of credit, and whether that security interest is perfected;

(iv) An explanation of the basis upon which the loan was made or the line of credit established, if not made on the basis of either traditional collateral or the other sources of repayment described in 11 CFR 100.82(e)(1) and (2) and 100.142(e)(1) and (2); and

(v) A certification from the lending institution that the borrower's responses to paragraphs (d)(1)(i)–(iv) of this section are accurate, to the best of the lending institution's knowledge; that the loan was made or the line of credit established on terms and conditions (including interest rate) no more favorable at the time than those imposed for similar extensions of credit to other borrowers of comparable credit worthiness; and that the lending institution is aware of the requirement that a loan or a line of credit must be made on a basis which assures repayment and that the lending institution has complied with Commission regulations at 11 CFR 100.82(a) through (d) and 100.142(a) through (d).

(2) The political committee shall submit a copy of the loan or line of credit agreement which describes the terms and conditions of the loan or line of credit when it files Schedule C-1 or C-P-1. This paragraph (d)(2) shall not

apply to any Schedule C-1 or C-P-1 that is filed pursuant to paragraph (d)(4) of this section.

(3) The political committee shall file in the next due report a Schedule C-1 or C-P-1 each time a draw is made on a line of credit, and each time a loan or line of credit is restructured to change the terms of repayment. This paragraph (d)(3) shall not apply to any Schedule C-1 or C-P-1 that is filed pursuant to paragraph (d)(4) of this section.

(4) When a candidate obtains a bank loan or loan of money derived from an advance on the candidate's brokerage account, credit card, home equity line of credit, or other line of credit described in 11 CFR 100.83 and 100.143 for use in connection with the candidate's campaign, the candidate's principal campaign committee shall disclose in the report covering the period when the loan was obtained, the following information on Schedule C-1 or C-P-1:

(i) The date, amount, and interest rate of the loan, advance, or line of credit;

(ii) The name and address of the lending institution; and

(iii) The types and value of collateral or other sources of repayment that secure the loan, advance, or line of credit, if any.

(e) *Use of pseudonyms.* (1) To determine whether the names and addresses of its contributors are being used in violation of 11 CFR 104.15 to solicit contributions or for commercial purposes, a political committee may submit up to ten (10) pseudonyms on each report filed.

(2) For purposes of this section, a pseudonym is a wholly fictitious name which does not represent the name of an actual contributor to a committee.

(3) If a committee uses pseudonyms it shall subtract the total dollar amount of the fictitious contributions from the total amount listed as a memo entry on line 11(a) of the Detailed Summary page, *Unitemized contributions from individual persons other than political committees.* Thus, the committee will, for this purpose only, be overstating the amount of itemized contributions received and understating the amount of unitemized contributions received.

(4) No authorized committee of a candidate shall attribute more than $1,000 in contributions to the same pseudonym for each election and no other political committee shall attribute more than $5,000 in contributions to the same pseudonym in any calendar year.

(5) A committee using pseudonyms shall send a list of such pseudonyms under separate cover directly to the Reports Analysis Division, Federal Election Commission, at the street address identified in the definition of "Commission" in § 1.2, on or before the date on which any report containing such pseudonyms is filed with the Secretary of the Senate or the Commission. The Commission shall maintain the list, but shall exclude it from the public record. A committee shall not send any list of pseudonyms to the Secretary of the Senate or to any Secretary of State or equivalent state officer.

(6) A political committee shall not use pseudonyms for the purpose of circumventing the reporting requirements or the limitations and prohibitions of the Act.

(f) *Consolidated reports.* Each principal campaign committee shall consolidate in each report those reports required to be filed with it. Such consolidated reports shall include: (1) Reports submitted to it by any authorized committees and (2) the principal campaign committee's own report. Such consolidation shall be made on FEC Form 3-Z and shall be submitted with the reports of the principal campaign committee and with the reports, or applicable portions thereof, of the committees shown on the consolidation.

(g) *Building funds.* (1) A political party committee must report gifts, subscriptions, loans, advances, deposits of money, or anything of value that are used by the political party committee's Federal accounts to defray the costs of construction or purchase of the committee's office building. See 11 CFR 300.35. Such a receipt is a contribution subject to the limitations and prohibitions of the Act and reportable as a contribution, regardless of whether the contributor has designated the funds or things of value for such purpose and regardless of whether such funds are deposited in a separate Federal account dedicated to that purpose.

(2) Gifts, subscriptions, loans, advances, deposits of money, or anything of value that are donated to a non-Federal account of a State or local party committee and are used by that party committee for the purchase or construction of its office building are not contributions subject to the reporting requirements of the Act. The reporting of such funds or things of value is subject to State law.

(3) Gifts, subscriptions, loans, advances, deposits of money, or anything of value that are used by a national committee of a political party to defray the costs of construction or purchase of the national committee's office building are contributions subject to the requirements of paragraph (g)(1) of this section.

(h) *Legal and accounting services.* A committee which receives legal or accounting services pursuant to 11 CFR 100.85 and 100.86 shall report as a memo entry, on Schedule A, the amounts paid for these services by the regular employer of the person(s) providing such services; the date(s) such services were performed; and the name of each person performing such services.

(i) *Cumulative reports.* The reports required to be filed under §104.5 shall be cumulative for the calendar year (or for the election cycle, in the case of an authorized committee) to which they relate, but if there has been no change in a category reported in a previous report during that year (or during that election cycle, in the case of an authorized committee), only the amount thereof need be carried forward.

(j) *Earmarked contributions.* Earmarked contributions shall be reported in accordance with 11 CFR 110.6. *See also* 11 CFR 102.8(c).

(k) *Reporting Election Cycle Activity Occurring Prior to January 1, 2001.* The aggregate of each category of receipt listed in paragraph (a)(3) of this section, except those in paragraphs (a)(3)(i)(A) and (B) of this section, and for each category of disbursement listed in paragraph (b)(2) of this section shall include amounts received or disbursed on or after the day after the

last general election for the seat or office for which the candidate is running through December 31, 2000.

[45 FR 15108, Mar. 7, 1980]

EDITORIAL NOTE: For FEDERAL REGISTER citations affecting §104.3, see the List of CFR Sections Affected, which appears in the Finding Aids section of the printed volume and at *www.fdsys.gov.*

§104.4 **Independent expenditures by political committees (52 U.S.C. 30104(b), (d), and (g)).**

(a) *Regularly scheduled reporting.* Every political committee that makes independent expenditures must report all such independent expenditures on Schedule E in accordance with 11 CFR 104.3(b)(3)(vii). Every person that is not a political committee must report independent expenditures in accordance with paragraphs (e) and (f) of this section and 11 CFR 109.10.

(b) *Reports of independent expenditures made at any time up to and including the 20th day before an election*—(1) *Independent expenditures aggregating less than $10,000 in a calendar year.* For each election in which a political committee makes independent expenditures, the political committee shall aggregate its independent expenditures made in each calendar year to determine its reporting obligation. When a committee makes independent expenditures aggregating less than $10,000 for an election in any calendar year, up to and including the 20th day before an election, the committee must report those independent expenditures on Schedule E of FEC Form 3X, at the time of its regular reports in accordance with 11 CFR 104.3, 104.5, and 104.9.

(2) *Independent expenditures aggregating $10,000 or more in a calendar year.* For each election in which a political committee makes independent expenditures, the political committee shall aggregate its independent expenditures made in each calendar year to determine its reporting obligation. When a committee makes independent expenditures aggregating $10,000 or more for an election in any calendar year, up to and including the 20th day before an election, it must report those independent expenditures on Schedule E of FEC Form 3X. Political committees

must ensure that the Commission receives these reports by 11:59 p.m. Eastern Standard/Daylight Time on the second day following the date on which a communication that constitutes an independent expenditure is publicly distributed or otherwise publicly disseminated. Each time subsequent independent expenditures relating to the same election aggregate an additional $10,000 or more, the political committee must ensure that the Commission receives a new 48-hour report of the subsequent independent expenditures by 11:59 p.m. Eastern Standard/Daylight Time on the second day following the date on which the communication is publicly distributed or otherwise publicly disseminated. (See paragraph (f) of this section for aggregation.) Each 48-hour report must contain the information required by 11 CFR 104.3(b)(3)(vii) indicating whether the independent expenditure is made in support of, or in opposition to, the candidate involved. In addition to other permissible means of filing, a political committee may file the 48-hour reports under this section by any of the means permissible under 11 CFR 100.19(d)(3).

(c) *Reports of independent expenditures made less than 20 days, but more than 24 hours before the day of an election.* Political committees must ensure that the Commission receives reports of independent expenditures aggregating $1,000 or more with respect to a given election, after the 20th day, but more than 24 hours before 12:01 a.m. of the day of the election, by 11:59 p.m. Eastern Standard/Daylight Time on the day following the date on which a communication is publicly distributed or otherwise publicly disseminated. Each time subsequent independent expenditures relating to the same election aggregate an additional $1,000 or more, the political committee must ensure that the Commission receives a new 24-hour report of the subsequent independent expenditures by 11:59 p.m. Eastern Standard/Daylight Time on the day following the date on which a communication that constitutes an independent expenditure is publicly distributed or otherwise publicly disseminated. (See paragraph (f) of this section for aggregation.) Each 24-hour report shall contain the information

required by 11 CFR 104.3(b)(3)(vii) indicating whether the independent expenditure is made in support of, or in opposition to, the candidate involved. Political committees may file reports under this section by any of the means permissible under 11 CFR 100.19(d)(3).

(d) *Verification.* Political committees must verify reports of independent expenditures filed under paragraph (b) or (c) of this section by one of the methods stated in paragraph (d)(1) or (2) of this section. Any report verified under either of these methods shall be treated for all purposes (including penalties for perjury) in the same manner as a document verified by signature.

(1) For reports filed on paper (e.g., by hand-delivery, U.S. Mail or facsimile machine), the treasurer of the political committee that made the independent expenditure must certify, under penalty of perjury, the independence of the expenditure by handwritten signature immediately following the certification required by 11 CFR 104.3(b)(3)(vii).

(2) For reports filed by electronic mail, the treasurer of the political committee that made the independent expenditure shall certify, under penalty of perjury, the independence of the expenditure by typing the treasurer's name immediately following the certification required by 11 CFR 104.3(b)(3)(vii).

(e) *Where to file.* Reports of independent expenditures under this section and 11 CFR 109.10(b) shall be filed as follows:

(1) For independent expenditures in support of, or in opposition to, a candidate for President or Vice President: with the Commission and the Secretary of State for the State in which the expenditure is made.

(2) For independent expenditures in support of, or in opposition to, a candidate for the Senate:

(i) For regularly scheduled reports, with the Secretary of the Senate and the Secretary of State for the State in which the candidate is seeking election; or

(ii) For 24-hour and 48-hour reports, with the Commission and the Secretary of State for the State in which the candidate is seeking election.

(3) For independent expenditures in support of, or in opposition to, a candidate for the House of Representatives: with the Commission and the Secretary of State for the State in which the candidate is seeking election.

(4) Notwithstanding the requirements of paragraphs (e)(1), (2), and (3) of this section, political committees and other persons shall not be required to file reports of independent expenditures with the Secretary of State if that State has obtained a waiver under 11 CFR 108.1(b).

(f) *Aggregating independent expenditures for reporting purposes.* For purposes of determining whether 24-hour and 48-hour reports must be filed in accordance with paragraphs (b) and (c) of this section and 11 CFR 109.10(c) and (d), aggregations of independent expenditures must be calculated as of the first date on which a communication that constitutes an independent expenditure is publicly distributed or otherwise publicly disseminated, and as of the date that any such communication with respect to the same election is subsequently publicly distributed or otherwise publicly disseminated. Every person must include in the aggregate total all disbursements during the calendar year for independent expenditures, and all enforceable contracts, either oral or written, obligating funds for disbursements during the calendar year for independent expenditures, where those independent expenditures are made with respect to the same election for Federal office.

[68 FR 417, Jan. 3, 2003, as amended at 81 FR 34863, June 1, 2016]

§104.5 Filing dates (52 U.S.C. 30104(a)(2)).

(a) *Principal campaign committee of House of Representatives or Senate candidate.* Each treasurer of a principal campaign committee of a candidate for the House of Representatives or for the Senate must file quarterly reports on the dates specified in paragraph (a)(1) of this section in both election years and non-election years, and must file additional reports on the dates specified in paragraph (a)(2) of this section in election years.

(1) *Quarterly reports.* (i) Quarterly reports must be filed no later than the 15th day following the close of the immediately preceding calendar quarter (on April 15, July 15, and October 15), except that the report for the final calendar quarter of the year must be filed no later than January 31 of the following calendar year.

(ii) The report must be complete as of the last day of each calendar quarter.

(iii) The requirement for a quarterly report shall be waived if, under paragraph (a)(2) of this section, a pre-election report is required to be filed during the period beginning on the 5th day after the close of the calendar quarter and ending on the 15th day after the close of the calendar quarter.

(2) *Additional reports in the election year.* (i) *Pre-election reports.* (A) Pre-election reports for the primary and general election must be filed no later than 12 days before any primary or general election in which the candidate seeks election. If sent by registered or certified mail, Priority Mail or Express Mail with a delivery confirmation, or with an overnight delivery service and scheduled to be delivered the next business day after the date of deposit and recorded in the overnight delivery service's on-line tracking system, the postmark on the report must be dated no later than the 15th day before any election.

(B) The pre-election report must disclose all receipts and disbursements as of the 20th day before a primary or general election.

(ii) *Post-general election report.* (A) The post-general election report must be filed no later than 30 days after any general election in which the candidate seeks election.

(B) The post-general election report must be complete as of the 20th day after the general election.

(b) *Principal campaign committee of Presidential candidate.* Each treasurer of a principal campaign committee of a candidate for President shall file reports on the dates specified at 11 CFR 104.5(b) (1) and (2).

(1) *Election year reports.* (i) If on January 1 of the election year, the committee has received or anticipates receiving contributions aggregating

$100,000 or more, or has made or anticipates making expenditures aggregating $100,000 or more, it shall file monthly reports.

(A) Each report shall be filed no later than the 20th day after the last day of each month.

(B) The report shall be complete as of the last day of each month.

(C) In lieu of the monthly reports due in November and December, a pre-election report shall be filed as prescribed at paragraph (a)(2)(i) of this section, a post-general election report shall be filed as prescribed at paragraph (a)(2)(ii) of this section, and a year-end report shall be filed no later than January 31 of the following calendar year.

(ii) If on January 1 of the election year, the committee does not anticipate receiving and has not received contributions aggregating $100,000 and does not anticipate making and has not made expenditures aggregating $100,000, the committee shall file a preelection report or reports, a post general election report, and quarterly reports, as prescribed in paragraphs (a)(1) and (2) of this section.

(iii) If during the election year, a committee filing under 11 CFR 104.5(b)(1)(ii) receives contributions aggregating $100,000 or makes expenditures aggregating $100,000, the treasurer shall begin filing monthly reports at the next reporting period.

(2) *Non-election year reports.* During a non-election year, the treasurer shall file either monthly reports as prescribed by paragraph (b)(1)(i) of this section or quarterly reports as prescribed by paragraph (a)(1) of this section. A principal campaign committee of a Presidential candidate may elect to change the frequency of its reporting from monthly to quarterly or vice versa during a non-election year only after notifying the Commission in writing of its intention at the time it files a required report under its pre-existing filing frequency. The committee will then be required to file the next required report under its new filing frequency. The committee may change its filing frequency no more than once per calendar year.

(c) *Political committees that are not authorized committees of candidates.* Except as provided in paragraph (c)(4) of this section, each political committee that is not the authorized committee of a candidate must file either: Election year and non-election year reports in accordance with paragraphs (c)(1) and (2) of this section; or monthly reports in accordance with paragraph (c)(3) of this section. A political committee reporting under paragraph (c) of this section may elect to change the frequency of its reporting from monthly to quarterly and semi-annually or *vice versa.* A political committee reporting under this paragraph (c) may change the frequency of its reporting only after notifying the Commission in writing of its intention at the time it files a required report under its current filing frequency. Such political committee will then be required to file the next required report under its new filing frequency. A political committee may change its filing frequency no more than once per calendar year.

(1) *Election year reports—*(i) *Quarterly reports.* (A) Quarterly reports shall be filed no later than the 15th day following the close of the immediately preceding calendar quarter, (on April 15, July 15, and October 15), except that the report for the final calendar quarter of the year shall be filed on January 31 of the following calendar year.

(B) The reports shall be complete as of the last day of the calendar quarter for which the report is filed.

(C) The requirement for a quarterly report shall be waived if under 11 CFR 104.5(c)(1)(ii) a pre-election report is required to be filed during the period beginning on the fifth day after the close of the calendar quarter and ending on the fifteenth day after the close of the calendar quarter.

(ii) *Pre-election reports.* (A) Pre-election reports for the primary and general election shall be filed by a political committee which makes contributions or expenditures in connection with any such election if such disbursements have not been previously disclosed. Pre-election reports shall be filed no later than 12 days before any primary or general election. If sent by registered or certified mail, Priority Mail or Express Mail with a delivery confirmation, or with an overnight delivery service and scheduled to be delivered the next business day after the date of deposit and recorded in the overnight delivery service's on-line tracking system, the postmark on the report shall be dated no later than the 15th day before any election.

(B) The report shall disclose all receipts and disbursements as of the 20th day before a primary or general election.

(iii) *Post-general election reports.* (A) A post-general election report shall be filed no later than 30 days after any general election.

(B) The report shall be complete as of the 20th day after the general election.

(2) *Non-election year reports*—(i) *Semiannual reports.* (A) The first report shall cover January 1 through June 30, and shall be filed no later than July 31.

(B) The second report shall cover July 1 through December 31, and shall be filed no later than January 31 of the following year.

(3) *Monthly reports.* (i) Except as provided at 11 CFR 104.5(c)(3)(ii), monthly reports shall be filed no later than 20 days after the last day of the month.

(ii) In lieu of the monthly reports due in November and December, in any year in which a regularly scheduled general election is held, a pre-election report shall be filed as prescribed at 11 CFR 104.5(a)(2)(i), a post general election report shall be filed as prescribed at 11 CFR 104.5(a)(2)(ii), and a year-end report shall be filed no later than January 31 of the following calendar year.

(4) *National party committee reporting.* Notwithstanding anything to the contrary in this paragraph, a national committee of a political party, including a national Congressional campaign committee, must report monthly in accordance with paragraph (c)(3) of this section in both election and non-election years.

(d) *Committees supporting Vice Presidential candidates.* The treasurer of a committee supporting a candidate for the office of Vice President (other than a nominee of a political party) shall file reports on the same basis that the principal campaign committee of a Presidential candidate must file reports under 11 CFR 104.5(b).

(e) *Date of filing.* A designation, report or statement, other than those addressed in paragraphs (f), (g), and (j) of this section, sent by registered or cer-

tified mail, Priority Mail or Express Mail with a delivery confirmation, or with an overnight delivery service and scheduled to be delivered the next business day after the date of deposit and recorded in the overnight delivery service's on-line tracking system, shall be considered filed on the date of the postmark except that a twelve day pre-election report sent by such mail or overnight delivery service must have a postmark dated no later than the 15th day before any election. Designations, reports or statements, other than those addressed in paragraphs (f), (g), and (j) of this section, sent by first class mail, or by any means other than those listed in this paragraph (e), must be received by the close of business on the prescribed filing date to be timely filed. Designations, reports or statements electronically filed must be received and validated at or before 11:59 p.m., eastern standard/daylight time on the prescribed filing date to be timely filed.

(f) *48-hour notification of contributions.* If any contribution of $1,000 or more is received by any authorized committee of a candidate after the 20th day, but more than 48 hours, before 12:01 a.m. of the day of the election, the principal campaign committee of that candidate shall notify the Commission, the Secretary of the Senate and the Secretary of State, as appropriate, within 48 hours of receipt of the contribution. The notification shall be in writing and shall include the name of the candidate and office sought by the candidate, the identification of the contributor, and the date of receipt and amount of the contribution. The notification shall be filed in accordance with 11 CFR 100.19. The notification shall be in addition to the reporting of these contributions on the post-election report.

(g) *Reports of independent expenditures*—(1) *48-hour reports of independent expenditures.* Every person that must file a 48-hour report under 11 CFR 104.4(b) must ensure the Commission receives the report by 11:59 p.m. Eastern Standard/Daylight Time on the second day following the date on which a communication that constitutes an independent expenditure is publicly distributed or otherwise publicly disseminated. Each time subsequent independent expenditures by that person relating to the same election as that to which the previous report relates aggregate $10,000 or more, that person must ensure that the Commission receives a new 48-hour report of the subsequent independent expenditures by 11:59 p.m. Eastern Standard/Daylight Time on the second day following the date on which the $10,000 threshold is reached or exceeded. (*See* 11 CFR 104.4(f) for aggregation.)

(2) *24-hour reports of independent expenditures.* Every person that must file a 24-hour report under 11 CFR 104.4(c) must ensure that the Commission receives the report by 11:59 p.m. Eastern Standard/Daylight Time on the day following the date on which a communication that constitutes an independent expenditure is publicly distributed or otherwise publicly disseminated. Each time subsequent independent expenditures by that person relating to the same election as that to which the previous report relates aggregate $1,000 or more, that person must ensure that the Commission receives a 24-hour report of the subsequent independent expenditures by 11:59 p.m. Eastern Standard/Daylight Time on the day following the date on which the $1,000 threshold is reached or exceeded. (*See* 11 CFR 104.4(f) for aggregation.)

(3) Each 24-hour or 48-hour report of independent expenditures filed under this section shall contain the information required by 11 CFR 104.3(b)(3)(vii) indicating whether the independent expenditure is made in support of, or in opposition to, the candidate involved.

(4) For purposes of this part and 11 CFR part 109, a communication that is mailed to its intended audience is publicly disseminated when it is relinquished to the U.S. Postal Service.

(h) *Special election reports.* (1) Within 5 days of the setting of a special election, the Commission shall set filing dates for reports to be filed by principal campaign committees of candidates seeking election, or nomination for election, in special elections and for political committees, other than authorized committees, which make contributions to or expenditures

on behalf of a candidate or candidates in special elections. The Commission shall publish such reporting dates in the FEDERAL REGISTER and shall notify the principal campaign committees of all candidates in such election of the reporting dates. The Commission shall not require such committees to file more than one pre-election report for each election and one post-election report for the election which fills the vacancy.

(2) Reports required to be filed under 11 CFR 104.5(a) or (c) may be waived by the Commission for committees filing special election reports if a report under 11 CFR 104.5(a) or (c) is due within 10 days of the date a special election report is due. The Commission shall notify all appropriate committees of reports so waived.

(i) Committees should retain proof of mailing or other means of transmittal of the reports to the Commission.

(j) *24-hour statements of electioneering communications.* Every person who has made a disbursement or who has executed a contract to make a disbursement for the direct costs of producing or airing electioneering communications as defined in 11 CFR 100.29 aggregating in excess of $10,000 during any calendar year shall file a statement with the Commission by 11:59 p.m. Eastern Standard/Daylight Time on the day following the disclosure date. The statement shall be filed under penalty of perjury and in accordance with 11 CFR 104.20.

[45 FR 15108, Mar. 7, 1980, as amended at 61 FR 3549, Feb. 1, 1996; 65 FR 31794, May 19, 2000; 65 FR 38423, June 21, 2000; 67 FR 12839, Mar. 20, 2002; 68 FR 418, Jan. 3, 2003; 68 FR 47414, Aug. 8, 2003; 69 FR 68238, Nov. 24, 2004; 70 FR 13091, Mar. 18, 2005; 79 FR 16663, Mar. 26, 2014]

§ 104.6 Form and content of internal communications reports (52 U.S.C. 30101(9)(B)(iii)).

(a) *Form.* Every membership organization or corporation which makes disbursements for communications pursuant to 11 CFR 100.134(a) and 114.3 shall report to the Commission on FEC Form 7 such costs which are directly attributable to any communication expressly advocating the election or defeat of a clearly identified candidate (other than a communication primarily devoted to subjects other than the election or defeat of a clearly identified candidate), if such costs exceed $2,000 for any election.

(1) For the purposes of 11 CFR 104.6(a), *election* means two separate processes in a calendar year, to each of which the $2,000 threshold described above applies separately. The first process is comprised of all primary elections for federal office, wherever and whenever held; the second process is comprised of all general elections for federal office, wherever and whenever held.

(2) The term election shall also include each special election held to fill a vacancy in a Federal office (11 CFR 100.2(f)) or each runoff election (11 CFR 100.2(d)).

(b) *Filing dates.* Organizations required to report under 11 CFR 104.6(a) shall file such reports during a calendar year in which a regularly scheduled general election is held. Such reports shall be filed quarterly in accordance with 11 CFR 104.5(a)(1) and, with respect to any general election, in accordance with 11 CFR 104.5(a)(2)(i). The organization shall be required to file reports beginning with the first reporting period during which the aggregate cost for such communications exceeds $2,000 per election as defined in 11 CFR 104.6(a)(1), and for each quarter thereafter in which the organization makes additional disbursements in connection with the same election.

(c) Each report filed under 11 CFR 104.6 shall include, for each communication:

(1) The type of communication (such as direct mail, telephone or telegram);

(2) The date(s) of the communication;

(3) The name of the candidate, the office sought (and the district and state of the office, if applicable), and whether the communication was for the primary or general election;

(4) Whether the communication was in support of or in opposition to, a particular candidate; and

(5) The cost of the communication.

[45 FR 15108, Mar. 7, 1980, as amended at 67 FR 78680, Dec. 26, 2002; 79 FR 16663, Mar. 26, 2014]

§104.7 Best efforts (52 U.S.C. 30102(i)).

(a) When the treasurer of a political committee shows that best efforts have been used to obtain, maintain and submit the information required by the Act for the political committee, any report of such committee shall be considered in compliance with the Act.

(b) With regard to reporting the identification as defined at 11 CFR 100.12 of each person whose contribution(s) to the political committee and its affiliated political committees aggregate in excess of $200 in a calendar year (or in an election cycle in the case of an authorized committee) (pursuant to 11 CFR 104.3(a)(4)), the treasurer and the political committee will only be deemed to have exercised best efforts to obtain, maintain and report the required information if:

(1)(i) All written solicitations for contributions include a clear request for the contributor's full name, mailing address, occupation and name of employer, and include an accurate statement of Federal law regarding the collection and reporting of individual contributor identifications.

(A) The following are examples of acceptable statements for unauthorized committees, but are not the only allowable statements: "Federal law requires us to use our best efforts to collect and report the name, mailing address, occupation and name of employer of individuals whose contributions exceed $200 in a calendar year;" and "To comply with Federal law, we must use best efforts to obtain, maintain, and submit the name, mailing address, occupation and name of employer of individuals whose contributions exceed $200 per calendar year."

(B) The following are examples of acceptable statements for authorized committees, but are not the only allowable statements: "Federal law requires us to use our best efforts to collect and report the name, mailing address, occupation and name of employer of individuals whose contributions exceed $200 in an election cycle;" and "To comply with Federal law, we must use best efforts to obtain, maintain, and submit the name, mailing address, occupation and name of employer of individuals whose contributions exceed $200 per election cycle."

(ii) The request and statement shall appear in a clear and conspicuous manner on any response material included in a solicitation. The request and statement are not clear and conspicuous if they are in small type in comparison to the solicitation and response materials, or if the printing is difficult to read or if the placement is easily overlooked.

(2) For each contribution received aggregating in excess of $200 per calendar year (or per election cycle, in the case of an authorized committee) which lacks required contributor information, such as the contributor's full name, mailing address, occupation or name of employer, the treasurer makes at least one effort after the receipt of the contribution to obtain the missing information. Such effort shall consist of either a written request sent to the contributor or an oral request to the contributor documented in writing. The written or oral request must be made no later than thirty (30) days after receipt of the contribution. The written or oral request shall not include material on any other subject or any additional solicitation, except that it may include language solely thanking the contributor for the contribution. The request must clearly ask for the missing information, and must include the statement set forth in paragraph (b)(1) of this section. Written requests must include this statement in a clear and conspicuous manner. If the request is written, it shall be accompanied by a pre-addressed return post card or envelope for the response material;

(3) The treasurer reports all contributor information not provided by the contributor, but in the political committee's possession, or in its connected organization's possession, regarding contributor identifications, including information in contributor records, fundraising records and previously filed reports, in the same two-year election cycle in accordance with 11 CFR 104.3; and

(4)(i) If any of the contributor information is received after the contribution has been disclosed on a regularly scheduled report, the political committee shall either:

(A) File with its next regularly scheduled report, an amended memo Schedule A listing all contributions for which contributor identifications have been received during the reporting period covered by the next regularly scheduled report together with the dates and amounts of the contribution(s) and an indication of the previous report(s) to which the memo Schedule A relates; or

(B) File on or before its next regularly scheduled reporting date, amendments to the report(s) originally disclosing the contribution(s), which include the contributor identifications together with the dates and amounts of the contribution(s).

(ii) Amendments must be filed for all reports that cover the two-year election cycle in which the contribution was received and that disclose itemizable contributions from the same contributor. However, political committees are not required to file amendments to reports covering previous election cycles.

[45 FR 15108, Mar. 7, 1980, as amended at 58 FR 57729, Oct. 27, 1993; 62 FR 23336, Apr. 30, 1997; 65 FR 42624, July 11, 2000]

§ 104.8 Uniform reporting of receipts.

(a) A reporting political committee shall disclose the identification of each individual who contributes an amount in excess of $200 to the political committee's federal account(s). This identification shall include the individual's name, mailing address, occupation, the name of his or her employer, if any, and the date of receipt and amount of any such contribution. If an individual contributor's name is known to have changed since an earlier contribution reported during the calendar year (or during the election cycle, in the case of an authorized committee), the exact name or address previously used shall be noted with the first reported contribution from that contributor subsequent to the name change.

(b) In each case where a contribution received from an individual in a reporting period is added to previously unitemized contributions from the same individual and the aggregate exceeds $200 in a calendar year (or in an election cycle, in the case of an authorized committee) the reporting political committee shall disclose the identification of such individual along with the date of receipt and amount of any such contribution. Except for contributions by payroll deduction, each additional contribution from the individual shall be separately itemized. In the case of a political committee other than an authorized committee which receives contributions through a payroll deduction plan, such committee is not required to separately itemize each additional contribution received from the contributor during the reporting period. In lieu of separate itemization, such committee may report: the aggregate amount of contributions received from the contributor through the payroll deduction plan during the reporting period; the identification of the individual; and a statement of the amount deducted per pay period.

(c) Absent evidence to the contrary, any contribution made by check, money order, or other written instrument shall be reported as a contribution by the last person signing the instrument prior to delivery to the candidate or committee.

(d)(1) If an itemized contribution is made by more than one person in a single written instrument, the treasurer shall report the amount to be attributed to each contributor.

(2)(i) If a contribution is redesignated by a contributor, in accordance with 11 CFR 110.1(b) or 110.2(b), the treasurer of the authorized political committee receiving the contribution shall report the redesignation in a memo entry on Schedule A of the report covering the reporting period in which the redesignation is received. The memo entry for each redesignated contribution shall be reported in the following manner—

(A) The first part of the memo entry shall disclose all of the information for the contribution as it was originally reported on Schedule A;

(B) The second part of the memo entry shall disclose all of the information for the contribution as it was redesignated by the contributor, including the election for which the contribution was redesignated and the date on which the redesignation was received.

(ii) If a contribution from a political committee is redesignated by the contributing political committee in accordance with 11 CFR 110.1(b) or 110.2(b), the treasurer of such political committee shall report the redesignation in a memo entry on Schedule B of the report covering the reporting period in which the redesignation is made. The memo entry for each redesignated contribution shall be reported in the following manner—

(A) The first part of the memo entry shall disclose all of the information for the contribution as it was originally reported on Schedule B;

(B) The second part of the memo entry shall disclose all of the information for the contribution as it was redesignated by the contributing political committee, including the election for which the contribution was redesignated and the date on which the redesignation was made.

(3) If an itemized contribution is reattributed by the contributor(s) in accordance with 11 CFR 110.1(k), the treasurer shall report the reattribution in a memo entry on Schedule A of the report covering the reporting period in which the reattribution is received. The memo entry for each reattributed contribution shall be reported in the following manner—

(i) The first part of the memo entry shall disclose all of the information for the contribution as it was originally reported on Schedule A;

(ii) The second part of the memo entry shall disclose all of the information for the contribution as it was reattributed by the contributors, including the date on which the reattribution was received.

(4) If a contribution is refunded to the contributor, the treasurer of the political committee making the refund shall report the refund on Schedule B of the report covering the reporting period in which the refund is made, in accordance with 11 CFR 103.3(b)(5) and 104.3(b). If a contribution is refunded to a political committee, the treasurer of the political committee receiving the refund shall report the refund on Schedule A of the report covering the reporting period in which the refund is received, in accordance with 11 CFR 104.3(a).

(e) For reports covering activity on or before December 31, 2002, national party committees shall disclose in a memo Schedule A information about each individual, committee, corporation, labor organization, or other entity that donates an aggregate amount in excess of $200 in a calendar year to the committee's non-Federal account(s). This information shall include the donating individual's or entity's name, mailing address, occupation or type of business, and the date of receipt and amount of any such donation. If a donor's name is known to have changed since an earlier donation reported during the calendar year, the exact name or address previously used shall be noted with the first reported donation from that donor subsequent to the name change. The memo entry shall also include, where applicable, the information required by paragraphs (b) through (d) of this section.

(f) For reports covering activity on or before December 31, 2002, national party committees shall also disclose in a memo Schedule A information about each individual, committee, corporation, labor organization, or other entity that donates an aggregate amount in excess of $200 in a calendar year to the committee's building fund account(s). This information shall include the donating individual's or entity's name, mailing address, occupation or type of business, and the date of receipt and amount of any such donation. If a donor's name is known to have changed since an earlier donation reported during the calendar year, the exact name or address previously used shall be noted with the first reported donation from that donor subsequent to the name change. The memo entry shall also include, where applicable, the information required by paragraphs (b) through (d) of this section.

(g) The principal campaign committee of the candidate shall report the receipt of any bank loan obtained by the candidate or loan of money derived from an advance on a candidate's brokerage account, credit card, home equity line of credit, or other lines of credit described in 11 CFR 100.83 and 100.143, as an itemized entry of Schedule A as follows:

(1) The amount of the loan that is used in connection with the candidate's campaign shall be reported as an itemized entry on Schedule A.

(2) *See* 11 CFR 100.83(c) for special reporting rules regarding certain loans used for a candidate's routine living expenses.

[45 FR 15108, Mar. 7, 1980, as amended at 52 FR 774, Jan. 9, 1987; 55 FR 26067, June 26, 1990; 65 FR 42624, July 11, 2000; 67 FR 38360, June 4, 2002; 67 FR 49112, July 29, 2002; 75 FR 31, Jan. 4, 2010]

§ 104.9 Uniform reporting of disbursements.

(a) Political committees shall report the full name and mailing address of each person to whom an expenditure in an aggregate amount or value in excess of $200 within the calendar year (or within the election cycle, in the case of an authorized committee) is made from the reporting political committee's federal account(s), together with the date, amount and purpose of such expenditure, in accordance with paragraph (b) of this section. As used in this section, *purpose* means a brief statement or description as to the reasons for the expenditure. *See* 11 CFR 104.3(b)(3)(i)(A).

(b) In each case when an expenditure made to a recipient in a reporting period is added to previously unitemized expenditures to the same recipient and the total exceeds $200 for the calendar year (or for the election cycle, in the case of an authorized committee), the reporting political committee shall disclose the recipient's full name and mailing address on the prescribed reporting forms, together with the date, amount and purpose of such expenditure. As used in this section, *purpose* means a brief statement or description as to the reason for the disbursement as defined at 11 CFR 104.3(b)(3)(i)(A).

(c) For reports covering activity on or before March 31, 2003, national party committees shall report in a memo Schedule B the full name and mailing address of each person to whom a disbursement in an aggregate amount or value in excess of $200 within the calendar year is made from the committee's non-Federal account(s), together with the date, amount, and purpose of such disbursement, in accordance with paragraph (b) of this section. As used in this section, *purpose* means a brief statement or description as to the reasons for the disbursement. *See* 11 CFR 104.3(b)(3)(i)(A).

(d) For reports covering activity on or before March 31, 2003, national party committees shall report in a memo Schedule B the full name and mailing address of each person to whom a disbursement in an aggregate amount or value in excess of $200 within the calendar year is made from the committee's building fund account(s), together with the date, amount, and purpose of such disbursement, in accordance with paragraph (b) of this section. As used in this section, *purpose* means a brief statement or description as to the reasons for the disbursement. *See* 11 CFR 104.3(b)(3)(i)(A).

(e) For reports covering activity on or before December 31, 2002, national party committees shall report in a memo Schedule B each transfer from their non-Federal account(s) to the non-Federal accounts of a State or local party committee.

(f) The principal campaign committee of the candidate shall report its repayment to the candidate or lending institution of any bank loan obtained by the candidate or loan of money derived from an advance on a candidate's brokerage account, credit card, home equity line of credit, or other lines of credit described in 11 CFR 100.83 and 100.143 as an itemized entry on Schedule B.

[45 FR 15108, Mar. 7, 1980, as amended at 55 FR 26067, June 26, 1990; 65 FR 42624, July 11, 2000; 67 FR 38361, June 4, 2002; 67 FR 49113, July 29, 2002; 79 FR 16663, Mar. 26, 2014]

§ 104.10 Reporting by separate segregated funds and nonconnected committees of expenses allocated among candidates and activities.

(a) *Expenses allocated among candidates.* A political committee that is a separate segregated fund or a nonconnected committee making an expenditure on behalf of more than one clearly identified candidate for Federal office shall allocate the expenditure among the candidates pursuant to 11 CFR part 106. Payments involving both expenditures on behalf of one or more clearly identified Federal candidates and disbursements on behalf of one or more clearly identified non-Federal can-

didates shall also be allocated pursuant to 11 CFR part 106. For allocated expenditures, the committee shall report the amount of each in-kind contribution, independent expenditure, or coordinated expenditure attributed to each Federal candidate. If a payment also includes amounts attributable to one or more non-Federal candidates, and is made by a political committee with separate Federal and non-Federal accounts, then the payment shall be made according to the procedures set forth in 11 CFR 106.6(e), but shall be reported pursuant to paragraphs (a)(1) through (a)(4) of this section, as follows:

(1) *Reporting of allocation of expenses attributable to specific Federal and non-Federal candidates.* In each report disclosing a payment that includes both expenditures on behalf of one or more Federal candidates and disbursements on behalf of one or more non-Federal candidates, the committee shall assign a unique identifying title or code to each program or activity conducted on behalf of such candidates, shall state the allocation ratio calculated for the program or activity, and shall explain the manner in which the ratio was derived. The committee shall also summarize the total amounts attributed to each candidate, to date, for each joint program or activity.

(2) *Reporting of transfers between accounts for the purpose of paying expenses attributable to specific Federal and non-Federal candidates.* A political committee that pays allocable expenses in accordance with 11 CFR 106.6(e) shall report each transfer of funds from its non-Federal account to its Federal account or to its separate allocation account for the purpose of paying such expenses. In the report covering the period in which each transfer occurred, the committee shall explain in a memo entry the allocable expenses to which the transfer relates and the date on which the transfer was made. If the transfer includes funds for the allocable costs of more than one program or activity, the committee shall itemize the transfer, showing the amounts designated for each program or activity conducted on behalf of one

or more clearly identified Federal candidates and one or more clearly identified non-Federal candidates.

(3) *Reporting of allocated disbursements attributable to specific Federal and non-Federal candidates.* A political committee that pays allocable expenses in accordance with 11 CFR 106.6(e) shall also report each disbursement from its Federal account or its separate allocation account in payment for a program or activity conducted on behalf of one or more clearly identified Federal candidates and one or more clearly identified non-Federal candidates. In the report covering the period in which the disbursement occurred, the committee shall state the full name and address of each person to whom the disbursement was made, and the date, amount, and purpose of each such disbursement. If the disbursement includes payment for the allocable costs of more than one program or activity, the committee shall itemize the disbursement, showing the amounts designated for payment of each program or activity conducted on behalf of one or more clearly identified Federal candidates and one or more clearly identified non-Federal candidates. The committee shall also report the amount of each in-kind contribution, independent expenditure, or coordinated expenditure attributed to each Federal candidate, and the total amount attributed to the non-Federal candidate(s). In addition, the committee shall report the total amount expended by the committee that year, to date, for each joint program or activity.

(4) *Recordkeeping.* The treasurer shall retain all documents supporting the committee's allocation on behalf of specific Federal and non-Federal candidates, in accordance with 11 CFR 104.14.

(b) *Expenses allocated among activities.* A political committee that is a separate segregated fund or a nonconnected committee and that has established separate Federal and non-Federal accounts under 11 CFR 102.5(a)(1)(i) shall allocate between those accounts its administrative expenses and its costs for fundraising, generic voter drives, and certain public communications according to 11 CFR 106.6, and shall report those allocations according to para-

graphs (b)(1) through (5) of this section, as follows:

(1) *Reporting of allocation of administrative expenses and costs of generic voter drives and public communications that refer to any political party.* In each report disclosing a disbursement for administrative expenses, generic voter drives, or public communications that refer to any political party, but do not refer to any clearly identified candidates, as described in 11 CFR 106.6(b)(1)(i), (b)(1)(iii) and (b)(1)(iv), as applicable, the committee shall state the allocation ratio to be applied to each category of activity according to 11 CFR 106.6(c).

(2) *Reporting of allocation of the direct costs of fundraising.* In each report disclosing a disbursement for the direct costs of a fundraising program, as described in 11 CFR 106.6(b), the committee shall assign a unique identifying title or code to each such program or activity, shall state the allocation ratio calculated for the program or activity according to 11 CFR 106.6(d), and shall explain the manner in which the ratio was derived. The committee shall also summarize the total amounts spent by the Federal and non-Federal accounts that year, to date, for each such program or activity.

(3) *Reporting of transfers between accounts for the purpose of paying allocable expenses.* A political committee that pays allocable expenses in accordance with 11 CFR 106.6(e) shall report each transfer of funds from its non-Federal account to its Federal account or to its separate allocation account for the purpose of paying such expenses. In the report covering the period in which each transfer occurred, the committee shall explain in a memo entry the allocable expenses to which the transfer relates and the date on which the transfer was made. If the transfer includes funds for the allocable costs of more than one activity, the committee shall itemize the transfer, showing the amounts designated for administrative expenses and generic voter drives, and for each fundraising program, as described in 11 CFR 106.6(b).

(4) *Reporting of allocated disbursements.* A political committee that pays allocable expenses in accordance with

11 CFR 106.6(e) shall also report each disbursement from its Federal account or its separate allocation account in payment for a joint Federal and non-Federal expense or activity. In the report covering the period in which the disbursement occurred, the committee shall state the full name and address of each person to whom the disbursement was made, and the date, amount, and purpose of each such disbursement. If the disbursement includes payment for the allocable costs of more than one activity, the committee shall itemize the disbursement, showing the amounts designated for payment of administrative expenses and generic voter drives, and for each fundraising program, as described in 11 CFR 106.6(b). The committee shall also report the total amount expended by the committee that year, to date, for each category of activity.

(5) *Recordkeeping.* The treasurer shall retain all documents supporting the committee's allocated disbursements for three years, in accordance with 11 CFR 104.14.

[67 FR 49113, July 29, 2002, as amended at 69 FR 68067, Nov. 23, 2004]

§ 104.11 Continuous reporting of debts and obligations.

(a) Debts and obligations owed by or to a political committee which remain outstanding shall be continuously reported until extinguished. See 11 CFR 104.3(d). These debts and obligations shall be reported on separate schedules together with a statement explaining the circumstances and conditions under which each debt and obligation was incurred or extinguished. Where such debts and obligations are settled for less than their reported amount or value, the reporting committee shall include a statement as to the circumstances and conditions under which the debt or obligation was extinguished and the amount paid.

(b) A debt or obligation, including a loan, written contract, written promise or written agreement to make an expenditure, the amount of which is $500 or less, shall be reported as of the time payment is made or not later than 60 days after such obligation is incurred, whichever comes first. A debt or obligation, including a loan, written contract, written promise or written agreement to make an expenditure, the amount of which is over $500 shall be reported as of the date on which the debt or obligation is incurred, except that any obligation incurred for rent, salary or other regularly reoccurring administrative expense shall not be reported as a debt before the payment due date. *See* 11 CFR 116.6. If the exact amount of a debt or obligation is not known, the report shall state that the amount reported is an estimate. Once the exact amount is determined, the political committee shall either amend the report(s) containing the estimate or indicate the correct amount on the report for the reporting period in which such amount is determined.

[45 FR 15108, Mar. 7, 1980, as amended at 55 FR 26386, June 27, 1990]

§ 104.12 Beginning cash on hand for political committees.

Political committees which have cash on hand at the time of registration shall disclose on their first report the source(s) of such funds, including the information required by 11 CFR 104.3(a)(1). The cash on hand balance is assumed to be composed of those contributions most recently received by the committee. The committee shall exclude from funds to be used for Federal elections any contributions not permissible under the Act. See 11 CFR parts 110, 114, and 115.

§ 104.13 Disclosure of receipt and consumption of in-kind contributions.

(a)(1) The amount of an in-kind contribution shall be equal to the usual and normal value on the date received. Each in-kind contribution shall be reported as a contribution in accordance with 11 CFR 104.3(a).

(2) Except for items noted in 11 CFR 104.13(b), each in-kind contribution shall also be reported as an expenditure at the same usual and normal value and reported on the appropriate expenditure schedule, in accordance with 11 CFR 104.3(b).

(b) Contributions of stocks, bonds, art objects, and other similar items to be liquidated shall be reported as follows:

(1) If the item has not been liquidated at the close of a reporting period, the

committee shall record as a memo entry (not as cash) the item's fair market value on the date received, including the name and mailing address (and, where in excess of $200, the occupation and name of employer) of the contributor.

(2) When the item is sold, the committee shall record the proceeds. It shall also report the (i) name and mailing address (and, where in excess of $200, the occupation and name of employer) of the purchaser, if purchased directly from the candidate or committee (as the purchaser shall be considered to have made a contribution to the committee), and (ii) the identification of the original contributor.

§ 104.14 Formal requirements regarding reports and statements.

(a) Each individual having the responsibility to file a designation, report or statement required under this subchapter shall sign the original designation, report or statement except that:

(1) Reports or statements of independent expenditures filed by facsimile machine or electronic mail under 11 CFR 104.4(b) or 11 CFR 109.10 must be verified in accordance with those sections; and

(2) Reports, designations, or statements filed electronically under 11 CFR 104.18 must follow the signature requirements of 11 CFR 104.18(g).

(b) Each political committee or other person required to file any report or statement under this subchapter shall maintain all records as follows:

(1) Maintain records, including bank records, with respect to the matters required to be reported, including vouchers, worksheets, receipts, bills and accounts, which shall provide in sufficient detail the necessary information and data from which the filed reports and statements may be verified, explained, clarified, and checked for accuracy and completeness;

(2) Preserve a copy of each report or statement required to be filed under 11 CFR parts 102 and 104, and all records relevant to such reports or statements;

(3) Keep all reports required to be preserved under this section available for audit, inspection, or examination by the Commission or its authorized

representative(s) for a period of not less that 3 years after the report or statement is filed (*See* 11 CFR 102.9(c) for requirements relating to preservation of records and accounts); and

(4) Candidates, who obtain bank loans or loans derived from an advance from the candidate's brokerage account, credit card, home equity line of credit, or other lines of credit available to the candidate, must preserve the following records for three years after the date of the election for which they were a candidate:

(i) Records to demonstrate the ownership of the accounts or assets securing the loans;

(ii) Copies of the executed loan agreements and all security and guarantee statements;

(iii) Statements of account for all accounts used to secure any loan for the period the loan is outstanding such as brokerage accounts or credit card accounts, and statements on any line of credit account that was used for the purpose of influencing the candidate's election for Federal office;

(iv) For brokerage loans or other loans secured by financial assets, documentation to establish the source of the funds in the account at the time of the loan; and

(v) Documentation for all payments made on the loan by any person.

(c) Acknowledgements by the Commission or the Secretary of the Senate, of the receipt of Statements of Organization, reports or other statements filed under 11 CFR parts 101, 102 and 104 are intended solely to inform the person filing the report of its receipt and neither the acknowledgement nor the acceptance of a report or statement shall constitute express or implied approval, or in any manner indicate that the contents of any report or statement fulfill the filing or other requirements of the Act or of these regulations.

(d) Each treasurer of a political committee, and any other person required to file any report or statement under these regulations and under the Act, shall be personally responsible for the timely and complete filing of the report or statement and for the accuracy of any information or statement contained in it.

[45 FR 15108, Mar. 7, 1980, as amended at 61 FR 3549, Feb. 1, 1996; 67 FR 12840, Mar. 20, 2002; 67 FR 38361, June 4, 2002; 79 FR 16663, Mar. 26, 2014]

§ 104.15 Sale or use restriction (52 U.S.C. 30111(a)(4)).

(a) Any information copied, or otherwise obtained, from any report or statement, or any copy, reproduction, or publication thereof, filed under the Act, shall not be sold or used by any person for the purpose of soliciting contributions or for any commercial purpose, except that the name and address of any political committee may be used to solicit contributions from such committee.

(b) For purposes of 11 CFR 104.15, *soliciting contributions* includes soliciting any type of contribution or donation, such as political or charitable contributions.

(c) The use of information, which is copied or otherwise obtained from reports filed under 11 CFR part 104, in newspapers, magazines, books or other similar communications is permissible as long as the principal purpose of such communications is not to communicate any contributor information listed on such reports for the purpose of soliciting contributions or for other commercial purposes.

[45 FR 15108, Mar. 7, 1980, as amended at 61 FR 3549, Feb. 1, 1996]

§ 104.16 Audits (52 U.S.C. 30111(b)).

(a) The Commission may conduct audits of any political committee required to register under 11 CFR part 102 and to report under 11 CFR part 104. Prior to conducting any such audit or investigation, the Commission shall conduct an internal review of reports filed by selected committees to determine whether reports filed by a particular committee meet thresholds established by the Commission for substantial compliance with the Act. Such thresholds may vary according to the type of political committee being reviewed.

(b) The Commission may, upon affirmative vote of four members, conduct an audit and field investigation of any committee which meets the thresholds established pursuant to 11 CFR 104.16(a). All such audits and investigations shall commence within 30 days of such vote except that any audit or investigation of an authorized committee of a candidate shall be commenced within 6 months of the election for which such committee was authorized.

(c) The Commission may, upon affirmative vote of four members, conduct an audit and field investigation of any committee pursuant to 11 CFR 111.10.

(d) All audits and field investigations concerning the verification for and the receipt and use of payments under chapters 95 and 96 of title 26 shall be given priority over any audit or investigation of committees not receiving such payments.

§ 104.17 Reporting of allocable expenses by party committees.

(a) *Expenses allocated among candidates.* A national party committee making an expenditure on behalf of more than one clearly identified candidate for Federal office must report the allocation between or among the named candidates. A national party committee making expenditures and disbursements on behalf of one or more clearly identified Federal candidates and on behalf of one or more clearly identified non-Federal candidates must report the allocation among all named candidates. These payments shall be allocated among candidates pursuant to 11 CFR part 106, but only Federal funds may be used for such payments. A State, district, or local party committee making expenditures and disbursements for Federal election activity as defined at 11 CFR 100.24 on behalf of one or more clearly identified Federal and one or more clearly identified non-Federal candidates must make the payments from its Federal account and must report the allocation among all named candidates. A State, district, or local party committee making expenditures and disbursements on behalf of one or more clearly identified Federal and one or more clearly identified non-Federal candidates where the activity is not a Federal election activity may allocate the payments between its Federal and non-Federal account and must report the allocation among all named candidates. For allocated expenditures, the committee must report the amount of each in-kind contribution, independent expenditure, or coordinated expenditure attributed to each candidate. If a payment also includes amounts attributable to one or more non-Federal candidates, and is made by a State, district, or local party committee with separate Federal and non-Federal accounts, and is not for a Federal election activity, then the payment shall be made according to the procedures set forth in 11 CFR 106.7(f), but shall be reported pursuant to paragraphs (a)(1) through (a)(4) of this section, as follows:

(1) *Reporting of allocation of expenses attributable to specific Federal and non-Federal candidates.* In each report disclosing a payment that includes both expenditures on behalf of one or more Federal candidates and disbursements on behalf of one or more non-Federal candidates, the committee must assign a unique identifying title or code to each program or activity conducted on behalf of such candidates, state the allocation ratio calculated for the program or activity, and explain the manner in which the ratio applied to each candidate was derived. The committee must also summarize the total amounts attributed to each candidate, to date, for each program or activity.

(2) *Reporting of transfers between accounts for the purpose of paying expenses attributable to specific Federal and non-Federal candidates.* A State, district, or local party committee that pays allocable expenses in accordance with 11 CFR 106.7(f) shall report each transfer of funds from its non-Federal account to its Federal account or to its separate allocation account for the purpose of paying such expenses. In the report covering the period in which each transfer occurred, the State, district, or local party committee shall explain in a memo entry the allocable expenses to which the transfer relates and the date on which the transfer was made. If the transfer includes funds for the allocable costs of more than one program or activity, the State, district, or local party committee must itemize the transfer, showing the amounts designated for each program or activity

conducted on behalf of one or more clearly identified Federal candidates and one or more clearly identified non-Federal candidates.

(3) *Reporting of allocated disbursements attributable to specific Federal and non-Federal candidates.* A State, district, or local committee that pays allocable expenses in accordance with 11 CFR 106.7(f) shall also report each disbursement from its Federal account or its separate allocation account in payment for a program or activity conducted on behalf of one or more clearly identified Federal candidates and one or more clearly identified non-Federal candidates. In the report covering the period in which the disbursement occurred, the State, district, or local party committee shall state the full name and address of each person to whom the disbursement was made, and the date, amount, and purpose of each such disbursement. If the disbursement includes payment for the allocable costs of more than one program or activity, the committee shall itemize the disbursement, showing the amounts designated for payment of each program or activity conducted on behalf of one or more clearly identified Federal candidates and one or more clearly identified non-Federal candidates. The State, district, or local party committee must also report the amount of each in-kind contribution, independent expenditure, or coordinated expenditure attributed to each Federal candidate, and the total amount attributed to the non-Federal candidate(s). In addition, the State, district, or local party committee must report the total amount expended by the committee that year, to date, for each joint program or activity.

(4) *Recordkeeping.* The treasurer of a State, district, or local party committee must retain all documents supporting the committee's allocations on behalf of specific Federal and non-Federal candidates, in accordance with 11 CFR 104.14.

(b) *Allocation of activities that are not Federal election activities.* A State, district, or local committee of a political party that has established separate Federal and non-Federal accounts, including related allocation accounts, under 11 CFR 102.5 must report all payments that are allocable between these accounts pursuant to the allocation rules in 11 CFR 106.7. Disbursements for activities that are allocable between Federal and Levin accounts, including related allocation accounts, must be reported pursuant to 11 CFR 300.36.

(1) *Reporting of allocations of expenses for activities that are not Federal election activities.* (i) In the first report in a calendar year disclosing a disbursement allocable pursuant to 11 CFR 106.7, a State, district, or local committee shall state and explain the allocation percentages to be applied to each category of allocable activity (e.g., 36% Federal/64% non-Federal in Presidential and Senate election years) pursuant to 11 CFR 106.7(d).

(ii) In each subsequent report in the calendar year itemizing an allocated disbursement, the State, district, or local party committee shall state the category of activity for which each allocated disbursement was made, and shall summarize the total amounts expended from Federal and non-Federal accounts, or from allocation accounts, that year to date for each such category.

(iii) In each report disclosing disbursements for allocable activities as described in 11 CFR 106.7, the State, district, or local party committee shall assign a unique identifying title or code to each such program or activity, and shall state the applicable Federal/non-Federal percentage for any direct costs of fundraising. Unique identifying titles or codes are not required for salaries and wages pursuant to 11 CFR 106.7(c)(1), or for other administrative costs allocated pursuant to 11 CFR 106.7(c)(2).

(2) *Reporting of transfers between the accounts of State, district, and local party committees and into allocation accounts for allocable expenses.* A State, district, or local committee of a political party that pays allocable expenses in accordance with 11 CFR 106.7 shall report each transfer of funds from its non-Federal account to its Federal account, or each transfer from its Federal account and its non-Federal account into an allocation account, for the purpose of payment of such expenses. In the report covering the period in which each transfer occurred, the State, district, or local party committee must explain in a memo entry the allocable expenses to which the transfer relates and the date on which the transfer was made. If the transfer includes funds for the allocable costs of more than one activity, the State, district, or local party committee must itemize the transfer, showing the amounts designated for each category of expense as described in 11 CFR 106.7.

(3) *Reporting of allocated disbursements for certain allocable activity that is not Federal election activity.* (i) A State, district, or local committee of a political party that pays allocable expenses in accordance with 11 CFR 106.7 shall report each disbursement from its Federal account for allocable expenses, or each payment from an allocation account for such activity. In the report covering the period in which the disbursement occurred, the State, district, or local committee shall state the full name and address of each individual or vendor to which the disbursement was made, the date, amount, and purpose of each such disbursement, and the amounts allocated to Federal and non-Federal portions of the allocable activity. If the disbursement includes payment for the allocable costs of more than one activity, the State, district, or local party committee must itemize the disbursement, showing the amounts designated for payments of particular categories of activity as described in 11 CFR 106.7. The State, district, or local party committee must also report the total amount paid that calendar year to date for each category of allocable activity.

(ii) A State, district, or local committee of a political party that pays allocable expenses from a Federal account and a Levin account in accordance with 11 CFR 300.33 shall report disbursements from those accounts according to the requirements of 11 CFR 300.36.

(4) *Recordkeeping.* The treasurer of a State, district, or local party committee must retain all documents supporting the committee's allocations of expenditures and disbursements for the costs and activities cited at paragraph

(b) of this section, in accordance with 11 CFR 104.14.

[67 FR 49114, July 29, 2002]

§ 104.18 Electronic filing of reports (52 U.S.C. 30102(d) and 30104(a)(11)).

(a) *Mandatory.* (1) Political committees and other persons required to file reports with the Commission, as provided in 11 CFR Parts 105 and 107, must file reports in an electronic format that meets the requirements of this section if—

(i) The political committee or other person has received contributions or has reason to expect to receive contributions aggregating in excess of $50,000 in any calendar year; or

(ii) The political committee or other person has made expenditures or has reason to expect to make expenditures aggregating in excess of $50,000 in any calendar year.

(2) Once any political committee or other person described in paragraph (a)(1) of this section exceeds or has reason to expect to exceed the appropriate threshold, the political committee or person must file electronically all subsequent reports covering financial activity for the remainder of the calendar year. All electronically filed reports must pass the Commission's validation program in accordance with paragraph (e) of this section. Reports filed on paper do not satisfy a political committee's or other person's filing obligations.

(3) *Have reason to expect to exceed.* (i) A political committee or other person shall have reason to expect to exceed the threshold stated in paragraph (a)(1) of this section for two calendar years following the calendar year in which the political committee or other person exceeds the threshold unless—

(A) The committee is an authorized committee, and has $50,000 or less in net debts outstanding on January 1 of the year following the general election, and anticipates terminating prior to January 1 of the next election year; and

(B) The candidate has not qualified as a candidate for the next election and does not intend to become a candidate for federal office in the next election.

(ii) New political committees or other persons with no history of campaign finance activity shall have reason to expect to exceed the threshold stated in paragraph (a)(1) of this section within the calendar year if—

(A) It receives contributions or makes expenditures that exceed one quarter of the threshold amount in the first calendar quarter of the calendar year; or

(B) It receives contributions or makes expenditures that exceed one-half of the threshold amount in the first half of the calendar year.

(b) *Voluntary.* A political committee or other person who files reports with the Commission, as provided in 11 CFR part 105, and who is not required to file electronically under paragraph (a) of this section, may choose to file its reports in an electronic format that meets the requirements of this section (internet forms included). If a political committee or other person chooses to file its reports electronically, all electronically filed reports must pass the Commission's validation program in accordance with paragraph (e) of this section. The committee or other person must continue to file in an electronic format all reports covering financial activity for that calendar year, unless the Commission determines that extraordinary and unforeseeable circumstances have made it impracticable for the political committee or other person to continue filing electronically.

(c) *Definition of report.* For purposes of this section, *report* means any statement, designation or report required by the Act to be filed with the Commission.

(d) *Format specifications.* Reports filed electronically shall conform to the technical specifications described in the Federal Election Commission's Electronic Filing Specifications Requirements. The data contained in the computerized magnetic media provided to the Commission shall be organized in the order specified by the Electronic Filing Specifications Requirements.

(e) *Acceptance of reports filed in electronic format; validation program.* (1) Each political committee or other person who submits an electronic report shall check the report against the Commission's validation program before it is submitted, to ensure that the files submitted meet the Commission's format specifications and can be read by the Commission's computer system. Each report submitted in an electronic format under this section shall also be checked upon receipt against the Commission's validation program. The Commission's validation program and the Electronic Filing Specification Requirement are available on request and at no charge.

(2) A report that does not pass the validation program will not be accepted by the Commission and will not be considered filed. If a political committee or other person submits a report that does not pass the validation program, the Commission will notify the political committee or other person that the report has not been accepted.

(f) *Amended reports.* If a political committee or other person files an amendment to a report that was filed electronically, the political committee or other person shall also submit the amendment in an electronic format. The political committee or other person shall submit a complete version of the report as amended, rather than just those portions of the report that are being amended. In addition, amendments must be filed in accordance with the Electronic Filing Specification Requirements.

(g) *Signature requirements.* The political committee's treasurer, or any other person having the responsibility to file a designation, report or statement under this subchapter, shall verify the report in one of the following ways: by submitting a signed certification on paper that is submitted with the computerized media; or by submitting a digitized copy of the signed certification as a separate file in the electronic submission; or by submitting a signed certification on a Commission internet form. Each verification submitted under this section shall certify that the treasurer or other signatory has examined the report or statement and, to the best of the signatory's knowledge and belief, it is true, correct and complete. Any verification under this section shall be treated for all purposes (including penalties for perjury) in the same manner

as a verification by signature on a report submitted in a paper format.

(h) *Schedules and forms with special requirements.* (1) The following are schedules and forms that require the filing of additional documents and that have special signature requirements:

(i) Schedules C-1 and C-P-1, Loans and Lines of Credit From Lending Institutions (see 11 CFR 104.3(d)); and

(ii) Form 8, Debt Settlement Plan (see 11 CFR 116.7(e)).

(2) If a person files a report electronically by submitting a diskette to the Commission and is required to file any of the schedules or forms listed in paragraph (h)(1) of this section, the person shall file a paper copy of the required schedule or form with the electronic submission, or a digitized version as a separate file in the electronic submission, by the close of business on the prescribed filing date.

(3) If a person files a report electronically by uploading the data to the Commission's electronic filing system and is required to file any schedules or forms listed in paragraph (h)(1) of this section, the person shall file a paper copy or a digitized version of the required schedule or form by the close of business on the prescribed filing date.

(i) *Preservation of reports.* For any report filed in electronic format under this section, the treasurer or other person required to file any report under the Act shall retain a machine-readable copy of the report as the copy preserved under 11 CFR 104.14(b)(2). In addition, the treasurer or other person required to file any report under the Act shall retain the original signed version of any documents submitted in a digitized format under paragraphs (g) and (h) of this section.

[65 FR 38423, June 21, 2000, as amended at 67 FR 12840, Mar. 20, 2002; 81 FR 34863, June 1, 2016]

§104.19 [Reserved]

§104.20 Reporting electioneering communications (52 U.S.C. 30104 (f)).

(a) *Definitions*—(1) *Disclosure date* means:

(i) The first date on which an electioneering communication is publicly distributed provided that the person making the electioneering communication has made one or more disbursements, or has executed one or more contracts to make disbursements, for the direct costs of producing or airing one or more electioneering communications aggregating in excess of $10,000; or

(ii) Any other date during the same calendar year on which an electioneering communication is publicly distributed provided that the person making the electioneering communication has made one or more disbursements, or has executed one or more contracts to make disbursements, for the direct costs of producing or airing one or more electioneering communications aggregating in excess of $10,000 since the most recent disclosure date during such calendar year.

(2) *Direct costs of producing or airing electioneering communications* means the following:

(i) Costs charged by a vendor, such as studio rental time, staff salaries, costs of video or audio recording media, and talent; or

(ii) The cost of airtime on broadcast, cable or satellite radio and television stations, studio time, material costs, and the charges for a broker to purchase the airtime.

(3) *Persons sharing or exercising direction or control* means officers, directors, executive directors or their equivalent, partners, and in the case of unincorporated organizations, owners, of the entity or person making the disbursement for the electioneering communication.

(4) *Identification* has the same meaning as in 11 CFR 100.12.

(5) *Publicly distributed* has the same meaning as in 11 CFR 100.29(b)(3).

(b) *Who must report and when.* Every person who has made an electioneering communication, as defined in 11 CFR 100.29, aggregating in excess of $10,000 during any calendar year shall file a statement with the Commission by 11:59 p.m. Eastern Standard/Daylight Time on the day following the disclosure date. The statement shall be filed under penalty of perjury, shall contain the information set forth in paragraph (c) of this section, and shall be filed on FEC Form 9. Political committees that make communications that are de-

scribed in 11 CFR 100.29(a) must report such communications as expenditures or independent expenditures under 11 CFR 104.3 and 104.4, and not under this section.

(c) *Contents of statement.* Statements of electioneering communications filed under paragraph (b) of this section shall disclose the following information:

(1) The identification of the person who made the disbursement, or who executed a contract to make a disbursement, and, if the person is not an individual, the person's principal place of business;

(2) The identification of any person sharing or exercising direction or control over the activities of the person who made the disbursement or who executed a contract to make a disbursement;

(3) The identification of the custodian of the books and accounts from which the disbursements were made;

(4) The amount of each disbursement, or amount obligated, of more than $200 during the period covered by the statement, the date the disbursement was made, or the contract was executed, and the identification of the person to whom that disbursement was made;

(5) All clearly identified candidates referred to in the electioneering communication and the elections in which they are candidates;

(6) The disclosure date, as defined in paragraph (a) of this section;

(7) If the disbursements were paid exclusively from a segregated bank account consisting of funds provided solely by persons other than national banks, corporations organized by authority of any law of Congress, or foreign nationals as defined in 11 CFR 110.20(a)(3), the name and address of each donor who donated an amount aggregating $1,000 or more to the segregated bank account, aggregating since the first day of the preceding calendar year.

(8) If the disbursements were not paid exclusively from a segregated bank account described in paragraph (c)(7) of this section and were not made by a corporation or labor organization, the name and address of each donor who donated an amount aggregating $1,000

or more to the person making the disbursement, aggregating since the first day of the preceding calendar year.

(9) If the disbursements were made by a corporation or labor organization and were not paid exclusively from a segregated bank account described in paragraph (c)(7) of this section, the name and address of each person who made a donation aggregating $1,000 or more to the corporation or labor organization, aggregating since the first day of the preceding calendar year, which was made for the purpose of furthering electioneering communications.

(d) *Recordkeeping.* All persons who make electioneering communications or who accept donations for the purpose of making electioneering communications must maintain records in accordance with 11 CFR 104.14.

(e) *State waivers.* Statements of electioneering communications that must be filed with the Commission must also be filed with the Secretary of State of the appropriate State if the State has not obtained a waiver under 11 CFR 108.1(b).

[68 FR 419, Jan. 3, 2003; 68 FR 5075, Jan. 31, 2003, as amended at 72 FR 72913, Dec. 26, 2007; 80 FR 62816, Oct. 21, 2014]

§ 104.21 **Reporting by inaugural committees.**

(a) *Definitions*—(1) *Inaugural committee.* Inaugural committee means the committee appointed by the President-elect to be in charge of the Presidential inaugural ceremony and functions and activities connected with the inaugural ceremony.

(2) *Donation.* For purposes of this section, donation has the same meaning as in 11 CFR 300.2(e).

(b) *Initial letter-filing by inaugural committees.* (1) In order to be considered the inaugural committee under 36 U.S.C. Chapter 5, within 15 days of appointment by the President-elect, the appointed committee must file a signed letter with the Commission containing the following:

(i) The name and address of the inaugural committee;

(ii) The name of the chairperson, or the name and title of another officer who will serve as the point of contact; and

(iii) A statement agreeing to comply with paragraphs (c) and (d) of this section and with 11 CFR 110.20(j).

(2) Upon receipt of the letter filed under this paragraph (b), the Commission will assign a FEC committee identification number to the inaugural committee. The inaugural committee must include this FEC committee identification number on all reports and supplements thereto required under paragraph (c) of this section, as well as on all communications with the Commission concerning the letter filed under this paragraph (b).

(c) *Reporting requirements for inaugural committees*—(1) *Who must report.* The chairperson or other officer identified in the letter-filing required by paragraph (b) of this section must file a report and any supplements thereto as required by this paragraph (c). Such person must sign the report and any supplements thereto in accordance with 11 CFR 104.14(a). The signature on the report and any supplements thereto certifies that the contents are true, correct, and complete, to the best of knowledge of the chairperson or other officer identified in the letter-filing required by paragraph (b) of this section.

(2) *When to file.* A report, and any supplements thereto, must be timely filed in accordance with 11 CFR 100.19 as follows:

(i) *Report.* An inaugural committee must file a report with the Commission no later than the 90th day following the date on which the Presidential inaugural ceremony is held.

(ii) *Supplements to the report.* (A) An inaugural committee must file a supplement to its report if it accepts a reportable donation, or makes a refund during the 90 days following the end of the covering period of its original report or its most recent supplement.

(B) Any supplement must be filed no later than the 90th day following the filing date of an original report, or if a supplement has already been filed, the filing date of the most recent supplement.

(3) *Where to file.* All letters, reports, and any supplements thereto, as required under this section, shall be filed with the Federal Election Commission at the street address identified in the definition of "Commission" in §1.2.

(4) *How to file.* An inaugural committee must file its letter, report, and any supplements thereto, in original form; however, an inaugural committee may choose to file its reports in an electronic format that meets the requirements of 11 CFR 104.18.

(5) *Form.* An inaugural committee must file the report required by this paragraph on FEC Form 13.

(6) *Content of report.* Each report, and any supplements thereto, filed with the Commission under this section must contain the following:

(i) Covering period beginning and ending dates, as follows:

(A) The covering period of a report means the period of time beginning on the date of the inaugural committee's appointment by the President-elect and ending no earlier than 15 days before the day on which the inaugural committee files its report with the Commission.

(B) The covering period of a supplement to the report means the period of time beginning on the day after the ending date of the covering period of the original report, or the most recent supplement thereto, and ending no earlier than 15 days before the day on which the inaugural committee files such supplement with the Commission.

(ii) Cumulative totals from the date of the inaugural committee's appointment by the President-elect for all:

(A) Donations reported under paragraph (c)(6)(iii) of this section;

(B) Refunds reported under paragraph (c)(6)(iv) of this section; and

(C) Net reported donations;

(iii) Itemization of previously unreported donations of $200 or more, and donations that aggregate $200 or more, including:

(A) The full name of each person who made such a donation, including first name, middle name or initial, if available, and last name, in the case of an individual;

(B) The address of each such person;

(C) The amount of each such donation; and

(D) The date of receipt of each such donation; and

(iv) Itemization of previously unreported refunds of previously, or contemporaneously, reported donations, including:

(A) The full name of each person to whom such a refund was made, including first name, middle name or initial, if available, and last name, in the case of an individual;

(B) The address of each such person;

(C) The amount of each such refund; and

(D) The date of each such refund.

(d) *Recordkeeping.* All inaugural committees must maintain records in accordance with 11 CFR 104.14.

[69 FR 59779, Oct. 6, 2004, as amended at 82 FR 60853, Dec. 26, 2017]

§ 104.22 Disclosure of bundling by Lobbyist/Registrants and Lobbyist/Registrant PACs (52 U.S.C. 30104(i)).

(a) *Definitions.* (1) *Reporting Committee. Reporting committee* means:

(i) An authorized committee of a Federal candidate as defined at 11 CFR 100.5(f)(1);

(ii) A leadership PAC as defined at 11 CFR 100.5(e)(6); or

(iii) A party committee as defined at 11 CFR 100.5(e)(4).

(2) *Lobbyist/Registrant. Lobbyist/registrant* means a person who, at the time a contribution is forwarded to, or is received by, a reporting committee, is:

(i) A current registrant under Section 4(a) of the Lobbying Disclosure Act of 1995 (2 U.S.C. 1603(a)); or

(ii) An individual who is named on a current registration or current report filed under Section 4(b)(6) or 5(b)(2)(C) of the Lobbying Disclosure Act of 1995 (2 U.S.C. 1603(b)(6) or 1604(b)(2)(C)).

(3) *Lobbyist/Registrant PAC. Lobbyist/registrant PAC* means any political committee that a lobbyist/registrant "established or controls," as defined in paragraph (a)(4) of this section.

(4) *Established or Controls.* (i) For purposes of this section only, a lobbyist/registrant established or controls any political committee that the lobbyist/registrant is required to disclose to the Secretary of the U. S. Senate or Clerk of the U.S. House of Representatives as being established or controlled by that lobbyist/registrant under Section 203 of the Honest Leadership and Open Government Act of 2007, amending the Lobbying Disclosure Act of 1995 (2 U.S.C. 1604(d)(1)(C)).

(ii) If, after consulting guidance from the offices of the Secretary of the Senate or Clerk of the U.S House of Representatives, or communicating with such offices, a political committee is unable to ascertain whether it is established or controlled by a lobbyist/registrant, a lobbyist/registrant will be deemed to have established or to control a political committee if:

(A) The political committee is a separate segregated fund with a current registrant under Section 4(a) of the Lobbying Disclosure Act (2 U.S.C. 1603(a)) as its connected organization; or

(B) The political committee meets either of the following criteria:

(1) A lobbyist/registrant had a primary role in the establishment of the political committee, excluding the provision of legal or compliance services or advice; or

(2) A lobbyist/registrant directs the governance or operations of the political committee, excluding the provision of legal or compliance services or advice.

(5) *Covered Period. Covered period* means:

(i) *Semi-annually.* The semi-annual periods of January 1 through June 30, and July 1 through December 31; and the period described in paragraph (a)(5)(ii), (iii) or (iv), below, that applies to the reporting committee.

(ii) *Quarterly.* For reporting committees that file campaign finance reports under 11 CFR 104.5 on a quarterly basis, the covered period also includes the quarters beginning on January 1, April 1, July 1, and October 1 of each calendar year and the applicable pre- and post-election reporting periods in election years; in a nonelection year, reporting committees not authorized by a candidate need only observe the semi-annual period described in paragraph (a)(5)(i) above; or

(iii) *Monthly.* For reporting committees that file monthly campaign finance reports under 11 CFR 104.5, the covered period also includes each month in the calendar year, except that in election years the pre- and post-general election reporting periods shall constitute the covered period in lieu of the monthly November and December reporting periods.

(iv) *Alternative for monthly filers.* Any reporting committee that files monthly campaign finance reports under 11 CFR 104.5 may choose to file reports pursuant to the quarterly covered period in paragraph (a)(5)(ii) of this section instead of the monthly covered period in paragraph (a)(5)(iii) of this section. It shall do so by notifying the Commission in writing of its intention to do so at the time the reporting committee files a monthly report under paragraph (a)(5)(iii) of this section. The reporting committee will be required to file its next report under the new filing frequency. The reporting committee may change its filing frequency no more than once per calendar year.

(v) *Runoffs and Special Elections.* For special elections and runoff elections set by State law, the covered period shall be the same as the reporting periods set under 11 CFR 104.5(h).

(6) *Bundled Contribution. Bundled contribution* means any contribution that meets the definition set forth in either paragraph (i) or (ii) below:

(i) *Forwarded contribution* means a contribution delivered or transmitted, by physical or electronic means, to the reporting committee by a lobbyist/registrant or lobbyist/registrant PAC, or by any person that the reporting committee knows to be forwarding such contribution on behalf of a lobbyist/registrant or lobbyist/registrant PAC.

(ii) *Received and credited contribution* means a contribution received by the reporting committee from the contributor or contributors, and credited by the reporting committee or candidate involved to a lobbyist/registrant or lobbyist/registrant PAC through records, designations, or other means of recognizing that a certain amount of money has been raised by the lobbyist/registrant or lobbyist/registrant PAC.

(A) *Records, designations, or other means of recognizing. Records* means written evidence (including writings, charts, computer files, tables, spreadsheets, databases, or other data or data compilations stored in any medium from which information can be obtained) that the reporting committee or candidate involved attributes to a lobbyist/registrant or lobbyist/registrant PAC contributions raised by that person or entity and received by the reporting committee.

Designations or other means of recognizing bundled contributions means benefits given by the reporting committee to persons for raising a certain amount of contributions, including but not limited to:

(1) Titles that the reporting committee assigns to persons who have raised a certain amount of contributions;

(2) Tracking identifiers that the reporting committee assigns and that are included on contributions or contributions-related materials (for example, contributor response devices, cover letters, or Internet Web site solicitation pages) for the purpose of maintaining information about the amounts of contributions that a person raises;

(3) Access (including offers or attendance) to events or activities given to the lobbyist/registrant or lobbyist/registrant PAC by the reporting committee as a result of raising a certain amount of contributions; and

(4) Mementos, such as photographs with the candidate or autographed copies of books authored by the candidate, given by the reporting committee to persons who have raised a certain amount of contributions.

(B) *The candidate involved.* The *candidate involved* means the candidate by whom the authorized committee is authorized; the candidate or individual holding Federal office who directly or indirectly established, finances, maintains or controls the leadership PAC; or the chairman of the committee in the case of a political party committee.

(iii) Bundled contributions do not include contributions made by the lobbyist/registrant PAC or from the personal funds of the lobbyist/registrant that forwards or is credited with raising the contributions or the personal funds of that person's spouse.

(b) *Reporting requirement for reporting committees*—(1) *FEC Form 3L.* Each reporting committee must file FEC Form 3L (Report of Contributions Bundled by Lobbyist/Registrants and Lobbyist/Registrant PACs) if it has received two or more bundled contributions (*see* paragraph (a)(6)) forwarded by or received and credited to a person reasonably known by the reporting committee to be a lobbyist/registrant or lobbyist/registrant PAC aggregating in excess of $15,000 during the covered period. The form shall set forth:

(i) The name of each lobbyist/registrant or lobbyist/registrant PAC;

(ii) The address of each lobbyist/registrant or lobbyist/registrant PAC;

(iii) The employer of each lobbyist/registrant; and

(iv) The aggregate amount of bundled contributions forwarded by or received and credited to each lobbyist/registrant or lobbyist/registrant PAC by the reporting committee during the covered period.

(2) *Determining whether a person is reasonably known to be a lobbyist/registrant or lobbyist/registrant PAC.* (i) In order to comply with paragraph (b)(1) of this section, a reporting committee must consult, in a manner reasonably calculated to find the name of each person who is a lobbyist/registrant or lobbyist/registrant PAC, the Web sites maintained by the Clerk of the House of Representatives, the Secretary of the Senate, and the Federal Election Commission to determine whether, at the time a contribution was forwarded to, or received by, the reporting committee:

(A) The person was listed as a current registrant under Section 4(a) of the Lobbying Disclosure Act of 1995 (2 U.S.C. 1603(a));

(B) The person was an individual listed on a current registration filed under Section 4(b)(6) or a current report filed under Section 5(b)(2)(C) of the Lobbying Disclosure Act of 1995 (2 U.S.C. 1603 or 1604);

(C) The person identified itself as a lobbyist/registrant PAC on its Statement of Organization, FEC Form 1, filed with the Commission; or

(D) The person was listed as a political committee established or controlled by a lobbyist or registrant on a report filed under Sec. 203(a) of the Honest Leadership and Open Government Act of 2007, amending the Lobbying Disclosure Act of 1995 (2 U.S.C. 1604).

(ii) A manner reasonably calculated to find the name of each person who is a lobbyist/registrant or lobbyist/registrant PAC may be demonstrated by the reporting committee producing a computer printout or screen capture from a Web browser indicating that the name of the person sought was not listed in the results of the Web site consultations performed in accordance with paragraph (b)(2)(i) of this section. Such a computer printout or screen capture shall constitute conclusive evidence that the reporting committee has consulted such Web sites and not found the name of the person sought, but shall not be the exclusive means by which the reporting committee may provide evidence that it has consulted such Web sites and not found the name of the person sought.

(iii) A reporting committee shall be subject to the reporting requirement under paragraph (b)(1) of this section if it had actual knowledge that, at the time a contribution was forwarded or received, the person whose name is sought was required to be listed on any registration or report described in paragraph (b)(2)(i) of this section.

(c) *Lobbyist/Registrant PAC reporting requirements.* Any political committee that is a lobbyist/registrant PAC as defined in paragraph (a)(3) of this section must identify itself as such on FEC Form 1 either upon registration with the Commission if it is a new political committee, or by amendment in accordance with 11 CFR 102.2(a)(2) if it is a political committee registered with the Commission.

(d) *Where to file.* Reporting committees shall file either with the Secretary of the Senate or with the Federal Election Commission in accordance with 11 CFR part 105.

(e) *When to file.* Reporting committees must file the forms required under this section with the first report that they file under 11 CFR 104.5 following the end of each covered period.

(f) *Recordkeeping.* In addition to any requirements to maintain records and accounts under 11 CFR 102.8, 102.9 and 110.6, each reporting committee must maintain for three years after the filing of the report to which the information relates a record of any bundled contributions (*see* 11 CFR 104.22(a)(6)) provided by a lobbyist/registrant or lobbyist/registrant PAC that aggregate in excess of $15,000 for any covered period. The information required to be maintained is:

(1) The name and address of the lobbyist/registrant or lobbyist/registrant PAC;

(2) The employer of the lobbyist/registrant; and

(3) The aggregate amount of bundled contributions forwarded by or received and credited to each lobbyist/registrant or lobbyist/registrant PAC by the reporting committee during the covered period.

(g) *Price index increase.* (1) The threshold for reporting bundled contributions established in paragraph (b)(1) of this section shall be increased by the percent difference between the price index as defined at 11 CFR 110.17(d), as certified to the Commission by the Secretary of Labor, for the 12 months preceding the beginning of the calendar year and the price index for the base period.

(2) Each contribution bundling threshold so increased shall be the threshold in effect for that calendar year.

(3) For purposes of this paragraph (g), the term base period means calendar year 2006.

(4) If any amount after the increases under this paragraph (g) is not a multiple of $100, such amount shall be rounded to the nearest multiple of $100.

[74 FR 7302, Feb. 17, 2009]

PART 105—DOCUMENT FILING (52 U.S.C. 30102(g))

Sec.

AUTHORITY: 52 U.S.C. 30102(g), 30104, 30111(a)(8).

SOURCE: 45 FR 15116, Mar. 7, 1980, unless otherwise noted.

§ 105.1 Place of filing; House candidates and their authorized committees (52 U.S.C. 30102(g)(1)).

All designations, statements, reports, and notices, as well as any modification(s) or amendment(s) thereto, required to be filed under 11 CFR parts 101, 102, and 104 by a candidate for nomination or election to the office of Representative in, or Delegate or Resident Commissioner to, the Congress, by his or her authorized committee(s), shall be filed in original form with, and received by, the Federal Election Commission.

[61 FR 3550, Feb. 1, 1996]

§ 105.2 Place of filing; Senate candidates, their principal campaign committees, and committees supporting only Senate candidates (52 U.S.C. 30102(g), 30104(g)(3)).

(a) *General Rule.* Except as provided in paragraph (b) of this section, all designations, statements, reports, and notices as well as any modification(s) or amendment(s) thereto, required to be filed under 11 CFR parts 101, 102, and 104 by a candidate for nomination or election to the office of United States Senator, by his or her principal campaign committee or by any other political committee(s) that supports only candidates for nomination for election or election to the Senate of the United States shall be filed in original form with, and received by, the Secretary of the Senate, as custodian for the Federal Election Commission.

(b) *Exceptions.* 24-hour and 48-hour reports of independent expenditures must be filed with the Commission and not with the Secretary of the Senate, even if the communication refers to a Senate candidate.

[68 FR 420, Jan. 3, 2003]

§ 105.3 Place of filing; Presidential candidates and their principal campaign committees (52 U.S.C. 30102(g)(4)).

All designations, statements, reports, and notices, as well as any modification(s) or amendment(s) thereto, required to be filed under 11 CFR parts 101, 102 and 104 by a candidate for nom-

ination for election or election to the office of President or Vice President of the United States or by his or her principal campaign committee shall be filed in original form with the Federal Election Commission.

§ 105.4 Place of filing; political committees and other persons (52 U.S.C. 30102(g)(4)).

All designations, statements, reports, and notices, as well as any modifications or amendments thereto, required to be filed under 11 CFR parts 101, 102, and 104 by a political committee other than any principal campaign committee or any committee referred to in 11 CFR 105.2 or 105.3, by persons other than political committees making independent expenditures under 11 CFR part 109, and by persons required to report the cost of communications under 11 CFR 104.6, shall be filed in original form with the Federal Election Commission.

[45 FR 15116, Mar. 7, 1980, as amended at 61 FR 3550, Feb. 1, 1996]

§ 105.5 Transmittal of microfilm copies and photocopies of original reports filed with the Secretary of the Senate to the Commission (52 U.S.C. 30102(g)(3)).

(a) Either a microfilmed copy or photocopy of all original designations, statements, reports, modifications or amendments required to be filed pursuant to 11 CFR 105.2 shall be transmitted by the Secretary of the Senate to the Commission as soon as possible, but in any case no later than two (2) working days after receiving such designations, statements, reports, modifications, or amendments.

(b) The Secretary of the Senate shall then forward to the Commission a microfilm copy and a photocopy of each designation, statement, and report, or any modification or amendment thereto, filed with the Secretary pursuant to 11 CFR 105.2.

(c) The Secretary of the Senate shall place a time and date stamp on each original designation, statement, report, modification or amendment received.

[61 FR 3550, Feb. 1, 1996]

PART 106—ALLOCATIONS OF CANDIDATE AND COMMITTEE ACTIVITIES

AUTHORITY: 52 U.S.C. 30111(a)(8), 30116(b), 30116(g).

§106.1 Allocation of expenses between candidates.

(a) *General rule.* (1) Expenditures, including in-kind contributions, independent expenditures, and coordinated expenditures made on behalf of more than one clearly identified Federal candidate shall be attributed to each such candidate according to the benefit reasonably expected to be derived. For example, in the case of a publication or broadcast communication, the attribution shall be determined by the proportion of space or time devoted to each candidate as compared to the total space or time devoted to all candidates. In the case of a fundraising program or event where funds are collected by one committee for more than one clearly identified candidate, the attribution shall be determined by the proportion of funds received by each candidate as compared to the total receipts by all candidates. In the case of a phone bank, the attribution shall be determined by the number of questions or statements devoted to each candidate as compared to the total number of questions or statements devoted to all candidates. These methods shall

also be used to allocate payments involving both expenditures on behalf of one or more clearly identified Federal candidates and disbursements on behalf of one or more clearly identified non-Federal candidates.

(2) An expenditure made on behalf of more than one clearly identified Federal candidate shall be reported pursuant to 11 CFR 104.10(a) or 104.17(a), as appropriate. A payment that also includes amounts attributable to one or more non-Federal candidates, and that is made by a political committee with separate Federal and non-Federal accounts, shall be made according to the procedures set forth in 11 CFR 106.6(e) or 106.7(f), but shall be reported pursuant to 11 CFR 104.10(a) or 104.17(a). If a State, district, or local party committee's payment on behalf of both a Federal candidate and a non-Federal candidate is for a Federal election activity, only Federal funds may be used for the entire payment. For Federal election activities, the provisions of 11 CFR 300.33 and 104.17(a) will apply to payments attributable to candidates.

(b) An authorized expenditure made by a candidate or political committee on behalf of another candidate shall be reported as a contribution in-kind (transfer) to the candidate on whose behalf the expenditure was made, except that expenditures made by party committees pursuant to §109.32 or 109.33 need only be reported as an expenditure.

(c) *Exceptions:* (1) Expenditures for rent, personnel, overhead, general administrative, fund-raising, and other day-to-day costs of political committees need not be attributed to individual candidates, unless these expenditures are made on behalf of a clearly identified candidate and the expenditure can be directly attributed to that candidate.

(2) Expenditures for educational campaign seminars, for training of campaign workers, and for registration or get-out-the-vote drives of committees need not be attributed to individual candidates unless these expenditures are made on behalf of a clearly identified candidate, and the expenditure can be directly attributed to that candidate.

(3) Payments made for the cost of certain voter registration and get-out-the-vote activities conducted by State or local party organizations on behalf of any Presidential or Vice-Presidential candidate(s) are exempt from the definition of a contribution or an expenditure under 11 CFR 100.89 and 100.149. If the State or local party organization includes references to any candidate(s) seeking nomination or election to the House of Representatives or Senate of the United States the portion of the cost of such activities allocable to such candidate(s) shall be considered a contribution to or an expenditure on behalf of such candidate(s), unless such reference is incidental to the overall activity. If such reference is incidental to the overall activity, such costs shall not be considered a contribution to or expenditure on behalf of any candidate(s).

(d) For purposes of this section, *clearly identified* shall have the same meaning as set forth at 11 CFR 100.17.

(e) State, district, and local party committees, separate segregated funds, and nonconnected committees that make mixed Federal/non-Federal payments for activities other than an activity entailing an expenditure for a Federal candidate and disbursement for a non-Federal candidate, or that make mixed Federal/Levin fund payments, shall allocate those expenses in accordance with 11 CFR 106.6, 106.7, or 300.33, as appropriate.

(52 U.S.C. 30111(a)(8))

[41 FR 35944, Aug. 25, 1976, as amended at 45 FR 15117, Mar. 7, 1980; 45 FR 21209, Apr. 1, 1980; 55 FR 26069, June 26, 1990; 60 FR 35305, July 6, 1995; 67 FR 49115, July 29, 2002; 67 FR 78681, Dec. 26, 2002]

§ 106.2 State allocation of expenditures incurred by authorized committees of Presidential primary candidates receiving matching funds.

(a) *General*—(1) This section applies to Presidential primary candidates receiving or expecting to receive federal matching funds pursuant to 11 CFR parts 9031 *et seq.* The expenditures described in 11 CFR 106.2(b)(2) shall be allocated to a particular State if incurred by a candidate's authorized committee(s) for the purpose of influencing the nomination of that can-

didate for the office of President with respect to that State. An expenditure shall not necessarily be allocated to the State in which the expenditure is incurred or paid. In the event that the Commission disputes the candidate's allocation or claim of exemption for a particular expense, the candidate shall demonstrate, with supporting documentation, that his or her proposed method of allocation or claim of exemption was reasonable. Expenditures required to be allocated to the primary election under 11 CFR 9034.4(e) shall also be allocated to particular states in accordance with this section.

(2) Disbursements made prior to the time an individual becomes a candidate for the purpose of determining whether that individual should become a candidate pursuant to 11 CFR 100.72(a) and 100.131(a), *i.e.*, payments for testing the waters, shall be allocable expenditures under this section if the individual becomes a candidate.

(b) *Method of allocating expenditures among States*—(1) *General allocation method.* Unless otherwise specified under 11 CFR 106.2(b)(2), an expenditure described in 11 CFR 106.2(b)(2) and incurred by a candidate's authorized committee(s) for the purpose of influencing the nomination of that candidate in more than one State shall be allocated to each State on a reasonable and uniformly applied basis. The total amount allocated to a particular State may be reduced by the amount of exempt fundraising expenses for that State, as specified in 11 CFR 110.8(c)(2).

(2) *Specific allocation methods.* Expenditures that fall within the categories listed below shall be allocated based on the following methods. The method used to allocate a category of expenditures shall be based on consistent data for each State to which an allocation is made.

(i) *Media expenditures*—(A) *Print media.* Except for expenditures exempted under 11 CFR 106.2(b)(2)(i) (E) and (F), allocation of expenditures for the publication and distribution of newspaper, magazine and other types of printed advertisements distributed in more than one State shall be made using relative circulation percentages in each State or an estimate thereof. For purposes of this section, allocation to a particular State will not be required if less than 3% of the total estimated readership of the publication is in that State.

(B) *Broadcast media.* Except for expenditures exempted under 11 CFR 106.2(b)(2)(i) (E) and (F), expenditures for radio, television and similar types of advertisements purchased in a particular media market that covers more than one State shall be allocated to each State in proportion to the estimated audience. This allocation of expenditures, shall be made using industry market data. If industry market data is not available, the committee shall obtain market data from the media carrier transmitting the advertisement(s).

(C) *Refunds for media expenditures.* Refunds for broadcast time or advertisement space, purchased but not used, shall be credited to the States on the same basis as the original allocation.

(D) *Limits on allocation of media expenditures.* No allocation of media expenditures shall be made to any State in which the primary election has already been held.

(E) *National advertising.* Expenditures incurred for advertisements on national networks, national cable or in publications distributed nationwide need not be allocated to any State.

(F) *Media production costs.* Expenditures incurred for production of media advertising, whether or not that advertising is used in more than one State, need not be allocated to any State.

(G) *Commissions.* Expenditures for commissions, fees and other compensation for the purchase of broadcast or print media need not be allocated to any State.

(ii) *Expenditures for mass mailings and other campaign materials.* Expenditures for mass mailings of more than 500 pieces to addresses in the same State, and expenditures for shipping campaign materials to a State, including pins, bumperstickers, handbills, brochures, posters and yardsigns, shall be allocated to that State. For purposes of this section, *mass mailing* includes newsletters and other materials in which the content of the materials is substantially identical. Records supporting the committee's allocations under this section shall include: For each mass mailing, documentation showing the total number of pieces mailed and the number mailed to each state or zip code; and, for other campaign materials acquired for use outside the State of purchase, records relating to any shipping costs incurred for transporting these items to each State.

(iii) *Overhead expenditures—(A) Overhead expenditures of State offices and other facilities.* Except for expenditures exempted under 11 CFR 106.2(b)(2)(iii)(C), overhead expenditures of committee offices whose activities are directed at a particular State, and the costs of other facilities used for office functions and campaign events, shall be allocated to that State. An amount that does not exceed 10% of office overhead expenditures for a particular State may be treated as exempt compliance expenses, and may be excluded from allocation to that State.

(B) *Overhead expenditures of regional offices.* Except for expenditures exempted under 11 CFR 106.2(b)(2)(iii)(C), overhead expenditures of a committee regional office or any committee office with responsibilities in two or more States shall be allocated to the State holding the next primary election, caucus or convention in the region. The committee shall maintain records to demonstrate that an office operated on a regional basis. These records should show, for example, the kinds of programs conducted from the office, the number and nature of contacts with other States in the region, and the amount of time devoted to regional programs by staff working in the regional office.

(C) *Overhead expenditures of national campaign headquarters.* Expenditures incurred for administrative, staff, and overhead expenditures of the national campaign headquarters need not be allocated to any State, except as provided in paragraph (b)(2)(iv) of this section.

(D) *Definition of overhead expenditures.* For purposes of 11 CFR 106.2(b)(2)(iii), overhead expenditures include, but are not limited to, rent, utilities, equipment, furniture, supplies, and telephone service base charges. "Telephone service base charges" include any regular monthly charges for committee

127

phone service, and charges for phone installation and intrastate phone calls other than charges related to a special program under 11 CFR 106.2(b)(2)(iv). Inter-state calls are not included in "telephone service base charges." Overhead expenditures also include the costs of temporary offices established while the candidate is traveling in the State or in the final weeks before the primary election, as well as expenses paid by campaign staff and subsequently reimbursed by the committee, such as miscellaneous supplies, copying, printing and telephone expenses. See 11 CFR 116.5.

(iv) *Expenditures for special telephone programs.* Expenditures for special telephone programs targeted at a particular State, including the costs of designing and operating the program, the costs of installing or renting telephone lines and equipment, toll charges, personnel costs, consultants' fees, related travel costs, and rental of office space, including a *pro rata* portion of national, regional or State office space used for such purposes, shall be allocated to that State based on the percentage of telephone calls made to that State. Special telephone programs include voter registration, get out the vote efforts, fundraising, and telemarketing efforts conducted on behalf of the candidate. A special telephone program is targeted at a particular State if 10% or more of the total telephone calls made each month are made to that State. Records supporting the committee's allocation of each special telephone program under this section shall include either the telephone bills showing the total number of calls made in that program and the number made to each State; or, a copy of the list used to make the calls, from which these numbers can be determined.

(v) *Public opinion poll expenditures.* Expenditures incurred for the taking of a public opinion poll covering only one State shall be allocated to that State. Except for expenditures incurred in conducting a public opinion poll on a nationwide basis, expenditures incurred for the taking of a public opinion poll covering two or more States shall be allocated to those States based on the number of people interviewed in each State. Expenditures incurred for the taking of a public opinion poll include consultant's fees, travel costs and other expenses associated with designing and conducting the poll. Records supporting the committee's allocation under this section shall include documentation showing the total number of people contacted for each poll and the number contacted in each State.

(3) *National consulting fees.* Expenditures for consultants' fees need not be allocated to any State if the fees are charged for consulting on national campaign strategy. Expenditures for consultants' fees charged for conducting special telephone programs and public opinion polls shall be allocated in accordance with paragraphs (b)(2) (iv) and (v) of this section.

(c) *Reporting.* All expenditures allocated under this section shall be reported on FEC Form 3P, page 3.

(d) *Recordkeeping.* All assumptions and supporting calculations for allocations made under this section shall be documented and retained for Commission inspection. In addition to the records specified in paragraph (b) of this section, the treasurer shall retain records supporting the committee's allocations of expenditures to particular States and claims of exemption from allocation under this section. If the records supporting the allocation or claim of exemption are not retained, the expenditure shall be considered allocable and shall be allocated to the State holding the next primary election, caucus or convention after the expenditure is incurred.

[56 FR 35909, July 29, 1991, as amended at 60 FR 31872, June 16, 1995; 67 FR 78681, Dec. 26, 2002]

§ 106.3 Allocation of expenses between campaign and non-campaign related travel.

(a) This section applies to allocation for expenses between campaign and non-campaign related travel with respect to campaigns of candidates for Federal office, other than Presidential and Vice Presidential candidates who receive federal funds pursuant to 11 CFR part 9005 or 9036. (See 11 CFR 9004.7 and 9034.7) All expenditures for campaign-related travel paid for by a candidate from a campaign account or by his or her authorized committees or by any other political committee shall be reported.

(b)(1) Travel expenses paid for by a candidate from personal funds, or from a source other than a political committee, shall constitute reportable expenditures if the travel is campaign-related.

(2) Where a candidate's trip involves both campaign-related and non-campaign-related stops, the expenditures allocable for campaign purposes are reportable, and are calculated on the actual cost-per-mile of the means of transportation actually used, starting at the point of origin of the trip, via every campaign-related stop and ending at the point of origin.

(3) Where a candidate conducts any campaign-related activity in a stop, the stop is a campaign-related stop and travel expenditures made are reportable. Campaign-related activity shall not include any incidental contacts.

(c)(1) Where an individual, other than a candidate, conducts campaign-related activities on a trip, the portion of the trip attributed to each candidate shall be allocated on a reasonable basis.

(2) Travel expenses of a candidate's spouse and family are reportable as expenditures only if the spouse or family members conduct campaign-related activities.

(d) Costs incurred by a candidate for the United States Senate or House of Representatives for travel between Washington, DC, and the State or district in which he or she is a candidate need not be reported herein unless the costs are paid by the candidate's authorized committee(s), or by any other political committee(s).

(e) Notwithstanding paragraphs (b) and (c) of this section, the reportable expenditure for a candidate who uses government accommodations for travel that is campaign-related is the rate for comparable accommodations. The reportable expenditure for a candidate who uses a government conveyance for travel that is campaign-related is the applicable rate for a comparable commercial conveyance set forth in 11 CFR 100.93(e). In the case of a candidate authorized by law or required by national security to be accompanied by staff

and equipment, the allocable expenditures are the costs of facilities sufficient to accommodate the party, less authorized or required personnel and equipment. If such a trip includes both campaign and noncampaign stops, equivalent costs are calculated in accordance with paragraphs (b) and (c) of this section.

(52 U.S.C. 30111(a)(8))

[41 FR 35944, Aug. 25, 1976, as amended at 45 FR 15117, Mar. 7, 1980; 45 FR 43387, June 27, 1980; 48 FR 5234, Feb. 4, 1983; 68 FR 69595, Dec. 15, 2003]

§106.4 Allocation of polling expenses.

(a) The purchase of opinion poll results by a candidate or a candidate's authorized political committee or agent is an expenditure by the candidate. Regarding the purchase of opinion poll results for the purpose of determining whether an individual should become a candidate, see 11 CFR 100.131(a).

(b) The purchase of opinion poll results by a political committee or other person not authorized by a candidate to make expenditures and the subsequent acceptance of the poll results by a candidate or a candidate's authorized political committee or agent or by another unauthorized political committee is a contribution in-kind by the purchaser to the candidate or other political committee and an expenditure by the candidate or other political committee. Regarding the purchase of opinion poll results for the purpose of determining whether an individual should become a candidate, see 11 CFR 100.72(a). The poll results are accepted by a candidate or other political committee if the candidate or the candidate's authorized political committee or agent or the other unauthorized political committee—

(1) Requested the poll results before their receipt;

(2) Uses the poll results; or

(3) Does not notify the contributor that the results are refused.

(c) The acceptance of any part of a poll's results which part, prior to receipt, has been made public without any request, authorization, prearrangement, or coordination by the candidate-recipient or political committee-recipient, shall not be treated as a contribution in-kind and expenditure under paragraph (b) of this section.

(d) The purchase of opinion poll results by an unauthorized political committee for its own use, in whole or in part, is an overhead expenditure by the political committee under § 106.1(c)(1) to the extent of the benefit derived by the committee.

(e) The amount of a contribution under paragraph (b) of this section or of any expenditure under paragraphs (a) and (b) of this section attributable to each candidate-recipient or political committee-recipient shall be—

(1) That share of the overall cost of the poll which is allocable to each candidate (including State and local candidates) or political committee, based upon the cost allocation formula of the polling firm from which the results are purchased. Under this method the size of the sample, the number of computer column codes, the extent of computer tabulations, and the extent of written analysis and verbal consultation, if applicable, may be used to determine the shares; or

(2) An amount computed by dividing the overall cost of the poll equally among candidates (including State and local candidates) or political committees receiving the results; or

(3) A proportion of the overall cost of the poll equal to the proportion that the number of question results received by the candidate or political committee bears to the total number of question results received by all candidates (including State and local candidates) and political committees; or

(4) An amount computed by any other method which reasonably reflects the benefit derived.

(f) The first candidate(s) or committee(s) receiving poll results under paragraph (b) or (d) of this section and any candidate or political committee receiving poll results under paragraph (b) of this section within 15 days after receipt by the initial recipient(s) shall compute the amount of the contribution in-kind and the expenditure as provided in paragraph (e) of this section.

(g) The amount of the contribution and expenditure reported by a candidate or a political committee receiving poll results under paragraph (b) of this section more than 15 days after receipt of such poll results by the initial recipient(s) shall be—

(1) If the results are received during the period 16 to 60 days following receipt by the initial recipient(s), 50 percent of the amount allocated to an initial recipient of the same results;

(2) If the results are received during the period 61 to 180 days after receipt by the initial recipient(s), 5 percent of the amount allocated to an initial recipient of the same results;

(3) If the results are received more than 180 days after receipt by the initial recipient(s), no amount need be allocated.

(h) A contributor of poll results under paragraph (b) of this section shall maintain records sufficient to support the valuation of the contribution(s) in-kind and shall inform the candidate-recipient(s) or political committee-recipient(s) of the value of the contribution(s).

[41 FR 35944, Aug. 25, 1976, as amended at 45 FR 21209, Apr. 1, 1980; 67 FR 78681, Dec. 26, 2002]

§ 106.5 Allocation of expenses between federal and non-federal activities by national party committees.

(a) *General rules*—(1) *Disbursements from Federal and non-Federal accounts.* National party committees that make disbursements in connection with Federal and non-Federal elections shall make those disbursements entirely from funds subject to the prohibitions and limitations of the Act, or from accounts established pursuant to 11 CFR 102.5. Political committees that have established separate Federal and non-Federal accounts under 11 CFR 102.5(a)(1)(i) shall allocate expenses between those accounts according to this section. Organizations that are not political committees but have established separate Federal and non-Federal accounts under 11 CFR 102.5(b)(1)(i), or that make Federal and non-Federal disbursements from a single account under 11 CFR 102.5(b)(1)(ii), shall also allocate their Federal and non-Federal expenses according to this section. This section covers:

(i) General rules regarding allocation of Federal and non-Federal expenses by party committees;

(ii) Percentages to be allocated for administrative expenses and costs of generic voter drives by national party committees;

(iii) Methods for allocation of administrative expenses, costs of generic voter drives, and of fundraising costs by national party committees; and

(iv) Procedures for payment of allocable expenses. Requirements for reporting of allocated disbursements are set forth in 11 CFR 104.10.

(2) *Costs to be allocated.* National party committees that make disbursements in connection with Federal and non-Federal elections shall allocate expenses according to this section for the following categories of activity:

(i) Administrative expenses including rent, utilities, office supplies, and salaries, except for such expenses directly attributable to a clearly identified candidate;

(ii) The direct costs of a fundraising program or event including disbursements for solicitation of funds and for planning and administration of actual fundraising events, where Federal and non-Federal funds are collected by one committee through such program or event; and

(iii) [Reserved]

(iv) Generic voter drives including voter identification, voter registration, and get-out-the-vote drives, or any other activities that urge the general public to register, vote or support candidates of a particular party or associated with a particular issue, without mentioning a specific candidate.

(b) *National party committees other than Senate or House campaign committees; fixed percentages for allocating administrative expenses and costs of generic voter drives*—(1) *General rule.* Each national party committee other than a Senate or House campaign committee shall allocate a fixed percentage of its administrative expenses and costs of generic voter drives, as described in paragraph (a)(2) of this section, to its Federal and non-Federal account(s) each year. These percentages shall differ according to whether or not the allocable expenses were incurred in a presidential election year. Such com-

mittees shall allocate the costs of each combined Federal and non-Federal fundraising program or event according to paragraph (f) of this section, with no fixed percentages required.

(2) *Fixed percentages according to type of election year.* National party committees other than the Senate or House campaign committees shall allocate their administrative expenses and costs of generic voter drives according to paragraphs (b)(2) (i) and (ii) as follows:

(i) *Presidential election years.* In presidential election years, national party committees other than the Senate or House campaign committees shall allocate to their Federal accounts at least 65% each of their administrative expenses and costs of generic voter drives.

(ii) *Non-presidential election years.* In all years other than presidential election years, national party committees other than the Senate or House campaign committees shall allocate to their Federal accounts at least 60% each of their administrative expenses and costs of generic voter drives.

(c) *Senate and House campaign committees of a national party; method and minimum Federal percentage for allocating administrative expenses and costs of generic voter drives*—(1) *Method for allocating administrative expenses and costs of generic voter drives.* Subject to the minimum percentage set forth in paragraph (c)(2) of this section, each Senate or House campaign committee of a national party shall allocate its administrative expenses and costs of generic voter drives, as described in paragraph (a)(2) of this section, according to the funds expended method, described in paragraphs (c)(1)(i) and (ii) as follows:

(i) Under this method, expenses shall be allocated based on the ratio of Federal expenditures to total Federal and non-Federal disbursements made by the committee during the two-year Federal election cycle. This ratio shall be estimated and reported at the beginning of each Federal election cycle, based upon the committee's Federal and non-Federal disbursements in a prior comparable Federal election cycle or upon the committee's reasonable prediction of its disbursements for the coming two years. In calculating its Federal expenditures, the committee shall include only amounts contributed to or otherwise spent on behalf of specific federal candidates. Calculation of total Federal and non-Federal disbursements shall also be limited to disbursements for specific candidates, and shall not include overhead or other generic costs.

(ii) On each of its periodic reports, the committee shall adjust its allocation ratio to reconcile it with the ratio of actual Federal and non-Federal disbursements made, to date. If the non-Federal account has paid more than its allocable share, the committee shall transfer funds from its Federal to its non-Federal account, as necessary, to reflect the adjusted allocation ratio. The committee shall make note of any such adjustments and transfers on its periodic reports, submitted pursuant to 11 CFR 104.5.

(2) *Minimum Federal percentage for administrative expenses and costs of generic voter drives.* Regardless of the allocation ratio calculated under paragraph (c)(1) of this section, each Senate or House campaign committee of a national party shall allocate to its Federal account at least 65% each of its administrative expenses and costs of generic voter drives each year. If the committee's own allocation calculation under paragraph (c)(1) of this section yields a Federal share greater than 65%, then the higher percentage shall be applied. If such calculation yields a Federal share lower than 65%, then the committee shall report its calculated ratio according to 11 CFR 104.10(b), and shall apply the required minimum Federal percentage.

(3) *Allocation of fundraising costs.* Senate and House campaign committees shall allocate the costs of each combined Federal and non-Federal fundraising program or event according to paragraph (f) of this section, with no minimum percentages required.

(d)–(e) [Reserved]

(f) *National party committees; method for allocating direct costs of fundraising.* (1) If Federal and non-Federal funds are collected by one committee through a joint activity, that committee shall allocate its direct costs of fundraising, as described in paragraph (a)(2) of this section, according to the funds received

method. Under this method, the committee shall allocate its fundraising costs based on the ratio of funds received into its Federal account to its total receipts from each fundraising program or event. This ratio shall be estimated prior to each such program or event based upon the committee's reasonable prediction of its Federal and non-Federal revenue from that program or event, and shall be noted in the committee's report for the period in which the first disbursement for such program or event occurred, submitted pursuant 11 CFR 104.5. Any disbursements for fundraising costs made prior to the actual program or event shall be allocated according to this estimated ratio.

(2) No later than the date 60 days after each fundraising program or event from which both Federal and non-Federal funds are collected, the committee shall adjust the allocation ratio for that program or event to reflect the actual ratio of funds received. If the non-Federal account has paid more than its allocable share, the committee shall transfer funds from its Federal to its non-Federal account, as necessary, to reflect the adjusted allocation ratio. If the Federal account has paid more than its allocable share, the committee shall make any transfers of funds from its non-federal to its federal account to reflect the adjusted allocation ratio within the 60-day time period established by this paragraph. The committee shall make note of any such adjustments and transfers in its report for any period in which a transfer was made, and shall also report the date of the fundraising program or event that serves as the basis for the transfer. In the case of a telemarketing or direct mail campaign, the date for purposes of this paragraph is the last day of the telemarketing campaign, or the day on which the final direct mail solicitations are mailed.

(g) *Payment of allocable expenses by committees with separate Federal and non-Federal accounts—*(1) *Payment options.* Committees that have established separate Federal and non-Federal accounts under 11 CFR 102.5(a)(1)(i) or (b)(1)(i) shall pay the expenses of joint Federal and non-Federal activities described in paragraph (a)(2) of this section according to either paragraph (g)(1)(i) or (ii), as follows:

(i) *Payment by Federal account; transfers from non-Federal account to Federal account.* The committee shall pay the entire amount of an allocable expense from its Federal account and shall transfer funds from its non-Federal account to its Federal account solely to cover the non-Federal share of that allocable expense.

(ii) *Payment by separate allocation account; transfers from Federal and non-Federal accounts to allocation account.* (A) The committee shall establish a separate allocation account into which funds from its Federal and non-Federal accounts shall be deposited solely for the purpose of paying the allocable expenses of joint Federal and non-Federal activities. Once a committee has established a separate allocation account for this purpose, all allocable expenses shall be paid from that account for as long as the account is maintained.

(B) The committee shall transfer funds from its Federal and non-Federal accounts to its allocation account in amounts proportionate to the Federal or non-Federal share of each allocable expense.

(C) No funds contained in the allocation account may be transferred to any other account maintained by the committee.

(2) *Timing of transfers between accounts.* (i) Under either payment option described in paragraphs (g)(1)(i) or (ii) of this section, the committee shall transfer funds from its non-Federal account to its Federal account or from its Federal and non-Federal accounts to its separate allocation account following determination of the final cost of each joint Federal and non-Federal activity, or in advance of such determination if advance payment is required by the vendor and if such payment is based on a reasonable estimate of the activity's final cost as determined by the committee and the vendor(s) involved.

(ii) Funds transferred from a committee's non-Federal account to its Federal account or its allocation account are subject to the following requirements:

(A) For each such transfer, the committee must itemize in its reports the allocable activities for which the transferred funds are intended to pay, as required by 11 CFR 104.10(b)(3); and

(B) Except as provided in paragraph (f)(2) of this section, such funds may not be transferred more than 10 days before or more than 60 days after the payments for which they are designated are made.

(iii) Any portion of a transfer from a committee's non-Federal account to its Federal account or its allocation account that does not meet the requirements of paragraph (g)(2)(ii) of this section shall be presumed to be a loan or contribution from the non-Federal account to a Federal account, in violation of the Act.

(3) *Reporting transfers of funds and allocated disbursements.* A political committee that transfers funds between accounts and pays allocable expenses according to this section shall report each such transfer and disbursement pursuant to 11 CFR 104.10(b).

(h) *Sunset provision.* This section applies from November 6, 2002, to December 31, 2002. After December 31, 2002, *see* 11 CFR 106.7(a).

[67 FR 49116, July 29, 2002]

§ **106.6 Allocation of expenses between federal and non-federal activities by separate segregated funds and nonconnected committees.**

(a) *General rule.* Separate segregated funds and nonconnected committees that make disbursements in connection with federal and non-federal elections shall make those disbursements either entirely from funds subject to the prohibitions and limitations of the Act, or from accounts established pursuant to 11 CFR 102.5. Separate segregated funds and nonconnected committees that have established separate federal and non-federal accounts under 11 CFR 102.5 (a)(1)(i), or that make federal and non-federal disbursements from a single account under 11 CFR 102.5(a)(1)(ii), shall allocate their federal and non-federal expenses according to paragraphs (c), (d), and (f) of this section. For purposes of this section, "nonconnected committee" includes any committee which conducts activities in connection with an election, but which is not a party committee, an authorized committee of any candidate for federal election, or a separate segregated fund.

(b) *Payments for administrative expenses, voter drives and certain public communications*—(1) *Costs to be allocated.* Separate segregated funds and nonconnected committees that make disbursements in connection with Federal and non-Federal elections shall allocate expenses for the following categories of activity in accordance with paragraphs (c) or (d) of this section:

(i) Administrative expenses including rent, utilities, office supplies, and salaries not attributable to a clearly identified candidate, except that for a separate segregated fund such expenses may be paid instead by its connected organization;

(ii) The direct costs of a fundraising program or event including disbursements for solicitation of funds and for planning and administration of actual fundraising events, where Federal and non-Federal funds are collected through such program or event, except that for a separate segregated fund such expenses may be paid instead by its connected organization;

(iii) Generic voter drives including voter identification, voter registration, and get-out-the-vote drives, or any other activities that urge the general public to register, vote or support candidates of a particular party or associated with a particular issue, without mentioning a specific candidate; and

(iv) Public communications that refer to a political party, but do not refer to any clearly identified Federal or non-Federal candidate;

(2) *Costs not subject to allocation.* Separate segregated funds and nonconnected committees that make disbursements for the following categories of activity shall pay for those activities in accordance with paragraph (f) of this section:

(i) Voter drives, including voter identification, voter registration, and get-out-the-vote drives, in which the printed materials or scripted messages refer to, or the written instructions direct the separate segregated fund's or nonconnected committee's employee or volunteer to refer to:

(A) One or more clearly identified Federal candidates, but do not refer to

any clearly identified non-Federal candidates; or

(B) One or more clearly identified Federal candidates and also refer to candidates of a particular party or associated with a particular issue, but do not refer to any clearly identified non-Federal candidates;

(ii) Voter drives, including voter identification, voter registration, and get-out-the-vote drives, in which the printed materials or scripted messages refer to, or the written instructions direct the separate segregated fund's or nonconnected committee's employee or volunteer to refer to:

(A) One or more clearly identified non-Federal candidates, but do not refer to any clearly identified Federal candidates; or

(B) One or more clearly identified non-Federal candidates and also refer to candidates of a particular party or associated with a particular issue, but do not refer to any clearly identified Federal candidates;

(iii) Public communications that refer to one or more clearly identified Federal candidates, regardless of whether there is reference to a political party, but do not refer to any clearly identified non-Federal candidates; and

(iv) Public communications that refer to a political party, and refer to one or more clearly identified non-Federal candidates, but do not refer to any clearly identified Federal candidates.

(c) [Reserved]

(d) *Method for allocating direct costs of fundraising.* (1) If federal and non-federal funds are collected by one committee through a joint activity, that committee shall allocate its direct costs of fundraising, as described in paragraph (b)(1) of this section, according to the funds received method. Under this method, the committee shall allocate its fundraising costs based on the ratio of funds received into its federal account to its total receipts from each fundraising program or event. This ratio shall be estimated prior to each such program or event based upon the committee's reasonable prediction of its federal and non-federal revenue from that program or event, and shall be noted in the committee's report for the period in which the first disbursement for such program or event occurred, submitted pursuant to 11 CFR 104.5. Any disbursements for fundraising costs made prior to the actual program or event shall be allocated according to this estimated ratio.

(2) No later than the date 60 days after each fundraising program or event from which both federal and nonfederal funds are collected, the committee shall adjust the allocation ratio for that program or event to reflect the actual ratio of funds received. If the non-federal account has paid more than its allocable share, the committee shall transfer funds from its federal to its non-federal account, as necessary, to reflect the adjusted allocation ratio. If the federal account has paid more than its allocable share, the committee shall make any transfers of funds from its non-federal to its federal account to reflect the adjusted allocation ratio within the 60-day time period established by this paragraph. The committee shall make note of any such adjustments and transfers in its report for any period in which a transfer was made, and shall also report the date of the fundraising program or event which serves as the basis for the transfer. In the case of a telemarketing or direct mail campaign, the "date" for purposes of this paragraph is the last day of the telemarketing campaign, or the day on which the final direct mail solicitations are mailed.

(e) *Payment of allocable expenses by committees with separate federal and non-federal accounts—*(1) *Payment options.* Nonconnected committees and separate segregated funds that have established separate federal and non-federal accounts under 11 CFR 102.5 (a)(1)(i) shall pay the expenses of joint federal and non-federal activities described in paragraph (b) of this section according to either paragraph (e)(1)(i) or (ii), as follows:

(i) *Payment by federal account; transfers from non-federal account to federal account.* The committee shall pay the entire amount of an allocable expense from its federal account and shall transfer funds from its non-federal account to its federal account solely to cover the non-federal share of that allocable expense.

(ii) *Payment by separate allocation account; transfers from federal and non-federal accounts to allocation account.* (A) The committee shall establish a separate allocation account into which funds from its federal and non-federal accounts shall be deposited solely for the purpose of paying the allocable expenses of joint federal and non-federal activities. Once a committee has established an allocation account for this purpose, all allocable expenses shall be paid from that account for as long as the account is maintained.

(B) The committee shall transfer funds from its federal and non-federal accounts to its allocation account in amounts proportionate to the federal or non-federal share of each allocable expense.

(C) No funds contained in the allocation account may be transferred to any other account maintained by the committee.

(2) *Timing of transfers between accounts.* (i) Under either payment option described in paragraphs (e)(1) (i) or (ii) of this section, the committee shall transfer funds from its non-federal account or from its federal and non-federal accounts to its separate allocation account following determination of the final cost of each joint federal and non-federal activity, or in advance of such determination if advance payment is required by the vendor and if such payment is based on a reasonable estimate of the activity's final cost as determined by the committee and the vendor(s) involved.

(ii) Funds transferred from a committee's non-federal account to its federal account or its allocation account are subject to the following requirements:

(A) For each such transfer, the committee must itemize in its reports the allocable activities for which the tranferred funds are intended to pay, as required by 11 CFR 104.10(b)(3); and

(B) Except as provided in paragraph (d)(2) of this section, such funds may not be transferred more than 10 days before or more than 60 days after the payments for which they are designated are made.

(iii) Any portion of a transfer from a committee's non-federal account to its federal account or its allocation account that does not meet the requirements of paragraph (e)(2)(ii) of this section shall be presumed to be a loan or contribution from the non-federal account to a federal account, in violation of the Act.

(3) *Reporting transfers of funds and allocated disbursements.* A political committee that transfers funds between accounts and pays allocable expenses according to this section shall report each such transfer and disbursement pursuant to 11 CFR 104.10(b).

(f) [Reserved]

NOTE TO 11 CFR 106.6: On November 30, 2009, the United States District Court for the District of Columbia ordered that paragraphs (c) and (f) of §106.6 are vacated. *See Final Order, EMILY's List* v. *FEC,* No. 05-0049 (D.D.C. Nov. 30, 2009).

[55 FR 26071, June 26, 1990, as amended at 57 FR 8993, Mar. 13, 1992; 69 FR 68067, Nov. 23, 2004; 74 FR 68662, Dec. 29, 2009; 75 FR 13224, Mar. 19, 2010; 81 FR 34863, June 1, 2016]

§ 106.7 Allocation of expenses between Federal and non-Federal accounts by party committees, other than for Federal election activities.

(a) National party committees are prohibited from raising or spending non-Federal funds. Therefore, these committees shall not allocate expenditures and disbursements between Federal and non-Federal accounts. All disbursements by a national party committee must be made from a Federal account.

(b) State, district, and local party committees that make expenditures and disbursements in connection with both Federal and non-Federal elections for activities that are not Federal election activities pursuant to 11 CFR 100.24 may use only funds subject to the prohibitions and limitations of the Act, or they may allocate such expenditures and disbursements between their Federal and their non-Federal accounts. State, district, and local party committees that are political committees that have established separate Federal and non-Federal accounts under 11 CFR 102.5(a)(1)(i) shall allocate expenses between those accounts according to paragraphs (c) and (d) of this section. Party organizations that are not political committees but have established separate Federal and non-Federal ac-

counts, or that make Federal and non-Federal disbursements from a single account, shall also allocate their Federal and non-Federal expenses according to paragraphs (c) and (d) of this section. In lieu of establishing separate accounts, party organizations that are not political committees may choose to use a reasonable accounting method approved by the Commission (including any method embedded in software provided or approved by the Commission) pursuant to 11 CFR 102.5 and 300.30.

(c) *Costs allocable by State, district, and local party committees between Federal and non-Federal accounts*—(1) *Salaries, wages, and fringe benefits.* State, district, and local party committees must either pay salaries, wages, and fringe benefits for employees who spend 25% or less of their time in a given month on Federal election activity or activity in connection with a Federal election with funds from their Federal account, or with a combination of funds from their Federal and non-Federal accounts, in accordance with paragraph (d)(2) of this section. *See* 11 CFR 300.33(d)(1).

(2) *Administrative costs.* State, district, and local party committees may either pay administrative costs, including rent, utilities, office equipment, office supplies, postage for other than mass mailings, and routine building maintenance, upkeep and repair, from their Federal account, or allocate such expenses between their Federal and non-Federal accounts, except that any such expenses directly attributable to a clearly identified Federal candidate must be paid only from the Federal account.

(3) *Exempt party activities that are not Federal election activities.* State, district, and local party committees may pay expenses for party activities that are exempt from the definitions of contribution and expenditure under 11 CFR 100.80, 100.87 or 100.89, and 100.140, 100.147 or 100.149, that are conducted in conjunction with non-Federal activity, and that are not Federal election activities pursuant to 11 CFR 100.24, from their Federal accounts, or may allocate these expenses between their Federal and non-Federal accounts.

(4) *Certain fundraising costs.* State, district, and local party committees

may allocate the direct costs of joint fundraising programs or events between their Federal and non-Federal accounts according to the funds received method described in paragraph (d)(4) of this section. The direct costs of a fundraising program or event include expenses for the solicitation of funds and for the planning and administration of actual fundraising programs and events.

(5) *Voter-drive activities that do not qualify as Federal election activities and that are not party exempt activities.* Expenses for voter identification, voter registration, and get-out-the-vote drives, and any other activities that urge the general public to register or vote, or that promote or oppose a political party, without promoting or opposing a candidate or non-Federal candidate, that do not qualify as Federal election activities and that are not exempt party activities, must be paid with Federal funds or may be allocated between the committee's Federal and non-Federal accounts.

(d) *Allocation percentages, ratios, and record-keeping*—(1) *Salaries and wages.* Committees must keep a monthly log of the percentage of time each employee spends in connection with a Federal election. Allocations of salaries and wages shall be undertaken as follows:

(i) Except as provided in paragraph (d)(1)(iii) of this section, salaries, wages, and fringe benefits paid for employees who spend 25% or less of their compensated time in a given month on Federal election activities or on activities in connection with a Federal election must either be paid only from the Federal account or be allocated as administrative costs under paragraph (d)(2) of this section.

(ii) Salaries, wages, and fringe benefits paid for employees who spend more than 25% of their compensated time in a given month on Federal election activities or on activities in connection with a Federal election must be paid only from a Federal account. *See* 11 CFR 300.33(d)(2), and paragraph (e)(2) of this section.

(iii) Salaries, wages, and fringe benefits paid for employees who spend none of their compensated time in a given month on Federal election activities or on activities in connection with a Federal election may be paid entirely with funds that comply with State law.

(2) *Administrative costs.* State, district, and local party committees that choose to allocate administrative expenses may do so subject to the following requirements:

(i) *Presidential election years.* In any even year in which a Presidential candidate, but no Senate candidate appears on the ballot, and in the preceding year, State, district, and local party committees must allocate at least 28% of administrative expenses to their Federal accounts.

(ii) *Presidential and Senate election year.* In any even year in which a Presidential candidate and a Senate candidate appear on the ballot, and in the preceding year, State, district, and local party committees must allocate at least 36% of administrative expenses to their Federal accounts.

(iii) *Senate election year.* In any even year in which a Senate candidate, but no Presidential candidate, appears on the ballot, and in the preceding year, State, district, and local party committees must allocate at least 21% of administrative expenses to their Federal account.

(iv) *Non-Presidential and non-Senate year.* In any even year in which neither a Presidential nor a Senate candidate appears on the ballot, and in the preceding year, State, district, and local party committees must allocate at least 15% of administrative expenses to their Federal account.

(3) *Exempt party activities and voter drive activities that are not Federal election activities.* State, district, and local party committees that choose to allocate expenses for exempt activities conducted in conjunction with non-Federal activities and voter drive activities, that are not Federal election activities, must do so subject to the following requirements:

(i) *Presidential election years.* In any even year in which a Presidential candidate, but no Senate candidate appears on the ballot, and in the preceding year, State, district, and local party committees must allocate at least 28% of these expenses to their Federal accounts.

(ii) *Presidential and Senate election year.* In any even year in which a Presidential candidate and a Senate candidate appear on the ballot, and in the preceding year, State, district, and local party committees must allocate at least 36% of these expenses to their Federal accounts.

(iii) *Senate election year.* In any even year in which a Senate candidate, but no Presidential candidate, appears on the ballot, and in the preceding year, State, district, and local party committees must allocate at least 21% of these expenses to their Federal account.

(iv) *Non-Presidential and non-Senate year.* In any even year in which neither a Presidential nor a Senate candidate appears on the ballot, and in the preceding year, State, district, and local party committee must allocate at least 15% of these expenses to their Federal account.

(4) *Fundraising for Federal and non-Federal accounts.* If Federal and non-Federal funds are collected by a State, district, or local party committee through a joint fundraising activity, that committee must allocate its direct fundraising costs using the funds received method and according to the following procedures:

(i) The committee must allocate its fundraising costs based on the ratio of funds received into its Federal account to its total receipts from each fundraising program or event. This ratio shall be estimated prior to each such program or event based upon the committee's reasonable prediction of its Federal and non-Federal revenue from that program or event, and must be noted in the committee's report for the period in which the first disbursement for such program or event occurred, submitted pursuant to 11 CFR 104.5. Any disbursements for fundraising costs made prior to the actual program or event must be allocated according to this estimated ratio.

(ii) No later than the date 60 days after each fundraising program or event from which both Federal and non-Federal funds are collected, the committee shall adjust the allocation ratio for that program or event to reflect the actual ratio of funds received. If the non-Federal account has paid more than its allocable share, the committee shall transfer funds from its Federal to its non-Federal account, as necessary, to reflect the adjusted allocation ratio. If the Federal account has paid more than its allocable share, the committee shall make any transfers of funds from its non-Federal to its Federal account to reflect the adjusted allocation ratio within the 60-day time period established by this paragraph. The committee shall make note of any such adjustments and transfers in its report for any period in which a transfer was made, and shall also report the date of the fundraising program or event that serves as the basis for the transfer. In the case of a telemarketing or direct mail campaign, the date for purposes of this paragraph is the last day of the telemarketing campaign, or the day on which the final direct mail solicitations are mailed.

(e) *Costs not allocable by State, district, and local party committees between Federal and non-Federal accounts.* The following costs incurred by State, district, and local party committees shall be paid only with Federal funds:

(1) Disbursements for State, district, and local party committees for activities that refer only to one or more candidates for Federal office must not be allocated. All such disbursements must be made from a Federal account.

(2) *Salaries and wages.* Salaries and wages for employees who spend more than 25% of their compensated time in a given month on activities in connection with a Federal election must not be allocated. All such disbursements must be made from a Federal account. *See* 11 CFR 300.33(d)(2).

(3) *Federal election activities.* Activities that are Federal election activities pursuant to 11 CFR 100.24 must not be allocated between Federal and non-Federal accounts. Only Federal funds, or a mixture of Federal funds and Levin funds, as provided in 11 CFR 300.33, may be used.

(f) *Transfers between accounts to cover allocable expenses.* State, district, and local party committees may transfer funds from their non-Federal to their Federal accounts or to an allocation account solely to meet allocable expenses under this section and only pursuant to the following requirements:

(1) *Payments from Federal accounts or from allocation accounts.* (i) State, district, and local party committees must pay the entire amount of an allocable expense from their Federal accounts and transfer funds from their non-Federal account to the Federal account solely to cover the non-Federal share of that allocable expense; or

(ii) State, district, or local party committees may establish a separate allocation account into which funds from its Federal and non-Federal accounts may be deposited solely for the purpose of paying the allocable expenses of joint Federal and non-Federal activities.

(2) *Timing.* (i) If a Federal or allocation account is used to make allocable expenditures and disbursements, State, district, and local party committees must transfer funds from their non-Federal to their Federal or allocation account to meet allocable expenses no more than 10 days before and no more than 60 days after the payments for which they are designated are made from a Federal or allocation account, except that transfers may be made more than 10 days before a payment is made from the Federal or allocation account if advance payment is required by the vendor(s) and if such payment is based on a reasonable estimate of the activity's final costs as determined by the committee and the vendor(s) involved.

(ii) Any portion of a transfer from a committee's non-Federal account to its Federal or allocation account that does not meet the requirement of paragraph (f)(2)(i) of this section shall be presumed to be a loan or contribution from the non-Federal account to the Federal or allocation account, in violation of the Act.

[67 FR 49118, July 29, 2002, as amended at 67 FR 78681, Dec. 26, 2002; 70 FR 75384, Dec. 20, 2005; 81 FR 34863, June 1, 2016]

§ 106.8 **Allocation of expenses for political party committee phone banks that refer to a clearly identified Federal candidate.**

(a) *Scope.* This section applies to the costs of a phone bank conducted by a national, State, district, or local committee or organization of a political party where—

(1) The communication refers to a clearly identified Federal candidate;

(2) The communication does not refer to any other clearly identified Federal or non-Federal candidate;

(3) The communication includes another reference that generically refers to other candidates of the Federal candidate's party without clearly identifying them;

(4) The communication does not solicit a contribution, donation, or any other funds from any person; and

(5) The phone bank is not exempt from the definition of "contribution" under 11 CFR 100.89 and is not exempt from the definition of "expenditure" under 11 CFR 100.149.

(b) *Attribution.* Each disbursement for the costs of a phone bank described in paragraph (a) of this section shall be attributed as follows:

(1) Fifty percent of the disbursement is not attributable to any other Federal or non-Federal candidate, but must be paid for entirely with Federal funds; and

(2) Fifty percent of the disbursement is attributed to the clearly identified Federal candidate and must be paid for entirely with Federal funds. This disbursement may be one or a combination of the following:

(i) An in-kind contribution, subject to the limitations set forth in 11 CFR 110.1 or 110.2; or

(ii) A coordinated expenditure or an independent expenditure, subject to the limitations, restrictions, and requirements of 11 CFR 109.10, 109.32, and 109.33; or

(iii) Reimbursed by the clearly identified Federal candidate or his or her authorized committee.

[68 FR 64520, Nov. 14, 2003, as amended at 69 FR 63920, Nov. 3, 2004]

PART 107—PRESIDENTIAL NOMINATING CONVENTION, REGISTRATION AND REPORTS

AUTHORITY: 52 U.S.C. 30105, 30111(a)(8).

SOURCE: 59 FR 33615, June 29, 1994, unless otherwise noted.

§ 107.1 Registration and reports by political parties.

Each convention committee established under 11 CFR 9008.3(a)(2) by a national committee of a political party and each committee or other organization, including a national committee, which represents a political party in making arrangements for that party's convention held to nominate a presidential or vice presidential candidate shall register and report in accordance with 11 CFR 9008.3(b).

§ 107.2 Registration and reports by host committees and municipal funds.

Each host committee and municipal fund shall register and report in accordance with 11 CFR 9008.51. The reports shall contain the information specified in 11 CFR part 104.

[68 FR 47414, Aug. 8, 2003]

PART 108—FILING COPIES OF REPORTS AND STATEMENTS WITH STATE OFFICERS (52 U.S.C. 30113)

Sec.
108.1 Filing requirements (52 U.S.C. 30113(a)(1)).
108.2 Filing copies of reports and statements in connection with the campaign of any candidate seeking nomination for election to the Office of President or Vice-President (52 U.S.C. 30113(a)(2)).
108.3 Filing copies of reports and statements in connection with the campaign of any congressional candidate (52 U.S.C. 30113(a)(2)).
108.4 Filing copies of reports by committees other than principal campaign committees (52 U.S.C. 30113(a)(2)).
108.5 Time and manner of filing copies (52 U.S.C. 30104(a)(2)).
108.6 Duties of State officers (52 U.S.C. 30113(b)).
108.7 Effect on State law (52 U.S.C. 30143).
108.8 Exemption for the District of Columbia.

AUTHORITY: 52 U.S.C. 30104(a)(2), 30111(a)(8), 30113, 30143.

SOURCE: 45 FR 15117, Mar. 7, 1980, unless otherwise noted.

§ 108.1 Filing requirements (52 U.S.C. 30113(a)(1)).

(a) Except as provided in paragraph (b) of this section, a copy of each report and statement required to be filed by any person under the Act shall be filed either with the Secretary of State of the appropriate State or with the State officer who is charged by State law with maintaining state election campaign reports. In States where reports are to be filed with a designated officer other than the Secretary of State, the chief executive officer of that State shall notify the Commission of such designation.

(b) The filing requirements and duties of State officers under this part 108 shall not apply to a State if the Commission has determined that the State maintains a system that can electronically receive and duplicate reports and statements filed with the Commission. Once a State has obtained a waiver pursuant to this paragraph, the waiver shall apply to all reports that can be electronically accessed and duplicated from the Commission, regardless of whether the report or statement was originally filed with the Commission. The list of States that have obtained waivers under this section is available on the Commission's website.

[45 FR 15117, Mar. 7, 1980, as amended at 65 FR 15223, Mar. 22, 2000; 68 FR 420, Jan. 3, 2003]

§ 108.2 Filing copies of reports and statements in connection with the campaign of any candidate seeking nomination for election to the Office of President or Vice-President (52 U.S.C. 30113(a)(2)).

Except as provided in § 108.1(b), a copy of each report and statement required to be filed under the Act (including 11 CFR part 104) by a Presidential or Vice Presidential candidate's principal campaign committee, or under 11 CFR 104.4 or part 109 by any other person making independent expenditures, in connection with a candidate seeking nomination for election to the office of President or Vice-President, shall be filed with the State officer of each State in which an expenditure is made in connection with the campaign of a candidate seeking nomination for election to the office of President or Vice-President. The report and statement shall contain all transactions pertaining to that State during the reporting period. Any committee, other than a Presidential or Vice Presidential candidate's principal campaign committee and the candidate's authorized committee(s) shall also file a copy of each report and statement with the appropriate State officer of the State in which such committee has its headquarters pursuant to 11 CFR 108.4.

[45 FR 15117, Mar. 7, 1980, as amended at 65 FR 15224, Mar. 22, 2000]

§ 108.3 Filing copies of reports and statements in connection with the campaign of any congressional candidate (52 U.S.C. 30113(a)(2)).

(a) Except as provided in § 108.1(b), a copy of each report and statement required to be filed under 11 CFR part 104 by candidates, and the authorized committees of candidates, for nomination for election or election to the office of Senator; by other committees that support only such candidates; and by the National Republican Senatorial Committee and the Democratic Senatorial Campaign Committees shall be filed with the appropriate State officer of that State in which an expenditure is made in connection with the campaign.

(b) Except as provided in § 108.1(b), a copy of each report and statement required to be filed under 11 CFR part 104 by candidates, and authorized committees of candidates, for nomination for election or election to the office of Representative in, Delegate or Resident Commissioner to the Congress, or by unauthorized committees, or by any other person under 11 CFR part 109, in connection with these campaigns shall be filed with the appropriate State officer of that State in which an expenditure is made in connection with the campaign.

(c) Unauthorized committees that file reports pursuant to paragraph (b) of this section are required to file, and the Secretary of State is required to retain, only that portion of the report applicable to candidates seeking election in that State.

[65 FR 15224, Mar. 22, 2000]

§ 108.4 Filing copies of reports by committees other than principal campaign committees (52 U.S.C. 30113(a)(2)).

Except as provided in § 108.1(b), any unauthorized committee that makes contributions in connection with a Presidential election and that is required to file a report(s) and statement(s) under the Act shall file a copy of such report(s) and statement(s) with the State officer of the State in which both the recipient and contributing committees have their headquarters.

[65 FR 15224, Mar. 22, 2000]

§ 108.5 Time and manner of filing copies (52 U.S.C. 30104(a)(2)).

A copy of any report or statement required to be filed with a State officer under 11 CFR part 108 shall be filed at the same time as the original report is filed. Each copy of such report or statement shall be a complete, true, and legible copy of the original report or statement filed.

§ 108.6 Duties of State officers (52 U.S.C. 30113(b)).

Except as provided in § 108.1(b), the Secretary of State, or the equivalent State officer, shall carry out the duties set forth in paragraphs (a) through (e) of this section:

(a) Receive and maintain in an orderly manner all reports and statements required to be filed;

(b) Preserve such reports and statements (either in original form or in facsimile copy by microfilm or otherwise) filed under the Act for a period of 2 years from the date of receipt, except that reports and statements that can be accessed and duplicated electronically from the Commission need not be so preserved;

(c) Make the reports and statements filed available as soon as practicable (but within 48 hours of receipt) for public inspection and copying during office hours and permit copying of any such reports or statements by hand or by duplicating machine, at the request of any person except that such copying shall be at the expense of the person making the request and at a reasonable fee;

(d) Compile and maintain a current list of all reports and statements or parts of such reports and statements pertaining to each candidate; and

(e) If the State has received a waiver of these filing requirements pursuant to § 108.1(b), allow access to and duplication of reports and statements covered by that waiver, except that such access and duplication shall be at the expense of the person making the request and at a reasonable fee.

[45 FR 15117, Mar. 7, 1980, as amended at 65 FR 15224, Mar. 22, 2000]

§ 108.7 Effect on State law (52 U.S.C. 30143).

(a) The provisions of the Federal Election Campaign Act of 1971, as amended, and rules and regulations issued thereunder, supersede and preempt any provision of State law with respect to election to Federal office.

(b) Federal law supersedes State law concerning the—

(1) Organization and registration of political committees supporting Federal candidates;

(2) Disclosure of receipts and expenditures by Federal candidates and political committees; and

(3) Limitation on contributions and expenditures regarding Federal candidates and political committees.

(c) The Act does not supersede State laws which provide for the—

(1) Manner of qualifying as a candidate or political party organization;

(2) Dates and places of elections;

(3) Voter registration;

(4) Prohibition of false registration, voting fraud, theft of ballots, and similar offenses;

(5) Candidate's personal financial disclosure; or

(6) Application of State law to the funds used for the purchase or construction of a State or local party office building to the extent described in 11 CFR 300.35.

[45 FR 15117, Mar. 7, 1980, as amended at 67 FR 49119, July 29, 2002]

§ 108.8 Exemption for the District of Columbia.

Any copy of a report required to be filed with the equivalent officer in the District of Columbia shall be deemed to be filed if the original has been filed with the Secretary or the Commission, as appropriate.

[45 FR 15117, Mar. 7, 1980, as amended at 61 FR 6095, Feb. 16, 1996]

PART 109—COORDINATED AND INDEPENDENT EXPENDITURES (52 U.S.C. 30101(17), 30116(a) AND (d), AND PUB. L. 107-155 SEC. 214(C))

Sec.

Subpart A—Scope and Definitions

109.1   When will this part apply?
109.2   [Reserved]
109.3   Definitions.

Subpart B—Independent Expenditures

109.10   How do political committees and other persons report independent expenditures?
109.11   When is a "non-authorization notice" (disclaimer) required?

Subpart C—Coordination

109.20   What does "coordinated" mean?
109.21   What is a "coordinated communication"?
109.22   Who is prohibited from making coordinated communications?
109.23   Dissemination, distribution, or republication of candidate campaign materials.

Subpart D—Special Provisions for Political Party Committees

109.30   How are political party committees treated for purposes of coordinated and independent expenditures?
109.31   [Reserved]
109.32   What are the coordinated party expenditure limits?
109.33   May a political party committee assign its coordinated party expenditure authority to another political party committee?
109.34   When may a political party committee make coordinated party expenditures?
109.35   [Reserved]
109.36   Are there circumstances under which a political party committee is prohibited from making independent expenditures?
109.37   What is a "party coordinated communication"?

AUTHORITY: 52 U.S.C. 30101(17), 30104(c), 30111(a)(8), 30116, 30120; Sec. 214(c), Pub. L. 107-155, 116 Stat. 81.

SOURCE: 68 FR 451, Jan. 3, 2003, unless otherwise noted.

Subpart A—Scope and Definitions

§109.1 When will this part apply?

This part applies to expenditures that are made independently from a candidate, an authorized committee, a political party committee, or their agents, and to those payments that are made in coordination with a candidate, an authorized committee, a political party committee, or their agents. The rules in this part explain how these types of payments must be reported and how they must be treated by candidates, authorized committees, and political party committees. In addition, subpart D of part 109 describes procedures and limits that apply only to payments, transfers, and assignments made by political party committees.

§109.2 [Reserved]

§109.3 Definitions.

For the purposes of 11 CFR part 109 only, agent means any person who has actual authority, either express or implied, to engage in any of the following activities on behalf of the specified persons:

(a) In the case of a national, State, district, or local committee of a political party, any one or more of the activities listed in paragraphs (a)(1) through (a)(5) of this section:

(1) To request or suggest that a communication be created, produced, or distributed.

(2) To make or authorize a communication that meets one or more of the content standards set forth in 11 CFR 109.21(c).

(3) To create, produce, or distribute any communication at the request or suggestion of a candidate.

(4) To be materially involved in decisions regarding:

(i) The content of the communication;

(ii) The intended audience for the communication;

(iii) The means or mode of the communication;

(iv) The specific media outlet used for the communication;

(v) The timing or frequency of the communication; or,

(vi) The size or prominence of a printed communication, or duration of a communication by means of broadcast, cable, or satellite.

(5) To make or direct a communication that is created, produced, or distributed with the use of material or information derived from a substantial discussion about the communication with a candidate.

(b) In the case of an individual who is a Federal candidate or an individual holding Federal office, any one or more of the activities listed in paragraphs (b)(1) through (b)(6) of this section:

(1) To request or suggest that a communication be created, produced, or distributed.

(2) To make or authorize a communication that meets one or more of the content standards set forth in 11 CFR 109.21(c).

(3) To request or suggest that any other person create, produce, or distribute any communication.

(4) To be materially involved in decisions regarding:

(i) The content of the communication;

(ii) The intended audience for the communication;

(iii) The means or mode of the communication;

(iv) The specific media outlet used for the communication;

(v) The timing or frequency of the communication;

(vi) The size or prominence of a printed communication, or duration of a communication by means of broadcast, cable, or satellite.

(5) To provide material or information to assist another person in the creation, production, or distribution of any communication.

(6) To make or direct a communication that is created, produced, or distributed with the use of material or information derived from a substantial discussion about the communication with a different candidate.

Subpart B—Independent Expenditures

§ 109.10 How do political committees and other persons report independent expenditures?

(a) Political committees, including political party committees, must report independent expenditures under 11 CFR 104.4.

(b) Every person that is not a political committee and that makes independent expenditures aggregating in excess of $250 with respect to a given election in a calendar year shall file a verified statement or report on FEC Form 5 in accordance with 11 CFR 104.4(e) containing the information required by paragraph (e) of this section. Every person filing a report or statement under this section shall do so in accordance with the quarterly reporting schedule specified in 11 CFR 104.5(a)(1)(i) and (ii) and shall file a report or statement for any quarterly period during which any such independent expenditures that aggregate in excess of $250 are made and in any quarterly reporting period thereafter in which additional independent expenditures are made.

(c) For each election in which a person who is not a political committee makes independent expenditures, the person shall aggregate its independent expenditures made in each calendar year to determine its reporting obligation. When such a person makes independent expenditures aggregating $10,000 or more for an election in any calendar year, up to and including the 20th day before an election, the person must report the independent expenditures on FEC Form 5, or by signed statement if the person is not otherwise required to file electronically under 11 CFR 104.18. (See 11 CFR 104.4(f) for aggregation.) The person making the independent expenditures aggregating $10,000 or more must ensure that the Commission receives the report or statement by 11:59 p.m. Eastern Standard/Daylight Time on the second day following the date on which a communication is publicly distributed or otherwise publicly disseminated. Each time subsequent independent expenditures relating to the same election aggregate an additional $10,000 or more,

the person making the independent expenditures must ensure that the Commission receives a new 48-hour report of the subsequent independent expenditures. Each 48-hour report must contain the information required by paragraph (e)(1) of this section.

(d) Every person making, after the 20th day, but more than 24 hours before 12:01 a.m. of the day of an election, independent expenditures aggregating $1,000 or more with respect to a given election must report those independent expenditures and ensure that the Commission receives the report or signed statement by 11:59 p.m. Eastern Standard/Daylight Time on the day following the date on which a communication is publicly distributed or otherwise publicly disseminated. Each time subsequent independent expenditures relating to the same election aggregate $1,000 or more, the person making the independent expenditures must ensure that the Commission receives a new 24-hour report of the subsequent independent expenditures. (See 11 CFR 104.4(f) for aggregation.) Such report or statement shall contain the information required by paragraph (e) of this section.

(e) Content of verified reports and statements and verification of reports and statements.

(1) *Contents of verified reports and statement.* If a signed report or statement is submitted, the report or statement shall include:

(i) The reporting person's name, mailing address, occupation, and the name of his or her employer, if any;

(ii) The identification (name and mailing address) of the person to whom the expenditure was made;

(iii) The amount, date, and purpose of each expenditure;

(iv) A statement that indicates whether such expenditure was in support of, or in opposition to a candidate, together with the candidate's name and office sought;

(v) A verified certification under penalty of perjury as to whether such expenditure was made in cooperation, consultation, or concert with, or at the request or suggestion of a candidate, a candidate's authorized committee, or their agents, or a political party committee or its agents; and

(vi) The identification of each person who made a contribution in excess of $200 to the person filing such report, which contribution was made for the purpose of furthering the reported independent expenditure.

(2) *Verification of independent expenditure statements and reports.* Every person shall verify reports and statements of independent expenditures filed pursuant to the requirements of this section by one of the methods stated in paragraph (e)(2)(i) or (ii) of this section. Any report or statement verified under either of these methods shall be treated for all purposes (including penalties for perjury) in the same manner as a document verified by signature.

(i) For reports or statements filed on paper (e.g., by hand-delivery, U.S. Mail, or facsimile machine), the person who made the independent expenditure shall certify, under penalty of perjury, the independence of the expenditure by handwritten signature immediately following the certification required by paragraph (e)(1)(v) of this section.

(ii) For reports or statements filed by electronic mail, the person who made the independent expenditure shall certify, under penalty of perjury, the independence of the expenditure by typing the treasurer's name immediately following the certification required by paragraph (e)(1)(v) of this section.

[68 FR 451, Jan. 3, 2003, as amended at 81 FR 34863, June 1, 2016]

§109.11 When is a "non-authorization notice" (disclaimer) required?

Whenever any person makes an independent expenditure for the purpose of financing communications expressly advocating the election or defeat of a clearly identified candidate, such person shall comply with the requirements of 11 CFR 110.11.

Subpart C—Coordination

§109.20 What does "coordinated" mean?

(a) *Coordinated* means made in cooperation, consultation or concert with, or at the request or suggestion of, a candidate, a candidate's authorized committee, or a political party committee. For purposes of this subpart C, any reference to a candidate, or a candidate's authorized committee, or a political party committee includes an agent thereof.

(b) Any expenditure that is coordinated within the meaning of paragraph (a) of this section, but that is not made for a coordinated communication under 11 CFR 109.21 or a party coordinated communication under 11 CFR 109.37, is either an in-kind contribution to, or a coordinated party expenditure with respect to, the candidate or political party committee with whom or with which it was coordinated and must be reported as an expenditure made by that candidate or political party committee, unless otherwise exempted under 11 CFR part 100, subparts C or E.

[68 FR 451, Jan. 3, 2003, as amended at 71 FR 33208, June 8, 2006]

§109.21 What is a "coordinated communication"?

(a) *Definition.* A communication is coordinated with a candidate, an authorized committee, a political party committee, or an agent of any of the foregoing when the communication:

(1) Is paid for, in whole or in part, by a person other than that candidate, authorized committee, or political party committee;

(2) Satisfies at least one of the content standards in paragraph (c) of this section; and

(3) Satisfies at least one of the conduct standards in paragraph (d) of this section.

(b) *Treatment as an in-kind contribution and expenditure; Reporting*—(1) *General rule.* A payment for a coordinated communication is made for the purpose of influencing a Federal election, and is an in-kind contribution under 11 CFR 100.52(d) to the candidate, authorized committee, or political party committee with whom or which it is coordinated, unless excepted under 11 CFR part 100, subpart C, and must be reported as an expenditure made by that candidate, authorized committee, or political party committee under 11 CFR 104.13, unless excepted under 11 CFR part 100, subpart E.

(2) *In-kind contributions resulting from conduct described in paragraphs (d)(4) or (d)(5) of this section.* Notwithstanding paragraph (b)(1) of this section, the candidate, authorized committee, or

political party committee with whom or which a communication is coordinated does not receive or accept an in-kind contribution, and is not required to report an expenditure, that results from conduct described in paragraphs (d)(4) or (d)(5) of this section, unless the candidate, authorized committee, or political party committee engages in conduct described in paragraphs (d)(1) through (d)(3) of this section.

(3) *Reporting of coordinated communications.* A political committee, other than a political party committee, that makes a coordinated communication must report the payment for the communication as a contribution made to the candidate or political party committee with whom or which it was coordinated and as an expenditure in accordance with 11 CFR 104.3(b)(1)(v). A candidate, authorized committee, or political party committee with whom or which a communication paid for by another person is coordinated must report the usual and normal value of the communication as an in-kind contribution in accordance with 11 CFR 104.13, meaning that it must report the amount of the payment as a receipt under 11 CFR 104.3(a) and as an expenditure under 11 CFR 104.3(b).

(c) *Content standards.* Each of the types of content described in paragraphs (c)(1) through (c)(5) of this section satisfies the content standard of this section.

(1) A communication that is an electioneering communication under 11 CFR 100.29.

(2) A public communication, as defined in 11 CFR 100.26, that disseminates, distributes, or republishes, in whole or in part, campaign materials prepared by a candidate or the candidate's authorized committee, unless the dissemination, distribution, or republication is excepted under 11 CFR 109.23(b). For a communication that satisfies this content standard, see paragraph (d)(6) of this section.

(3) A public communication, as defined in 11 CFR 100.26, that expressly advocates, as defined in 11 CFR 100.22, the election or defeat of a clearly identified candidate for Federal office.

(4) A public communication, as defined in 11 CFR 100.26, that satisfies

paragraph (c)(4)(i), (ii), (iii), or (iv) of this section:

(i) *References to House and Senate candidates.* The public communication refers to a clearly identified House or Senate candidate and is publicly distributed or otherwise publicly disseminated in the clearly identified candidate's jurisdiction 90 days or fewer before the clearly identified candidate's general, special, or runoff election, or primary or preference election, or nominating convention or caucus.

(ii) *References to Presidential and Vice Presidential candidates.* The public communication refers to a clearly identified Presidential or Vice Presidential candidate and is publicly distributed or otherwise publicly disseminated in a jurisdiction during the period of time beginning 120 days before the clearly identified candidate's primary or preference election in that jurisdiction, or nominating convention or caucus in that jurisdiction, up to and including the day of the general election.

(iii) *References to political parties.* The public communication refers to a political party, does not refer to a clearly identified Federal candidate, and is publicly distributed or otherwise publicly disseminated in a jurisdiction in which one or more candidates of that political party will appear on the ballot.

(A) When the public communication is coordinated with a candidate and it is publicly distributed or otherwise publicly disseminated in that candidate's jurisdiction, the time period in paragraph (c)(4)(i) or (ii) of this section that would apply to a communication containing a reference to that candidate applies;

(B) When the public communication is coordinated with a political party committee and it is publicly distributed or otherwise publicly disseminated during the two-year election cycle ending on the date of a regularly scheduled non-Presidential general election, the time period in paragraph (c)(4)(i) of this section applies;

(C) When the public communication is coordinated with a political party committee and it is publicly distributed or otherwise publicly disseminated during the two-year election cycle ending on the date of a Presidential general election, the time period in paragraph (c)(4)(ii) of this section applies.

(iv) *References to both political parties and clearly identified Federal candidates.* The public communication refers to a political party and a clearly identified Federal candidate, and is publicly distributed or otherwise publicly disseminated in a jurisdiction in which one or more candidates of that political party will appear on the ballot.

(A) When the public communication is coordinated with a candidate and it is publicly distributed or otherwise publicly disseminated in that candidate's jurisdiction, the time period in paragraph (c)(4)(i) or (ii) of this section that would apply to a communication containing a reference to that candidate applies;

(B) When the public communication is coordinated with a political party committee and it is publicly distributed or otherwise publicly disseminated in the clearly identified candidate's jurisdiction, the time period in paragraph (c)(4)(i) or (ii) of this section that would apply to a communication containing only a reference to that candidate applies;

(C) When the public communication is coordinated with a political party committee and it is publicly distributed or otherwise publicly disseminated outside the clearly identified candidate's jurisdiction, the time period in paragraph (c)(4)(iii)(B) or (C) of this section that would apply to a communication containing only a reference to a political party applies.

(5) A public communication, as defined in 11 CFR 100.26, that is the functional equivalent of express advocacy. For purposes of this section, a communication is the functional equivalent of express advocacy if it is susceptible of no reasonable interpretation other than as an appeal to vote for or against a clearly identified Federal candidate.

(d) *Conduct standards.* Any one of the following types of conduct satisfies the conduct standard of this section whether or not there is agreement or formal collaboration, as defined in paragraph (e) of this section:

(1) *Request or suggestion.* (i) The communication is created, produced, or distributed at the request or suggestion of a candidate, authorized committee, or political party committee; or

(ii) The communication is created, produced, or distributed at the suggestion of a person paying for the communication and the candidate, authorized committee, or political party committee assents to the suggestion.

(2) *Material involvement.* This paragraph, (d)(2), is not satisfied if the information material to the creation, production, or distribution of the communication was obtained from a publicly available source. A candidate, authorized committee, or political party committee is materially involved in decisions regarding:

(i) The content of the communication;

(ii) The intended audience for the communication;

(iii) The means or mode of the communication;

(iv) The specific media outlet used for the communication;

(v) The timing or frequency of the communication; or

(vi) The size or prominence of a printed communication, or duration of a communication by means of broadcast, cable, or satellite.

(3) *Substantial discussion.* This paragraph, (d)(3), is not satisfied if the information material to the creation, production, or distribution of the communication was obtained from a publicly available source. The communication is created, produced, or distributed after one or more substantial discussions about the communication between the person paying for the communication, or the employees or agents of the person paying for the communication, and the candidate who is clearly identified in the communication, or the candidate's authorized committee, the candidate's opponent, the opponent's authorized committee, or a political party committee. A discussion is substantial within the meaning of this paragraph if information about the candidate's or political party committee's campaign plans, projects, activities, or needs is conveyed to a person paying for the communication, and that information is material to the creation, production, or distribution of the communication.

(4) *Common vendor.* All of the following statements in paragraphs (d)(4)(i) through (d)(4)(iii) of this section are true:

(i) The person paying for the communication, or an agent of such person, contracts with or employs a commercial vendor, as defined in 11 CFR 116.1(c), to create, produce, or distribute the communication;

(ii) That commercial vendor, including any owner, officer, or employee of the commercial vendor, has provided any of the following services to the candidate who is clearly identified in the communication, or the candidate's authorized committee, the candidate's opponent, the opponent's authorized committee, or a political party committee, during the previous 120 days:

(A) Development of media strategy, including the selection or purchasing of advertising slots;

(B) Selection of audiences;

(C) Polling;

(D) Fundraising;

(E) Developing the content of a public communication;

(F) Producing a public communication;

(G) Identifying voters or developing voter lists, mailing lists, or donor lists;

(H) Selecting personnel, contractors, or subcontractors; or

(I) Consulting or otherwise providing political or media advice; and

(iii) This paragraph, (d)(4)(iii), is not satisfied if the information material to the creation, production, or distribution of the communication used or conveyed by the commercial vendor was obtained from a publicly available source. That commercial vendor uses or conveys to the person paying for the communication:

(A) Information about the campaign plans, projects, activities, or needs of the clearly identified candidate, the candidate's opponent, or a political party committee, and that information is material to the creation, production, or distribution of the communication; or

(B) Information used previously by the commercial vendor in providing services to the candidate who is clearly identified in the communication, or the candidate's authorized committee, the candidate's opponent, the oppo-

nent's authorized committee, or a political party committee, and that information is material to the creation, production, or distribution of the communication.

(5) *Former employee or independent contractor.* Both of the following statements in paragraphs (d)(5)(i) and (d)(5)(ii) of this section are true:

(i) The communication is paid for by a person, or by the employer of a person, who was an employee or independent contractor of the candidate who is clearly identified in the communication, or the candidate's authorized committee, the candidate's opponent, the opponent's authorized committee, or a political party committee, during the previous 120 days; and

(ii) This paragraph, (d)(5)(ii), is not satisfied if the information material to the creation, production, or distribution of the communication used or conveyed by the former employee or independent contractor was obtained from a publicly available source. That former employee or independent contractor uses or conveys to the person paying for the communication:

(A) Information about the campaign plans, projects, activities, or needs of the clearly identified candidate, the candidate's opponent, or a political party committee, and that information is material to the creation, production, or distribution of the communication; or

(B) Information used by the former employee or independent contractor in providing services to the candidate who is clearly identified in the communication, or the candidate's authorized committee, the candidate's opponent, the opponent's authorized committee, or a political party committee, and that information is material to the creation, production, or distribution of the communication.

(6) *Dissemination, distribution, or republication of campaign material.* A communication that satisfies the content standard of paragraph (c)(2) of this section or 11 CFR 109.37(a)(2)(i) shall only satisfy the conduct standards of paragraphs (d)(1) through (d)(3) of this section on the basis of conduct by the candidate, the candidate's authorized committee, or the agents of any of the foregoing, that occurs after the original

preparation of the campaign materials that are disseminated, distributed, or republished. The conduct standards of paragraphs (d)(4) and (d)(5) of this section may also apply to such communications as provided in those paragraphs.

(e) *Agreement or formal collaboration.* Agreement or formal collaboration between the person paying for the communication and the candidate clearly identified in the communication, or the candidate's authorized committee, the candidate's opponent, the opponent's authorized committee, or a political party committee, is not required for a communication to be a coordinated communication. *Agreement* means a mutual understanding or meeting of the minds on all or any part of the material aspects of the communication or its dissemination. *Formal collaboration* means planned, or systematically organized, work on the communication.

(f) *Safe harbor for responses to inquiries about legislative or policy issues.* A candidate's or a political party committee's response to an inquiry about that candidate's or political party committee's positions on legislative or policy issues, but not including a discussion of campaign plans, projects, activities, or needs, does not satisfy any of the conduct standards in paragraph (d) of this section.

(g) *Safe harbor for endorsements and solicitations by Federal candidates.* (1) A public communication in which a candidate for Federal office endorses another candidate for Federal or non-Federal office is not a coordinated communication with respect to the endorsing Federal candidate unless the public communication promotes, supports, attacks, or opposes the endorsing candidate or another candidate who seeks election to the same office as the endorsing candidate.

(2) A public communication in which a candidate for Federal office solicits funds for another candidate for Federal or non-Federal office, a political committee, or organizations as permitted by 11 CFR 300.65, is not a coordinated communication with respect to the soliciting Federal candidate unless the public communication promotes, supports, attacks, or opposes the soliciting

candidate or another candidate who seeks election to the same office as the soliciting candidate.

(h) *Safe harbor for establishment and use of a firewall.* The conduct standards in paragraph (d) of this section are not met if the commercial vendor, former employee, or political committee has established and implemented a firewall that meets the requirements of paragraphs (h)(1) and (h)(2) of this section. This safe harbor provision does not apply if specific information indicates that, despite the firewall, information about the candidate's or political party committee's campaign plans, projects, activities, or needs that is material to the creation, production, or distribution of the communication was used or conveyed to the person paying for the communication.

(1) The firewall must be designed and implemented to prohibit the flow of information between employees or consultants providing services for the person paying for the communication and those employees or consultants currently or previously providing services to the candidate who is clearly identified in the communication, or the candidate's authorized committee, the candidate's opponent, the opponent's authorized committee, or a political party committee; and

(2) The firewall must be described in a written policy that is distributed to all relevant employees, consultants, and clients affected by the policy.

(i) *Safe harbor for commercial transactions.* A public communication in which a Federal candidate is clearly identified only in his or her capacity as the owner or operator of a business that existed prior to the candidacy is not a coordinated communication with respect to the clearly identified candidate if:

(1) The medium, timing, content, and geographic distribution of the public communication are consistent with public communications made prior to the candidacy; and

(2) The public communication does not promote, support, attack, or oppose that candidate or another candidate who seeks the same office as that candidate.

[68 FR 451, Jan. 3, 2003, as amended at 71 FR 33208, June 8, 2006; 75 FR 55961, Sept. 15, 2010]

§ 109.22 Who is prohibited from making coordinated communications?

Any person who is otherwise prohibited from making contributions or expenditures under any part of the Act or Commission regulations is prohibited from paying for a coordinated communication.

§ 109.23 Dissemination, distribution, or republication of candidate campaign materials.

(a) *General rule.* The financing of the dissemination, distribution, or republication, in whole or in part, of any broadcast or any written, graphic, or other form of campaign materials prepared by the candidate, the candidate's authorized committee, or an agent of either of the foregoing shall be considered a contribution for the purposes of contribution limitations and reporting responsibilities of the person making the expenditure. The candidate who prepared the campaign material does not receive or accept an in-kind contribution, and is not required to report an expenditure, unless the dissemination, distribution, or republication of campaign materials is a coordinated communication under 11 CFR 109.21 or a party coordinated communication under 11 CFR 109.37.

(b) *Exceptions.* The following uses of campaign materials do not constitute a contribution to the candidate who originally prepared the materials:

(1) The campaign material is disseminated, distributed, or republished by the candidate or the candidate's authorized committee who prepared that material;

(2) The campaign material is incorporated into a communication that advocates the defeat of the candidate or party that prepared the material;

(3) The campaign material is disseminated, distributed, or republished in a news story, commentary, or editorial exempted under 11 CFR 100.73 or 11 CFR 100.132;

(4) The campaign material used consists of a brief quote of materials that demonstrate a candidate's position as part of a person's expression of its own views; or

(5) A national political party committee or a State or subordinate political party committee pays for such dissemination, distribution, or republication of campaign materials using coordinated party expenditure authority under 11 CFR 109.32.

[68 FR 451, Jan. 3, 2003, as amended at 71 FR 33210, June 8, 2006]

Subpart D—Special Provisions for Political Party Committees

§ 109.30 How are political party committees treated for purposes of coordinated and independent expenditures?

Political party committees may make independent expenditures subject to the provisions in this subpart. *See* 11 CFR 109.36. Political party committees may also make coordinated party expenditures in connection with the general election campaign of a candidate, subject to the limits and other provisions in this subpart. *See* 11 CFR 109.32 through 11 CFR 109.34.

[69 FR 63920, Nov. 3, 2004]

§ 109.31 [Reserved]

§ 109.32 What are the coordinated party expenditure limits?

(a) *Coordinated party expenditures in Presidential elections.* (1) The national committee of a political party may make coordinated party expenditures in connection with the general election campaign of any candidate for President of the United States affiliated with the party.

(2) The coordinated party expenditures shall not exceed an amount equal to two cents multiplied by the voting age population of the United States. See 11 CFR 110.18. This limitation shall be increased in accordance with 11 CFR 110.17.

(3) Any coordinated party expenditure under paragraph (a) of this section shall be in addition to—

(i) Any expenditure by a national committee of a political party serving as the principal campaign committee of a candidate for President of the United States; and

(ii) Any contribution by the national committee to the candidate permissible under 11 CFR 110.1 or 110.2.

(4) Any coordinated party expenditures made by the national committee

of a political party pursuant to paragraph (a) of this section, or made by any other party committee under authority assigned by a national committee of a political party under 11 CFR 109.33, on behalf of that party's Presidential candidate shall not count against the candidate's expenditure limitations under 11 CFR 110.8.

(b) *Coordinated party expenditures in other Federal elections.* (1) The national committee of a political party, and a State committee of a political party, including any subordinate committee of a State committee, may each make coordinated party expenditures in connection with the general election campaign of a candidate for Federal office in that State who is affiliated with the party.

(2) The coordinated party expenditures shall not exceed:

(i) In the case of a candidate for election to the office of Senator, or of Representative from a State which is entitled to only one Representative, the greater of—

(A) Two cents multiplied by the voting age population of the State (see 11 CFR 110.18); or

(B) Twenty thousand dollars.

(ii) In the case of a candidate for election to the office of Representative, Delegate, or Resident Commissioner in any other State, $10,000.

(3) The limitations in paragraph (b)(2) of this section shall be increased in accordance with 11 CFR 110.17.

(4) Any coordinated party expenditure under paragraph (b) of this section shall be in addition to any contribution by a political party committee to the candidate permissible under 11 CFR 110.1 or 110.2.

§109.33 May a political party committee assign its coordinated party expenditure authority to another political party committee?

(a) *Assignment.* The national committee of a political party and a State committee of a political party, including any subordinate committee of a State committee, may assign its authority to make coordinated party expenditures authorized by 11 CFR 109.32 to another political party committee. Such an assignment must be made in writing, must state the amount of the

authority assigned, and must be received by the assignee committee before any coordinated party expenditure is made pursuant to the assignment.

(b) *Compliance.* For purposes of the coordinated party expenditure limits, *State committee* includes a subordinate committee of a State committee and includes a district or local committee to which coordinated party expenditure authority has been assigned. State committees and subordinate State committees and such district or local committees combined shall not exceed the coordinated party expenditure limits set forth in 11 CFR 109.32. The State committee shall administer the limitation in one of the following ways:

(1) The State committee shall be responsible for insuring that the coordinated party expenditures of the entire party organization are within the coordinated party expenditure limits, including receiving reports from any subordinate committee of a State committee or district or local committee making coordinated party expenditures under 11 CFR 109.32, and filing consolidated reports showing all coordinated party expenditures in the State with the Commission; or

(2) Any other method, submitted in advance and approved by the Commission, that permits control over coordinated party expenditures.

(c) *Recordkeeping.* (1) A political party committee that assigns its authority to make coordinated party expenditures under this section must maintain the written assignment for at least three years in accordance with 11 CFR 104.14.

(2) A political party committee that is assigned authority to make coordinated party expenditures under this section must maintain the written assignment for at least three years in accordance with 11 CFR 104.14.

[68 FR 451, Jan. 3, 2003, as amended at 69 FR 63920, Nov. 3, 2004]

§109.34 When may a political party committee make coordinated party expenditures?

A political party committee authorized to make coordinated party expenditures may make such expenditures in connection with the general election campaign before or after its candidate has been nominated. All pre-nomination coordinated party expenditures shall be subject to the coordinated party expenditure limitations of this subpart, whether or not the candidate on whose behalf they are made receives the party's nomination.

§ 109.35　[Reserved]

§ 109.36　Are there circumstances under which a political party committee is prohibited from making independent expenditures?

The national committee of a political party must not make independent expenditures in connection with the general election campaign of a candidate for President of the United States if the national committee of that political party is designated as the authorized committee of its Presidential candidate pursuant to 11 CFR 9002.1(c).

§ 109.37　What is a "party coordinated communication"?

(a) *Definition.* A political party communication is coordinated with a candidate, a candidate's authorized committee, or agent of any of the foregoing, when the communication satisfies the conditions set forth in paragraphs (a)(1), (a)(2), and (a)(3) of this section.

(1) The communication is paid for by a political party committee or its agent.

(2) The communication satisfies at least one of the content standards described in paragraphs (a)(2)(i) through (a)(2)(iii) of this section.

(i) A public communication that disseminates, distributes, or republishes, in whole or in part, campaign materials prepared by a candidate, the candidate's authorized committee, or an agent of any of the foregoing, unless the dissemination, distribution, or republication is excepted under 11 CFR 109.23(b). For a communication that satisfies this content standard, see 11 CFR 109.21(d)(6).

(ii) A public communication that expressly advocates the election or defeat of a clearly identified candidate for Federal office.

(iii) A public communication, as defined in 11 CFR 100.26, that satisfies paragraphs (a)(2)(iii)(A) or (B) of this section:

(A) *References to House and Senate candidates.* The public communication refers to a clearly identified House or Senate candidate and is publicly distributed or otherwise publicly disseminated in the clearly identified candidate's jurisdiction 90 days or fewer before the clearly identified candidate's general, special, or runoff election, or primary or preference election, or nominating convention or caucus.

(B) *References to Presidential and Vice Presidential candidates.* The public communication refers to a clearly identified Presidential or Vice Presidential candidate and is publicly distributed or otherwise publicly disseminated in a jurisdiction during the period of time beginning 120 days before the clearly identified candidate's primary or preference election in that jurisdiction, or nominating convention or caucus in that jurisdiction, up to and including the day of the general election.

(3) The communication satisfies at least one of the conduct standards in 11 CFR 109.21(d)(1) through (d)(6), subject to the provisions of 11 CFR 109.21(e), (g), and (h). A candidate's response to an inquiry about that candidate's positions on legislative or policy issues, but not including a discussion of campaign plans, projects, activities, or needs, does not satisfy any of the conduct standards in 11 CFR 109.21(d)(1) through (d)(6). Notwithstanding paragraph (b)(1) of this section, the candidate with whom a party coordinated communication is coordinated does not receive or accept an in-kind contribution, and is not required to report an expenditure that results from conduct described in 11 CFR 109.21(d)(4) or (d)(5), unless the candidate, authorized committee, or an agent of any of the foregoing, engages in conduct described in 11 CFR 109.21(d)(1) through (d)(3).

(b) *Treatment of a party coordinated communication.* A payment by a political party committee for a communication that is coordinated with a candidate, and that is not otherwise exempted under 11 CFR part 100, subpart C or E, must be treated by the political party committee making the payment as either:

(1) An in-kind contribution for the purpose of influencing a Federal election under 11 CFR 100.52(d) to the candidate with whom it was coordinated, which must be reported under 11 CFR part 104; or

(2) A coordinated party expenditure pursuant to coordinated party expenditure authority under 11 CFR 109.32 in connection with the general election campaign of the candidate with whom it was coordinated, which must be reported under 11 CFR part 104.

[68 FR 451, Jan. 3, 2003, as amended at 71 FR 33210, June 8, 2006]

PART 110—CONTRIBUTION AND EXPENDITURE LIMITATIONS AND PROHIBITIONS

AUTHORITY: 52 U.S.C. 30101(8), 30101(9), 30102(c)(2), 30104(1)(3), 30111(a)(8), 30116, 30118, 30120, 30121, 30122, 30123, 30124, and 36 U.S.C. 510.

§110.1 Contributions by persons other than multicandidate political committees (52 U.S.C. 30116(a)(1)).

(a) *Scope.* This section applies to all contributions made by any person as defined in 11 CFR 100.10, except multicandidate political committees as defined in 11 CFR 100.5(e)(3) or entities and individuals prohibited from making contributions under 11 CFR 110.20 and 11 CFR parts 114 and 115.

(b) *Contributions to candidates; designations; and redesignations.* (1) No person shall make contributions to any candidate, his or her authorized political committees or agents with respect to any election for Federal office that, in the aggregate, exceed $2,000.

(i) The contribution limitation in the introductory text of paragraph (b)(1) of this section shall be increased by the percent difference in the price index in accordance with 11 CFR 110.17.

(ii) The increased contribution limitation shall be in effect for the 2-year period beginning on the first day following the date of the last general election in the year preceding the year in which the contribution limitation is increased and ending on the date of the next general election. For example, an increase in the contribution limitation made in January 2005 is effective from November 3, 2004 to November 7, 2006.

(iii) In every odd numbered year, the Commission will publish in the FEDERAL REGISTER the amount of the contribution limitation in effect and place such information on the Commission's Web site.

(2) For purposes of this section, *with respect to any election* means—

(i) In the case of a contribution designated in writing by the contributor for a particular election, the election so designated. Contributors to candidates are encouraged to designate their contributions in writing for particular elections. See 11 CFR 110.1(b)(4).

(ii) In the case of a contribution not designated in writing by the contributor for a particular election, the next election for that Federal office after the contribution is made.

(3)(i) A contribution designated in writing for a particular election, but made after that election, shall be made only to the extent that the contribution does not exceed net debts outstanding from such election. To the extent that such contribution exceeds net debts outstanding, the candidate or the candidate's authorized political committee shall return or deposit the contribution within ten days from the date of the treasurer's receipt of the contribution as provided by 11 CFR 103.3(a), and if deposited, then within sixty days from the date of the treasurer's receipt the treasurer shall take the following action, as appropriate:

(A) Refund the contribution using a committee check or draft; or

(B) Obtain a written redesignation by the contributor for another election in accordance with 11 CFR 110.1(b)(5); or

(C) Obtain a written reattribution to another contributor in accordance with 11 CFR 110.1(k)(3).

If the candidate is not a candidate in the general election, all contributions made for the general election shall be either returned or refunded to the contributors or redesignated in accordance with 11 CFR 110.1(b)(5), or reattributed in accordance with 11 CFR 110.1(k)(3), as appropriate.

(ii) In order to determine whether there are net debts outstanding from a particular election, the treasurer of the candidate's authorized political committee shall calculate net debts outstanding as of the date of the election. For purposes of this section, *net debts outstanding* means the total amount of unpaid debts and obligations incurred with respect to an election, including the estimated cost of raising funds to liquidate debts incurred with respect to the election and, if the candidate's authorized committee terminates or if the candidate will not be a candidate for the next election, estimated necessary costs associated with termination of political activity, such as the costs of complying with the post-election requirements of the Act and other necessary administrative costs associated with winding down the campaign, including office space rental, staff salaries and office supplies, less the sum of:

(A) The total cash on hand available to pay those debts and obligations, including: currency; balances on deposit in banks, savings and loan institutions, and other depository institutions; trav-

eler's checks; certificates of deposit; treasury bills; and any other committee investments valued at fair market value;

(B) The total amounts owed to the candidate or political committee in the form of credits, refunds of deposits, returns, or receivables, or a commercially reasonable amount based on the collectibility of those credits, refunds, returns, or receivables; and

(C) The amount of personal loans, as defined in 11 CFR 116.11(b), that in the aggregate exceed $250,000 per election.

(iii) The amount of the net debts outstanding shall be adjusted as additional funds are received and expenditures are made. The candidate and his or her authorized political committee(s) may accept contributions made after the date of the election if:

(A) Such contributions are designated in writing by the contributor for that election;

(B) Such contributions do not exceed the adjusted amount of net debts outstanding on the date the contribution is received; and

(C) Such contributions do not exceed the contribution limitations in effect on the date of such election.

(iv) This paragraph shall not be construed to prevent a candidate who is a candidate in the general election or his or her authorized political committee(s) from paying primary election debts and obligations with funds which represent contributions made with respect to the general election.

(4) For purposes of this section, a contribution shall be considered to be designated in writing for a particular election if—

(i) The contribution is made by check, money order, or other negotiable instrument which clearly indicates the particular election with respect to which the contribution is made;

(ii) The contribution is accompanied by a writing, signed by the contributor, which clearly indicates the particular election with respect to which the contribution is made; or

(iii) The contribution is redesignated in accordance with 11 CFR 110.1(b)(5).

(5)(i) The treasurer of an authorized political committee may request a written redesignation of a contribution by the contributor for a different election if—

(A) The contribution was designated in writing for a particular election, and the contribution, either on its face or when aggregated with other contributions from the same contributor for the same election, exceeds the limitation on contributions set forth in 11 CFR 110.1(b)(1);

(B) The contribution was designated in writing for a particular election and the contribution was made after that election and the contribution cannot be accepted under the net debts outstanding provisions of 11 CFR 110.1(b)(3);

(C) The contribution was not designated in writing for a particular election, and the contribution exceeds the limitation on contributions set forth in 11 CFR 110.1(b)(1); or

(D) The contribution was not designated in writing for a particular election, and the contribution was received after the date of an election for which there are net debts outstanding on the date the contribution is received.

(ii)(A) A contribution shall be considered to be redesignated for another election if—

(1) The treasurer of the recipient authorized political committee requests that the contributor provide a written redesignation of the contribution and informs the contributor that the contributor may request the refund of the contribution as an alternative to providing a written redesignation; and

(2) Within sixty days from the date of the treasurer's receipt of the contribution, the contributor provides the treasurer with a written redesignation of the contribution for another election, which is signed by the contributor.

(B) Notwithstanding paragraph (b)(5)(ii)(A) of this section or any other provision of this section, the treasurer of the recipient authorized political committee may treat all or part of the amount of the contribution that exceeds the contribution limits in paragraph (b)(1) of this section as made with respect to the general election, provided that:

(1) The contribution was made before the primary election;

(2) The contribution was not designated for a particular election;

(3) The contribution would exceed the limitation on contributions set forth in paragraph (b)(1) of this section if it were treated as a contribution made for the primary election;

(4) Such redesignation would not cause the contributor to exceed any of the limitations on contributions set forth in paragraph (b)(1) of this section;

(5) The treasurer of the recipient authorized political committee notifies the contributor of the amount of the contribution that was redesignated and that the contributor may request a refund of the contribution; and

(6) Within sixty days from the date of the treasurer's receipt of the contribution, the treasurer shall provide notification required in paragraph (b)(5)(ii)(B)(5) of this section to the contributor by any written method including electronic mail.

(C) Notwithstanding paragraph (b)(5)(ii)(A) of this section or any other provision of this section, the treasurer of the recipient authorized political committee may treat all or part of the amount of the contribution that exceeds the contribution limits in paragraph (b)(1) of this section as made with respect to the primary election, provided that:

(1) The contribution was made after the primary election but before the general election;

(2) The contribution was not designated for a particular election;

(3) The contribution would exceed the limitation on contributions set forth in paragraph (b)(1) of this section if it were treated as a contribution made for the general election;

(4) Such redesignation would not cause the contributor to exceed any of the limitations on contributions set forth in paragraph (b)(1) of this section;

(5) The contribution does not exceed the committee's net debts outstanding for the primary election;

(6) The treasurer of the recipient authorized political committee notifies the contributor of how the contribution was redesignated and that the contributor may request a refund of the contribution; and

(7) Within sixty days from the date of the treasurer's receipt of the contribution, the treasurer shall provide notification required in paragraph (b)(5)(ii)(C)(6) of this section to the contributor by any written method, including electronic mail.

(iii) A contribution redesignated for another election shall not exceed the limitations on contributions made with respect to that election. A contribution redesignated for a previous election shall be subject to the requirements of 11 CFR 110.1(b)(3) regarding net debts outstanding.

(6) For the purposes of this section, a contribution shall be considered to be made when the contributor relinquishes control over the contribution. A contributor shall be considered to relinquish control over the contribution when it is delivered by the contributor to the candidate, to the political committee, or to an agent of the political committee. A contribution that is mailed to the candidate, or to the political committee or to an agent of the political committee, shall be considered to be made on the date of the postmark. See 11 CFR 110.1(l)(4). An in-kind contribution shall be considered to be made on the date that the goods or services are provided by the contributor.

(c) *Contributions to political party committees.* (1) No person shall make contributions to the political committees established and maintained by a national political party in any calendar year that in the aggregate exceed $25,000.

(i) The contribution limitation in paragraph (c)(1) of this section shall be increased by the percent difference in the price index in accordance with 11 CFR 110.17.

(ii) The increased contribution limitation shall be in effect for the two calendar years starting on January 1 of the year in which the contribution limitation is increased.

(iii) In every odd-numbered year, the Commission will publish in the FEDERAL REGISTER the amount of the contribution limitation in effect and place such information on the Commission's Web site.

(2) For purposes of this section, *political committees established and maintained by a national political party* means—

(i) The national committee;

(ii) The House campaign committee; and

(iii) The Senate campaign committee.

(3) Each recipient committee referred to in 11 CFR 110.1(c)(2) may receive up to the $25,000 limitation from a contributor.

(4) The recipient committee shall not be an authorized political committee of any candidate, except as provided in 11 CFR 9002.1(c).

(5) On or after January 1, 2003, no person shall make contributions to a political committee established and maintained by a State committee of a political party in any calendar year that, in the aggregate, exceed $10,000.

(d) *Contributions to other political committees.* No person shall make contributions to any other political committee in any calendar year which, in the aggregate, exceed $5,000.

(e) *Contributions by partnerships.* A contribution by a partnership shall be attributed to the partnership and to each partner—

(1) In direct proportion to his or her share of the partnership profits, according to instructions which shall be provided by the partnership to the political committee or candidate; or

(2) By agreement of the partners, as long as—

(i) Only the profits of the partners to whom the contribution is attributed are reduced (or losses increased), and

(ii) These partners' profits are reduced (or losses increased) in proportion to the contribution attributed to each of them.

A contribution by a partnership shall not exceed the limitations on contributions in 11 CFR 110.1 (b), (c), and (d). No portion of such contribution may be made from the profits of a corporation that is a partner.

(f) *Contributions to candidates for more than one Federal office.* If an individual is a candidate for more than one Federal office, a person may make contributions which do not exceed $2,000 to the candidate, or his or her authorized political committees for each election for each office, as long as—

(1) Each contribution is designated in writing by the contributor for a particular office;

(2) The candidate maintains separate campaign organizations, including separate principal campaign committees and separate accounts; and

(3) No principal campaign committee or other authorized political committee of that candidate for one election for one Federal office transfers funds to, loans funds to, makes contributions to, or makes expenditures on behalf of another principal campaign committee or other authorized political committee of that candidate for another election for another Federal office, except as provided in 11 CFR 110.3(c)(4).

(g) *Contributions by limited liability companies ("LLC")*—(1) *Definition.* A limited liability company is a business entity that is recognized as a limited liability company under the laws of the State in which it is established.

(2) A contribution by an LLC that elects to be treated as a partnership by the Internal Revenue Service pursuant to 26 CFR 301.7701–3, or does not elect treatment as either a partnership or a corporation pursuant to that section, shall be considered a contribution from a partnership pursuant to 11 CFR 110.1(e).

(3) An LLC that elects to be treated as a corporation by the Internal Revenue Service, pursuant to 26 CFR 301.7701–3, or an LLC with publicly-traded shares, shall be considered a corporation pursuant to 11 CFR Part 114.

(4) A contribution by an LLC with a single natural person member that does not elect to be treated as a corporation by the Internal Revenue Service pursuant to 26 CFR 301.7701–3 shall be attributed only to that single member.

(5) An LLC that makes a contribution pursuant to paragraph (g)(2) or (g)(4) of this section shall, at the time it makes the contribution, provide information to the recipient committee as to how the contribution is to be attributed, and affirm to the recipient committee that it is eligible to make the contribution.

(h) *Contributions to committees supporting the same candidate.* A person may contribute to a candidate or his or her authorized committee with respect to a particular election and also contribute to a political committee which has supported, or anticipates supporting, the same candidate in the same election, as long as—

(1) The political committee is not the candidate's principal campaign committee or other authorized political committee or a single candidate committee;

(2) The contributor does not give with the knowledge that a substantial portion will be contributed to, or expended on behalf of, that candidate for the same election; and

(3) The contributor does not retain control over the funds.

(i) *Contributions by spouses.* The limitations on contributions of this section shall apply separately to contributions made by each spouse even if only one spouse has income.

(j) *Application of limitations to elections.* (1) The limitations on contributions of this section shall apply separately with respect to each election as defined in 11 CFR 100.2, except that all elections held in a calendar year for the office of President of the United States (except a general election for that office) shall be considered to be one election.

(2) An election in which a candidate is unopposed is a separate election for the purposes of the limitations on contributions of this section.

(3) A primary or general election which is not held because a candidate is unopposed or received a majority of votes in a previous election is a separate election for the purposes of the limitations on contributions of this section. The date on which the election would have been held shall be considered to be the date of the election.

(4) A primary election which is not held because a candidate was nominated by a caucus or convention with authority to nominate is not a separate election for the purposes of the limitations on contributions of this section.

(k) *Joint contributions and reattributions.* (1) Any contribution made by more than one person, except for a contribution made by a partnership, shall include the signature of each contributor on the check, money order, or other negotiable instrument or in a separate writing.

(2) If a contribution made by more than one person does not indicate the amount to be attributed to each contributor, the contribution shall be attributed equally to each contributor.

(3)(i) If a contribution to a candidate or political committee, either on its face or when aggregated with other contributions from the same contributor, exceeds the limitations on contributions set forth in 11 CFR 110.1 (b), (c) or (d), as appropriate, the treasurer of the recipient political committee may ask the contributor whether the contribution was intended to be a joint contribution by more than one person.

(ii)(A) A contribution shall be considered to be reattributed to another contributor if—

(1) The treasurer of the recipient political committee asks the contributor whether the contribution is intended to be a joint contribution by more than one person, and informs the contributor that he or she may request the return of the excessive portion of the contribution if it is not intended to be a joint contribution; and

(2) Within sixty days from the date of the treasurer's receipt of the contribution, the contributor provides the treasurer with a written reattribution of the contribution, which is signed by each contributor, and which indicates the amount to be attributed to each contributor if equal attribution is not intended.

(B)(1) Notwithstanding paragraph (k)(3)(ii)(A) of this section or any other provision of this section, any excessive portion of a contribution described in paragraph (k)(3)(i) of this section that was made by a written instrument that is imprinted with the names of more than one individual may be attributed among the individuals listed unless a different instruction is on the instrument or in a separate writing signed by the contributor(s), provided that such attribution would not cause any contributor to exceed any of the limitations on contributions set forth in paragraph (b)(1) of this section.

(2) The treasurer of the recipient political committee shall notify each contributor of how the contribution was attributed and that the contributor may request the refund of the excessive portion of the contribution if it is not intended to be a joint contribution.

(3) Within sixty days from the date of the treasurer's receipt of the contribution, the treasurer shall provide such notification to each contributor by any written method, including electronic mail.

(l) *Supporting evidence.* (1) If a political committee receives a contribution designated in writing for a particular election, the treasurer shall retain a copy of the written designation, as required by 11 CFR 110.1(b)(4) or 110.2(b)(4), as appropriate. If the written designation is made on a check or other written instrument, the treasurer shall retain a full-size photocopy of the check or written instrument.

(2) If a political committee receives a written redesignation of a contribution for a different election, the treasurer shall retain the written redesignation provided by the contributor, as required by 11 CFR 110.1(b)(5) or 110.2(b)(5), as appropriate.

(3) If a political committee receives a written reattribution of a contribution to a different contributor, the treasurer shall retain the written reattribution signed by each contributor, as required by 11 CFR 110.1(k).

(4)(i) If a political committee chooses to rely on a postmark as evidence of the date on which a contribution was made, the treasurer shall retain the envelope or a copy of the envelope containing the postmark and other identifying information; and

(ii) If a political committee chooses to rely on the redesignation presumption in 11 CFR 110.1(b)(5)(ii)(B) or (C) or the reattribution presumption in 11 CFR 110.1(k)(3)(ii)(B), the treasurer shall retain a full-size photocopy of the check or written instrument, of any signed writings that accompanied the contribution, and of the notices sent to the contributors as required by 11 CFR 110.1(b)(5)(ii)(B) and (k)(3)(ii)(B).

(5) If a political committee does not retain the written records concerning designation required under 11 CFR 110.1(l)(1), the contribution shall not be considered designated in writing for a

particular election, and the provisions of 11 CFR 110.1(b)(2)(ii) or 11 CFR 110.2(b)(2)(ii) shall apply. If a political committee does not retain the written records concerning redesignation or reattribution required under 11 CFR 110.1(l)(2), (3), (4)(ii) or (6), including the contributor notices, the redesignation or reattribution shall not be effective, and the original designation or attribution shall control.

(6) For each written redesignation or written reattribution of a contribution described in paragraph (b)(5) or paragraph (k)(3) of this section, the political committee shall retain documentation demonstrating when the written redesignation or written reattribution was received. Such documentation shall consist of:

(i) A copy of the envelope bearing the postmark and the contributor's name, or return address or other identifying code; or

(ii) A copy of the written redesignation or written reattribution with a date stamp indicating the date of the committee's receipt; or

(iii) A copy of the written redesignation or written reattribution dated by the contributor.

(m) *Contributions to delegates and delegate committees.* (1) Contributions to delegates for the purpose of furthering their selection under 11 CFR 110.14 are not subject to the limitations of this section.

(2) Contributions to delegate committees under 11 CFR 110.14 are subject to the limitations of this section.

(n) *Contributions to committees making independent expenditures.* The limitations on contributions of this section also apply to contributions made to political committees making independent expenditures under 11 CFR Part 109.

[52 FR 769, Jan. 9, 1987]

EDITORIAL NOTE: For FEDERAL REGISTER citations affecting § 110.1, see the List of CFR Sections Affected, which appears in the Finding Aids section of the printed volume and at *www.fdsys.gov.*

§ 110.2 Contributions by multi-candidate political committees (52 U.S.C. 30116(a)(2)).

(a)(1) *Scope.* This section applies to all contributions made by any multicandidate political committee as de-

fined in 11 CFR 100.5(e)(3). See 11 CFR 102.2(a)(3) for multicandidate political committee certification requirements. A political committee becomes a multicandidate committee at the time the political committee meets the requirements of 11 CFR 100.5(e)(3) or becomes affiliated with an existing multicandidate committee, whether or not the political committee has certified its status as a multicandidate committee with the Commission in accordance with 11 CFR 102.2(a)(3).

(2) *Notice to recipients.* Each multicandidate committee that makes a contribution under this section shall notify the recipient in writing of its status as a multicandidate committee.

(b) *Contributions to candidates; designations; and redesignations.* (1) No multicandidate political committee shall make contributions to any candidate, his or her authorized political committees or agents with respect to any election for Federal office which, in the aggregate, exceed $5,000.

(2) For purposes of this section, *with respect to any election* means—

(i) In the case of a contribution designated in writing by the contributor for a particular election, the election so designated. Multicandidate political committees making contributions to candidates are encouraged to designate their contributions in writing for particular elections. *See* 11 CFR 110.2(b)(4).

(ii) In the case of a contribution not designated in writing by the contributor for a particular election, the next election for that Federal office after the contribution is made.

(3)(i) A contribution designated in writing for a particular election, but made after that election, shall be made only to the extent that the contribution does not exceed net debts outstanding from such election. To the extent that such contribution exceeds net debts outstanding, the candidate or the candidate's authorized political committee shall return or deposit the contribution within ten days from the date of the treasurer's receipt of the contribution as provided by 11 CFR 103.3(a), and if deposited, then within sixty days from the date of the treasurer's receipt the treasurer shall take the following action, as appropriate:

(A) Refund the contribution using a committee check or draft; or

(B) Obtain a written redesignation by the contributor for another election in accordance with 11 CFR 110.2(b)(5).

If the candidate is not a candidate in the general election, all contributions made for the general election shall be either returned or refunded to the contributors or redesignated in accordance with 11 CFR 110.2(b)(5).

(ii) The treasurer of the candidate's authorized political committee shall calculate net debts outstanding in accordance with 11 CFR 110.1(b)(3)(ii). The amount of the net debts outstanding shall be adjusted as additional funds are received and expenditures are made. The candidate and his or her authorized political committee(s) may accept contributions made after the date of the election if such contributions are designated in writing by the contributor for that election and if such contributions do not exceed the adjusted amount of net debts outstanding on the date the contribution is received.

(4) For purposes of this section, a contribution shall be considered to be designated in writing for a particular election if—

(i) The contribution is made by check, money order, or other negotiable instrument which clearly indicates the particular election with respect to which the contribution is made;

(ii) The contribution is accompanied by a writing, signed by the contributor, which clearly indicates the particular election with respect to which the contribution is made; or

(iii) The contribution is redesignated in accordance with 11 CFR 110.2(b)(5).

(5)(i) The treasurer of an authorized political committee may request a written redesignation of a contribution by the contributor for a different election if—

(A) The contribution was designated in writing for a particular election, and the contribution, either on its face or when aggregated with other contributions from the same contributor for the same election, exceeds the limitation on contributions set forth in 11 CFR 110.2(b)(1);

(B) The contribution was designated in writing for a particular election and the contribution was made after that election and the contribution cannot be accepted under the net debts outstanding provisions of 11 CFR 110.2(b)(3);

(C) The contribution was not designated in writing for a particular election, and the contribution exceeds the limitation on contributions set forth in 11 CFR 110.2(b)(1); or

(D) The contribution was not designated in writing for a particular election and the contribution was received after the date of an election for which there are net debts outstanding on the date the contribution is received.

(ii) A contribution shall be considered to be redesignated for another election if—

(A) The treasurer of the recipient authorized political committee requests that the contributor provide a written redesignation of the contribution and informs the contributor that the contributor may request the refund of the contribution as an alternative to providing a written redesignation; and

(B) Within sixty days from the date of the treasurer's receipt of the contribution, the contributor provides the treasurer with a written redesignation of the contribution for another election, which is signed by the contributor.

(iii) A contribution redesignated for another election shall not exceed the limitations on contributions made with respect to that election. A contribution redesignated for a previous election shall be subject to the requirements of 11 CFR 110.2(b)(3) regarding net debts outstanding.

(6) For the purposes of this section, a contribution shall be considered to be made when the contributor relinquishes control over the contribution. A contributor shall be considered to relinquish control over the contribution when it is delivered by the contributor to the candidate, to the political committee, or to an agent of the political committee. A contribution that is mailed to the candidate, or to the political committee or to an agent of the political committee, shall be considered to be made on the date of the postmark. See 11 CFR 110.1(1)(4). An in-kind

contribution shall be considered to be made on the date that the goods or services are provided by the contributor.

(c) *Contributions to political party committees.* (1) No multicandidate political committee shall make contributions to the political committees established and maintained by a national political party in any calendar year which, in the aggregate, exceed $15,000.

(2) For purposes of this section, *political committees established and maintained by a national political party* means—

(i) The national committee;

(ii) The House campaign committee; and

(iii) The Senate campaign committee.

(3) Each recipient committee referred to in 11 CFR 110.2(c)(2) may receive up to the $15,000 limitation from a multicandidate political committee.

(4) The recipient committee shall not be an authorized political committee of any candidate, except as provided in 11 CFR 9002.1(c).

(d) *Contributions to other political committees.* No multicandidate political committee shall make contributions to any other political committee in any calendar year which, in the aggregate, exceed $5,000.

(e) *Contributions by political party committees to Senatorial candidates.* (1) Notwithstanding any other provision of the Act, or of these regulations, the Republican and Democratic Senatorial campaign committees, or the national committee of a political party, may make contributions of not more than a combined total of $35,000 to a candidate for nomination or election to the Senate during the calendar year of the election for which he or she is a candidate. Any contribution made by such committee to a Senatorial candidate under this paragraph in a year other than the calendar year in which the election is held shall be considered to be made during the calendar year in which the election is held.

(2) The contribution limitation in paragraph (e)(1) of this section shall be increased by the percent difference in the price index in accordance with 11 CFR 110.17. The increased contribution limitation shall be in effect for the two calendar years starting on January 1 of the year in which the contribution limitation is increased. In every odd-numbered year, the Commission will publish in the FEDERAL REGISTER the amount of the contribution limitation in effect and place such information on the Commission's Web site.

(f) *Contributions to candidates for more than one Federal office.* If an individual is a candidate for more than one Federal office, a multicandidate political committee may make contributions which do not exceed $5,000 to the candidate, or his or her authorized political committees for each election for each office, provided that the requirements set forth in 11 CFR 110.1(f)(1), (2), and (3) are satisfied.

(g) *Contributions to retire pre-1975 debts.* Contributions made to retire debts resulting from elections held prior to January 1, 1975 are not subject to the limitations of 11 CFR part 110, as long as contributions and solicitations to retire these debts are designated in writing and used for that purpose. Contributions made to retire debts resulting from elections held after December 31, 1974 are subject to the limitations of 11 CFR part 110.

(h) *Contributions to committees supporting the same candidate.* A multicandidate political committee may contribute to a candidate or his or her authorized committee with respect to a particular election and also contribute to a political committee which has supported, or anticipates supporting, the same candidate in the same election, as long as—

(1) The recipient political committee is not the candidate's principal campaign committee or other authorized political committee or a single candidate committee;

(2) The multicandidate political committee does not give with the knowledge that a substantial portion will be contributed to, or expended on behalf of, that candidate for the same election; and

(3) The multicandidate political committee does not retain control over the funds.

(i) *Application of limitations to elections.* (1) The limitations on contributions of this section (other than paragraph (e) of this section) shall apply separately with respect to each election as defined in 11 CFR 100.2, except that all elections held in a calendar year for the office of President of the United States (except a general election for that office) shall be considered to be one election.

(2) An election in which a candidate is unopposed is a separate election for the purposes of the limitations on contributions of this section.

(3) A primary or general election which is not held because a candidate is unopposed or received a majority of votes in a previous election is a separate election for the purposes of the limitations on contributions of this section. The date on which the election would have been held shall be considered to be the date of the election.

(4) A primary election which is not held because a candidate was nominated by a caucus or convention with authority to nominate is not a separate election for the purposes of the limitations on contributions of this section.

(j) *Contributions to delegates and delegate committees.* (1) Contributions to delegates for the purpose of furthering their selection under 11 CFR 110.14 are not subject to the limitations of this section.

(2) Contributions to delegate committees under 11 CFR 110.14 are subject to the limitations of this section.

(k) *Contributions to multicandidate political committees making independent expenditures.* The limitations on contributions of this section also apply to contributions made to multicandidate political committees making independent expenditures under 11 CFR Part 109.

(1) *Pre-candidacy expenditures by multicandidate political committees deemed in-kind contributions; effect of reimbursement.* (1) A payment by a multicandidate political committee is deemed an in-kind contribution to and an expenditure by a Presidential candidate, even though made before the individual becomes a candidate under 11 CFR 100.3, if—

(i) The expenditure is made on or after January 1 of the year immediately following the last Presidential election year;

(ii) With respect to the goods or services involved, the candidate accepted or received them, requested or suggested their provision, was materially involved in the decision to provide them, or was involved in substantial discussions about their provision; and

(iii) The goods or services are—

(A) Polling expenses for determining the favorability, name recognition, or relative support level of the candidate involved;

(B) Compensation paid to employees, consultants, or vendors for services rendered in connection with establishing and staffing offices in States where Presidential primaries, caucuses, or preference polls are to be held, other than offices in the candidate's home state and in or near the District of Columbia;

(C) Administrative expenses, including rent, utilities, office supplies and equipment, in connection with establishing and staffing offices in States where Presidential primaries, caucuses, or preference polls are to be held, other than offices in the candidate's home state and in or near the District of Columbia; or

(D) Expenses of individuals seeking to become delegates in the Presidential nomination process.

(2) Notwithstanding paragraph (l)(1) of this section, if the candidate, through an authorized committee, reimburses the multicandidate political committee within 30 days of becoming a candidate, the payment shall not be deemed an in-kind contribution for either entity, and the reimbursement shall be an expenditure of the candidate.

[52 FR 772, Jan. 9, 1987, as amended at 52 FR 35534, Sept. 22, 1987; 58 FR 42173, Aug. 6, 1993; 67 FR 69948, Nov. 19, 2002; 68 FR 457, Jan. 3, 2003; 68 FR 47414, Aug. 8, 2003; 68 FR 64516, Nov. 14, 2003; 81 FR 34863, June 1, 2016]

§ 110.3 Contribution limitations for affiliated committees and political party committees; transfers (52 U.S.C. 30116(a)(4), 30116(a)(5)).

(a) *Contribution limitations for affiliated committees.* (1) For the purposes of the contribution limitations of 11 CFR 110.1 and 110.2, all contributions made or received by more than one affiliated committee, regardless of whether they are political committees under 11 CFR 100.5, shall be considered to be made or received by a single political committee. *See* 11 CFR 100.5(g). Application of this paragraph means that all contributions made or received by the following committees shall be considered to be made or received by a single political committee—

(i) Authorized committees of the same candidate for the same election to Federal office; or

(ii) Committees (including a separate segregated fund, *see* 11 CFR part 114) established, financed, maintained or controlled by the same corporation, labor organization, person or group of persons, including any parent, subsidiary, branch, division, department or local unit thereof. For the purposes of this section, *local unit* may include, in appropriate cases, a franchisee, licensee, or State or regional association.

(2) Affiliated committees sharing a single contribution limitation under paragraph (a)(1)(ii) of this section include all of the committees established, financed, maintained or controlled by—

(i) A single corporation and/or its subsidiaries;

(ii) A single national or international union and/or its local unions or other subordinate organizations;

(iii) An organization of national or international unions and/or all its State and local central bodies;

(iv) A membership organization, (other than political party committees, *see* paragraph (b) of this section) including trade or professional associations, *see* 11 CFR 114.8(a), and/or related State and local entities of that organization or group; or

(v) The same person or group of persons.

(3)(i) The Commission may examine the relationship between organizations that sponsor committees, between the committees themselves, or between one sponsoring organization and a committee established by another organization to determine whether committees are affiliated.

(ii) In determining whether committees not described in paragraphs (a)(2)(i)–(iv) of this section are affiliated, the Commission will consider the circumstantial factors described in paragraphs (a)(3)(ii) (A) through (J) of this section. The Commission will examine these factors in the context of the overall relationship between committees or sponsoring organizations to determine whether the presence of any factor or factors is evidence of one committee or organization having been established, financed, maintained or controlled by another committee or sponsoring organization. Such factors include, but are not limited to:

(A) Whether a sponsoring organization owns a controlling interest in the voting stock or securities of the sponsoring organization of another committee;

(B) Whether a sponsoring organization or committee has the authority or ability to direct or participate in the governance of another sponsoring organization or committee through provisions of constitutions, bylaws, contracts, or other rules, or through formal or informal practices or procedures;

(C) Whether a sponsoring organization or committee has the authority or ability to hire, appoint, demote or otherwise control the officers, or other decisionmaking employees or members of another sponsoring organization or committee;

(D) Whether a sponsoring organization or committee has a common or overlapping membership with another sponsoring organization or committee which indicates a formal or ongoing relationship between the sponsoring organizations or committees;

(E) Whether a sponsoring organization or committee has common or overlapping officers or employees with another sponsoring organization or committee which indicates a formal or ongoing relationship between the sponsoring organizations or committees;

(F) Whether a sponsoring organization or committee has any members, officers or employees who were members, officers or employees of another sponsoring organization or committee which indicates a formal or ongoing relationship between the sponsoring organizations or committees, or which indicates the creation of a successor entity;

(G) Whether a sponsoring organization or committee provides funds or goods in a significant amount or on an ongoing basis to another sponsoring organization or committee, such as through direct or indirect payments for administrative, fundraising, or other costs, but not including the transfer to a committee of its allocated share of proceeds jointly raised pursuant to 11 CFR 102.17;

(H) Whether a sponsoring organization or committee causes or arranges for funds in a significant amount or on an ongoing basis to be provided to another sponsoring organization or committee, but not including the transfer to a committee of its allocated share of proceeds jointly raised pursuant to 11 CFR 102.17;

(I) Whether a sponsoring organization or a committee or its agent had an active or significant role in the formation of another sponsoring organization or committee; and

(J) Whether the sponsoring organizations or committees have similar patterns of contributions or contributors which indicates a formal or ongoing relationshp between the sponsoring organizations or committees.

(b) *Contribution limitations for political party committees.* (1) For the purposes of the contribution limitations of 11 CFR 110.1 and 110.2, all contributions made or received by the following political committees shall be considered to be made or received by separate political committees—

(i) The national committee of a political party and any political committees established, financed, maintained, or controlled by the same national committee; and

(ii) The State committee of the same political party.

(2) Application of paragraph (b)(1)(i) of this section means that—

(i) The House campaign committee and the national committee of a political party shall have separate limitations on contributions under 11 CFR 110.1 and 110.2.

(ii) The Senate campaign committee and the national committee of a political party shall have separate limitations on contributions, except that contributions to a senatorial candidate made by the Senate campaign committee and the national committee of a political party are subject to a single contribution limitation under 11 CFR 110.2(e).

(3) All contributions made by the political committees established, financed, maintained, or controlled by a State party committee and by subordinate State party committees shall be presumed to be made by one political committee. This presumption shall not apply if—

(i) The political committee of the party unit in question has not received funds from any other political committee established, financed, maintained, or controlled by any party unit; and

(ii) The political committee of the party unit in question does not make its contributions in cooperation, consultation or concert with, or at the request or suggestion of any other party unit or political committee established, financed, maintained, or controlled by another party unit.

(c) *Permissible Transfers.* The contribution limitations of 11 CFR 110.1 and 110.2 shall not limit the transfers set forth below in 11 CFR 110.3(c) (1) through (6)—

(1) Transfers of funds between affiliated committees or between party committees of the same political party whether or not they are affiliated or by collecting agents to a separate segregated fund made pursuant to 11 CFR 102.6;

(2) Transfers of joint fundraising proceeds between organizations or committees participating in the joint fundraising activity provided that no participating committee or organization governed by 11 CFR 102.17 received more than its allocated share of the funds raised;

(3) Transfers of funds between the primary campaign and general election campaign of a candidate of funds unused for the primary;

(4) Transfers of funds between a candidate's previous Federal campaign committee and his or her current Federal campaign committee, or between previous Federal campaign committees, provided that the candidate is not a candidate for more than one Federal office at the same time, and provided

that the funds transferred are not composed of contributions that would be in violation of the Act. The cash on hand from which the transfer is made shall be considered to consist of the funds most recently received by the transferor committee. The transferor committee must be able to demonstrate that such cash on hand contains sufficient funds at the time of the transfer that comply with the limitations and prohibitions of the Act to cover the amount transferred.

(i) *Previous Federal campaign committee* means a principal campaign committee, or other authorized committee, that was organized to further the candidate's campaign in a Federal election that has already been held.

(ii) *Current Federal campaign committee* means a principal campaign committee, or other authorized committee, organized to further the candidate's campaign in a future Federal election.

(iii) For purposes of the contribution limits, a contribution made after an election has been held, or after an individual ceases to be a candidate in an election, shall be aggregated with other contributions from the same contributor for the next election unless the contribution is designated for the previous election, or is designated for another election, and the candidate has net debts outstanding for the election so designated pursuant to 11 CFR 110.1(b)(3).

(iv) For purposes of this section, an individual ceases to be a candidate in an election as of the earlier of the following dates—

(A) The date on which the candidate publicly announces that he or she will no longer be a candidate in that election for that office and ceases to conduct campaign activities with respect to that election; or

(B) The date on which the candidate is or becomes ineligible for nomination or election to that office by operation of law;

(5) Transfers of funds between the principal campaign committees of an individual seeking nomination or election to more than one Federal office, as long as the conditions in 11 CFR 110.3(c)(5) (i), (ii) and (iii) are met. An individual will be considered to be

seeking nomination or election to more than one Federal office if the individual is concurrently a candidate for more than one Federal office during the same or overlapping election cycles.

(i) The transfer shall not be made when the individual is actively seeking nomination or election to more than one Federal office. An individual will not be considered to be actively seeking nomination or election to a Federal office if:

(A) The individual publicly announces that he or she will no longer seek nomination or election to that office and ceases to conduct campaign activities with respect to that election, except in connection with the retirement of debts outstanding at the time of the announcement;

(B) The individual is or becomes ineligible for nomination or election to that office by operation of law;

(C) The individual has filed a proper termination report with the Commission under 11 CFR 102.3; or

(D) The individual has notified the Commission in writing that the individual and his or her authorized committees will conduct no further campaign activities with respect to that election, except in connection with the retirement of debts outstanding at the time of the notification;

(ii) The limitations on contributions by persons shall not be exceeded by the transfer. The cash on hand from which the transfer is made shall be considered to consist of the funds most recently received by the transferor committee. The transferor committee must be able to demonstrate that such cash on hand contains sufficient funds at the time of the transfer that comply with the limitations and prohibitions of the Act to cover the amount transferred. A contribution shall be excluded from the amount transferred to the extent that such contribution, when aggregated with other contributions from the same contributor to the transferee principal campaign committee, exceeds the contribution limits set forth at 11 CFR 110.1 or 110.2, as appropriate; and

(iii) The candidate has not elected to receive funds under 26 U.S.C. 9006 or 9037 for either election; or

(6) [Reserved]

(7) The authorized committees of a candidate for more than one Federal office, or for a Federal office and a nonfederal office, shall follow the requirements for separate campaign organizations set forth at 11 CFR 110.8(d).

(d) *Transfers from nonfederal to federal campaigns.* Transfers of funds or assets from a candidate's campaign committee or account for a nonfederal election to his or her principal campaign committee or other authorized committee for a federal election are prohibited. However, at the option of the nonfederal committee, the nonfederal committee may refund contributions, and may coordinate arrangements with the candidate's principal campaign committee or other authorized committee for a solicitation by such committee(s) to the same contributors. The full cost of this solicitation shall be paid by the Federal committee.

[54 FR 34110, Aug. 17, 1989, and 54 FR 48580, Nov. 24, 1989; 58 FR 3476, Jan. 8, 1993]

§ 110.4 Contributions in the name of another; cash contributions (52 U.S.C. 30122, 30123, 30102(c)(2)).

(a) [Reserved]

(b) *Contributions in the name of another.* (1) No person shall—

(i) Make a contribution in the name of another;

(ii) Knowingly permit his or her name to be used to effect that contribution;

(iii) Knowingly help or assist any person in making a contribution in the name of another; or

(iv) Knowingly accept a contribution made by one person in the name of another.

(2) Examples of *contributions in the name of another* include—

(i) Giving money or anything of value, all or part of which was provided to the contributor by another person (the true contributor) without disclosing the source of money or the thing of value to the recipient candidate or committee at the time the contribution is made, *see* 11 CFR 110.6; or

(ii) Making a contribution of money or anything of value and attributing as the source of the money or thing of value another person when in fact the contributor is the source.

(c) *Cash contributions.* (1) With respect to any campaign for nomination for election or election to Federal office, no person shall make contributions to a candidate or political committee of currency of the United States, or of any foreign country, which in the aggregate exceed $100.

(2) A candidate or committee receiving a cash contribution in excess of $100 shall promptly return the amount over $100 to the contributor.

(3) A candidate or committee receiving an anonymous cash contribution in excess of $50 shall promptly dispose of the amount over $50. The amount over $50 may be used for any lawful purpose unrelated to any Federal election, campaign, or candidate.

[54 FR 34112, Aug. 17, 1989, and 54 FR 48580, Nov. 24, 1989, as amended at 54 FR 48582, Nov. 24, 1989; 55 FR 1139, Jan. 11, 1990; 67 FR 69948, Nov. 19, 2002]

§ 110.5 [Reserved]

§ 110.6 Earmarked contributions 52 U.S.C. 30116(a)(8)).

(a) *General.* All contributions by a person made on behalf of or to a candidate, including contributions which are in any way earmarked or otherwise directed to the candidate through an intermediary or conduit, are contributions from the person to the candidate.

(b) *Definitions.* (1) For purposes of this section, *earmarked* means a designation, instruction, or encumbrance, whether direct or indirect, express or implied, oral or written, which results in all or any part of a contribution or expenditure being made to, or expended on behalf of, a clearly identified candidate or a candidate's authorized committee.

(2) For purposes of this section, *conduit or intermediary* means any person who receives and forwards an earmarked contribution to a candidate or a candidate's authorized committee, except as provided in paragraph (b)(2)(i) of this section.

(i) For purposes of this section, the following persons shall not be considered to be conduits or intermediaries:

(A) An individual who is an employee or a full-time volunteer working for the candidate's authorized committee, provided that the individual is not acting in his or her capacity as a representative of an entity prohibited from making contributions;

(B) A fundraising representative conducting joint fundraising with the candidate's authorized committee pursuant to 11 CFR 102.17 or 9034.8;

(C) An affiliated committee, as defined in 11 CFR 100.5(g);

(D) A commercial fundraising firm retained by the candidate or the candidate's authorized committee to assist in fundraising; and

(E) An individual who is expressly authorized by the candidate or the candidate's authorized committee to engage in fundraising, and who occupies a significant position within the candidate's campaign organization, provided that the individual is not acting in his or her capacity as a representative of an entity prohibited from making contributions.

(ii) Any person who is prohibited from making contributions or expenditures in connection with an election for Federal office shall be prohibited from acting as a conduit for contributions earmarked to candidates or their authorized committees. The provisions of this section shall not restrict the ability of an organization or committee to serve as a collecting agent for a separate segregated fund pursuant to 11 CFR 102.6.

(iii) Any person who receives an earmarked contribution shall forward such earmarked contribution to the candidate or authorized committee in accordance with 11 CFR 102.8, except that—

(A) A fundraising representative shall follow the joint fundraising procedures set forth at 11 CFR 102.17.

(B) A person who is prohibited from acting as a conduit pursuant to paragraph (b)(2)(ii) of this section shall return the earmarked contribution to the contributor.

(c) *Reporting of earmarked contributions—(1) Reports by conduits and intermediaries.* (i) The intermediary or conduit of the earmarked contribution shall report the original source and the recipient candidate or authorized committee to the Commission or the Secretary of the Senate, as appropriate

(see 11 CFR part 105), and to the recipient candidate or authorized committee.

(ii) The report to the Commission or Secretary shall be included in the conduit's or intermediary's report for the reporting period in which the earmarked contribution was received, or, if the conduit or intermediary is not required to report under 11 CFR part 104, by letter to the Commission within thirty days after forwarding the earmarked contribution.

(iii) The report to the recipient candidate or authorized committee shall be made when the earmarked contribution is forwarded to the recipient candidate or authorized committee pursuant to 11 CFR 102.8.

(iv) The report by the conduit or intermediary shall contain the following information:

(A) The name and mailing address of each contributor and, for each earmarked contribution in excess of $200, the contributor's occupation and the name of his or her employer;

(B) The amount of each earmarked contribution, the date received by the conduit, and the intended recipient as designated by the contributor; and

(C) The date each earmarked contribution was forwarded to the recipient candidate or authorized committee and whether the earmarked contribution was forwarded in cash or by the contributor's check or by the conduit's check.

(v) For each earmarked contribution passed through the conduit's or intermediary's account, the information specified in paragraph (c)(1)(iv) (A) through (C) of this section shall be itemized on the appropriate schedules of receipts and disbursements attached to the conduit's or intermediary's report, or shall be disclosed by letter, as appropriate. For each earmarked contribution forwarded in the form of the contributor's check or other written instrument, the information specified in paragraph (c)(1)(iv) (A) through (C) of this section shall be disclosed as a memo entry on the appropriate schedules of receipts and disbursements attached to the conduit's or intermediary's report, or shall be disclosed by letter, as appropriate.

(2) *Reports by recipient candidates and authorized committees.* (i) The recipient candidate or authorized committee shall report each conduit or intermediary who forwards one or more earmarked contributions which in the aggregate exceed $200 in any election cycle.

(ii) The report by the recipient candidate or authorized committee shall contain the following information:

(A) The identification of the conduit or intermediary, as defined in 11 CFR 100.12;

(B) The total amount of earmarked contributions received from the conduit or intermediary and the date of receipt; and

(C) The information required under 11 CFR 104.3(a) (3) and (4) for each earmarked contribution which in the aggregate exceeds $200 in any election cycle.

(iii) The information specified in paragraph (c)(2)(ii) (A) through (C) of this section shall be itemized on Schedule A attached to the report for the reporting period in which the earmarked contribution is received.

(d) *Direction or control.* (1) A conduit's or intermediary's contribution limits are not affected by the forwarding of an earmarked contribution except where the conduit or intermediary exercises any direction or control over the choice of the recipient candidate.

(2) If a conduit or intermediary exercises any direction or control over the choice of the recipient candidate, the earmarked contribution shall be considered a contribution by both the original contributor and the conduit or intermediary. If the conduit or intermediary exercises any direction or control over the choice of the recipient candidate, the report filed by the conduit or intermediary and the report filed by the recipient candidate or authorized committee shall indicate that the earmarked contribution is made by both the original contributor and the conduit or intermediary, and that the entire amount of the contribution is attributed to each.

[54 FR 34113, Aug. 17, 1989 and 54 FR 48580, Nov. 24, 1989; 61 FR 3550, Feb. 1, 1996; 81 FR 94240, Dec. 23, 2016]

§ 110.7 [Reserved]

§ 110.8 Presidential candidate expenditure limitations.

(a)(1) No candidate for the office of President of the United States who is eligible under 26 U.S.C. 9003 (relating to conditions for eligibility for payments) or under 26 U.S.C. 9033 (relating to eligibility for payments) to receive payments from the Secretary of the Treasury and has received payments, may make expenditures in excess of—

(i) $10,000,000 in the case of a campaign for nomination for election to the office, except the aggregate of expenditures under this paragraph in any one State shall not exceed the greater of 16 cents multiplied by the voting age population of the State or $200,000; or

(ii) $20,000,000 in the case of a campaign for election to the office.

(2) The expenditure limitations in paragraph (a)(1) of this section shall be increased in accordance with 11 CFR 110.17.

(3) Voting age population is defined at 11 CFR 110.18.

(b) The expenditure limitations shall not be considered violated if, after the date of the primary or general election, convention or caucus, receipt of refunds and rebates causes a candidate's expenditures to be within the limitations.

(c) For the State limitations in paragraph (a)(1) of this section—

(1) Expenditures made in a State after the date of the primary election, convention or caucus relating to the primary election, convention or caucus count toward that State's expenditure limitation;

(2) The candidate may treat an amount that does not exceed 50% of the candidate's total expenditures allocable to a particular State under 11 CFR 106.2 as exempt fundraising expenses, and may exclude this amount from the candidate's total expenditures attributable to the expenditure limitations for that State. The candidate may treat 100% of the cost of mass mailings as exempt fundraising expenses, unless the mass mailings were mailed within 28 days before the state's primary election, convention or caucus. The total of all amounts excluded for exempt fundraising expenses shall

not exceed 20% of the overall expenditure limitation under 11 CFR 9035.1.

(d)(1) If an individual is a candidate for more than one Federal office, or for a Federal office and a State office, he or she must designate separate principal campaign committees and establish completely separate campaign organizations.

(2) No funds, goods, or services, including loans and loan guarantees, may be transferred between or used by the separate campaigns, except as provided in 11 CFR 110.3(c)(5).

(3) Except for Presidential candidates receiving Presidential Primary Matching Funds, see 26 U.S.C. 9032, or General Election Public Financing, see 26 U.S.C. 9002, campaigns may share personnel and facilities, as long as expenditures are allocated between the campaigns, and the payment made from each campaign account reflects the allocation.

(e)(1) A political party may make reimbursement for the expenses of a candidate who is engaging in party-building activities, without the payment being considered a contribution to the candidate, and without the unreimbursed expense being considered an expenditure counting against the limitations in paragraph (a) (1) or (2) of this section, as long as—

(i) The event is a bona fide party event or appearance; and

(ii) No aspect of the solicitation for the event, the setting of the event, and the remarks or activities of the candidate in connection with the event were for the purpose of influencing the candidate's nomination or election.

(2)(i) An event or appearance meeting the requirements of paragraph (e)(1) of this section and occurring prior to January 1 of the year of the election for which the individual is a candidate is presumptively party-related;

(ii) Notwithstanding the requirements of paragraph (e)(1) of this section, an event or appearance occurring on or after January 1 of the year of the election for which the individual is a candidate is presumptively for the purpose of influencing the candidate's election, and any contributions or expenditures are governed by the contribution and expenditure limitations of this part 110.

(iii) The presumptions in paragraphs (e)(2) (i) and (ii) of this section may be rebutted by a showing to the Commission that the appearance or event was, or was not, party-related, as the case may be.

(f)(1) Expenditures made by or on behalf of any candidate nominated by a political party for election to the office of Vice President of the United States shall be considered to be expenditures made by or on behalf of the candidate of such party for election to the office of President of the United States.

(2) Expenditures from personal funds made by a candidate for Vice President shall be considered to be expenditures by the candidate for President, if the candidate is receiving General Election Public Financing, see §9003.2(c).

(g) An expenditure is made on behalf of a candidate, including a Vice-Presidential candidate, if it is made by—

(1) An authorized committee or any other agent of the candidate for purposes of making any expenditure;

(2) Any person authorized or requested by the candidate, an authorized committee of the candidate, or an agent of the candidate to make the expenditure; or

(3) A committee not authorized in writing, so long as it is requested by the candidate, an authorized committee of the candidate, or an agent of the candidate to make the expenditure.

[41 FR 35948, Aug. 25, 1976, as amended at 45 FR 21210, Apr. 1, 1980; 54 FR 34114, Aug. 17, 1989; 54 FR 48580, Nov. 24, 1989; 56 FR 35911, July 29, 1991; 68 FR 457, Jan. 3, 2003; 68 FR 6346, Feb. 7, 2003]

§110.9 Violation of limitations.

No candidate or political committee shall knowingly accept any contribution or make any expenditure in violation of the provisions of 11 CFR part 110. No officer or employee of a political committee shall knowingly accept a contribution made for the benefit or use of a candidate, or make any expenditure on behalf of a candidate, in violation of any limitation imposed on contributions and expenditures under this part 110.

[67 FR 69949, Nov. 19, 2002]

§ 110.10 Expenditures by candidates.

Except as provided in 11 CFR parts 9001, *et seq.* and 9031, *et seq.*, candidates for Federal office may make unlimited expenditures from personal funds as defined in 11 CFR 100.33.

[68 FR 3996, Jan. 27, 2003]

§ 110.11 Communications; advertising; disclaimers (52 U.S.C. 30120).

(a) *Scope.* The following communications must include disclaimers, as specified in this section:

(1) All public communications, as defined in 11 CFR 100.26, made by a political committee; electronic mail of more than 500 substantially similar communications when sent by a political committee; and all Internet websites of political committees available to the general public.

(2) All public communications, as defined in 11 CFR 100.26, by any person that expressly advocate the election or defeat of a clearly identified candidate.

(3) All public communications, as defined in 11 CFR 100.26, by any person that solicit any contribution.

(4) All electioneering communications by any person.

(b) *General content requirements.* A disclaimer required by paragraph (a) of this section must contain the following information:

(1) If the communication, including any solicitation, is paid for and authorized by a candidate, an authorized committee of a candidate, or an agent of either of the foregoing, the disclaimer must clearly state that the communication has been paid for by the authorized political committee;

(2) If the communication, including any solicitation, is authorized by a candidate, an authorized committee of a candidate, or an agent of either of the foregoing, but is paid for by any other person, the disclaimer must clearly state that the communication is paid for by such other person and is authorized by such candidate, authorized committee, or agent; or

(3) If the communication, including any solicitation, is not authorized by a candidate, authorized committee of a candidate, or an agent of either of the foregoing, the disclaimer must clearly state the full name and permanent street address, telephone number, or World Wide Web address of the person who paid for the communication, and that the communication is not authorized by any candidate or candidate's committee.

(c) *Disclaimer specifications*—(1) *Specifications for all disclaimers.* A disclaimer required by paragraph (a) of this section must be presented in a clear and conspicuous manner, to give the reader, observer, or listener adequate notice of the identity of the person or political committee that paid for and, where required, that authorized the communication. A disclaimer is not clear and conspicuous if it is difficult to read or hear, or if the placement is easily overlooked.

(2) *Specific requirements for printed communications.* In addition to the general requirement of paragraphs (b) and (c)(1) of this section, a disclaimer required by paragraph (a) of this section that appears on any printed public communication must comply with all of the following:

(i) The disclaimer must be of sufficient type size to be clearly readable by the recipient of the communication. A disclaimer in twelve (12)-point type size satisfies the size requirement of this paragraph (c)(2)(i) when it is used for signs, posters, flyers, newspapers, magazines, or other printed material that measure no more than twenty-four (24) inches by thirty-six (36) inches.

(ii) The disclaimer must be contained in a printed box set apart from the other contents of the communication.

(iii) The disclaimer must be printed with a reasonable degree of color contrast between the background and the printed statement. A disclaimer satisfies the color contrast requirement of this paragraph (c)(2)(iii) if it is printed in black text on a white background or if the degree of color contrast between the background and the text of the disclaimer is no less than the color contrast between the background and the largest text used in the communication.

(iv) The disclaimer need not appear on the front or cover page of the communication as long as it appears within the communication, except on communications, such as billboards, that contain only a front face.

(v) A communication that would require a disclaimer if distributed separately, that is included in a package of materials, must contain the required disclaimer.

(3) *Specific requirements for radio and television communications authorized by candidates.* In addition to the general requirements of paragraphs (b) and (c)(1) of this section, a communication that is authorized or paid for by a candidate or the authorized committee of a candidate (*see* paragraph (b)(1) or (b)(2) of this section) that is transmitted through radio or television, or through any broadcast, cable, or satellite transmission, must comply with the following:

(i) A communication transmitted through radio must include an audio statement by the candidate that identifies the candidate and states that he or she has approved the communication; or

(ii) A communication transmitted through television or through any broadcast, cable, or satellite transmission, must include a statement that identifies the candidate and states that he or she has approved the communication. The candidate shall convey the statement either:

(A) Through an unobscured, full-screen view of himself or herself making the statement, or

(B) Through a voice-over by himself or herself, accompanied by a clearly identifiable photographic or similar image of the candidate. A photographic or similar image of the candidate shall be considered clearly identified if it is at least eighty (80) percent of the vertical screen height.

(iii) A communication transmitted through television or through any broadcast, cable, or satellite transmission, must also include a similar statement that must appear in clearly readable writing at the end of the television communication. To be clearly readable, this statement must meet all of the following three requirements:

(A) The statement must appear in letters equal to or greater than four (4) percent of the vertical picture height;

(B) The statement must be visible for a period of at least four (4) seconds; and

(C) The statement must appear with a reasonable degree of color contrast between the background and the text of the statement. A statement satisfies the color contrast requirement of this paragraph (c)(3)(iii)(C) if it is printed in black text on a white background or if the degree of color contrast between the background and the text of the statement is no less than the color contrast between the background and the largest type size used in the communication.

(iv) The following are examples of acceptable statements that satisfy the spoken statement requirements of paragraph (c)(3) of this section with respect to a radio, television, or other broadcast, cable, or satellite communication, but they are not the only allowable statements:

(A) "I am [insert name of candidate], a candidate for [insert Federal office sought], and I approved this advertisement."

(B) "My name is [insert name of candidate]. I am running for [insert Federal office sought], and I approved this message."

(4) *Specific requirements for radio and television communications paid for by other persons and not authorized by a candidate.* In addition to the general requirements of paragraphs (b) and (c)(1) of this section, a communication not authorized by a candidate or a candidate's authorized committee that is transmitted through radio or television or through any broadcast, cable, or satellite transmission, must comply with the following:

(i) A communication transmitted through radio or television or through any broadcast, cable, or satellite transmission, must include the following audio statement, "XXX is responsible for the content of this advertising," spoken clearly, with the blank to be filled in with the name of the political committee or other person paying for the communication, and the name of the connected organization, if any, of the payor unless the name of the connected organization is already provided in the "XXX is responsible" statement; and

171

(ii) A communication transmitted through television, or through any broadcast, cable, or satellite transmission, must include the audio statement required by paragraph (c)(4)(i) of this section. That statement must be conveyed by an unobscured full-screen view of a representative of the political committee or other person making the statement, or by a representative of such political committee or other person in voice-over.

(iii) A communication transmitted through television or through any broadcast, cable, or satellite transmission, must also include a similar statement that must appear in clearly readable writing at the end of the communication. To be clearly readable, the statement must meet all of the following three requirements:

(A) The statement must appear in letters equal to or greater than four (4) percent of the vertical picture height;

(B) The statement must be visible for a period of at least four (4) seconds; and

(C) The statement must appear with a reasonable degree of color contrast between the background and the disclaimer statement. A disclaimer satisfies the color contrast requirement of this paragraph (c)(4)(iii)(C) if it is printed in black text on a white background or if the degree of color contrast between the background and the text of the disclaimer is no less than the color contrast between the background and the largest type size used in the communication.

(d) *Coordinated party expenditures and independent expenditures by political party committees.* (1)(i) For a communication paid for by a political party committee pursuant to 52 U.S.C. 30116(d), the disclaimer required by paragraph (a) of this section must identify the political party committee that makes the expenditure as the person who paid for the communication, regardless of whether the political party committee was acting in its own capacity or as the designated agent of another political party committee.

(ii) A communication made by a political party committee pursuant to 52 U.S.C. 30116(d) and distributed prior to the date the party's candidate is nominated shall satisfy the requirements of

this section if it clearly states who paid for the communication.

(2) For purposes of this section, a communication paid for by a political party committee, other than a communication covered by paragraph (d)(1)(ii) of this section, that is being treated as a coordinated expenditure under 52 U.S.C. 30116(d) and that was made with the approval of a candidate, a candidate's authorized committee, or the agent of either shall identify the political party that paid for the communication and shall state that the communication is authorized by the candidate or candidate's authorized committee.

(3) For a communication paid for by a political party committee that constitutes an independent expenditure under 11 CFR 100.16, the disclaimer required by this section must identify the political party committee that paid for the communication, and must state that the communication is not authorized by any candidate or candidate's authorized committee.

(e) *Exempt activities.* A public communication authorized by a candidate, authorized committee, or political party committee, that qualifies as an exempt activity under 11 CFR 100.140, 100.147, 100.148, or 100.149, must comply with the disclaimer requirements of paragraphs (a), (b), (c)(1), and (c)(2) of this section, unless excepted under paragraph (f)(1) of this section, but the disclaimer does not need to state whether the communication is authorized by a candidate, or any authorized committee or agent of any candidate.

(f) *Exceptions.* (1) The requirements of paragraphs (a) through (e) of this section do not apply to the following:

(i) Bumper stickers, pins, buttons, pens, and similar small items upon which the disclaimer cannot be conveniently printed;

(ii) Skywriting, water towers, wearing apparel, or other means of displaying an advertisement of such a nature that the inclusion of a disclaimer would be impracticable; or

(iii) Checks, receipts, and similar items of minimal value that are used for purely administrative purposes and do not contain a political message.

(2) For purposes of this section, whenever a separate segregated fund or

172

its connected organization solicits contributions to the fund from those persons it may solicit under the applicable provisions of 11 CFR part 114, or makes a communication to those persons, such communication shall not be considered a type of public communication and need not contain the disclaimer required by paragraphs (a) through (c) of this section.

(g) *Comparable rate for campaign purposes.* (1) No person who sells space in a newspaper or magazine to a candidate, an authorized committee of a candidate, or an agent of the candidate, for use in connection with the candidate's campaign for nomination or for election, shall charge an amount for the space which exceeds the comparable rate for the space for non-campaign purposes.

(2) For purposed of this section, comparable rate means the rate charged to a national or general rate advertiser, and shall include discount privileges usually and normally available to a national or general rate advertiser.

[67 FR 76975, Dec. 13, 2002, as amended at 71 FR 18613, Apr. 12, 2006; 79 FR 77847, Dec. 29, 2014]

§ 110.12 Candidate appearances on public educational institution premises.

(a) *Rental of facilities at usual and normal charge.* Any unincorporated public educational institution exempt from federal taxation under 26 U.S.C. 115, such as a school, college or university, may make its facilities available to any candidate or political committee in the ordinary course of business and at the usual and normal charge. In this event, the requirements of paragraph (b) of this section are not applicable.

(b) *Use of facilities at no charge or at less than the usual and normal charge.* An unincorporated public educational institution exempt from federal taxation under 26 U.S.C. 115, such as a school, college or university, may sponsor appearances by candidates, candidates' representatives or representatives of political parties at which such individuals address or meet the institution's academic community or the general public (whichever is invited) on the educational institution's

premises at no charge or at less than the usual and normal charge, if:

(1) The educational institution makes reasonable efforts to ensure that the appearances constitute speeches, question and answer sessions, or similar communications in an academic setting, and makes reasonable efforts to ensure that the appearances are not conducted as campaign rallies or events; and

(2) The educational institution does not, in conjunction with the appearance, expressly advocate the election or defeat of any clearly identified candidate(s) or candidates of a clearly identified political party, and does not favor any one candidate or political party over any other in allowing such appearances.

[60 FR 64273, Dec. 14, 1995]

§ 110.13 Candidate debates.

(a) *Staging organizations.* (1) Nonprofit organizations described in 26 U.S.C. 501 (c)(3) or (c)(4) and which do not endorse, support, or oppose political candidates or political parties may stage candidate debates in accordance with this section and 11 CFR 114.4(f).

(2) Broadcasters (including a cable television operator, programmer or producer), *bona fide* newspapers, magazines and other periodical publications may stage candidate debates in accordance with this section and 11 CFR 114.4(f), provided that they are not owned or controlled by a political party, political committee or candidate. In addition, broadcasters (including a cable television operator, programmer or producer), *bona fide* newspapers, magazines and other periodical publications, acting as press entities, may also cover or carry candidate debates in accordance with 11 CFR part 100, subparts B and C and part 100, subparts D and E.

(b) *Debate structure.* The structure of debates staged in accordance with this section and 11 CFR 114.4(f) is left to the discretion of the staging organizations(s), provided that:

(1) Such debates include at least two candidates; and

(2) The staging organization(s) does not structure the debates to promote or advance one candidate over another.

(c) *Criteria for candidate selection.* For all debates, staging organization(s) must use pre-established objective criteria to determine which candidates may participate in a debate. For general election debates, staging organizations(s) shall not use nomination by a particular political party as the sole objective criterion to determine whether to include a candidate in a debate. For debates held prior to a primary election, caucus or convention, staging organizations may restrict candidate participation to candidates seeking the nomination of one party, and need not stage a debate for candidates seeking the nomination of any other political party or independent candidates.

[61 FR 18051, Apr. 24, 1996; 61 FR 24533, May 15, 1996, as amended at 67 FR 78681, Dec. 26, 2002]

§ 110.14 Contributions to and expenditures by delegates and delegate committees.

(a) *Scope.* This section sets forth the prohibitions, limitations and reporting requirements under the Act applicable to all levels of a delegate selection process.

(b) *Definitions*—(1) *Delegate.* Delegate means an individual who becomes or seeks to become a delegate, as defined by State law or party rule, to a national nominating convention or to a State, district, or local convention, caucus or primary that is held to select delegates to a national nominating convention.

(2) *Delegate committee.* A delegate committee is a group of persons that receives contributions or makes expenditures for the sole purpose of influencing the selection of one or more delegates to a national nominating convention. The term *delegate committee* includes a group of delegates, a group of individuals seeking selection as delegates and a group of individuals supporting delegates. A delegate committee that qualifies as a political committee under 11 CFR 100.5 must register with the Commission pursuant to 11 CFR part 102 and report its receipts and disbursements in accordance with 11 CFR part 104.

(c) *Funds received and expended; Prohibited funds.* (1) Funds received or disbursements made for the purpose of

furthering the selection of a delegate to a national nominating convention are contributions or expenditures for the purpose of influencing a federal election, see 11 CFR 100.2 (c)(3) and (e), except that—

(i) Payments made by an individual to a State committee or subordinate State committee as a condition for ballot access as a delegate are not contributions or expenditures. Such payments are neither required to be reported under 11 CFR part 104 nor subject to limitation under 11 CFR 110.1; and

(ii) Payments made by a State committee or subordinate State party committee for administrative expenses incurred in connection with sponsoring conventions or caucuses during which delegates to a national nominating convention are selected are not contributions or expenditures. Such payments are neither required to be reported under 11 CFR part 104 nor subject to limitation under 11 CFR 110.1 and 110.2.

(2) All funds received or disbursements made for the purpose of furthering the selection of a delegate to a national nominating convention, including payments made under paragraphs (c)(1)(i) and (c)(1)(ii) of this section, shall be made from funds permissible under the Act. *See* 11 CFR parts 110, 114 and 115.

(d) *Contributions to a delegate.* (1) The limitations on contributions to candidates and political committees under 11 CFR 110.1 and 110.2 do not apply to contributions made to a delegate for the purpose of furthering his or her selection.

(2) Contributions to a delegate made by the authorized committee of a presidential candidate count against the presidential candidate's expenditure limitation under 11 CFR 110.8(a).

(3) A delegate is not required to report contributions received for the purpose of furthering his or her selection.

(e) *Expenditures by delegate to advocate only his or her selection.* (1) Expenditures by a delegate that advocate only his or her selection are neither contributions to a candidate, subject to limitation under 11 CFR 110.1, nor chargeable to the expenditure limits of any Presidential candidate under 11

CFR 110.8(a). Such expenditures may include, but are not limited to: Payments for travel and subsistence during the delegate selection process, including the national nominating convention, and payments for any communications advocating only the delegate's selection.

(2) A delegate is not required to report expenditures made to advocate only his or her selection.

(f) *Expenditures by a delegate referring to a candidate for public office*—(1) *Volunteer activities that do not use public political advertising.* (i) Expenditures by a delegate to defray the costs of certain campaign materials (such as pins, bumper stickers, handbills, brochures, posters and yard signs) that advocate his or her selection and also include information on or reference to a candidate for the office of President or any other public office are neither contributions to the candidate referred to nor subject to limitation under 11 CFR 110.1 provided that:

(A) The materials are used in connection with volunteer activities; and

(B) The expenditures are not for costs incurred in the use of broadcasting, newspapers, magazines, billboards, direct mail or similar types of general public communication or political advertising.

(ii) Such expenditures are not chargeable to the expenditure limitation of a presidential candidate under 11 CFR 110.8(a).

(iii) A delegate is not required to report expenditures made pursuant to this paragraph.

(2) *Use of public political advertising.* A delegate may make expenditures to defray costs incurred in the use of broadcasting, newspapers, magazines, billboards, direct mail or similar types of general public communication or political advertising to advocate his or her selection and also include information on or reference to a candidate for the office of President or any other public office.

(i) Such expenditures are in-kind contributions to a Federal candidate if they are coordinated communications under 11 CFR 109.21.

(A) The portion of the expenditure allocable to a Federal candidate is subject to the contribution limitations of 11 CFR 110.1.

(B) A Federal candidate's authorized committee must report the portion of the expenditure allocable to the candidate as a contribution pursuant to 11 CFR part 104.

(C) The portion of the expenditure allocable to a presidential candidate is chargeable to the presidential candidate's expenditure limitation under 11 CFR 110.8(a).

(ii) Such expenditures are independent expenditures under 11 CFR 100.16 if they are made for a communication expressly advocating the election or defeat of a clearly identified Federal candidate that is not a coordinated communication under 11 CFR 109.21.

(A) Such independent expenditures must be made in accordance with the requirements of 11 CFR part 109.

(B) The delegate shall report the portion of the expenditure allocable to the Federal candidate as an independent expenditure in accordance with 11 CFR 109.10.

(3) *Republication of candidate materials.* Expenditures made to finance the dissemination, distribution or republication, in whole or in part, of any broadcast or materials prepared by a Federal candidate are in-kind contributions to the candidate.

(i) Such expenditures are subject to the contribution limits of 11 CFR 110.1.

(ii) The Federal candidate must report the expenditure as a contribution pursuant to 11 CFR part 104.

(iii) Such expenditures are not chargeable to the presidential candidate's expenditure limitation under 11 CFR 110.8 unless they were coordinated communications under 11 CFR 109.21.

(4) For purposes of this paragraph, *direct mail* means any mailing(s) by commercial vendors or any mailing(s) made from lists that were not developed by the delegate.

(g) *Contributions made to and by a delegate committee.* (1) The limitations on contributions to political committees under 11 CFR 110.1 and 110.2 apply to contributions made to and by a delegate committee.

(2) A delegate committee shall report contributions it makes and receives pursuant to 11 CFR part 104.

(h) *Expenditures by a delegate committee to advocate only the selection of one or more delegates.* (1) Expenditures by a delegate committee that advocate only the selection of one or more delegates are neither contributions to a candidate, subject to limitation under 11 CFR 110.1 nor chargeable to the expenditure limits of any Presidential candidate under 11 CFR 110.8(a). Such expenditures may include but are not limited to: Payments for travel and subsistence during the delegate selection process, including the national nominating convention, and payments for any communications advocating only the selection of one or more delegates.

(2) A delegate committee shall report expenditures made pursuant to this paragraph.

(i) *Expenditures by a delegate committee referring to a candidate for public office—* (1) *Volunteer activities that do not use public political advertising.* (i) Expenditures by a delegate committee to defray the costs of certain campaign materials (such as pins, bumper stickers, handbills, brochures, posters and yard signs) that advocate the selection of a delegate and also include information on or reference to a candidate for the office of President or any other public office are neither contributions to the candidate referred to, nor subject to limitation under 11 CFR 110.1 provided that:

(A) The materials are used in connection with volunteer activities; and

(B) The expenditures are not for costs incurred in the use of broadcasting, newspapers, magazines, billboards, direct mail or similar types of general public communication or political advertising.

(ii) Such expenditures are not chargeable to the expenditure limitation of a presidential candidate under 11 CFR 110.8(a).

(iii) A delegate committee shall report expenditures made pursuant to this paragraph.

(2) *Use of public political advertising.* A delegate committee may make expenditures to defray costs incurred in the use of broadcasting, newspapers, maga-zines, billboards, direct mail or similar types of general public communication or political advertising to advocate the selection of one or more delegates and also include information on or reference to a candidate for the office of President or any other public office. If such expenditures are in-kind contributions or independent expenditures under paragraphs (i) or (ii) below, the delegate committee shall allocate the portion of the expenditures relating to the delegate(s) and candidate(s) referred to in the communications between them and report the portion allocable to each.

(i) Such expenditures are in-kind contributions to a Federal candidate if they are coordinated communications under 11 CFR 109.21.

(A) The portion of the expenditure allocable to a Federal candidate is subject to the contribution limitations of 11 CFR 110.1. The delegate committee shall report the portion allocable to the Federal candidate as a contribution in-kind.

(B) The Federal candidate's authorized committee shall report the portion of the expenditure allocable to the candidate as a contribution pursuant to 11 CFR part 104.

(C) The portion of the expenditure allocable to a presidential candidate is chargeable to the presidential candidate's expenditure limitation under 11 CFR 110.8(a).

(ii) Such expenditures are independent expenditures under 11 CFR 100.16 if they are made for a communication expressly advocating the election or defeat of a clearly identified Federal candidate that is not a coordinated communication under 11 CFR 109.21.

(A) Such independent expenditures must be made in accordance with the requirements of 11 CFR part 100.16.

(B) The delegate committee shall report the portion of the expenditure allocable to the Federal candidate as an independent expenditure in accordance with 11 CFR 109.10.

(3) *Republication of candidate materials.* Expenditures made to finance the dissemination, distribution or republication, in whole or in part, of any broadcast or materials prepared by a

Federal candidate are in-kind contributions to the candidate.

(i) Such expenditures are subject to the contribution limitations of 11 CFR 110.1. The delegate committee shall report the expenditure as a contribution in-kind.

(ii) The Federal candidate's authorized committee shall report the expenditure as a contribution pursuant to 11 CFR part 104.

(iii) Such expenditures are not chargeable to the presidential candidate's expenditure limitation under 11 CFR 110.8 unless they were coordinated communications under 11 CFR 109.21.

(4) For purposes of this paragraph, *direct mail* means any mailing(s) by commercial vendors or any mailing(s) made from lists that were not developed by the delegate committee or any participating delegate.

(j) *Affiliation of delegate committees with a Presidential candidate's authorized committee.* (1) For purposes of the contribution limits of 11 CFR 110.1 and 110.2, a delegate committee shall be considered to be affiliated with a Presidential candidate's authorized committee if both such committees are established, financed, maintained or controlled by the same person, such as the Presidential candidate, or the same group of persons.

(2) Factors the Commission may consider in determining whether a delegate committee is affiliated under paragraph (j)(1) of this section with a Presidential candidate's authorized committee may include, but are not limited to:

(i) Whether the Presidential candidate or any other person associated with the Presidential authorized committee played a significant role in the formation of the delegate committee;

(ii) Whether any delegate associated with a delegate committee is or has been a staff member of the Presidential authorized committee;

(iii) Whether the committees have common or overlapping officers or employees;

(iv) Whether the Presidential authorized committee provides funds or goods in a significant amount or on an ongoing basis to the delegate committee, such as through direct or indirect payments for administrative, fundraising, or other costs, but not including the transfer to a committee of its allocated share of proceeds jointly raised pursuant to 11 CFR 102.17 or 9034.8;

(v) Whether the Presidential candidate or any other person associated with the Presidential authorized committee suggested, recommended or arranged for contributions to be made to the delegate committee;

(vi) Similar patterns of contributions received by the committees;

(vii) Whether one committee provides a mailing list to the other committee;

(viii) Whether the Presidential authorized committee or any person associated with that committee provides ongoing administrative support to the other committee;

(ix) Whether the Presidential authorized committee or any person associated with that committee directs or organizes the specific campaign activities of the delegate committee; and

(x) Whether the Presidential authorized committee or any person associated with that committee files statements or reports on behalf of the delegate committee.

(k) *Affiliation between delegate committees.* Delegate committees will be considered to be affiliated with each other if they meet the criteria for affiliation set forth at 11 CFR 100.5(g).

[52 FR 35534, Sept. 22, 1987, as amended at 65 FR 76146, Dec. 6, 2000; 68 FR 457, Jan. 3, 2003; 68 FR 6346, Feb. 7, 2003; 75 FR 32, Jan. 4, 2010; 79 FR 62336, Oct. 17, 2014]

§ 110.15 [Reserved]

§ 110.16 Prohibitions on fraudulent misrepresentations.

(a) *In general.* No person who is a candidate for Federal office or an employee or agent of such a candidate shall—

(1) Fraudulently misrepresent the person or any committee or organization under the person's control as speaking or writing or otherwise acting for or on behalf of any other candidate or political party or employee or agent thereof in a matter which is damaging to such other candidate or political party or employee or agent thereof; or

(2) Willfully and knowingly participate in or conspire to participate in

any plan, scheme, or design to violate paragraph (a)(1) of this section.

(b) *Fraudulent solicitation of funds.* No person shall—

(1) Fraudulently misrepresent the person as speaking, writing, or otherwise acting for or on behalf of any candidate or political party or employee or agent thereof for the purpose of soliciting contributions or donations; or

(2) Willfully and knowingly participate in or conspire to participate in any plan, scheme, or design to violate paragraph (b)(1) of this section.

[67 FR 76977, Dec. 13, 2002]

§ 110.17 Price index increase.

(a) *Price index increases for party committee expenditure limitations and Presidential candidate expenditure limitations.* The limitations on expenditures established by 11 CFR 109.32 and 110.8 shall be increased by the percent difference between the price index, as certified to the Commission by the Secretary of Labor, for the 12 months preceding the beginning of the calendar year and the price index for the base period.

(1) Each expenditure limitation so increased shall be the expenditure limitation in effect for that calendar year.

(2) For purposes of this paragraph (a), the term *base period* means calendar year 1974.

(b) *Price index increases for contributions by persons and political party committees to Senatorial candidates.* The limitations on contributions established by 11 CFR 110.1(b) and (c) and 110.2(e) shall be increased only in odd-numbered years by the percent difference between the price index, as certified to the Commission by the Secretary of Labor, for the 12 months preceding the beginning of the calendar year and the price index for the base period.

(1) The increased contribution limitations shall be in effect as provided in 11 CFR 110.1(b)(1)(ii), 110.1(c)(1)(ii), and 110.2(e)(2).

(2) For purposes of this paragraph (b) the term *base period* means calendar year 2001.

(c) *Rounding of price index increases.* If any amount after the increases under paragraph (a) or (b) of this section is not a multiple of $100, such amount shall be rounded to the nearest multiple of $100.

(d) *Definition of price index.* For purposes of this section, the term *price index* means the average over a calendar year of the Consumer Price Index (all items—United States city average) published monthly by the Bureau of Labor Statistics.

(e) *Publication of price index increases*—(1) *Expenditure and Contribution Limitations.* In every odd-numbered year, the Commission will publish in the FEDERAL REGISTER the amount of the expenditure and contribution limitations in effect and place such information on the Commission's Web site.

(2) *Lobbyist/registrant and lobbyist/registrant PAC contribution bundling disclosure threshold.* In every calendar year, the Commission will publish in the FEDERAL REGISTER the amount of the lobbyist/registrant and lobbyist/registrant PAC contribution bundling disclosure threshold in effect and place such information on the Commission's Web site.

(f) *Price index increases for lobbyist/registrant and lobbyist/registrant PAC contribution bundling threshold.* The threshold for disclosure of lobbyists/registrants and lobbyist/registrant PACs that bundle contributions shall be indexed for each calendar year in accordance with 11 CFR 104.22(g).

[67 FR 69949, Nov. 19, 2002, as amended at 74 FR 7304, Feb. 17, 2009; 75 FR 32, Jan. 4, 2010; 79 FR 62336, Oct. 17, 2014]

§ 110.18 Voting age population.

There is annually published by the Department of Commerce in the FEDERAL REGISTER an estimate of the voting age population based on an estimate of the voting age population of the United States, of each State, and of each Congressional district. The term *voting age population* means resident population, 18 years of age or older.

[68 FR 457, Jan. 3, 2003]

§ 110.19 Contributions by minors.

An individual who is 17 years old or younger (a Minor) may make contributions to any candidate or political committee that in the aggregate do not exceed the limitations on contributions of 11 CFR 110.1, if—

(a) The decision to contribute is made knowingly and voluntarily by the Minor;

(b) The funds, goods, or services contributed are owned or controlled by the Minor, such as income earned by the Minor, the proceeds of a trust for which the Minor is the beneficiary, or funds withdrawn by the Minor from a financial account opened and maintained in the Minor's name; and

(c) The contribution is not made from the proceeds of a gift, the purpose of which was to provide funds to be contributed, or is not in any other way controlled by another individual.

[70 FR 5568, Feb. 3, 2005, as amended at 79 FR 62336, Oct. 17, 2014]

§110.20 **Prohibition on contributions, donations, expenditures, independent expenditures, and disbursements by foreign nationals (52 U.S.C. 30121, 36 U.S.C. 510).**

(a) *Definitions.* For purposes of this section, the following definitions apply:

(1) *Disbursement* has the same meaning as in 11 CFR 300.2(d).

(2) *Donation* has the same meaning as in 11 CFR 300.2(e).

(3) *Foreign national* means—

(i) A foreign principal, as defined in 22 U.S.C. 611(b); or

(ii) An individual who is not a citizen of the United States and who is not lawfully admitted for permanent residence, as defined in 8 U.S.C. 1101(a)(20); however,

(iii) *Foreign national* shall not include any individual who is a citizen of the United States, or who is a national of the United States as defined in 8 U.S.C. 1101(a)(22).

(4) *Knowingly* means that a person must:

(i) Have actual knowledge that the source of the funds solicited, accepted or received is a foreign national;

(ii) Be aware of facts that would lead a reasonable person to conclude that there is a substantial probability that the source of the funds solicited, accepted or received is a foreign national; or

(iii) Be aware of facts that would lead a reasonable person to inquire whether the source of the funds solicited, accepted or received is a foreign national,

but the person failed to conduct a reasonable inquiry.

(5) For purposes of paragraph (a)(4) of this section, pertinent facts include, but are not limited to:

(i) The contributor or donor uses a foreign passport or passport number for identification purposes;

(ii) The contributor or donor provides a foreign address;

(iii) The contributor or donor makes a contribution or donation by means of a check or other written instrument drawn on a foreign bank or by a wire transfer from a foreign bank; or

(iv) The contributor or donor resides abroad.

(6) *Solicit* has the same meaning as in 11 CFR 300.2(m).

(7) *Safe Harbor.* For purposes of paragraph (a)(4)(iii) of this section, a person shall be deemed to have conducted a reasonable inquiry if he or she seeks and obtains copies of current and valid U.S. passport papers for U.S. citizens who are contributors or donors described in paragraphs (a)(5)(i) through (iv) of this section. No person may rely on this safe harbor if he or she has actual knowledge that the source of the funds solicited, accepted, or received is a foreign national.

(b) *Contributions and donations by foreign nationals in connection with elections.* A foreign national shall not, directly or indirectly, make a contribution or a donation of money or other thing of value, or expressly or impliedly promise to make a contribution or a donation, in connection with any Federal, State, or local election.

(c) *Contributions and donations by foreign nationals to political committees and organizations of political parties.* A foreign national shall not, directly or indirectly, make a contribution or donation to:

(1) A political committee of a political party, including a national party committee, a national congressional campaign committee, or a State, district, or local party committee, including a non-Federal account of a State, district, or local party committee, or

(2) An organization of a political party whether or not the organization is a political committee under 11 CFR 100.5.

(d) *Contributions and donations by foreign nationals for office buildings.* A foreign national shall not, directly or indirectly, make a contribution or donation to a committee of a political party for the purchase or construction of an office building. *See* 11 CFR 300.10 and 300.35.

(e) *Disbursements by foreign nationals for electioneering communications.* A foreign national shall not, directly or indirectly, make any disbursement for an electioneering communication as defined in 11 CFR 100.29.

(f) *Expenditures, independent expenditures, or disbursements by foreign nationals in connection with elections.* A foreign national shall not, directly or indirectly, make any expenditure, independent expenditure, or disbursement in connection with any Federal, State, or local election.

(g) *Solicitation, acceptance, or receipt of contributions and donations from foreign nationals.* No person shall knowingly solicit, accept, or receive from a foreign national any contribution or donation prohibited by paragraphs (b) through (d) of this section.

(h) *Providing substantial assistance.* (1) No person shall knowingly provide substantial assistance in the solicitation, making, acceptance, or receipt of a contribution or donation prohibited by paragraphs (b) through (d), and (g) of this section.

(2) No person shall knowingly provide substantial assistance in the making of an expenditure, independent expenditure, or disbursement prohibited by paragraphs (e) and (f) of this section.

(i) *Participation by foreign nationals in decisions involving election-related activities.* A foreign national shall not direct, dictate, control, or directly or indirectly participate in the decision-making process of any person, such as a corporation, labor organization, political committee, or political organization with regard to such person's Federal or non-Federal election-related activities, such as decisions concerning the making of contributions, donations, expenditures, or disbursements in connection with elections for any Federal, State, or local office or decisions concerning the administration of a political committee.

(j) *Donations by foreign nationals to inaugural committees.* A foreign national shall not, directly or indirectly, make a donation to an inaugural committee, as defined in 11 CFR 104.21(a)(1). No person shall knowingly accept from a foreign national any donation to an inaugural committee.

[67 FR 69950, Nov. 19, 2002, as amended at 69 FR 59780, Oct. 6, 2004]

PART 111—COMPLIANCE PROCEDURE (52 U.S.C. 30109, 30107(a))

Subpart A—Enforcement

AUTHORITY: 52 U.S.C. 30102(i), 30109, 30107(a), 30111(a)(8); 28 U.S.C. 2461 note; 31 U.S.C. 3701, 3711, 3716–3719, and 3720A, as amended; 31 CFR parts 285 and 900–904.

SOURCE: 45 FR 15120, Mar. 7, 1980, unless otherwise noted.

Subpart A—Enforcement

§ 111.1   Scope (52 U.S.C. 30109).

These regulations provide procedures for processing possible violations of the Federal Election Campaign Act of 1971, as amended (52 U.S.C. 30101, *et seq.*) and chapters 95 and 96 of the Internal Revenue Code of 1954 (26 U.S.C. 9001, *et seq.* and 9031 *et seq.*).

[45 FR 15120, Mar. 7, 1980, as amended at 79 FR 77847, Dec. 29, 2014]

§ 111.2   Computation of time.

(a) *General rule.* In computing any period of time prescribed or allowed by this part, the day of the act, event, or default from which the designated period of time begins to run shall not be included. The last day of the period so computed shall be included, unless it is a Saturday, a Sunday, or a legal holiday. As used in this section, the term *legal holiday* includes New Year's Day, President's Day, Memorial Day, Independence Day, Labor Day, Columbus Day, Veterans Day, Thanksgiving Day, Christmas Day, and any other day appointed as a holiday for employees of the United States by the President or the Congress of the United States.

(b) *Special rule for periods less than seven days.* When the period of time prescribed or allowed is less than seven (7) days, intermediate Saturdays, Sundays, and legal holidays shall be excluded in the computation.

(c) *Special rule for service by mail.* Whenever the Commission or any person has the right or is required to do some act within a prescribed period after the service of any paper by or upon the Commission or such person and the paper is served by or upon Commission or such person by mail, three (3) days shall be added to the prescribed period.

§ 111.3   Initiation of compliance matters (52 U.S.C. 30109(a)(1), (2)).

(a) Compliance matters may be initiated by a complaint or on the basis of information ascertained by the Commission in the normal course of carrying out its supervisory responsibilities.

(b) Matters initiated by complaint are subject to the provisions of 11 CFR

111.4 through 111.7. Matters initiated on the basis of information ascertained by the Commission in the normal course of carrying out its supervisory responsibilities are subject to the provisions of 11 CFR 111.8. All compliance matters are subject to the provisions of 11 CFR 111.2 and 111.9 through 111.23.

§ 111.4 Complaints (52 U.S.C. 30109(a)(1)).

(a) Any person who believes that a violation of any statute or regulation over which the Commission has jurisdiction has occurred or is about to occur may file a complaint in writing to the General Counsel of the Federal Election Commission at the street address identified in the definition of "Commission" in § 1.2. If possible, three (3) copies should be submitted.

(b) A complaint shall comply with the following:

(1) It shall provide the full name and address of the complainant; and

(2) The contents of the complaint shall be sworn to and signed in the presence of a notary public and shall be notarized.

(c) All statements made in a complaint are subject to the statutes governing perjury and to 18 U.S.C. 1001. The complaint should differentiate between statements based upon personal knowledge and statements based upon information and belief.

(d) The complaint should conform to the following provisions:

(1) It should clearly identify as a respondent each person or entity who is alleged to have committed a violation;

(2) Statements which are not based upon personal knowledge should be accompanied by an identification of the source of information which gives rise to the complainants belief in the truth of such statements;

(3) It should contain a clear and concise recitation of the facts which describe a violation of a statute or regulation over which the Commission has jurisdiction; and

(4) It should be accompanied by any documentation supporting the facts alleged if such documentation is known of, or available to, the complainant.

[45 FR 15120, Mar. 7, 1980, as amended at 50 FR 50778, Dec. 12, 1985; 82 FR 60853, Dec. 26, 2017]

§ 111.5 Initial complaint processing; notification (52 U.S.C. 30109(a)(1)).

(a) Upon receipt of a complaint, the General Counsel shall review the complaint for substantial compliance with the technical requirements of 11 CFR 111.4, and, if it complies with those requirements shall within five (5) days after receipt notify each respondent that the complaint has been filed, advise them of Commission compliance procedures, and enclose a copy of the complaint.

(b) If a complaint does not comply with the requirements of 11 CFR 111.4, the General Counsel shall so notify the complainant and any person(s) or entity(ies) identified therein as respondent(s), within the five (5) day period specified in 11 CFR 111.5(a), that no action shall be taken on the basis of that complaint. A copy of the complaint shall be enclosed with the notification to each respondent.

§ 111.6 Opportunity to demonstrate that no action should be taken on complaint-generated matters (52 U.S.C. 30109 (a)(1)).

(a) A respondent shall be afforded an opportunity to demonstrate that no action should be taken on the basis of a complaint by submitting, within fifteen (15) days from receipt of a copy of the complaint, a letter or memorandum setting forth reasons why the Commission should take no action.

(b) The Commission shall not take any action, or make any finding, against a respondent other than action dismissing the complaint, unless it has considered such response or unless no such response has been served upon the Commission within the fifteen (15) day period specified in 11 CFR 111.6(a).

§ 111.7 General Counsel's recommendation on complaint-generated matters (52 U.S.C. 30109(a)(1).

(a) Following either the expiration of the fifteen (15) day period specified by 11 CFR 111.6(a) or the receipt of a response as specified by 11 CFR 111.6(a), whichever occurs first, the General Counsel may recommend to the Commission whether or not it should find reason to believe that a respondent has committed or is about to commit a violation of statutes or regulations over which the Commission has jurisdiction.

(b) The General Counsel may recommend that the Commission find that there is no reason to believe that a violation has been committed or is about to be committed, or that the Commission otherwise dismiss a complaint without regard to the provisions of 11 CFR 111.6(a).

§111.8 Internally generated matters; referrals (52 U.S.C. 30109(a)(2)).

(a) On the basis of information ascertained by the Commission in the normal course of carrying out its supervisory responsibilities, or on the basis of a referral from an agency of the United States or of any state, the General Counsel may recommend in writing that the Commission find reason to believe that a person or entity has committed or is about to commit a violation of statutes or regulations over which the Commission has jurisdiction.

(b) If the Commission finds reason to believe that a violation has occurred or is about to occur the notification to respondent required by 11 CFR 111.9(a) shall include a copy of a staff report setting forth the legal basis and the alleged facts which support the Commission's action.

(c) Prior to taking any action pursuant to this section against any person who has failed to file a disclosure report required by 11 CFR 104.5(a)(1)(iii) for the calendar quarter immediately preceding the election involved or by §104.5(a)(1)(i), the Commission shall notify such person of failure to file the required reports. If a satisfactory response is not received within four (4) business days, the Commission shall publish before the election the name of the person and the report or reports such person has failed to file.

(d) Notwithstanding §§111.9 through 111.19, for violations of 52 U.S.C. 30104(a),the Commission, when appropriate, may review internally generated matters under subpart B of this part.

[45 FR 15120, Mar. 7, 1980, as amended at 45 FR 21210, Apr. 1, 1980; 65 FR 31794, May 19, 2000; 79 FR 77848, Dec. 29, 2014]

§111.9 The reason to believe finding; notification (52 U.S.C. 30109(a)(2)).

(a) If the Commission, either after reviewing a complaint-generated recommendation as described in 11 CFR 111.7 and any response of a respondent submitted pursuant to 11 CFR 111.6, or after reviewing an internally-generated recommendation as described in 11 CFR 111.8, determines by an affirmative vote of four (4) of its members that it has reason to believe that a respondent has violated a statute or regulation over which the Commission has jurisdiction, its Chairman or Vice Chairman shall notify such respondent of the Commission's finding by letter, setting forth the sections of the statute or regulations alleged to have been violated and the alleged factual basis supporting the finding.

(b) If the Commission finds no reason to believe, or otherwise terminates its proceedings, the General Counsel shall so advise both complainant and respondent by letter.

§111.10 Investigation (52 U.S.C. 30109 (a)(2)).

(a) An investigation shall be conducted in any case in which the Commission finds reason to believe that a violation of a statute or regulation over which the Commission has jurisdiction has occurred or is about to occur.

(b) In its investigation, the Commission may utilize the provisions of 11 CFR 111.11 through 111.15. The investigation may include, but is not limited to, field investigations, audits, and other methods of information-gathering.

§111.11 Written questions under order (52 U.S.C. 30107(a)(1)).

The Commission may authorize its Chairman or Vice Chairman to issue an order requiring any person to submit sworn written answers to written questions and may specify a date by which such answers must be submitted.

§111.12 Subpoenas and subpoenas duces tecum; depositions (52 U.S.C. 30107(a)(3), (4)).

(a) The Commission may authorize its Chairman or Vice Chairman to issue subpoenas requiring the attendance and testimony of any person by deposition and to issue subpoenas duces tecum for the production of documentary or other tangible evidence in connection with a deposition or otherwise.

(b) If oral testimony is ordered to be taken by deposition or documents are ordered to be produced, the subpoena shall so state and shall advise the deponent or person subpoenaed that all testimony will be under oath. A deposition may be taken before any person having the power to administer oaths.

(c) The Federal Rules of Civil Procedure, Rule 30(e), shall govern the opportunity to review and sign depositions taken pursuant to this section.

§ 111.13 Service of subpoenas, orders and notifications (52 U.S.C. 30107(a)(3), (4)).

(a) Service of a subpoena, order or notification upon a person named therein shall be made by delivering a copy to that person in the manner described by 11 CFR 111.13 (b), (c), and (d). In the case of subpoenas, fees for one day's attendance and mileage shall be tendered as specified in 11 CFR 111.14.

(b) Whenever service is to be made upon a person who has advised the Commission of representation by an attorney pursuant to 11 CFR 111.23, the service shall be made upon the attorney by any of the methods specified in 11 CFR 111.13(c).

(c) Delivery of subpoenas, orders and notifications to a natural person may be made by handing a copy to the person, or leaving a copy at his or her office with the person in charge thereof, by leaving a copy at his or her dwelling place or usual place of abode with some person of suitable age and discretion residing therein, or by mailing a copy by registered or certified mail to his or her last known address, or by any other method whereby actual notice is given.

(d) When the person to be served is not a natural person delivery of subpoenas, orders and notifications may be made by mailing a copy by registered or certified mail to the person at its place of business or by handing a copy to a registered agent for service, or to any officer, director, or agent in charge of any office of such person, or by mailing a copy by registered or certified mail to such representative at his or her last known address, or by any other method whereby actual notice is given.

§ 111.14 Witness fees and mileage (52 U.S.C. 30107 (a)(5)).

Witnesses subpoenaed to appear for depositions shall be paid the same fees and mileage as witnesses in the courts of the United States. Such fees may be tendered at the time the witness appears for such deposition, or within a reasonable time thereafter.

§ 111.15 Motions to quash or modify a subpoena (52 U.S.C. 30107(a)(3), (4)).

(a) Any person to whom a subpoena is directed may, prior to the time specified therein for compliance, but in no event more than 5 days after the date of receipt of such subpoena, apply to the Commission to quash or modify such subpoena, accompanying such application with a brief statement of the reasons therefor. Motions to quash shall be filed with the General Counsel of the Federal Election Commission at the street address identified in the definition of "Commission" in §1.2. If possible, three (3) copies should be submitted.

(b) The Commission may deny the application or quash the subpoena or modify the subpoena.

(c) The person subpoenaed and the General Counsel may agree to change the date, time, or place of a deposition or for the production of documents without affecting the force and effect of the subpoena, but such agreements shall be confirmed in writing.

[45 FR 15120, Mar. 7, 1980, as amended at 50 FR 50778, Dec. 12, 1985; 82 FR 60853, Dec. 26, 2017]

§ 111.16 The probable cause to believe recommendation; briefing procedures (52 U.S.C. 30109 (a)(3)).

(a) Upon completion of the investigation, the General Counsel shall prepare a brief setting forth his or her position on the factual and legal issues of the case and containing a recommendation on whether or not the Commission should find probable cause to believe that a violation has occurred or is about to occur.

(b) The General Counsel shall notify each respondent of the recommendation and enclose a copy of his or her brief.

(c) Within fifteen (15) days from receipt of the General Counsel's brief, respondent may file a brief with the Commission Secretary, Federal Election Commission, at the street address identified in the definition of "Commission" in §1.2, setting forth respondent's position on the factual and legal issues of the case. If possible, ten (10) copies of such brief should be filed with the Commission Secretary and three (3) copies should be submitted to the General Counsel, Federal Election Commission, at the street address identified in the definition of "Commission" in §1.2.

(d) After reviewing the respondent's brief, the General Counsel shall advise the Commission in writing whether he or she intends to proceed with the recommendation or to withdraw the recommendation from Commission consideration.

[45 FR 15120, Mar. 7, 1980, as amended at 50 FR 50778, Dec. 12, 1985; 82 FR 60853, Dec. 26, 2017]

§111.17 The probable cause to believe finding; notification (52 U.S.C. 30109(a)(4)).

(a) If the Commission, after having found reason to believe and after following the procedures set forth in 11 CFR 111.16, determines by an affirmative vote of four (4) of its members that there is probable cause to believe that a respondent has violated a statute or regulation over which the Commission has jurisdiction, the Commission shall authorize the General Counsel to so notify the respondent by letter.

(b) If the Commission finds no probable cause to believe or otherwise orders a termination of Commission proceedings, it shall authorize the General Counsel to so notify both respondent and complainant by letter.

§111.18 Conciliation (52 U.S.C. 30109(a)(4)).

(a) Upon a Commission finding of probable cause to believe, the Office of General Counsel shall attempt to correct or prevent the violation by informal methods of conference conciliation and persuasion, and shall attempt to reach a tentative conciliation agreement with the respondent.

(b) A conciliation agreement is not binding upon either party unless and until it is signed by the respondent and by the General Counsel upon approval by the affirmative vote of four (4) members of the Commission.

(c) If the probable cause to believe finding is made within forty-five days prior to any election, such conciliation attempt shall continue for at least fifteen (15) days from the date of such finding. In all other cases such attempts by the Commission shall continue for at least thirty (30) days, not to exceed ninety (90) days.

(d) Nothing in these regulations shall be construed to prevent the Commission from entering into a conciliation agreement with a respondent prior to a Commission finding of probable cause if a respondent indicates by letter to the General Counsel a desire to enter into negotiations directed towards reaching such a conciliation agreement. However, the Commission is not required to enter into any negotiations directed towards reaching a conciliation agreement unless and until it makes a finding of probable cause to believe. Any conciliation agreement reached under this subsection is subject to the provisions of subsection (b) of this section and shall have the same force and effect as a conciliation agreement reached after a Commission finding of probable cause to believe.

(e) If a conciliation agreement is reached between the Commission and the respondent, the General Counsel shall send a copy of the signed agreement to both complainant and respondent.

§111.19 Civil proceedings (52 U.S.C. 30109(a)(6)).

(a) If no conciliation agreement is finalized within the applicable minimum period specified by 11 CFR 111.18(c) the General Counsel may recommend to the Commission that the Commission authorize a civil action for relief in an appropriate court of the United States.

(b) Upon recommendation of the General Counsel, the Commission may, by an affirmative vote of four (4) of its members, authorize the General Counsel to commence a civil action for relief in an appropriate court of the United States.

(c) The provisions of 11 CFR 111.18(c) shall not preclude the Commission upon request of a respondent, from entering into a conciliation agreement even after a recommendation to file a civil action has been made pursuant to this section. Any conciliation agreement reached under this subsection is subject to the provisions of 11 CFR 111.18(b) and shall have the same force and effect as a conciliation agreement reached under 11 CFR 111.18(c).

§ 111.20 Public disclosure of Commission action (52 U.S.C. 30109(a)(4)).

(a) If the Commission makes a finding of no reason to believe or no probable cause to believe or otherwise terminates its proceedings, it shall make public such action and the basis therefor no later than thirty (30) days from the date on which the required notifications are sent to complainant and respondent.

(b) If a conciliation agreement is finalized, the Commission shall make public such conciliation agreement forthwith.

(c) For any compliance matter in which a civil action is commenced, the Commission will make public the non-exempt 52 U.S.C. 30109 investigatory materials in the enforcement and litigation files no later than thirty (30) days from the date on which the Commission sends the complainant and the respondent(s) the required notification of the final disposition of the civil action. The final disposition may consist of a judicial decision which is not reviewed by a higher court.

[45 FR 15120, Mar. 7, 1980, as amended at 65 FR 31794, May 19, 2000; 79 FR 77848, Dec. 29, 2014]

§ 111.21 Confidentiality (52 U.S.C. 30109(a)(12)).

(a) Except as provided in 11 CFR 111.20, no complaint filed with the Commission, nor any notification sent by the Commission, nor any investigation conducted by the Commission, nor any findings made by the Commission shall be made public by the Commission or by any person or entity without the written consent of the respondent with respect to whom the complaint was filed, the notification sent, the investigation conducted, or the finding made.

(b) Except as provided in 11 CFR 111.20(b), no action by the Commission or by any person, and no information derived in connection with conciliation efforts pursuant to 11 CFR 111.18, may be made public by the Commission except upon a written request by respondent and approval thereof by the Commission.

(c) Nothing in these regulations shall be construed to prevent the introduction of evidence in the courts of the United States which could properly be introduced pursuant to the Federal Rules of Evidence or Federal Rules of Civil Procedure.

§ 111.22 Ex parte communications.

(a) In order to avoid the possibility of prejudice, real or apparent, to the public interest in enforcement actions pending before the Commission pursuant to 11 CFR part 111, except to the extent required for the disposition of ex parte matters as required by law (for example, during the normal course of an investigation or a conciliation effort), no interested person outside the agency shall make or cause to be made to any Commissioner or any member of any Commissioner's staff any ex parte communication relative to the factual or legal merits of any enforcement action, nor shall any Commissioner or member of any Commissioner's staff make or entertain any such ex parte communications.

(b) The prohibition of this regulation shall apply from the time a complaint is filed with the Commission pursuant to 11 CFR part 111 or from the time that the Commission determines on the basis of information ascertained in the normal course of its supervisory responsibilities that it has reason to believe that a violation has occurred or may occur pursuant to 11 CFR part 111, and remains in force until the Commission has finally concluded all action with respect to the enforcement matter in question.

(c) Nothing in this section shall be construed to prohibit contact between a respondent or respondent's attorney and any attorney or staff member of the Office of General Counsel in the course of representing the Commission or the respondent with respect to an enforcement proceeding or civil action. No statement made by such a Commission attorney or staff member during any such communication shall bind or estop the Commission in any way.

§ 111.23   Representation by counsel; notification.

(a) If a respondent wishes to be represented by counsel with regard to any matter pending before the Commission, respondent shall so advise the Commission by sending a letter of representation signed by the respondent, which letter shall state the following:

(1) The name, address, and telephone number of the counsel;

(2) A statement authorizing such counsel to receive any and all notifications and other communications from the Commission on behalf of respondent.

(b) Upon receipt of a letter of representation, the Commission shall have no contact with respondent except through the designated counsel unless authorized in writing by respondent.

§ 111.24   Civil Penalties (52 U.S.C. 30109(a)(5), (6), (12), 28 U.S.C. 2461 nt.).

(a) Except as provided in 11 CFR part 111, subpart B and in paragraph (b) of this section, a civil penalty negotiated by the Commission or imposed by a court for a violation of the Act or chapters 95 or 96 of title 26 (26 U.S.C.) shall be as follows:

(1) Except as provided in paragraph (a)(2) of this section, in the case of a violation of the Act or chapters 95 or 96 of title 26 (26 U.S.C.), the civil penalty shall not exceed the greater of $19,446 or an amount equal to any contribution or expenditure involved in the violation.

(2) *Knowing and willful violations.* (i) In the case of a knowing and willful violation of the Act or chapters 95 or 96 of title 26 (26 U.S.C.), the civil penalty shall not exceed the greater of $41,484 or an amount equal to 200% of any contribution or expenditure involved in the violation.

(ii) Notwithstanding paragraph (a)(2)(i) of this section, in the case of a knowing and willful violation of 52 U.S.C. 30122,the civil penalty shall not be less than 300% of the amount of any contribution involved in the violation and shall not exceed the greater of $68,027 or 1,000% of the amount of any contribution involved in the violation.

(b) Any Commission member or employee, or any other person, who in violation of 52 U.S.C. 30109(a)(12)(A) makes public any notification or investigation under 52 U.S.C. 30109 without receiving the written consent of the person receiving such notification, or the person with respect to whom such investigation is made, shall be fined not more than $5,817. Any such member, employee, or other person who knowingly and willfully violates this provision shall be fined not more than $14,543.

[62 FR 11317, Mar. 12, 1997; 62 FR 18167, Apr. 14, 1997; 65 FR 31794, May 19, 2000; 67 FR 76977, Dec. 13, 2002; 70 FR 34635, June 15, 2005; 74 FR 31347, July 1, 2009; 78 FR 44420, July 24, 2013; 79 FR 77848, Dec. 29, 2014; 81 FR 41199, June 24, 2016; 82 FR 8987, Feb. 2, 2017; 82 FR 61141, Dec. 27, 2017]

Subpart B—Administrative Fines

SOURCE: 65 FR 31794, May 19, 2000, unless otherwise noted.

§ 111.30   When will subpart B apply?

Subpart B applies to violations of the reporting requirements of 52 U.S.C. 30104(a) committed by political committees and their treasurers that relate to the reporting periods that begin on or after July 14, 2000, and that end on or before the date specified by 52 U.S.C. 30109(a)(4)(C)(v). This subpart, however, does not apply to reports that relate to reporting periods that end between January 1, 2014, and January 21, 2014.

[79 FR 3303, Jan. 21, 2014, as amended at 79 FR 77848, Dec. 29, 2014]

§ 111.31   Does this subpart replace subpart A of this part for violations of the reporting requirements of 52 U.S.C. 30104(a)?

(a) No; §§ 111.1 through 111.8 and 111.20 through 111.24 shall apply to all compliance matters. This subpart will apply, rather than §§ 111.9 through 111.19, when the Commission, on the basis of information ascertained by the Commission in the normal course of carrying out its supervisory responsibilities, and when appropriate, determines that the compliance matter should be subject to this subpart. If the Commission determines that the violation should not be subject to this subpart, then the violation will be subject to all sections of subpart A of this part.

(b) Subpart B will apply to compliance matters resulting from a complaint filed pursuant to 11 CFR 111.4 through 111.7 if the complaint alleges a violation of 52 U.S.C. 30104(a). If the complaint alleges violations of any other provision of any statute or regulation over which the Commission has jurisdiction, subpart A will apply to the alleged violations of these other provisions.

[65 FR 31794, May 19, 2000, as amended at 79 FR 77848, Dec. 29, 2014]

§ 111.32 How will the Commission notify respondents of a reason to believe finding and a proposed civil money penalty?

If the Commission determines, by an affirmative vote of at least four (4) of its members, that it has reason to believe that a respondent has violated 52 U.S.C. 30104(a), the Chairman or Vice-Chairman shall notify such respondent of the Commission's finding. The written notification shall set forth the following:

(a) The alleged factual and legal basis supporting the finding including the type of report that was due, the filing deadline, the actual date filed (if filed), and the number of days the report was late (if filed);

(b) The applicable schedule of penalties;

(c) The number of times the respondent has been assessed a civil money penalty under this subpart during the current two-year election cycle and the prior two-year election cycle;

(d) The amount of the proposed civil money penalty based on the schedules of penalties set forth in 11 CFR 111.43 or 111.44; and

(e) An explanation of the respondent's right to challenge both the reason to believe finding and the proposed civil money penalty.

[65 FR 31794, May 19, 2000, as amended at 79 FR 77848, Dec. 29, 2014]

§ 111.33 What are the respondent's choices upon receiving the reason to believe finding and the proposed civil money penalty?

The respondent must either send payment in the amount of the proposed civil money penalty pursuant to 11 CFR 111.34 or submit a written response pursuant to 11 CFR 111.35.

§ 111.34 If the respondent decides to pay the civil money penalty and not to challenge the reason to believe finding, what should the respondent do?

(a) The respondent shall transmit payment in the amount of the civil money penalty to the Commission within forty (40) days of the Commission's reason to believe finding.

(b) Upon receipt of the respondent's payment, the Commission shall send the respondent a final determination that the respondent has violated the statute or regulations and the amount of the civil money penalty and an acknowledgment of the respondent's payment.

§ 111.35 If the respondent decides to challenge the alleged violation or proposed civil money penalty, what should the respondent do?

(a) To challenge a reason to believe finding or proposed civil money penalty, the respondent must submit a written response to the Commission within forty (40) days of the Commission's reason to believe finding.

(b) The respondent's written response must assert at least one of the following grounds for challenging the reason to believe finding or proposed civil money penalty:

(1) The Commission's reason to believe finding is based on a factual error including, but not limited to, the committee was not required to file the report, or the committee timely filed the report in accordance with 11 CFR 100.19;

(2) The Commission improperly calculated the civil money penalty; or

(3) The respondent used best efforts to file in a timely manner in that:

(i) The respondent was prevented from filing in a timely manner by reasonably unforeseen circumstances that were beyond the control of the respondent; and

(ii) The respondent filed no later than 24 hours after the end of these circumstances.

(c) Circumstances that will be considered reasonably unforeseen and beyond the control of respondent include, but are not limited to:

(1) A failure of Commission computers or Commission-provided software despite the respondent seeking technical assistance from Commission personnel and resources;

(2) A widespread disruption of information transmissions over the Internet not caused by any failure of the Commission's or respondent's computer systems or Internet service provider; and

(3) Severe weather or other disaster-related incident.

(d) Circumstances that will not be considered reasonably unforeseen and beyond the control of respondent include, but are not limited to:

(1) Negligence;

(2) Delays caused by committee vendors or contractors;

(3) Illness, inexperience, or unavailability of the treasurer or other staff;

(4) Committee computer, software or Internet service provider failures;

(5) A committee's failure to know filing dates; and

(6) A committee's failure to use filing software properly.

(e) Respondent's written response must detail the factual basis supporting its challenge and include supporting documentation.

[72 FR 14667, Mar. 29, 2007]

§111.36 Who will review the respondent's written response?

(a) A reviewing officer shall review the respondent's written response. The reviewing officer shall be a person who has not been involved in the reason to believe finding.

(b) The reviewing officer shall review the reason to believe finding with supporting documentation and the respondent's written response with supporting documentation. The reviewing officer may request supplemental information from the respondent and/or the Commission staff. The respondent shall submit the supplemental information to the reviewing officer within a time specified by the reviewing officer. The reviewing officer will be entitled to draw an adverse inference from the failure by the respondent to submit the supplemental information.

(c) All documents required to be submitted by the respondents pursuant to this section and §111.35 should be submitted in the form of affidavits or declarations.

(d) If the Commission staff, after the respondent files a written response pursuant to §111.35, forwards any additional documents pertaining to the matter to the reviewing officer for his or her examination, the reviewing officer shall also furnish a copy of the document(s) to the respondents.

(e) Upon completion of the review, the reviewing officer shall forward a written recommendation to the Commission along with all documents required under this section and 11 CFR 111.32 and 111.35.

(f) The reviewing office shall also forward a copy of the recommendation to the respondent. The respondent may file with the Commission Secretary a written response to the recommendation within ten (10) days of transmittal of the recommendation. This response may not raise any arguments not raised in the respondent's original written response or not directly responsive to the reviewing officer's recommendation.

§111.37 What will the Commission do once it receives the respondent's written response and the reviewing officer's recommendation?

(a) If the Commission, after having found reason to believe and after reviewing the respondent's written response and the reviewing officer's recommendation, determines by an affirmative vote of at least four (4) of its members, that the respondent has violated 52 U.S.C. 30104(a) and the amount of the civil money penalty, the Commission shall authorize the reviewing officer to notify the respondent by letter of its final determination.

(b) If the Commission, after reviewing the reason to believe finding, the respondent's written response, and the reviewing officer's written recommendation, determines by an affirmative vote of at least four (4) of its members, that no violation has occurred (either because the Commission had based its reason to believe finding on a factual error or because the respondent used best efforts to file in a timely manner) or otherwise terminates its proceedings, the Commission shall authorize the reviewing officer to notify the respondent by letter of its final determination.

(c) The Commission will modify the proposed civil money penalty only if the respondent is able to demonstrate that the amount of the proposed civil money penalty was calculated on an incorrect basis.

(d) When the Commission makes a final determination under this section, the statement of reasons for the Commission action will, unless otherwise indicated by the Commission, consist of the reasons provided by the reviewing officer for the recommendation, if approved by the Commission, although statements setting forth additional or different reasons may also be issued. If the reviewing officer's recommendation is modified or not approved, the Commission will indicate the grounds for its action and one or more statements of reasons may be issued.

[65 FR 31794, May 19, 2000, as amended at 72 FR 14668, Mar. 29, 2007; 79 FR 77848, Dec. 29, 2014]

§ 111.38 Can the respondent appeal the Commission's final determination?

Yes; within thirty (30) days of receipt of the Commission's final determination under 11 CFR 111.37, the respondent may submit a written petition to the district court of the United States for the district in which the respondent resides, or transacts business, requesting that the final determination be modified or set aside. The respondent's failure to raise an argument in a timely fashion during the administrative process shall be deemed a waiver of the respondent's right to present such argument in a petition to the district court under 52 U.S.C. 30109.

[65 FR 31794, May 19, 2000, as amended at 79 FR 77848, Dec. 29, 2014]

§ 111.39 When must the respondent pay the civil money penalty?

(a) If the respondent does not submit a written petition to the district court of the United States, the respondent must remit payment of the civil money penalty within thirty (30) days of receipt of the Commission's final determination under 11 CFR 111.37.

(b) If the respondent submits a written petition to the district court of the United States and, upon the final disposition of the civil action, is required to pay a civil money penalty, the respondent shall remit payment of the civil money penalty to the Commission within thirty (30) days of the final disposition of the civil action. The final disposition may consist of a judicial decision which is not reviewed by a higher court.

(c) Failure to pay the civil money penalty may result in the commencement of collection action under 31 U.S.C. 3701 et seq. (1996), or a civil suit pursuant to 52 U.S.C. 30109(a)(6)(A), or any other legal action deemed necessary by the Commission.

[65 FR 31794, May 19, 2000, as amended at 79 FR 77848, Dec. 29, 2014]

§ 111.40 What happens if the respondent does not pay the civil money penalty pursuant to 11 CFR 111.34 and does not submit a written response to the reason to believe finding pursuant to 11 CFR 111.35?

(a) If the Commission, after the respondent has failed to pay the civil money penalty and has failed to submit a written response, determines by an affirmative vote of at least four (4) of its members that the respondent has violated 52 U.S.C. 30104(a) and determines the amount of the civil money penalty, the respondent shall be notified by letter of its final determination.

(b) The respondent shall transmit payment of the civil money penalty to the Commission within thirty (30) days of receipt of the Commission's final determination.

(c) Failure to pay the civil money penalty may result in the commencement of collection action under 31 U.S.C. 3701 et seq. (1996), or a civil suit pursuant to 52 U.S.C. 30109(a)(6)(A), or any other legal action deemed necessary by the Commission.

[65 FR 31794, May 19, 2000, as amended at 79 FR 77848, Dec. 29, 2014]

§ 111.41 [Reserved]

§ 111.42 Will the enforcement file be made available to the public?

(a) Yes; the Commission shall make the enforcement file available to the public.

(b) If neither the Commission nor the respondent commences a civil action, the Commission shall make the enforcement file available to the public pursuant to 11 CFR 4.4(a)(3).

(c) If a civil action is commenced, the Commission shall make the enforcement file available pursuant to 11 CFR 111.20(c).

§ 111.43 What are the schedules of penalties?

(a) The civil money penalty for all reports that are filed late or not filed, except election sensitive reports and pre-election reports under 11 CFR 104.5, shall be calculated in accordance with the following schedule of penalties:

If the level of activity in the report was:	And the report was filed late, the civil money penalty is:	Or the report was not filed, the civil money penalty is:
$1–4,999.99 [a]	[$34 + ($6 × Number of days late)] × [1 + (.25 × Number of previous violations)].	$333 × [1 + (.25 × Number of previous violations)].
$5,000–9,999.99	[$66 + ($6 × Number of days late)] × [1 + (.25 × Number of previous violations)].	$400 × [1 + (.25 × Number of previous violations)].
$10,000–24,999.99	[$142 + ($6 × Number of days late)] × [1 + (.25 × Number of previous violations)].	$667 × [1 + (.25 × Number of previous violations)].
$25,000–49,999.99	[$283 + ($27 × Number of days late)] × [1 + (.25 × Number of previous violations)].	$1200 × [1 + (.25 × Number of previous violations)].
$50,000–74,999.99	[$426 + ($107 × Number of days late)] × [1 + (.25 × Number of previous violations)].	$3828 × [1 + (.25 × Number of previous violations)].
$75,000–99,999.99	[$567 + ($142 × Number of days late)] × [1 + (.25 × Number of previous violations)].	$4961 × [1 + (.25 × Number of previous violations)].
$100,000–149,999.99	[$850 + ($178 × Number of days late)] × [1 + (.25 × Number of previous violations)].	$6380 × [1 + (.25 × Number of previous violations)].
$150,000–199,999.99	[$1135 + ($212 × Number of days late)] × [1 + (.25 × Number of previous violations)].	$7797 × [1 + (.25 × Number of previous violations)].
$200,000–249,999.99	[$1417 + ($248 × Number of days late)] × [1 + (.25 × Number of previous violations)].	$9214 × [1 + (.25 × Number of previous violations)].
$250,000–349,999.99	[$2127 + ($283 × Number of days late)] × [1 + (.25 × Number of previous violations)].	$11,341 × [1 + (.25 × Number of previous violations)].
$350,000–449,999.99	[$2836 + ($283 × Number of days late)] × [1 + (.25 × Number of previous violations)].	$12,758 × [1 + (.25 × Number of previous violations)].
$450,000–549,999.99	[$3544 + ($283 × Number of days late)] × [1 + (.25 × Number of previous violations)].	$13,466 × [1 + (.25 × Number of previous violations)].
$550,000–649,999.99	[$4253 + ($283 × Number of days late)] × [1 + (.25 × Number of previous violations)].	$14,177 × [1 + (.25 × Number of previous violations)].
$650,000–749,999.99	[$4961 + ($283 × Number of days late)] × [1 + (.25 × Number of previous violations)].	$14,885 × [1 + (.25 × Number of previous violations)].
$750,000–849,999.99	[$5670 + ($283 × Number of days late)] × [1 + (.25 × Number of previous violations)].	$15,594 × [1 + (.25 × Number of previous violations)].
$850,000–949,999.99	[$6380 + ($283 × Number of days late)] × [1 + (.25 × Number of previous violations)].	$16,302 × [1 + (.25 × Number of previous violations)].
$950,000 or over	[$7088 + ($283 × Number of days late)] × [1 + (.25 × Number of previous violations)].	$17,011 × [1 + (.25 × Number of previous violations)].

[a] The civil money penalty for a respondent who does not have any previous violations will not exceed the level of activity in the report.

(b) The civil money penalty for election sensitive reports that are filed late or not filed shall be calculated in accordance with the following schedule of penalties:

If the level of activity in the report was:	And the report was filed late, the civil money penalty is:	Or the report was not filed, the civil money penalty is:
$1–$4,999.99 [a]	[$66 + ($13 × Number of days late)] × [1 + (.25 × Number of previous violations)].	$667 × [1 + (.25 × Number of previous violations)].
$5,000–$9,999.99	[$134 + ($13 × Number of days late)] × [1 + (.25 × Number of previous violations)].	$800 × [1 + (.25 × Number of previous violations)].
$10,000–24,999.99	[$200 + ($13 × Number of days late)] × [1 + (.25 × Number of previous violations)].	$1200 × [1 + (.25 × Number of previous violations)].

If the level of activity in the report was:	And the report was filed late, the civil money penalty is:	Or the report was not filed, the civil money penalty is:
$25,000–49,999.99	[$426 + ($34 × Number of days late)] × [1 + (.25 × Number of previous violations)].	$1866 × [1 + (.25 × Number of previous violations)].
$50,000–74,999.99	[$638 + ($107 × Number of days late)] × [1 + (.25 × Number of previous violations)].	$4253 × [1 + (.25 × Number of previous violations)].
$75,000–99,999.99	[$850 + ($142 × Number of days late)] × [1 + (.25 × Number of previous violations)].	$5670 × [1 + (.25 × Number of previous violations)].
$100,000–149,999.99	[$1276 + ($178 × Number of days late)] × [1 + (.25 × Number of previous violations)].	$7088 × [1 + (.25 × Number of previous violations)].
$150,000–199,999.99	[$1701 + ($212 × Number of days late)] × [1 + (.25 × Number of previous violations)].	$8505 × [1 + (.25 × Number of previous violations)].
$200,000–249,999.99	[$2127 + ($248 × Number of days late)] × [1 + (.25 × Number of previous violations)].	$10,633 × [1 + (.25 × Number of previous violations)].
$250,000–349,999.99	[$3190 + ($283 × Number of days late)] × [1 + (.25 × Number of previous violations)].	$12,758 × [1 + (.25 × Number of previous violations)].
$350,000–449,999.99	[$4253 + ($283 × Number of days late)] × [1 + (.25 × Number of previous violations)].	$14,177 × [1 + (.25 × Number of previous violations)].
$450,000–549,999.99	[$5316 + ($283 × Number of days late)] × [1 + (.25 × Number of previous violations)].	$15,594 × [1 + (.25 × Number of previous violations)].
$550,000–649,999.99	[$6380 + ($283 × Number of days late)] × [1 + (.25 × Number of previous violations)].	$17,011 × [1 + (.25 × Number of previous violations)].
$650,000–749,999.99	[$7442 + ($283 × Number of days late)] × [1 + (.25 × Number of previous violations)].	$18,430 × [1 + (.25 × Number of previous violations)].
$750,000–849,999.99	[$8505 + ($283 × Number of days late)] × [1 + (.25 × Number of previous violations)].	$19,846 × [1 + (.25 × Number of previous violations)].
$850,000–949,999.99	[$9569 + ($283 × Number of days late)] × [1 + (.25 × Number of previous violations)].	$21,263 × [1 + (.25 × Number of previous violations)].
$950,000 or over	[$10,633 + ($283 × Number of days late)] × [1 + (.25 × Number of previous violations)].	$22,682 × [1 + (.25 × Number of previous violations)].

[a] The civil money penalty for a respondent who does not have any previous violations will not exceed the level of activity in the report.

(c) If the respondent fails to file a required report and the Commission cannot calculate the level of activity under paragraph (d) of this section, then the civil money penalty shall be $7,797.

(d) *Definitions.* For this section only, the following definitions will apply:

(1) *Election Sensitive Reports* means third quarter reports due on October 15th before the general election (for all committees required to file this report except committees of candidates who do not participate in that general election); monthly reports due October 20th before the general election (for all committees required to file this report except committees of candidates who do not participate in that general election); and pre-election reports for primary, general, and special elections under 11 CFR 104.5.

(2) *Estimated level of activity* means:

(i) For an authorized committee, total receipts and disbursements reported in the current two-year election cycle divided by the number of reports filed to date covering the activity in the current two-year election cycle. If the respondent has not filed a report covering activity in the current two-year election cycle, estimated level of activity for an authorized committee means total receipts and disbursements reported in the prior two-year election cycle divided by the number of reports filed covering the activity in the prior two-year election cycle.

(ii)(A) For an unauthorized committee, estimated level of activity is calculated as follows: [(Total receipts and disbursements reported in the current two-year cycle)—(Transfers received from non-Federal account(s) as reported on Line 18(a) of FEC Form 3X Disbursements for the non-Federal share of operating expenditures attributable to allocated Federal/non-Federal activity as reported on Line 21(a)(ii) of FEC Form 3X)] ÷ Number of reports filed to date covering the activity in the current two-year election cycle.

(B) If the unauthorized committee has not filed a report covering activity in the current two-year election cycle, the estimated level of activity is calculated as follows: [(Total receipts and disbursements reported in the prior two-year election cycle)—(Transfers received from non-Federal account(s) as reported on Line 18(a) of FEC Form 3X

Disbursements for the non-Federal share of operating expenditures attributable to allocated Federal/non-Federal activity as reported on Line 21(a)(ii) of FEC Form 3X)] ÷ Number of reports filed covering the activity in the prior two-year election cycle.

(3) *Level of activity* means:

(i) For an authorized committee, the total amount of receipts and disbursements for the period covered by the late report. If the report is not filed, the level of activity is the estimated level of activity as set forth in paragraph (d)(2)(i) of this section.

(ii) For an unauthorized committee, the total amount of receipts and disbursements for the period covered by the late report minus the total of: Transfers received from non-Federal account(s) as reported on Line 18(a) of FEC Form 3X and disbursements for the non-Federal share of operating expenditures attributable to allocated Federal/non-Federal activity as reported on Line 21(a)(ii) of FEC Form 3X for the period covered by the late report. If the report is not filed, the level of activity is the estimated level of activity as set forth in paragraph (d)(2)(ii) of this section.

(4) *Number of previous violations* means all prior final civil money penalties assessed under this subpart during the current two-year election cycle and the prior two-year election cycle.

(e) For purposes of the schedules of penalties in paragraphs (a) and (b) of this section,

(1) Reports that are not election sensitive reports are considered to be filed late if they are filed after their due dates but within thirty (30) days of their due dates. These reports are considered to be not filed if they are filed after thirty (30) days of their due dates or not filed at all.

(2) Election sensitive reports are considered to be filed late if they are filed after their due dates but prior to four (4) days before the primary election for pre-primary reports, prior to four (4) days before the special election for pre-special election reports, or prior to four (4) days before the general election for all other election sensitive reports. These reports are considered to be not filed if they are not filed prior to four (4) days before the primary

election for pre-primary reports, prior to four (4) days before the special election for pre-special election reports or prior to four (4) days before the general election for all other election sensitive reports.

[65 FR 31794, May 19, 2000, as amended at 68 FR 12577, Mar. 17, 2003; 70 FR 34636, June 15, 2005; 74 FR 31348, July 1, 2009; 74 FR 37161, July 28, 2009; 78 FR 44421, July 24, 2013; 81 FR 41199, June 24, 2016; 82 FR 8987, Feb. 2, 2017; 82 FR 61141, Dec. 27, 2017]

§111.44 What is the schedule of penalties for 48-hour notices that are not filed or are filed late?

(a) If the respondent fails to file timely a notice regarding contribution(s) received after the 20th day but more than 48 hours before the election as required under 52 U.S.C. 30104(a)(6), the civil money penalty will be calculated as follows:

(1) Civil money penalty = $142 + (.10 × amount of the contribution(s) not timely reported).

(2) The civil money penalty calculated in paragraph (a)(1) of this section shall be increased by twenty-five percent (25%) for each prior violation.

(b) For purposes of this section, prior violation means a final civil money penalty that has been assessed against the respondent under this subpart in the current two-year election cycle or the prior two-year election cycle.

[65 FR 31794, May 19, 2000, as amended at 70 FR 34636, June 15, 2005; 74 FR 31349, July 1, 2009; 79 FR 77848, Dec. 29, 2014; 81 FR 41200, June 24, 2016; 82 FR 8989, Feb. 2, 2017; 82 FR 61143, Dec. 27, 2017]

§111.45 [Reserved]

§111.46 How will the respondent be notified of actions taken by the Commission and the reviewing officer?

If a statement designating counsel has been filed in accordance with 11 CFR 111.23, all notifications and other communications to a respondent provided for in subpart B of this part will be sent to designated counsel. If a statement designating counsel has not been filed, all notifications and other communications to a respondent provided for in subpart B of this part will be sent to respondent political committee and its treasurer at the political committee's address as listed in the most recent Statement of Organization, or amendment thereto, filed with the Commission in accordance with 11 CFR 102.2.

[68 FR 12580, Mar. 17, 2003]

Subpart C—Collection of Debts Arising From Enforcement and Administration of Campaign Finance Laws

SOURCE: 75 FR 19876, Apr. 16, 2010, unless otherwise noted.

§ 111.50 Purpose and scope.

Subpart C prescribes standards and procedures under which the Commission will collect and dispose of certain debts owed to the United States, as described in 11 CFR 111.51. The regulations in this subpart implement the Debt Collection Improvement Act of 1996, 31 U.S.C. 3701, 3711, and 3716–3720A, as amended; and the Federal Claims Collection Standards, 31 CFR parts 900–904. The activities covered include: The collection of claims of any amount; compromising claims; suspending or terminating the collection of claims; and referring debts to the U.S. Department of the Treasury for collection action.

§ 111.51 Debts that are covered.

(a) The procedures of this subpart C of part 111 apply to claims for payment or debt arising from, or ancillary to, any action undertaken by or on behalf of the Commission in furtherance of efforts to ensure compliance with the Federal Election Campaign Act, 52 U.S.C. 30101 *et seq.*, as amended, and to administer the Presidential Election Campaign Fund Act, 26 U.S.C. 9001 *et seq.*, or the Presidential Primary Matching Payment Account Act, 26 U.S.C. 9031 *et seq.*, and Commission regulations, including:

(1) Negotiated civil penalties in enforcement matters and alternative dispute resolution matters;

(2) Civil money penalties assessed under the administrative fines program;

(3) Claims reduced to judgment in the courts and that are no longer in litigation;

(4) Repayments of public funds under the Presidential Election Campaign Fund Act, 26 U.S.C. 9001 *et seq.;* or

(5) Repayment of public funds under the Presidential Primary Matching Payment Account Act, 26 U.S.C. 9031 *et seq.*

(b) The procedures covered by this subpart do not apply to any of the following debts:

(1) Debts that result from administrative activities of the Commission that are governed by 11 CFR part 8.

(2) Debts involving criminal actions of fraud, the presentation of a false claim, or misrepresentation on the part of the debtor or any other person having an interest in the claim.

(3) Debts based in whole or in part on conduct in violation of the antitrust laws.

(4) Debts under the Internal Revenue Code of 1986.

(5) Debts between the Commission and another Federal agency. The Commission will attempt to resolve interagency claims by negotiation in accordance with Executive Order 12146, 3 CFR pp. 409–12 (1980 Comp.).

(6) Debts that have become subject to salary offset under 5 U.S.C. 5514.

[75 FR 19876, Apr. 16, 2010, as amended at 79 FR 16663, Mar. 26, 2014; 79 FR 77848, Dec. 29, 2014]

§ 111.52 Administrative collection of claims.

(a) The Commission shall act to collect all claims or debts. These collection activities will be undertaken promptly and follow up action will be taken as appropriate in accordance with 31 CFR 901.1.

(b) The Commission may take any and all appropriate collection actions authorized and required by the Debt Collection Act of 1982, as amended by the Debt Collection Improvement Act of 1996, 31 U.S.C. 3701 *et seq.* The U.S. Department of the Treasury regulations at 31 CFR 285.2, 285.4, 285.7, and 285.11, and the Federal Claims Collection Standards issued jointly by the Department of Justice and the U.S. Department of the Treasury at 31 CFR parts 900–904, also apply. The Commission has adopted these regulations by cross-reference.

(c) The Commission will refer to the Dept. of Treasury all debt that has been delinquent for more than 180 days, and may refer to the Dept. of Treasury any debt that has been delinquent for 180 days or less. On behalf of the Commission, the U.S. Department of the Treasury will attempt to collect the debt, in accordance with the statutory and regulatory requirements and authorities applicable to the debt and action. This may include referral to another debt collection center, or a private collection contractor. *See* 31 CFR 285.12 (Transfer of debts to Treasury for collection). This requirement does not apply to any debt that:

(1) Is in litigation or foreclosure;

(2) Will be disposed of under an approved asset sale program;

(3) Has been referred to a private collection contractor for a period of time acceptable to the U.S. Department of the Treasury; or

(4) Will be collected under internal offset procedures within three years after the debt first became delinquent.

(d) The U.S. Department of the Treasury is authorized to charge a fee for services rendered regarding referred or transferred debts. The Commission will add the fee to the debt as an administrative cost, in accordance with 11 CFR 111.55.

§ 111.53 **Litigation by the Commission.**

Nothing in this subpart C precludes the Commission from filing suit in the appropriate court to enforce compliance with a conciliation agreement under 52 U.S.C. 30109(a)(5)(D), seek a civil money penalty under 52 U.S.C. 30109(a)(6), petition the court for a contempt order under 52 U.S.C. 30109(a)(11), or otherwise exercise its authority to enforce or administer the statutes specified in 11 CFR 111.51(a).

[75 FR 19876, Apr. 16, 2010, as amended at 79 FR 77848, Dec. 29, 2014]

§ 111.54 **Bankruptcy claims.**

When the Commission learns that a bankruptcy petition has been filed by a debtor, before proceeding with further collection action, the Commission will take any necessary action in accordance with the provision of 31 CFR 901.2(h).

§ 111.55 **Interest, penalties, and administrative costs.**

(a) The Commission shall assess interest, penalties, and administrative costs on debts owed to the United States Government, pursuant to 31 U.S.C. 3717. Interest, penalties, and administrative costs will be assessed in accordance with 31 CFR 901.9.

(b) The Commission shall waive collection of interest and administrative costs on a debt or any portion of the debt that is paid within thirty days after the date on which the interest begins to accrue.

(c) The Commission may waive collection of interest, penalties, and administrative costs if it:

(1) Determines that collection is against equity and good conscience or not in the best interest of the United States, including when an administrative offset or installment agreement is in effect; or

(2) Determines that waiver is appropriate under the criteria for compromise of debts set forth at 31 CFR 902.2(a).

(d) The Commission is authorized to impose interest and related charges on debts not subject to 31 U.S.C. 3717, in accordance with common law.

PART 112—ADVISORY OPINIONS (52 U.S.C. 30108)

Sec.
112.1 Requests for advisory opinions (52 U.S.C. 30108(a)(1)).
112.2 Public availability of requests (52 U.S.C. 30108(d)).
112.3 Written comments on requests (52 U.S.C. 30108(d)).
112.4 Issuance of advisory opinions (52 U.S.C. 30108(a) and (b)).
112.5 Reliance on advisory opinions (52 U.S.C. 30108(c)).
112.6 Reconsideration of advisory opinions.

AUTHORITY: 52 U.S.C. 30108, 30111(a)(8).

SOURCE: 45 FR 15123, Mar. 7, 1980, unless otherwise noted.

§ 112.1 **Requests for advisory opinions (52 U.S.C. 30108(a)(1)).**

(a) Any person may request in writing an advisory opinion concerning the application of the Act, chapters 95 or 96 of the Internal Revenue Code of 1954, or any regulation prescribed by the Commission. An authorized agent of the requesting person may submit the advisory opinion request, but the agent shall disclose the identity of his or her principal.

(b) The written advisory opinion request shall set forth a specific transaction or activity that the requesting person plans to undertake or is presently undertaking and intends to undertake in the future. Requests presenting a general question of interpretation, or posing a hypothetical situation, or regarding the activities of third parties, do not qualify as advisory opinion requests.

(c) Advisory opinion requests shall include a complete description of all facts relevant to the specific transaction or activity with respect to which the request is made.

(d) The Office of General Counsel shall review all requests for advisory opinions submitted under 11 CFR 112.1. If the Office of General Counsel determines that a request for an advisory opinion is incomplete or otherwise not qualified under 11 CFR 112.1, it shall, within 10 calendar days of receipt of such request, notify the requesting person and specify the deficiencies in the request.

(e) Advisory opinion requests should be sent to the Federal Election Commission, Office of General Counsel, at the street address identified in the definition of "Commission" in § 1.2.

(f) Upon receipt by the Commission, each request which qualifies as an advisory opinion request (AOR) under 11 CFR 112.1 shall be assigned an AOR number for reference purposes.

[45 FR 15123, Mar. 7, 1980, as amended at 50 FR 50778, Dec. 12, 1985; 82 FR 60853, Dec. 26, 2017]

§ 112.2 Public availability of requests (52 U.S.C. 30108(d)).

(a) Advisory opinion requests which qualify under 11 CFR 112.1 shall be made public at the Commission promptly upon their receipt.

(b) A copy of the original request and any supplements thereto, shall be available for public inspection and purchase at the Public Disclosure and Media Relations Division of the Commission.

[45 FR 15123, Mar. 7, 1980, as amended at 81 FR 94240, Dec. 23, 2016]

§ 112.3 Written comments on requests (52 U.S.C. 30108(d)).

(a) Any interested person may submit written comments concerning advisory opinion requests made public at the Commission.

(b) The written comments shall be submitted within 10 calendar days following the date the request is made public at the Commission. However, if the 10th calendar day falls on a Saturday, Sunday, or Federal holiday, the 10 day period ends at the close of the business day next following the weekend or holiday. Additional time for submission of written comments may be granted upon written request for an extension by the person who wishes to submit comments or may be granted by the Commission without an extension request.

(c) Comments on advisory opinion requests should refer to the AOR number of the request, and statutory references should be to the United States Code citations, rather than to Public Law citations.

(d) Written comments and requests for additional time to comment shall be sent to the Federal Election Commission, Office of General Counsel, at the street address identified in the definition of "Commission" in § 1.2.

(e) Before it issues an advisory opinion the Commission shall accept and consider all written comments submitted within the 10 day comment period or any extension thereof.

[45 FR 15123, Mar. 7, 1980, as amended at 50 FR 50778, Dec. 12, 1985; 82 FR 60853, Dec. 26, 2017]

§ 112.4 Issuance of advisory opinions (52 U.S.C. 30108(a) and (b)).

(a) Within 60 calendar days after receiving an advisory opinion request that qualifies under 11 CFR 112.1, the Commission shall issue to the requesting person a written advisory opinion or shall issue a written response stating that the Commission was unable to approve an advisory opinion by the required affirmative vote of 4 members.

(b) The 60 calendar day period of 11 CFR 112.4(a) is reduced to 20 calendar days for an advisory opinion request qualified under 11 CFR 112.1 provided the request:

(1) Is submitted by any candidate, including any authorized committee of the candidate (or agent of either), within the 60 calendar days preceding the date of any election for Federal office in which the candidate is seeking nomination or election; and

(2) Presents a specific transaction or activity related to the election that may invoke the 20 day period if the connection is explained in the request.

(c) The 60 day and 20 day periods referred to in 11 CFR 112.4 (a) and (b) only apply when the Commission has received a qualified and complete advisory opinion request under 11 CFR 112.1, and when the 60th or 20th day occurs on a Saturday, Sunday or Federal holiday, the respective period ends at the close of the business day next following the weekend or holiday.

(d) The Commission may issue advisory opinions pertaining only to the Federal Election Campaign Act of 1971, as amended, chapters 95 or 96 of the Internal Revenue Code of 1954, or rules or regulations duly prescribed under those statutes.

(e) Any rule of law which is not stated in the Act or in chapters 95 or 96 of the Internal Revenue Code of 1954, or in a regulation duly prescribed by the Commission, may be initially proposed only as a rule or regulation pursuant to procedures established in 52 U.S.C. 30111(d) or 26 U.S.C. 9009(c) and 9039(c) as applicable.

(f) No opinion of an advisory nature may be issued by the Commission or any of its employees except in accordance with 11 CFR part 112; however, this limitation does not preclude distribution by the Commission of information consistent with the Act and chapters 95 or 96 of the Internal Revenue Code of 1954.

(g) When issued by the Commission, each advisory opinion or other response under 11 CFR 112.4(a) shall be made public and sent by mail, or personally delivered to the person who requested the opinion.

[45 FR 15123, Mar. 7, 1980, as amended at 79 FR 77849, Dec. 29, 2014]

§ 112.5 Reliance on advisory opinions (52 U.S.C. 30108(c)).

(a) An advisory opinion rendered by the Commission under 11 CFR part 112 may be relied upon by:

(1) Any person involved in the specific transaction or activity with respect to which such advisory opinion is rendered, and

(2) Any person involved in any specific transaction or activity which is indistinguishable in all its material aspects from the transaction or activity with respect to which such advisory opinion is rendered.

(b) Notwithstanding any other provision of law, any person who relies upon an advisory opinion in accordance with 11 CFR 112.5(a) and who acts in good faith in accordance with that advisory opinion shall not, as a result of any such act, be subject to any sanction provided by the Federal Election Campaign Act of 1971, as amended, or by chapters 95 or 96 of the Internal Revenue Code of 1954.

§ 112.6 Reconsideration of advisory opinions.

(a) The Commission may reconsider an advisory opinion previously issued if the person to whom the opinion was issued submits a written request for reconsideration within 30 calendar days of receipt of the opinion and if, upon the motion of a Commissioner who voted with the majority that originally approved the opinion, the Commission adopts the motion to reconsider by the affirmative vote of 4 members.

(b) The Commission may reconsider an advisory opinion previously issued if, upon the motion of a Commissioner who voted with the majority that originally approved the opinion and within 30 calendar days after the date the Commission approved the opinion, the Commission adopts the motion to reconsider by the affirmative vote of 4 members.

(c) In the event an advisory opinion is reconsidered pursuant to 11 CFR 112.6(b), the action taken in good faith reliance on that advisory opinion by the person to whom the opinion was issued shall not result in any sanction provided by the Act or chapters 95 or 96 of the Internal Revenue Code of 1954. 11 CFR 112.6(c) shall not be effective after the date when the person to whom the advisory opinion was issued has received actual notice of the Commission's decision to reconsider that advisory opinion.

(d) Adoption of a motion to reconsider vacates the advisory opinion to which it relates.

PART 113—PERMITTED AND PROHIBITED USES OF CAMPAIGN ACCOUNTS

Sec.
113.1 Definitions (52 U.S.C. 30114).
113.2 Permissible non-campaign use of funds (52 U.S.C. 30114).
113.3 Deposits of funds donated to a Federal or State officeholder (52 U.S.C. 30102(h)).
113.4 Contribution and expenditure limitations (52 U.S.C. 30116).
113.5 Restrictions on use of campaign funds for flights on noncommercial aircraft (52 U.S.C. 30114(c)).

AUTHORITY: 52 U.S.C. 30102(h), 30111(a)(8), 30114, and 30116.

SOURCE: 45 FR 15124, Mar. 7, 1980, unless otherwise noted.

§ 113.1 Definitions (52 U.S.C. 30114).

When used in this part—

(a) *Funds donated. Funds donated* means all funds, including, but not limited to, gifts, loans, advances, credits or deposits of money which are donated for the purpose of supporting the activities of a Federal or State officeholder; but does not mean funds appropriated by Congress, a State legislature, or another similar public appropriating body, or personal funds of the officeholder donated to an account containing only those personal funds.

(b) *Office account.* Office account means an account established for the purposes of supporting the activities of a Federal or State officeholder which contains campaign funds and funds donated, but does not include an account used exclusively for funds appropriated by Congress, a State legislature, or another similar public appropriating body, or an account of the officeholder which contains only the personal funds of the officeholder.

(c) *Federal officeholder. Federal officeholder* means an individual elected to or serving in the office of President or Vice President of the United States; or a Senator or a Representative in, or Delegate or Resident Commissioner to, the Congress of the United States.

(d) *State officeholder. State officeholder* means an individual elected to or serving in any elected public office within a State of the United States, the District of Columbia, the Commonwealth of Puerto Rico or any subdivision thereof.

(e) [Reserved]

(f) *Qualified Member. Qualified Member* means an individual who was serving as a Senator or Representative in, or Delegate or Resident Commissioner to, Congress, on January 8, 1980.

(g) *Personal use. Personal use* means any use of funds in a campaign account of a present or former candidate to fulfill a commitment, obligation or expense of any person that would exist irrespective of the candidate's campaign or duties as a Federal officeholder.

(1)(i) Personal use includes but is not limited to the use of funds in a campaign account for any item listed in paragraphs (g)(1)(i)(A) through (J) of this section:

(A) Household food items or supplies.

(B) Funeral, cremation or burial expenses except those incurred for a candidate (as defined in 11 CFR 100.3) or an employee or volunteer of an authorized committee whose death arises out of, or in the course of, campaign activity.

(C) Clothing, other than items of *de minimis* value that are used in the campaign, such as campaign "T-shirts" or caps with campaign slogans.

(D) Tuition payments, other than those associated with training campaign staff.

(E) Mortgage, rent or utility payments—

(*1*) For any part of any personal residence of the candidate or a member of the candidate's family; or

(*2*) For real or personal property that is owned by the candidate or a member of the candidate's family and used for campaign purposes, to the extent the payments exceed the fair market value of the property usage.

(F) Admission to a sporting event, concert, theater or other form of entertainment, unless part of a specific campaign or officeholder activity.

(G) Dues, fees or gratuities at a country club, health club, recreational facility or other nonpolitical organization, unless they are part of the costs of a specific fundraising event that takes place on the organization's premises.

(H) Salary payments to a member of the candidate's family, unless the family member is providing *bona fide* services to the campaign. If a family member provides *bona fide* services to the campaign, any salary payment in excess of the fair market value of the services provided is personal use.

(I) Salary payments by a candidate's principal campaign to a candidate in excess of the lesser of: the minimum salary paid to a Federal officeholder holding the Federal office that the candidate seeks; or the earned income that the candidate received during the year prior to becoming a candidate. Any earned income that a candidate receives from salaries or wages from any other source shall count against the foregoing limit of the minimum salary paid to a Federal officeholder holding the Federal office that the candidate seeks. The candidate must provide income tax records from the relevant years and other evidence of earned income upon the request of the Commission. Salary shall not be paid to a candidate before the filing deadline for access to the primary election ballot for the Federal office that the candidate seeks, as determined by State law, or in those states that do not conduct primaries, on January 1 of each even-numbered year. *See* 11 CFR 100.24(a)(1)(i). If the candidate wins the primary election, his or her principal campaign committee may pay him or her a salary from campaign funds through the date of the general election, up to and including the date of any general election runoff. If the candidate loses the primary, withdraws from the race, or otherwise ceases to be a candidate, no salary payments may be paid beyond the date he or she is no longer a candidate. In odd-numbered years in which a special election for a Federal office occurs, the principal campaign committee of a candidate for that office may pay him or her a salary from campaign funds starting on the date the special election is set and end-

ing on the day of the special election. *See* 11 CFR 100.24(a)(1)(ii). During the time period in which a principal campaign committee may pay a salary to a candidate under this paragraph, such payment must be computed on a pro-rata basis. A Federal officeholder, as defined in paragraph (c) of this section, must not receive salary payments as a candidate from campaign funds.

(J) A vacation.

(ii) The Commission will determine, on a case-by-case basis, whether other uses of funds in a campaign account fulfill a commitment, obligation or expense that would exist irrespective of the candidate's campaign or duties as a Federal officeholder, and therefore are personal use. Examples of such other uses include:

(A) Legal expenses;

(B) Meal expenses;

(C) Travel expenses, including subsistence expenses incurred during travel. If a committee uses campaign funds to pay expenses associated with travel that involves both personal activities and campaign or officeholder-related activities, the incremental expenses that result from the personal activities are personal use, unless the person(s) benefiting from this use reimburse(s) the campaign account within thirty days for the amount of the incremental expenses, and

(D) Vehicle expenses, unless they are a *de minimis* amount. If a committee uses campaign funds to pay expenses associated with a vehicle that is used for both personal activities beyond a *de minimis* amount and campaign or officeholder-related activities, the portion of the vehicle expenses associated with the personal activities is personal use, unless the person(s) using the vehicle for personal activities reimburse(s) the campaign account within thirty days for the expenses associated with the personal activities.

(2) *Charitable donations.* Donations of campaign funds or assets to an organization described in section 170(c) of Title 26 of the United States Code are not personal use, unless the candidate receives compensation from the organization before the organization has expended the entire amount donated for purposes unrelated to his or her personal benefit.

(3) *Transfers of campaign assets.* The transfer of a campaign committee asset is not personal use so long as the transfer is for fair market value. Any depreciation that takes place before the transfer must be allocated between the committee and the purchaser based on the useful life of the asset.

(4) *Gifts.* Gifts of nominal value and donations of a nominal amount made on a special occasion such as a holiday, graduation, marriage, retirement, or death are not personal use, unless made to a member of the candidate's family.

(5) *Political or officially connected expenses.* The use of campaign funds for an expense that would be a political expense under the rules of the United States House of Representatives or an officially connected expense under the rules of the United States Senate is not personal use to the extent that the expense is an expenditure under subpart D of part 100 or an ordinary and necessary expense incurred in connection with the duties of a holder of Federal office. Any use of funds that would be personal use under paragraph (g)(1) of this section will not be considered an expenditure under subpart D of part 100 or an ordinary and necessary expense incurred in connection with the duties of a holder of Federal office.

(6) *Third party payments.* Notwithstanding that the use of funds for a particular expense would be a personal use under this section, payment of that expense by any person other than the candidate or the campaign committee shall be a contribution under subpart B of part 100 to the candidate unless the payment would have been made irrespective of the candidacy. Examples of payments considered to be irrespective of the candidacy include, but are not limited to, situations where—

(i) The payment is a donation to a legal expense trust fund established in accordance with the rules of the United States Senate or the United States House of Representatives;

(ii) The payment is made from funds that are the candidate's personal funds as defined in 11 CFR 100.33, including an account jointly held by the candidate and a member of the candidate's family;

(iii) Payments for that expense were made by the person making the payment before the candidate became a candidate. Payments that are compensation shall be considered contributions unless—

(A) The compensation results from *bona fide* employment that is genuinely independent of the candidacy;

(B) The compensation is exclusively in consideration of services provided by the employee as part of this employment; and

(C) The compensation does not exceed the amount of compensation which would be paid to any other similarly qualified person for the same work over the same period of time.

(7) *Members of the candidate's family.* For the purposes of paragraph (g) of this section, the candidate's family includes:

(i) The spouse of the candidate;

(ii) Any child, step-child, parent, grandparent, sibling, half-sibling or step-sibling of the candidate or the candidate's spouse;

(iii) The spouse of any child, step-child, parent, grandparent, sibling, half-sibling or step-sibling of the candidate; and

(iv) A person who shares a residence with the candidate.

(8) *Recordkeeping.* For those uses of campaign funds described in paragraphs (g)(1)(i) and (g)(1)(ii) of this section that involve both personal use and either campaign or office-holder use, a contemporaneous log or other record must be kept to document the dates and expenses related to the personal use of the campaign funds. The log must be updated whenever campaign funds are used for personal expenses, as described in paragraph (g)(1) of this section, rather than for campaign or office-holder expenses. The log or other record must also be maintained and preserved for 3 years after the report disclosing the disbursement is filed, pursuant to 11 CFR 102.9 and 104.14(b).

[45 FR 15124, Mar. 7, 1980, as amended at 56 FR 34126, July 25, 1991; 60 FR 7874, Feb. 9, 1995; 67 FR 38361, June 4, 2002; 67 FR 76978, Dec. 13, 2002; 73 FR 79602, Dec. 30, 2008; 75 FR 32, Jan. 4, 2010; 79 FR 77849, Dec. 29, 2014; 81 FR 34863, June 1, 2016]

§113.2 Permissible non-campaign use of funds (52 U.S.C. 30114).

In addition to defraying expenses in connection with a campaign for federal office, funds in a campaign account or an account described in 11 CFR 113.3:

(a) May be used to defray any ordinary and necessary expenses incurred in connection with the recipient's duties as a holder of Federal office, if applicable, including:

(1) The costs of travel by the recipient Federal officeholder and an accompanying spouse to participate in a function directly connected to *bona fide* official responsibilities, such as a fact-finding meeting or an event at which the officeholder's services are provided through a speech or appearance in an official capacity; and

(2) The costs of winding down the office of a former Federal officeholder for a period of 6 months after he or she leaves office; or

(b) May be contributed to any organization described in section 170(c) of Title 26, of the United States Code; or

(c) May be transferred without limitation to any national, State, or local committee of any political party; or

(d) May be donated to State and local candidates subject to the provisions of State law; or

(e) May be used for any other lawful purpose, unless such use is personal use under 11 CFR 113.1(g).

(f) Nothing in this section modifies or supersedes other Federal statutory restrictions or relevant State laws that may apply to the use of campaign or donated funds by candidates or Federal officeholders.

[45 FR 15124, Mar. 7, 1980, as amended at 56 FR 34126, July 25, 1991; 60 FR 7875, Feb. 9, 1995; 67 FR 76979, Dec. 13, 2002; 72 FR 56247, Oct. 3, 2007; 81 FR 94240, Dec. 23, 2016]

§113.3 Deposits of funds donated to a Federal or State officeholder (52 U.S.C. 30102(h)).

All funds donated to a federal officeholder, or State officeholder who is a candidate for federal office, shall be deposited into one of the following accounts:

(a) An account of the officeholder's principal campaign committee or other authorized committee pursuant to 11 CFR part 103;

(b) An account to which only funds donated to an individual to support his or her activities as a holder of federal office are deposited (including an office account).

§113.4 Contribution and expenditure limitations (52 U.S.C. 30116).

(a) Any contributions to, or expenditures from an office account which are made for the purpose of influencing a federal election shall be subject to 52 U.S.C. 30116 and 11 CFR part 110 of these regulations.

(b) If any treasury funds of a corporation or labor organization are donated to an office account, no funds from that office account may be transferred to a political committee account or otherwise used in connection with a federal election.

[45 FR 15124, Mar. 7, 1980, as amended at 79 FR 77849, Dec. 29, 2014]

§113.5 Restrictions on use of campaign funds for flights on non-commercial aircraft (52 U.S.C. 30114(c)).

(a) *Presidential, vice-presidential and Senate candidates.* Notwithstanding any other provision of the Act or Commission regulations, a presidential, vice-presidential, or Senate candidate, and any authorized committee of such candidate, shall not make any expenditure for travel on an aircraft unless the flight is:

(1) Commercial travel as provided in 11 CFR 100.93(a)(3)(iv);

(2) Noncommercial travel as provided in 11 CFR 100.93(a)(3)(v), and the pro rata share per campaign traveler of the normal and usual charter fare or rental charge for travel on a comparable aircraft of comparable size, as provided in 11 CFR 100.93(c), is paid by the candidate, the authorized committee, or other political committee on whose behalf the travel is conducted, to the owner, lessee, or other person who provides the aircraft within seven calendar days after the date the flight began, except as provided in 11 CFR 100.93(b)(3); or

(3) Provided by the Federal government or by a State or local government.

(b) *House candidates and their leadership PACs.* Notwithstanding any other provision of the Act or Commission regulations, a candidate for the office of Representative in, or Delegate or Resident Commissioner to, the Congress, and any authorized committee or leadership PAC of such candidate, shall not make any expenditures, or receive any in-kind contribution, for travel on an aircraft unless the flight is:

(1) Commercial travel as provided in 11 CFR 100.93(a)(3)(iv); or

(2) Provided by the Federal government or by a State or local government.

(c) *Exception for aircraft owned or leased by candidates and immediate family members of candidates.* (1) Paragraphs (a) and (b) of this section do not apply to flights on aircraft owned or leased by the candidate, or by an immediate family member of the candidate, provided that the candidate does not use the aircraft more than the candidate's or immediate family member's proportional share of ownership, as defined by 11 CFR 100.93(g)(3), allows.

(2) A candidate, or an immediate family member of the candidate, will be considered to own or lease an aircraft under the conditions described in 11 CFR 100.93(g)(2).

(3) An "immediate family member" is defined in 11 CFR 100.93(g)(4).

(d) *In-kind contribution.* Except as provided in 11 CFR 100.79, the unreimbursed value of transportation provided to any campaign traveler is an in-kind contribution from the service provider to the candidate or political committee on whose behalf, or with whom, the campaign traveler traveled. Such contributions are subject to the reporting requirements, limitations and prohibitions of the Act.

[74 FR 63967, Dec. 7, 2009, as amended at 79 FR 77849, Dec. 29, 2014]

PART 114—CORPORATE AND LABOR ORGANIZATION ACTIVITY

AUTHORITY: 52 U.S.C. 30101(8), 30101(9), 30102, 30104, 30107(a)(8), 30111(a)(8), 30118.

§114.1   Definitions.

(a) For purposes of part 114—

(1) The terms *contribution* and *expenditure* shall include any direct or indirect payment, distribution, loan, advance, deposit, or gift of money, or any services, or anything of value (except a loan of money by a State bank, a federally chartered depository institution (including a national bank) or a depository institution whose deposits and accounts are insured by the Federal Deposit Insurance Corporation or the National Credit Union Administration, if such loan is made in accordance with 11 CFR 100.82(a) through (d)) to any candidate, political party or committee, organization, or any other person in connection with any election to any of the offices referred to in 11 CFR 114.2 (a) or (b) as applicable.

(2) The terms *contribution* and *expenditure* shall *not* include—

(i) Communications by a corporation to its stockholders and executive or administrative personnel and their families or by a labor organization to its members and executive or administrative personnel, and their families, on any subject;

(ii) Registration and get-out-the-vote campaigns by a corporation aimed at its stockholders and executive or administrative personnel, and their families, or by a labor organization aimed at its members and executive or administrative personnel, and their families, as described in 11 CFR 114.3(c)(4)(ii);

(iii) The establishment, administration, and solicitation of contributions to a separate segregated fund to be utilized for political purposes by a corporation, labor organization, membership organization, cooperative, or corporation without capital stock;

(iv) [Reserved]

(v) The sale of any food or beverage by a corporate vendor for use in a candidate's campaign or for use by a political committee of a political party at a charge less than the normal or comparable commercial rate, if the charge is at least equal to the costs of such food or beverage to the vendor, to the extent that: The aggregate value of such discount by the vendor on behalf of a single candidate does not exceed $1,000 with respect to any single election; and on behalf of all political committees of each political party does not exceed $2,000 in a calendar year.

(vi) The payment for legal or accounting services rendered to or on behalf of any political committee of a political party other than services attributable to activities which directly further the election of a designated candidate or candidates for Federal office if the corporation or labor organization paying for the services is the regular employer of the individual rendering the services. This exclusion shall not be applicable if additional employees are hired for the purpose of rendering services or if additional employees are hired in order to make regular employees available;

(vii) The payment for legal or accounting services rendered to or on behalf of an authorized committee of a candidate or any other political committee solely for the purpose of ensuring compliance with this Act or chapter 95 or 96 of the Internal Revenue Code of 1954 if the corporation or labor organization paying for the services is the regular employer of the individual rendering the services, but amounts paid or incurred for these services shall be reported in accordance with part 104. This exclusion shall not be applicable if additional employees are hired for the purpose of rendering services or if additional employees are hired in order to make regular employees available;

(viii) Activity permitted under 11 CFR 9008.9, 9008.52 and 9008.53 with respect to a presidential nominating convention;

(ix) Donations to a State or local party committee used for the purchase or construction of its office building are subject to 11 CFR 300.35. No exception applies to contributions or donations to a national party committee that are made or used for the purchase or construction of any office building or facility; or

(x) Any activity that is specifically permitted by part 114, but this exception does not apply to activities permitted by 11 CFR 114.3(c)(4), 114.4(a), (c)(1)–(6), and (d), and 114.10(a), other than as provided specifically in those sections.

(b) *Establishment, administration, and solicitation costs* means the cost of office space, phones, salaries, utilities, supplies, legal and accounting fees, fund-raising and other expenses incurred in setting up and running a separate segregated fund established by a corporation, labor organization, membership organization, cooperative, or corporation without capital stock.

(c) *Executive or administrative personnel* means individuals employed by a corporation or labor organization who are paid on a salary rather than hourly basis and who have policymaking, managerial, professional, or supervisory responsibilities.

(1) This definition includes—

(i) The individuals who run the corporation's business such as officers, other executives, and plant, division, and section managers; and

(ii) Individuals following the recognized professions, such as lawyers and engineers.

(2) This definition does *not* include—

(i) Professionals who are represented by a labor organization;

(ii) Salaried foremen and other salaried lower level supervisors having direct supervision over hourly employees;

(iii) Former or retired personnel who are not stockholders; or

(iv) Individuals who may be paid by the corporation or labor organization, such as consultants, but who are not employees, within the meaning of 26 CFR 31.3401(c)–1, of the corporation or labor organization for the purpose of income withholding tax on employee wages under Internal Revenue Code of 1954, section 3402.

(3) Individuals on commission may be considered executive or administrative personnel if they have policymaking, managerial, professional, or supervisory responsibility and if the individuals are employees, within the meaning of 26 CFR 31.3401(c)–1 of the corporation for the purpose of income withholding tax on employee wages under the Internal Revenue Code of 1954, section 3402.

(4) The Fair Labor Standards Act, 29 U.S.C. 201, *et seq.* and the regulations issued pursuant to that Act, 29 CFR part 541, may serve as a guideline in determining whether individuals have policymaking, managerial, professional, or supervisory responsibilities.

(d) *Labor organization* means any organization of any kind, or any agency or employee representative committee or plan, in which employees participate and which exists for the purpose, in whole or in part, of dealing with employers concerning grievances, labor disputes, wages, rates of pay, hours of employment, or conditions of work.

(e)(1) For purposes of this part *membership organization* means a trade association, cooperative, corporation without capital stock, or a local, national, or international labor organization that:

(i) Is composed of members, some or all of whom are vested with the power and authority to operate or administer the organization, pursuant to the organization's articles, bylaws, constitution or other formal organizational documents;

(ii) Expressly states the qualifications and requirements for membership in its articles, bylaws, constitution or other formal organizational documents;

(iii) Makes its articles, bylaws, constitution, or other formal organizational documents available to its members upon request;

(iv) Expressly solicits persons to become members;

(v) Expressly acknowledges the acceptance of membership, such as by sending a membership card or including the member's name on a membership newsletter list; and

(vi) Is not organized primarily for the purpose of influencing the nomination for election, or election, of any individual to Federal office.

(2) For purposes of this part, the term *members* includes all persons who are currently satisfying the requirements for membership in a membership organization, affirmatively accept the membership organization's invitation to become a member, and either:

(i) Have some significant financial attachment to the membership organization, such as a significant investment or ownership stake; or

(ii) Pay membership dues at least annually, of a specific amount predetermined by the organization; or

(iii) Have a significant organizational attachment to the membership organization which includes: affirmation of membership on at least an annual basis; and direct participatory rights in the governance of the organization. For example, such rights could include the right to vote directly or indirectly for at least one individual on the membership organization's highest governing board; the right to vote directly for organization officers; the right to vote on policy questions where the highest governing body of the membership organization is obligated to abide by the results; the right to approve the organization's annual budget; or the right to participate directly in similar aspects of the organization's governance.

(3) Notwithstanding the requirements of paragraph (e)(2) of this section, the Commission may determine, on a case-by-case basis, that persons who do not precisely meet the requirements of the general rule, but have a relatively enduring and independently significant financial or organizational attachment to the organization, may be considered members for purposes of this section. For example, student members who pay a lower amount of dues while in school, long term dues paying members who qualify for lifetime membership status with little or no dues obligation, and retired members of the organization may be considered members for purposes of these rules.

(4) Notwithstanding the requirements of paragraphs (e)(2)(i) through (iii) of this section, members of a local union are considered to be members of any national or international union of which the local union is a part and of any federation with which the local, national, or international union is affiliated.

(5) In the case of a membership organization which has a national federation structure or has several levels, including, for example, national, state, regional and/or local affiliates, a person who qualifies as a member of any entity within the federation or of any affiliate by meeting the requirements of paragraphs (e)(2)(i), (ii), or (iii) of this section shall also qualify as a member of all affiliates for purposes of this part. The factors set forth at 11 CFR 100.5 (g)(2), (3) and (4) shall be used to determine whether entities are affiliated for purposes of this paragraph.

(6) The status of a membership organization, and of members, for purposes of this part, shall be determined pursuant to paragraph (e)(1) of this section and not by provisions of state law governing trade associations, cooperatives, corporations without capital stock, or labor organizations.

(f) *Method of facilitating the making of contributions* means the manner in which the contributions are received or collected such as, but not limited to, payroll deduction or checkoff systems, other periodic payment plans, or return envelopes enclosed in a solicitation request.

(g) *Method of soliciting voluntary contributions* means the manner in which the solicitation is undertaken including, but not limited to, mailings, oral requests for contributions, and hand distribution of pamphlets.

(h) *Stockholder* means a person who has a vested beneficial interest in stock, has the power to direct how that stock shall be voted, if it is voting stock, and has the right to receive dividends.

(i) *Voluntary contributions* are contributions which have been obtained by the separate segregated fund of a corporation or labor organization in a manner which is in compliance with §114.5(a) and which is in accordance with other provisions of the Act.

(j) *Restricted class.* A corporation's restricted class is its stockholders and executive or administrative personnel, and their families, and the executive and administrative personnel of its subsidiaries, branches, divisions, and departments and their families. A labor organization's restricted class is its members and executive or administrative personnel, and their families. For communications under 11 CFR 114.3, the restricted class of an incorporated membership organization, incorporated trade association, incorporated cooperative or corporation without capital stock is its members and executive or administrative personnel, and their families. (The solicitable class of a membership organization, cooperative, corporation without capital stock or trade association, as described in 11 CFR 114.7 and 114.8, may include some persons who are not considered part of the organization's restricted class, and may exclude some persons who are in the restricted class.)

(52 U.S.C. 30101(8)(B)(iii), 30102(c)(3), 30107(a)(8), 30111(a)(8), 30118)

[41 FR 35955, Aug. 25, 1976, as amended at 44 FR 63045, Nov. 1, 1979; 45 FR 15125, Mar. 7, 1980; 45 FR 21210, Apr. 1, 1980; 48 FR 50508, Nov. 2, 1983; 57 FR 1640, Jan. 15, 1992; 58 FR 45775, Aug. 30, 1993; 59 FR 33615, June 29, 1994; 60 FR 64273, Dec. 14, 1995; 64 FR 41273, July 30, 1999; 67 FR 49120, July 29, 2002; 67 FR 78681, Dec. 26, 2002; 79 FR 77849, Dec. 29, 2014; 80 FR 62817, Oct. 21, 2014]

§114.2 Prohibitions on contributions, expenditures and electioneering communications.

(a) National banks and corporations organized by authority of any law of Congress are prohibited from making a contribution, as defined in 11 CFR 114.1(a), in connection with any election to any political office, including local, State and Federal offices, or in connection with any primary election or political convention or caucus held to select candidates for any political office, including any local, State or Federal office. National banks and corporations organized by authority of any law of Congress are prohibited from making expenditures as defined in 11 CFR 114.1(a) for communications to those outside the restricted class expressly advocating the election or defeat of one or more clearly identified candidate(s) or the candidates of a clearly identified political party, with respect to an election to any political office, including any local, State, or Federal office.

(1) Such national banks and corporations may engage in the activities permitted by 11 CFR part 114, except to the extent that such activity constitutes a contribution, expenditure, or electioneering communication or is foreclosed by provisions of law other than the Act.

(2) The provisions of 11 CFR part 114 apply to the activities of a national bank, or a corporation organized by any law of Congress, in connection with local, State and Federal elections.

(b) Any corporation whatever or any labor organization is prohibited from making a contribution as defined in 11 CFR part 100, subpart B. Any corporation whatever or any labor organization is prohibited from making a contribution as defined in 11 CFR 114.1(a) in connection with any Federal election.

NOTE TO PARAGRAPH (b): Pursuant to *SpeechNow.org* v. *FEC*, 599 F.3d 686 (D.C. Cir. 2010) (en banc), and *Carey* v. *FEC*, 791 F. Supp. 2d 121 (D.D.C. 2011), corporations and labor organizations may make contributions to nonconnected political committees that make only independent expenditures, or to separate accounts maintained by nonconnected political committees for making only independent expenditures, notwithstanding 11 CFR 114.2(b) and 11 CFR 114.10(a). The Commission has not conducted a rulemaking in response to these cases.

(c) Disbursements by corporations and labor organizations for the election-related activities described in 11 CFR 114.3 and 114.4 will not cause those activities to be contributions when coordinated with any candidate, candidate's agent, candidate's authorized committee(s) or any party committee to the extent permitted in those sections. Coordination beyond that described in 11 CFR 114.3 and 114.4 shall not cause subsequent activities directed at the restricted class to be considered contributions. However, such coordination may be considered evidence that could negate the independence of subsequent communications to those outside the restricted class by the corporation, labor organization or its separate segregated fund, and could

result in an in-kind contribution. *See* 11 CFR 100.16 regarding independent expenditures and coordination with candidates.

(d) A candidate, political committee, or other person is prohibited from knowingly accepting or receiving any contribution prohibited by this section.

(e) No officer or director of any corporation or any national bank, and no officer of any labor organization shall consent to any contribution or expenditure by the corporation, national bank, or labor organization prohibited by this section.

(f) *Facilitating the making of contributions.* (1) Corporations and labor organizations (including officers, directors or other representatives acting as agents of corporations and labor organizations) are prohibited from facilitating the making of contributions to candidates or political committees, other than to the separate segregated funds of the corporations and labor organizations. Facilitation means using corporate or labor organization resources or facilities to engage in fundraising activities in connection with any federal election, such as activities which go beyond the limited exemptions set forth in 11 CFR part 100, subparts B and C, part 100, subparts D and E, 114.9(a) through (c) and 114.13. A corporation does not facilitate the making of a contribution to a candidate or political committee if it provides goods or services in the ordinary course of its business as a commercial vendor in accordance with 11 CFR part 116 at the usual and normal charge.

(2) Examples of facilitating the making of contributions include but are not limited to—

(i) Fundraising activities by corporations (except commercial vendors) or labor organizations that involve—

(A) Officials or employees of the corporation or labor organization ordering or directing subordinates or support staff (who therefore are not acting as volunteers) to plan, organize or carry out the fundraising project as a part of their work responsibilities using corporate or labor organization resources, unless the corporation or labor organization receives advance payment for the fair market value of such services;

(B) Failure to reimburse a corporation or labor organization within a commercially reasonable time for the use of corporate facilities described in 11 CFR 114.9(d) in connection with such fundraising activities;

(C) Using a corporate or labor organization list of customers, clients, vendors or others who are not in the restricted class to solicit contributions or distribute invitations to the fundraiser, unless the corporation or labor organization receives advance payment for the fair market value of the list;

(D) Using meeting rooms that are not customarily made available to clubs, civic or community organizations or other groups; or

(E) Providing catering or other food services operated or obtained by the corporation or labor organization, unless the corporation or labor organization receives advance payment for the fair market value of the services;

(ii) Providing materials for the purpose of transmitting or delivering contributions, such as stamps, envelopes addressed to a candidate or political committee other than the corporation's or labor organization's separate segregated fund, or other similar items which would assist in transmitting or delivering contributions, but not including providing the address of the candidate or political committee;

(iii) Soliciting contributions earmarked for a candidate that are to be collected and forwarded by the corporation's or labor organizations's separate segregated fund, except to the extent such contributions also are treated as contributions to and by the separate segregated fund; or

(iv) Using coercion, such as the threat of a detrimental job action, the threat of any other financial reprisal, or the threat of force, to urge any individual to make a contribution or engage in fundraising activities on behalf of a candidate or political committee.

(3) Facilitating the making of contributions does not include the following activities if conducted by a separate segregated fund—

(i) Any activity specifically permitted under 11 CFR 110.1, 110.2, or 114.5 through 114.8, including soliciting contributions to a candidate or political committee, and making in kind

contributions to a candidate or political committee; and

(ii) Collecting and forwarding contributions earmarked to a candidate in accordance with 11 CFR 110.6.

(4) Facilitating the making of contributions also does not include the following activities if conducted by a corporation or labor organization—

(i) Enrolling members of a corporation's or labor organization's restricted class in a payroll deduction plan or check-off system which deducts contributions from dividend or payroll checks to make contributions to the corporation's or labor organization's separate segregated fund or an employee participation plan pursuant to 11 CFR 114.11;

(ii) Soliciting contributions to be sent directly to candidates if the solicitation is directed to the restricted class, *see* 11 CFR 114.1(a)(2)(i); and

(iii) Soliciting contributions earmarked for a candidate that are to be collected and forwarded by the corporation's or labor organization's separate segregated fund, to the extent such contributions also are treated as contributions to and by the separate segregated fund.

(5) Facilitating the making of contributions also does not include the provision of incidental services by a corporation to collect and forward contributions from its employee stockholders and executive and administrative personnel to the separate segregated fund of a trade association of which the corporation is a member, including collection through a payroll deduction or check-off system, pursuant to 11 CFR 114.8(e)(4).

[60 FR 64274, Dec. 14, 1995, as amended at 67 FR 65211, Oct. 23, 2002; 67 FR 78681, Dec. 26, 2002; 70 FR 41944, July 21, 2005; 72 FR 72913, Dec. 26, 2007; 79 FR 62817, Oct. 21, 2014; 81 FR 34864, June 1, 2016]

§ 114.3 Disbursements for communications to the restricted class in connection with a Federal election.

(a) *General.* (1) Corporations and labor organizations may make communications on any subject, including communications containing express advocacy, to their restricted class or any part of that class. Corporations and labor organizations may also make the communications permitted under 11 CFR 114.4 to their restricted class or any part of that class. The activities permitted under this section may involve election-related coordination with candidates and political committees. See 11 CFR 100.16 and 114.2(c) regarding independent expenditures and coordination with candidates.

(2) Incorporated membership organizations, incorporated trade associations, incorporated cooperatives and corporations without capital stock may make communications to their restricted class, or any part of that class as permitted in paragraphs (a)(1) and (c) of this section.

(b) *Reporting communications containing express advocacy to the restricted class.* Disbursements for communications expressly advocating the election or defeat of one or more clearly identified candidate(s) made by a corporation, including a corporation described in paragraph (a)(2) of this section, or labor organization to its restricted class shall be reported in accordance with 11 CFR 100.134(a) and 104.6.

(c) *Communications containing express advocacy.* Communications containing express advocacy which may be made to the restricted class include, but are not limited to, the examples set forth in paragraphs (c)(1) through (c)(4) of this section.

(1) *Publications.* Printed material expressly advocating the election or defeat of one or more clearly identified candidate(s) or candidates of a clearly identified political party may be distributed by a corporation or by a labor organization to its restricted class, provided that:

(i) The material is produced at the expense of the corporation or labor organization; and

(ii) The material constitutes a communication of the views of the corporation or the labor organization, and is not the republication or reproduction, in whole or in part, of any broadcast, transcript or tape or any written, graphic, or other form of campaign materials prepared by the candidate, his or her campaign committees, or their authorized agents. A corporation or labor organization may, under this section, use brief quotations from speeches or other materials of a candidate that demonstrate the candidate's position as part of the corporation's or labor organization's expression of its own views.

(2) *Candidate and party appearances.* (i) A corporation may allow a candidate, candidate's representative or party representative to address its restricted class at a meeting, convention or other function of the corporation, but is not required to do so. A labor organization may allow a candidate or party representative to address its restricted class at a meeting, convention, or other function of the labor organization, but is not required to do so. A corporation or labor organization may bar other candidates for the same office or a different office and their representatives, and representatives of other parties addressing the restricted class. A corporation or labor organization may allow the presence of employees outside the restricted class of the corporation or labor organization who are necessary to administer the meeting, other guests of the corporation or labor organization who are being honored or speaking or participating in the event, and representatives of the news media.

(ii) The candidate, candidate's representative or party representative may ask for contributions to his or her campaign or party, or ask that contributions to the separate segregated fund of the corporation or labor organization be designated for his or her campaign or party. The incidental solicitation of persons outside the corporation's or labor organization's restricted class who may be present at the meeting as permitted by this section will not be a violation of 11 CFR part 114. The candidate's representative or party representative (other than an officer, director or other representative of a corporation or official, member or employee of a labor organization) or the candidate, may accept contributions before, during or after the appearance at the meeting, convention or other function of the corporation or labor organization.

(iii) The corporation or labor organization may suggest that members of its restricted class contribute to the candidate or party committee, but the collection of contributions by any officer, director or other representative of the corporation or labor organization before, during, or after the appearance while at the meeting, is an example of a prohibited facilitation of contributions under 11 CFR 114.2(f).

(iv) If the corporation or labor organization permits more than one candidate for the same office, or more than one candidate's representative or party representative, to address its restricted class, and permits the news media to cover or carry an appearance by one candidate or candidate's representative or party representative, the corporation or labor organization shall also permit the news media to cover or carry the appearances by the other candidate(s) for that office, or the other candidates' representatives or party representatives. If the corporation or labor organization permits a representative of the news media to cover or carry a candidate or candidate's representative or party representative appearance, the corporation or labor organization shall provide all other representatives of the news media with equal access for covering or carrying that appearance. Equal access is provided by—

(A) Providing advance information regarding the appearance to the representatives of the news media whom the corporation or labor organization customarily contacts and other representatives of the news media upon request; and

(B) Allowing all representatives of the news media to cover or carry the appearance, through the use of pooling arrangements if necessary.

(3) *Phone banks.* A corporation or a labor organization may establish and operate phone banks to communicate with its restricted class, urging them to register and/or vote for a particular candidate or candidates, or to register with a particular political party.

(4) *Registration and get-out-the-vote drives.* (i) A corporation or labor organization may conduct voter registration and get-out-the-vote drives aimed at its restricted class, except as provided in paragraph (c)(4)(iii) of this section. Voter registration and get-out-the-vote drives include providing transportation to the place of registration and to the polls. Such drives may in-

clude communications containing express advocacy, such as urging individuals to register with a particular party or to vote for a particular candidate or candidates.

(ii) Disbursements for a voter registration or get-out-the-vote drive conducted under paragraph (c)(4)(i) of this section are not contributions or expenditures if the drive is nonpartisan. *See* 52 U.S.C. 30118(b)(2)(B). A drive is nonpartisan if it is conducted so that information and other assistance regarding registering or voting, including transportation and other services offered, is not withheld or refused on the basis of support for or opposition to particular candidates or a particular political party.

(iii) A corporation or labor organization may make disbursements to conduct voter registration and get-out-the-vote drives that are aimed at its restricted class and that do not qualify as nonpartisan under paragraph (c)(4)(ii) of this section, provided that the disbursements do not constitute coordinated expenditures as defined in 11 CFR 109.20, coordinated communications as defined in 11 CFR 109.21, or contributions as defined in 11 CFR part 100, subpart B. *See also* note to 11 CFR 114.2(b), 114.10(a).

[60 FR 64275, Dec. 14, 1995, as amended at 67 FR 78681, Dec. 26, 2002; 79 FR 77849, Dec. 29, 2014; 79 FR 62817, Oct. 21, 2014]

§ 114.4 Disbursements for communications by corporations and labor organizations beyond the restricted class in connection with a Federal election.

(a) *General.* A corporation or labor organization may communicate beyond the restricted class in accordance with this section. Communications that a corporation or labor organization may make only to its employees (including its restricted class) and their families, but not to the general public, are set forth in paragraph (b) of this section. Any communications that a corporation or labor organization may make to the general public under paragraph (c) of this section may also be made to the corporation's or labor organization's restricted class and to other employees and their families. Communications that a corporation or labor organization may make only to its restricted class are set forth at 11 CFR 114.3. The activities described in paragraphs (b) and (c) of this section may be coordinated with candidates and political committees only to the extent permitted by this section. For the otherwise applicable regulations regarding independent expenditures and coordination with candidates, see 11 CFR 100.16, 109.21, and 114.2(c). Voter registration and get-out-the-vote drives as described in paragraph (d) of this section must not include coordinated expenditures as defined in 11 CFR 109.20, coordinated communications as defined in 11 CFR 109.21, or contributions as defined in 11 CFR part 100, subpart B. *See also* note to 11 CFR 114.2(b), 114.10(a). Incorporated membership organizations, incorporated trade associations, incorporated cooperatives, and corporations without capital stock will be treated as corporations for the purpose of this section.

(b) *Communications by a corporation or labor organization to employees beyond its restricted class*—(1) *Candidate and party appearances on corporate premises or at a meeting, convention or other function.* Corporations may permit candidates, candidates' representatives or representatives of political parties on corporate premises or at a meeting, convention, or other function of the corporation to address or meet its restricted class and other employees of the corporation and their families, in accordance with the conditions set forth in paragraphs (b)(1)(i) through (b)(1)(viii) of this section. Other guests of the corporation who are being honored or speaking or participating in the event and representatives of the news media may be present. A corporation may bar all candidates, candidates' representatives and representatives of political parties from addressing or meeting its restricted class and other employees of the corporation and their families on corporate premises or at any meeting, convention or other function of the corporation.

(i) If a candidate for the House or Senate or a candidate's representative is permitted to address or meet employees, all candidates for that seat who request to appear must be given a similar opportunity to appear;

(ii) If a Presidential or Vice Presidential candidate or candidate's representative is permitted to address or meet employees, all candidates for that office who are seeking the nomination or election, and who meet pre-established objective criteria under 11 CFR 110.13(c), and who request to appear must be given a similar opportunity to appear;

(iii) If representatives of a political party are permitted to address or meet employees, representatives of all political parties which had a candidate or candidates on the ballot in the last general election or which are actively engaged in placing or will have a candidate or candidates on the ballot in the next general election and who request to appear must be given a similar opportunity to appear;

(iv) The candidate's representative or party representative (other than an officer, director or other representative of a corporation) or the candidate, may ask for contributions to his or her campaign or party, or ask that contributions to the separate segregated fund of the corporation be designated for his or her campaign or party. The candidate, candidate's representative or party representative shall not accept contributions before, during or after the appearance while at the meeting, convention or other function of the corporation, but may leave campaign materials or envelopes for members of the audience. A corporation, its restricted class, or other employees of the corporation or its separate segregated fund shall not, either orally or in writing, solicit or direct or control contributions by members of the audience to any candidate or party in conjunction with any appearance by any candidate or party representative under this section, and shall not facilitate the making of contributions to any such candidate or party (see 11 CFR 114.2(f));

(v) A corporation or its separate segregated fund shall not, in conjunction with any candidate, candidate representative or party representative appearance under this section, expressly advocate the election or defeat of any clearly identified candidate(s) or candidates of a clearly identified political party and shall not promote or encourage express advocacy by employees;

(vi) No candidate, candidate's representative or party representative shall be provided with more time or a substantially better location than other candidates, candidates' representatives or party representatives who appear, unless the corporation is able to demonstrate that it is clearly impractical to provide all candidates, candidates' representatives and party representatives with similar times or locations;

(vii) Coordination with each candidate, candidate's agent, and candidate's authorized committee(s) may include discussions of the structure, format and timing of the candidate appearance and the candidate's positions on issues, but shall not include discussions of the candidate's plans, projects, or needs relating to the campaign; and

(viii) Representatives of the news media may be allowed to be present during a candidate, candidate representative or party representative appearance under this section, in accordance with the procedures set forth at 11 CFR 114.3(c)(2)(iv).

(2) *Candidate and party appearances on labor organization premises or at a meeting, convention or other function.* A labor organization may permit candidates, candidates' representatives or representatives of political parties on the labor organization's premises or at a meeting, convention, or other function of the labor organization to address or meet its restricted class and other employees of the labor organization, and their families, in accordance with the conditions set forth in paragraphs (b)(1) (i) through (iii), (vi) through (viii), and paragraphs (b)(2) (i) and (ii) of this section. Other guests of the labor organization who are being honored or speaking or participating in the event and representatives of the news media may be present. A labor organization may bar all candidates, candidates' representatives and representatives of political parties from addressing or meeting its restricted class and other employees of the labor organization and their families on the labor organization's premises or at any meeting, convention or other function of the labor organization.

(i) The candidate's representative or party representative (other than an official, member or employee of a labor organization) or the candidate, may ask for contributions to his or her campaign or party, or ask that contributions to the separate segregated fund of the labor organization be designated for his or her campaign or party. The candidate, candidate's representative or party representative shall not accept contributions before, during or after the appearance while at the meeting, convention or other function of the labor organization, but may leave campaign materials or envelopes for members of the audience. No official, member, or employee of a labor organization or its separate segregated fund shall, either orally or in writing, solicit or direct or control contributions by members of the audience to any candidate or party representative under this section, and shall not facilitate the making of contributions to any such candidate or party. See 11 CFR 114.2(f).

(ii) A labor organization or its separate segregated fund shall not, in conjunction with any candidate or party representative appearance under this section, expressly advocate the election or defeat of any clearly identified candidate(s), and shall not promote or encourage express advocacy by its members or employees.

(c) *Communications by a corporation or labor organization to the general public—* (1) *General.* A corporation or labor organization may make independent expenditures or electioneering communications pursuant to 11 CFR 114.10. This section addresses specific communications, described in paragraphs (c)(2) through (c)(7) of this section, that a corporation or labor organization may make to the general public. The general public includes anyone who is not in the corporation's or labor organization's restricted class. The preparation, contents, and distribution of any of the communications described in paragraphs (2) through (6) below must not include coordinated expenditures as defined in 11 CFR 109.20, coordinated communications as defined in 11 CFR 109.21, or contributions as defined in 11 CFR part 100, subpart B. *See also* note to 11 CFR 114.2(b), 114.10(a).

(2) *Voter registration and get-out-the-vote communications.* (i) A corporation or labor organization may make voter registration and get-out-the-vote communications to the general public.

(ii) Disbursements for the activity described in paragraph (c)(2)(i) of this section are not contributions or expenditures, provided that:

(A) The voter registration and get-out-the-vote communications to the general public do not expressly advocate the election or defeat of any clearly identified candidate(s) or candidates of a clearly identified political party; and

(B) The preparation and distribution of voter registration and get-out-the-vote communications is not coordinated with any candidate(s) or political party.

(3) *Official registration and voting information.* (i) A corporation or labor organization may distribute to the general public, or reprint in whole and distribute to the general public, any registration or voting information, such as instructional materials, that has been produced by the official election administrators.

(ii) A corporation or labor organization may distribute official registration-by-mail forms to the general public. A corporation or labor organization may distribute absentee ballots to the general public if permitted by the applicable State law.

(iii) A corporation or labor organization may donate funds to State or local government agencies responsible for the administration of elections to help defray the costs of printing or distributing voter registration or voting information and forms.

(iv) Disbursements for the activity described in paragraphs (c)(3)(i) through (iii) of this section are not contributions or expenditures, provided that:

(A) The corporation or labor organization does not, in connection with any such activity, expressly advocate the election or defeat of any clearly identified candidate(s) or candidates of a clearly identified political party and does not encourage registration with any particular political party; and

(B) The reproduction and distribution of registration or voting information

and forms is not coordinated with any candidate(s) or political party.

(4) *Voting records.* (i) A corporation or labor organization may prepare and distribute to the general public the voting records of Members of Congress.

(ii) Disbursements for the activity described in paragraph (c)(4)(i) of this section are not contributions or expenditures, provided that:

(A) The voting records of Members of Congress and all communications distributed with it do not expressly advocate the election or defeat of any clearly identified candidate(s) or candidates of a clearly identified political party; and

(B) The decision on content and the distribution of voting records is not coordinated with any candidate, group of candidates, or political party.

(5) *Voter guides.* (i) A corporation or labor organization may prepare and distribute to the general public voter guides, including voter guides obtained from a nonprofit organization that is described in 26 U.S.C. 501(c)(3) or (c)(4).

(ii) Disbursements for the activity described in paragraph (c)(5)(i) of this section are not contributions or expenditures, provided that the voter guides comply with either paragraph (c)(5)(ii)(A) or (c)(5)(ii)(B)(*1*) through (*5*) of this section:

(A) The corporation or labor organization does not act in cooperation, consultation, or concert with or at the request or suggestion of the candidates, the candidates' committees or agents regarding the preparation, contents and distribution of the voter guide, and no portion of the voter guide expressly advocates the election or defeat of one or more clearly identified candidate(s) or candidates of any clearly identified political party; or

(B)(*1*) The corporation or labor organization does not act in cooperation, consultation, or concert with or at the request or suggestion of the candidates, the candidates' committees or agents regarding the preparation, contents and distribution of the voter guide;

(*2*) All of the candidates for a particular seat or office are provided an equal opportunity to respond, except that in the case of Presidential and

Vice Presidential candidates the corporation or labor organization may choose to direct the questions only to those candidates who—

(*i*) Are seeking the nomination of a particular political party in a contested primary election; or

(*ii*) Appear on the general election ballot in the state(s) where the voter guide is distributed or appear on the general election ballot in enough states to win a majority of the electoral votes;

(*3*) No candidate receives greater prominence in the voter guide than other participating candidates, or substantially more space for responses;

(*4*) The voter guide and its accompanying materials do not contain an electioneering message; and

(*5*) The voter guide and its accompanying materials do not score or rate the candidates' responses in such a way as to convey an electioneering message.

(*6*) *Endorsements.* (i) A corporation or labor organization may endorse a candidate, and may communicate the endorsement to the restricted class and the general public. The Internal Revenue Code and regulations promulgated thereunder should be consulted regarding restrictions or prohibitions on endorsements by nonprofit corporations described in 26 U.S.C. 501(c)(3).

(ii) Disbursements for announcements of endorsements to the general public are not contributions or expenditures, provided that:

(A) The public announcement is not coordinated with a candidate, a candidate's authorized committee, or their agents; and

(B) Disbursements for any press release or press conference to announce the endorsement are de minimis. Such disbursements shall be considered de minimis if the press release and notice of the press conference are distributed only to the representatives of the news media that the corporation or labor organization customarily contacts when issuing non-political press releases or holding press conferences for other purposes.

(iii) Disbursements for announcements of endorsements to the restricted class may be coordinated pursuant to 114.3(a) and are not contribu-

tions or expenditures provided that no more than a *de minimis* number of copies of the publication that includes the endorsement are circulated beyond the restricted class.

(7) *Candidate appearances on educational institution premises*—(i) *Rental of facilities at usual and normal charge.* Any incorporated nonprofit educational institution exempt from federal taxation under 26 U.S.C. 501(c)(3), such as a school, college or university, may make its facilities available to any candidate or political committee in the ordinary course of business and at the usual and normal charge. In this event, the requirements of paragraph (c)(7)(ii) of this section are not applicable.

(ii) *Use of facilities at no charge or at less than the usual and normal charge.* An incorporated nonprofit educational institution exempt from federal taxation under 26 U.S.C. 501(c)(3), such as a school, college or university, may sponsor appearances by candidates, candidates' representatives or representatives of political parties at which such individuals address or meet the institution's academic community or the general public (whichever is invited) on the educational institution's premises at no charge or at less than the usual and normal charge, if:

(A) The educational institution makes reasonable efforts to ensure that the appearances constitute speeches, question and answer sessions, or similar communications in an academic setting, and makes reasonable efforts to ensure that the appearances are not conducted as campaign rallies or events; and

(B) The educational institution does not, in conjunction with the appearance, expressly advocate the election or defeat of any clearly identified candidate(s) or candidates of a clearly identified political party, and does not favor any one candidate or political party over any other in allowing such appearances.

(d) *Voter registration and get-out-the-vote drives*—(1) *Voter registration and get-out-the-vote drives permitted.* A corporation or labor organization may support or conduct voter registration and get-out-the-vote drives that are aimed at employees outside its restricted class and the general public. Voter registration and get-out-the-vote drives include providing transportation to the polls or to the place of registration.

(2) *Disbursements for certain voter registration and get-out-the-vote drives not expenditures.* Voter registration or get-out-the-vote drives that are conducted in accordance with paragraphs (d)(2)(i) through (d)(2)(v) of this section are not expenditures.

(i) The corporation or labor organization shall not make any communication expressly advocating the election or defeat of any clearly identified candidate(s) or candidates of a clearly identified political party as part of the voter registration or get-out-the-vote drive.

(ii) The voter registration drive shall not be directed primarily to individuals previously registered with, or intending to register with, the political party favored by the corporation or labor organization. The get-out-the-vote drive shall not be directed primarily to individuals currently registered with the political party favored by the corporation or labor organization.

(iii) These services shall be made available without regard to the voter's political preference. Information and other assistance regarding registering or voting, including transportation and other services offered, shall not be withheld or refused on the basis of support for or opposition to particular candidates or a particular political party.

(iv) Individuals conducting the voter registration or get-out-the-vote drive shall not be paid on the basis of the number of individuals registered or transported who support one or more particular candidates or political party.

(v) The corporation or labor organization shall notify those receiving information or assistance of the requirements of paragraph (d)(2)(iii) of this section. The notification shall be made in writing at the time of the registration or get-out-the-vote drive.

(e) *Incorporated membership organizations, incorporated trade associations, incorporated cooperatives and corporations without capital stock.* An incorporated membership organization, incorporated trade association, incorporated cooperative or corporation without capital stock may permit candidates, candidates' representatives or representatives of political parties to address or meet members and employees of the organization, and their families, on the organization's premises or at a meeting, convention or other function of the organization, in accordance with the conditions set forth in paragraphs (b)(1) (i) through (viii) of this section.

(f) *Candidate debates.* (1) A nonprofit organization described in 11 CFR 110.13(a)(1) may use its own funds and may accept funds donated by corporations or labor organizations under paragraph (f)(3) of this section to defray costs incurred in staging candidate debates held in accordance with 11 CFR 110.13.

(2) A broadcaster (including a cable television operator, programmer or producer), *bona fide* newspaper, magazine or other periodical publication may use its own funds to defray costs incurred in staging public candidate debates held in accordance with 11 CFR 110.13.

(3) A corporation or labor organization may donate funds to nonprofit organizations qualified under 11 CFR 110.13(a)(1) to stage candidate debates held in accordance with 11 CFR 110.13 and 114.4(f).

[60 FR 64276, Dec. 14, 1995, as amended at 61 FR 18051, Apr. 24, 1996; 67 FR 78681, Dec. 26, 2002; 68 FR 457, Jan. 3, 2003; 72 FR 72913, Dec. 26, 2007; 79 FR 62817, Oct. 21, 2014]

§ 114.5   Separate segregated funds.

(a) *Voluntary contributions to a separate segregated fund.* (1) A separate segregated fund is prohibited from making a contribution or expenditure by utilizing money or anything of value secured by physical force, job discrimination, financial reprisals, or the threat of force, job discrimination, or financial reprisal; or by dues, fees, or other monies required as a condition of membership in a labor organization or as a condition of employment or by monies obtained in any commercial transaction. For purposes of this section, fees or monies paid as a condition of acquiring or retaining membership or employment are monies required as a condition of membership or employment even though they are refundable upon request of the payor.

(2) A guideline for contributions may be suggested by a corporation or a labor organization, or the separate segregated fund of either, provided that the person soliciting or the solicitation informs the persons being solicited—

(i) That the guidelines are merely suggestions; and

(ii) That an individual is free to contribute more or less than the guidelines suggest and the corporation or labor organization will not favor or disadvantage anyone by reason of the amount of their contribution or their decision not to contribute.

A corporation or labor organization or the separate segregated fund of either may not enforce any guideline for contributions.

(3) Any person soliciting an employee or member for a contribution to a separate segregated fund must inform such employee or member of the political purposes of the fund at the time of the solicitation.

(4) Any persons soliciting an employee or member for a contribution to a separate segregated fund must inform the employee or member at the time of such solicitation of his or her right to refuse to so contribute without any reprisal.

(5) Any written solicitation for a contribution to a separate segregated fund which is addressed to an employee or member must contain statements which comply with the requirements of paragraphs (a) (3) and (4) of this section, and if a guideline is suggested, statements which comply with the requirements of paragraph (a)(2) of this section.

(b) *Use of treasury monies.* Corporations, labor organizations, membership organizations, cooperatives, or corporations without capital stock may use general treasury monies, including monies obtained in commercial transactions and dues monies or membership fees, for the establishment, administration, and solicitation of contributions to its separate segregated fund. A corporation, labor organization, membership organization, cooperative, or corporation without capital stock may not use the establishment, administration, and solicitation process as a means of exchanging treasury monies for voluntary contributions.

(1) A contributor may not be paid for his or her contribution through a bonus, expense account, or other form of direct or indirect compensation.

(2) A corporation, labor organization, membership organization, cooperative, or corporation without capital stock may, subject to the provisions of 39 U.S.C. 3005 and chapter 61, title 18, United States Code, utilize a raffle or other fundraising device which involves a prize, so long as State law permits and the prize is not disproportionately valuable. Dances, parties, and other types of entertainment may also be used as fundraising devices. When using raffles or entertainment to raise funds, a reasonable practice to follow is for the separate segregated fund to reimburse the corporation or labor organization for costs which exceed one-third of the money contributed.

(3) If the separate segregated fund pays any solicitation or other administrative expense from its own account, which expense could be paid for as an administrative expense by the collecting agent, the collecting agent may reimburse the separate segregated fund no later than 30 calendar days after the expense was paid by the separate segregated fund.

(c) *Membership in separate segregated funds.* (1) A separate segregated fund established by a corporation, labor organization, membership organization, cooperative, or corporation without capital stock may provide that persons who contribute a certain amount to its separate segregated fund will become *members* of its separate segregated fund, so long as—

(i) The fund accepts contributions of all amounts, subject to the limitations of part 110;

(ii) Subject to paragraph (c)(1)(iii) of this section, nothing of value may be given in return for or in the course of membership;

(iii) The fund may use membership status for intangible privileges such as allowing members only to choose the candidates to whom the fund will contribute.

215

(2) The fact that the separate segregated fund of a corporation, labor organization, membership organization, cooperative, or corporation without capital stock is a *membership group* does not provide the corporation, labor organization, membership organization, cooperative, or corporation without capital stock with any greater right of communication or solicitation than the corporation, labor organization, membership organization, cooperative, or corporation without capital stock is otherwise granted under this part.

(d) *Control of funds.* A corporation, membership organization, cooperative, corporation without capital stock, or labor organization may exercise control over its separate segregated fund.

(e) *Disclosure.* Separate segregated funds are subject to the following disclosure requirements:

(1) A corporation or labor organization is not required to report any payment made or obligation incurred which is not a contribution or expenditure, as defined in § 114.1(a), except those reporting requirements specifically set forth in this section.

(2) A membership organization or corporation is not required to report the cost of any communication to its members or stockholders or executive or administrative personnel, if such membership organization or corporation is not organized primarily for the purpose of influencing the nomination for election, or election, of any person to Federal office, except that—

(i) The costs incurred by a membership organization, including a labor organization, or by a corporation, directly attributable to a communication expressly advocating the election or defeat of a clearly identified candidate (other than a communication primarily devoted to subjects other than the express advocacy of the election or defeat of a clearly identified candidate) shall, if those costs exceed $2,000 per election, be reported in accordance with 11 CFR 100.134(a); and

(ii) The amounts paid or incurred for legal or accounting services rendered to or on behalf of a candidate or political committee solely for the purpose of ensuring compliance with the provisions of the Act or chapter 95 or 96 of the Internal Revenue Code of 1954 paid by a corporation or labor organization which is the regular employer of the individual rendering such services, shall be reported in accordance with the provisions of part 104.

(3) A separate segregated fund is subject to all other disclosure requirements of political committees as set forth in part 104.

(f) *Contribution limits.* Separate segregated funds are subject to the contribution limitations for political committees set forth in part 110. (See particularly § 110.3).

(g) *Solicitations.* Except as specifically provided in §§ 114.6, 114.7, and 114.8, a corporation and/or its separate segregated fund or a labor organization and/or its separate segregated fund is subject to the following limitations on solicitations:

(1) A corporation or a separate segregated fund established by a corporation is prohibited from soliciting contributions to such fund from any person other than its stockholders and their families and its executive or administrative personnel and their families. A corporation may solicit the executive or administrative personnel of its subsidiaries, branches, divisions, and affiliates and their families. For purposes of this section, the factors set forth at 11 CFR 100.5(g)(4) shall be used to determine whether an organization is an affiliate of a corporation.

(2) A labor organization, or a separate segregated fund established by a labor organization is prohibited from soliciting contributions to such a fund from any person other than its members and executive or administrative personnel, and their families.

(h) *Accidental or inadvertent solicitation.* Accidental or inadvertent solicitation by a corporation or labor organization, or the separate segregated fund of either, of persons apart from and beyond those whom it is permitted to solicit will not be deemed a violation, provided that such corporation or labor organization or separate segregated fund has used its best efforts to comply with the limitations regarding the persons it may solicit and that the method of solicitation is corrected forthwith after the discovery of such erroneous solicitation.

(i) *Communications paid for with voluntary contributions.* A separate segregated fund may, using voluntary contributions, communicate with the general public, except that such communications may not solicit contributions to a separate segregated fund established by a corporation, labor organization, membership organization, cooperative, or corporation without capital stock, unless such solicitation is permitted under paragraph (g) of this section.

(j) *Acceptance of contributions.* A separate segregated fund may accept contributions from persons otherwise permitted by law to make contributions.

(k) *Availability of methods.* Any corporation, including its subsidiaries, branches, divisions, and affiliates, that uses a method of soliciting voluntary contributions or facilitating the making of voluntary contributions from its stockholders or executive or administrative personnel and their families, shall make that method available to a labor organization representing any members working for the corporation, its subsidiaries, branches, divisions, and affiliates for soliciting voluntary contributions or facilitating the making of voluntary contributions from its members and their families. Such method shall be made available on the written request of the labor organization and at a cost sufficient only to reimburse the corporation for the expenses incurred thereby. For example—

(1) If a corporation, including its subsidiaries, branches, divisions, or affiliates utilizes a payroll deduction plan, check-off system, or other plan which deducts contributions from the dividend or payroll checks of stockholders or executive or administrative personnel, the corporation shall, upon written request of the labor organization, make that method available to members of the labor organization working for the corporation, its subsidiaries, branches, divisions, or affiliates, who wish to contribute to the separate segregated fund of the labor organization representing any members working for the corporation, or any of its subsidiaries, branches, divisions, or affiliates. The corporation shall make the payroll deduction plan available to the labor organization at a cost suffi-cient only to reimburse the corporation for the actual expenses incurred thereby.

(2) If a corporation uses a computer for addressing envelopes or labels for a solicitation to its stockholders or executive or administrative personnel, the corporation shall, upon written request, program the computer to enable the labor organization to solicit its members. The corporation shall charge the labor organization a cost sufficient only to reimburse the corporation for the actual expenses incurred in programming the computers and the allocated cost of employee time relating to the work, and the materials used.

(3) If a corporation uses corporate facilities, such as a company dining room or cafeteria, for meetings of stockholders or executive or administrative personnel at which solicitations are made, the corporation shall upon written request of the labor organization allow that labor organization to use existing corporate facilities for meetings to solicit its members. The labor organization shall be required to reimburse the corporation for any actual expenses incurred thereby, such as any increase in the overhead to the corporation and any cost involved in setting up the facilities.

(4) If a corporation uses no method to solicit voluntary contributions or to facilitate the making of voluntary contributions from stockholders or executive or administrative personnel, it is not required by law to make any method available to the labor organization for its members. The corporation and the labor organization may agree upon making any lawful method available even though such agreement is not required by the Act.

(5) The availability of methods of twice yearly solicitations is subject to the provisions of § 114.6(e).

(l) *Methods permitted by law to labor organizations.* Notwithstanding any other law, any method of soliciting voluntary contributions or of facilitating the making of voluntary contributions to a separate segregated fund established by a corporation, permitted by law to corporations with regard to stockholders and executive or administrative personnel, shall also be permitted to labor organizations with regard to their members and executive or administrative personnel.

(52 U.S.C. 30118, 30107(a)(8))

[41 FR 35955, Aug. 25, 1976, as amended at 45 FR 21210, Apr. 1, 1980; 48 FR 26303, June 7, 1983; 48 FR 50508, Nov. 2, 1983; 54 FR 34114, Aug. 17, 1989; 54 FR 48580, Nov. 24, 1989; 67 FR 78681, Dec. 26, 2002]

§ 114.6 Twice yearly solicitations.

(a) A corporation and/or its separate segregated fund may make a total of two written solicitations for contributions to its separate segregated fund per calendar year of its employees other than stockholders, executive or administrative personnel, and their families. Employees as used in this section does not include former or retired employees who are not stockholders. Nothing in this paragraph shall limit the number of solicitations a corporation may make of its stockholders and executive or administrative personnel under § 114.5(g).

(b) A labor organization and/or its separate segregated fund may make a total of two written solicitations per calendar year of employees who are not members of the labor organization, executive or administrative personnel, or stockholders (and their families) of a corporation in which the labor organization represents members working for the corporation. Nothing in this paragraph shall limit the number of solicitations a labor organization may make of its members under § 114.5(g).

(c) *Written solicitation.* A solicitation under this section may be made only by mail addressed to stockholders, executive or administrative personnel, or employees at their residences. All written solicitations must inform the recipient—

(1) Of the existence of the custodial arrangement described hereinafter;

(2) That the corporation, labor organization, or the separate segregated fund of either cannot be informed of persons who do not make contributions; and

(3) That persons who, in a calendar year make a single contribution of $50 or less, or multiple contributions aggregating $200 or less may maintain their anonymity by returning their contributions to the custodian.

(d) *The custodial arrangement.* In order to maintain the anonymity of persons who do not wish to contribute and of persons who wish to respond with a single contribution of $50 or less, or multiple contributions aggregating $200 or less in a calendar year, and to satisfy the recordkeeping provisions, the corporation, labor organization, or separate segregated fund of either shall establish a custodial arrangement for collecting the contributions under this section.

(1) The custodian for a separate segregated fund established by a corporation shall not be a stockholder, officer, executive or administrative personnel, or employee of the corporation, or an officer, or employee of its separate segregated fund. The custodian for a separate segregated fund established by a labor organization shall not be a member, officer or employee of the labor organization or its separate segregated fund.

(2) The custodian shall keep the records of contributions received in accordance with the requirements of part 102 and shall also—

(i) Establish a separate account and deposit contributions in accordance with the provisions of part 103;

(ii) Provide the fund with the identification of any person who makes a single contribution of more than $50 and the identification of any person who makes multiple contributions aggregating more than $200. The custodian must provide this information within a reasonable time prior to the reporting date of the fund under part 104;

(iii) Periodically forward all funds in the separate account, by check drawn on that account, to the separate segregated fund; and

(iv) Treat all funds which appear to be illegal in accordance with the provisions of § 103.3(b).

(3) The custodian shall not—

(i) Make the records of persons making a single contribution of $50 or less, or multiple contributions aggregating $200 or less, in a calendar year, available to any person other than representatives of the Federal Election Commission or the Secretary of the

Senate, as appropriate, and law enforcement officials or judicial bodies.

(ii) Provide the corporation or labor organization or the separate segregated fund of either with any information pertaining to persons who, in a calendar year, make a single contribution of $50 or less or multiple contributions aggregating $200 or less except that the custodian may forward to the corporation, labor organization or separate segregated fund of either the total number of contributions received; or

(iii) Provide the corporation, labor organization, or the separate segregated fund of either with any information pertaining to persons who have not contributed.

(4) The corporation, labor organization, or the separate segregated fund of either shall provide the custodian with a list of all contributions, indicating the contributor's identification and amount contributed, which have been made directly to the separate segregated fund by any person within the group of persons solicited under this section.

(5) Notwithstanding the prohibitions of paragraph (d)(1) of this section, the custodian may be employed by the separate segregated fund as its treasurer and may handle all of its contributions, provided that the custodian preserves the anonymity of the contributors as required by this section. The custodian shall file the required reports with the Federal Election Commission or the Secretary of the Senate, as appropriate. A custodian who serves as treasurer is subject to all of the duties, responsibilities, and liabilities of a treasurer under the Act, and may not participate in the decision making process whereby the separate segregated fund makes contributions and expenditures.

(e) *Availability of methods.* (1) A corporation or labor organization or the separate segregated fund of either may not use a payroll deduction plan, a check-off system, or other plan which deducts contributions from an employee's paycheck as a method of facilitating the making of contributions under this section.

(2) The twice yearly solicitation may only be used by a corporation or labor organization to solicit contributions to its separate segregated fund and may not be used for any other purpose.

(3) A corporation is required to make available to a labor organization representing any members working for the corporation or its subsidiaries, branches, divisions, or affiliates the method which the corporation uses to solicit employees under this section during any calendar year.

(i) If the corporation uses a method to solicit any employees under this section, the corporation is required to make that method available to the labor organization to solicit the employees of the corporation who are not represented by that labor organization, and the executive or administrative personnel and the stockholders of the corporation and their families.

(ii) If the corporation does not wish to disclose the names and addresses of stockholders or employees, the corporation shall make the names and addresses of stockholders and employees available to an independent mailing service which shall be retained to make the mailing for *both* the corporation and the labor organization for any mailings under this section.

(iii) If the corporation makes no solicitation of employees under this section during the calendar year, the corporation is not required to make any method or any names and addresses available to any labor organization.

(4) The corporation shall notify the labor organization of its intention to make a solicitation under this section during a calendar year and of the method it will use, within a reasonable time prior to the solicitation, in order to allow the labor organization opportunity to make a similar solicitation.

(5) If there are several labor organizations representing members employed at a single corporation, its subsidiaries, branches, divisions, or affiliates, the labor organizations, either singularly or jointly, may not make a combined total of more than two written solicitations per calendar year. A written solicitation may contain a request for contributions to each separate fund established by the various

219

labor organizations making the combined mailing.

(52 U.S.C. 30101(8)(B)(iii), 30102(c)(3), 30111(a)(8))

[41 FR 35955, Aug. 25, 1976, as amended at 45 FR 15125, Mar. 7, 1980; 61 FR 3550, Feb. 1, 1996]

§ 114.7 Membership organizations, cooperatives, or corporations without capital stock.

(a) Membership organizations, cooperatives, or corporations without capital stock, or separate segregated funds established by such persons may solicit contributions to the fund from members and executive or administrative personnel, and their families, of the organization, cooperative, or corporation without capital stock.

(b) Nothing in this section waives the prohibition on contributions to the separate segregated fund by corporations, national banks, or labor organizations which are members of a membership organization, cooperative, or corporation without capital stock.

(c) A trade association whose membership is made up in whole or in part of corporations is subject to the provisions of § 114.8 when soliciting any stockholders or executive or administrative personnel of member corporations. A trade association which is a membership organization may solicit its noncorporate members under the provisions of this section.

(d) The question of whether a professional organization is a corporation is determined by the law of the State in which the professional organization exists.

(e) There is no limitation upon the number of times an organization under this section may solicit its members and executive or administrative personnel, and their families.

(f) There is no limitation under this section on the method of solicitation or the method of facilitating the making of voluntary contributions which may be used.

(g) A membership organization, cooperative, or corporation without capital stock and the separate segregated funds of the organizations are subject to the provisions in § 114.5(a).

(h) A membership organization, cooperative, or corporation without capital stock may communicate with its members and executive or administrative personnel, and their families, under the provisions of § 114.3.

(i) A mutual life insurance company may solicit its policyholders if the policyholders are members within the organizational structure.

(j) A membership organization, including a trade association, cooperative, or corporation without capital stock or a separate segregated fund established by such organization may not solicit contributions from the separate segregated funds established by its members. The separate segregated fund established by a membership organization, including a trade association, cooperative, or corporation without capital stock may, however, accept unsolicited contributions from the separate segregated funds established by its members.

(k)(1) A federated cooperative as defined in the Agricultural Marketing Act of 1929, 12 U.S.C. 1141j, or a rural cooperative eligible for assistance under chapter 31 or title 7 of the United States Code, may solicit the members of the cooperative's regional, state or local affiliates, provided that all of the political committees established, financed, maintained or controlled by the cooperative and its regional, State or local affiliates are considered one political committee for the purposes of the limitations in 11 CFR 110.1 and 110.2.

(2) A cooperative as described in paragraph (k)(1) of this section may make communications to its members under the provisions of 11 CFR 114.3.

(52 U.S.C. 30118, 30107(a)(8))

[41 FR 35955, Aug. 25, 1976, as amended at 48 FR 50508, Nov. 2, 1983; 58 FR 45775, Aug. 30, 1993]

§ 114.8 Trade associations.

(a) *Definition.* A trade association is generally a membership organization of persons engaging in a similar or related line of commerce, organized to promote and improve business conditions in that line of commerce and not to engage in a regular business of a kind ordinarily carried on for profit, and no part of the net earnings of which inures to the benefit of any member.

(b) *Prohibition.* Nothing in this section waives the prohibition on contributions by corporations which are members of a trade association.

(c) *Limitations.* A trade association or a separate segregated fund established by a trade association may solicit contributions from the stockholders and executive or administrative personnel of the member corporations of such trade association and the families of such stockholders and personnel if—

(1) The member corporation involved has separately and specifically approved the solicitations; and

(2) The member corporation has not approved a solicitation by any other trade association for the same calendar year.

(d) *Separate and specific approval.* (1) The member corporation must knowingly and specifically approve any solicitation for a trade association, whether the solicitation is done by the trade association, its separate segregated fund, or the corporation or any of its personnel, for contributions to the trade association's separate segregated fund.

(2) A copy of each approved request received by a trade association or its separate segregated fund shall be maintained by the trade association or its fund for three years from the year for which the approval is given.

(3) The request for approval may contain a copy of solicitation materials which will be used if approval is granted. Such a mailing must specifically indicate the requirement of approval and the limitation of paragraph (c)(2) of this section, and approval must be granted to the trade association or its separate segregated fund prior to the time any solicitation is made of the stockholders or executive or administrative personnel by the trade association, its separate segregated fund, or by the corporation for contributions to the separate segregated fund of the trade association. (The request for approval may be sent to the representatives of the corporation with whom the trade association normally conducts the association's activities.)

(4) A separate authorization specifically allowing a trade association to solicit its corporate member's stockholders, and executive or administra-

tive personnel applies through the calendar year for which it is designated. A separate authorization by the corporate member must be designated for each year during which the solicitation is to occur. This authorization may be requested and may also be received prior to the calendar year in which the solicitation is to occur.

(5) In its request to a member corporation, a trade association may indicate that it intends to solicit, for example, a limited class of the executive or administrative personnel of the member corporation, or only the executive or administrative personnel but not the stockholders of the member corporation. Moreover, in its approval, a member corporation may similarly limit any solicitation by the trade association or its separate segregated fund. In any event, a member corporation, once it has approved any solicitation—even to a limited extent—of its personnel or stockholders by a trade association or its separate segregated fund, is precluded from approving any such solicitation by another trade association or its separate segregated fund and the corporation and its personnel are precluded from soliciting the corporation's executive or administrative personnel or stockholders on behalf of another trade association or its separate segregated fund.

(e) *Solicitation.* (1) After a trade association has obtained the approval required in paragraph (c) of this section, there is no limit on the number of times the trade association or its separate segregated fund may solicit the persons approved by the member corporation during the calendar year to which the approval applies. The member corporation may, however, in its approval limit the number of times solicitations may be made.

(2) A member corporation which grants permission to a trade association to solicit is in no way restricted in its rights under §114.5(g) to solicit its stockholders or executive or administrative personnel and their families for contributions to the corporation's own separate segregated fund.

(3) There is no limitation on the method of soliciting voluntary contributions or the method of facilitating

the making of voluntary contributions which a trade association may use.

(4) A corporation may provide incidental services to collect and forward contributions from its employee stockholders and executive and administrative personnel to the separate segregated fund of a trade association of which the corporation is a member, including a payroll deduction or check-off system, upon written request of the trade association. Any corporation that provides such incidental services, and the corporation's subsidiaries, branches, divisions, and affiliates, shall make those incidental services available to a labor organization representing any members working for the corporation or the corporation's subsidiaries, branches, divisions, or affiliates, upon written request of the labor organization and at a cost sufficient only to reimburse the corporation or the corporation's subsidiaries, branches, divisions, and affiliates, for the expenses incurred thereby.

(5) A trade association and/or its separate segregated fund is subject to the provisions of § 114.5(a).

(f) *Solicitation of a subsidiary corporation.* If a parent corporation is a member of the trade association but its subsidiary is not, the trade association or its separate segregated fund may only solicit the parent's executive or administrative personnel and their families and the parent's stockholders and their families; it may not solicit the subsidiary's executive or administrative personnel or stockholders or their families. If a subsidiary is a member of the trade association but the parent corporation is not, the trade association or its separate segregated fund may only solicit the subsidiary's executive or administrative personnel and their families and the subsidiary's stockholders and their families; it may not solicit the parent's executive or administrative personnel or stockholders or their families. If both parent and subsidiary are members of the trade association, the executive or administrative personnel and their families and the stockholders and their families of each may be solicited.

(g) *Federations of trade associations.* (1) A federation of trade associations is an organization representing trade associations involved in the same or allied line of commerce. Such a federation may, subject to the following limitations, solicit the members of the federation's regional, State or local affiliates or members, provided that all of the political committees established, financed, maintained or controlled by the federation and its regional, State, or local affiliates or members are considered one political committee for the purposes of the limitations in §§ 110.1 and 110.2. The factors set forth at § 100.5(g)(4) shall be used to determine whether an entity is a regional, State or local affiliate of a federation of trade associations.

(i) The federation and its member associations may engage in a joint solicitation; or

(ii) The member association may delegate its solicitation rights to the federation.

(2) A federation is subject to the provisions of this section when soliciting the stockholders and executive or administrative personnel of the corporate members of its member associations.

(h) *Communications other than solicitations.* A trade association may make communications, other than solicitations, to its members and their families under the provisions of § 114.3. When making communications to a member which is a corporation, the trade association may communicate with the representatives of the corporation with whom the trade association normally conducts the association's activities.

(i) *Trade association employees.* (1) A trade association may communicate with its executive or administrative personnel and their families under the provisions of § 114.3; a trade association may communicate with its other employees under the provisions of § 114.4.

(2) A trade association may solicit its executive or administrative personnel and their families under the provisions

of §114.5(g); a trade association may solicit its other employees under the provisions of §114.6.

(52 U.S.C. 30118, 30107(a)(8))

[41 FR 35955, Aug. 25, 1976, as amended at 48 FR 48650, Oct. 20, 1983; 48 FR 50508, Nov. 2, 1983; 54 FR 10622, Mar. 15, 1989; 54 FR 27154, June 28, 1989, 54 FR 34114, Aug. 17, 1989; 54 FR 48580, Nov. 24, 1989; 55 FR 2281, Jan. 23, 1990; 70 FR 41944, July 21, 2005]

§114.9 Use of corporate or labor organization facilities.

(a) *Use of corporate facilities for individual volunteer activity by stockholders and employees.* (1) Stockholders and employees of the corporation may, subject to the rules and practices of the corporation and 11 CFR 100.54, make occasional, isolated, or incidental use of the facilities of a corporation for individual volunteer activity in connection with a Federal election and will be required to reimburse the corporation only to the extent that the overhead or operating costs of the corporation are increased. A corporation may not condition the availability of its facilities on their being used for political activity, or on support for or opposition to any particular candidate or political party. As used in this paragraph, *occasional, isolated, or incidental use* generally means—

(i) When used by employees during working hours, an amount of activity which does not prevent the employee from completing the normal amount of work which that employee usually carries out during such work period; or

(ii) When used by stockholders other than employees during the working period, such use does not interfere with the corporation in carrying out its normal activities.

(2) *Safe harbor.* For the purposes of paragraph (a)(1) of this section, the following shall be considered occasional, isolated, or incidental use of corporate facilities:

(i) Any individual volunteer activity that does not exceed one hour per week or four hours per month, regardless of whether the activity is undertaken during or after normal working hours; or

(ii) Any such activity that constitutes voluntary individual Internet activities (as defined in 11 CFR 100.94),

in excess of one hour per week or four hours per month, regardless of whether the activity is undertaken during or after normal working hours, provided that:

(A) As specified in 11 CFR 100.54, the activity does not prevent the employee from completing the normal amount of work for which the employee is paid or is expected to perform;

(B) The activity does not increase the overhead or operating costs of the corporation; and

(C) The activity is not performed under coercion.

(3) A stockholder or employee who makes more than occasional, isolated, or incidental use of a corporation's facilities for individual volunteer activities in connection with a Federal election is required to reimburse the corporation within a commercially reasonable time for the normal and usual rental charge, as defined in 11 CFR 100.52(d)(2), for the use of such facilities.

(b) *Use of labor organization facilities for individual volunteer activity by officials, members, and employees.* (1) The officials, members, and employees of a labor organization may, subject to the rules and practices of the labor organization and 11 CFR 100.54, make occasional, isolated, or incidental use of the facilities of a labor organization for individual volunteer activity in connection with a Federal election and will be required to reimburse the labor organization only to the extent that the overhead or operating costs of the labor organization are increased. A labor organization may not condition the availability of its facilities on their being used for political activity, or on support for or opposition to any particular candidate or political party. As used in this paragraph, *occasional, isolated, or incidental use* generally means—

(i) When used by employees during working hours, an amount of activity during any particular work period which does not prevent the employee from completing the normal amount of work which that employee usually carries out during such work period; or

(ii) When used by members other than employees during the working period, such use does not interfere with the labor organization in carrying out its normal activities.

(2) *Safe harbor.* For the purposes of paragraph (b)(1) of this section, the following shall be considered occasional, isolated, or incidental use of labor organization facilities:

(i) Any individual volunteer activity that does not exceed one hour per week or four hours per month, regardless of whether the activity is undertaken during or after normal working hours; or

(ii) Any such activity that constitutes voluntary individual Internet activities (as defined in 11 CFR 100.94), in excess of one hour per week or four hours per month, regardless of whether the activity is undertaken during or after normal working hours, provided that:

(A) As specified in 11 CFR 100.54, the activity does not prevent the employee from completing the normal amount of work for which the employee is paid or is expected to perform;

(B) The activity does not increase the overhead or operating costs of the labor organization; and

(C) The activity is not performed under coercion.

(3) The officials, members, and employees who make more than occasional, isolated, or incidental use of a labor organization's facilities for individual volunteer activities in connection with a Federal election are required to reimburse the labor organization within a commercially reasonable time for the normal and usual rental charge, as defined in 11 CFR 100.52(d)(2), for the use of such facilities.

(c) *Use of corporate or labor organization facilities to produce materials.* Any person who uses the facilities of a corporation or labor organization to produce materials in connection with a Federal election is required to reimburse the corporation or labor organization within a commercially reasonable time for the normal and usual charge for producing such materials in the commercial market.

(d) *Use or rental of corporate or labor organization facilities by other persons.* Persons, other than those specifically mentioned in paragraphs (a) and (b) of this section, who make any use of cor-

porate or labor organization facilities, such as by using telephones or typewriters or borrowing office furniture, for activity in connection with a Federal election are required to reimburse the corporation or labor organization within a commercially reasonable time in the amount of the normal and usual rental charge, as defined in 11 CFR 100.52(d)(2), for the use of the facilities.

(e) Nothing in this section shall be construed to alter the provisions in 11 CFR Part 114 regarding communications to and beyond a restricted class.

[41 FR 35955, Aug. 25, 1976, as amended at 45 FR 21210, Apr. 1, 1980; 67 FR 78681, 78682, Dec. 26, 2002; 68 FR 69595, Dec. 15, 2003; 71 FR 18614, Apr. 4, 2006]

§ 114.10 **Corporations and labor organizations making independent expenditures and electioneering communications.**

(a) *General.* Corporations and labor organizations may make independent expenditures, as defined in 11 CFR 100.16, and electioneering communications, as defined in 11 CFR 100.29. Corporations and labor organizations are prohibited from making coordinated expenditures as defined in 11 CFR 109.20, coordinated communications as defined in 11 CFR 109.21, or contributions as defined in 11 CFR part 100, subpart B.

NOTE TO PARAGRAPH (a): Pursuant to *SpeechNow.org* v. *FEC*, 599 F.3d 686 (D.C. Cir. 2010) (en banc), and *Carey* v. *FEC*, 791 F. Supp. 2d 121 (D.D.C. 2011), corporations and labor organizations may make contributions to nonconnected political committees that make only independent expenditures, or to separate accounts maintained by nonconnected political committees for making only independent expenditures, notwithstanding 11 CFR 114.2(b) and 11 CFR 114.10(a). The Commission has not conducted a rulemaking in response to these cases.

(b) *Reporting independent expenditures and electioneering communications.* (1) Corporations and labor organizations that make independent expenditures aggregating in excess of $250 with respect to a given election in a calendar year shall file reports as required by 11 CFR part 114, 104.4(a), and 109.10(b)–(e).

(2) Corporations and labor organizations that make electioneering communications aggregating in excess of $10,000 in a calendar year shall file the

statements required by 11 CFR 104.20(b).

(c) *Non-authorization notice.* Corporations or labor organizations making independent expenditures or electioneering communications shall comply with the requirements of 11 CFR 110.11.

(d) *Segregated bank account.* A corporation or labor organization may, but is not required to, establish a segregated bank account into which it deposits only funds donated or otherwise provided by persons other than national banks, corporations organized by authority of any law of Congress, or foreign nationals (as defined in 11 CFR 110.20(a)(3)), as described in 11 CFR 104.20(c)(7), from which it makes disbursements for electioneering communications.

(e) *Activities prohibited by the Internal Revenue Code.* Nothing in this section shall be construed to authorize any organization exempt from taxation under 26 U.S.C. 501(a) to carry out any activity that it is prohibited from undertaking by the Internal Revenue Code, 26 U.S.C. 501, *et seq.*

[79 FR 62819, Oct. 21, 2014, as amended at 81 FR 34864, June 1, 2016]

§114.11 Employee participation plans.

(a) A corporation may establish and administer an employee participation plan (*i.e.*, a *trustee plan*) which is a political giving program in which a corporation pays the cost of establishing and administering separate bank accounts for any employee who wishes to participate. The cost of administering and establishing includes the payment of costs for a payroll deduction or check-off plan and the cost of maintaining the separate bank accounts.

(1) The employees must exercise complete control and discretion over the disbursement of the monies in their accounts.

(2) The trustee, bank, or other administrator shall not provide the corporation or its separate segregated fund any report of the source or recipient of any contribution(s) or donation(s) into or out of any account or of the amount any employee has in an account.

(3) The trustee, bank, or other administrator may provide the corporation or its separate segregated fund with a periodic report limited to information about the total number of employees in the program, the total number of funds in all the accounts combined, and the total amount of contributions made to all candidates and committees combined.

(4) No stockholder, director, or employee of the corporation or its separate segregated fund may exert pressure of any kind to induce participation in the program.

(5) No stockholder, director, or employee of the corporation or its separate segregated fund may exercise any direction or control, either oral or written, over contributions by participants in the program to any candidate, group of candidates, political party, or other person.

(b) An employee participation plan must be made available to all employees including members of a labor organization who are employees of the corporation. Communications about participation in the plan may be conducted by either the corporation or the labor organization or both.

(c) A labor organization may establish and administer an employee participation plan subject to the above provisions, except that the cost shall be borne by the labor organization.

(d) The method used to transmit employee or member contributions to the candidate or political committee may not in any manner identify the corporation or labor organization which established the employee participation plan.

[41 FR 35955, Aug. 25, 1976]

§114.12 Incorporation of political committees; payment of fringe benefits.

(a) An organization may incorporate and not be subject to the provisions of this part if the organization incorporates for liability purposes only, and if the organization is a political committee as defined in 11 CFR 100.5. Notwithstanding the corporate status of the political committee, the treasurer of an incorporated political committee remains personally responsible for carrying out their respective duties under the Act.

(b) [Reserved]

(c)(1) A corporation or labor organization may not pay the employer's share of the cost of fringe benefits, such as health and life insurance and retirement, for employees or members on leave-without-pay to participate in political campaigns of Federal candidates. The separate segregated fund of a corporation or a labor organization may pay the employer's share of fringe benefits, and such payment would be a contribution in-kind to the candidate. An employee or member may, out of unreimbursed personal funds, assure the continuity of his or her fringe benefits during absence from work for political campaigning, and such payment would not be a contribution in-kind.

(2) Service credit for periods of leave-without-pay is not considered compensation for purposes of this section if the employer normally gives identical treatment to employees placed on leave-without-pay for nonpolitical purposes.

[41 FR 35955, Aug. 25, 1976, as amended at 45 FR 21210, Apr. 1, 1980; 60 FR 31382, June 15, 1995; 60 FR 64279, Dec. 14, 1995; 79 FR 16663, Mar. 26, 2014]

§ 114.13 Use of meeting rooms.

Notwithstanding any other provisions of part 114, a corporation or labor organization which customarily makes its meeting rooms available to clubs, civic or community organizations, or other groups may make such facilities available to a political committee or candidate if the meeting rooms are made available to any candidate or political committee upon request and on the same terms given to other groups using the meeting rooms.

[60 FR 64279, Dec. 14, 1995]

§§ 114.14–114.15 [Reserved]

PART 115—FEDERAL CONTRACTORS

AUTHORITY: 52 U.S.C. 30107(a)(8), 30111(a)(8), and 30119.

SOURCE: 41 FR 35963, Aug. 25, 1976, unless otherwise noted.

§ 115.1 Definitions.

(a) *A Federal contractor* means a person, as defined in 11 CFR 100.10 who—

(1) Enters into any contract with the United States or any department or agency thereof either for—

(i) The rendition of personal services; or

(ii) Furnishing any material, supplies, or equipment; or

(iii) Selling any land or buildings;

(2) If the payment for the performance of the contract or payment for the material, supplies, equipment, land, or building is to be made in whole or in part from funds appropriated by the Congress.

(b) The period during which a person is prohibited from making a contribution or expenditure is the time between the earlier of the commencement of negotiations or when the requests for proposals are sent out, and the later of—

(1) The completion of performance under; or

(2) The termination of negotiations for, the contract or furnishing of material, supplies, equipment, land, or buildings, or the rendition of personal services.

(c) For purposes of this part, a contract includes

(1) A sole source, negotiated, or advertised procurement conducted by the United States or any of its agencies;

(2) A written (except as otherwise authorized) contract, between any person and the United States or any of its departments or agencies, for the furnishing of personal property, real property, or personal services; and

(3) Any modification of a contract.

(d) The basic contractual relationship must be with the United States or any department or agency thereof. A person who contracts with a State or local jurisdiction or entity other than the United States or any department or agency thereof is not subject to this part, even if the State or local jurisdiction or entity is funded in whole or in part from funds appropriated by the Congress. The third party beneficiary of a Federal contract is not subject to the prohibitions of this part.

(e) The term labor organization has the meaning given it by § 114.1(a).

[41 FR 35963, Aug. 25, 1976, as amended at 45 FR 21210, Apr. 1, 1980]

§ 115.2 Prohibition.

(a) It shall be unlawful for a Federal contractor, as defined in § 115.1(a), to make, either directly or indirectly, any contribution or expenditure of money or other thing of value, or to promise expressly or impliedly to make any such contribution or expenditure to any political party, committee, or candidate for Federal office or to any person for any political purpose or use. This prohibition does not apply to contributions or expenditures in connection with State or local elections.

(b) This prohibition runs for the time period set forth in § 115.1(b).

(c) It shall be unlawful for any person knowingly to solicit any such contribution from a Federal contractor.

§ 115.3 Corporations, labor organizations, membership organizations, cooperatives, and corporations without capital stock.

(a) Corporations, labor organizations, membership organizations, cooperatives, and corporations without capital stock to which this part applies may expend treasury monies to establish, administer, and solicit contributions to any separate segregated fund subject to the provisions of part 114. Each specific prohibition, allowance, and duty applicable to a corporation, labor organization, or separate segregated fund under part 114 applies to a corporation, labor organization, or separate segregated fund to which this part applies.

(b) The question of whether a professional organization is a corporation is determined by the law of the State in which the professional organization exists.

§ 115.4 Partnerships.

(a) The assets of a partnership which is a Federal contractor may not be used to make contributions or expenditures in connection with Federal elections.

(b) Individual partners may make contributions or expenditures in their own names from their personal assets.

(c) Nothing in this part prohibits an employee of a partnership which is a Federal contractor from making contributions or expenditures from his or her personal assets.

§ 115.5 Individuals and sole proprietors.

Individuals or sole proprietors who are Federal contractors are prohibited from making contributions or expenditures from their business, personal, or other funds under their dominion or control. The spouse of an individual or sole proprietor who is a Federal contractor is not prohibited from making a personal contribution or expenditure in his or her name.

§ 115.6 Employee contributions or expenditures.

Nothing in this part shall prohibit the stockholders, officers, or employees of a corporation, the employees, officers, or members of an unincorporated association, cooperative, membership organization, labor organization, or other group or organization which is a Federal contractor from making contributions or expenditures from their personal assets.

PART 116—DEBTS OWED BY CANDIDATES AND POLITICAL COMMITTEES

116.11 Restriction on an authorized committee's repayment of personal loans exceeding $250,000 made by the candidate to the authorized committee.
116.12 Repayment of candidate loans of $250,000 or less.

AUTHORITY: 52 U.S.C. 30103(d), 30104(b)(8), 30111(a)(8), 30116, 30118, and 30141.

SOURCE: 55 FR 26386, June 27, 1990, unless otherwise noted.

§ 116.1 Definitions.

(a) *Terminating committee.* For purposes of this part, *terminating committee* means any political committee that is winding down its political activities in preparation for filing a termination report, and that would be able to terminate under 11 CFR 102.3 except that it has outstanding debts or obligations. A political committee will be considered to be winding down its political activities if it has ceased to make or accept contributions and expenditures, other than contributions accepted for debt retirement purposes and expenditures representing payments of debts or obligations previously incurred or payments for the costs associated with the termination of political activity, such as the costs of complying with the post election requirements of the Act, if applicable, and other necessary administrative costs associated with winding down a campaign or winding down committee activities, including office space rental, staff salaries and office supplies.

(b) *Ongoing committee.* For purposes of this part, *ongoing committee* means any political committee that has not terminated and does not qualify as a terminating committee.

(c) *Commercial vendor.* For purposes of this part, *commercial vendor* means any persons providing goods or services to a candidate or political committee whose usual and normal business involves the sale, rental, lease or provision of those goods or services.

(d) *Disputed debt.* For purposes of this part, *disputed debt* means an actual or potential debt or obligation owed by a political committee, including an obligation arising from a written contract, promise or agreement to make an expenditure, where there is a bona fide disagreement between the creditor and the political committee as to the exist-ence or amount of the obligation owed by the political committee.

(e) *Extension of credit.* For purposes of this part, *extension of credit* includes but is not limited to:

(1) Any agreement between the creditor and political committee that full payment is not due until after the creditor provides goods or services to the political committee;

(2) Any agreement between the creditor and the political committee that the political committee will have additional time to pay the creditor beyond the previously agreed to due date; and

(3) The failure of the political committee to make full payment to the creditor by a previously agreed to due date.

(f) *Creditor.* For purposes of this part, *creditor* means any person or entity to whom a debt is owed.

[55 FR 26386, June 27, 1990; 55 FR 34007, Aug. 20, 1990]

§ 116.2 Debts owed by terminating committees, ongoing committees, and authorized committees.

(a) *Terminating committees.* A terminating committee may settle outstanding debts provided that the terminating committee files a debt settlement plan and the requirements of 11 CFR 116.7 are satisfied. The Commission will review each debt settlement plan filed to determine whether or not the terminating committee appears to have complied with the requirements set forth in this part, and whether or not the proposed debt settlement plan would result in an apparent violation of the Act or the Commission's regulations.

(b) *Ongoing committees.* Ongoing committees shall not settle any outstanding debts for less than the entire amount owed, but may request a Commission determination that such debts are not payable under 11 CFR 116.9, and may resolve disputed debts under 11 CFR 116.10. Creditors may forgive debts owed by ongoing committees under the limited circumstances provided in 11 CFR 116.8.

(c) *Authorized committees.* (1) An authorized committee shall not settle any outstanding debts for less than the entire amount owed if any other authorized committee of the same candidate has permissible funds available to pay part or all of the amount outstanding. Except as provided in paragraph (c)(3), of this section, an authorized committee shall not terminate under 11 CFR 102.3 if—

(i) It has any outstanding debts or obligations; or

(ii) It has any funds or assets available to pay part or all of the outstanding debts or obligations owed by another authorized committee of the same candidate and that other authorized committee is unable to pay such debts or obligations.

(2) No transfers of funds may be made from a candidate's authorized committee to another authorized committee of the same candidate if the transferor committee has net debts outstanding at the time of the transfer under the formula described in 11 CFR 110.1(b)(3)(ii).

(3) An authorized committee that qualifies as a terminating committee may assign debts to another authorized committee of the same candidate to the extent permitted under applicable state law provided that the authorized committee assigning the debts has no cash on hand or assets available to pay any part of the outstanding debts, and provided that the authorized committee assigning the debts was not organized to further the candidate's campaign in an election not yet held. If a Presidential candidate elects to receive federal funds pursuant to 11 CFR part 9001 *et seq.* or 11 CFR part 9031 *et seq.*, the authorized committee(s) of the Presidential candidate shall not assign debts or receive assigned debts until after the authorized committee(s) or the Presidential candidate has made all required repayments pursuant to 11 CFR parts 9007 and 9038 and has paid all civil penalties pursuant to 52 U.S.C. 30109. An authorized committee that has assigned all its outstanding debts may terminate if—

(i) The authorized committee that has assigned the debts otherwise qualifies for termination under 11 CFR 102.3; and

(ii) The authorized committee that received the assigned debts notifies the Commission in writing that it has as-

sumed the obligation to pay the entire amount owed and that it has assumed the obligation to report the debts, and any contributions received for retirement of the assigned debts, in accordance with 11 CFR part 104. The assigned debts shall be disclosed on a separate schedule of debts and obligations attached to the authorized committee's reports. Contributions received for retirement of the assigned debts shall be disclosed on a separate schedule of receipts attached to the authorized committee's reports. *See* 11 CFR 110.1 (b)(3) and (b)(4) and 110.2 (b)(3) and (b)(4). The authorized committee that has assigned the debts shall notify each creditor in writing of the assignment no later than thirty days before the assignment takes effect and shall include the name and address of the authorized committee that will receive the assigned debts.

[55 FR 26386, June 27, 1990, as amended at 79 FR 77849, Dec. 29, 2014]

§116.3 Extensions of credit by commercial vendors.

(a) *Unincorporated vendor.* A commercial vendor that is not a corporation may extend credit to a candidate, a political committee or another person on behalf of a candidate or political committee. An extension of credit will not be considered a contribution to the candidate or political committee provided that the credit is extended in the ordinary course of the commercial vendor's business and the terms are substantially similar to extensions of credit to nonpolitical debtors that are of similar risk and size of obligation.

(b) *Incorporated vendor.* A corporation in its capacity as a commercial vendor may extend credit to a candidate, a political committee or another person on behalf of a candidate or political committee provided that the credit is extended in the ordinary course of the corporation's business and the terms are substantially similar to extensions of credit to nonpolitical debtors that are of similar risk and size of obligation.

(c) *Ordinary course of business.* In determining whether credit was extended in the ordinary course of business, the Commission will consider—

(1) Whether the commercial vendor followed its established procedures and its past practice in approving the extension of credit;

(2) Whether the commercial vendor received prompt payment in full if it previously extended credit to the same candidate or political committee; and

(3) Whether the extension of credit conformed to the usual and normal practice in the commercial vendor's trade or industry.

(d) *Extension of credit by regulated industries.* The Commission may rely on the regulations prescribed by the Federal Communications Commission, the Interstate Commerce Commission, and the Department of Transportation on behalf of the Civil Aeronautics Board, issued pursuant to 52 U.S.C. 30141 and any other regulations prescribed by other Federal agencies to determine whether extensions of credit by the entities regulated by those Federal agencies were made in the ordinary course of business.

[55 FR 26386, June 27, 1990, as amended at 79 FR 77849, Dec. 29, 2014]

§ 116.4 Forgiveness or settlement of debts owed to commercial vendors.

(a) *Unincorporated vendor.* A commercial vendor that is not a corporation may forgive or settle a debt incurred by a candidate, a political committee or another person on behalf of a candidate or political committee for less than the entire amount owed on the debt. The amount forgiven will not be considered a contribution by the commercial vendor to the candidate or political committee if—

(1) The amount forgiven is exempted from the definition of contribution in 11 CFR part 100, subpart C; or

(2) The commercial vendor has treated the debt in a commercially reasonable manner and the requirements of 11 CFR 116.7 or 116.8, as appropriate, are satisfied.

(b) *Incorporated vendor.* A corporation may not forgive or settle a debt incurred by a candidate, a political committee or another person on behalf of a candidate or political committee for less than the entire amount owed on the debt unless—

(1) The amount forgiven is exempted from the definition of contribution in 11 CFR part 100, subpart C; or

(2) The corporation has treated the debt in a commercially reasonable manner and the requirements of 11 CFR 116.7 or 116.8, as appropriate, are satisfied.

(c) *Reasonable efforts by a political committee.* A debt or obligation owed by a candidate or a political committee may be totally forgiven (*see* 11 CFR 116.8), or settled (*see* 11 CFR 116.7), provided that—

(1) The amount forgiven is exempted from the definition of contribution in 11 CFR part 100, subpart C; or

(2) The candidate and the political committee have undertaken all reasonable efforts to satisfy the outstanding debt and the requirements of 11 CFR 116.7 or 116.8, as appropriate, including the submission of the information specified in those sections and Commission review, are satisfied.

(d) *Commercially reasonable.* The Commission will determine that a debt settlement between a political committee and a commercial vendor is commercially reasonable if—

(1) The initial extension of credit was made in accordance with 11 CFR 116.3;

(2) The candidate or political committee has undertaken all reasonable efforts to satisfy the outstanding debt. Such efforts may include, but are not limited to, the following—

(i) Engaging in fundraising efforts;

(ii) Reducing overhead and administrative costs; and

(iii) Liquidating assets; and

(3) The commercial vendor has pursued its remedies as vigorously as it would pursue its remedies against a nonpolitical debtor in similar circumstances. Such remedies may include, but are not limited to, the following—

(i) Oral and written requests for payment;

(ii) Withholding delivery of additional goods or services until overdue debts are satisfied;

(iii) Imposition of additional charges or penalties for late payment;

(iv) Referral of overdue debts to a commercial debt collection service; and

(v) Litigation.

(e) *Settlement or forgiveness not required.* The provisions of this part shall not be construed to require a commercial vendor to forgive or settle the debt for less than the entire amount owed.

(f) *Reporting.* The political committee shall continue to report the debt in accordance with 11 CFR 104.3(d) and 104.11 until the Commission has completed a review of the debt settlement plan pursuant to 11 CFR 116.7(f) or until the Commission has completed a review of the request to forgive the debt pursuant to 11 CFR 116.8, or until the political committee pays the debt, whichever occurs first.

[55 FR 26386, June 27, 1990, as amended at 67 FR 78682, Dec. 26, 2002]

§ 116.5 **Advances by committee staff and other individuals.**

(a) *Scope.* This section applies to individuals who are not acting as commercial vendors. Individuals who are acting as commercial vendors shall follow the requirements of 11 CFR 116.3 and 116.4.

(b) *Treatment as contributions.* The payment by an individual from his or her personal funds, including a personal credit card, for the costs incurred in providing goods or services to, or obtaining goods or services that are used by or on behalf of, a candidate or a political committee is a contribution unless the payment is exempted from the definition of contribution under 11 CFR 100.79. If the payment is not exempted under 11 CFR 100.79, it shall be considered a contribution by the individual unless—

(1) The payment is for the individual's transportation expenses incurred while traveling on behalf of a candidate or political committee of a political party or for usual and normal subsistence expenses incurred by an individual, other than a volunteer, while traveling on behalf of a candidate or political committee of a political party; and

(2) The individual is reimbursed within sixty days after the closing date of the billing statement on which the charges first appear if the payment was made using a personal credit card, or within thirty days after the date on which the expenses were incurred if a personal credit card was not used. For purposes of this section, the closing date shall be the date indicated on the billing statement which serves as the cutoff date for determining which charges are included on that billing statement. In addition, "subsistence expenses" include only expenditures for personal living expenses related to a particular individual traveling on committee business, such as food or lodging.

(c) *Treatment as debts.* A political committee shall treat the obligation arising from a payment described in paragraph (b) of this section as an outstanding debt until reimbursed.

(d) *Settlement or forgiveness of the debt.* The individual and the political committee may agree to the total forgiveness of the debt (*See* 11 CFR 116.8) or a settlement of the debt for less than the entire amount owed (*See* 11 CFR 116.7), provided that the requirements of 11 CFR 116.7 or 116.8, as appropriate, including the submission of the information specified in these sections and Commission review, are satisfied. The provisions of this part shall not be construed to require the individual to forgive or settle the debt for less than the entire amount owed.

(e) *Reporting.* The political committee shall continue to report the obligation arising from the payment as a debt in accordance with 11 CFR 104.3(d) and 104.11 until the Commission has completed a review of the debt settlement plan pursuant to 11 CFR 116.7(f) or until the Commission has completed a review of the request to forgive the debt pursuant to 11 CFR 116.8, or until the political committee pays the debt, whichever occurs first.

[55 FR 26386, June 27, 1990, as amended at 56 FR 35911, July 29, 1991; 67 FR 78682, Dec. 26, 2002]

§ 116.6 **Salary payments owed to employees.**

(a) *Treatment as debts or volunteer services.* If a political committee does not pay an employee for services rendered to the political committee in accordance with an employment contract or a formal or informal agreement to do so, the unpaid amount either may be treated as a debt owed by the political committee to the employee or, provided that the employee signs a written statement agreeing to be considered a volunteer, converted to a volunteer services arrangement under 11 CFR 100.74. The unpaid amount shall not be treated as a contribution under 11 CFR part 100, subparts B and C.

(b) *Settlement or forgiveness of the debt.* If the unpaid amount is treated as a debt, the employee and the political committee may agree to a settlement of the debt for less than the entire amount owed pursuant to 11 CFR 116.7. The provisions of this part shall not be construed to require the employee to settle the debt for less than the entire amount owed.

(c) *Reporting.* If the unpaid amount is treated as a debt, the political committee shall continue to report the debt in accordance with 11 CFR 104.3(d) and 104.11 until the Commission has completed a review of the debt settlement plan pursuant to 11 CFR 116.7(f) or until the employee agrees to be considered a volunteer, or until the political committee pays the debt, whichever occurs first.

[55 FR 26386, June 27, 1990, as amended at 67 FR 78682, Dec. 26, 2002]

§ 116.7 Debt settlement plans filed by terminating committees; Commission review.

(a) *Procedures for filing debt settlement plans.* Every terminating committee as defined in 11 CFR 116.1(a) shall file at least one debt settlement plan with the Commission prior to filing its termination report under 11 CFR 102.3. The terminating committee shall file a debt settlement plan after the creditors included in the debt settlement plan have agreed to the settlement or forgiveness of the particular debt(s) owed to each of them. The terminating committee shall not make any payments to the creditors included in the debt settlement plan until completion of Commission review. The Commission encourages terminating committees to include as many debt settlement agreements as possible in a debt settlement plan. The terminating committee shall not file its termination report under 11 CFR 102.3 and shall not terminate until each debt or obligation owed either:

(1) Has been paid in full;

(2) Has been settled and the requirements of this section, including Commission review, have been satisfied;

(3) Has been forgiven by the creditor and the requirements of 11 CFR 116.8, including Commission review, have been satisfied;

(4) Has been determined not to be payable pursuant to 11 CFR 116.9; or

(5) Has been otherwise extinguished or discharged.

(b) *Debts subject to settlement.* Debts and obligations subject to the debt settlement and Commission review requirements and procedures set forth in this section include:

(1) Amounts owed to commercial vendors (*See* 11 CFR 116.3 and 116.4);

(2) Debts arising from advances by committee staff and other individuals (*See* 11 CFR 116.5);

(3) Salary owed to committee employees (*See* 11 CFR 116.6); and

(4) Debts arising from loans from political committees or individuals, including candidates, to the extent permitted under 11 CFR part 110.

(c) *Debts that shall not be settled; Disputed debts.* (1) Debts and obligations that shall not be forgiven or settled for less than the entire amount owed include repayment obligations pursuant to 11 CFR 9007.2, 9008.10, 9008.11, 9038.2 or 9038.3 of funds received from the Presidential Election Campaign Fund or the Presidential Primary Matching Payment Account.

(2) Disputed debts are not subject to the debt settlement and Commission review requirements and procedures. (*See* CFR 116.10).

(d) *Reporting.* The terminating committee shall continue to report each outstanding debt or obligation included in a debt settlement plan in accordance with 11 CFR 104.3(d) and 104.11 until the Commission has completed a review of the debt settlement plan pursuant to paragraph (f) of this section. The terminating committee shall continue to report all remaining debts and obligations not included in the debt settlement plan in accordance with 11 CFR 104.3 and 104.11.

(e) *Contents of debt settlement plans.* (1) The debt settlement plan shall provide the following information on each debt covered by the plan—

(i) The terms of the initial extension of credit and a description of the terms under which the creditor has extended credit to nonpolitical debtors of similar risk and size of obligation;

(ii) A description of the efforts made by the candidate or the terminating committee to satisfy the debt;

(iii) A description of the remedies pursued by the creditor to obtain payment of the debt and a comparison to the remedies customarily pursued by the creditor in similar circumstances involving nonpolitical debtors; and

(iv) The terms of the debt settlement and a comparison to the terms of the creditor's other debt settlements involving nonpolitical debtors in similar circumstances, if any.

(2) Each debt settlement plan filed under this section shall include a signed statement from each creditor covered indicating agreement to the terms of the settlement of the debt owed to that creditor.

(3) The debt settlement plan shall include a statement as to whether the terminating committee has sufficient cash on hand to pay the total amount indicated in the debt settlement plan, and if not, a statement as to what steps the terminating committee will take to obtain the funds needed to make the payments.

(4) If a debt settlement plan does not include settlements for all of the terminating committee's outstanding debts and obligations, the debt settlement plan shall include a separate list of all of the terminating committee's remaining debts and obligations, including debts that are not subject to debt settlement as set forth in paragraph (c) of this section. The debt settlement plan shall indicate—

(i) Whether the terminating committee intends to pay the entire amount still owed on each remaining debt or obligation or to settle such debts and obligations, and if settlement is contemplated, the terms that were or will be offered to the creditor(s); and

(ii) Whether the terminating committee has sufficient cash on hand to pay such remaining debts and obligations, or to pay a lesser portion of such amounts, and if not, what steps the terminating committee will take to ob-

tain the funds needed to make such payments.

(5) If the terminating committee expects to have residual funds or assets after disposing of all its outstanding debts and obligations, the debt settlement plan shall include a statement as to the purpose for which such residual funds or assets will be used. *See* 11 CFR 110.1(b)(3)(iii) regarding contributions received to pay net debts outstanding owed by authorized committees.

(6) The political committee filing the debt settlement plan shall demonstrate in the debt settlement plan that such political committee qualifies as a terminating committee under 11 CFR 116.1(a) and shall state when the political committee expects to file a termination report under 11 CFR 102.3.

(7) Upon the Commission's request, the candidate, the terminating committee or the creditor shall provide such additional information as the Commission may require to review the debt settlement plan. The Commission may also require the submission of additional debt settlement agreements prior to Commission review of the debt settlement plan.

(f) *Commission review of debt settlement plans.* In reviewing the debt settlement plan, the Commission will consider—

(1) The information provided by the terminating committee and the creditors under this section;

(2) The amount of each debt that remains unpaid and the length of time each debt has been overdue;

(3) The amount and percentage of each debt that would be forgiven under the plan;

(4) The total amount of debts and obligations owed by the terminating committee to all creditors, compared to the total amount of cash on hand and other amounts available to pay those debts and obligations;

(5) The year to date expenditures and receipts of the terminating committee; and

(6) Whether the total percentage that was or will be repaid on any loans made by the candidate to the terminating committee is comparable to the total percentage that was or will be paid to other creditors.

(g) *Debts dischargeable in bankruptcy.* If a terminating committee is released from debts or obligations pursuant to a discharge under 11 U.S.C. chapter 7, the terminating committee's debt settlement plan shall include a copy of the order issued by the Bankruptcy Court of the United States so indicating, and a list of all debts and obligations from which the terminating committee is released, in lieu of the information specified in paragraphs (e)(1), (e)(2), and (e)(3) of this section.

§ 116.8 Creditor forgiveness of debts owed by ongoing committees; Commission review.

(a) *General requirements.* A creditor may forgive the outstanding balance of a debt owed by an ongoing committee if the creditor and the ongoing committee have satisfied the requirements of 11 CFR 116.3 or 116.5, as appropriate, regarding extensions of credit by commercial vendors and advances by committee staff and other individuals, and the debt has been outstanding for at least twenty-four months, and—

(1) The creditor has exercised reasonable diligence in attempting to locate the ongoing committee and has been unable to do so; or

(2) The ongoing committee—

(i) Does not have sufficient cash on hand to pay the creditor;

(ii) Has receipts of less than $1000 during the previous twenty-four months;

(iii) Has disbursements of less than $1000 during the previous twenty-four months; and

(iv) Owes debts to other creditors of such magnitude that the creditor could reasonably conclude that the ongoing committee will not pay this particular debt.

(b) *Procedures for forgiving debts.* A creditor that intends to forgive a debt owed by an ongoing committee shall notify the Commission by letter of its intent. The letter shall demonstrate that the requirements set forth in paragraph (a) of this section are satisfied. The letter shall provide the following information—

(1) The terms of the initial extension of credit and a description of the terms under which the creditor has extended credit to nonpolitical debtors of similar risk and size of obligation;

(2) A description of the efforts made by the candidate or the ongoing committee to satisfy the debt;

(3) A description of the remedies pursued by the creditor to obtain payment of the debt and a comparison to the remedies customarily pursued by the creditor in similar circumstances involving nonpolitical debtors; and

(4) An indication that the creditor has forgiven other debts involving nonpolitical debtors in similar circumstances, if any.

(c) *Commission review.* Upon the Commission's request, the ongoing committee or the creditor shall provide such additional information as the Commission may require to review the creditor's request. The Commission will review each request to forgive a debt to determine whether the candidate, the ongoing committee, and the creditor have complied with the requirements of 11 CFR part 116, and whether or not the forgiveness of the debt would result in an apparent violation of the Act or the Commission's regulations.

§ 116.9 Creditors that cannot be found or that are out of business.

(a) *General requirements.* A political committee may request that the Commission determine that a debt owed to a creditor is not payable for purposes of the Act if the debt has been outstanding for at least twenty-four months, and the requirements of paragraph (b) or (c) of this section, as appropriate, have been satisfied, and—

(1) The creditor has gone out of business and no other entity has a right to be paid the amount owed; or

(2) The political committee has exercised reasonable diligence in attempting to locate the creditor and has been unable to do so. *Reasonable diligence in attempting to locate the creditor* means the political committee has attempted to ascertain the current address and telephone number, and has attempted to contact the creditor by registered or certified mail, and either in person or by telephone.

(b) *Terminating committees.* If the political committee making the request is a terminating committee, the terminating committee shall include the request in a debt settlement plan filed with the Commission, and shall demonstrate that the requirements of 11 CFR 116.3, 116.5 or 116.6, as appropriate, and 116.9(a) are satisfied. The terminating committee shall continue to disclose the debt on its schedules of outstanding debts and obligations until the Commission has completed its review of the debt settlement plan pursuant to 11 CFR 116.7(f) and has determined that the debt is not payable for purposes of the Act.

(c) *Ongoing committees.* If the political committee making the request is an ongoing committee, the ongoing committee shall make the request in writing and shall demonstrate that the requirements of 11 CFR 116.3, 116.5 or 116.6, as appropriate, and 116.9(a) are satisfied. The Commission will review the request to determine whether the ongoing committee and the creditor have complied with the requirements of 11 CFR part 116, and to determine whether reporting the debt as not payable would result in an apparent violation of the Act or the Commission's regulations. The ongoing committee shall continue to disclose the debt on its schedules of outstanding debts and obligations until the Commission has completed its review of the request and has determined that the debt is not payable for purposes of the Act.

(d) *Reporting.* Upon notification that the Commission has determined that the debt is not payable for purposes of the Act, the political committee may list the debt as not payable on the next due report. Notwithstanding 11 CFR 104.11, the debt does not have to be included in subsequent reports unless the status of the debt changes. The presence of a debt that the Commission has determined is not payable shall not bar the political committee from terminating its registration pursuant to 11 CFR 102.3.

§116.10 Disputed debts.

(a) *Reporting disputed debts.* A political committee shall report a disputed debt in accordance with 11 CFR 104.3(d) and 104.11 if the creditor has provided something of value to the political committee. Until the dispute is resolved, the political committee shall disclose on the appropriate reports any amounts paid to the creditor, any

amount the political committee admits it owes and the amount the creditor claims is owed. The political committee may also note on the appropriate reports that the disclosure of the disputed debt does not constitute an admission of liability or a waiver of any claims the political committee may have against the creditor. (*See also* 11 CFR 9035.1(a)(2) regarding the effect of disputed debts on a candidate's expenditure limitations under 11 CFR part 9035.)

(b) *Disputed debts owed by terminating committees.* If a terminating committee and a creditor have been unable to resolve a disputed debt, and the terminating committee files a debt settlement plan covering other debts or other creditors, the terminating committee shall include in the debt settlement plan a brief description as to the nature of the dispute and the status of the terminating committee's efforts to resolve the dispute. The debt settlement plan need not include a signed affidavit from the creditor involved in the dispute pursuant to 11 CFR 116.7(e)(2).

§116.11 Restriction on an authorized committee's repayment of personal loans exceeding $250,000 made by the candidate to the authorized committee.

(a) For purposes of this part, personal loans mean a loan or loans, including advances, made by a candidate, using personal funds, as defined in 11 CFR 100.33, to his or her authorized committee where the proceeds of the loan were used in connection with the candidate's campaign for election. Personal loans also include loans made to a candidate's authorized committee that are endorsed or guaranteed by the candidate or that are secured by the candidate's personal funds.

(b) For personal loans that, in the aggregate, exceed $250,000 in connection with an election, the authorized committee:

(1) May repay the entire amount of the personal loans using contributions to the candidate or the candidate's authorized committee provided that those contributions were made on the day of the election or before;

(2) May repay up to $250,000 of the personal loans from contributions

made to the candidate or the candidate's authorized committee after the date of the election; and

(3) Must not repay, directly or indirectly, the aggregate amount of the personal loans that exceeds $250,000, from contributions to the candidate or the candidate's authorized committee if those contributions were made after the date of the election.

(c) If the aggregate outstanding balance of the personal loans exceeds $250,000 after the election, the authorized political committee must comply with the following conditions:

(1) If the authorized committee uses the amount of cash on hand as of the day after the election to repay all or part of the personal loans, it must do so within 20 days of the election.

(2) Within 20 days of the election date, the authorized committee must treat the portion of the aggregate outstanding balance of the personal loans that exceeds $250,000 minus the amount of cash on hand as of the day after the election used to repay the loan as a contribution by the candidate.

(3) The candidate's principal campaign committee must report the transactions in paragraphs (c)(1) and (c)(2) of this section in the first report scheduled to be filed after the election pursuant to 11 CFR 104.5(a) or (b).

(d) This section applies separately to each election.

[68 FR 3996, Jan. 27, 2003]

§ 116.12 Repayment of candidate loans of $250,000 or less.

(a) A candidate's authorized committee may repay to the candidate a personal loan, as defined in 11 CFR 116.11(a), of up to $250,000 where the proceeds of the loan were used in connection with the candidate's campaign for election. The repayment may be made from contributions to the candidate or the candidate's authorized committee at any time before, on, or after the date of the election.

(b) This section applies separately to each election.

(c) Nothing in this section shall supersede 11 CFR 9035.2 regarding the limitations on expenditures from personal funds or family funds of a presidential candidate who accepts matching funds.

[68 FR 3996, Jan. 27, 2003]

SUBCHAPTER B—ADMINISTRATIVE REGULATIONS

PART 200—PETITIONS FOR RULEMAKING

Sec.
200.1 Purpose of scope.
200.2 Procedural requirements.
200.3 Processing of petitions.
200.4 Disposition of petitions.
200.5 Agency considerations.
200.6 Administrative record.

AUTHORITY: 52 U.S.C. 30107(a)(8), 30111(a)(8); 5 U.S.C. 553(e).

SOURCE: 57 FR 34510, Aug. 5, 1992, unless otherwise noted.

§ 200.1 Purpose and scope.

This part prescribes the procedures for the submission, consideration, and disposition of petitions filed with the Federal Election Commission. It establishes the conditions under which the Commission may identify and respond to petitions for rulemaking, and informs the public of the procedures the agency follows in response to such petitions.

[57 FR 34510, Aug. 5, 1992; 57 FR 39743, Sept. 1, 1992]

§ 200.2 Procedural requirements.

(a) Any interested person may file with the Commission a written petition for the issuance, amendment, or repeal of a rule implementing any of the following statutes:

(1) The Federal Election Campaign Act of 1971, as amended, 52 U.S.C. 30101 et seq.;

(2) The Presidential Election Campaign Fund Act, as amended, 26 U.S.C. 9001 et seq.;

(3) The Presidential Primary Matching Payment Account Act, as amended, 26 U.S.C. 9031 et seq.;

(4) The Freedom of Information Act, 5 U.S.C. 552; or

(5) Any other law that the Commission is required to implement and administer.

(b) The petition shall—

(1) Include the name and address of the petitioner or agent. An authorized agent of the petitioner may submit the petition, but the agent shall disclose the identity of his or her principal;

(2) Identify itself as a petition for the issuance, amendment, or repeal of a rule;

(3) Identify the specific section(s) of the regulations to be affected;

(4) Set forth the factual and legal grounds on which the petitioner relies, in support of the proposed action; and

(5) Be addressed and submitted to the Federal Election Commission, Office of General Counsel, at the street address identified in the definition of "Commission" in § 1.2.

(c) The petition may include draft regulatory language that would effectuate the petitioner's proposal.

(d) The Commission may, in its discretion, treat a document that fails to conform to the format requirements of paragraph (b) of this section as a basis for a sua sponte rulemaking. For example, the Commission may consider whether to initiate a rulemaking project addressing issues raised in an advisory opinion request submitted under 11 CFR 112.1 or in a complaint filed under 11 CFR 111.4. However, the Commission need not follow the procedures of 11 CFR 200.3 in these instances.

[57 FR 34510, Aug. 5, 1992, as amended at 79 FR 77849, Dec. 29, 2014; 82 FR 60854, Dec. 26, 2017]

§ 200.3 Processing of petitions.

(a) If a document qualifies as a petition under 11 CFR 200.2, the Commission, upon the recommendation of the Office of General Counsel, will—

(1) Publish a Notice of Availability in the FEDERAL REGISTER, stating that the petition is available for public inspection in the Commission's Public Records Office and that statements in support of or in opposition to the petition may be filed within a stated period after publication of the notice;

(2) Send a letter to the Commissioner of Internal Revenue, pursuant to 52 U.S.C. 30111(f), seeking the IRS's comments on the petition; and

(3) Send a letter to the petitioner, acknowledging receipt of the petition and informing the petitioner of the above actions.

(b) If the petition does not comply with the requirements of 11 CFR

200.2(b), the Office of General Counsel may notify the petitioner of the nature of any discrepancies.

(c) If the Commission decides that a Notice of Inquiry, Advance Notice of Proposed Rulemaking, or a public hearing on the petition would contribute to its determination whether to commence a rulemaking proceeding, it will publish an appropriate notice in the FEDERAL REGISTER, to advise interested persons and to invite their participation.

(d) The Commission will not consider the merits of the petition before the expiration of the comment period on the Notice of Availability.

(e) The Commission will consider all comments filed within the comment period prescribed in the relevant FEDERAL REGISTER notice. The Commission may, at its discretion, consider comments received after the close of the comment period.

[57 FR 34510, Aug. 5, 1992, as amended at 79 FR 77849, Dec. 29, 2014]

§ 200.4   Disposition of petitions.

(a) After considering the comments that have been filed within the comment period(s) and any other information relevant to the subject matter of the petition, the Commission will decide whether to initiate a rulemaking based on the filed petition.

(b) If the Commission decides not to initiate a rulemaking, it will give notice of this action by publishing a Notice of Disposition in the FEDERAL REGISTER and sending a letter to the petitioner. The Notice of Disposition will include a brief statement of the grounds for the Commission's decision, except in an action affirming a prior denial.

(c) The Commission may reconsider a petition for rulemaking previously denied if the petitioner submits a written request for reconsideration within 30 calendar days after the date of the denial and if, upon the motion of a Commissioner who voted with the majority that originally denied the petition, the Commission adopts the motion to reconsider by the affirmative vote of four members.

§ 200.5   Agency considerations.

The Commission's decision on the petition for rulemaking may include, but will not be limited to, the following considerations—

(a) The Commission's statutory authority;

(b) Policy considerations;

(c) The desirability of proceeding on a case-by-case-basis;

(d) The necessity or desirability of statutory revision;

(e) Available agency resources.

§ 200.6   Administrative record.

(a) The agency record for the petition process consists of the following:

(1) The petition, including all attachments on which it relies, filed by the petitioner.

(2) Written comments on the petition which have been circulated to and considered by the Commission, including attachments submitted as a part of the comments.

(3) Agenda documents, in the form they are circulated to and considered by the Commission in the course of the petition process.

(4) All notices published in the FEDERAL REGISTER, including the Notice of Availability and Notice of Disposition. If a Notice of Inquiry or Advance Notice of Proposed Rulemaking was published it will also be included.

(5) The transcripts or audio tapes of any public hearing(s) on the petition.

(6) All correspondence between the Commission and the petitioner, other commentators and state or federal agencies pertaining to Commission consideration of the petition.

(7) The Commission's decision on the petition, including all documents identified or filed by the Commission as part of the record relied on in reaching its final decision.

(b) The administrative record specified in paragraph (a) of this section is the exclusive record for the Commission's decision.

PART 201—EX PARTE COMMUNICATIONS

Sec.

201.3 Public funding, audits and litigation: Ex parte contacts prohibited.
201.4 Rulemaking proceedings and advisory opinions: Ex parte contacts reported.
201.5 Sanctions.

AUTHORITY: 52 U.S.C. 30107(a)(8), 30108, 30111(a)(8), and 30111(b); 26 U.S.C. 9007, 9008, 9009(b), 9038, and 9039(b).

SOURCE: 58 FR 59645, Nov. 10, 1993, unless otherwise noted.

§201.1 Purpose and scope.

This part prescribes procedures for handling ex parte communications made in connection with public funding, Commission audits, litigation, rulemaking proceedings and the advisory opinion process. Rules governing such communications made in connection with Commission enforcement actions are found at 11 CFR 111.22, while provisions setting forth employee responsibilities under the Commission's Standards of Conduct rules are found at 11 CFR 7.8.

[58 FR 59645, Nov. 10, 1993, as amended at 76 FR 70331, Nov. 14, 2011]

§201.2 Definitions.

As used in this part:

(a) *Ex parte communication* means any written or oral communication by any person outside the agency to any Commissioner or any member of a Commissioner's staff which imparts information or argument regarding prospective Commission action or potential action concerning:

(1) Any candidate or committee applying for or participating in the public funding process, or

(2) Any ongoing audit, or

(3) Any pending litigation matter, or

(4) Any pending rulemaking, or

(5) Any pending advisory opinion request.

(b) Ex parte communications does not include the following communications.

(1) Statements by any person publicly made in a public forum; or

(2) Statements or inquiries by any person limited to the procedural status of an open proceeding involving an application for public funding, a rulemaking, an advisory opinion request, an audit being conducted pursuant to 26 U.S.C. 9007 (a) and (b), 9008 (g) and

(h), or 9038 (a) and (b), or a litigation matter.

(c) *Commissioner* means an individual appointed to the Federal Election Commission pursuant to 52 U.S.C. 30106(a).

(d) *Commissioner's staff* means all individuals working under the personal supervision of a Commissioner including executive assistants and executive secretaries.

[58 FR 59645, Nov. 10, 1993, as amended at 75 FR 32, Jan. 4, 2010; 79 FR 77849, Dec. 29, 2014]

§201.3 Public funding, audits and litigation: Ex parte contacts prohibited.

(a) In order to avoid the possibility of prejudice, real or apparent, to the public interest in Commission decision-making during the public funding process, in audits undertaken by the Commission, and in any litigation to which the Commission is a party, no person outside the agency shall make or cause to be made to any Commissioner or any member of any Commissioner's staff any ex parte communication regarding any candidate or committee's eligibility for or entitlement to public funding; any audit; or any pending or prospective Commission decision regarding litigation, including whether to initiate, settle, appeal, or seek certiorari, or any other decision concerning a litigation matter; nor shall any Commissioner or member of any Commissioner's staff entertain any such ex parte communications.

(b) The requirements of this section apply:

(1) In the case of public funding, from the time a primary election candidate submits to the Commission the letter required by 11 CFR 9033.1(a), Presidential and Vice Presidential candidates submit to the Commission the letter required by 11 CFR 9003.1, or a committee seeking convention funding registers with the Commission as required by 11 CFR 9008.12(a)(1) or 9008.12(b)(1), until the start of the audit process.

(2)(i) In the case of an audit undertaken pursuant to 26 U.S.C. 9007 (a) and (b), 9008 (g) and (h), or 9038 (a) and (b), from the date of the Commission's letter to a presidential campaign committee, a convention committee, or a host committee asking that it make a pre-inventory check of its records, prior to the commencement of audit fieldwork by the Commission, through the end of the audit process; and

(ii) In the case of an audit undertaken pursuant to 52 U.S.C. 30111(b), from the date the Commission's staff circulates a document for Commission approval containing a proposed referral to undertake an audit, until the Commission publicly issues the final audit report.

(c)(1) A Commissioner or member of a Commissioner's staff who receives an oral ex parte communication concerning any matters addressed in paragraph (a) or (b) of this section shall attempt to prevent the communication. If unsuccessful in preventing the communication, the Commissioner or staff member shall advise the person making the communication that he or she will not consider the communication and shall, as soon after the communication as is reasonably possible but no later than three business days after the communication, unless special circumstances make this impracticable; or prior to the next Commission discussion of the matter, whichever is earlier, prepare a statement setting forth the substance and circumstances of the communication, and deliver the statement to the Designated Agency Ethics Official for placement in the file of the matching fund request, audit or litigation case.

(2) A Commissioner or member of a Commissioner's staff who receives a written ex parte communication concerning any Commission action or potential action concerning any candidate or committee's eligibility for or entitlement to public funding, or any audit, or any prospective Commission decision or action concerning any pending litigation case, during the period described in paragraph (b) of this section shall, as soon after the communication as is reasonably possible but no later than three business days after the communication, unless special circumstances make this impracticable; or prior to the next Commission discussion of the matter, whichever is earlier, deliver a copy of the communication to the Designated Agency Ethics

Official for placement in the file of the audit or litigation case.

[58 FR 59645, Nov. 10, 1993, as amended at 79 FR 77850, Dec. 29, 2014]

§ 201.4 Rulemaking proceedings and advisory opinions: Ex parte contacts reported.

(a) A Commissioner or member of a Commissioner's staff who receives an ex parte communication concerning any rulemaking or advisory opinion during the period described in paragraph (b) of this section shall, as soon after the communication as is reasonably possible but no later than three business days after the communication unless special circumstances make this impracticable, or prior to the next Commission discussion of the matter, whichever is earlier, provide a copy of a written communication or a written summary of an oral communication to the Commission Secretary for placement in the public file of the rulemaking or advisory opinion. The Commissioner or staff member shall advise any person making an oral communication that a written summary of the conversation will be made part of the public record.

(b) The requirements of paragraph (a) of this section apply:

(1) In the case of a rulemaking proceeding, from the date a petition for rulemaking is circulated to Commissioners' offices, or the date on which a proposed rulemaking document is first circulated to the Commission or placed on an agenda of a Commission public meeting, through final Commission action on that rulemaking.

(2) In the case of an advisory opinion, from the date a request for an advisory opinion is circulated to Commissioner's offices through the date on which the advisory opinion is issued, and during any period of reconsideration pursuant to 11 CFR 112.6.

§ 201.5 Sanctions.

Any person who becomes aware of a possible violation of this part shall notify the Designated Agency Ethics Official in writing of the facts and circumstances of the alleged violation. The Designated Agency Ethics Official shall recommend to the Commission the appropriate action to be taken. The

Commission shall determine the appropriate action by at least four votes.

SUBCHAPTER C—BIPARTISAN CAMPAIGN REFORM ACT OF 2002—(BCRA) REGULATIONS

PART 300—NON-FEDERAL FUNDS

Sec.
300.1 Scope, effective date, and organization.
300.2 Definitions.

Subpart A—National Party Committees

300.10 General prohibitions on raising and spending non-Federal funds (52 U.S.C. 30125(a) and (c)).
300.11 Prohibitions on fundraising for and donating to certain tax-exempt organizations (52 U.S.C. 30125(d)).
300.12 [Reserved]
300.13 Reporting (52 U.S.C. 30101 note and 30104(e)).

Subpart B—State, District, and Local Party Committees and Organizations

300.30 Accounts.
300.31 Receipt of Levin funds.
300.32 Expenditures and disbursements.
300.33 Allocation of costs of Federal election activity.
300.34 Transfers.
300.35 Office buildings.
300.36 Reporting Federal election activity; recordkeeping.
300.37 Prohibitions on fundraising for and donating to certain tax-exempt organizations (52 U.S.C. 30125(d)).

Subpart C—Tax-Exempt Organizations

300.50 Prohibited fundraising by national party committees (52 U.S.C. 30125(d)).
300.51 Prohibited fundraising by State, district, or local party committees (52 U.S.C. 30125(d)).
300.52 Fundraising by Federal candidates and Federal officeholders (52 U.S.C. 30125(e)(1) and (4)).

Subpart D—Federal Candidates and Officeholders

300.60 Scope (52 U.S.C. 30125(e)(1)).
300.61 Federal elections (52 U.S.C. 30125(e)(1)(A)).
300.62 Non-Federal elections (52 U.S.C. 30125(e)(1)(B)).
300.63 Exception for State candidates (52 U.S.C. 30125(e)(2)).
300.64 Participation by Federal candidates and officeholders at non-Federal fundraising events (52 U.S.C. 30125(e)(1) and (3)).
300.65 Exceptions for certain tax-exempt organizations (52 U.S.C. 30125(e)(1) and (4)).

Subpart E—State and Local Candidates

300.70 Scope (52 U.S.C. 30125(f)(1)).
300.71 Federal funds required for certain public communications (52 U.S.C. 30125(f)(1)).
300.72 Federal funds not required for certain communications (52 U.S.C. 30125(f)(2)).

AUTHORITY: 52 U.S.C. 30104(e), 30111(a)(8), 30116(a), 30125, and 30143.

SOURCE: 67 FR 49120, July 29, 2002, unless otherwise noted.

§ 300.1 Scope and effective date, and organization.

(a) *Introduction.* This part implements changes to the Federal Election Campaign Act of 1971, as amended ("FECA" or the "Act"), enacted by Title I of the Bipartisan Campaign Finance Reform Act of 2002 ("BCRA"). Public Law 107–155. Unless expressly stated to the contrary, nothing in this part alters the definitions, restrictions, liabilities, and obligations imposed by sections 30101 to 30145 of Title 52, United States Code, or regulations prescribed thereunder (11 CFR parts 100 to 116).

(b) *Effective dates.* (1) Except as otherwise specifically provided in this part, this part shall take effect on November 6, 2002. However, subpart B of this part shall not apply with respect to runoff elections, recounts, or election contests resulting from elections held prior to such date.

(2) The increase in individual contribution limits to State committees of political parties, as described in 11 CFR 110.1(c)(5), shall apply to contributions made on or after January 1, 2003.

(c) *Organization of part.* Part 300, which generally addresses non-Federal funds and closely related topics, is organized into five subparts. Each subpart is oriented to the perspective of a category of persons facing issues related to non-Federal funds.

(1) Subpart A of this part prescribes rules pertaining to national party committees, including general non-Federal

funds prohibitions, fundraising, and donation prohibitions with regard to certain tax-exempt organizations, and reporting.

(2) Subpart B of this part pertains to State, district, and local political party committees and organizations. Subpart B of this part focuses on "Levin Amendment" to BCRA; office buildings; and fundraising and donation prohibitions with regard to certain tax-exempt organizations.

(3) Subpart C of this part addresses non-Federal funds from the perspective of tax-exempt organizations, setting out rules about prohibited fundraising for certain tax-exempt organizations by national party committees, State, district, and local party committees, and Federal candidates and officeholders.

(4) Subpart D of this part includes regulations pertaining to soliciting non-Federal funds from the perspective of Federal candidates and officeholders in Federal and non-Federal elections; including exceptions for those who are also State candidates and exemptions for those attending, speaking, and appearing as featured guests at fundraising events, or who solicit for certain tax-exempt organizations.

(5) Subpart E of this part focuses on State and local candidates, including regulations about using Federal funds for certain public communications, and exceptions for entirely non-Federal communications.

(6) For rules pertaining to convention and host committees, see 11 CFR part 9008.

[67 FR 49120, July 29, 2002, as amended at 79 FR 77850, Dec. 29, 2014; 81 FR 94240, Dec. 23, 2016]

§300.2 Definitions.

(a) *501(c) organization that makes expenditures or disbursements in connection with a Federal election.* A 501(c) organization *that makes expenditures or disbursements in connection with a Federal election* as that term is used in 11 CFR 300.11, 300.37, 300.50, and 300.51 includes an organization that, within the current election cycle, plans to:

(1) Make expenditures or disbursements in connection with an election for Federal office including for Federal election activity; or

(2) Pay a debt incurred from the making of expenditures or disbursements in connection with an election for Federal office (including for Federal election activity) in a prior election cycle.

(b) *Agent.* For the purposes of part 300 of chapter I, agent means any person who has actual authority, either express or implied, to engage in any of the following activities on behalf of the specified persons:

(1) In the case of a national committee of a political party:

(i) To solicit, direct, or receive any contribution, donation, or transfer of funds; or,

(ii) To solicit any funds for, or make or direct any donations to, an organization that is described in 26 U.S.C 501(c) and exempt from taxation under 26 U.S.C. 501(a) (or has submitted an application for determination of tax exempt status under 26 U.S.C. 501(a)), or an organization described in 26 U.S.C. 527 (other than a political committee, a State, district, or local committee of a political party, or the authorized campaign committee of a candidate for State or local office).

(2) In the case of a State, district, or local committee of a political party:

(i) To expend or disburse any funds for Federal election activity; or

(ii) To transfer, or accept a transfer of, funds to make expenditures or disbursements for Federal election activity; or

(iii) To engage in joint fundraising activities with any person if any part of the funds raised are used, in whole or in part, to pay for Federal election activity; or

(iv) To solicit any funds for, or make or direct any donations to, an organization that is described in 26 U.S.C. 501(c) and exempt from taxation under 26 U.S.C. 501(a) (or has submitted an application for determination of tax exempt status under 26 U.S.C. 501(a)), or an organization described in 26 U.S.C. 527 (other than a political committee, a State, district, or local committee of a political party, or the authorized campaign committee of a candidate for State or local office).

(3) In the case of an individual who is a Federal candidate or an individual

holding Federal office, to solicit, receive, direct, transfer, or spend funds in connection with any election.

(4) In the case of an individual who is a candidate for State or local office, to spend funds for a public communication (*see* 11 CFR 100.26).

(c) *Directly or indirectly establish, finance, maintain, or control.* (1) This paragraph (c) applies to national, State, district, and local committees of a political party, candidates, and holders of Federal office, including an officer, employee, or agent of any of the foregoing persons, which shall be referred to as "sponsors" in this section.

(2) To determine whether a sponsor directly or indirectly established, finances, maintains, or controls an entity, the factors described in paragraphs (c)(2)(i) through (x) of this section must be examined in the context of the overall relationship between sponsor and the entity to determine whether the presence of any factor or factors is evidence that the sponsor directly or indirectly established, finances, maintains, or controls the entity. Such factors include, but are not limited to:

(i) Whether a sponsor, directly or through its agent, owns controlling interest in the voting stock or securities of the entity;

(ii) Whether a sponsor, directly or through its agent, has the authority or ability to direct or participate in the governance of the entity through provisions of constitutions, bylaws, contracts, or other rules, or through formal or informal practices or procedures;

(iii) Whether a sponsor, directly or through its agent, has the authority or ability to hire, appoint, demote, or otherwise control the officers, or other decision-making employees or members of the entity;

(iv) Whether a sponsor has a common or overlapping membership with the entity that indicates a formal or ongoing relationship between the sponsor and the entity;

(v) Whether a sponsor has common or overlapping officers or employees with the entity that indicates a formal or ongoing relationship between the sponsor and the entity;

(vi) Whether a sponsor has any members, officers, or employees who were members, officers or employees of the entity that indicates a formal or ongoing relationship between the sponsor and the entity, or that indicates the creation of a successor entity;

(vii) Whether a sponsor, directly or through its agent, provides funds or goods in a significant amount or on an ongoing basis to the entity, such as through direct or indirect payments for administrative, fundraising, or other costs, but not including the transfer to a committee of its allocated share of proceeds jointly raised pursuant to 11 CFR 102.17, and otherwise lawfully;

(viii) Whether a sponsor, directly or through its agent, causes or arranges for funds in a significant amount or on an ongoing basis to be provided to the entity, but not including the transfer to a committee of its allocated share of proceeds jointly raised pursuant to 11 CFR 102.17, and otherwise lawfully;

(ix) Whether a sponsor, directly or through its agent, had an active or significant role in the formation of the entity; and

(x) Whether the sponsor and the entity have similar patterns of receipts or disbursements that indicate a formal or ongoing relationship between the sponsor and the entity.

(3) *Safe harbor.* On or after November 6, 2002, an entity shall not be deemed to be directly or indirectly established, maintained, or controlled by another entity unless, based on the entities' actions and activities solely after November 6, 2002, they satisfy the requirements of this section. If an entity receives funds from another entity prior to November 6, 2002, and the recipient entity disposes of the funds prior to November 6, 2002, the receipt of such funds prior to November 6, 2002 shall have no bearing on determining whether the recipient entity is financed by the sponsoring entity within the meaning of this section.

(4) *Determinations by the Commission.* (i) A sponsor or entity may request an advisory opinion of the Commission to determine whether the sponsor is no longer directly or indirectly financing, maintaining, or controlling the entity for purposes of this part. The request for such an advisory opinion must meet the requirements of 11 CFR part 112 and must demonstrate that the entity

is not directly or indirectly financed, maintained, or controlled by the sponsor.

(ii) Notwithstanding the fact that a sponsor may have established an entity within the meaning of paragraph (c)(2) of this section, the sponsor or the entity may request an advisory opinion of the Commission determining that the relationship between the sponsor and the entity has been severed. The request for such an advisory opinion must meet the requirements of 11 CFR part 112, and must demonstrate that all material connections between the sponsor and the entity have been severed for two years.

(iii) Nothing in this section shall require entities that are separate organizations on November 6, 2002 to obtain an advisory opinion to operate separately from each other.

(d) *Disbursement. Disbursement* means any purchase or payment made by:

(1) A political committee; or

(2) Any other person, including an organization that is not a political committee, that is subject to the Act.

(e) *Donation.* For purposes of part 300, *donation* means a payment, gift, subscription, loan, advance, deposit, or anything of value given to a person, but does not include contributions.

(f) *Federal account. Federal account* means an account at a campaign depository that contains funds to be used in connection with a Federal election.

(g) *Federal Funds. Federal funds* mean funds that comply with the limitations, prohibitions, and reporting requirements of the Act.

(h) *Levin account. Levin account* means an account at a campaign depository established by a State, district, or local committee of a political party pursuant to 11 CFR 300.30, for purposes of making expenditures or disbursements for Federal election activity or non-Federal activity (subject to State law) under 11 CFR 300.32.

(i) *Levin funds* mean funds that are raised pursuant to 11 CFR 300.31 and are or will be disbursed pursuant to 11 CFR 300.32.

(j) *Non-Federal account* means an account that contains funds to be used in connection with a State or local election or allocable expenses under 11 CFR 106.7, 300.30, or 300.33.

(k) *Non-Federal funds* mean funds that are not subject to the limitations and prohibitions of the Act.

(l) [Reserved]

(m) *To solicit.* For the purposes of part 300, *to solicit* means to ask, request, or recommend, explicitly or implicitly, that another person make a contribution, donation, transfer of funds, or otherwise provide anything of value. A solicitation is an oral or written communication that, construed as reasonably understood in the context in which it is made, contains a clear message asking, requesting, or recommending that another person make a contribution, donation, transfer of funds, or otherwise provide anything of value. A solicitation may be made directly or indirectly. The context includes the conduct of persons involved in the communication. A solicitation does not include mere statements of political support or mere guidance as to the applicability of a particular law or regulation.

(1) The following types of communications constitute solicitations:

(i) A communication that provides a method of making a contribution or donation, regardless of the communication. This includes, but is not limited to, providing a separate card, envelope, or reply device that contains an address to which funds may be sent and allows contributors or donors to indicate the dollar amount of their contribution or donation to the candidate, political committee, or other organization.

(ii) A communication that provides instructions on how or where to send contributions or donations, including providing a phone number specifically dedicated to facilitating the making of contributions or donations. However, a communication does not, in and of itself, satisfy the definition of "to solicit" merely because it includes a mailing address or phone number that is not specifically dedicated to facilitating the making of contributions or donations.

(iii) A communication that identifies a Web address where the Web page displayed is specifically dedicated to facilitating the making of a contribution or donation, or automatically redirects the Internet user to such a page, or exclusively displays a link to such a page. However, a communication does not, in and of itself, satisfy the definition of "to solicit" merely because it includes the address of a Web page that is not specifically dedicated to facilitating the making of a contribution or donation.

(2) The following statements constitute solicitations:

(i) "Please give $100,000 to Group X."

(ii) "It is important for our State party to receive at least $100,000 from each of you in this election."

(iii) "Group X has always helped me financially in my elections. Keep them in mind this fall."

(iv) "X is an effective State party organization; it needs to obtain as many $100,000 donations as possible."

(v) "Giving $100,000 to Group X would be a very smart idea."

(vi) "Send all contributions to the following address * * *."

(vii) "I am not permitted to ask for contributions, but unsolicited contributions will be accepted at the following address * * *."

(viii) "Group X is having a fundraiser this week; you should go."

(ix) "You have reached the limit of what you may contribute directly to my campaign, but you can further help my campaign by assisting the State party."

(x) A candidate hands a potential donor a list of people who have contributed to a group and the amounts of their contributions. The candidate says, "I see you are not on the list."

(xi) "I will not forget those who contribute at this crucial stage."

(xii) "The candidate will be very pleased if we can count on you for $10,000."

(xiii) "Your contribution to this campaign would mean a great deal to the entire party and to me personally."

(xiv) Candidate says to potential donor: "The money you will help us raise will allow us to communicate our message to the voters through Labor Day."

(xv) "I appreciate all you've done in the past for our party in this State. Looking ahead, we face some tough elections. I'd be very happy if you could maintain the same level of finan-

cial support for our State party this year."

(xvi) The head of Group X solicits a contribution from a potential donor in the presence of a candidate. The donor asks the candidate if the contribution to Group X would be a good idea and would help the candidate's campaign. The candidate nods affirmatively.

(3) The following statements do not constitute solicitations:

(i) During a policy speech, the candidate says: "Thank you for your support of the Democratic Party."

(ii) At a ticket-wide rally, the candidate says: "Thank you for your support of my campaign."

(iii) At a Labor Day rally, the candidate says: "Thank you for your past financial support of the Republican Party."

(iv) At a GOTV rally, the candidate says: "Thank you for your continuing support."

(v) At a ticket-wide rally, the candidate says: "It is critical that we support the entire Democratic ticket in November."

(vi) A Federal officeholder says: "Our Senator has done a great job for us this year. The policies she has vigorously promoted in the Senate have really helped the economy of the State."

(vii) A candidate says: "Thanks to your contributions we have been able to support our President, Senator and Representative during the past election cycle."

(n) *To direct.* For the purposes of part 300, *to direct* means to guide, directly or indirectly, a person who has expressed an intent to make a contribution, donation, transfer of funds, or otherwise provide anything of value, by identifying a candidate, political committee or organization, for the receipt of such funds, or things of value. The contribution, donation, transfer, or thing of value may be made or provided directly or through a conduit or intermediary. Direction does not include merely providing information or guidance as to the applicability of a particular law or regulation.

(o) *Individual holding Federal office.* *Individual holding Federal office* means an individual elected to or serving in the office of President or Vice President of the United States; or a Senator or a Representative in, or Delegate or Resident Commissioner to, the Congress of the United States.

[67 FR 49120, July 29, 2002, as amended at 67 FR 78682, Dec. 26, 2002; 71 FR 13933, Mar. 20, 2006]

Subpart A—National Party Committees

§ 300.10 General prohibitions on raising and spending non-Federal funds (52 U.S.C. 30125(a) and (c)).

(a) *Prohibitions.* A national committee of a political party, including a national congressional campaign committee, must not:

(1) Solicit, receive, or direct to another person a contribution, donation, or transfer of funds, or any other thing of value that is not subject to the prohibitions, limitations and reporting requirements of the Act;

(2) Spend any funds that are not subject to the prohibitions, limitations, and reporting requirements of the Act; or

(3) Solicit, receive, direct, or transfer to another person, or spend, Levin funds.

(b) *Fundraising costs.* A national committee of a political party, including a national congressional campaign committee, must use only Federal funds to raise funds that are used, in whole or in part, for expenditures and disbursements for Federal election activity.

(c) *Application.* This section also applies to:

(1) An officer or agent acting on behalf of a national party committee or a national congressional campaign committee; and

(2) An entity that is directly or indirectly established, financed, maintained, or controlled by a national party committee or a national congressional campaign committee.

§ 300.11 Prohibitions on fundraising for and donating to certain tax-exempt organizations (52 U.S.C. 30125(d)).

(a) *Prohibitions.* A national committee of a political party, including a national congressional campaign committee, must not solicit any funds for, or make or direct any donations of

non-Federal funds to, the following organizations:

(1) An organization that is described in 26 U.S.C. 501(c) and exempt from taxation under section 26 U.S.C. 501(a) and that makes expenditures or disbursements in connection with an election for Federal office, including expenditures or disbursements for Federal election activity;

(2) An organization that has submitted an application for tax-exempt status under 26 U.S.C. 501(c) and that makes expenditures or disbursements in connection with an election for Federal office, including expenditures or disbursements for Federal election activity; or

(3) An organization described in 26 U.S.C. 527, unless the organization is:

(i) A political committee under 11 CFR 100.5;

(ii) A State, district, or local committee of a political party; or

(iii) The authorized campaign committee of a State or local candidate;

(b) *Application.* This section also applies to:

(1) An officer or agent acting on behalf of a national party committee, including a national congressional campaign committee;

(2) An entity that is directly or indirectly established, financed, maintained, or controlled by a national party committee, including a national congressional campaign committee, or an officer or agent acting on behalf of such an entity; or

(3) An entity that is directly or indirectly established, financed, maintained or controlled by an agent of a national committee of a political party, including a national congressional campaign committee.

(c) *Determining whether a section 501(c) organization makes expenditures or disbursements in connection with Federal elections.* In determining whether a section 501(c) organization is one that makes expenditures or disbursements in connection with a Federal election, including expenditures or disbursements for Federal election activity, pursuant to paragraphs (a)(1) and (2) of this section, a national committee of a political party, including a national congressional campaign committee, or any other person described in paragraph (b) of this section, may obtain and rely upon a certification from the organization that satisfies the criteria described in paragraph (d) of this section.

(d) *Certification.* A national committee of a political party, including a national congressional campaign committee, or any person described in paragraph (b) of this section, may rely upon a certification that meets all of the following criteria:

(1) The certification is a signed written statement by an officer or other authorized representative of the organization with knowledge of the organization's activities;

(2) The certification states that within the current election cycle, the organization has not made, and does not intend to make, expenditures or disbursements in connection with an election for Federal office (including for Federal election activity); and

(3) The certification states that the organization does not intend to pay debts incurred from the making of expenditures or disbursements in connection with an election for Federal office (including for Federal election activity) in a prior election cycle.

(e) If a national committee of a political party or any person described in paragraph (b) of this section has actual knowledge that the certification is false, the certification may not be relied upon.

(f) It is not prohibited for a national party or its agent to respond to a request for information about a tax-exempt group that shares the party's political or philosophical goals.

[67 FR 49120, July 29, 2002, as amended at 70 FR 12789, Mar. 16, 2005]

§ 300.12   [Reserved]

§ 300.13   Reporting (52 U.S.C. 30101 note and 30104(e)).

The national committee of a political party, any national congressional campaign committee of a political party, and any subordinate committee of either, shall report all receipts and disbursements during the reporting period.

[67 FR 49120, July 29, 2002, as amended at 79 FR 77850, Dec. 29, 2014; 81 FR 94240, Dec. 23, 2016]

Subpart B—State, District, and Local Party Committees and Organizations

§ 300.30   Accounts.

(a) *Scope and introduction.* This section applies to State, district, or local committees or organizations of a political party, whether or not the committee is a political committee under 11 CFR 100.5, that have receipts or make disbursements for Federal election activity. Paragraph (b) of this section describes and explains the types of accounts available to a political party committee or organization covered by this section. Paragraph (c) of this section sets out the account structure that must be maintained by a political party committee or organization covered by this section.

(b) *Types of accounts.* Each State, district, and local party organization or committee that has receipts or makes disbursements for Federal election activity must establish one or more of the following types of accounts, pursuant to paragraph (c) of this section.

(1) *Non-Federal accounts.* The funds deposited into this account are governed by State law. Disbursements, contributions, and expenditures made wholly or in part in connection with Federal elections must not be made from any non-Federal account, except as permitted by paragraph (c)(3)(ii) of this section, 11 CFR 102.5(a)(4), 11 CFR 106.7(d)(1)(i), 11 CFR 300.33 and 11 CFR 300.34.

(2) *Levin account.* The funds deposited into this account must comply with 11 CFR 300.31. Such funds may be used for the categories of activities described at 11 CFR 300.32(b).

(3) *Federal account.* Federal accounts may be used for the deposit of contributions and the making of expenditures pursuant to the following conditions:

(i) Only contributions that are permissible pursuant to the limitations and prohibitions of the Act may be deposited into any Federal account, regardless of whether such contributions are for use in connection with Federal or non-Federal elections. *See* 11 CFR 103.3 regarding impermissible funds.

(ii) Only contributions solicited and received pursuant to the following conditions may be deposited in a Federal account:

(A) Contributions must be designated by the contributors for the Federal account;

(B) The solicitation must expressly state that contributions may be used wholly or in part in connection with a Federal election; or

(C) The contributor must be informed that all contributions are subject to the limitations and prohibitions of the Act.

(iii) All disbursements, contributions, and expenditures made wholly or in part by any State, district, or local party organization or committee in connection with a Federal election must be made from either:

(A) A Federal account, except as permitted by 11 CFR 300.32; or

(B) A separate allocation account (*see* paragraph (b)(4) of this section).

(iv) If all payments in connection with a Federal election, including payments for Federal election activities, are to be made from a Federal account, expenditures and disbursements for costs that are allocable pursuant to 11 CFR 106.7 or 11 CFR 300.33 must be made from the Federal account in their entirety, with the shares of a non-Federal account or of a Levin account being transferred to the Federal account pursuant to 11 CFR 106.7 and 11 CFR 300.33.

(v) No transfers may be made to a Federal account from any other account(s) maintained by a State, district, or local party committee or organization from any other party organization or committee at any level for the purpose of financing activity in connection with Federal elections, except as provided by paragraph (b)(3)(iv) of this section or 11 CFR 300.33 and 300.34.

(4) *Allocation accounts.* At the discretion of the party committee or organization, separate allocation accounts may be established for purposes of making allocable expenditures and disbursements.

(i) Only funds from the party organization's or committee's Federal and non-Federal accounts may be deposited into an allocation account used to make allocable expenditures and disbursements for activities in connection with Federal and non-Federal elections.

(ii) Only funds from the party organization's or committee's Federal account and Levin funds from its non-Federal or Levin account(s) may be deposited into an allocation account used to make allocable expenditures and disbursements for activities undertaken pursuant to 11 CFR 300.32(b).

(iii) Once a party organization or committee has established a separate allocation account for activities in connection with Federal and non-Federal elections and a separate account for activities undertaken pursuant to 11 CFR 300.32(b), all allocable expenses must be paid from the appropriate allocation account for as long as that account is maintained.

(iv) The party organization or committee must transfer to the appropriate allocation account funds from its Federal and non-Federal or Levin accounts in amounts proportionate to the Federal, non-Federal and Levin shares of each allocable expense pursuant to 11 CFR 106.7 and 11 CFR 300.33. The transfers must be made pursuant to 11 CFR 300.33 and 300.34.

(v) No funds contained in an allocation account may be transferred to any other account maintained by the party committee or organization.

(vi) For reporting purposes, all allocation accounts must be treated as Federal accounts.

(c) *Required account or accounts.* Each State, district, and local party organization or committee that has receipts or makes disbursements for Federal election activity must establish its accounts in accordance with paragraphs (c)(1), or (c)(2), or (c)(3) of this section.

(1) One or more Federal accounts in a campaign depository, in accordance with 11 CFR part 103, which must be treated as a separate political committee and be required to comply with the requirements of the Act including

the registration and reporting requirements of 11 CFR part 102 and part 104. State, district, and local party organizations or committees may choose to make non-Federal disbursements, subject to State law, and disbursements for Federal election activity from a Federal account provided that such disbursements are reported pursuant to 11 CFR 104.17 and 11 CFR 300.36, and provided that contributors of the Federal funds so used were notified that their contributions were subject to the limitations and prohibitions of the Act.

(2) Establish at least three separate accounts in depositories as follows—

(i) One or more Federal accounts;

(ii) One or more Levin accounts; and

(iii) One or more Non-Federal accounts.

(3) Establish two separate accounts in depositories as follows:

(i) One or more Federal accounts, and;

(ii) An account that must function as both a Non-Federal account and a Levin account. If such an account is used, the State, district, and local party must demonstrate through a reasonable accounting method approved by the Commission (including any method embedded in software provided or approved by the Commission) that whenever such organization makes a disbursement for activities undertaken pursuant to 11 CFR 300.32(b), that organization had received sufficient contributions or Levin funds to make such disbursement.

(d) *Recordkeeping.* All party organizations or committees must keep records of deposits into and disbursements from such accounts, and, upon request, must make such records available for examination by the Commission.

§ 300.31 Receipt of Levin funds.

(a) *General rule.* Levin funds expended or disbursed by any State, district, or local committee must be raised solely by the committee that expends or disburses them.

(b) *Compliance with State law.* Each donation of Levin funds solicited or accepted by a State, district, or local committee of a political party must be lawful under the laws of the State in which the committee is organized.

(c) *Donations from sources permitted by State law but prohibited by the Act.* If the laws of the State in which a State, district, or local committee of a political party is organized permit donations to the committee from a source prohibited by the Act and this chapter, other than 52 U.S.C. 30121, the committee may solicit and accept donations of Levin funds from that source, subject to paragraph (d) of this section.

(d) *Donation amount limitation—*(1) *General rule.* A State, district, or local committee of a political party must not solicit or accept from any person (including any entity established, financed, maintained, or controlled by such person) one or more donations of Levin funds aggregating more than $10,000 in a calendar year.

(2) *Effect of different State limitations.* If the laws of the State in which a State, district, or local committee of a political party is organized limit donations to that committee to less than the amount specified in paragraph (d)(1) of this section, then the State law amount limitations shall control. If the laws of the State in which a State, district, or local committee of a political party is organized permit donations to that committee in amounts greater than the amount specified in paragraph (d)(1) of this section, then the amount limitations in paragraph (d)(1) of this section shall control.

(3) *No affiliation of committees for purposes of this paragraph.* For purposes of determining compliance with paragraph (d) of this section only, State, district, and local committees of the same political party shall not be considered affiliated. Subject to the amount limitations specified in paragraphs (d)(1) and (d)(2) of this section, a person (including any entity directly or indirectly established, financed, maintained, or controlled by such person) may donate without additional limitation to each and every State, district, and local committee of a political party.

(e) *No Levin funds from a national party committee or a Federal candidate or officeholder.* A State, district, or local committee of a political party disbursing Levin funds pursuant to 11 CFR 300.32 must not accept or use for such purposes any donations or other funds that are solicited, received, directed, transferred, or spent by or in the name of any of the following persons:

(1) A national committee of a political party (including a national congressional campaign committee of a political party), any officer or agent acting on behalf of such a national party committee, or any entity that is directly or indirectly established, financed, maintained, or controlled by such a national party committee. Notwithstanding 11 CFR 102.17, a State, district, or local committee of a political party must not raise Levin funds by means of joint fundraising with a national committee of a political party, any officer or agent acting on behalf of such a national party committee, or any entity that is directly or indirectly established, financed, maintained, or controlled by such a national party committee. Nothing in this section shall be construed to prohibit a State, district, or local committee of a political party from jointly raising, under 11 CFR 102.17, Federal funds not to be used for Federal election activity with a national committee of a political party, or its agent, or any entity directly or indirectly established, financed, maintained, or controlled by such a national party committee.

(2) A Federal candidate, or an individual holding Federal office, or an agent of a Federal candidate or officeholder, or an entity directly or indirectly established, financed, maintained, or controlled by, or acting on behalf of, one or more Federal candidates or individuals holding Federal office. Notwithstanding 11 CFR 102.17, a State, district, or local committee of a political party must not raise Levin funds by means of joint fundraising with a Federal candidate, an individual holding Federal office, or an entity directly or indirectly established, financed, maintained, or controlled by, or acting on behalf of, one or more candidates or individuals holding Federal office. A Federal candidate or individual holding Federal office may attend, speak, or be a featured guest at a fundraising event for a State, district, or local committee of a political party at which Levin funds are raised. *See* 11 CFR 300.64.

(f) *Certain joint fundraising prohibited.* Notwithstanding 11 CFR 102.17, a State, district, or local committee of a political party must not raise Levin funds by means of any joint fundraising activity with any other State, district, or local committee of any political party, the agent of such a committee, or an entity directly or indirectly established, financed, maintained, or controlled by such a committee. This prohibition includes State, district, and local committees of a political party organized in another State. Nothing in this section shall be construed to prohibit two or more State, district, or local committees of a political party from jointly raising, under 11 CFR 102.17, Federal funds not to be used for Federal election activity.

(g) *Safe Harbor.* The use of a common vendor for fundraising by more than one State, district, or local committee of a political party, or the agent of such a committee, does not constitute joint fundraising within the meaning of this section.

[67 FR 49120, July 29, 2002, as amended at 75 FR 32, Jan. 4, 2010; 79 FR 77850, Dec. 29, 2014]

§ 300.32 Expenditures and disbursements.

(a) *Federal funds.* (1) An association or similar group of candidates for State or local office, or an association or similar group of individuals holding State or local office, must make any expenditures or disbursements for Federal election activity solely with Federal funds.

(2) Except as provided in this part, a State, district, or local committee of a political party that makes expenditures or disbursements for Federal election activity must use Federal funds for that purposes, subject to the provisions of this chapter.

(3) State, district, and local party committees that raise Federal funds through an activity where only Federal funds are raised, must pay the direct costs of such fundraising only with Federal funds. State, district, and local party committees that raise Federal funds and non-Federal funds through a joint fundraising activity under 11 CFR 106.7(d)(4) or a joint fundraiser under 11 CFR 102.17, where the Federal funds are

to be used, in whole or in part, for Federal election activities, must either pay the direct costs of such fundraising only with Federal funds or allocate the direct costs in accordance with the funds received method described in 11 CFR 106.7(d)(4). The direct costs of a fundraising program or event include expenses for the solicitation of funds and for the planning and administration of actual fundraising programs and events.

(4) State, district, and local party committees that raise Levin funds to be used, in whole or in part, for Federal election activity must pay the direct costs of such fundraising with either Federal or Levin funds. The direct costs of a fundraising program or event include expenses for the solicitation of funds and for the planning and administration of actual fundraising programs and events.

(b) *Levin funds.* A State, district, or local committee of a political party may spend Levin funds in accordance with this part on the following types of activity:

(1) Subject to the conditions set out in paragraph (c) of this section, only the following types of Federal election activity:

(i) Voter registration activity during the period that begins on the date that is 120 days before the date a regularly scheduled Federal election is held and ends on the date of the election; and

(ii) Voter identification, get-out-the-vote activity, or generic campaign activity conducted in connection with an election in which a candidate for Federal office appears on the ballot (regardless of whether a candidate for State or local office also appears on the ballot).

(2) Any use that is lawful under the laws of the State in which the committee is organized, other than the Federal election activities defined in 11 CFR 100.24(b)(3) and (4). A disbursement of Levin funds under this paragraph need not comply with paragraphs (c)(1) and (c)(2) of this section, except as required by State law.

(c) *Conditions and restrictions on spending Levin funds.* (1) The Federal election activity for which the disbursement is made must not refer to a clearly identified candidate for Federal office.

(2) The disbursement must not pay for any part of the costs of any broadcasting, cable, or satellite communication, other than a communication that refers solely to a clearly identified candidate for State or local office.

(3) The disbursement must be made from funds raised in accordance with 11 CFR 300.31.

(4) The disbursements for allocable Federal election activity must be paid for either entirely with Federal funds or by allocating between Federal funds and Levin funds according to 11 CFR 300.33.

(d) *Non-Federal activities.* A State, district, or local committee of a political party that makes disbursements for non-Federal activity may make those disbursements from its Federal, Levin, or non-Federal funds, subject to the laws of the State in which it is organized. A State, district, or local party committee that engages in fundraising for solely non-Federal funds may pay the costs related to such fundraising from any account, subject to State law, including a Federal account.

[67 FR 49120, July 29, 2002, as amended at 70 FR 69632, Nov. 17, 2005; 70 FR 75384, Dec. 20, 2005]

§ 300.33 Allocation of costs of Federal election activity.

(a) *Costs of Federal election activity allocable by State, district, and local party committees and organizations*—(1) *Costs of voter registration.* Subject to the conditions of 11 CFR 300.32(c), State, district, and local party committees and organizations may allocate disbursements or expenditures, except salaries and wages for employees, between Federal funds and Levin funds for voter registration activity, as defined in 11 CFR 100.24(a)(2), that takes place during the period that begins on the date that is 120 days before the date of a regularly scheduled Federal election and that ends on the date of the election, provided that the activity does not refer to a clearly identified Federal candidate.

(2) *Costs of voter identification, get-out-the-vote activity, or generic campaign activities within certain time periods.* Subject to the conditions of 11 CFR

300.32(c), State, district, and local party committees and organizations may allocate disbursements or expenditures, except salaries and wages for employees, between Federal funds and Levin funds for voter identification, get-out-the-vote activity, or generic campaign activities, as defined in 11 CFR 100.24(a)(3) and (4) and 11 CFR 100.25, that are conducted in connection with an election in which a candidate for Federal office is on the ballot and within the time periods set forth in 11 CFR 100.24(a)(1), provided that the activity does not refer to a clearly identified Federal candidate.

(b) *Allocation percentages.* State, district, and local party committees and organizations that choose to allocate between Federal funds and Levin funds their expenditures and disbursements, except for salaries and wages, in connection with activities described in paragraph (a) of this section that take place within the time periods set forth in 11 CFR 100.24(a)(1) or paragraph (a) of this section must allocate the following minimum percentages to their Federal funds:

(1) *Presidential election years.* If a Presidential candidate, but no Senate candidate appears on the ballot, State, district, and local party committees and organizations must allocate at least 28% of expenses for activities described in paragraph (a) of this section to their Federal funds.

(2) *Presidential and Senate election year.* If a Presidential candidate and a Senate candidate appear on the ballot, State, district, and local party committees and organizations must allocate at least 36% of expenses for activities described in paragraph (a) of this section to their Federal funds.

(3) *Senate election year.* If a Senate candidate, but no Presidential candidate, appears on the ballot, State, district, and local party committees and organizations must allocate at least 21% of expenses for activities described in paragraph (a) of this section to their Federal funds.

(4) *Non-Presidential and non-Senate year.* If neither a Presidential nor a Senate candidate appears on the ballot, State, district, and local party committees and organizations must allocate at least 15% of expenses for activi-

ties described in paragraph (a) of this section to their Federal funds.

(c) *Costs of public communications.* Expenditures for public communications as defined in 11 CFR 100.26 by State, district, and local party committees and organizations that refer to a clearly identified candidate for Federal office and that promote, support, attack, or oppose any such candidate for Federal office must not be allocated between or among Federal, non-Federal, and Levin accounts. Only Federal funds may be used.

(d) *Costs of salaries, wages, and fringe benefits.* (1) Except as provided in paragraph (d)(3) of this section, salaries, wages, and fringe benefits paid for employees who spend 25% or less of their compensated time in a given month on Federal election activities or on activities in connection with a Federal election must either be paid only from the Federal account or be allocated as administrative costs under 11 CFR 106.7(d)(2).

(2) Salaries, wages, and fringe benefits paid for employees who spend more than 25% of their compensated time in a given month on Federal election activities or on activities in connection with a Federal election must be paid only from a Federal account.

(3) Salaries, wages, and fringe benefits paid for employees who spend none of their compensated time in a given month on Federal election activities or on activities in connection with a Federal election may be paid entirely with funds that comply with State law. *See* 11 CFR 106.7(c)(1) and (d)(1).

(e) *Transfers between accounts to cover allocable expenses.* State, district, and local party committees and organizations may transfer Levin funds from their Levin or non-Federal accounts to their Federal accounts or to allocation accounts solely to meet expenses allocable pursuant to paragraphs (a)(1) and (2) of this section and only pursuant to the following methods:

(1) *Payments from Federal accounts or from allocation accounts.* (i) If Federal accounts are used to make payments for allocable activities, State, district, and local party committees and organizations must pay the entire amount of allocable expenses from their Federal accounts and transfer Levin funds from

their Levin or non-Federal accounts to their Federal accounts solely to cover the portions of the expenses for which Levin funds may be used; or

(ii) State, district, and local party committees and organizations may establish separate allocation accounts into which Federal funds and Levin funds may be deposited solely for the purpose of paying allocable expenses.

(2) *Timing.* (i) If Federal or allocation accounts are used to make allocable expenditures and disbursements, State, district, and local party committees and organizations must transfer Levin funds to their Federal or allocation accounts to meet allocable expenses no more than 10 days before and no more than 60 days after the payments for which they are designated are made from a Federal or allocation account, except that transfers may be made more than 10 days before a payment is made from the Federal or allocation account if advance payment is required by the vendor(s) and if such payment is based on a reasonable estimate of the activity's final costs as determined by the committee and the vendor(s) involved.

(ii) Any portion of a transfer of Levin funds to a party committee or organization's Federal or allocation account that does not meet the requirement of paragraph (e)(2)(i) of this section shall be presumed to be a loan or contribution from the Levin or non-Federal account to the Federal or allocation account, in violation of the Act.

[67 FR 49120, July 29, 2002, as amended at 70 FR 75385, Dec. 20, 2005]

§ 300.34   Transfers.

(a) *Federal funds.* (1) Notwithstanding 11 CFR 102.6(a)(1)(ii), a State, district, or local committee of a political party must not use any Federal funds transferred to it from, or otherwise accepted by it from, any of the persons enumerated in paragraphs (b)(1) and (b)(2) of this section as the Federal component of an expenditure or disbursement for Federal election activity under 11 CFR 300.32. A State, district, or local committee of a political party must itself raise the Federal component of an expenditure or disbursement allocated between Federal funds and Levin funds under 11 CFR 300.32 and 300.33.

(2) A State, district, or local committee of a political party that makes an expenditure or disbursement of Federal funds for Federal election activities must demonstrate through a reasonable accounting method approved by the Commission (including any method embedded in software provided or approved by the Commission) that the Federal funds used to make the expenditure or disbursement do not include Federal funds transferred to the committee in violation of this section. Alternatively, a State, district, or local committee of a political party may establish a separate Federal account into which the committee deposits its only Federal funds raised by the committee itself, and from which all expenditures or disbursement of Federal funds for Federal election activities are made.

(b) *Levin funds.* Levin funds must be raised solely by the State, district, or local committee of a political party that expends or disburses the funds. A State, district, or local committee of a political party must not use as Levin funds any funds transferred or otherwise provided to the committee by:

(1) Any other State, district, or local committee of any political party, any officer or agent acting on behalf of such a committee, or any entity directly or indirectly established, financed, maintained or controlled by such a committee; or,

(2) The national committee of any political party (including a national congressional campaign committee of a political party), any officer or agent acting on behalf of such a committee, or any entity directly or indirectly established, financed, maintained, or controlled by such a committee.

(c) *Allocation transfers.* Transfers of Levin funds between the accounts of a State, district, or local committee of a political party for allocation purposes must comply with 11 CFR 300.30 and 11 CFR 300.33.

§ 300.35   Office buildings.

(a) *General provision.* For the purchase or construction of its office building, a State or local party committee may spend Federal funds or non-Federal funds that are not subject to the limitations, prohibitions, and disclosure provisions of the Act, so long as such funds are not contributed or donated by a foreign national. *See* 52 U.S.C. 30121. If non-Federal funds are used, they are subject to State law. An office building must not be purchased or constructed for the purpose of influencing the election of any candidate in any particular election for Federal office. For purposes of this section, the term *local party committee* shall include a *district party committee*.

(b) *Application of State law.* Non-Federal funds received by a State or local party committee that are spent for the purchase or construction of its office building are subject to State law as set forth in paragraphs (b)(1) and (2) of this section.

(1) *Non-Federal account.* If a State or local party committee uses non-Federal funds, Federal law does not pre-empt or supersede State law as to the source of funds used, the permissibility of the disbursements, or the reporting of the receipt and disbursement of such funds, except as provided in paragraph (a) of this section.

(2) *Levin funds.* Levin funds may be used for the purchase or construction of a State or local party committee office building, if permitted by State law.

(c) *Leasing a portion of the party office building.* A State or local party committee may lease a portion of its office building to others to generate income at the usual and normal charge. If the building is purchased or constructed in whole or in part with non-Federal funds, all rental income shall be deposited in the committee's non-Federal account and used only for non-Federal purposes. Such rental income and its use must also comply with State law. If the building is purchased or constructed solely with Federal funds, the rental income may be deposited in the Federal account. The receipt of such funds shall be reported in compliance with 11 CFR 104.3(a)(4)(vi).

(d) *Transitional Provisions for State Party Building or Facility Account.* Up to and including November 5, 2002, the State committee of a political party may accept funds into its party office building or facility account, established pursuant to repealed 2 U.S.C. 431(8)(B)(viii), designated for the purchase or construction of an office building. Starting on November 6, 2002, the funds in the account may not be used for Federal account or Levin account purposes, but may be used for any non-Federal purposes, as permitted under State law.

[67 FR 49120, July 29, 2002, as amended at 79 FR 77850, Dec. 29, 2014]

§ 300.36 **Reporting Federal election activity; recordkeeping.**

(a) *Requirements for a State, district, or local committee of a political party, or an association or similar group of candidates for State or local office or of individuals holding State or local office, that is not a political committee.* (1) A State, district, or local committee of a political party, or an association or similar group of candidates for State or local office or of individuals holding State or local office, that is not a political committee (*see* 11 CFR 100.5) must demonstrate through a reasonable accounting method that whenever it makes a payment of Federal funds or Levin funds (if it is permitted to spend Levin funds) for Federal election activity (*see* 11 CFR 300.32 and 300.33) it has received sufficient funds subject to the limitations and prohibitions of the Act to make the payment. Such an organization must keep records of amounts received or expended under this paragraph and, upon request, shall make such records available for examination by the Commission.

(2) Notwithstanding the foregoing, a payment of Federal funds or Levin funds for Federal election activity shall not constitute an expenditure for purposes of determining whether a State, district, or local committee of a political party, or an association or similar group of candidates for State or local office or of individuals holding State or local office, qualifies as a political committee under 11 CFR 100.5, unless the payment otherwise qualifies as an expenditure under 52 U.S.C. 30101(9). A payment of Federal funds for Federal election activity that refers to a clearly identified Federal candidate and that meets the criteria of 11 CFR 100.140, 100.147, or 100.149 (*exempt activities*) shall be treated as a payment for exempt activity in accordance with all applicable provisions of this chapter,

including, but not limited to, 52 U.S.C. 30121.

(b) *Requirements for a State, district, or local committee of a political party, or an association or similar group of candidates for State or local office or of individuals holding State or local office, that is a political committee*—(1) *Requirements for a State, district, or local committee of a political party that has less than $5,000 of aggregate receipts and disbursements for Federal election activity in a calendar year, and for an association or similar group of candidates for State or local office or of individuals holding State or local office at all times.* This paragraph applies to a State, district, or local committee of a political party that is a political committee, and that has less than $5,000 of aggregate receipts and disbursements for Federal election activity in a calendar year; and, at all times, to an association or similar group of candidates for State or local office or of individuals holding State or local office that is a political committee (*see* 11 CFR 100.5). Such a party committee or association of candidates or officeholders must report all receipts and disbursements of Federal funds for Federal election activity, including the Federally allocated portion of a payment for Federal election activity. A disbursement of Federal funds or Levin funds for Federal election activity (*see* 11 CFR 300.32 and 300.33) by either such a party committee or association of candidates or officeholders shall not be deemed an expenditure and reported as such pursuant to 11 CFR part 104, unless the disbursement otherwise qualifies as an expenditure under 2 U.S.C. 431(9).

(2) *Requirements for a State, district, or local committee of a political party that has $5,000 or more of aggregate receipts and disbursements for Federal election activity in a calendar year.* A State, district, or local committee of a political party that is a political committee (*see* 11 CFR 100.5) must report all receipts and disbursements made for Federal election activity if the aggregate amount of such receipts and disbursements is $5,000 or more during the calendar year. The disclosure required by this paragraph must include receipts and disbursements of Federal funds and

of Levin funds used for Federal election activity.

(i) *Reporting of allocation of expenses between Federal funds and Levin funds.* A State, district, or local committee of a political party that makes a disbursement for Federal election activity that is allocated between Federal funds and Levin funds (*see* 11 CFR 300.33) must report for each such disbursement:

(A) In the first report of a calendar year disclosing an allocated disbursement for Federal election activity, the committee must state the allocation percentages to be applied for allocable Federal election activity pursuant to 11 CFR 300.33(b).

(B) In each subsequent report in the calendar year itemizing an allocated disbursement for Federal election activity, the committee must state the category of Federal election activity (*see* 11 CFR 100.24(b)) for which each allocated disbursement was made, and must disclose the total amounts disbursed from Federal funds and Levin funds for that year to date for each such category.

(ii) *Reporting of allocation transfers.* A committee that makes allocated disbursements for Federal election activities in accordance with 11 CFR 300.33(e) shall report each transfer of Levin funds from its Levin or non-Federal account, to its Federal account, and each transfer from its Federal account and its Levin or non-Federal account into an allocation account, for the purpose of making such disbursements. In the report covering the period in which each transfer occurred, the committee must explain in a memo entry the allocated disbursement to which the transfer relates and the date on which the transfer was made. If the transfer includes funds for the allocable costs of more than one category of Federal election activity, the committee must itemize the transfer, showing the amounts designated for each category.

(iii) *Reporting of allocated disbursements.* For each disbursement allocated between Federal funds and Levin funds, the committee must report the full name and address of each person to whom the disbursement was made, the date of the disbursement, amount, and purpose of the disbursement. If the disbursement is for the allocable costs of more than one category of Federal election activity, the committee must itemize the disbursement, showing the amounts designated for each category. The committee must also disclose the total amount disbursed from Federal funds and Levin funds for Federal election activity that calendar year, to date, for each category of Federal election activity.

(iv) *Itemization.* The disclosure required by paragraph (b)(2) of this section must include, in addition to any other applicable reporting requirement of this chapter, the itemized disclosure of receipts and disbursements of $200 or more to or from any person for Federal election activities.

(3) *Reporting of disbursements allocated between Federal funds and non-Federal funds, other than Levin funds.* A State, district, or local committee of a political party that makes a disbursement for costs allocable between Federal and non-Federal funds, other than the costs of Federal election activity that is allocated between Federal funds and Levin funds under 11 CFR 300.33, must comply with 11 CFR 104.17.

(c) *Filing*—(1) *Schedule.* A State, district, or local committee of a political party, or an association or similar group of candidates for State or local office or of individuals holding State or local office, that must file reports under paragraph (b) of this section must comply with the monthly filing schedule in 11 CFR 104.5(c)(3).

(2) *Electronic filing.* Receipts of Federal funds for Federal election activity that constitute contributions under 11 CFR part 100, subpart B, and disbursements of Federal funds for Federal election activity that constitute expenditures under 11 CFR part 100, subpart D, apply when determining whether a political committee must file reports in an electronic format under 11 CFR 104.18.

(d) *Recordkeeping.* A State, district, or local committee of a political party, or an association or similar group of candidates for State or local office or of individuals holding State or local office, that must file reports under para-

graph (b) of this section must comply with the requirements of 11 CFR 104.14.

[67 FR 49120, July 29, 2002, as amended at 67 FR 78682, Dec. 26, 2002; 70 FR 75385, Dec. 20, 2005; 79 FR 77850, Dec. 29, 2014]

§300.37 Prohibitions on fundraising for and donating to certain tax-exempt organizations (52 U.S.C. 30125(d)).

(a) *Prohibitions.* A State, district or local committee of a political party must not solicit any funds for, or make or direct any donations of non-Federal funds, including Levin funds, to:

(1) An organization that is described in 26 U.S.C. 501(c) and exempt from taxation under section 26 U.S.C. 501(a) and that makes expenditures or disbursements in connection with an election for Federal office, including expenditures or disbursements for Federal election activity;

(2) An organization that has submitted an application for tax-exempt status under 26 U.S.C. 501(c) and that makes expenditures or disbursements in connection with an election for Federal office, including expenditures or disbursements for Federal election activity; or

(3) An organization described in 26 U.S.C. 527, unless the organization is:

(i) A political committee under 11 CFR 100.5;

(ii) A State, district, or local committee of a political party;

(iii) The authorized campaign committee of a State or local candidate; or

(iv) A political committee under State law, that supports only State or local candidates and that does not make expenditures or disbursements in connection with an election for Federal office, including expenditures or disbursements for Federal election activity.

(b) *Application.* This section also applies to:

(1) An officer or agent acting on behalf of a State, district, or local committee of a political party;

(2) An entity that is directly or indirectly established, financed, maintained or controlled by a State, district or local committee of a political party or an officer or agent acting on behalf of such an entity; or

(3) An entity that is directly or indirectly established, financed, maintained, or controlled by an agent of a State, district, or local committee of a political party.

(c) *Determining whether an organization makes expenditures or disbursements in connection with a Federal election.* (1) In determining whether a section 501(c) organization is one that makes expenditures or disbursements in connection with a Federal election, including expenditures or disbursements for Federal election activity, pursuant to paragraphs (a)(1) and (2) of this section, a State, district, or local committee of a political party or any other person described in paragraph (b) of this section, may obtain and rely upon a certification from the organization that satisfies the criteria described in paragraph (d) of this section.

(2) In determining whether a section 527 organization is a State-registered political committee that supports only State or local candidates and does not make expenditures or disbursements in connection with an Federal election, including expenditures or disbursements for Federal election activity, pursuant to paragraph (a)(3)(iv) of this section, a State, district, or local committee of a political party or any other person described in paragraph (b) of this section, may obtain and rely upon a certification from the organization that satisfies the criteria described in paragraph (d) of this section.

(d) *Certification.* A State, district, or local committee of a political party or any person described in paragraph (b) of this section may rely upon a certification that meets all of the following criteria:

(1) The certification is a signed written statement by an officer or other authorized representative of the organization with knowledge of the organization's activities or by the treasurer of the State-registered political committee described in paragraph (a)(3)(iv) of this section;

(2) The certification states that within the current election cycle, the organization or political committee has not made, and does not intend to make, expenditures or disbursements in connection with an election for Federal office

(including for Federal election activity); and

(3) The certification states that the organization or political committee does not intend to pay debts incurred from the making of expenditures or disbursements in connection with an election for Federal office (including for Federal election activity) in a prior election cycle.

(e) If a State, district, or local committee of a political party or any person described in paragraph (b) of this section has actual knowledge that the certification is false, the certification may not be relied upon.

(f) It is not prohibited for a State, district, or local committee of a political party or its agents to respond to a request for information about a tax-exempt group that shares the party's political or philosophical goals.

[67 FR 49120, July 29, 2002, as amended at 70 FR 12789, Mar. 16, 2005; 79 FR 77850, Dec. 29, 2014]

Subpart C—Tax-Exempt Organizations

§ 300.50 Prohibited fundraising by national party committees (52 U.S.C. 30125(d)).

(a) *Prohibitions on fundraising and donations.* A national committee of a political party, including a national congressional campaign committee, must not solicit any funds for, or make or direct any donations of non-Federal funds to the following organizations:

(1) An organization that is described in 26 U.S.C. 501(c) and exempt from taxation under section 26 U.S.C. 501(a) and that makes expenditures or disbursements in connection with an election for Federal office, including expenditures or disbursements for Federal election activity;

(2) An organization that has submitted an application for tax-exempt status under 26 U.S.C. 501(c) and that makes expenditures or disbursements in connection with an election for Federal office, including expenditures or disbursements for Federal election activity; or

(3) An organization described in 26 U.S.C. 527, unless the organization is:

(i) A political committee under 11 CFR 100.5;

(ii) A State, district, or local committee of a political party; or

(iii) The authorized campaign committee of a State or local candidate;

(b) *Application.* This section also applies to:

(1) An officer or agent acting on behalf of a national party committee, including a national congressional campaign committee;

(2) An entity that is directly or indirectly established, financed, maintained, or controlled by a national party committee, including a national congressional campaign committee, or an officer or agent acting on behalf of such an entity; or

(3) An entity that is directly or indirectly established, financed, maintained or controlled by an agent of a national committee of a political party, including a national congressional campaign committee.

(c) *Determining whether a section 501(c) organization makes expenditures or disbursements in connection with Federal elections.* In determining whether a section 501(c) organization is one that makes expenditures or disbursements in connection with a Federal election, including expenditures or disbursements for Federal election activity, pursuant to paragraphs (a)(1) and (2) of this section, a national committee of a political party, including a national congressional campaign committee, or any other person described in paragraph (b) of this section, may obtain and rely upon a certification from the organization that satisfies the criteria described in paragraph (d) of this section.

(d) *Certification.* A national committee of a political party, including a national congressional campaign committee, or any person described in paragraph (b) of this section, may rely upon a certification that meets all of the following criteria:

(1) The certification is a signed written statement by an officer or other authorized representative of the organization with knowledge of the organization's activities;

(2) The certification states that within the current election cycle, the organization has not made, and does not intend to make, expenditures or disbursements in connection with an election

for Federal office (including for Federal election activity); and

(3) The certification states that the organization or political committee does not intend to pay debts incurred from the making of expenditures or disbursements in connection with an election for Federal office (including for Federal election activity) in a prior election cycle.

(e) *Reliance on false certification.* If a national committee of a political party or any person described in paragraph (b) of this section has actual knowledge that the certification is false, the certification may not be relied upon.

(f) *Requests for information.* It is not prohibited for a national party or its agent to respond to a request for information about a tax-exempt group that shares the party's political or philosophical goals.

[67 FR 49120, July 29, 2002, as amended at 70 FR 12789, Mar. 16, 2005]

§ 300.51 **Prohibited fundraising by State, district, or local party committees (52 U.S.C. 30125(d)).**

(a) *Prohibitions.* A State, district or local committee of a political party must not solicit any funds for, or make or direct any donations of non-Federal funds, including Levin funds, to:

(1) An organization that is described in 26 U.S.C. 501(c) and exempt from taxation under section 26 U.S.C. 501(a) and that makes expenditures or disbursements in connection with an election for Federal office, including expenditures or disbursements for Federal election activity;

(2) An organization that has submitted an application for tax-exempt status under 26 U.S.C. 501(c) and that makes expenditures or disbursements in connection with an election for Federal office, including expenditures or disbursements for Federal election activity; or

(3) An organization described in 26 U.S.C. 527, unless the organization is:

(i) A political committee under 11 CFR 100.5;

(ii) A State, district, or local committee of a political party;

(iii) The authorized campaign committee of a State or local candidate; or

(iv) A political committee under State law, that supports only State or local candidates and that does not make expenditures or disbursements in connection with an election for Federal office, including expenditures or disbursements for Federal election activity.

(b) *Application.* This section also applies to:

(1) An officer or agent acting on behalf of a State, district, or local committee of a political party;

(2) An entity that is directly or indirectly established, financed, maintained or controlled by a State, district or local committee of a political party or an officer or agent acting on behalf of such an entity; or

(3) An entity that is directly or indirectly established, financed, maintained, or controlled by an agent of a State, district, or local committee of a political party.

(c) *Determining whether an organization makes expenditures or disbursements in connection with a Federal election.* (1) In determining whether a section 501(c) organization is one that makes expenditures or disbursements in connection with a Federal election, including expenditures or disbursements for Federal election activity, pursuant to paragraphs (a)(1) and (2) of this section, a State, district, or local committee of a political party or any other person described in paragraph (b) of this section, may obtain and rely upon a certification from the organization that satisfies the criteria described in paragraph (d) of this section.

(2) In determining whether a section 527 organization is a State-registered political committee that supports only State or local candidates and does not make expenditures or disbursements in connection with a Federal election, including expenditures or disbursements for Federal election activity, pursuant to paragraph (a)(3)(iv) of this section, a State, district, or local committee of a political party or any other person described in paragraph (b) of this section, may obtain and rely upon a certification from the organization that satisfies the criteria described in paragraph (d) of this section.

(d) *Certification.* A State, district, or local committee of a political party or any person described in paragraph (b) of this section may rely upon a certifi-

cation that meets all of the following criteria:

(1) The certification is a signed written statement by an officer or other authorized representative of the organization with knowledge of the organization's activities or by the treasurer of the State-registered political committee described in paragraph (a)(3)(iv) of this section;

(2) The certification states that within the current election cycle, the organization or political committee has not made, and does not intend to make, expenditures or disbursements in connection with an election for Federal office (including for Federal election activity); and

(3) The certification states that the organization does not intend to pay debts incurred from the making of expenditures or disbursements in connection with an election for Federal office (including for Federal election activity) in a prior election cycle.

(e) If a State, district, or local committee of a political party or any person described in paragraph (b) of this section has actual knowledge that the certification is false, the certification may not be relied upon.

(f) It is not prohibited for a State, district, or local committee of a political party or its agents to respond to a request for information about a tax-exempt group that shares the party's political or philosophical goals.

[67 FR 49120, July 29, 2002, as amended at 70 FR 12789, Mar. 16, 2005; 79 FR 77850, Dec. 29, 2014]

§ 300.52 **Fundraising by Federal candidates and Federal officeholders (52 U.S.C. 30125(e)(1) and (4)).**

A Federal candidate, an individual holding Federal office, and an individual agent acting on behalf of either may make the following solicitations of funds on behalf of any organization described in 26 U.S.C. 501(c) and exempt from taxation under 26 U.S.C. 501(a), or an organization that has submitted an application for determination of tax-exempt status under 26 U.S.C. 501(c):

(a) *General solicitations.* A Federal candidate, an individual holding Federal office, or an individual agent acting on behalf of either, may make a general solicitation of funds, without regard to source or amount limitation, if:

(1) The organization does not engage in activities in connection with an election, including any activity described in paragraph (c) of this section; or

(2)(i) The organization conducts activities in connection with an election, but the organization's principal purpose is not to conduct election activities or any activity described in paragraph (c) of this section; and

(ii) The solicitation is not to obtain funds for activities in connection with an election or any activity described in paragraph (c) of this section.

(b) *Specific solicitations.* A Federal candidate, an individual holding Federal office, or an individual agent acting on behalf of either, may make a solicitation explicitly to obtain funds for any activity described in paragraph (c) of this section or for an organization whose principal purpose is to conduct that activity, if:

(1) The solicitation is made only to individuals; and

(2) The amount solicited from any individual does not exceed $20,000 during any calendar year.

(c) *Voter registration, voter identification, get-out-the-vote activity and generic campaign activity.* This section applies to only the following types of Federal election activity:

(1) Voter registration activity, as described in 11 CFR 100.24(a)(2), during the period that begins on the date that is 120 days before the date a regularly scheduled Federal election is held and ends on the date of the election; or

(2) The following activities conducted in connection with an election in which one or more Federal candidates appear on the ballot (*see* 11 CFR 100.24(a)(1)), regardless of whether one or more State candidates also appears on the ballot:

(i) Voter identification as described in 11 CFR 100.24(a)(4);

(ii) Get-out-the-vote activity as described in 11 CFR 100.24(a)(3); or

(iii) Generic campaign activity as defined in 11 CFR 100.25.

(d) *Prohibited solicitations.* A Federal candidate, an individual holding Federal office, and an individual who is an agent acting on behalf of either, must not make any solicitation on behalf of any organization described in 26 U.S.C. 501(c) and exempt from taxation under 26 U.S.C. 501(a), or an organization that has submitted an application for determination of tax-exempt status under 26 U.S.C. 501(c) for any election activity other than a Federal election activity as described in paragraph (c) of this section.

(e) *Safe Harbor.* In determining whether a 501(c) organization is one whose principal purpose is to conduct election activities, including activity described in paragraph (c) of this section, a Federal candidate, an individual holding Federal office, or an individual agent acting on behalf of either, may obtain and rely upon a certification from the organization that satisfies the following criteria:

(1) The certification is a signed written statement by an officer or other authorized representative of the organization with knowledge of the organization's activities;

(2) The certification states that the organization's principal purpose is not to conduct election activities, including election activity described in paragraph (c) of this section; and

(3) The certification states that the organization does not intend to pay debts incurred from the making of expenditures or disbursements in connection with an election for Federal office (including for Federal election activity) in a prior election cycle.

(f) If a Federal candidate, an individual holding Federal office, or an individual agent acting on behalf of either has actual knowledge that the certification is false, the certification may not be relied upon.

[67 FR 49120, July 29, 2002, as amended at 79 FR 77850, Dec. 29, 2014]

Subpart D—Federal Candidates and Officeholders

§ 300.60 Scope (52 U.S.C. 30125(e)(1)).

This subpart applies to:

(a) Federal candidates;

(b) Individuals holding Federal office (*see* 11 CFR 300.2(o));

(c) Agents acting on behalf of a Federal candidate or individual holding Federal office; and

(d) Entities that are directly or indirectly established, financed, maintained, or controlled by, or acting on behalf of, one or more Federal candidates or individuals holding Federal office.

§ 300.61 Federal elections (52 U.S.C. 30125(e)(1)(A)).

No person described in 11 CFR 300.60 shall solicit, receive, direct, transfer, spend, or disburse funds in connection with an election for Federal office, including funds for any Federal election activity as defined in 11 CFR 100.24, unless the amounts consist of Federal funds that are subject to the limitations, prohibitions, and reporting requirements of the Act.

§ 300.62 Non-Federal elections (52 U.S.C. 30125(e)(1)(B)).

A person described in 11 CFR 300.60 may solicit, receive, direct, transfer, spend, or disburse funds in connection with any non-Federal election, only in amounts and from sources that are consistent with State law, and that do not exceed the Act's contribution limits or come from prohibited sources under the Act.

§ 300.63 Exception for State candidates (52 U.S.C. 30125(e)(2)).

Section 300.62 shall not apply to a Federal candidate or individual holding Federal office who is a candidate for State or local office, if the solicitation, receipt or spending of funds is permitted under State law; and refers only to that State or local candidate, to any other candidate for that same State or local office, or both. If an individual is simultaneously running for both Federal and State or local office, the individual must raise, accept, and spend only Federal funds for the Federal election.

§ 300.64 Participation by Federal candidates and officeholders at non-Federal fundraising events (52 U.S.C. 30125(e)(1) and (3)).

(a) *Scope.* This section covers participation by Federal candidates and officeholders at fundraising events in connection with an election for Federal office or any non-Federal election at which funds outside the amount limita-

tions and source prohibitions of the Act or Levin funds are solicited. This section also covers participation by Federal candidates and officeholders in publicity related to such non-Federal fundraising events. This section applies even if funds that comply with the amount limitations and source prohibitions of the Act are also solicited at the event. Nothing in this section shall be construed to alter the fundraising exception for State candidates at 11 CFR 300.63 or the fundraising exceptions for certain tax-exempt organizations at 11 CFR 300.65.

(b) *Participation at non-Federal fundraising events.* A Federal candidate or officeholder may:

(1) Attend, speak at, or be a featured guest at a non-Federal fundraising event.

(2) Solicit funds at a non-Federal fundraising event, provided that the solicitation is limited to funds that comply with the amount limitations and source prohibitions of the Act and that are consistent with State law.

(i) A Federal candidate or officeholder may limit such a solicitation by displaying at the fundraising event a clear and conspicuous written notice, or making a clear and conspicuous oral statement, that the solicitation is not for Levin funds (when applicable), does not seek funds in excess of $[Federally permissible amount], and does not seek funds from corporations, labor organizations, national banks, federal government contractors, or foreign nationals.

(ii) A written notice or oral statement is not clear and conspicuous if it is difficult to read or hear or if its placement is easily overlooked by any significant number of those in attendance.

(c) *Publicity for non-Federal fundraising events.* For the purposes of this paragraph, publicity for a non-Federal fundraising event includes, but is not limited to, advertisements, announcements, or pre-event invitation materials, regardless of format or medium of communication.

(1) *Publicity not containing a solicitation.* A Federal candidate, officeholder, or an agent of either may approve, authorize, agree to, or consent to the use of the Federal candidate's or officeholder's name or likeness in publicity

for a non-Federal fundraising event that does not contain a solicitation.

(2) *Publicity containing a solicitation limited to funds that comply with the amount limitations and source prohibitions of the Act.* A Federal candidate, officeholder, or an agent of either may approve, authorize, agree to, or consent to the use of the Federal candidate's or officeholder's name or likeness in publicity for a non-Federal fundraising event that solicits only funds that comply with the amount limitations and source prohibitions of the Act.

(3) *Publicity containing a solicitation of funds outside the amount limitations and source prohibitions of the Act.* (i) A Federal candidate, officeholder, or an agent of either may approve, authorize, agree to, or consent to the use of the Federal candidate's or officeholder's name or likeness in publicity for a non-Federal fundraising event that contains a solicitation of funds outside the amount limitations and source prohibitions of the Act or Levin funds only if:

(A) The Federal candidate or officeholder is identified as a featured guest, honored guest, special guest, featured speaker, or honored speaker, or in any other manner not specifically related to fundraising; and

(B) The publicity includes a clear and conspicuous disclaimer that the solicitation is not being made by the Federal candidate or officeholder.

(ii) The disclaimer required in paragraph (c)(3)(i)(B) of this section must meet the requirements in 11 CFR 110.11(c)(2) if the publicity is written.

(iii) Where publicity is disseminated by non-written means, the disclaimer described in paragraph (c)(3)(i)(B) of this section is required only if the publicity is recorded or follows any form of written script or is conducted according to a structured or organized program.

(iv) Examples of disclaimers that satisfy paragraph (c)(3)(i)(B) of this section include, but are not limited to:

(A) "[Name of Federal candidate/officeholder] is appearing at this event only as a featured speaker. [Federal candidate/officeholder] is not asking for funds or donations"; or

(B) "All funds solicited in connection with this event are by [name of non-

Federal candidate or entity], and not by [Federal candidate/officeholder]."

(v) A Federal candidate, officeholder, or an agent of either may not approve, authorize, agree to, or consent to the use of the Federal candidate's or officeholder's name or likeness in publicity for a non-Federal fundraising event that contains a solicitation of funds outside the amount limitations and source prohibitions of the Act or Levin funds if:

(A) The Federal candidate or officeholder is identified as serving in a position specifically related to fundraising, such as honorary chairperson or member of a host committee, or is identified in the publicity as extending an invitation to the event, even if the communication contains a written disclaimer as described in paragraph (c)(3)(i)(B) of this section; or

(B) The Federal candidate or officeholder signs the communication, even if the communication contains a written disclaimer as described in paragraph (c)(3)(i)(B) of this section.

(vi) A Federal candidate, officeholder, or an agent of either, may not disseminate publicity for a non-Federal fundraising event that contains a solicitation of funds outside the amount limitations and source prohibitions of the Act or Levin funds by someone other than the Federal candidate or officeholder.

[75 FR 24383, May 5, 2010]

§300.65 **Exceptions for certain tax-exempt organizations (52 U.S.C. 30125(e)(1) and (4)).**

A Federal candidate, an individual holding Federal office, and an individual agent acting on behalf of either may make the following solicitations of funds on behalf of any organization described in 26 U.S.C. 501(c) and exempt from taxation under 26 U.S.C. 501(a), or an organization that has submitted an application for determination of tax-exempt status under 26 U.S.C. 501(c):

(a) *General solicitations.* A Federal candidate, an individual holding Federal office or an individual agent acting on behalf of either, may make a general solicitation of funds, without regard to source or amount limitation, if:

(1) The organization does not engage in activities in connection with an election, including any activity described in paragraph (c) of this section; or

(2)(i) The organization conducts activities in connection with an election, but the organization's principal purpose is not to conduct election activities or any activity described in paragraph (c) of this section; and

(ii) The solicitation is not to obtain funds for activities in connection with an election or any activity described in paragraph (c) of this section.

(b) *Specific solicitations.* A Federal candidate, an individual holding Federal office, or an individual agent acting on behalf of either, may make a solicitation explicitly to obtain funds for any activity described in paragraph (c) of this section or for an organization whose principal purpose is to conduct that activity, if:

(1) The solicitation is made only to individuals; and

(2) The amount solicited from any individual does not exceed $20,000 during any calendar year.

(c) *Voter registration, voter identification, get-out-the-vote activity and generic campaign activity.* This section applies to only the following types of Federal election activity:

(1) Voter registration activity, as described in 11 CFR 100.24(a)(2), during the period that begins on the date that is 120 days before the date a regularly scheduled Federal election is held and ends on the date of the election; or

(2) The following activities conducted in connection with an election in which one or more Federal candidates appear on the ballot (see 11 CFR 100.24(a)(1)), regardless of whether one or more State candidates also appears on the ballot:

(i) Voter identification as described in 11 CFR 100.24(a)(4);

(ii) Get-out-the-vote activity as described in 11 CFR 100.24(a)(3); or

(iii) Generic campaign activity as defined in 11 CFR 100.25.

(d) *Prohibited solicitations.* A Federal candidate, an individual holding Federal office, and an individual who is an agent acting on behalf of either, must not make any solicitation on behalf of any organization described in 26 U.S.C.

501(c) and exempt from taxation under 26 U.S.C. 501(a), or an organization that has submitted an application for determination of tax-exempt status under 26 U.S.C. 501(c) for any election activity other than a Federal election activity, as described in paragraph (c) of this section.

(e) *Safe Harbor.* In determining whether a 501(c) organization is one whose principal purpose is to conduct election activities, including activity described in paragraph (c) of this section, a Federal candidate, an individual holding Federal office, or an individual agent acting on behalf of either may obtain and rely upon a certification from the organization that satisfies the following criteria:

(1) The certification is a signed written statement by an officer or other authorized representative of the organization with knowledge of the organization's activities;

(2) The certification states that the organization's principal purpose is not to conduct election activities, including election activities described in paragraphs (c) of this section.

(3) The certification states that the organization does not intend to pay debts incurred from the making of expenditures or disbursements in connection with an election for Federal office (including for Federal election activity) in a prior election cycle.

(f) If a Federal candidate, an individual holding Federal office, or an individual agent acting on behalf of either has actual knowledge that the certification is false, the certification may not be relied upon.

Subpart E—State and Local Candidates

§ 300.70   Scope (52 U.S.C. 30125(f)(1)).

This subpart applies to any candidate for State or local office, individual holding State or local office, or an agent acting on behalf of any such candidate or individual. For example, this subpart applies to an individual holding Federal office who is a candidate for State or local office. This subpart does not apply to an association or similar group of candidates for State or local office or of individuals holding State or local office.

§ 300.71 Federal funds required for certain public communications (52 U.S.C. 30125(f)(1)).

No individual described in 11 CFR 300.70 shall spend any funds for a public communication that refers to a clearly identified candidate for Federal office (regardless of whether a candidate for State or local office is also mentioned or identified), and that promotes or supports any candidate for that Federal office, or attacks or opposes any candidate for that Federal office (regardless of whether the communication expressly advocates a vote for or against a candidate) unless the funds consist of Federal funds that are subject to the limitations, prohibitions, and reporting requirements of the Act. *See* definition of *public communication* at 11 CFR 100.26

§ 300.72 Federal funds not required for certain communications (52 U.S.C. 30125(f)(2)).

The requirements of section 11 CFR 300.71 shall not apply if the public communication is in connection with an election for State or local office, and refers to one or more candidates for State or local office or to a State or local officeholder but does not promote, support, attack, or oppose any candidate for Federal office.

SUBCHAPTER D [RESERVED]

SUBCHAPTER E—PRESIDENTIAL ELECTION CAMPAIGN FUND: GENERAL ELECTION FINANCING

PART 9001—SCOPE

AUTHORITY: 26 U.S.C. 9009(b).

§ 9001.1 Scope.

This subchapter governs entitlement to and use of funds certified from the Presidential Election Campaign Fund under 26 U.S.C. 9001 *et seq.* The definitions, restrictions, liabilities and obligations imposed by this subchapter are in addition to those imposed by sections 30101–30145 of Title 52, United States Code, and regulations prescribed thereunder (11 CFR parts 100 through 300). Unless expressly stated to the contrary, this subchapter does not alter the effect of any definitions, restrictions, obligations and liabilities imposed by sections 30101–30145 of Title 52, United States Code, or regulations prescribed thereunder (11 CFR parts 100 through 300).

[56 FR 35911, July 29, 1991, as amended at 68 FR 47414, Aug. 8, 2003; 73 FR 79602, Dec. 30, 2008; 79 FR 77850, Dec. 29, 2014]

PART 9002—DEFINITIONS

Sec.
9002.1 Authorized committee.
9002.2 Candidate.
9002.3 Commission.
9002.4 Eligible candidates.
9002.5 Fund.
9002.6 Major party.
9002.7 Minor party.
9002.8 New party.
9002.9 Political committee.
9002.10 Presidential election.
9002.11 Qualified campaign expense.
9002.12 Expenditure report period.
9002.13 Contribution.
9002.14 Secretary.
9002.15 Political party.

AUTHORITY: 26 U.S.C. 9002 and 9009(b).

SOURCE: 56 FR 35911, July 29, 1991, unless otherwise noted.

§ 9002.1 Authorized committee.

(a) Notwithstanding the definition at 11 CFR 100.5, *authorized committee* means with respect to a candidate (as defined at 11 CFR 9002.2) of a political party for President and Vice President, any political committee that is authorized by a candidate to incur expenses on behalf of such candidate. The term "authorized committee" includes the candidate's principal campaign committee designated in accordance with 11 CFR 102.12, any political committee authorized in writing by the candidate in accordance with 11 CFR 102.13, and any political committee not disavowed by the candidate pursuant to 11 CFR 100.3(a)(3). If a party has nominated a Presidential and a Vice Presidential candidate, all political committees authorized by that party's Presidential candidate shall also be authorized committees of the Vice Presidential candidate and all political committees authorized by the Vice Presidential candidate shall also be authorized committees of the Presidential candidate.

(b) Any withdrawal of an authorization shall be in writing and shall be addressed and filed in the same manner provided for at 11 CFR 102.12 or 102.13.

(c) Any candidate nominated by a political party may designate the national committee of that political party as that candidate's authorized committee in accordance with 11 CFR 102.12(c).

(d) For purposes of this subchapter, references to the "candidate" and his or her responsibilities under this subchapter shall also be deemed to refer to the candidate's authorized committee(s).

§ 9002.2 Candidate.

(a) For the purposes of this subchapter, *candidate* means with respect to any presidential election, an individual who—

(1) Has been nominated by a major party for election to the office of President of the United States or the office of Vice President of the United States; or

(2) Has qualified or consented to have his or her name appear on the general election ballot (or to have the names of electors pledged to him or her on such ballot) as the candidate of a political

266

party for election to either such office in 10 or more States. For the purposes of this section, *political party* shall be defined in accordance with 11 CFR 9002.15.

(b) An individual who is no longer actively conducting campaigns in more than one State pursuant to 11 CFR 9004.8 shall cease to be a candidate for the purpose of this subchapter.

§9002.3 Commission.

Commission means the Federal Election Commission.

[56 FR 35911, July 29, 1991, as amended at 82 FR 60854, Dec. 26, 2017]

§9002.4 Eligible candidates.

Eligible candidates means those Presidential and Vice Presidential candidates who have met all applicable conditions for eligibility to receive payments from the Fund under 11 CFR part 9003.

§9002.5 Fund.

Fund means the Presidential Election Campaign Fund established by 26 U.S.C. 9006(a).

§9002.6 Major party.

Major party means a political party whose candidate for the office of President in the preceding Presidential election received, as a candidate of such party, 25 percent or more of the total number of popular votes received by all candidates for such office. For the purposes of 11 CFR 9002.6, *candidate* means, with respect to any preceding Presidential election, an individual who received popular votes for the office of President in such election.

§9002.7 Minor party.

Minor party means a political party whose candidate for the office of President in the preceding Presidential election received, as a candidate of such party, 5 percent or more, but less than 25 percent, of the total number of popular votes received by all candidates for such office. For the purposes of 11 CFR 9002.7, *candidate* means with respect to any preceding Presidential election, an individual who received popular votes for the office of President in such election.

§9002.8 New party.

New party means a political party which is neither a major party nor a minor party.

§9002.9 Political committee.

For purposes of this subchapter, *political committee* means any committee, club, association, organization or other group of persons (whether or not incorporated) which accepts contributions or makes expenditures for the purpose of influencing, or attempting to influence, the election of any candidate to the office of President or Vice President of the United States.

§9002.10 Presidential election.

Presidential election means the election of Presidential and Vice Presidential electors.

§9002.11 Qualified campaign expense.

(a) *Qualified campaign expense* means any expenditure, including a purchase, payment, distribution, loan, advance, deposit, or gift of money or anything of value—

(1) Incurred to further a candidate's campaign for election to the office of President or Vice President of the United States;

(2) Incurred within the expenditure report period, as defined under 11 CFR 9002.12, or incurred before the beginning of such period in accordance with 11 CFR 9003.4 to the extent such expenditure is for property, services or facilities to be used during such period; and

(3) Neither the incurrence nor the payment of such expenditure constitutes a violation of any law of the United States, any law of the State in which such expense is incurred or paid, or any regulation prescribed under such Federal or State law, except that any State law which has been preempted by the Federal Election Campaign Act of 1971, as amended, shall not be considered a State law for purposes of this subchapter. An expenditure which constitutes such a violation shall nevertheless count against the candidate's expenditure limitation if the expenditure meets the conditions set forth at 11 CFR 9002.11(a) (1) and (2).

(b)(1) An expenditure is made to further a Presidential or Vice Presidential candidate's campaign if it is incurred by or on behalf of such candidate or his or her authorized committee. For purposes of 11 CFR 9002.11(b)(1), any expenditure incurred by or on behalf of a Presidential candidate of a political party will also be considered an expenditure to further the campaign of the Vice Presidential candidate of that party. Any expenditure incurred by or on behalf of the Vice Presidential candidate will also be considered an expenditure to further the campaign of the Presidential candidate of that party.

(2) An expenditure is made on behalf of a candidate if it is made by—

(i) Any authorized committee or any other agent of the candidate for the purpose of making an expenditure; or

(ii) Any person authorized or requested by the candidate, by the candidate's authorized committee(s), or by an agent of the candidate or his or her authorized committee(s) to make an expenditure; or

(iii) A committee which has been requested by the candidate, the candidate's authorized committee(s), or an agent thereof to make the expenditure, even though such committee is not authorized in writing.

(3) Expenditures that further the election of other candidates for any public office shall be allocated in accordance with 11 CFR 106.1(a) and will be considered qualified campaign expenses only to the extent that they specifically further the election of the candidate for President or Vice President. A candidate may make expenditures under this section in conjunction with other candidates for any public office, but each candidate shall pay his or her proportionate share of the cost in accordance with 11 CFR 106.1(a).

(4) Expenditures by a candidate's authorized committee(s) pursuant to 11 CFR 9004.6 for the travel and related ground service costs of media shall be qualified campaign expenses. Any reimbursement for travel and related services costs received by a candidate's authorized committee shall be subject to the provisions of 11 CFR 9004.6.

(5) Legal and accounting services which are provided solely to ensure compliance with 52 U.S.C. 30101 *et seq.* or 26 U.S.C. 9001, *et seq.* shall be qualified campaign expenses which may be paid from payments received from the Fund. If federal funds are used to pay for such services, the payments will count against the candidate's expenditure limitation. Payments for such services may also be made from an account established in accordance with 11 CFR 9003.3 or may be provided to the committee in accordance with 11 CFR 100.86 and 100.146. If payments for such services are made from an account established in accordance with 11 CFR 9003.3, the payments do not count against the candidate's expenditure limitation. If payments for such services are made by a minor or new party candidate from an account containing private contributions, the payments do not count against that candidate's expenditure limitation. The amount paid by the committee shall be reported in accordance with 11 CFR part 9006. Amounts paid by the regular employer of the person providing such services pursuant to 11 CFR 100.86 and 100.146 shall be reported by the recipient committee in accordance with 11 CFR 104.3(h).

(c) Except as provided in 11 CFR 9034.4(e), expenditures incurred either before the beginning of the expenditure report period or after the last day of a candidate's eligibility will be considered qualified campaign expenses if they meet the provisions of 11 CFR 9004.4(a). Expenditures described under 11 CFR 9004.4(b) will not be considered qualified campaign expenses.

[56 FR 35911, July 29, 1991, as amended at 60 FR 31872, June 16, 1995; 67 FR 78682, Dec. 26, 2002; 79 FR 77850, Dec. 29, 2014]

§ 9002.12　Expenditure report period.

Expenditure report period means, with respect to any Presidential election, the period of time described in either paragraph (a) or (b) of this section, as appropriate.

(a) In the case of a major party, the expenditure report period begins on September 1 before the election or on the date on which the major party's presidential nominee is chosen, whichever is earlier; and the period ends 30 days after the Presidential election.

(b) In the case of a minor or new party, the period will be the same as that of the major party with the shortest expenditure report period for that Presidential election as determined under paragraph (a) of this section.

§ 9002.13 Contribution.

Contribution has the same meaning given the term under 52 U.S.C. 30101(8), 30118, and 30119, and under 11 CFR part 100, subparts B and C, and 11 CFR parts 114 and 115.

[56 FR 35911, July 29, 1991, as amended at 67 FR 78682, Dec. 26, 2002; 79 FR 77850, Dec. 29, 2014]

§ 9002.14 Secretary.

Secretary means the Secretary of the Treasury.

§ 9002.15 Political party.

Political party means an association, committee, or organization which nominates or selects an individual for election to any Federal office, including the office of President or Vice President of the United States, whose name appears on the general election ballot as the candidate of such association, committee, or organization.

PART 9003—ELIGIBILITY FOR PAYMENTS

Sec.
9003.1 Candidate and committee agreements.
9003.2 Candidate certifications.
9003.3 Allowable contributions; General election legal and accounting compliance fund.
9003.4 Expenses incurred prior to the beginning of the expenditure report period or prior to receipt of Federal funds.
9003.5 Documentation of disbursements.
9003.6 Production of computer information.

AUTHORITY: 26 U.S.C. 9003 and 9009(b).

SOURCE: 56 FR 35913, July 29, 1991, unless otherwise noted.

§ 9003.1 Candidate and committee agreements.

(a) *General.* (1) To become eligible to receive payments under 11 CFR part 9005, the Presidential and Vice Presidential candidates of a political party shall agree in a letter signed by the candidates to the Commission that they and their authorized committee(s) shall comply with the conditions set forth in 11 CFR 9003.1(b).

(2) Major party candidates shall sign and submit such letter to the Commission within 14 days after receiving the party's nomination for election. Minor and new party candidates shall sign and submit such letter within 14 days after such candidates have qualified to appear on the general election ballot in 10 or more states pursuant to 11 CFR 9002.2(a)(2). The Commission, on written request by a minor or new party candidate, at any time prior to the date of the general election, may extend the deadline for filing such letter except that the deadline shall be a date prior to the date of the general election.

(b) *Conditions.* The candidates shall:

(1) Agree that they have the burden of proving that disbursements made by them or any authorized committee(s) or agent(s) thereof are qualified campaign expenses as defined in 11 CFR 9002.11.

(2) Agree that they and their authorized committee(s) shall comply with the documentation requirements set forth at 11 CFR 9003.5.

(3) Agree that they and their authorized committee(s) shall provide an explanation, in addition to complying with the documentation requirements, of the connection between any disbursements made by the candidates or the authorized committee(s) of the candidates and the campaign if requested by the Commission.

(4) Agree that they and their authorized committee(s) will keep and furnish to the Commission all documentation relating to receipts and disbursements including any books, records (including bank records for all accounts), all documentation required by this subchapter (including those required to be maintained under 11 CFR 9003.5), and other information that the Commission may request. If the candidate or the candidate's authorized committee maintains or uses computerized information containing any of the categories of data listed in 11 CFR 9003.6(a), the committee will provide computerized magnetic media, such as magnetic tapes or magnetic diskettes,

containing the computerized information that meets the requirements of 11 CFR 9003.6(b) at the times specified in 11 CFR 9007.1(b)(1). Upon request, documentation explaining the computer system's software capabilities shall be provided, and such personnel as are necessary to explain the operation of the computer system's software and the computerized information prepared or maintained by the committee shall also be made available.

(5) Agree that they and their authorized committee(s) shall obtain and furnish to the Commission upon request all documentation relating to funds received and disbursements made on the candidate's behalf by other political committees and organizations associated with the candidate.

(6) Agree that they and their authorized committee(s) shall permit an audit and examination pursuant to 11 CFR part 9007 of all receipts and disbursements including those made by the candidate, all authorized committees and any agent or person authorized to make expenditures on behalf of the candidate or committee(s). The candidate and authorized committee(s) shall facilitate the audit by making available in one central location, office space, records and such personnel as are necessary to conduct the audit and examination, and shall pay any amounts required to be repaid under 11 CFR part 9007.

(7) Submit the name and mailing address of the person who is entitled to receive payments from the Fund on behalf of the candidates; the name and address of the depository designated by the candidates as required by 11 CFR part 103 and 11 CFR 9005.2; and the name under which each account is held at the depository at which the payments from the Fund are to be deposited.

(8) Agree that they and their authorized committee(s) shall comply with the applicable requirements of 52 U.S.C. 30101 *et seq.*, 26 U.S.C. 9001 *et seq.*, and the Commission's regulations at 11 CFR parts 100–300, and 9001–9012.

(9) Agree that they and their authorized committee(s) shall pay any civil penalties included in a conciliation agreement or otherwise imposed under 52 U.S.C. 30109 against the candidates,

any authorized committees of the candidates or any agent thereof.

(10) Agree that any television commercial prepared or distributed by the candidate or the candidate's authorized committee(s) will be prepared in a manner which ensures that the commercial contains or is accompanied by closed captioning of the oral content of the commercial to be broadcast in line 21 of the vertical blanking interval, or is capable of being viewed by deaf and hearing impaired individuals via any comparable successor technology to line 21 of the vertical blanking interval.

[56 FR 35913, July 29, 1991, as amended at 60 FR 31872, June 16, 1995; 63 FR 45680, Aug. 27, 1998; 65 FR 38424, June 21, 2000; 68 FR 47414, Aug. 8, 2003; 73 FR 79602, Dec. 30, 2008; 79 FR 77850, Dec. 29, 2014]

§ 9003.2 Candidate certifications.

(a) *Major party candidates.* To be eligible to receive payments under 11 CFR part 9005, each Presidential and Vice Presidential candidate of a major party shall, under penalty of perjury, certify to the Commission:

(1) That the candidate and his or her authorized committee(s) have not incurred and will not incur qualified campaign expenses in excess of the aggregate payments to which they will be entitled under 11 CFR part 9004.

(2) That no contributions have been or will be accepted by the candidate or his or her authorized committee(s); except as contributions specifically solicited for, and deposited to, the candidate's legal and accounting compliance fund established under 11 CFR 9003.3(a); or except to the extent necessary to make up any deficiency in payments received from the Fund due to the application of 11 CFR 9005.2(b).

(b) *Minor and new party candidates.* To be eligible to receive any payments under 11 CFR part 9005, each Presidential and Vice Presidential candidate of a minor or new party shall, under penalty of perjury, certify to the Commission:

(1) That the candidate and his or her authorized committee(s) have not incurred and will not incur qualified campaign expenses in excess of the aggregate payments to which the eligible

candidates of a major party are entitled under 11 CFR 9004.1.

(2) That no contributions to defray qualified campaign expenses have been or will be accepted by the candidate or his or her authorized committee(s) except to the extent that the qualified campaign expenses incurred exceed the aggregate payments received by such candidate from the Fund under 11 CFR 9004.2.

(c) *All candidates.* To be eligible to receive any payment under 11 CFR 9004.2, the Presidential candidate of each major, minor or new party shall certify to the Commission, under penalty of perjury, that such candidate will not knowingly make expenditures from his or her personal funds, or the personal funds of his or her immediate family, in connection with his or her campaign for the office of President in excess of $50,000 in the aggregate.

(1) For purposes of this section, the term *immediate family* means a candidate's spouse, and any child, parent, grandparent, brother, half-brother, sister, or half-sister of the candidate, and the spouses of such persons.

(2) Expenditures from personal funds made under this paragraph shall not apply against the expenditure limitations.

(3) For purposes of this section, the terms *personal funds* and *personal funds of his or her immediate family* mean:

(i) Any assets which, under applicable state law, at the time he or she became a candidate, the candidate had legal right of access to or control over, and with respect to which the candidate had either:

(A) Legal and rightful title, or

(B) An equitable interest.

(ii) Salary and other earned income from bona fide employment; dividends and proceeds from the sale of the candidate's stocks or other investments; bequests to the candidate; income from trusts established before candidacy; income from trusts established by bequest after candidacy of which the candidate is a beneficiary; gifts of a personal nature which had been customarily received prior to candidacy; proceeds from lotteries and similar legal games of chance.

(iii) A candidate may use a portion of assets jointly owned with his or her spouse as personal funds. The portion of the jointly owned assets that shall be considered as personal funds of the candidate shall be that portion which is the candidate's share under the instrument(s) of conveyance or ownership. If no specific share is indicated by any instrument of conveyance or ownership, the value of one-half of the property used shall be considered as personal funds of the candidate.

(4) For purposes of this section, expenditures from personal funds made by a candidate of a political party for the office of Vice President shall be considered to be expenditures made by the candidate of such party for the office of President.

(5) Contributions made by members of a candidate's family from funds which do not meet the definition of personal funds under 11 CFR 9003.2(c)(3) shall not count against such candidate's $50,000 expenditure limitation under 11 CFR 9003.2(c).

(6) Personal funds expended pursuant to this section shall be first deposited in an account established in accordance with 11 CFR 9003.3 (b) or (c).

(7) The provisions of this section shall not operate to limit the candidate's liability for, nor the candidate's ability to pay, any repayments required under 11 CFR part 9007. If the candidate or his or her committee knowingly incurs expenditures in excess of the limitations of 11 CFR 110.8(a), the Commission may seek civil penalties under 11 CFR part 111 in addition to any repayment determinations made on the basis of such excessive expenditures.

(8) Expenditures made using a credit card for which the candidate is jointly or solely liable will count against the limits of this section to the extent that the full amount due, including any finance charge, is not paid by the committee within 60 days after the closing date of the billing statement on which the charges first appear. For purposes of this section, the "closing date" shall be the date indicated on the billing statement which serves as the cutoff date for determining which charges are included on that billing statement.

(d) *Form.* Major party candidates shall submit the certifications required under 11 CFR 9003.2 in a letter which shall be signed and submitted within 14 days after receiving the party's nomination for election. Minor and new party candidates shall sign and submit such letter within 14 days after such candidates have qualified to appear on the general election ballot in 10 or more States pursuant to 11 CFR 9002.2(a)(2). The Commission, upon written request by a minor or new party candidate made at any time prior to the date of the general election, may extend the deadline for filing such letter, except that the deadline shall be a date prior to the day of the general election.

§ 9003.3 Allowable contributions; General election legal and accounting compliance fund.

(a) *Legal and accounting compliance fund—major party candidates*—(1) *Sources.* (i) A major party candidate, or an individual who is seeking the nomination of a major party, may accept contributions to a legal and accounting compliance fund if such contributions are received and disbursed in accordance with this section. A general election legal and accounting compliance fund ("GELAC") may be established by such individual prior to being nominated or selected as the candidate of a political party for the office of President or Vice President of the United States. Before April 1 of the calendar year in which a Presidential general election is held, contributions may only be deposited in the GELAC if they are made for the primary and exceed the contributor's contribution limits for the primary and are lawfully redesignated for the GELAC pursuant to 11 CFR 110.1.

(A) All solicitations for contributions to the GELAC shall clearly state that Federal law prohibits private contributions from being used for the candidate's election and that contributions will be used solely for legal and accounting services to ensure compliance with Federal law, and shall clearly state how contribution checks should be made payable. Contributions shall not be solicited for the GELAC before April 1 of the calendar year in which a Presidential general election is held. If the candidate does not become the nominee, all contributions accept-

ed for the GELAC, including redesignated contributions, shall be refunded within sixty (60) days after the candidate's date of ineligibility.

(B) Contributions to the GELAC shall be subject to the limitations and prohibitions of 11 CFR parts 110, 114, and 115.

(C) Contributions shall be deposited in the GELAC only if they are designated in writing for the GELAC, or transferred pursuant to paragraph (a)(1) (ii), (iii), (iv) or (v) of this section. Any contribution which otherwise could be matched pursuant to 11 CFR 9034.2 shall not be considered designated in writing for the GELAC unless the contributor specifically redesignates it for the GELAC or unless it is accompanied by a proper designation for the GELAC. Any contribution that is designated in writing or redesignated for the GELAC shall not be matched pursuant to 11 CFR 9034.2.

(ii)(A) Contributions made during the matching payment period that do not exceed the contributor's limit for the primary election may be redesignated for the GELAC and subsequently transferred to the GELAC before the nomination only if—

(1) The contributions represent funds in excess of any amount needed to pay remaining primary expenses;

(2) The contributions have not been submitted for matching;

(3) The written redesignations are received within 60 days of the Treasurer's receipt of the contributions; and

(4) The requirements of 11 CFR 110.1(b)(5)(i) and (ii)(A) and 110.1(l) regarding redesignation are satisfied.

(B) All contributions redesignated and deposited pursuant to paragraph (a)(1)(ii)(A) of this section shall be subject to the contribution limitations applicable for the general election pursuant to 11 CFR 110.1(b)(2)(i).

(iii) Funds received during the matching payment period that are remaining in a candidate's primary election account after the nomination may be transferred to the GELAC without regard to the contribution limitations of 11 CFR part 110 and used for any purpose permitted under this section, only if the funds are in excess of any amount needed to pay remaining net outstanding campaign obligations under 11 CFR 9034.1(b) and any amount required to be reimbursed to the Presidential Primary Matching Payment Account under 11 CFR 9038.2. The excess funds so transferred may include contributions made before the beginning of the expenditure report period, which contributions do not exceed the contributor's limit for the primary election. Such contributions need not be redesignated by the contributors for the GELAC.

(iv) Contributions that are made after the beginning of the expenditure report period but that are not designated in writing for the GELAC are considered made with respect to the primary election and may be redesignated for the GELAC and transferred to the GELAC only if—

(A) The funds are in excess of any amount needed to pay remaining net outstanding campaign obligations under 11 CFR 9034.1(b) and any amount required to be reimbursed to the Presidential Primary Matching Payment Account under 11 CFR 9038.2;

(B) The contributions have not been submitted for matching; and

(C) The candidate obtains the contributor's written redesignation in accordance with 11 CFR 110.1.

(v) Contributions made with respect to the primary election that exceed the contributor's limit for the primary election may be redesignated for the GELAC and transferred to the GELAC if the candidate redesignates the contribution for the GELAC in accordance with 11 CFR 110.1(b)(5)(i) and (ii)(A) or (ii)(B). For purposes of this section only, 11 CFR 110.1(b)(5)(ii)(B)(*1*) shall not apply.

(vi) For purposes of this section, a contribution shall be considered to be designated in writing for the GELAC if—

(A) The contribution is made by check, money order, or other negotiable instrument which clearly indicates that it is made with respect to the GELAC; or

(B) The contribution is accompanied by a writing, signed by the contributor, which clearly indicates that it is made with respect to the GELAC.

(2) *Uses.* (i) Contributions to the GELAC shall be used only for the following purposes:

(A) To defray the cost of legal and accounting services provided solely to ensure compliance with 52 U.S.C. 30101 *et seq.* and 26 U.S.C. 9001 *et seq.* in accordance with paragraph (a)(2)(ii) of this section;

(B) To defray in accordance with paragraph (a)(2)(ii)(A) of this section, that portion of expenditures for payroll, overhead, and computer services related to ensuring compliance with 52 U.S.C. 30101 *et seq.* and 26 U.S.C. 9001 *et seq.;*

(C) To defray any civil or criminal penalties imposed pursuant to 52 U.S.C. 30109 or 26 U.S.C. 9012;

(D) To make repayments under 11 CFR 9007.2, 9038.2, or 9038.3;

(E) To defray the cost of soliciting contributions to the GELAC;

(F) To defray the cost of producing, delivering and explaining the computerized information and materials provided pursuant to 11 CFR 9003.6 and explaining the operation of the computer system's software;

(G) To make a loan to an account established pursuant to 11 CFR 9003.4 to defray qualified campaign expenses incurred prior to the expenditure report period or prior to receipt of Federal funds, provided that the amounts so loaned are restored to the GELAC;

(H) To defray unreimbursed costs incurred in providing transportation and services for the Secret Service and national security staff pursuant to 11 CFR 9004.6; and

(I) To defray winding down expenses for legal and accounting compliance activities incurred after the end of the expenditure report period by either the candidate's primary election committee, general election committee, or both committees. For purposes of this section, 100% of salary, overhead and computer expenses incurred after the end of the expenditure report period shall be considered winding down expenses for legal and accounting compliance activities payable from GELAC funds, and will be presumed to be solely to ensure compliance with 52 U.S.C. 30101 *et seq.* and 26 U.S.C. 9001 *et seq.*

(ii)(A) Expenditures for payroll (including payroll taxes), overhead and computer services, a portion of which are related to ensuring compliance with Title 52 of the United States Code and Chapter 95 of Title 26 of the United States Code, shall be initially paid from the candidate's Federal fund account under 11 CFR 9005.2 and may be later reimbursed by the compliance fund. For purposes of paragraph (a)(2)(i)(B) of this section, a candidate may use contributions to the GELAC to reimburse his or her Federal fund account an amount equal to 10% of the payroll and overhead expenditures of his or her national campaign headquarters and state offices.

(B) Overhead expenditures include, but are not limited to rent, utilities, office equipment, furniture, supplies and all telephone charges except for telephone charges related to a special use such as voter registration and get out the vote efforts.

(C) If the candidate wishes to claim a larger compliance exemption for payroll or overhead expenditures, the candidate shall establish allocation percentages for each individual who spends all or a portion of his or her time to perform duties which are considered necessary to ensure compliance with Title 52 of the United States Code or chapter 95 of title 26 of the United States Code. The candidate shall keep detailed records to support the derivation of each percentage. Such records shall indicate which duties are considered compliance and the percentage of time each person spends on such activity.

(D) In addition, a candidate may use contributions to the GELAC to reimburse his or her Federal fund account an amount equal to 50% of the costs (other than payroll) associated with computer services. Such costs include but are not limited to rental and maintenance of computer equipment, data entry services not performed by committee personnel, and related supplies.

(E) If the candidate wishes to claim a larger compliance exemption for costs associated with computer services, the candidate shall establish allocation percentages for each computer function that is considered necessary, in whole or in part, to ensure compliance with 52 U.S.C. 30101 *et seq.*, and 26 U.S.C. 9001 *et seq*. The allocation shall be based on a reasonable estimate of the costs associated with each computer function, such as the costs for

data entry services performed by persons other than committee personnel and processing time. The candidate shall keep detailed records to support such calculations. The records shall indicate which computer functions are considered compliance-related and shall reflect which costs are associated with each computer function.

(F) The Commission's Financial Control and Compliance Manual for General Election Candidates Receiving Public Funding contains some accepted alternative allocation methods for determining the amount of salaries and overhead expenditures that may be considered exempt compliance costs.

(G) Reimbursement from the GELAC may be made to the separate account maintained for federal funds under 11 CFR 9005.2 for legal and accounting compliance services disbursements that are initially paid from the separate federal funds account. Such reimbursement must be made prior to any repayment determination by the Commission pursuant to 11 CFR 9007.2. Any amounts so reimbursed to the Federal funds account may not subsequently be transferred back to the GELAC.

(iii) Amounts paid from the GELAC for the purposes permitted by paragraphs (a)(2)(i) (A) through (F), (H) and (I) of this section shall not be subject to the expenditure limits of 52 U.S.C. 30116(b) and 11 CFR 110.8. (*See also* 11 CFR 100.146.) When the proceeds of loans made in accordance with paragraph (a)(2)(i)(G) of this section are expended on qualified campaign expenses, such expenditures shall count against the candidate's expenditure limit.

(iv) Contributions to and funds deposited in the GELAC may not be used to retire debts remaining from the presidential primaries, except that, after payment of all expenses set out in paragraph (a)(2)(i) of this section, and the completion of the audit and repayment process, including the making of all repayments owed to the United States Treasury by both the candidate's primary and general election committees, funds remaining in the GELAC may be used for any purpose permitted under 52 U.S.C. 30114 and 11

CFR part 113, including payment of primary election debts, which shall remain subject to the primary expenditure limit under 11 CFR 9035.1.

(3) *Deposit and disclosure.* (i) Amounts received pursuant to paragraph (a)(1) of this section shall be deposited and maintained in a GELAC account separate from the account described in 11 CFR 9005.2 and shall not be commingled with any money paid to the candidate by the Secretary pursuant to 11 CFR 9005.2.

(ii) The receipts to and disbursements from the GELAC account shall be reported in a separate report in accordance with 11 CFR 9006.1(b)(2). All contributions made to the GELAC account shall be recorded in accordance with 11 CFR 102.9. Disbursements made from the GELAC account shall be documented in the same manner provided in 11 CFR 9003.5.

(b) *Contributions to defray qualified campaign expenses—major party candidates.* (1) A major party candidate or his or her authorized committee(s) may solicit contributions to defray qualified campaign expenses to the extent necessary to make up any deficiency in payments received from the Fund due to the application of 11 CFR 9005.2(b).

(2) Such contributions may be deposited in a separate account or may be deposited with federal funds received under 11 CFR 9005.2. Disbursements from this account shall be made only to defray qualified campaign expenses and to defray the cost of soliciting contributions to such account. All disbursements from this account shall be documented in accordance with 11 CFR 9003.5 and shall be reported in accordance with 11 CFR 9006.1.

(3) A candidate may make transfers to this account from his or her GELAC, or from the candidate's primary election account in accordance with paragraph (a)(1)(iii) of this section.

(4) The contributions received under this section shall be subject to the limitations and prohibitions of 11 CFR parts 110, 114 and 115 and shall be aggregated with all contributions made by the same persons to the candidate's GELAC under paragraph (a) of this section for the purposes of such limitations.

(5) Any costs incurred for soliciting contributions to this account shall not be considered expenditures to the extent that the aggregate of such costs does not exceed 20 percent of the expenditure limitation under 11 CFR 9003.2(a)(1). These costs shall, however, be reported as disbursements in accordance with 11 CFR part 104 and 11 CFR 9006.1. For purposes of this section, a candidate may exclude from the expenditure limitation an amount equal to 10% of the payroll (including payroll taxes) and overhead expenditures of his or her national campaign headquarters and state offices as exempt fundraising costs. The candidate may claim a larger fundraising exemption by establishing allocation percentages for employees using the method described in paragraph (a)(2)(ii)(C) of this section.

(6) Any costs incurred for legal and accounting services which are provided solely to ensure compliance with 52 U.S.C. 30101 *et seq.* and 26 U.S.C. 9001 *et seq.* shall not count against the candidate's expenditure limitation. A candidate may exclude from the expenditure limitation the amounts described in paragraphs (a)(2)(ii) (A) and (D) of this section for payroll, overhead or computer costs or a larger amount under paragraphs (a)(2)(ii) (C) and (E) of this section.

(7) The Commission's Financial Control and Compliance Manual for General Election Candidates Receiving Public Funding contains some accepted alternative allocation methods for determining the amount of salaries and overhead expenditures that may be considered exempt compliance costs or exempt fundraising costs.

(c) *Contributions to defray qualified campaign expenses—minor and new party candidates.* (1) A minor or new party candidate may solicit contributions to defray qualified campaign expenses which exceed the amount received by such candidate from the Fund, subject to the limits of 11 CFR 9003.2(b).

(2) The contributions received under this section shall be subject to the limitations and prohibitions of 11 CFR parts 110, 114 and 115.

(3) Such contributions may be deposited in a separate account or may be deposited with federal funds received under 11 CFR 9005.2. Disbursements

from this account shall be made only for the following purposes:

(i) To defray qualified campaign expenses;

(ii) To make repayments under 11 CFR 9007.2;

(iii) To defray the cost of soliciting contributions to such account;

(iv) To defray the cost of legal and accounting services provided solely to ensure compliance with 52 U.S.C. 30101 *et seq.* and 26 U.S.C. 9001 *et seq.;*

(v) To defray the cost of producing, delivering and explaining the computerized information and materials provided pursuant to 11 CFR 9003.6 and explaining the operation of the computer system's software.

(4) All disbursements from this account shall be documented in accordance with 11 CFR 9003.5 and shall be reported in accordance with 11 CFR part 104 and § 9006.1. The candidate shall keep and maintain a separate record of disbursements made to defray exempt legal and accounting costs under paragraphs (c) (6) and (7) of this section and shall report such disbursements in accordance with 11 CFR part 104 and 11 CFR 9006.1.

(5) Any costs incurred for soliciting contributions to this account shall not be considered expenditures to the extent that the aggregate of such costs does not exceed 20 percent of the expenditure limitation under 11 CFR 9003.2(a)(1). These costs shall, however, be reported as disbursements in accordance with 11 CFR part 104 and 9006.1. For purposes of this section, a candidate may exclude from the expenditure limitation the amount of payroll costs described in paragraph (b)(5) of this section.

(6) Any costs incurred for legal and accounting services which are provided solely to ensure compliance with 52 U.S.C. 30101 *et seq.* and 26 U.S.C. 9001 *et seq.* shall not count against the candidate's expenditure limitation. A candidate may exclude from the expenditure limitation the amounts described in paragraphs (a)(2)(ii) (A) and (D) of this section for payroll, overhead or computer costs or a larger amount under paragraphs (a)(2)(ii) (C) and (E) of this section.

(7) The Commission's Financial Control and Compliance Manual for General Election Candidates Receiving Public Funding contains some accepted alternative allocation methods for determining the amount of salaries and overhead expenditures that may be considered exempt compliance costs or exempt fundraising costs.

[60 FR 31872, June 16, 1995, as amended at 60 FR 57537, Nov. 16, 1995; 64 FR 49362, Sept. 13, 1999; 67 FR 78682, Dec. 26, 2002; 68 FR 47414, Aug. 8, 2003; 79 FR 77850, Dec. 29, 2014]

§ 9003.4 Expenses incurred prior to the beginning of the expenditure report period or prior to receipt of Federal funds.

(a) *Permissible expenditures.* (1) A candidate may incur expenditures before the beginning of the expenditure report period, as defined at 11 CFR 9002.12, if such expenditures are for property, services or facilities which are to be used in connection with his or her general election campaign and which are for use during the expenditure report period. Such expenditures will be considered qualified campaign expenses. Examples of such expenditures include but are not limited to: Expenditures for establishing financial accounting systems and expenditures for organizational planning. Expenditures for polling that are incurred before the start of the expenditure report period are attributed as provided in 11 CFR 9034.4(e)(2).

(2) A candidate may incur qualified campaign expenses prior to receiving payments under 11 CFR part 9005.

(b) *Sources.* (1) A candidate may obtain a loan which meets the requirements of 11 CFR 100.82 for loans in the ordinary course of business to defray permissible expenditures described in 11 CFR 9003.4(a). A candidate receiving payments equal to the expenditure limitation in 11 CFR 110.8 shall make full repayment of principal and interest on such loans from payments received by the candidate under 11 CFR part 9005 within 15 days of receiving such payments.

(2) A major party candidate may borrow from his or her legal and accounting compliance fund for the purposes of defraying permissible expenditures described in 11 CFR 9003.4(a). All amounts borrowed from the legal and accounting compliance fund must be restored

to such fund after the beginning of the expenditure report period either from federal funds received under 11 CFR part 9005 or private contributions received under 11 CFR 9003.3(b). For candidates receiving federal funds, restoration shall be made within 15 days after receipt of such funds.

(3) A minor or new party candidate may defray such expenditures from contributions received in accordance with 11 CFR 9003.3(c).

(4)(i) A candidate who has received federal funding under 11 CFR part 9031 *et seq.*, may borrow from his or her primary election committee(s) an amount not to exceed the residual balance projected to remain in the candidate's primary account(s) on the basis of the formula set forth at 11 CFR 9038.3(c). A major party candidate receiving payments equal to the expenditure limitation shall reimburse amounts borrowed from his or her primary committee(s) from payments received by the candidate under 11 CFR part 9005 within 15 days of such receipt.

(ii) A candidate who has not received federal funding during the primary campaign may borrow at any time from his or her primary account(s) to defray such expenditures, provided that a major party candidate receiving payments equal to the expenditure limitation shall reimburse all amounts borrowed from his or her primary committee(s) from payments received by the candidate under 11 CFR part 9005 within 15 days of such receipt.

(5) A candidate may use personal funds in accordance with 11 CFR 9003.2(c), up to his or her $50,000 limit, to defray such expenditures.

(c) *Deposit and disclosure.* Amounts received or borrowed by a candidate under 11 CFR 9003.4(b) to defray expenditures permitted under 11 CFR 9003.4(a) shall be deposited in a separate account to be used only for such expenditures. All receipts and disbursements from such account shall be reported pursuant to 11 CFR 9006.1(a) and documented in accordance with 11 CFR 9003.5

[56 FR 35913, July 29, 1991, as amended at 60 FR 31874, June 16, 1995; 67 FR 78682, Dec. 26, 2002]

§ 9003.5 Documentation of disbursements.

(a) *Burden of proof.* Each candidate shall have the burden of proving that disbursements made by the candidate or his or her authorized committee(s) or persons authorized to make expenditures on behalf of the candidate or authorized committee(s) are qualified campaign expenses as defined in 11 CFR 9002.11. The candidate and his or her authorized committee(s) shall obtain and furnish to the Commission on request any evidence regarding qualified campaign expenses made by the candidate, his or her authorized committees and agents or persons authorized to make expenditures on behalf of the candidate or committee(s) as provided in paragraph (b) of this section.

(b) *Documentation required.* (1) For disbursements in excess of $200 to a payee, the candidate shall present a canceled check negotiated by the payee and either:

(i) A receipted bill from the payee that states that purpose of the disbursement; or

(ii) If such a receipt is not available,

(A) One of the following documents generated by the payee: a bill, invoice, or voucher that states the purpose of the disbursement; or

(B) Where the documents specified in paragraph (b)(1)(ii)(A) of this section are not available, a voucher or contemporaneous memorandum from the candidate or the committee that states the purpose of the disbursement; or

(iii) Where the supporting documentation required in paragraphs (b)(1) (i) or (ii) of this section is not available, the candidate or committee may present collateral evidence to document the qualified campaign expense. Such collateral evidence may include, but is not limited to:

(A) Evidence demonstrating that the expenditure is part of an identifiable program or project which is otherwise sufficiently documented such as a disbursement which is one of a number of documented disbursements relating to a campaign mailing or to the operation of a campaign office; or

(B) Evidence that the disbursement is covered by a pre-established written campaign committee policy, such as a daily travel expense policy.

(iv) If the purpose of the disbursement is not stated in the accompanying documentation, it must be indicated on the canceled check negotiated by the payee.

(2) For all other disbursements, the candidate shall present:

(i) A record disclosing the full name and mailing address of the payee, the amount, date and purpose of the disbursement, if made from a petty cash fund; or

(ii) A canceled check negotiated by the payee that states the full name and mailing address of the payee, and the amount, date and purpose of the disbursement.

(3) For purposes of this section:

(i) *Payee* means the person who provides the goods or services to the candidate or committee in return for the disbursement; except that an individual will be considered a payee under this section if he or she receives $1000 or less advanced for travel and/or subsistence and if the individual is the recipient of the goods or services purchased.

(ii) *Purpose* means the full name and mailing address of the payee, the date and amount of the disbursement, and a brief description of the goods or services purchased. Examples of acceptable and unacceptable descriptions of goods and services purchased are listed at 11 CFR 104.3(b)(3)(i)(B).

(4) The documentation requirements of 11 CFR 102.9(b) shall also apply to disbursements.

(c) *Retention of records.* The candidate shall retain records with respect to each disbursement and receipt, including bank records, vouchers, worksheets, receipts, bills and accounts, journals, ledgers, fundraising solicitation material, accounting systems documentation, and any related materials documenting campaign receipts and disbursements, for a period of three years pursuant to 11 CFR 102.9(c), and shall present these records to the Commission on request.

(d) *List of capital and other assets*—(1) *Capital assets* The candidate or committee shall maintain a list of all capital assets whose purchase price exceeded $2000 when acquired by the campaign. The list shall include a brief description of each capital asset, the purchase price, the date it was acquired, the method of disposition and the amount received in disposition. For purposes of this section, "capital asset" shall be defined in accordance with 11 CFR 9004.9(d)(1).

(2) *Other assets.* The candidate or committee shall maintain a list of other assets acquired for use in fundraising or as collateral for campaign loans, if the aggregate value of such assets exceeds $5000. The list shall include a brief description of each such asset, the fair market value of each asset, the method of disposition and the amount received in disposition. The fair market value of other assets shall be determined in accordance with 11 CFR 9004.9(d)(2).

[60 FR 31874, June 16, 1995, as amended at 64 FR 49362, Sept. 13, 1999; 68 FR 47415, Aug. 8, 2003; 79 FR 77851, Dec. 29, 2014]

§ 9003.6 Production of computer information.

(a) *Categories of computerized information to be provided.* If the candidate or the candidate's authorized committee maintains or uses computerized information containing any of the categories of data listed in paragraphs (a)(1) through (a)(9) of this section, the committee shall provide computerized magnetic media, such as magnetic tapes or magnetic diskettes, containing the computerized information at the times specified in 11 CFR 9007.1(b)(1):

(1) Information required by law to be maintained regarding the committee's receipts or disbursements;

(2) Receipts by and disbursements from a legal and accounting compliance fund under 11 CFR 9003.3(a), including the allocation of payroll and overhead expenditures;

(3) Receipts and disbursements under 11 CFR 9003.3 (b) or (c) to defray the costs of soliciting contributions or to defray the costs of legal and accounting services, including the allocation of payroll and overhead expenditures;

(4) Records relating to the costs of producing broadcast communications and purchasing airtime;

(5) Records used to prepare statements of net outstanding qualified campaign expenses;

(6) Records used to reconcile bank statements;

(7) Disbursements made and reimbursements received for the cost of transportation, ground services and facilities made available to media personnel, including records relating to how costs charged to media personnel were determined;

(8) Records relating to the acquisition, use and disposition of capital assets or other assets; and

(9) Any other information that may be used during the Commission's audit to review the committee's receipts, disbursements, loans, debts, obligations, bank reconciliations or statements of net outstanding qualified campaign expenses.

(b) *Organization of computerized information and technical specifications.* The computerized magnetic media shall be prepared and delivered at the committee's expense and shall conform to the technical specifications, including file requirements, described in the Federal Election Commission's Computerized Magnetic Media Requirements for title 26 Candidates/Committees Receiving Federal Funding. The data contained in the computerized magnetic media provided to the Commission shall be organized in the order specified by the Computerized Magnetic Media Requirements.

(c) *Additional materials and assistance.* Upon request, the committee shall produce documentation explaining the computer system's software capabilities, such as user guides, technical manuals, formats, layouts and other materials for processing and analyzing the information requested. Upon request, the committee shall also make available such personnel as are necessary to explain the operation of the computer system's software and the computerized information prepared or maintained by the committee.

PART 9004—ENTITLEMENT OF ELIGIBLE CANDIDATES TO PAYMENTS; USE OF PAYMENTS

AUTHORITY: 26 U.S.C. 9004 and 9009(b).

SOURCE: 56 FR 35919, July 29, 1991, unless otherwise noted.

§9004.1 Major parties.

The eligible candidates of each major party in a Presidential election shall be entitled to equal payments under 11 CFR part 9005 in an amount which, in the aggregate, shall not exceed $20,000,000 as adjusted by the Consumer Price Index in the manner described in 11 CFR 110.17(a).

[56 FR 35919, July 29, 1991, as amended at 67 FR 78683, Dec. 26, 2002]

§9004.2 Pre-election payments for minor and new party candidates.

(a) *Candidate of a minor party in the preceding election.* An eligible candidate of a minor party is entitled to pre-election payments:

(1) If he or she received at least 5% of the total popular vote as the candidate of a minor party in the preceding election whether or not he or she is the same minor party's candidate in this election.

(2) In an amount which is equal, in the aggregate, to a proportionate share of the amount to which major party candidates are entitled under 11 CFR 9004.1.

The aggregate amount received by a minor party candidate shall bear the same ratio to the amount received by the major party candidates as the number of popular votes received by the minor party Presidential candidate in the preceding Presidential election bears to the average number of popular votes received by all major party candidates in that election.

(b) *Candidate of a minor party in the current election.* The eligible candidate

279

of a minor party whose candidate for the office of President in the preceding election received at least 5% but less than 25% of the total popular vote is eligible to receive pre-election payments. The amount which a minor party candidate is entitled to receive under this section shall be computed pursuant to 11 CFR 9004.2(a) based on the number of popular votes received by the minor party's candidate in the preceding Presidential election; however, the amount to which the minor party candidate is entitled under this section shall be reduced by the amount to which the minor party's Presidential candidate in this election is entitled under 11 CFR 9004.2(a), if any.

(c) *New party candidate.* A candidate of a new party who was a candidate for the office of President in at least 10 States in the preceding election may be eligible to receive pre-election payments if he or she received at least 5% but less than 25% of the total popular vote in the preceding election. The amount which a new party candidate is entitled to receive under this section shall be computed pursuant to 11 CFR 9004.2(a) based on the number of popular votes received by the new party candidate in the preceding election. If a new party candidate is entitled to payments under this section, the amount of the entitlement shall be reduced by the amount to which the candidate is entitled under 11 CFR 9004.2(a), if any.

§ 9004.3 Post-election payments.

(a) *Minor and new party candidates.* Eligible candidates of a minor party or of a new party who, as candidates, receive 5 percent or more of the total number of popular votes cast for the office of President in the election shall be entitled to payments under 11 CFR part 9005 equal, in the aggregate, to a proportionate share of the amount allowed for major party candidates under 11 CFR 9004.1. The amount to which a minor or new party candidate is entitled shall bear the same ratio to the amount received by the major party candidates as the number of popular votes received by the minor or new party candidate in the Presidential election bears to the average number of popular votes received by the major

party candidates for President in that election.

(b) *Amount of entitlement.* The aggregate payments to which an eligible candidate shall be entitled shall not exceed an amount equal to the lower of:

(1) The amount of qualified campaign expenses incurred by such eligible candidate and his or her authorized committee(s), reduced by the amount of contributions which are received to defray qualified campaign expenses by such eligible candidate and such committee(s); or

(2) The aggregate payments to which the eligible candidates of a major party are entitled under 11 CFR 9004.1, reduced by the amount of contributions received by such eligible candidates and their authorized committees to defray qualified campaign expenses in the case of a deficiency in the Fund.

(c) *Amount of entitlement limited by pre-election payment.* If an eligible candidate is entitled to payment under 11 CFR 9004.2, the amount allowable to that candidate under this section shall also be limited to the amount, if any, by which the entitlement under 11 CFR 9004.3(a) exceeds the amount of the entitlement under 11 CFR 9004.2.

§ 9004.4 Use of payments; examples of qualified campaign expenses and non-qualified campaign expenses.

(a) *Qualified campaign expenses.* An eligible candidate shall use payments received under 11 CFR part 9005 only for the following purposes:

(1) To defray qualified campaign expenses;

(2) To repay loans that meet the requirements of 11 CFR 100.52(b) or 100.82 or to otherwise restore funds (other than contributions received pursuant to 11 CFR 9003.3 (b) or (c) and expended to defray qualified campaign expenses) used to defray qualified campaign expenses;

(3) To restore funds expended in accordance with 11 CFR 9003.4 for qualified campaign expenses incurred by the candidate prior to the beginning of the expenditure report period;

(4) To defray winding down costs pursuant to 11 CFR 9004.11;

(5) To defray costs associated with the candidate's general election campaign paid after the end of the expenditure report period, but incurred by the candidate prior to the end of the expenditure report period, for which written arrangement or commitment was made on or before the close of the expenditure report period for goods and services received during the expenditure reporting period; and

(6) Monetary bonuses paid after the date of the election and gifts shall be considered qualified campaign expenses, provided that:

(i) All monetary bonuses paid after the date of the election for committee employees and consultants in recognition of campaign-related activities or services:

(A) Are provided for pursuant to a written contract made prior to the date of the election; and

(B) Are paid during the expenditure report period; and

(ii) Gifts for committee employees, consultants and volunteers in recognition of campaign-related activities or services do not exceed $150 total per individual and the total of all gifts does not exceed $20,000.

(b) *Non-qualified campaign expenses—* (1) *General.* The following are examples of disbursements that are not qualified campaign expenses.

(2) *Excessive expenditures.* An expenditure which is in excess of any of the limitations under 11 CFR 9003.2 shall not be considered a qualified campaign expense. The Commission will calculate the amount of expenditures attributable to these limitations using the full amounts originally charged for goods and services rendered to the committee and not the amounts for which such obligations were later settled and paid, unless the committee can demonstrate that the lower amount paid reflects a reasonable settlement of a bona fide dispute with the creditor.

(3) *Expenditures incurred after the close of the expenditure report period.* Except for accounts payable pursuant to paragraph (a)(5) of this section and winding down costs pursuant to 11 CFR 9004.11, any expenditures incurred after the close of the expenditure report period,

as defined in 11 CFR 9002.12, are not qualified campaign expenses.

(4) *Civil or criminal penalties.* Civil or criminal penalties paid pursuant to the Federal Election Campaign Act are not qualified campaign expenses and cannot be defrayed from payments received under 11 CFR part 9005. Penalties may be paid from contributions in the candidate's legal and accounting compliance fund, in accordance with 11 CFR 9003.3(a)(2)(i)(C). Additional amounts may be received and expended to pay such penalties, if necessary. These funds shall not be considered contributions or expenditures but all amounts so received shall be subject to the prohibitions of the Act. Amounts received and expended under this section shall be reported in accordance with 11 CFR part 104.

(5) *Solicitation expenses.* Any expenses incurred by a major party candidate to solicit contributions to a legal and accounting compliance fund established pursuant to 11 CFR 9003.3(a) are not qualified campaign expenses and cannot be defrayed from payments received under 11 CFR part 9005.

(6) *Payments to candidate.* Payments made to the candidate by his or her committee, other than to reimburse funds advanced by the candidate for qualified campaign expenses, are not qualified campaign expenses.

(7) *Payments to other authorized committees.* Payments, including transfers, contributions and loans, to other committees authorized by the same candidate for a different election are not qualified campaign expenses.

(8) *Lost, misplaced, or stolen items.* The cost of lost, misplaced, or stolen items may be considered a nonqualified campaign expense. Factors considered by the Commission in making this determination shall include, but not be limited to, whether the committee demonstrates that it made conscientious efforts to safeguard the missing equipment; whether the committee sought or obtained insurance on the items; whether the committee filed a police report; the type of equipment involved;

and the number and value of items that were lost.

[56 FR 35919, July 29, 1991, as amended at 60 FR 31875, June 16, 1995; 64 FR 49362, Sept. 13, 1999; 67 FR 78683, Dec. 26, 2002; 68 FR 47415, Aug. 8, 2003]

§ 9004.5 Investment of public funds; other uses resulting in income.

Investment of public funds or any other use of public funds that results in income is permissible, provided that an amount equal to all net income derived from such a use, less Federal, State and local taxes paid on such income, shall be paid to the Secretary. Any net loss from an investment or other use of public funds will be considered a non-qualified campaign expense and an amount equal to the amount of such loss shall be repaid to the United States Treasury as provided under 11 CFR 9007.2(b)(2)(i).

[60 FR 31876, June 16, 1995]

§ 9004.6 Expenditures for transportation and services made available to media personnel; reimbursements.

(a) *General.* (1) Expenditures by an authorized committee for transportation, ground services or facilities (including air travel, ground transportation, housing, meals, telephone service, typewriters, and computers) provided to media personnel, Secret Service personnel or national security staff will be considered qualified campaign expenses, and, except for costs relating to Secret Service personnel or national security staff, will be subject to the overall expenditure limitations of 11 CFR 9003.2(a)(1) and (b)(1).

(2) Subject to the limitations in paragraphs (b) and (c) of this section, committees may seek reimbursement from the media for the expenses described in paragraph (a)(3) of this section, and may deduct reimbursements received from media representatives from the amount of expenditures subject to the overall expenditure limitation of 11 CFR § 9003.2(a)(1) and (b)(1). Expenses for which the committee receives no reimbursement will be considered qualified campaign expenses, and, with the exception of those expenses relating to Secret Service personnel and na-

tional security staff, will be subject to the overall expenditure limitation.

(3) Committees may seek reimbursement from the media only for the billable items specified in the White House Press Corps Travel Policies and Procedures issued by the White House Travel Office.

(b) *Reimbursement limits; billing.* (1) The amount of reimbursement sought from a media representative under paragraph (a)(2) of this section shall not exceed 110% of the media representative's pro rata share (or a reasonable estimate of the media representative's pro rata share) of the actual cost of the transportation and services made available. Any reimbursement received in excess of this amount shall be disposed of in accordance with paragraph (d)(1) of this section.

(2) For the purposes of this section, a media representative's pro rata share shall be calculated by dividing the total actual cost of the transportation and services provided by the total number of individuals to whom such transportation and services are made available. For purposes of this calculation, the total number of individuals shall include committee staff, media personnel, Secret Service personnel, national security staff and any other individuals to whom such transportation and services are made available, except that, when seeking reimbursement for transportation costs paid by the committee under 11 CFR 9004.7(b)(5)(i), the total number of individuals shall not include national security staff.

(3) No later than sixty (60) days of the campaign trip or event, the committee shall provide each media representative attending the event with an itemized bill that specifies the amounts charged for air and ground transportation for each segment of the trip, housing, meals, telephone service, and other billable items specified in the White House Press Corps Travel Policies and Procedures issued by the White House Travel Office. Payments shall be due sixty (60) days from the date of the bill, unless the media representative disputes the charges.

(c) *Deduction of reimbursements from expenditures subject to the overall expenditure limitation.* (1) The committee may deduct from the amount of expenditures subject to the overall expenditure limitation:

(i) The amount of reimbursements received from media representatives in payment for the transportation and services described in paragraph (a) of this section, up to the actual cost of the transportation and services provided to media representatives; and

(ii) An additional amount of the reimbursements received from media representatives, representing the administrative costs incurred by the committee in providing these services to the media representative and seeking reimbursement for them, equal to:

(A) Three percent of the actual cost of transportation and services provided to the media representatives under this section; or

(B) An amount in excess of 3% representing the administrative costs actually incurred by the committee in providing services to the media representatives, provided that the committee is able to document the total amount of administrative costs actually incurred.

(2) For the purpose of this paragraph, "administrative costs" includes all costs incurred by the committee in making travel arrangements and seeking reimbursement, whether these services are performed by committee staff or by independent contractors.

(d) *Disposal of excess reimbursements.* If the committee receives reimbursements in excess of the amount deductible under paragraph (c) of this section, it shall dispose of the excess amount in the following manner:

(1) Any reimbursement received in excess of 110% of the actual pro rata cost of the transportation and services made available to a media representative shall be returned to the media representative.

(2) Any amount in excess of the amount deductible under paragraph (c) of this section that is not required to be returned to the media representative under paragraph (d)(1) of this section shall be paid to the Treasury.

(e) *Reporting.* The total amount paid by an authorized committee for the services and facilities described in paragraph (a)(1) of this section, plus the administrative costs incurred by the committee in providing these services and facilities and seeking reimbursement for them, shall be reported as an expenditure in accordance with 11 CFR 104.3(b)(2)(i). Any reimbursement received by such committee under paragraph (b)(1) of this section shall be reported in accordance with 11 CFR 104.3(a)(3)(ix).

[60 FR 31876, June 16, 1995, as amended at 64 FR 42583, Aug. 5, 1999; 68 FR 69595, Dec. 15, 2003; 81 FR 34864, June 1, 2016]

§ 9004.7 **Allocation of travel expenditures.**

(a) Notwithstanding the provisions of 11 CFR 106.3, expenditures for travel relating to a Presidential or Vice Presidential candidate's campaign by any individual, including a candidate, shall, pursuant to the provisions of paragraph (b) of this section, be qualified campaign expenses and be reported by the candidate's authorized committee(s) as expenditures.

(b)(1) For a trip which is entirely campaign-related, the total cost of the trip shall be a qualified campaign expense and a reportable expenditure.

(2) For a trip which includes campaign-related and non-campaign related stops, that portion of the cost of the trip allocable to campaign activity shall be a qualified campaign expense and a reportable expenditure. Such portion shall be determined by calculating what the trip would have cost from the point of origin of the trip to the first campaign-related stop and from the stop through each subsequent campaign-related stop to the point of origin. If any campaign activity, other than incidental contacts, is conducted at a stop, that stop shall be considered campaign-related. Campaign activity includes soliciting, making, or accepting contributions, and expressly advocating the election or defeat of the candidate. Other factors, including the setting, timing and statements or expressions of the purpose of an event, and the substance of the remarks or speech made, will also be considered in determining whether a stop is campaign-related.

(3) For each trip, an itinerary shall be prepared and such itinerary shall be made available by the committee for Commission inspection. The itinerary

shall show the time of arrival and departure and the type of events held.

(4) For trips by government conveyance or by charter, a list of all passengers on such trip, along with a designation of which passengers are and which are not campaign-related, shall be made available for Commission inspection. When required to be created, a copy of the government's or charter company's official manifest shall also be maintained and made available by the committee.

(5)(i) If any individual, including a candidate, uses a government aircraft for campaign-related travel, the candidate's authorized committee shall pay the appropriate government entity an amount equal to the applicable rate set forth in 11 CFR 100.93(e).

(ii) [Reserved]

(iii) If any individual, including a candidate, uses a government conveyance, other than an aircraft, for campaign-related travel, the candidate's authorized committee shall pay the appropriate government entity an amount equal to the amount required under 11 CFR 100.93(d).

(iv) If any individual, including a candidate, uses accommodations, including lodging and meeting rooms, during campaign-related travel, and the accommodations are paid for by a government entity, the candidate's authorized committee shall pay the appropriate government entity an amount equal to the usual and normal charge for the accommodations, and shall maintain documentation supporting the amount paid.

(v) For travel by aircraft, the committee shall maintain documentation as required by 11 CFR 100.93(j)(1) in addition to any other documentation required in this section. For travel by other conveyances, the committee shall maintain documentation of the commercial rental rate as required by 11 CFR 100.93(j)(3) in addition to any other documentation required in this section.

(6) Travel expenses of a candidate's spouse and family when accompanying the candidate on campaign-related travel may be treated as qualified campaign expenses and reportable expenditures. If the spouse or family members conduct campaign-related activities, their travel expenses shall be qualified campaign expenses and reportable expenditures.

(7) If any individual, including a candidate, incurs expenses for campaign-related travel, other than by use of government conveyance or accommodations, an amount equal to that portion of the actual cost of the conveyance or accommodations which is allocable to all passengers, including the candidate, who are traveling for campaign purposes shall be a qualified campaign expense and shall be reported by the committee as an expenditure.

(i) If the trip is by charter, the actual cost for each passenger shall be determined by dividing the total operating cost for the charter by the total number of passengers transported. The amount which is a qualified campaign expense and a reportable expenditure shall be calculated in accordance with the formula set forth at 11 CFR 9004.7(b)(2) on the basis of the actual cost per passenger multiplied by the number of passengers traveling for campaign purposes.

(ii) If the trip is by non-charter commercial transportation, the actual cost shall be calculated in accordance with the formula set forth at 11 CFR 9004.7(b)(2) on the basis of the commercial fare. Such actual cost shall be a qualified campaign expense and a reportable expenditure.

(8) Non-commercial travel, as defined in 11 CFR 100.93(a)(3)(v), on aircraft, and travel on other means of transportation not operated for commercial passenger service, is governed by 11 CFR 100.93.

[60 FR 31876, June 16, 1995, as amended at 68 FR 69595, Dec. 15, 2003; 74 FR 63967, Dec. 7, 2009]

§ 9004.8 Withdrawal by candidate.

(a) Any individual who is not actively conducting campaigns in more than one State for the office of President or Vice President shall cease to be a candidate under 11 CFR 9002.2.

(b) An individual who ceases to be a candidate under this section shall:

(1) No longer be eligible to receive any payments under 11 CFR 9005.2 except to defray qualified campaign expenses as provided in 11 CFR 9004.4.

(2) Submit a statement, within 30 calendar days after he or she ceases to be a candidate, setting forth the information required under 11 CFR 9004.9(c).

§ 9004.9 Net outstanding qualified campaign expenses.

(a) *Candidates receiving post-election funding.* A candidate who is eligible to receive post-election payments under 11 CFR 9004.3 shall file, no later than 20 calendar days after the date of the election, a preliminary statement of that candidate's net outstanding qualified campaign expenses. The candidate's net outstanding qualified campaign expenses under this section equal the difference between 11 CFR 9004.9(a) (1) and (2).

(1) The total of:

(i) All outstanding obligations for qualified campaign expenses as of the date of the election; plus

(ii) An estimate of the amount of qualified campaign expenses that will be incurred by the end of the expenditure report period; plus

(iii) An estimate of the necessary winding down costs, as defined under 11 CFR 9004.4(a)(4), submitted in the format required by paragraph (a)(4) of this section; less

(2) The total of:

(i) Cash on hand as of the close of business on the day of the election, including: All contributions dated on or before that date; currency; balances on deposit in banks, savings and loan institutions, and other depository institutions; traveler's checks; certificates of deposit; treasury bills; and any other committee investments valued at fair market value;

(ii) The fair market value of capital assets and other assets on hand; and

(iii) Amounts owed to the candidate's authorized committee(s) in the form of credits, refunds of deposits, returns, receivables, or rebates of qualified campaign expenses; or a commercially reasonable amount based on the collectibility of those credits, returns, receivables or rebates.

(3) The amount submitted as the total of outstanding campaign obligations under paragraph (a)(1) of this section shall not include any accounts payable for non-qualified campaign expenses nor any amounts determined or anticipated to be required as a repayment under 11 CFR part 9007 or any amounts paid to secure a surety bond under 11 CFR 9007.5(c).

(4) The amount submitted as an estimate of necessary winding down costs under paragraph (a)(1)(iii) of this section shall be broken down by expense category and quarterly or monthly time period. This breakdown shall include estimated costs for office space rental, staff salaries, legal expenses, accounting expenses, office supplies, equipment rental, telephone expenses, postage and other mailing costs, printing and storage. The breakdown shall estimate the costs that will be incurred in each category from the time the statement is submitted until the expected termination of the committee's political activity.

(b) *All candidates.* Each candidate, except for individuals who have withdrawn pursuant to 11 CFR 9004.8, shall submit a statement of net outstanding qualified campaign expenses no later than 30 calendar days after the end of the expenditure report period. The statement shall contain the information required by 11 CFR 9004.9(a) (1) and (2), except that the amount of outstanding obligations under 11 CFR 9004.9(a)(1)(i) and the amount of cash on hand, assets and receivables under 11 CFR 9004.9(a)(2) shall be complete as of the last day of the expenditure report period.

(c) *Candidates who withdraw.* An individual who ceases to be a candidate pursuant to 11 CFR 9004.8 shall file a statement of net outstanding qualified campaign expenses no later than 30 calendar days after he or she ceases to be a candidate. The statement shall contain the information required under 11 CFR 9004.9(a) (1) and (2), except that the amount of outstanding obligations under 11 CFR 9004.9(a)(1)(i) and the amount of cash on hand, assets and receivables under 11 CFR 9004.9(a)(2) shall be complete as of the day on which the individual ceased to be a candidate.

(d)(1) *Capital assets and assets purchased from the primary election committee.* (i) For purposes of this section, the term *capital asset* means any property used in the operation of the campaign whose purchase price exceeded $2000 when acquired by the committee.

Property that must be valued as capital assets under this section includes, but is not limited to, office equipment, furniture, vehicles and fixtures acquired for use in the operation of the candidate's campaign, but does not include property defined as "other assets" under paragraph (d)(2) of this section. Capital assets include items such as computer systems and telecommunications systems, if the equipment is used together and if the total cost of all components that are used together exceeds $2000. A list of all capital assets shall be maintained by the committee in accordance with 11 CFR 9003.5(d)(1). The fair market value of capital assets shall be considered to be 60% of the total original cost of such items when acquired, except that items received after the end of the expenditure report period must be valued at their fair market value on the date acquired. A candidate may claim a lower fair market value for a capital asset by listing that capital asset on the statement separately and demonstrating, through documentation, the lower fair market value.

(ii) If capital assets are obtained from the candidate's primary election committee, the purchase price shall be considered to be 60% of the original cost of such assets to the candidate's primary election committee. For purposes of the statement of net outstanding qualified campaign expenses filed after the end of the expenditure report period, the fair market value of capital assets obtained from the candidate's primary election committee shall be considered to be 20% of the original cost of such assets to the candidate's primary election committee.

(iii) Items purchased from the primary election committee that are not capital assets, and also are not other assets under paragraph (d)(2) of this section, shall be listed on an inventory that states their valuation.

(2) *Other assets.* The term *other assets* means any property acquired by the committee for use in raising funds or as collateral for campaign loans. "Other assets" must be included on the candidate's statement of net outstanding qualified campaign expenses if the aggregate value of such assets exceeds $5000. The value of "other as-

sets" shall be determined by the fair market value of each item on the last day of the expenditure report period or the day on which the individual ceased to be a candidate, whichever is earlier, unless the item is acquired after these dates, in which case the item shall be valued on the date it is acquired. A list of other assets shall be maintained by the committee in accordance with 11 CFR 9003.5(d)(2).

(e) *Collectibility of accounts receivable.* If the committee determines that an account receivable of $500 or more, including any credit, refund, return or rebate, is not collectible in whole or in part, the committee shall demonstrate through documentation that the determination was commercially reasonable. The documentation shall include records showing the original amount of the account receivable, copies of correspondence and memoranda of communications with the debtor showing attempts to collect the amount due, and an explanation of how the lesser amount or full write-off was determined.

(f) *Review of candidate statement*—(1) *General.* The Commission will review the statement filed by each candidate under this section. The Commission may request further information with respect to statements filed pursuant to 11 CFR 9004.9(b) during the audit of that candidate's authorized committee(s) under 11 CFR part 9007.

(2) *Candidate eligible for post-election funding.* (i) If, in reviewing the preliminary statement of a candidate eligible to receive post-election funding, the Commission receives information indicating that substantial assets of that candidate's authorized committee(s) have been undervalued or not included in the statement or that the amount of outstanding qualified campaign expenses has been otherwise overstated in relation to committee assets, the Commission may decide to temporarily postpone its certification of funds to that candidate pending a final determination of whether the candidate is entitled to all or a portion of the funds for which he or she is eligible based on the percentage of votes the candidate received in the general election.

(ii) *Initial determination.* In making a determination   under   11   CFR

9004.9(f)(2)(i), the Commission will notify the candidate within 10 business days after its receipt of the statement of its initial determination that the candidate is not entitled to receive the full amount for which the candidate may be eligible. The notice will give the legal and factual reasons for the initial determination and advise the candidate of the evidence on which the Commission's initial determination is based. The candidate will be given the opportunity to revise the statement or to submit, within 10 business days, written legal or factual materials to demonstrate that the candidate has net outstanding qualified campaign expenses that entitle the candidate to post-election funds. Such materials may be submitted by counsel if the candidate so desires.

(iii) *Final determination.* The Commission will consider any written legal or factual materials submitted by the candidate before making its final determination. A final determination that the candidate is entitled to receive only a portion or no post-election funding will be accompanied by a written statement of reasons for the Commission's action. This statement will explain the legal and factual reasons underlying the Commission's determination and will summarize the results of any investigation on which the determination is based.

(iv) If the candidate demonstrates that the amount of outstanding qualified campaign expenses still exceeds committee assets, the Commission will certify the payment of post-election funds to which the candidate is entitled.

(v) *Petitions for rehearing.* The candidate may file a petition for rehearing of a final determination under this section in accordance with 11 CFR 9007.5(a).

[56 FR 35919, July 29, 1991, as amended at 60 FR 31877, June 16, 1995; 64 FR 49363, Sept. 13, 1999]

§9004.10 Sale of assets acquired for fundraising purposes.

(a) *General.* A minor or new party candidate may sell assets donated to the candidate's authorized committee(s) or otherwise acquired for fundraising purposes subject to the limitations and prohibitions of 11 CFR 9003.2, Title 52, United States Code, and 11 CFR parts 110 and 114. This section will only apply to major party candidates to the extent that they sell assets acquired either for fundraising purposes in connection with his or her legal and accounting compliance fund or when it is necessary to make up any deficiency in payments received from the Fund due to the application of 11 CFR 9005.2(b).

(b) *Sale after end of expenditure report period.* A minor or new party candidate, or a major party candidate in the event of a deficiency in the payments received from the Fund due to the application of 11 CFR 9005.2(b), whose outstanding debts exceed the cash on hand after the end of the expenditure report period as determined under 11 CFR 9002.12, may dispose of assets acquired for fundraising purposes in a sale to a wholesaler or other intermediary who will in turn sell such assets to the public provided that the sale to the wholesaler or intermediary is an arms-length transaction. Sales made under this subsection will not be subject to the limitations and prohibitions of Title 52, United States Code and 11 CFR parts 110 and 114.

[56 FR 35919, July 29, 1991, as amended at 79 FR 77851, Dec. 29, 2014]

§9004.11 Winding down costs.

(a) *Winding down costs. Winding down costs* are costs associated with the termination of the candidate's general election campaign such as complying with the post-election requirements of the Federal Election Campaign Act and the Presidential Election Campaign Fund Act, and other necessary administrative costs associated with ending the campaign, including office space rental, staff salaries, and office supplies. Winding down costs are qualified campaign expenses.

(b) *Winding down limitation.* The total amount of winding down costs that may be paid for with public funds shall not exceed the lesser of:

(1) 2.5% of the expenditure limitation pursuant to 11 CFR 110.8(a)(2); or

(2) 2.5% of the total of:

(i) The candidate's expenditures subject to the expenditure limitation as of the end of the expenditure report period; plus

(ii) The candidate's expenses exempt from the expenditure limitation as of the end of the expenditure report period; except that

(iii) The winding down limitation shall be no less than $100,000.

(c) *Allocation of primary and general election winding down costs.* A candidate who runs in both the primary and general election may divide winding down expenses between his or her primary and general election committees using any reasonable allocation method. An allocation method is reasonable if it divides the total winding down costs between the primary and general election committees and results in no less than one third of total winding down costs allocated to each committee. A candidate may demonstrate that an allocation method is reasonable even if either the primary or the general election committee is allocated less than one third of total winding down costs.

[68 FR 47416, Aug. 8, 2003]

PART 9005—CERTIFICATION BY COMMISSION

Sec.
9005.1 Certification of payments for candidates.
9005.2 Payments to eligible candidates from the Fund.

AUTHORITY: 26 U.S.C. 9005, 9006 and 9009(b).

SOURCE: 56 FR 35923, July 29, 1991, unless otherwise noted.

§ 9005.1 Certification of payments for candidates.

(a) *Certification of payments for major party candidates.* Not later than 10 days after the Commission determines that the Presidential and Vice Presidential candidates of a major party have met all applicable conditions for eligibility to receive payments under 11 CFR 9003.1 and 9003.2, the Commission shall certify to the Secretary that payment in full of the amounts to which such candidates are entitled under 11 CFR part 9004 should be made pursuant to 11 CFR 9005.2.

(b) *Certification of pre-election payments for minor and new party candidates.* (1) Not later than 10 days after

a minor or new party candidate has met all applicable conditions for eligibility to receive payments under 11 CFR 9003.1, 9003.2 and 9004.2, the Commission will make an initial determination of the amount, if any, to which the candidate is entitled. The Commission will base its determination on the percentage of votes received in the official vote count certified in each State. In notifying the candidate, the Commission will give the legal and factual reasons for its determination and advise the candidate of the evidence on which the determination is based.

(2) The candidate may submit, within 15 days after the Commission's initial determination, written legal or factual materials to demonstrate that a redetermination is appropriate. Such materials may be submitted by counsel if the candidate so desires.

(3) The Commission will consider any written legal or factual materials timely submitted by the candidate in making its final determination. A final determination of certification by the Commission will be accompanied by a written statement of reasons for the Commission's action. This statement will explain the reasons underlying the Commission's determination and will summarize the results of any investigation on which the determination is based.

(c) *Certification of minor and new party candidates for post-election payments.* (1) Not later than 30 days after the general election, the Commission will determine whether a minor or new party candidate is eligible for post-election payments.

(2) The Commission's determination of eligibility will be based on the following factors:

(i) The candidate has received at least 5% or more of the total popular vote based on unofficial vote results in each State;

(ii) The candidate has filed a preliminary statement of his or her net outstanding qualified campaign expenses pursuant to 11 CFR 9004.9(a); and

(iii) The candidate has met all applicable conditions for eligibility under 11 CFR 9003.1 and 9003.2.

(3) The Commission will notify the candidate of its initial determination

of the amount, if any, to which the candidate is entitled, give the legal and factual reasons for its determination and advise the candidate of the evidence on which the determination is based. The Commission will also notify the candidate that it will deduct a percentage of the amount to which the candidate is entitled based on the unofficial vote results when the Commission certifies an amount for payment to the Secretary. This deduction will be based on the average percentage differential between the unofficial and official vote results for all candidates who received public funds in the preceding Presidential general election.

(4) The candidate may submit within 15 days after the Commission's initial determination written legal or factual materials to demonstrate that a redetermination is appropriate. Such materials may be submitted by counsel if the candidate so desires.

(5) The Commission will consider any written legal or factual materials timely submitted by the candidate in making its final determination. A final determination of certification by the Commission will be accompanied by a written statement of reasons for the Commission's action. This statement will explain the reasons underlying the Commission's determination and will summarize the results of any investigation on which the determination is based.

(d) All certifications made by the Commission pursuant to this section shall be final and conclusive, except to the extent that they are subject to examination and audit by the Commission under 11 CFR part 9007 and judicial review under 26 U.S.C. 9011.

[56 FR 35923, July 29, 1991; 56 FR 55972, Oct. 30, 1991]

§ 9005.2 Payments to eligible candidates from the Fund.

(a) Upon receipt of a certification from the Commission under 11 CFR 9005.1 for payment to the eligible Presidential and Vice Presidential candidates of a political party, the Secretary shall pay to such candidates out of the Fund the amount certified by the Commission. Amounts paid to a candidate shall be under the control of that candidate.

(b)(1) If at the time of a certification from the Commission under 11 CFR 9005.1, the Secretary determines that the monies in the Fund are not, or may not be, sufficient to satisfy the full entitlements of the eligible candidates of all political parties, he or she shall withhold an amount which is determined to be necessary to assure that the eligible candidates of each political party will receive their pro rata share.

(2) Amounts withheld under 11 CFR 9005.2(b)(1) shall be paid when the Secretary determines that there are sufficient monies in the Fund to pay such amounts, or pro rata portions thereof, to all eligible candidates from whom amounts have been withheld.

(c) Payments received from the Fund by a major party candidate shall be deposited in a separate account maintained by his or her authorized committee, unless there is a deficiency in the Fund as provided under 11 CFR 9005.2(b)(1). In the case of a deficiency, the candidate may establish a separate account for payments from the Fund or may deposit such payments with contributions received pursuant to 11 CFR 9003.3(b). The account(s) shall be maintained at a State bank, federally chartered depository institution or other depository institution, the deposits or accounts of which are insured by the Federal Deposit Insurance Corporation.

(d) No funds other than the payments received from the Treasury, reimbursements, or income generated through use of public funds in accordance with 11 CFR 9004.5, shall be deposited in the account described in 11 CFR 9005.2(c). "Reimbursements" shall include, but are not limited to, refunds of deposits, vendor refunds, reimbursements for travel expenses under 11 CFR 9004.6 and 9004.7 and reimbursements for legal and accounting costs under 11 CFR 9003.3(a)(2)(ii)(B).

PART 9006—REPORTS AND RECORDKEEPING

AUTHORITY: 52 U.S.C. 30104; 26 U.S.C. 9009(b).

SOURCE: 56 FR 35924, July 29, 1991, unless otherwise noted.

§ 9006.1 Separate reports.

(a) The authorized committee(s) of a candidate shall report all expenditures to further the candidate's general election campaign in reports separate from reports of any other expenditures made by such committee(s) with respect to other elections. Such reports shall be filed pursuant to the requirements of 11 CFR part 104.

(b) The authorized committee(s) of a candidate shall file separate reports as follows:

(1) One report shall be filed which lists all receipts and disbursements of:

(i) Contributions and loans received by a major party candidate pursuant to 11 CFR part 9003 to make up deficiencies in Fund payments due to the application of 11 CFR part 9005;

(ii) Contributions and loans received pursuant to 11 CFR 9003.2(b)(2) by a minor, or new party for use in the general election;

(iii) Receipts for expenses incurred before the beginning of the expenditure report period pursuant to 11 CFR 9003.4;

(iv) Personal funds expended in accordance with 11 CFR 9003.2(c); and

(v) Payments received from the Fund.

(2) A second report shall be filed which lists all receipts of and disbursements from, contributions received for the candidate's legal and accounting compliance fund in accordance with 11 CFR 9003.3(a).

§ 9006.2 Filing dates.

The reports required to be filed under 11 CFR 9006.1 shall be filed during an election year on a monthly or quarterly basis as prescribed at 11 CFR 104.5(b)(1). During a non-election year, the candidate's principal campaign committee may elect to file reports either on a monthly or quarterly basis in accordance with 11 CFR 104.5(b)(2).

§ 9006.3 Alphabetized schedules.

If the authorized committee(s) of a candidate file a schedule of itemized receipts, disbursements, or debts and obligations pursuant to 11 CFR 104.3 that was generated directly or indirectly from computerized files or

records, the schedule shall list in alphabetical order the sources of the receipts, the payees or the creditors, as appropriate. In the case of individuals, such schedule shall list all contributors, payees, and creditors in alphabetical order by surname.

[60 FR 31877, June 16, 1995]

PART 9007—EXAMINATIONS AND AUDITS; REPAYMENTS

AUTHORITY: 26 U.S.C. 9007 and 9009(b).

SOURCE: 56 FR 35924, July 29, 1991, unless otherwise noted.

§ 9007.1 Audits.

(a) *General.* (1) After each Presidential election, the Commission will conduct a thorough examination and audit of the receipts, disbursements, debts and obligations of each candidate, his or her authorized committee(s), and agents of such candidates or committees. Such examination and audit will include, but will not be limited to, expenditures pursuant to 11 CFR 9003.4 prior to the beginning of the expenditure report period, contributions to and expenditures made from the legal and accounting compliance fund established under 11 CFR 9003.3(a), contributions received to supplement any payments received from the Fund, and qualified campaign expenses.

(2) In addition, the Commission may conduct other examinations and audits from time to time as it deems necessary to carry out the provisions of this subchapter.

(3) Information obtained pursuant to any audit and examination conducted under 11 CFR 9007.1(a) (1) and (2) may be used by the Commission as the basis, or partial basis, for its repayment determinations under 11 CFR 9007.2.

(b) *Conduct of fieldwork.* (1) If the candidate or the candidate's authorized committee does not maintain or use any computerized information containing the data listed in 11 CFR 9003.6, the Commission will give the candidate's authorized committee at least two weeks' notice of the Commission's intention to commence fieldwork on the audit and examination. The fieldwork shall be conducted at a site provided by the committee. If the candidate or the candidate's authorized committee maintains or uses computerized information containing any of the data listed in 11 CFR 9003.6, the Commission generally will request such information prior to commencement of audit fieldwork. Such request will be made in writing. The committee shall produce the computerized information no later than 15 calendar days after service of such request. Upon receipt of the computerized information requested and compliance with the technical specifications of 11 CFR 9003.6(b), the Commission will give the candidate's authorized committee at least two weeks' notice of the Commission's intention to commence fieldwork on the audit and examination. The fieldwork shall be conducted at a site provided by the committee. During or after audit fieldwork, the Commission may request additional or updated computerized information which expands the coverage dates of computerized information previously provided, and which may be used for purposes including, but not limited to, updating a statement of net outstanding qualified campaign expenses. During or after audit fieldwork, the Commission may also request additional computerized information which was created by or becomes available to the committee that is of assistance in the Commission's audit. The committee shall produce the additional or updated computerized information no later than 15 calendar days after service of the Commission's request.

(i) *Office space and records.* On the date scheduled for the commencement of fieldwork, the candidate or his or her authorized committee(s) shall provide Commission staff with office space and committee records in accordance with the candidate and committee agreement under 11 CFR 9003.1(b)(6).

(ii) *Availability of committee personnel.* On the date scheduled for the commencement of fieldwork, the candidate or his or her authorized committee(s) shall have committee personnel present at the site of the fieldwork. Such personnel shall be familiar with the committee's records and operation and shall be available to Commission staff to answer questions and to aid in locating records.

(iii) *Failure to provide staff, records or office space.* If the candidate or his or her authorized committee(s) fail to provide adequate office space, personnel or committee records, the Commission may seek judicial intervention under 52 U.S.C. 30107 or 26 U.S.C. 9010(c) to enforce the candidate and committee agreement made under 11 CFR 9003.1(b). Before seeking judicial intervention, the Commission will notify the candidate of his or her failure to comply with the agreement and will recommend corrective action to bring the candidate into compliance. Upon receipt of the Commission's notification, the candidate will have ten (10) calendar days in which to take the corrective action indicated or to otherwise demonstrate to the Commission in writing that he or she is complying with the candidate and committee agreements.

(iv) If, in the course of the audit process, a dispute arises over the documentation sought or other requirements of the candidate agreement, the candidate may seek review by the Commission of the issues raised. To seek review, the candidate shall submit a written statement within 10 days after the disputed Commission staff request is made, describing the dispute and indicating the candidate's proposed alternative(s).

(v) If the candidate or his or her authorized committee fails to produce particular records, materials, evidence or other information requested by the Commission, the Commission may issue an order pursuant to 52 U.S.C. 30107(a)(1) or a subpoena or subpoena duces tecum pursuant to 52 U.S.C. 30107(a)(3). The procedures set forth in 11 CFR 111.11 through 111.15, as appropriate, shall apply to the production of such records, materials, evidence or other information as specified in the order, subpoena or subpoena duces tecum.

(2) Fieldwork will include the following steps designed to keep the candidate and committee informed as to the progress of the audit and to expedite the process:

(i) *Entrance conference.* At the outset of the fieldwork, Commission staff will hold an entrance conference, at which the candidate's representatives will be advised of the purpose of the audit and the general procedures to be followed. Future requirements of the candidate and his or her authorized committee, such as possible repayments to the United States Treasury, will also be discussed. Committee representatives shall provide information and records necessary to conduct the audit, and Commission staff will be available to answer committee questions.

(ii) *Review of records.* During the fieldwork, Commission staff will review committee records and may conduct interviews of committee personnel. Commission staff will be available to explain aspects of the audit and examination as it progresses. Additional meetings between Commission staff and committee personnel may be held from time to time during the fieldwork to discuss possible audit findings and to resolve issues arising during the course of the audit.

(iii) *Exit conference.* At the conclusion of the fieldwork, Commission staff will hold an exit conference to discuss with committee representatives the staff's preliminary findings and recommendations that the staff anticipates it will present to the Commission for approval. Commission staff will advise committee representatives at this conference of the committee's opportunity to respond to these preliminary findings; the projected timetables regarding the issuance of the Preliminary Audit Report, the Audit Report, and any repayment determination; the committee's opportunity for an administrative review of any repayment determination; and the procedures involved in Commission repayment determinations under 11 CFR 9007.2.

(3) Commission staff may conduct additional fieldwork after the completion of the fieldwork conducted pursuant to 11 CFR 9007.1(b) (1) and (2). Factors that may necessitate such follow-up fieldwork include, but are not limited to, the following:

(i) Committee response to audit findings;

(ii) Financial activity of the committee subsequent to the fieldwork conducted pursuant to 11 CFR 9007.1(b)(1);

(iii) Committee responses to Commission repayment determinations made under 11 CFR 9007.2.

(4) The Commission will notify the candidate and his or her authorized committee if follow-up fieldwork is necessary. The provisions of 11 CFR 9007.1(b) (1) and (2) will apply to any additional fieldwork conducted.

(c) *Preliminary Audit Report: Issuance by Commission and committee response.* (1) Commission staff will prepare a written Preliminary Audit Report, which will be provided to the committee after it is approved by an affirmative vote of four (4) members of the Commission. The Preliminary Audit Report may include—

(i) An evaluation of procedures and systems employed by the candidate and committee to comply with applicable provisions of the Federal Election Campaign Act, the Presidential Election Campaign Fund Act and Commission regulations;

(ii) The accuracy of statements and reports filed with the Commission by the candidate and committee; and

(iii) Preliminary calculations regarding future repayments to the United States Treasury.

(2) The candidate and his or her authorized committee may submit in writing within 60 calendar days after receipt of the Preliminary Audit Report, legal and factual materials disputing or commenting on the proposed findings contained in the Preliminary Audit Report. In addition, the committee shall submit any additional documentation requested by the Commission. Such materials may be submitted by counsel if the candidate so desires.

(d) *Approval and issuance of the audit report.* (1) Before voting on whether to approve and issue an audit report, the Commission will consider any written legal and factual materials timely submitted by the candidate or his or her authorized committee in accordance with paragraph (c) of this section. The Commission-approved audit report may address issues other than those contained in the Preliminary Audit Report. In addition, this report will contain a repayment determination made by the Commission pursuant to 11 CFR 9007.2(c)(1).

(2) The audit report may contain issues that warrant referral to the Office of General Counsel for possible enforcement proceedings under 52 U.S.C. 30109 and 11 CFR part 111.

(3) Addenda to the audit report may be approved and issued by the Commission from time to time as circumstances warrant and as additional information becomes available. Such addenda may be based on follow-up fieldwork conducted under paragraph (b)(3) of this section, and/or information ascertained by the Commission in the normal course of carrying out its supervisory responsibilities. The procedures set forth in paragraphs (c) and (d) (1) and (2) of this section will be followed in preparing such addenda. The addenda will be placed on the public record as set forth in paragraph (e) of this section. Such addenda may also include additional repayment determination(s).

(e) *Public release of audit report.* (1) The Commission will consider the audit report in an open session agenda document. The Commission will provide the candidate and the committee with copies of any agenda document to be considered in an open session 24 hours prior to releasing the agenda document to the public.

(2) Following Commission approval of the audit report, the report will be forwarded to the committee and released to the public. The Commission will provide the candidate and committee with copies of the audit report approved by the Commission 24 hours before releasing the report to the public.

(f)(1) *Sampling.* In conducting an audit of contributions pursuant to this section, the Commission may utilize generally accepted statistical sampling techniques to quantify, in whole or in part, the dollar value of related audit findings. A projection of the total amount of violations based on apparent violations identified in such a sample

may become the basis, in whole or in part, of any audit finding.

(2) A committee in responding to a sample-based finding shall respond only to the specific sample items used to make the projection. If the committee demonstrates that any apparent errors found among the sample items were not errors, the Commission shall make a new projection based on the reduced number of errors in the sample.

(3) Within 30 days of service of the Final Audit Report, the committee shall submit a check to the United States Treasury for the total amount of any excessive or prohibited contributions not refunded, reattributed or redesignated in a timely manner in accordance with 11 CFR 103.3(b) (1), (2) or (3); or take any other action required by the Commission with respect to sample-based findings.

[56 FR 35924, July 29, 1991; 56 FR 42380, Aug. 27, 1991; 60 FR 31878, June 16, 1995; 64 FR 61780, Nov. 15, 1999; 79 FR 77851, Dec. 29, 2014]

§ 9007.2 Repayments.

(a) *General.* (1) A candidate who has received payments from the Fund under 11 CFR part 9005 shall pay the United States Treasury any amounts which the Commission determines to be repayable under this section. In making repayment determinations under this section, the Commission may utilize information obtained from audits and examinations conducted pursuant to 11 CFR 9007.1 or otherwise obtained by the Commission in carrying out its responsibilities under this subchapter.

(2) The Commission will notify the candidate of any repayment determinations made under this section as soon as possible, but not later than 3 years after the day of the presidential election. The Commission's issuance of the audit report to the candidate under 11 CFR 9007.1(d) will constitute notification for purposes of this section.

(3) Once the candidate receives notice of the Commission's repayment determination under this section, the candidate should give preference to the repayment over all other outstanding obligations of his or her committee, except for any federal taxes owed by the committee.

(4) Repayments may be made only from the following sources: personal funds of the candidate (without regard to the limitations of 11 CFR 9003.2(c)), contributions and federal funds in the committee's account(s), and any additional funds raised subject to the limitations and prohibitions of the Federal Election Campaign Act of 1971, as amended.

(b) *Bases for repayment.* The Commission may determine that an eligible candidate of a political party who has received payments from the Fund must repay the United States Treasury under any of the circumstances described below.

(1) *Payments in excess of candidate's entitlement.* If the Commission determines that any portion of the payments made to the candidate was in excess of the aggregate payments to which such candidate was entitled, it will so notify the candidate, and such candidate shall pay to the United States Treasury an amount equal to such portion.

(2) *Use of funds for non-qualified campaign expenses.* (i) If the Commission determines that any amount of any payment to an eligible candidate from the Fund was used for purposes other than those described in paragraphs (b)(2)(i) (A) through (C) of this section, it will notify the candidate of the amount so used, and such candidate shall pay to the United States Treasury an amount equal to such amount.

(A) To defray qualified campaign expenses;

(B) To repay loans, the proceeds of which were used to defray qualified campaign expenses; and

(C) To restore funds (other than contributions which were received and expended by minor or new party candidates to defray qualified campaign expenses) which were used to defray qualified campaign expenses.

(ii) Examples of Commission repayment determinations under 11 CFR 9007.2(b)(2) include, but are not limited to the following:

(A) Determinations that a candidate, a candidate's authorized committee(s) or agent(s) have incurred expenses in excess of the aggregate payments to which an eligible major party candidate is entitled;

(B) Determinations that amounts spent by a candidate, a candidate's authorized committee(s) or agent(s) from the Fund were not documented in accordance with 11 CFR 9003.5;

(C) Determinations that any portion of the payments made to a candidate from the Fund was expended in violation of State or Federal law; and

(D) Determinations that any portion of the payments made to a candidate from the Fund was used to defray expenses resulting from a violation of State or Federal law, such as the payment of fines or penalties.

(iii) In the case of a candidate who has received contributions pursuant to 11 CFR 9003.3 (b) or (c), the amount of any repayment sought under this section shall bear the same ratio to the total amount determined to have been used for non-qualified campaign expenses as the amount of payments certified to the candidate from the Fund bears to the total deposits, as of December 31 of the Presidential election year. For purposes of this section, total deposits means all deposits to all candidate accounts minus transfers between accounts, refunds, rebates, reimbursements, checks returned for insufficient funds, proceeds of loans and other similar amounts.

(3) *Surplus.* If the Commission determines that a portion of payments from the Fund remains unspent after all qualified campaign expenses have been paid, it shall so notify the candidate, and such candidate shall pay the United States Treasury that portion of surplus funds.

(4) *Income on investment or other use of payments from the Fund.* If the Commission determines that a candidate received any income as a result of an investment or other use of payments from the fund pursuant to 11 CFR 9004.5, it shall so notify the candidate, and such candidate shall pay to the United States Treasury an amount equal to the amount determined to be income, less any Federal, State or local taxes on such income.

(5) *Unlawful acceptance of contributions by an eligible candidate of a major party.* If the Commission determines that an eligible candidate of a major

party, the candidate's authorized committee(s) or agent(s) accepted contributions to defray qualified campaign expenses (other than contributions to make up deficiencies in payments from the Fund, or to defray expenses incurred for legal and accounting services in accordance with 11 CFR 9003.3(a)), it shall notify the candidate of the amount of contributions so accepted, and the candidate shall pay to the United States Treasury an amount equal to such amount.

(c) *Repayment determination procedures.* The Commission's repayment determination will be made in accordance with the procedures set forth at paragraphs (c)(1) through (c)(4) of this section.

(1) *Repayment determination.* The Commission will provide the candidate with a written notice of its repayment determination(s). This notice will be included in the Commission's audit report prepared pursuant to 11 CFR 9007.1(d) and will set forth the legal and factual reasons for such determination(s), as well as the evidence upon which any such determination is based. The candidate shall repay to the United States Treasury in accordance with paragraph (d) of this section, the amount which the Commission has determined to be repayable.

(2) *Administrative review of repayment determination.* If a candidate disputes the Commission's repayment determination(s), he or she may request an administrative review of the determination(s) as set forth in paragraph (c)(2)(i) of this section.

(i) *Submission of written materials.* A candidate who disputes the Commission's repayment determination(s) shall submit in writing, within 60 calendar days after service of the Commission's notice, legal and factual materials demonstrating that no repayment, or a lesser repayment, is required. Such materials may be submitted by counsel if the candidate so desires. The candidate's failure to timely raise an issue in written materials presented pursuant to this paragraph will be deemed a waiver of the candidate's right to raise the issue at any future stage of proceedings including any petition for review filed under 26 U.S.C. 9011(a).

(ii) *Oral hearing.* A candidate who submits written materials pursuant to paragraph (c)(2)(i) of this section may at the same time request in writing that the Commission provide such candidate with an opportunity to address the Commission in open session to demonstrate that no repayment, or a lesser repayment, is required. The candidate should identify in this request the repayment issues he or she wants to address at the oral hearing. If the Commission decides by an affirmative vote of four (4) of its members to grant the candidate's request, it will inform the candidate of the date and time set for the oral hearing. At the date and time set by the Commission, the candidate or candidate's designated representative will be allotted an amount of time in which to make an oral presentation to the Commission based upon the legal and factual materials submitted under paragraph (c)(2)(ii) of this section. The candidate or representative will also have the opportunity to answer any questions from individual members of the Commission.

(3) *Repayment determination upon review.* In deciding whether to revise any repayment determination(s) following an administrative review pursuant to paragraph (c)(2) of this section, the Commission will consider any submission made under paragraph (c)(2)(i) of this section and any oral hearing conducted under paragraph (c)(2)(ii) of this section, and may also consider any new or additional information from other sources. A determination following an administrative review that a candidate must repay a certain amount will be accompanied by a written statement of reasons supporting the Commission's determination(s). This statement will explain the legal and factual reasons underlying the Commission's determination(s) and will summarize the results of any investigation(s) upon which the determination(s) are based.

(d) *Repayment period.* (1) Within 90 calendar days of service of the notice of the Commission's repayment determination(s), the candidate shall repay to the United States Treasury the amounts which the Commission has determined to be repayable. Upon application by the candidate, the Commission may grant an extension of up to 90 calendar days in which to make repayment.

(2) If the candidate requests an administrative review of the Commission's repayment determination(s) under paragraph (c)(2) of this section, the time for repayment will be suspended until the Commission has concluded its administrative review of the repayment determination(s). Within 30 calendar days after service of the notice of the Commission's post-administrative review repayment determination(s), the candidate shall repay to the United States Treasury the amounts which the Commission has determined to be repayable. Upon application by the candidate, the Commission may grant an extension of up to 90 calendar days in which to make repayment.

(3) Interest shall be assessed on all repayments made after the initial 90-day repayment period established at paragraph (d)(1) of this section or the 30-day repayment period established at paragraph (d)(2) of this section. The amount of interest due shall be the greater of:

(i) An amount calculated in accordance with 28 U.S.C. 1961 (a) and (b); or

(ii) The amount actually earned on the funds set aside or to be repaid under this section.

(e) *Computation of time.* The time periods established by this section shall be computed in accordance with 11 CFR 111.2.

(f) *Additional repayments.* Nothing in this section will prevent the Commission from making additional repayment determinations on one or more of the bases set forth at 11 CFR 9007.2(b) after it has made a repayment determination on any such basis. The Commission may make additional repayment determinations where there exist facts not used as the basis for any previous determination. Any such additional repayment determination will be made in accordance with the provisions of this section.

(g) *Newly-discovered assets.* If, after any repayment determination made under this section, a candidate or his or her authorized committee(s) receives or becomes aware of assets not previously included in any statement of net outstanding qualified campaign expenses submitted pursuant to 11 CFR 9004.9, the candidate or his or her authorized committee(s) shall promptly notify the Commission of such newly-discovered assets. Newly-discovered assets may include refunds, rebates, late-arriving receivables, and actual receipts for capital assets in excess of the value specified in any previously-submitted statement of net outstanding qualified campaign expenses. Newly-discovered assets may serve as a basis for additional repayment determinations under 11 CFR 9007.2(f).

(h) *Limit on repayment.* No repayment shall be required from the eligible candidates of a political party under 11 CFR 9007.2 to the extent that such repayment, when added to other repayments required from such candidates under 11 CFR 9007.2, exceeds the amount of payments received by such candidates under 11 CFR 9005.2.

(i) *Petitions for rehearing; stays pending appeal.* The candidate may file a petition for rehearing of a repayment determination in accordance with 11 CFR 9007.5(a). The candidate may request a stay of a repayment determination in accordance with 11 CFR 9007.5(c) pending the candidate's appeal of that repayment determination.

[56 FR 35924, July 29, 1991, as amended at 60 FR 31878, June 16, 1995]

§ 9007.3 Extensions of time.

(a) It is the policy of the Commission that extensions of time under 11 CFR part 9007 will not be routinely granted.

(b) Whenever a candidate has a right or is required to take action within a period of time prescribed by 11 CFR part 9007 or by notice given thereunder, the candidate may apply in writing to the Commission for an extension of time in which to exercise such right or take such action. The candidate shall demonstrate in the application for extension that good cause exists for his or her request.

(c) An application for extension of time shall be made at least 7 calendar days prior to the expiration of the time period for which the extension is sought. The Commission may, upon a showing of good cause, grant an extension of time to a candidate who has applied for such extension in a timely manner. The length of time of any extension granted hereunder shall be decided by the Commission and may be less than the amount of time sought by the candidate in his or her application. If a candidate seeks an extension of any 60-day response period under 11 CFR part 9007, the Commission may grant no more than one extension to that candidate, which extension shall not exceed 15 days.

(d) If a candidate fails to seek an extension of time, exercise a right or take a required action prior to the expiration of a time period prescribed by 11 CFR part 9007, the Commission may, on the candidate's showing of excusable neglect:

(1) Permit such candidate to exercise his or her right(s), or take such required action(s) after the expiration of the prescribed time period; and

(2) Take into consideration any information obtained in connection with the exercise of any such right or taking of any such action before making decisions or determinations under 11 CFR part 9007.

[56 FR 35924, July 29, 1991, as amended at 60 FR 31880, June 16, 1995]

§9007.4 Additional audits.

In accordance with 11 CFR 104.16(c), the Commission, pursuant to 11 CFR 111.10, may upon affirmative vote of four members conduct an audit and field investigation of any committee in any case in which the Commission finds reason to believe that a violation of a statute or regulation over which the Commission has jurisdiction has occurred or is about to occur.

§9007.5 Petitions for rehearing; stays of repayment determinations.

(a) *Petitions for rehearing.* (1) Following the Commission's repayment determination or a final determination that a candidate is not entitled to all or a portion of post-election funding under 11 CFR 9004.9(f), the candidate may file a petition for rehearing setting forth the relief desired and the legal and factual basis in support. To be considered by the Commission, petitions for rehearing must:

(i) Be filed within 20 calendar days following service of the Commission's

repayment determination or final determination;

(ii) Raise new questions of law or fact that would materially alter the Commission's repayment determination or final determination; and

(iii) Set forth clear and convincing grounds why such questions were not and could not have been presented during the original determination process.

(2) If a candidate files a timely petition under this section challenging a Commission repayment determination, the time for repayment will be suspended until the Commission serves notice on the candidate of its determination on the petition. The time periods for making repayment under 11 CFR 9007.2(d) shall apply to any amounts determined to be repayable following the Commission's consideration of a petition for rehearing under this section.

(b) *Effect of failure to raise issues.* The candidate's failure to raise an argument in a timely fashion during the original determination process or in a petition for rehearing under this section, as appropriate, shall be deemed a waiver of the candidate's right to present such arguments in any future stage of proceedings including any petition for review filed under 26 U.S.C. 9011(a). An issue is not timely raised in a petition for rehearing if it could have been raised earlier in response to the Commission's original determination.

(c) *Stay of repayment determination pending appeal.* (1)(i) The candidate may apply to the Commission for a stay of all or a portion of the amount determined to be repayable under this section or under 11 CFR 9007.2 pending the candidate's appeal of that repayment determination pursuant to 26 U.S.C. 9011(a). The repayment amount requested to be stayed shall not exceed the amount at issue on appeal.

(ii) A request for a stay shall be made in writing and shall be filed within 30 calendar days after service of the Commission's decision on a petition for rehearing under paragraph (a) of this section or, if no petition for rehearing is filed, within 30 calendar days after service of the Commission's repayment determination under 11 CFR 9007.2(c).

(2) The Commission's approval of a stay request will be conditioned upon

the candidate's presentation of evidence in the stay request that he or she:

(i) Has placed the entire amount at issue in a separate interest-bearing account pending the outcome of the appeal and that withdrawals from the account may only be made with the joint signatures of the candidate or his or her agent and a Commission representative; or

(ii) Has posted a surety bond guaranteeing payment of the entire amount at issue plus interest; or

(iii) Has met the following criteria:

(A) He or she will suffer irreparable injury in the absence of a stay; and, if so, that

(B) He or she has made a strong showing of the likelihood of success on the merits of the judicial action.

(C) Such relief is consistent with the public interest; and

(D) No other party interested in the proceedings would be substantially harmed by the stay.

(3) In determining whether the candidate has made a strong showing of the likelihood of success on the merits under paragraph (c)(2)(iii)(B) of this section, the Commission may consider whether the issue on appeal presents a novel or admittedly difficult legal question and whether the equities of the case suggest that the status quo should be maintained.

(4) All stays shall require the payment of interest on the amount at issue. The amount of interest due shall be calculated from the date 30 days after service of the Commission's repayment determination under 11 CFR 9007.2(c)(4) and shall be the greater of:

(i) An amount calculated in accordance with 28 U.S.C. 1961 (a) and (b); or

(ii) The amount actually earned on the funds set aside under this section.

[56 FR 35924, July 29, 1991, as amended at 60 FR 31880, June 16, 1995]

§ 9007.6 Stale-dated committee checks.

If the committee has checks outstanding to creditors or contributors that have not been cashed, the committee shall notify the Commission. The committee shall inform the Commission of its efforts to locate the payees, if such efforts have been necessary, and its efforts to encourage the payees

to cash the outstanding checks. The committee shall also submit a check for the total amount of such outstanding checks, payable to the United States Treasury.

§ 9007.7 Administrative record.

(a) The Commission's administrative record for final determinations under 11 CFR 9004.9 and 9005.1, and for repayment determinations under 11 CFR 9007.2, consists of all documents and materials submitted to the Commission for its consideration in making those determinations. The administrative record will include the certification of the Commission's vote(s), the audit report that is sent to the committee (for repayment determinations), the statement(s) of reasons, and the candidate agreement. The committee may include documents or materials in the administrative record by submitting them within the time periods set forth at 11 CFR 9004.9(f)(2)(ii), 9005.1(b)(2), 9005.1(c)(4), 9007.1(c) and 9007.2(c)(2), as appropriate.

(b) The Commission's administrative record for determinations under 11 CFR 9004.9, 9005.1 and 9007.2 does not include:

(1) Documents and materials in the files of individual Commissioners or employees of the Commission that do not constitute a basis for the Commission's decisions because they were not circulated to the Commission and were not referenced in documents that were circulated to the Commission;

(2) Transcripts or audio tapes of Commission discussions other than transcripts or audio tapes of oral hearings pursuant to 11 CFR 9007.2(c)(2), although such transcripts or tapes may be made available under 11 CFR parts 4 or 5; or

(3) Documents properly subject to privileges such as an attorney-client privilege, or items constituting attorney work product.

(c) The administrative record identified in paragraph (a) of this section is the exclusive record for the Commission's determinations under 11 CFR 9004.9, 9005.1 and 9007.2

[60 FR 31880, June 16, 1995]

PART 9008—FEDERAL FINANCING OF PRESIDENTIAL NOMINATING CONVENTIONS

Subpart A—Expenditures by National Committees and Convention Committees

Subpart B—Host Committees and Municipal Funds Representing a Convention City

AUTHORITY: 52 U.S.C. 30105, 30111(a)(8), 30125; 26 U.S.C. 9008, 9009(b).

SOURCE: 59 FR 33616, June 29, 1994, unless otherwise noted.

Subpart A—Expenditures by National Committees and Convention Committees

§ 9008.1 Scope.

(a) This part interprets 52 U.S.C. 30105 and 26 U.S.C. 9008. Under 26 U.S.C. 9008(b), the national committees of both major and minor parties are entitled to public funds to defray expenses incurred with respect to a Presidential Nominating convention. Under 26 U.S.C. 9008(d), expenditures with regard to such a convention by a national committee receiving public funds are limited to $4,000,000, as adjusted by the Consumer Price Index. New parties are not entitled to receive any public funds to defray convention expenses.

(b) Under 52 U.S.C. 30105, each committee or organization which represents a national party in making arrangements for that party's presidential nominating convention is required to file disclosure reports. This reporting obligation extends to all such committees or organizations, regardless of whether or not public funds are used or available to defray convention expenses.

[59 FR 33616, June 29, 1994, as amended at 79 FR 77851, Dec. 29, 2014]

§ 9008.2 Definitions.

(a) *Commission* means the Federal Election Commission.

(b) *Fund* means the Presidential Election Campaign Fund established by 26 U.S.C. 9006(a).

(c) *Major party* means, with respect to any presidential election, a political party whose candidate for the office of President in the preceding presidential election received, as the candidate of such party, 25 percent or more of the total number of popular votes received by all candidates for such office.

(d) *Minor party* means, with respect to any presidential election, a political party whose candidate for the office of President in the preceding presidential election received, as the candidate of such party, 5 percent or more, but less than 25 percent, of the total number of popular votes received by all candidates for such office.

(e) *National committee* means the organization which, by virtue of the bylaws of the political party, is responsible for the day to day operation of that party at the national level.

(f) *New party* means, with respect to any presidential election, a political party which is neither a major party nor a minor party.

(g) *Nominating convention* means a convention, caucus or other meeting which is held by a political party at the national level and which chooses the presidential nominee of the party through selection by delegates to that convention or through other similar means.

(h) *Secretary* means the Secretary of the Treasury of the United States.

[59 FR 33616, June 29, 1994, as amended at 82 FR 60854, Dec. 26, 2017]

§ 9008.3 Eligibility for payments; registration and reporting.

(a) *Eligibility requirements.* (1) To qualify for entitlement under 11 CFR 9008.4 and 9008.5, the national committee of a major or minor political party shall establish a convention committee pursuant to paragraph (a)(2) of this section and shall file an application statement pursuant to paragraph (a)(3) of this section. The convention committee, in conjunction with the national committee, shall file an agreement to comply with the conditions set forth at paragraph (a)(4) of this section.

(2) The national committee shall establish a convention committee which shall be responsible for conducting the day to day arrangements and operations of that party's presidential nominating convention. The convention committee shall register with the Commission as a political committee pursuant to 11 CFR part 102. The convention committee shall receive all public funds to which the national committee is entitled under 11 CFR 9008.4 and 9008.5 and all private contributions made for the purpose of defraying convention expenses. All expenditures on behalf of the national committee for convention expenses shall be made by the convention committee.

(3) The national committee shall file with the Commission an application statement. Any changes in the information provided in the application statement must be reported to the Commission within 10 days following the change. The application statement shall include:

(i) The name and address of the national committee;

(ii) The name and address of the convention committee and of the officers of that committee;

(iii) The name of the city where the convention is to be held and the approximate dates;

(iv) The name, address, and position of the convention committee officers

designated by the national committee to sign requests for payments; and

(v) The name and address of the depository of the convention committee.

(4) The convention committee shall, by letter to the Commission, agree to the conditions set forth in paragraph (a)(4) (i) through (viii) of this section. This agreement shall also be binding upon the national committee.

(i) The convention committee shall agree to comply with the applicable expenditure limitation set forth at 11 CFR 9008.8.

(ii) The convention committee shall agree to file convention reports as required under 52 U.S.C. 30105 and 11 CFR 9008.3(b).

(iii) The convention committee shall agree to establish one or more accounts into which all public funds received under 11 CFR 9008.4 and 9008.5 must be deposited and from which all expenditures for convention expenses must be made. Such account(s) shall contain only public funds except as provided in 11 CFR 9008.6(a)(3).

(iv) The convention committee shall agree to keep and furnish to the Commission all documentation of convention disbursements made by the committee as required under 11 CFR 9008.10. The convention committee has the burden of proving that disbursements by the convention committee were for purposes of defraying convention expenses as set forth at 11 CFR 9008.7(a)(4).

(v) The convention committee shall agree to furnish to the Commission any books, records (including bank records for all accounts), a copy of any contract which the national committee enters into with a host committee or convention city or vendor, a copy of documentation provided by commercial vendors in accordance with 11 CFR 9008.9(b), and any other information that the Commission may request. If the convention committee maintains or uses computerized information containing any of the categories of data listed in 11 CFR 9008.10(h)(1) (i) through (iv), the convention committee will provide computerized magnetic media, such as magnetic tapes or magnetic diskettes, containing the computerized information at the times specified in 11

CFR 9008.10(h)(2) that meet the requirements of 11 CFR 102.9 and 9008.10 (a) and (b). Upon request, documentation explaining the computer system's software capabilities shall be provided, and such personnel as are necessary to explain the operation of the computer system's software and the computerized information prepared or maintained by the convention committee shall also be made available.

(vi) The convention committee shall agree to permit an audit and examination pursuant to 26 U.S.C. 9008(g) and 11 CFR 9008.11 of all convention expenses; to facilitate such audit by making available office space, records, and such personnel as is necessary to the conduct of the audit and examination; and to pay any amounts required to be paid under 26 U.S.C. 9008(h) and 11 CFR 9008.12.

(vii) The convention committee shall agree to comply with the applicable requirements of 52 U.S.C. 30101 et seq., 26 U.S.C. 9008, and the Commission's regulations at 11 CFR parts 100–116 and 9008.

(viii) The convention committee shall pay any civil penalties included in a conciliation agreement or imposed under 52 U.S.C. 30109.

(5) The application statement and agreement may be filed at any time after June 1 of the calendar year preceding the year in which a Presidential nominating convention of the political party is held, but no later than the first day of the convention.

(b) *Registration and reports by political parties*—(1) *Registration.* (i) Each convention committee established by a national committee under paragraph (a)(2) of this section shall register with the Commission on FEC Form 1 as a political committee pursuant to 11 CFR part 102 and shall file reports with the Commission as required at paragraph (b)(2) of this section. Each report filed by the committee shall contain the information required by 11 CFR part 104.

(ii) Each convention committee established by a national committee under paragraph (a)(2) of this section shall submit to the Commission a copy of any and all written contracts or agreements that the convention committee has entered into with the city, county, or State hosting the conven-

tion, a host committee, or a municipal fund, including subsequent written modifications to previous contracts or agreements. Each such contract, agreement or modification shall be filed with the report covering the reporting period in which the contract or agreement or modification is executed.

(iii) A State party committee or a subordinate committee of a State party committee which only assists delegates and alternates to the convention from that State with travel expenses and arrangements, or which sponsors caucuses, receptions, and similar activities at the convention site, need not register or report under this section.

(2) *Quarterly and post convention reports; content and time of filing.* Each committee required to register under paragraph (b)(1) of this section shall file reports as follows:

(i) The first quarterly report shall be filed on FEC Form 4 no later than 15 days following the end of the calendar quarter in which the committee either receives payment under 11 CFR 9008.6, or for parties which do not accept public funds, no later than 15 days after the calendar quarter in which the committee receives contributions or makes expenditures to defray convention expenses. The committee shall continue to file reports on a quarterly basis no later than the 15th day following the close of each calendar quarter, except that the report for the final calendar quarter of the year shall be filed on January 31 of the following calendar year. Quarterly reports shall be completed as of the close of the quarter and shall continue to be filed until the committee ceases activity in connection with that party's presidential nominating convention.

(ii) Any quarterly report due within 20 days before or after the convention shall be suspended and the committee shall in lieu of such quarterly report file a post convention report. The post convention report shall be filed on the earlier of: 60 days following the last day the convention is officially in session; or 20 days prior to the presidential general election. The post convention report shall be complete as of 15 days prior to the date on which the report must be filed.

(c) *Cessation of activity.* A convention committee which has received payments under 11 CFR 9008.6 shall cease activity no later than 24 months after the convention, unless the committee has been granted an extension of time. The Commission may grant any extension of time it deems appropriate upon request of the committee at least 30 days prior to the close of the 24 month period.

[59 FR 33616, June 29, 1994, as amended at 68 FR 47416, Aug. 8, 2003; 79 FR 77851, Dec. 29, 2014]

§ 9008.4 Entitlement to payments from the fund.

(a) *Major parties.* Subject to the provisions of this part, the national committee of a major party shall be entitled to receive payments under 11 CFR 9008.6 with respect to any presidential nominating convention, in amounts which, in the aggregate, shall not exceed $4 million, as adjusted by the Consumer Price Index under 11 CFR 9008.5(a).

(b) *Minor parties.* Subject to the provisions of this part, the national committee of a minor party shall be entitled to payments under 11 CFR 9008.6 with respect to any presidential nominating convention in amounts which, in the aggregate, shall not exceed an amount which bears the same ratio to the amount which the national committee of a major party is entitled to receive under 11 CFR 9008.5 as the number of popular votes received in the preceding presidential election by that minor party's presidential candidate bears to the average number of popular votes received in the preceding presidential election by all of the major party presidential candidates.

(c) *Limitation on payments.* Payments to the national committee of a major party or a minor party under 11 CFR 9008.6 from the account designated for such committee shall be limited to the amounts in such account at the time of payment.

§ 9008.5 Adjustment of entitlement.

(a) The entitlements established by 11 CFR 9008.4 shall be adjusted on the basis of the Consumer Price Index pursuant to the provisions of 52 U.S.C. 30116(c).

(b) The entitlements established by 11 CFR 9008.4 shall be adjusted so as not to exceed the difference between the expenditure limitations of 11 CFR 9008.8(a) and the amount of private contributions received under 11 CFR 9008.6(a) by the national committee of a political party. Except as provided in 11 CFR 9008.12(b)(7), in calculating these adjustments, amounts expended by Government agencies and municipal corporations in accordance with 11 CFR 9008.53; in-kind donations by businesses to the national committee or convention committee in accordance with 11 CFR 9008.9; expenditures by host committees in accordance with 11 CFR 9008.52; expenditures to participate in or attend the convention under 11 CFR 9008.8(b)(2); and legal and accounting services rendered in accordance with 11 CFR 9008.8(b)(4) will not be considered private contributions or expenditures counting against the limitation.

[59 FR 33616, June 29, 1994, as amended at 79 FR 77851, Dec. 29, 2014]

§ 9008.6 Payment and certification procedures.

(a) *Optional payments; private contributions.* (1) The national committee of a major or minor party may elect to receive all, part, or none of the amounts to which it is entitled under 11 CFR 9008.4 and 9008.5.

(2) If a national committee of a major or minor party elects to receive part of the amounts to which it is entitled under 11 CFR 9008.4 and 9008.5, or if the Secretary determines there is a deficiency in the Fund under 26 U.S.C. 9008(b)(4), the national committee may receive and use private contributions, so long as the sum of the contributions which are used to defray convention expenses and the amount of entitlements elected to be received does not exceed the total expenditure limitation under 11 CFR 9008.8.

(3) All private contributions received by the national committee to defray convention expenses shall be subject to all reporting requirements, limitations and prohibitions of Title 52, United States Code. The convention committee may establish a separate account for private contributions or may

deposit such contributions with payments received from the Fund pursuant to paragraph (d) of this section. The account(s) shall be maintained at a State bank, federally chartered depository institution or other depository institution, the deposits or accounts of which are insured by the Federal Deposit Insurance Corporation.

(b) *Increase in certified amount.* If the application statement is filed before it is possible to determine the cost of living increase for the year preceding the convention, that amount determined by the increase shall be paid to the national committee promptly after the increase has been determined.

(c) *Availability of payments.* The national committee of a major or minor party may receive payments under this section beginning on July 1 of the calendar year immediately preceding the calendar year in which a Presidential nominating convention of the political party involved is held.

(d) *Certification of payment.* After a national committee has properly submitted its application statement and agreement as required under 11 CFR 9008.3(a) (3) and (4), and upon receipt of a written request, payment of the committee's entitlement will be certified by the Commission to the Secretary of the Treasury.

[59 FR 33616, June 29, 1994, as amended at 79 FR 77851, Dec. 29, 2014]

§9008.7 Use of funds.

(a) *Permissible uses.* Any payment made under 11 CFR 9008.6 shall be used only for the following purposes:

(1) Such payment may be used to defray convention expenses (including the payment of deposits) incurred by or on behalf of the national committee receiving such payments; or

(2) Such payment may be used to repay the principal and interest, at a commercially reasonable rate, on loans the proceeds of which were used to defray convention expenses; or

(3) Such payment may be used to restore funds (including advances from the national committee to the convention committee), other than contributions to the committee for the purpose of defraying convention expenses, where such funds were used to defray convention expenses.

(4) "Convention expenses" include all expenses incurred by or on behalf of a political party's national committee or convention committee with respect to and for the purpose of conducting a presidential nominating convention or convention-related activities. Such expenses include, but are not limited to:

(i) Expenses for preparing, maintaining, and dismantling the physical site of the convention, including rental of the hall, platforms and seating, decorations, telephones, security, convention hall utilities, and other related costs;

(ii) Salaries and expenses of convention committee employees, volunteers and similar personnel, whose responsibilities involve planning, management or otherwise conducting the convention;

(iii) Salary or portion of the salary of any national committee employee for any period of time during which, as a major responsibility, that employee performs services related to the convention;

(iv) Expenses of national committee employees, volunteers or other similar personnel if those expenses were incurred in the performance of services for the convention in addition to the services normally rendered to the national committee by such personnel;

(v) Expenses for conducting meetings of or related to committees dealing with the conduct and operation of the convention, such as rules, credentials, platform, site, contests, call, arrangements and permanent organization committees, including printing materials and rental costs for meeting space.

(vi) Expenses incurred in securing a convention city and facility;

(vii) Expenses incurred in providing a transportation system in the convention city for use by delegates and other persons attending or otherwise connected with the convention;

(viii) Expenses for entertainment activities which are part of the official convention activity sponsored by the national committee, including but not limited to dinners, concerts, and receptions; except that expenses for the following activities are excluded:

(A) Entertainment activities sponsored by or on behalf of candidates for nomination to the office of President or Vice President, or State delegations;

(B) Entertainment activities sponsored by the national committee if the purpose of the activity is primarily for national committee business, such as fund-raising events, or selection of new national committee officers;

(C) Entertainment activities sponsored by persons other than the national committee; and

(D) Entertainment activities prohibited by law;

(ix) Expenses for printing convention programs, a journal of proceedings, agendas, tickets, badges, passes, and other similar publications;

(x) Administrative and office expenses for conducting the convention, including stationery, office supplies, office machines, and telephone charges; but excluded from these expenses are the cost of any services supplied by the national committee at its headquarters or principal office if such services are incidental to the convention and not utilized primarily for the convention;

(xi) Payment of the principal and interest, at a commercially reasonable rate, on loans the proceeds of which were used to defray convention expenses;

(xii) Expenses for monetary bonuses paid after the last date of the convention or gifts for national committee or convention committee employees, consultants, volunteers and convention officials in recognition of convention-related activities or services, provided that:

(A) Gifts for committee employees, consultants, volunteers and convention officials in recognition of convention-related activities or services do not exceed $150 total per individual and the total of all gifts does not exceed $20,000; and

(B) All monetary bonuses paid after the last date of the convention for committee employees and consultants in recognition of convention-related activities or services are provided for pursuant to a written contract made prior to the date of the convention and are paid no later than 30 days after the convention; and

(xiii) Expenses for producing biographical films, or similar materials, for use at the convention, about candidates for nomination or election to the office of President or Vice President, but any other political committee(s) that use part or all of the biographical films or materials shall pay the convention committee for the reasonably allocated cost of the biographical films or materials used.

(5) Any investment of public funds or any other use of public funds to generate income is permissible only if the income so generated is used to defray convention expenses. Such income, less any tax paid on it, shall be repaid to the United States Treasury as provided under 11 CFR 9008.12(b)(6).

(b) *Prohibited uses.* (1) No part of any payment made under 11 CFR 9008.6 shall be used to defray the expenses of any candidate, delegate, or alternate delegate who is participating in any presidential nominating convention except that the expenses of a person participating in the convention as official personnel of the national party may be defrayed with public funds even though that person is simultaneously participating as a delegate or candidate to the convention. This part shall not prohibit candidates, delegates or alternate delegates who are participating in a presidential nominating convention from attending official party convention activities including but not limited to dinners, concerts and receptions, where such activities are paid for with public funds.

(2) Public funds shall not be used to defray any expense the incurring or payment of which violates any law of the United States or any law of the State in which such expense is incurred or paid, or any regulation prescribed under federal or State laws.

(3) Public funds shall not be used to pay civil or criminal penalties required or agreed to be paid pursuant to 52 U.S.C. 30109. Any amounts received or expended by the national committee or convention committee of a political party to pay such penalties shall not be considered contributions or expenditures, except that such amounts shall be reported in accordance with 11 CFR part 104 and shall be subject to the prohibitions of 11 CFR 110.4, 110.19(b)(2), and 110.20 and parts 114 and 115.

(c) *Lost, misplaced, or stolen items.* The cost of lost, misplaced, or stolen items may not be defrayed with public funds under certain circumstances. Factors considered by the Commission in making this determination shall include, but not be limited to, whether the committee demonstrates that it made conscientious efforts to safeguard the missing equipment; whether the committee sought or obtained insurance on the items; whether the committee filed a police report; the type of equipment involved; and the number and value of items that were lost.

[59 FR 33616, June 29, 1994, as amended at 64 FR 49363, Sept. 13, 1999; 67 FR 78683, Dec. 26, 2002; 68 FR 47416, Aug. 8, 2003; 79 FR 77851, Dec. 29, 2014]

§ 9008.8   Limitation of expenditures.

(a) *National party limitations*—(1) *Major parties*. Except as provided in paragraph (a)(3) of this section, the national committee of a major party may not incur convention expenses with respect to a Presidential nominating convention which, in the aggregate, exceed the amount to which such committee is entitled under 11 CFR 9008.4 and 9008.5.

(2) *Minor parties*. Except as provided by paragraph (a)(3) of this section, the national committee of a minor party may not incur convention expenses with respect to a Presidential nominating convention which, in the aggregate, exceed the amount to which the national committee of a major party is entitled under 11 CFR 9008.4 and 9008.5.

(3) *Authorization to exceed limitation*. The Commission may authorize the national committee of a major party or minor party to make expenditures for convention expenses, which expenditures exceed the limitation established by paragraph (a) (1) or (2) of this section. This authorization shall be based upon a determination by the Commission that, due to extraordinary and unforeseen circumstances, the expenditures are necessary to assure the effective operation of the Presidential nominating convention by the committee. Examples of "extraordinary and unforeseen circumstances" include, but are not limited to, a natural disaster or a catastrophic occurrence at the convention site. In no case, however, will such authorization entitle a national committee to receive public

funds greater than the entitlement specified under 11 CFR 9008.4 and 9008.5. All private contributions received to defray expenditures under this paragraph shall be subject to all reporting requirements, limitations (except for limitations imposed by paragraphs (a) (1) and (2) of this section) and prohibitions of the Federal Election Campaign Act (52 U.S.C. 30101 *et seq.*).

(b) *Payments not subject to limit*—(1) *Host committee expenditures*. Expenditures made by the host committee shall not be considered expenditures by the national committee and shall not count against the expenditure limitations of this section provided the funds are spent in accordance with 11 CFR 9008.52.

(2) *Expenditures by government agencies and municipal funds*. Expenditures made by government agencies and municipal funds shall not be considered expenditures by the national committee and shall not count against the expenditure limitations of this section if the funds are spent in accordance with the requirements of 11 CFR 9008.53.

(3) *Expenditures to participate in or attend convention*. Expenditures made by presidential candidates from campaign accounts, by delegates, or by any other individual from his or her personal funds for the purpose of attending or participating in the convention or convention related activities, including, but not limited to the costs of transportation, lodging and meals, or by State or local committees of a political party on behalf of such delegates or individuals shall not be considered expenditures made by or on behalf of the national party, and shall therefore not be subject to the overall expenditure limitations of this section.

(4) *Legal and accounting services*. (i) The payment of compensation to an individual by his or her regular employer for legal and accounting services rendered to or on behalf of the national committee shall not be considered an expenditure and shall not count against the expenditure limitations of this section.

(ii) The payment by the national committee of compensation to any individual for legal and accounting services rendered to or on behalf of the national committee in connection with the presidential nominating convention or convention-related activities shall not be considered an expenditure and shall not count against the expenditure limitations of this section provided that:

(A) The legal and accounting services relate solely to compliance with the Federal Election Campaign Act (52 U.S.C. 30101, *et seq.*) and the Presidential Election Campaign Fund Act (26 U.S.C. Chapter 95); and

(B) The contributions raised to pay for the legal and accounting services comply with the limitations and prohibitions of 11 CFR parts 110, 114 and 115. These contributions, when aggregated with other contributions from the same contributor to the political committees established and maintained by the national political party, shall not exceed the amounts permitted under 11 CFR 110.1(c) and 110.2(c), as applicable.

(iii) The convention committee shall report contributions received to pay for legal and accounting services on a separate Schedule A, and shall report payments for legal and accounting services on a separate Schedule B, attached to its reports.

(5) *Computerized information.* Payments to defray the costs of producing, delivering and explaining the computerized information and materials provided pursuant to 11 CFR 9008.10(h), and explaining the operation of the computer system's software, shall not be considered expenditures and shall not count against the expenditure limitations of this section, provided that the contributions raised to pay these expenses comply with the limitations and prohibitions of 11 CFR parts 110, 114 and 115.

[59 FR 33616, June 29, 1994, as amended at 68 FR 47416, Aug. 8, 2003; 79 FR 77851, Dec. 29, 2014]

§ 9008.9   Receipt of goods and services from commercial vendors.

Commercial vendors may sell, lease, rent or provide their goods or services to the national committee with respect to a presidential nominating convention at reduced or discounted rates, or at no charge, provided that the requirements of either paragraph (a), paragraph (b), or paragraph (c) of this section are met. For purposes of this section, *commercial vendor* shall have the same meaning as provided in 11 CFR 116.1(c).

(a) *Standard reductions or discounts.* A commercial vendor may provide reductions or discounts in the ordinary course of business. A reduction or discount shall be considered in the ordinary course of business if the commercial vendor has an established practice of providing the same reductions or discounts for the same amount of its goods or services to non-political clients, or if the reduction or discount is consistent with established practice in the commercial vendor's trade or industry. Examples of reductions or discounts made in the ordinary course of business include standard volume discounts and reduced rates for corporate, governmental or preferred customers. Reductions or discounts provided under paragraph (a) of this section need not be reported.

(b) *Items provided for promotional consideration.* (1) A commercial vendor may provide goods or services in exchange for promotional consideration provided that doing so is in the ordinary course of business.

(2) The provision of goods or services shall be considered in the ordinary course of business under this paragraph:

(i) If the commercial vendor has an established practice of providing goods or services on a similar scale and on similar terms to non-political clients, or

(ii) If the terms and conditions under which the goods or services are provided are consistent with established practice in the commercial vendor's trade or industry in similar circumstances.

(3) In all cases, the value of the goods or services provided shall not exceed the commercial benefit reasonably expected to be derived from the unique promotional opportunity presented by the national nominating convention.

(4) The convention committee shall maintain documentation showing: the goods or services provided; the date(s)

on which the goods or services were provided, the terms and conditions of the arrangement; and what promotional consideration was provided. In addition, the convention committee shall disclose in its report covering the period the goods or services are received, in a memo entry, a description of the goods or services provided for promotional consideration, the name and address of the commercial vendor, and the dates on which the goods or services were provided (e.g., "Generic Motor Co., Detroit, Michigan—ten automobiles for use 7/15–7/20, received on 7/14", or "Workers Inc., New York, New York—five temporary secretarial assistants for use 8/1–8/30, received on 8/1").

(c) *Items of de minimis value.* Commercial vendors (including banks) may sell at nominal cost, or provide at no charge, items of *de minimis* value, such as samples, discount coupons, maps, pens, pencils, or other items included in tote bags for those attending the convention. The items of *de minimis* value may be distributed by or with the help of persons employed by the commercial vendor, or employed by or volunteering for the national party or a host committee. The value of the items of *de minimis* value provided under this paragraph need not be reported.

(d) *Expenditure Limits.* The value of goods or services provided pursuant to this section will not count toward the national party's expenditure limitation under 11 CFR 9008.8(a).

§9008.10 Documentation of disbursements; net outstanding convention expenses.

In addition to the requirements set forth at 11 CFR 102.9(b), the convention committee must include as part of the evidence of convention expenses the following documentation:

(a) For disbursements in excess of $200 to a payee, either:

(1) A receipted bill from the payee that states the purpose of the disbursement; or

(2) If such a receipted bill is not available, the following documents;

(i) A canceled check negotiated by the payee; plus

(ii) One of the following documents generated by the payee—a bill, invoice, voucher or contemporaneous memorandum that states the purpose of the disbursement;

(iii) Where the documents specified at paragraph (a)(2)(ii) of this section are not available, a voucher or contemporaneous memorandum from the committee that states the purpose of the disbursement;

(3) If neither a receipted bill nor the supporting documentation specified in paragraph (a)(2) (ii) or (iii) of this section is available, a canceled check negotiated by the payee that states purpose of the disbursement.

(4) Where the supporting documentation required above is not available, the committee may present a canceled check and collateral evidence to document the convention expense. Such collateral evidence may include but is not limited to:

(i) Evidence demonstrating that the disbursement is part of an identifiable program or project which is otherwise sufficiently documented, such as a disbursement which is one of a number of documented disbursements relating to the operation of a committee office;

(ii) Evidence that the disbursement is covered by a preestablished written committee policy, such as a daily travel expense policy.

(b) For all other disbursements:

(1) If from the petty cash fund, a record that states the full name and mailing address of the payee and the amount, date and purpose of the disbursement; or

(2) A canceled check which has been negotiated by the payee and states the identification of the payee, and the amount and date of the disbursement.

(c) For purposes of this section, *payee* means the person who provides the goods or services to the committee in return for the disbursement, except that an individual will be considered a payee under this section if he or she receives $2,000 or less advanced for travel and/or subsistence and if he or she is the recipient of the goods or services purchased.

(d) For purposes of this section, the term *purpose* means the full name and mailing address of the payee, the date and amount of the disbursement, and a brief description of the goods or services purchased.

(e) Upon the request of the Commission the convention committee shall supply an explanation of the connection between the disbursement and the convention.

(f) The committee shall retain records with respect to each disbursement and receipt, including bank records, vouchers, worksheets, receipts, bills and accounts, journals, ledgers, fundraising solicitation material, accounting systems documentation, and any related material documenting campaign receipts and disbursements, for a period of three years pursuant to 11 CFR 102.9(c), and shall present these records to the Commission on request.

(g) *Net outstanding convention expenses.* A convention committee that is eligible to receive payments under 11 CFR 9008.3 shall file, no later than sixty days after the last day of the convention, a statement of that committee's net outstanding convention expenses. The convention committee shall file a revised statement of net outstanding convention expenses which shall reflect the financial position of the convention committee as of the end of the ninth month following the last day of the convention. The revised statement shall be filed no later than 30 calendar days after the end of the ninth month following the last day of the convention, and shall be accompanied by the interim repayment, if required under 11 CFR 9008.12(b)(5)(ii). The committee's net outstanding convention expenses under this section equal the difference between paragraphs (g) (1) and (2) of this section:

(1) The total of:

(i) All outstanding obligations for convention expenses as of 45 days after the last day of the convention; plus

(ii) An estimate of the amount of convention expenses that will be incurred after the 45th day and before the end of the ninth month following the last day of the convention; plus

(iii) An estimate of necessary winding down costs; less

(2) The total of:

(i) Cash on hand as of 45 days after the last day of the convention, including: all receipts dated on or before that date; currency; balances on deposit in banks, savings and loan institutions, and other depository institutions; traveler's checks; certificates of deposit; treasury bills; and any other committee investments valued at fair market value;

(ii) The fair market value of capital assets and other assets on hand; and

(iii) Amounts owed to the committee in the form of credits, refunds of deposits, returns, receivables, or rebates of convention expenses; or a commercially reasonable amount based on the collectibility of those credits, returns, receivables or rebates.

(3) The amount submitted as the total of outstanding convention obligations under paragraph (g)(1) of this section shall not include any accounts payable for non-convention expenses nor any amounts determined or anticipated to be required as a repayment under 11 CFR 9008.12 or any amounts paid to secure a surety bond under 11 CFR 9008.14(c).

(4) *Capital assets.* For purposes of this section, the term *capital asset* means any property used in the operation of the convention whose purchase price exceeded $2000 when acquired by the committee. Property that must be valued as capital assets under this section includes, but is not limited to, office equipment, furniture, vehicles and fixtures acquired for use in the operation of the convention, but does not include property defined as "other assets" under 11 CFR 9008.10(g)(5). A list of all capital assets shall be maintained by the committee, which shall include a brief description of each capital asset, the purchase price, the date it was acquired, the method of disposition and the amount received in disposition. The fair market value of capital assets may be considered to be the total original cost of such items when acquired less 40%, to account for depreciation. If the committee wishes to claim a higher depreciation percentage for an item, it must list that capital asset on the statement separately and demonstrate, through documentation, the fair market value of each such asset.

(5) *Other assets.* The term *other assets* means any property acquired by the committee for use in raising funds or as collateral for loans. "Other assets"

must be included on the committee's statement of net outstanding convention expenses if the aggregate value of such assets exceeds $5000. The value of "other assets" shall be determined by the fair market value of each item as of 45 days after the last day of the convention, unless the item is acquired after this date, in which case the item shall be valued on the date it is acquired. A list of other assets shall be maintained by the committee, which shall include a brief description of each such asset, the fair market value of each asset, the method of disposition and the amount received in disposition.

(6) *Collectibility of accounts receivable.* If the committee determines that an account receivable of $500 or more, including any credit, refund, return or rebate, is not collectible in whole or in part, the committee shall demonstrate through documentation that the determination was commercially reasonable. The documentation shall include records showing the original amount of the account receivable, copies of correspondence and memoranda of communications with the debtor showing attempts to collect the amount due, and an explanation of how the lesser amount or full write-off was determined.

(7) *Winding down costs.* The term *winding down costs* means:

(i) Costs associated with the termination of the convention such as complying with the post-convention requirements of the Act and other necessary administrative costs associated with winding down the convention, including office space rental, staff salaries and office supplies; and

(ii) Costs incurred by the convention committee prior to 45 days after the last day of the convention for which written arrangements or commitment was made on or before that date.

(8) *Review of convention committee statement.* The Commission will review the statement filed by each convention committee under this section. The Commission may request further information with respect to statements filed pursuant to 11 CFR 9008.10 during the audit of that committee under 11 CFR 9008.11.

(h) *Production of computer information*—(1) *Categories of computerized infor-*

mation to be provided. If the convention committee maintains or uses computerized information containing any of the categories of data listed in paragraphs (h)(1)(i) through (h)(1)(iv) of this section, the committee shall provide computerized magnetic media, such as magnetic tapes or magnetic diskettes, containing the computerized information at the times specified in paragraph (h)(2) of this section:

(i) Information required by law to be maintained regarding the committee's receipts or disbursements;

(ii) Records used to reconcile bank statements;

(iii) Records relating to the acquisition, use and disposition of capital assets; and

(iv) Any other information that may be used during the Commission's audit to review the committee's receipts, disbursements, loans, debts, obligations, or bank reconciliations.

(2) *Time for Production.* If the committee maintains or uses computerized information containing any of the data listed in paragraph (h)(1) of this section, the Commission generally will request such information prior to commencement of audit fieldwork. Such request will be made in writing. The committee shall produce the computerized information no later than 15 calendar days after service of such request. During or after audit fieldwork, the Commission may request additional or updated computerized information which expands the coverage dates of computerized information previously provided. During or after audit fieldwork, the Commission may also request additional computerized information which was created by or becomes available to the committee that is of assistance in the Commission's audit. The committee shall produce the additional or updated computerized information no later than 15 calendar days after service of the Commission's request.

(3) *Organization of computerized information and technical specifications.* The computerized magnetic media shall be prepared and delivered at the committee's expense and shall conform to the technical specifications, including file requirements, described in the Federal Election Commission's Computerized

Magnetic Media Requirements for Title 26 Candidates/Committees Receiving Federal Funding. The data contained in the computerized magnetic media provided to the Commission shall be organized in the order specified by the Computerized Magnetic Media Requirements.

(4) *Additional materials and assistance.* Upon request, the committee shall produce documentation explaining the computer system's software capabilities, such as user guides, technical manuals, formats, layouts and other materials for processing and analyzing the information request. Upon request, the committee shall also make available such personnel as are necessary to explain the operation of the computer system's software and the computerized information prepared or maintained by the committee.

[59 FR 33616, June 29, 1994, as amended at 68 FR 47416, Aug. 8, 2003]

§ 9008.11   Examinations and audits.

The Commission shall conduct an examination and audit of the convention committee no later than December 31 of the calendar year of the convention and may at any time conduct other examinations and audits as it deems necessary. The Commission will follow the same procedures during the audit, and will afford the committee the same right to respond, as are provided for audits of publicly funded candidates under 11 CFR 9007.1 and 9038.1.

§ 9008.12   Repayments.

(a) *General.* (1) A national committee that has received payments from the Fund under 11 CFR part 9008 shall pay the United States Treasury any amounts which the Commission determines to be repayable under this section. In making repayment determinations under this section, the Commission may utilize information obtained from audits and examinations conducted pursuant to 11 CFR 9008.11 or otherwise obtained by the Commission in carrying out its responsibilities under this subchapter.

(2) The Commission will notify the committee of any repayment determinations made under this section as soon as possible, but not later than 3 years after the last day of the Presidential nominating convention. The Commission's issuance of an audit report to the committee will constitute notification for purposes of the three year period.

(3) Once the committee receives notice of the Commission's final repayment determination under this section, the committee should give preference to the repayment over all other outstanding obligations of the committee, except for any federal taxes owed by the committee.

(b) *Bases for repayment.* The Commission may determine that the national committee of a political party that has received payments from the Fund must repay the United States Treasury under any of the circumstances described below.

(1) *Excess payments.* If the Commission determines that any portion of the payments to the national committee or convention committee under 11 CFR 9008.6(b) was in excess of the aggregate payments to which the national committee was entitled under 11 CFR 9008.4 and 9008.5, it shall so notify the national committee, and the national committee shall pay to the Secretary an amount equal to such portion.

(2) *Excessive expenditures.* If the Commission determines that the national committee or convention committee incurred convention expenses in excess of the limitations under 11 CFR 9008.8(a), it shall notify the national committee of the amount of such excessive expenditures, and the national committee shall pay to the Secretary an amount equal to the amount specified.

(3) *Excessive contributions.* If the Commission determines that the national committee accepted contributions to defray convention expenses which, when added to the amount of payments received, exceeds the expenditure limitation of such party, it shall notify the national committee of the amount of the contributions so accepted, and the national committee shall pay to the Secretary an amount equal to the amount specified.

(4) *Improper usage or documentation.* If the Commission determines that any amount of any payment to the national committee or convention committee under 11 CFR 9008.6(b) was used for any

purposes other than the purposes authorized at 11 CFR 9008.7 or was not documented in accordance with 11 CFR 9008.10, it shall notify the national committee of the amount improperly used or documented and the national committee shall pay to the Secretary an amount equal to the amount specified.

(5) *Unspent funds.* (i) If any portion of the payment under 11 CFR 9008.4 remains unspent after all convention expenses have been paid, that portion shall be returned to the Secretary of the Treasury.

(ii) The national committee or convention committee shall make an interim repayment of unspent funds based on the financial position of the committee as of the end of the ninth month following the last day of the convention, allowing for a reasonable amount as determined by the Commission to be withheld for unanticipated contingencies. The interim repayment shall be made no later than 30 calendar days after the end of the ninth month following the last day of the convention. If, after written request by the national committee or convention committee, the Commission determines, upon review of evidence presented by either committee, that amounts previously refunded are needed to defray convention expenses, the Commission shall certify such amount for payment.

(iii) All unspent funds shall be repaid to the U.S. Treasury no later than 24 months after the last day of the convention, unless the national committee has been granted an extension of time. The Commission may grant any extension of time it deems appropriate upon request of the national committee.

(6) *Income on investments of payments from the Fund.* If the Commission determines that the national committee or the convention committee received any income as a result of investment or other use of payments from the Fund pursuant to 11 CFR 9008.7(a)(5), it shall so notify the committee and the committee shall pay to the United States Treasury an amount equal to the amount determined to be income, less any Federal, State or local taxes on such income.

(7) The Commission may seek repayment, or may initiate an enforcement action, if the convention committee knowingly helps, assists or participates in the making of a convention expenditure by the host committee, government agency or municipal fund that is not in accordance with 11 CFR 9008.52 or 9008.53, or the acceptance of a contribution by the host committee or government agency or municipal fund from an impermissible source.

(c) *Repayment determination procedures.* The Commission will follow the same repayment determination procedures, and the committee has the same rights and obligations as are provided for repayment determinations involving publicly funded candidates under 11 CFR 9007.2 (c) through (h).

[59 FR 33616, June 29, 1994, as amended at 60 FR 31880, June 16, 1995; 68 FR 47417, Aug. 8, 2003]

§9008.13 Additional audits.

In accordance with 11 CFR 104.16(c), the Commission, pursuant to 11 CFR 111.10, may upon affirmative vote of four members conduct an audit and field investigation of any committee in any case in which the Commission finds reason to believe that a violation of a statute or regulation over which the Commission has jurisdiction has occurred or is about to occur.

§9008.14 Petitions for rehearing; stays of repayment determinations.

Petitions for rehearing following the Commission's repayment determination and requests for stays of repayment determinations will be governed by the procedures set forth at 11 CFR 9007.5 and 9038.5. The Commission will afford convention committees the same rights as are provided to publicly funded candidates under 11 CFR 9007.5 and 9038.5.

[64 FR 49363, Sept. 13, 1999]

§9008.15 Extensions of time.

(a) It is the policy of the Commission that extensions of time under 11 CFR part 9008 will not be routinely granted.

(b) Whenever a committee has a right or is required to take action within a period of time prescribed by 11 CFR part 9008 or by notice given thereunder, the committee may apply in writing to the Commission for an extension of time in which to exercise such right or take such action. The committee shall demonstrate in the application for extension that good cause exists for its request.

(c) An application for extension of time shall be made at least 7 calendar days prior to the expiration of the time period for which the extension is sought. The Commission may, upon a showing of good cause, grant an extension of time to a committee that has applied for such extension in a timely manner. The length of time of any extension granted hereunder shall be decided by the Commission and may be less than the amount of time sought by the committee in its application.

(d) If a committee fails to seek an extension of time, exercise a right or take a required action prior to the expiration of a time period prescribed by 11 CFR part 9008, the Commission may, on the committee's showing of excusable neglect:

(1) Permit such committee to exercise its right(s), or take such required action(s) after the expiration of the prescribed time period; and

(2) Take into consideration any information obtained in connection with the exercise of any such right or taking of any such action before making decisions or determinations under 11 CFR part 9008.

§ 9008.16 Stale-dated committee checks.

If the committee has checks outstanding that have not been cashed, the committee shall notify the Commission. The committee shall inform the Commission of its efforts to locate the payees, if such efforts have been necessary, and its efforts to encourage the payees to cash the outstanding checks. The committee shall also submit a check for the total amount of such outstanding checks, payable to the United States Treasury.

Subpart B—Host Committees and Municipal Funds Representing a Convention City

§ 9008.50 Scope and definitions.

(a) *Scope.* This subpart B governs registration and reporting by host committees and municipal funds representing convention cities. Unsuccessful efforts to attract a convention need not be reported by any city, committee or other organization. Subpart B also describes permissible sources of funds and other permissible donations to host committees and municipal funds. In addition, subpart B describes permissible disbursements by host committees and municipal funds to defray convention expenses and to promote the convention city and its commerce.

(b) *Definition of host committee.* A *host committee* is any local organization, such as a local civic association, business league, chamber of commerce, real estate board, board of trade, or convention bureau, that satisfies all of the following conditions:

(1) It is not organized for profit;

(2) Its net earnings do not inure to the benefit of any private shareholder or individual; and

(3) Its principal purpose is the encouragement of commerce in the convention city, as well as the projection of a favorable image of the city to convention attendees.

(c) *Definition of municipal fund.* A *municipal fund* is any fund or account of a government agency, municipality, or municipal corporation whose principal purpose is the encouragement of commerce in the municipality and whose receipt and use of funds is subject to the control of officials of the State or local government.

[68 FR 47417, Aug. 8, 2003]

§ 9008.51 Registration and reports.

(a) *Registration by host committees and municipal funds.* (1) Each host committee and municipal fund shall register with the Commission by filing a *Statement of Organization* on FEC Form 1 within 10 days of the date on which such party chooses the convention city, or within 10 days after the formation of the host committee or municipal fund, whichever is later. In addition to the information already required to be provided on FEC Form 1, the following information shall be disclosed by the registering entity on FEC Form 1: The name and address; the name and address of its officers; and a list of the activities that the registering entity plans to undertake in connection with the convention.

(2) Any such committee, organization or group which is unsuccessful in its efforts to attract the convention to a city need not register under this section.

(3) Each host committee and municipal fund required to register with the Commission under paragraph (a) of this section, shall submit to the Commission a copy of any and all written contracts or agreements that it has entered into with the city, county, or State hosting the convention, a host committee, a municipal fund, or a convention committee, including subsequent written modifications to previous contracts or agreements, unless such contracts, agreements or modifications have already been submitted to the Commission by the convention committee. Each such contract or agreement or modification shall be filed with the first report due under paragraph (b) of this section after the contract or agreement or modification is executed.

(b) *Post-convention and quarterly reports by host committees and municipal funds; content and time of filing.* (1) Each host committee or municipal fund required to register with the Commission pursuant to paragraph (a) of this section shall file a post convention report on FEC Form 4. The report shall be filed on the earlier of: 60 days following the last day the convention is officially in session; or 20 days prior to the presidential general election. This report shall be complete as of 15 days prior to the date on which the report must be filed and shall disclose all the information required by 11 CFR part 104 with respect to all activities related to a presidential nominating convention.

(2) If such host committee or municipal fund has receipts or makes disbursements after the completion date

of the post convention report, it shall begin to file quarterly reports no later than 15 days after the end of the following calendar quarter. This report shall disclose all transactions completed as of the close of that calendar quarter. Quarterly reports shall be filed thereafter until the host committee or municipal fund ceases all activity that must be reported under this section.

(3) Such host committee or municipal fund shall file a final report with the Commission not later than 10 days after it ceases activity that must be reported under this section, unless such status is reflected in either the post-convention report or a quarterly report.

(c) *Post-convention statements by State and local government agencies.* Each government agency of a State, municipality, or other political subdivision that provides facilities or services related to a Presidential nominating convention shall file, by letter, a statement with the Commission reporting the total amount spent to provide facilities and services for the convention under 11 CFR 9008.52(b), a list of the categories of facilities and services the government agency provided for the convention, the total amount spent for each category of facilities and services provided, and the total amount defrayed from general revenues. This statement shall be filed on the earlier of: 60 days following the last day the convention is officially in session; or 20 days prior to the presidential general election. Categories of facilities and services may include construction, security, communications, transportation, utilities, clean up, meeting rooms and accommodations. This paragraph (c) does not apply to any activities of a State or local government agency through a municipal fund that are reported pursuant to paragraph (b) of this section.

[59 FR 33616, June 29, 1994, as amended at 68 FR 47417, Aug. 8, 2003]

§9008.52 **Receipts and disbursements of host committees.**

(a) *Receipt of goods or services from commercial vendors.* Host committees may accept goods or services from commercial vendors under the same terms and conditions (including reporting requirements) set forth at 11 CFR 9008.9 for convention committees.

(b) *Receipt of donations from businesses, organizations, and individuals.* Businesses (including banks), labor organizations, and other organizations or individuals may donate funds or make in-kind donations to a host committee to be used for the following purposes:

(1) To defray those expenses incurred for the purpose of promoting the suitability of the city as a convention site;

(2) To defray those expenses incurred for welcoming the convention attendees to the city, such as expenses for information booths, receptions, and tours;

(3) To defray those expenses incurred in facilitating commerce, such as providing the convention and attendees with shopping and entertainment guides and distributing the samples and promotional material specified in 11 CFR 9008.9(c);

(4) To defray the administrative expenses incurred by the host committee, such as salaries, rent, travel, and liability insurance;

(5) To provide the national committee use of an auditorium or convention center and to provide construction and convention related services for that location such as: construction of podiums; press tables; false floors; camera platforms; additional seating; lighting, electrical, air conditioning and loudspeaker systems; offices; office equipment; and decorations;

(6) To defray the costs of various local transportation services, including the provision of buses and automobiles;

(7) To defray the costs of law enforcement services necessary to assure orderly conventions;

(8) To defray the cost of using convention bureau personnel to provide central housing and reservation services;

(9) To provide hotel rooms at no charge or a reduced rate on the basis of the number of rooms actually booked for the convention;

(10) To provide accommodations and hospitality for committees of the parties responsible for choosing the sites of the conventions; and

(11) To provide other similar convention-related facilities and services.

[68 FR 47418, Aug. 8, 2003]

§ 9008.53 **Receipts and disbursements of municipal funds.**

(a) *Receipt of goods and services provided by commercial vendors.* Municipal funds may accept goods or services from commercial vendors for convention uses under the same terms and conditions (including reporting requirements) set forth at 11 CFR 9008.9 for convention committees.

(b) *Receipt and use of donations to a municipal fund.* Businesses (including banks), labor organizations, and other organizations and individuals may donate funds or make in-kind donations to a municipal fund to pay for expenses listed in 11 CFR 9008.52(b).

[68 FR 47418, Aug. 8, 2003]

§ 9008.54 **Examinations and audits.**

The Commission shall conduct an examination and audit of each host committee registered under 11 CFR 9008.51. The Commission will follow the same procedures during the audit, and will afford the committee the same right to respond, as are provided for audits of publicly funded candidates under 11 CFR 9007.1 and 9038.1, except that Commission will not make any repayment calculations under this section.

§ 9008.55 **Funding for convention committees, host committees and municipal funds.**

(a) Convention committees, including any established pursuant to 11 CFR 9008.3(a)(2), are subject to 11 CFR 300.10, except that convention committees may accept in-kind donations from host committees and municipal funds provided that the in-kind donations are in accordance with the requirements of 11 CFR 9008.52 and 9008.53.

(b) Host committees and municipal funds are not "agents" of national committees of political parties or convention committees, unless they satisfy the prerequisites of 11 CFR 300.2(b)(1).

(c) Host committees and municipal funds are not "directly or indirectly established, financed, maintained, or controlled" by national committees of political parties or convention committees, unless they satisfy the prerequisites of 11 CFR 300.2(c).

(d) In accordance with 52 U.S.C. 30125(e)(4)(A), a person described in 11 CFR 300.60 may make a general solicitation of funds, without regard to source or amount limitation, for or on behalf of any host committee or municipal fund that is described in 26 U.S.C. 501(c) and exempt from taxation under 26 U.S.C. 501(a) (or has submitted an application for determination of tax exempt status under such section) where such solicitation does not specify how the funds will or should be spent.

[68 FR 47418, Aug. 8, 2003, as amended at 79 FR 77851, Dec. 29, 2014]

PARTS 9009–9011 [RESERVED]

PART 9012—UNAUTHORIZED EXPENDITURES AND CONTRIBUTIONS

Sec.
9012.1 Excessive expenses.
9012.2 Unauthorized acceptance of contributions.
9012.3 Unlawful use of payments received from the Fund.
9012.4 Unlawful misrepresentations and falsification of statements, records or other evidence to the Commission; refusal to furnish books and records.
9012.5 Kickbacks and illegal payments.

AUTHORITY: 26 U.S.C. 9012.

SOURCE: 56 FR 35928, July 29, 1991, unless otherwise noted.

§9012.1 Excessive expenses.

(a) It shall be unlawful for an eligible candidate of a political party for President and Vice President in a Presidential election or the candidate's authorized committee(s) knowingly and willfully to incur qualified campaign expenses in excess of the aggregate payments to which the eligible candidates of a major party are entitled under 11 CFR part 9004 with respect to such election.

(b) It shall be unlawful for the national committee of a major or minor party knowingly and willfully to incur expenses with respect to a presidential nominating convention in excess of the expenditure limitation applicable with respect to such committee under 11 CFR part 9008, unless the incurring of such expenses is authorized by the Commission under 11 CFR 9008.7(a)(3).

§9012.2 Unauthorized acceptance of contributions.

(a) It shall be unlawful for an eligible candidate of a major party in a Presidential election or any of his or her authorized committees knowingly and willfully to accept any contribution to defray qualified campaign expenses, except to the extent necessary to make up any deficiency in payments received from the Fund due to the application of 11 CFR 9005.2(b), or to defray expenses which would be qualified campaign expenses but for 11 CFR 9002.11(a)(3).

(b) It shall be unlawful for an eligible candidate of a political party (other than a major party) in a Presidential election or any of his or her authorized committees knowingly and willfully to accept and expend or retain contributions to defray qualified campaign expenses in an amount which exceeds the qualified campaign expenses incurred in that election by that eligible candidate or his or her authorized committee(s).

§9012.3 Unlawful use of payments received from the Fund.

(a) It shall be unlawful for any person who receives any payment under 11 CFR part 9005, or to whom any portion of any payment so received is transferred, knowingly and willfully to use, or authorize the use of, such payment or any portion thereof for any purpose other than—

(1) To defray the qualified campaign expenses with respect to which such payment was made; or

(2) To repay loans the proceeds of which were used, or otherwise to restore funds (other than contributions to defray qualified campaign expenses which were received and expended) which were used, to defray such qualified campaign expenses.

(b) It shall be unlawful for the national committee of a major or minor party which receives any payment under 11 CFR part 9008 to use, or authorize the use of, such payment for any purpose other than a purpose authorized by 11 CFR 9008.6.

§ 9012.4 **Unlawful misrepresentations and falsification of statements, records or other evidence to the Commission; refusal to furnish books and records.**

It shall be unlawful for any person knowingly and willfully—

(a) To furnish any false, fictitious, or fraudulent evidence, books or information to the Commission under 11 CFR parts 9001–9008, or to include in any evidence, books or information so furnished any misrepresentation of a material fact, or to falsify or conceal any evidence, books or information relevant to a certification by the Commission or any examination and audit by the Commission under 11 CFR parts 9001 *et seq.*; or

(b) To fail to furnish to the Commission any records, books or information requested by the Commission for purposes of 11 CFR parts 9001 *et seq.*

§ 9012.5 **Kickbacks and illegal payments.**

(a) It shall be unlawful for any person knowingly and willfully to give or accept any kickback or any illegal payment in connection with any qualified campaign expenses of any eligible candidate or his or her authorized committee(s).

(b) It shall be unlawful for the national committee of a major or minor party knowingly and willfully to give or accept any kickback or any illegal payment in connection with any expense incurred by such committee with respect to a Presidential nominating convention.

SUBCHAPTER F—PRESIDENTIAL ELECTION CAMPAIGN FUND: PRESIDENTIAL PRIMARY MATCHING FUND

PART 9031—SCOPE

AUTHORITY: 26 U.S.C. 9031 and 9039(b).

§ 9031.1 Scope.

This subchapter governs entitlement to and use of funds certified from the Presidential Primary Matching Payment Account under 26 U.S.C. 9031 *et seq.* The definitions, restrictions, liabilities and obligations imposed by this subchapter are in addition to those imposed by sections 30101–30145 of Title 52, United States Code, and regulations prescribed thereunder (11 CFR part 100 through 300). Unless expressly stated to the contrary, this subchapter does not alter the effect of any definitions, restrictions, obligations and liabilities imposed by sections 30101–30145 of Title 52, United States Code, or regulations prescribed thereunder (11 CFR parts 100 through 300).

[56 FR 35929, July 29, 1991, as amended at 68 FR 47418, Aug. 8, 2003; 68 FR 66699, Nov. 28, 2003; 73 FR 79602, Dec. 30, 2008; 79 FR 77851, Dec. 29, 2014]

PART 9032—DEFINITIONS

Sec.
9032.1 Authorized committee.
9032.2 Candidate.
9032.3 Commission.
9032.4 Contribution.
9032.5 Matching payment account.
9032.6 Matching payment period.
9032.7 Primary election.
9032.8 Political committee.
9032.9 Qualified campaign expense.
9032.10 Secretary.
9032.11 State.

AUTHORITY: 26 U.S.C. 9032 and 9039(b).

SOURCE: 56 FR 35929, July 29, 1991, unless otherwise noted.

§ 9032.1 Authorized committee.

(a) Notwithstanding the definition at 11 CFR 100.5, *authorized committee* means with respect to candidates (as defined at 11 CFR 9032.2) seeking the nomination of a political party for the office of President, any political committee that is authorized by a candidate to solicit or receive contributions or to incur expenditures on behalf of the candidate. The term *authorized committee* includes the candidate's principal campaign committee designated in accordance with 11 CFR 102.12, any political committee authorized in writing by the candidate in accordance with 11 CFR 102.13, and any political committee not disavowed by the candidate in writing pursuant to 11 CFR 100.3(a)(3).

(b) Any withdrawal of an authorization shall be in writing and shall be addressed and filed in the same manner provided for at 11 CFR 102.12 or 102.13.

(c) For the purposes of this subchapter, references to the "candidate" and his or her responsibilities under this subchapter shall also be deemed to refer to the candidate's authorized committee(s).

(d) An expenditure by an authorized committee on behalf of the candidate who authorized the committee cannot qualify as an independent expenditure.

(e) A delegate committee, as defined in 11 CFR 100.5(e)(5), is not an authorized committee of a candidate unless it also meets the requirements of 11 CFR 9032.1(a). Expenditures by delegate committees on behalf of a candidate may count against that candidate's expenditure limitation under the circumstances set forth in 11 CFR 110.14.

§ 9032.2 Candidate.

Candidate means an individual who seeks nomination for election to the office of President of the United States. An individual is considered to seek nomination for election if he or she—

(a) Takes the action necessary under the law of a State to qualify for a caucus, convention, primary election or run-off election;

(b) Receives contributions or incurs qualified campaign expenses;

(c) Gives consent to any other person to receive contributions or to incur qualified campaign expenses on his or her behalf; or

(d) Receives written notification from the Commission that any other person is receiving contributions or making expenditures on the individual's behalf and fails to disavow that activity by letter to the Commission within 30 calendar days after receipt of notification.

§ 9032.3 Commission.

Commission means the Federal Election Commission.

[56 FR 35929, July 29, 1991, as amended at 82 FR 60854, Dec. 26, 2017]

§ 9032.4 Contribution.

For purposes of this subchapter, *contribution* has the same meaning given the term under 52 U.S.C. 30101(8)(A) and 11 CFR part 100, subparts B and C, except as provided at 11 CFR 9034.4(b)(4).

[56 FR 35929, July 29, 1991, as amended at 67 FR 78683, Dec. 26, 2002; 79 FR 77851, Dec. 29, 2014]

§ 9032.5 Matching payment account.

Matching payment account means the Presidential Primary Matching Payment Account established by the Secretary of the Treasury under 26 U.S.C. 9037(a).

§ 9032.6 Matching payment period.

Matching payment period means the period beginning January 1 of the calendar year in which a Presidential general election is held and may not exceed one of the following dates:

(a) For a candidate seeking the nomination of a party which nominates its Presidential candidate at a national convention, the date on which the party nominates its candidate.

(b) For a candidate seeking the nomination of a party which does not make its nomination at a national convention, the earlier of—

(1) The date the party nominates its Presidential candidate, or

(2) The last day of the last national convention held by a major party in the calendar year.

§ 9032.7 Primary election.

(a) *Primary election* means an election held by a State or a political party, including a run-off election, or a nominating convention or a caucus—

(1) For the selection of delegates to a national nominating convention of a political party;

(2) For the expression of a preference for the nomination of Presidential candidates;

(3) For the purposes stated in both paragraphs (a) (1) and (2) of this section; or

(4) To nominate a Presidential candidate.

(b) If separate primary elections are held in a State by the State and a political party, the primary election for the purposes of this subchapter will be the election held by the political party.

§ 9032.8 Political committee.

Political committee means any committee, club, association, organization or other group of persons (whether or not incorporated) which accepts contributions or incurs qualified campaign expenses for the purpose of influencing, or attempting to influence, the nomination of any individual for election to the office of President of the United States.

§ 9032.9 Qualified campaign expense.

(a) *Qualified campaign expense* means a purchase, payment, distribution, loan, advance, deposit, or gift of money or anything of value—

(1) Incurred by or on behalf of a candidate or his or her authorized committees from the date the individual becomes a candidate through the last day of the candidate's eligibility as determined under 11 CFR 9033.5;

(2) Made in connection with his or her campaign for nomination; and

(3) Neither the incurrence nor payment of which constitutes a violation of any law of the United States or of any law of any State in which the expense is incurred or paid, or of any regulation prescribed under such law of the United States or of any State, except that any State law which has been preempted by the Federal Election Campaign Act of 1971, as amended, will not be considered a State law for purposes of this subchapter.

(b) An expenditure is made on behalf of a candidate, including a Vice Presidential candidate, if it is made by—

(1) An authorized committee or any other agent of the candidate for purposes of making an expenditure;

(2) Any person authorized or requested by the candidate, an authorized committee of the candidate, or an agent of the candidate to make the expenditure; or

(3) A committee which has been requested by the candidate, by an authorized committee of the candidate, or by an agent of the candidate to make the expenditure, even though such committee is not authorized in writing.

(c) Except as provided in 11 CFR 9034.4(e), expenditures incurred either prior to the date the individual becomes a candidate or after the last day of a candidate's eligibility will be considered qualified campaign expenses if they meet the provisions of 11 CFR 9034.4(a). Expenditures described under 11 CFR 9034.4(b) will not be considered qualified campaign expenses.

[56 FR 35929, July 29, 1991, as amended at 60 FR 31880, June 16, 1995; 68 FR 47418, Aug. 8, 2003]

§9032.10 Secretary.

For purposes of this subchapter, *Secretary* means the Secretary of the Treasury.

§9032.11 State.

State means each State of the United States, Puerto Rico, American Samoa, the Virgin Islands, the District of Columbia, and Guam.

[64 FR 49363, Sept. 13, 1999]

PART 9033—ELIGIBILITY FOR PAYMENTS

AUTHORITY: 26 U.S.C. 9003(e), 9033 and 9039(b).

SOURCE: 56 FR 35930, July 29, 1991, unless otherwise noted.

§9033.1 Candidate and committee agreements.

(a) *General.* (1) A candidate seeking to become eligible to receive Presidential primary matching fund payments shall agree in a letter signed by the candidate to the Commission that the candidate and the candidate's authorized committee(s) will comply with the conditions set forth in 11 CFR 9033.1(b). The candidate may submit the letter containing the agreements required by this section at any time after January 1 of the year immediately preceding the Presidential election year.

(2) The Commission will not consider a candidate's threshold submission until the candidate has submitted a candidate agreement that meets the requirements of this section.

(b) *Conditions.* The candidate shall agree that:

(1) The candidate has the burden of proving that disbursements by the candidate or any authorized committee(s) or agents thereof are qualified campaign expenses as defined at 11 CFR 9032.9.

(2) The candidate and the candidate's authorized committee(s) will comply with the documentation requirements set forth in 11 CFR 9033.11.

(3) The candidate and the candidate's authorized committee(s) will provide an explanation, in addition to complying with the documentation requirements, of the connection between any disbursements made by the candidate or authorized committee(s) of the candidate and the campaign if requested by the Commission.

(4) The candidate and the candidate's authorized committee(s) will keep and furnish to the Commission all documentation for matching fund submissions, any books, records (including bank records for all accounts), and supporting documentation and other information that the Commission may request.

(5) The candidate and the candidate's authorized committee(s) will keep and furnish to the Commission all documentation relating to disbursements and receipts including any books, records (including bank records for all accounts), all documentation required by this section (including those required to be maintained under 11 CFR 9033.11), and other information that the Commission may request. If the candidate or the candidate's authorized committee maintains or uses computerized information containing any of the categories of data listed in 11 CFR 9033.12(a), the committee will provide computerized magnetic media, such as magnetic tapes or magnetic diskettes, containing the computerized information at the times specified in 11 CFR 9038.1(b)(1) that meet the requirements of 11 CFR 9033.12(b). Upon request, documentation explaining the computer system's software capabilities shall be provided, and such personnel as are necessary to explain the operation of the computer system's software and the computerized information prepared or maintained by the committee shall be made available.

(6) The candidate and the candidate's authorized committee(s) will obtain and furnish to the Commission upon request all documentation relating to funds received and disbursements made on the candidate's behalf by other political committees and organizations associated with the candidate.

(7) The candidate and the candidate's authorized committee(s) will permit an audit and examination pursuant to 11 CFR part 9038 of all receipts and disbursements including those made by the candidate, all authorized committee(s) and any agent or person authorized to make expenditures on behalf of the candidate or committee(s). The candidate and the candidate's authorized committee(s) shall also provide any material required in connection with an audit, investigation, or examination conducted pursuant to 11 CFR part 9039. The candidate and authorized committee(s) shall facilitate the audit by making available in one central location, office space, records and such personnel as are necessary to conduct the audit and examination, and shall pay any amounts required to

be repaid under 11 CFR parts 9038 and 9039.

(8) The candidate and the candidate's authorized committee(s) will submit the name and mailing address of the person who is entitled to receive matching fund payments on behalf of the candidate and the name and address of the campaign depository designated by the candidate as required by 11 CFR part 103 and 11 CFR 9037.3. Changes in the information required by this paragraph shall not be effective until submitted to the Commission in a letter signed by the candidate or the Committee treasurer.

(9) The candidate and the candidate's authorized committee(s) will prepare matching fund submissions in accordance with the Federal Election Commission's Guideline for Presentation in Good Order.

(10) The candidate and the candidate's authorized committee(s) will comply with the applicable requirements of 52 U.S.C. 30101 *et seq.*; 26 U.S.C. 9031 *et seq.* and the Commission's regulations at 11 CFR parts 100–300, and 9031–9039.

(11) The candidate and the candidate's authorized committee(s) will pay any civil penalties included in a conciliation agreement or otherwise imposed under 52 U.S.C. 30109 against the candidate, any authorized committees of the candidate or any agent thereof.

(12) Any television commercial prepared or distributed by the candidate or the candidate's authorized committee(s) will be prepared in a manner which ensures that the commercial contains or is accompanied by closed captioning of the oral content of the commercial to be broadcast in line 21 of the vertical blanking interval, or is capable of being viewed by deaf and hearing impaired individuals via any comparable successor technology to line 21 of the vertical blanking interval.

[56 FR 35930, July 29, 1991, as amended at 60 FR 31880, June 16, 1995; 63 FR 45680, Aug. 27, 1998, 65 FR 38424, June 21, 2000; 68 FR 47418, Aug. 8, 2003; 73 FR 79602, Dec. 30, 2008; 79 FR 77851, Dec. 29, 2014]

§9033.2 Candidate and committee certifications; threshold submission.

(a) *General.* (1) A candidate seeking to become eligible to receive Presidential primary matching fund payments shall make the certifications set forth in 11 CFR 9033.2(b) to the Commission in a written statement signed by the candidate. The candidate may submit the letter containing the required certifications at any time after January 1 of the year immediately preceding the Presidential election year.

(2) The Commission will not consider a candidate's threshold submission until the candidate has submitted candidate certifications that meet the requirements of this section.

(b) *Certifications.* (1) The candidate shall certify that he or she is seeking nomination by a political party to the Office of President in more than one State. For purposes of this section, in order for a candidate to be deemed to be seeking nomination by a political party to the office of President, the party whose nomination the candidate seeks must have a procedure for holding a primary election, as defined in 11 CFR 9032.7, for nomination to that office. For purposes of this section, the term *political party* means an association, committee or organization which nominates an individual for election to the office of President. The fact that an association, committee or organization qualifies as a political party under this section does not affect the party's status as a national political party for purposes of 52 U.S.C. 30116(a)(1)(B) and 30116(a)(2)(B).

(2) The candidate and the candidate's authorized committee(s) shall certify that they have not incurred and will not incur expenditures in connection with the candidate's campaign for nomination, which expenditures are in excess of the limitations under 11 CFR part 9035.

(3) The candidate and the candidate's authorized committee(s) shall certify:

(i) That they have received matchable contributions totaling more than $5,000 in each of at least 20 States; and

(ii) That the matchable contributions are from individuals who are residents of the State for which their contributions are submitted.

(iii) A maximum of $250 of each individual's aggregate contributions will be considered as matchable contributions for the purpose of meeting the thresholds of this section.

(iv) For purposes of this section, contributions of an individual who maintains residences in more than one State may only be counted toward the $5,000 threshold for the State from which the earliest contribution was made by that contributor.

(c) *Threshold submission.* To become eligible to receive matching payments, the candidate shall submit documentation of the contributions described in 11 CFR 9033.2(b)(3) to the Commission for review. The submission shall follow the format and requirements of 11 CFR 9036.1.

[56 FR 35930, July 29, 1991, 79 FR 77851, Dec. 29, 2014]

§9033.3 Expenditure limitation certification.

(a) If the Commission makes an initial determination that a candidate or the candidate's authorized committee(s) have knowingly and substantially exceeded the expenditure limitations at 11 CFR part 9035 prior to that candidate's application for certification, the Commission may make an initial determination that the candidate is ineligible to receive matching funds.

(b) The Commission will notify the candidate of its initial determination, in accordance with the procedures outlined in 11 CFR 9033.10(b). The candidate may submit, within 20 calendar days after service of the Commission's notice, written legal or factual materials, in accordance with 11 CFR 9033.10(b), demonstrating that he or she has not knowingly and substantially exceeded the expenditure limitations at 11 CFR part 9035.

(c) A final determination of the candidate's ineligibility will be made by the Commission in accordance with the procedures outlined in 11 CFR 9033.10(c).

(d) A candidate who receives a final determination of ineligibility under 11 CFR 9033.3(c) shall be ineligible to receive matching fund payments under 11 CFR 9034.1.

§ 9033.4 Matching payment eligibility threshold requirements.

(a) The Commission will examine the submission made under 11 CFR 9033.1 and 9033.2 and either—

(1) Make a determination that the candidate has satisfied the minimum contribution threshold requirements under 11 CFR 9033.2(c); or

(2) Make an initial determination that the candidate has failed to satisfy the matching payment threshold requirements. The Commission will notify the candidate of its initial determination in accordance with the procedures outlined in 11 CFR 9033.10(b). The candidate may, within 30 calendar days after service of the Commission's notice, satisfy the threshold requirements or submit in accordance with 11 CFR 9033.10(b) written legal or factual materials to demonstrate that he or she has satisfied those requirements. A final determination by the Commission that the candidate has failed to satisfy threshold requirements will be made in accordance with the procedures outlined in 11 CFR 9033.10(c).

(b) The Commission will make its examination and determination under this section as soon as practicable. During the Presidential election year, the Commission will generally complete its review and make its determination within 15 business days.

[56 FR 35930, July 29, 1991, as amended at 60 FR 31881, June 16, 1995]

§ 9033.5 Determination of ineligibility date.

The candidate's date of ineligibility shall be whichever date by operation of 11 CFR 9033.5 (a), (b), or (c) occurs first. After the candidate's date of ineligibility, he or she may only receive matching payments to the extent that he or she has net outstanding campaign obligations as defined in 11 CFR 9034.5.

(a) *Inactive candidate.* The ineligibility date shall be the day on which an individual ceases to be a candidate because he or she is not actively conducting campaigns in more than one State in connection with seeking the Presidential nomination. This date shall be the earliest of—

(1) The date the candidate publicly announces that he or she will not be actively conducting campaigns in more than one State; or

(2) The date the candidate notifies the Commission by letter that he or she is not actively conducting campaigns in more than one State; or

(3) The date which the Commission determines under 11 CFR 9033.6 to be the date that the candidate is not actively seeking election in more than one State.

(b) *Insufficient votes.* The ineligibility date shall be the 30th day following the date of the second consecutive primary election in which such individual receives less than 10 percent of the number of popular votes cast for all candidates of the same party for the same office in that primary election, if the candidate permitted or authorized his or her name to appear on the ballot, unless the candidate certifies to the Commission at least 25 business days prior to the primary that he or she will not be an active candidate in the primary involved.

(1) The Commission may refuse to accept the candidate's certification if it determines under 11 CFR 9033.7 that the candidate is an active candidate in the primary involved.

(2) For purposes of this paragraph, if the candidate is running in two primary elections in different States on the same date, the highest percentage of votes the candidate receives in any one State will govern. Separate primary elections held in more than one State on the same date are not deemed to be consecutive primaries. If two primary elections are held on the same date in the same State (e.g., a primary to select delegates to a national nominating convention and a primary for the expression of preference for the nomination of candidates for election to the office of President), the highest percentage of votes a candidate receives in either election will govern. If two or more primaries are held in the same State on different dates, the earliest primary will govern.

(3) If the candidate certifies that he or she will not be an active candidate in a particular primary, and the Commission accepts the candidate's certification, the primary involved shall not be counted in determining the candidate's date of ineligibility under

paragraph (b) of this section, regardless of the percentage of popular votes cast for the candidate in that primary.

(c) *End of matching payment period.* The ineligibility date shall be the last day of the matching payment period for the candidate as specified in 11 CFR 9032.6.

(d) *Reestablishment of eligibility.* If the Commission has determined that a candidate is ineligible under 11 CFR 9033.5 (a) or (b), the candidate may reestablish eligibility to receive matching funds under 11 CFR 9033.8.

§9033.6 Determination of inactive candidacy.

(a) *General.* The Commission may, on the basis of the factors listed in 11 CFR 9033.6(b) below, make a determination that a candidate is no longer actively seeking nomination for election in more than one State. Upon a final determination by the Commission that a candidate is inactive, that candidate will become ineligible as provided in 11 CFR 9033.5.

(b) *Factors considered.* In making its determination of inactive candidacy, the Commission may consider, but is not limited to considering, the following factors:

(1) The frequency and type of public appearances, speeches, and advertisements;

(2) Campaign activity with respect to soliciting contributions or making expenditures for campaign purposes;

(3) Continued employment of campaign personnel or the use of volunteers;

(4) The release of committed delegates;

(5) The candidate urges his or her delegates to support another candidate while not actually releasing committed delegates;

(6) The candidate urges supporters to support another candidate.

(c) *Initial determination.* The Commission will notify the candidate of its initial determination in accordance with the procedures outlined in 11 CFR 9033.10(b) and will advise the candidate of the date on which active campaigning in more than one State ceased. The candidate may, within 15 business days after service of the Commission's notice, submit in accordance

with 11 CFR 9033.10(b) written legal or factual materials to demonstrate that he or she is actively campaigning in more than one State.

(d) *Final determination.* A final determination of inactive candidacy will be made by the Commission in accordance with the procedures outlined in 11 CFR 9033.10(c).

§9033.7 Determination of active candidacy.

(a) Where a candidate certifies to the Commission under 11 CFR 9033.5(b) that he or she will not be an active candidate in an upcoming primary, the Commission may, nevertheless, on the basis of factors listed in 11 CFR 9033.6(b), make an initial determination that the candidate is an active candidate in the primary involved.

(b) The Commission will notify the candidate of its initial determination within 10 business days of receiving the candidate's certification under 11 CFR 9033.5(b) or, if the timing of the activity does not permit notice during the 10 day period, as soon as practicable following campaign activity by the candidate in the primary state. The Commission's initial determination will be made in accordance with the procedures outlined in 11 CFR 9033.10(b). Within 10 business days after service of the Commission's notice the candidate may submit, in accordance with 11 CFR 9033.10(b), written legal or factual materials to demonstrate that he or she is not an active candidate in the primary involved.

(c) A final determination by the Commission that the candidate is active will be made in accordance with the procedures outlined in 11 CFR 9033.10(c).

§9033.8 Reestablishment of eligibility.

(a) *Candidates found to be inactive.* A candidate who has become ineligible under 11 CFR 9033.5(a) on the basis that he or she is not actively campaigning in more than one State may reestablish eligibility for matching payments by submitting to the Commission evidence of active campaigning in more than one State. In determining whether the candidate has reestablished eligibility, the Commission will consider, but is not limited to considering, the factors listed in 11 CFR 9033.6(b). The day the Commission determines to be the day the candidate becomes active again will be the date on which eligibility is reestablished.

(b) *Candidates receiving insufficient votes.* A candidate determined to be ineligible under 11 CFR 9033.5(b) by failing to obtain the required percentage of votes in two consecutive primaries may have his or her eligibility reestablished if the candidate receives at least 20 percent of the total number of votes cast for candidates of the same party for the same office in a primary election held subsequent to the date of the election which rendered the candidate ineligible.

(c) The Commission will make its determination under 11 CFR 9033.8 (a) or (b) without requiring the individual to reestablish eligibility under 11 CFR 9033.1 and 2. A candidate whose eligibility is reestablished under this section may submit, for matching payment, contributions received during ineligibility. Any expenses incurred during the period of ineligibility that would have been considered qualified campaign expenses if the candidate had been eligible during that time may be defrayed with matching payments.

§ 9033.9 Failure to comply with disclosure requirements or expenditure limitations.

(a) If the Commission receives information indicating that a candidate or his or her authorized committee(s) has knowingly and substantially failed to comply with the disclosure requirements of 52 U.S.C. 30104 and 11 CFR part 104, or that a candidate has knowingly and substantially exceeded the expenditure limitations at 11 CFR part 9035, the Commission may make an initial determination to suspend payments to that candidate.

(b) The Commission will notify the candidate of its initial determination in accordance with the procedures outlined in 11 CFR 9033.10(b). The candidate will be given an opportunity, within 20 calendar days after service of the Commission's notice, to comply with the above cited provisions or to submit in accordance with 11 CFR 9033.10(b) written legal or factual materials to demonstrate that he or she is not in violation of those provisions.

(c) Suspension of payments to a candidate will occur upon a final determination by the Commission to suspend payments. Such final determination will be made in accordance with the procedures outlined in 11 CFR 9033.10(c).

(d)(1) A candidate whose payments have been suspended for failure to comply with reporting requirements may become entitled to receive payments if he or she subsequently files the required reports and pays or agrees to pay any civil or criminal penalties resulting from failure to comply.

(2) A candidate whose payments are suspended for exceeding the expenditure limitations shall not be entitled to receive further matching payments under 11 CFR 9034.1.

[56 FR 35930, July 29, 1991, 79 FR 77851, Dec. 29, 2014]

§ 9033.10 Procedures for initial and final determinations.

(a) *General.* The Commission will follow the procedures set forth in this section when making an initial or final determination based on any of the following reasons.

(1) The candidate has knowingly and substantially exceeded the expenditure limitations of 11 CFR part 9035 prior to the candidate's application for certification, as provided in 11 CFR 9033.3;

(2) The candidate has failed to satisfy the matching payment threshold requirements, as provided in 11 CFR 9033.4;

(3) The candidate is no longer actively seeking nomination in more than one state, as provided in 11 CFR 9033.6;

(4) The candidate is an active candidate in an upcoming primary despite the candidate's assertion to the contrary, as provided in 11 CFR 9033.7;

(5) The Commission receives information indicating that the candidate has knowingly and substantially failed to comply with the disclosure requirements or exceeded the expenditure limits, as provided in 11 CFR 9033.9; or

(6) The Commission receives information indicating that substantial assets of the candidate's authorized committee have been undervalued or not

included in the candidate's statement of net outstanding campaign obligations or that the amount of outstanding campaign obligations has been otherwise overstated in relation to committee assets, as provided in 11 CFR 9034.5(g).

(b) *Initial determination*. If the Commission makes an initial determination that a candidate may not receive matching funds for one or more of the reasons indicated in 11 CFR 9033.10(a), the Commission will notify the candidate of its initial determination. The notification will give the legal and factual reasons for the determination and advise the candidate of the evidence on which the Commission's initial determination is based. The candidate will be given an opportunity to comply with the requirements at issue or to submit, within the time provided by the relevant section as referred to in 11 CFR 9033.10(a), written legal or factual materials to demonstrate that the candidate has satisfied those requirements. Such materials may be submitted by counsel if the candidate so desires.

(c) *Final determination*. The Commission will consider any written legal or factual materials timely submitted by the candidate before making its final determination. A final determination that the candidate has failed to satisfy the requirements at issue will be accompanied by a written statement of reasons for the Commission's action. This statement will explain the legal and factual reasons underlying the Commission's determination and will summarize the results of any investigation upon which the determination is based.

(d) *Effect on other determinations*. If the Commission makes an initial determination under this section, but decides to take no further action at that time, the Commission may use the legal and factual bases on which the initial determination was based in any future repayment determination under 11 CFR part 9038 or 9039. A determination by the Commission under this section may be independent of any Commission decision to institute an enforcement proceeding under 52 U.S.C. 30109.

(e) *Petitions for rehearing*. Following a final determination under this section, the candidate may file a petition for rehearing in accordance with 11 CFR 9038.5(a).

[56 FR 35930, July 29, 1991, 79 FR 77851, Dec. 29, 2014]

§ 9033.11 Documentation of disbursements.

(a) *Burden of proof*. Each candidate shall have the burden of proving that disbursements made by the candidate or his or her authorized committee(s) or persons authorized to make expenditures on behalf of the candidate or authorized committee(s) are qualified campaign expenses as defined in 11 CFR 9032.9. The candidate and his or her authorized committee(s) shall obtain and furnish to the Commission on request any evidence regarding qualified campaign expenses made by the candidate, his or her authorized committees and agents or persons authorized to make expenditures on behalf of the candidate or committee(s) as provided in paragraph (b) of this section.

(b) *Documentation required*. (1) For disbursements in excess of $200 to a payee, the candidate shall present a canceled check negotiated by the payee and either:

(i) A receipted bill from the payee that states the purpose of the disbursement; or

(ii) If such a receipt is not available,

(A) One of the following documents generated by the payee: a bill, invoice, or voucher that states the purpose of the disbursement; or

(B) Where the documents specified in paragraph (b)(1)(ii)(A) of this section are not available, a voucher or contemporaneous memorandum from the candidate or the committee that states the purpose of the disbursement; or

(iii) Where the supporting documentation required in paragraphs (b)(1)(i) or (ii) of this section is not available, the candidate or committee may present collateral evidence to document the qualified campaign expense. Such collateral evidence may include, but is not limited to:

(A) Evidence demonstrating that the expenditure is part of an identifiable program or project which is otherwise sufficiently documented such as a disbursement which is one of a number of documented disbursements relating to a campaign mailing or to the operation of a campaign office; or

(B) Evidence that the disbursement is covered by a pre-established written campaign committee policy, such as a daily travel expense policy.

(iv) If the purpose of the disbursement is not stated in the accompanying documentation, it must be indicated on the canceled check negotiated by the payee.

(2) For all other disbursements, the candidate shall present:

(i) A record disclosing the full name and mailing address of the payee, the amount, date and purpose of the disbursement, if made from a petty cash fund; or

(ii) A canceled check negotiated by the payee that states the full name and mailing address of the payee, and the amount, date and purpose of the disbursement.

(3) For purposes of this section:

(i) *Payee* means the person who provides the goods or services to the candidate or committee in return for the disbursement; except that an individual will be considered a payee under this section if he or she receives $1000 or less advanced for travel and/or subsistence and if the individual is the recipient of the goods or services purchased.

(ii) *Purpose* means the full name and mailing address of the payee, the date and amount of the disbursement, and a brief description of the goods or services purchased. Examples of acceptable and unacceptable descriptions of goods and services purchased are listed at 11 CFR 104.3(b)(3)(i)(B).

(4) The documentation requirements of 11 CFR 102.9(b) shall also apply to disbursements.

(c) *Retention of records.* The candidate shall retain records with respect to each disbursement and receipt, including bank records, vouchers, worksheets, receipts, bills and accounts, journals, ledgers, fundraising solicitation material, accounting systems documentation, and any related materials documenting campaign receipts and disbursements, for a period of three years pursuant to 11 CFR 102.9(c), and

shall present these records to the Commission on request.

(d) *List of capital and other assets*—(1) *Capital assets.* The candidate or committee shall maintain a list of all capital assets whose purchase price exceeded $2000 when acquired by the campaign. The list shall include a brief description of each capital asset, the purchase price, the date it was acquired, the method of disposition and the amount received in disposition. For purposes of this section, "capital asset" shall be defined in accordance with 11 CFR 9034.5(c)(1).

(2) *Other assets.* The candidate or committee shall maintain a list of other assets acquired for use in fundraising or as collateral for campaign loans, if the aggregate value of such assets exceeds $5000. The list shall include a brief description of each such asset, the fair market value of each asset, the method of disposition and the amount received in disposition. The fair market value of other assets shall be determined in accordance with 11 CFR 9034.5(c)(2).

[60 FR 31881, June 16, 1995, as amended at 64 FR 49363, Sept. 13, 1999; 68 FR 47418, Aug. 8, 2003]

§ 9033.12 Production of computerized information.

(a) *Categories of computerized information to be provided.* If the candidate or the candidate's authorized committee maintains or uses computerized information containing any of the categories of data listed in paragraphs (a)(1) through (a)(9) of this section, the committee shall provide computerized magnetic media, such as magnetic tapes or magnetic diskettes, containing the computerized information at the times specified in 11 CFR 9038.1(b)(1):

(1) Information required by law to be maintained regarding the committee's receipts or disbursements;

(2) Records of allocations of expenditures to particular state expenditure limits and to the overall expenditure limit;

(3) Disbursements for exempt fundraising and exempt compliance costs, including the allocation of salaries and overhead expenditures;

(4) Records of allocations of expenditures for the purchase of broadcast media;

(5) Records used to prepare statements of net outstanding campaign obligations;

(6) Records used to reconcile bank statements;

(7) Disbursements made and reimbursements received for the cost of transportation, ground services and facilities made available to media personnel, including records relating to how costs charged to media personnel were determined;

(8) Records relating to the acquisition, use and disposition of capital assets or other assets; and

(9) Any other information that may be used during the Commission's audit to review the committee's receipts, disbursements, loans, debts, obligations, bank reconciliations or statements of net outstanding campaign obligations.

(b) *Organization of computerized information and technical specifications.* The computerized magnetic media shall be prepared and delivered at the committee's expense and shall conform to the technical specifications, including file requirements, described in the Federal Election Commission's Computerized Magnetic Media Requirements for title 26 Candidates/Committees Receiving Federal Funding. The data contained in the computerized magnetic media provided to the Commission shall be organized in the order specified by the Computerized Magnetic Media Requirements.

(c) *Additional materials and assistance.* Upon request, the committee shall provide documentation explaining the computer system's software capabilities, such as user guides, technical manuals, formats, layouts and other materials for processing and analyzing the information requested. Upon request, the committee shall also make available such personnel as are necessary to explain the operation of the computer system's software and the computerized information prepared or maintained by the committee.

PART 9034—ENTITLEMENTS

AUTHORITY: 26 U.S.C. 9034 and 9039(b).

SOURCE: 56 FR 34132, July 25, 1991; 56 FR 35934, July 29, 1991, unless otherwise noted.

§9034.1 Candidate entitlements.

(a) A candidate who has been notified by the Commission under 11 CFR 9036.1 that he or she has successfully satisfied eligibility and certification requirements is entitled to receive payments under 26 U.S.C. 9037 and 11 CFR part 9037 in an amount equal to the amount of each matchable campaign contribution received by the candidate, except that a candidate who has become ineligible under 11 CFR 9033.5 may not receive further matching payments regardless of the date of deposit of the underlying contributions if he or she has no net outstanding campaign obligations as defined in 11 CFR 9034.5. See also 26 CFR parts 701 and 702 regarding payments by the Department of the Treasury.

(b) If on the date of ineligibility a candidate has net outstanding campaign obligations as defined under 11 CFR 9034.5, that candidate may continue to receive matching payments for matchable contributions received and deposited on or before December 31 of the Presidential election year provided that on the date of payment there are remaining net outstanding campaign obligations, *i.e.,* the sum of the contributions received on or after the date of ineligibility plus matching funds received on or after the date of ineligibility is less than the candidate's net outstanding campaign obligations.

This entitlement will be equal to the lesser of:

(1) The amount of contributions submitted for matching; or

(2) The remaining net outstanding campaign obligations.

(c) A candidate whose eligibility has been reestablished under 11 CFR 9033.8 or who after suspension of payments has met the conditions set forth at 11 CFR 9033.9(d) is entitled to receive payments for matchable contributions for which payments were not received during the ineligibility or suspension period.

(d) The total amount of payments to a candidate under this section shall not exceed 50% of the total expenditure limitation applicable under 11 CFR part 9035.

[56 FR 34132, July 25, 1991 and 56 FR 35934, July 29, 1991]

§ 9034.2 Matchable contributions.

(a) Contributions meeting the following requirements will be considered matchable campaign contributions.

(1) The contribution shall be a gift of money made: By an individual; by a written instrument and for the purpose of influencing the result of a primary election.

(2) Only a maximum of $250 of the aggregate amount contributed by an individual may be matched.

(3) Before a contribution may be submitted for matching, it must actually be received by the candidate or any of the candidate's authorized committees and deposited in a designated campaign depository maintained by the candidate's authorized committee.

(4) The written instrument used in making the contribution must be dated, physically received and deposited by the candidate or authorized committee on or after January 1 of the year immediately preceding the calendar year of the Presidential election, but no later than December 31 following the matching payment period as defined under 11 CFR 9032.6. Donations received by an individual who is testing the waters pursuant to 11 CFR 100.72(a) and 100.131(a) may be matched when the individual becomes a candidate if such donations meet the requirements of this section.

(b) For purposes of this section, the term *written instrument* means a check written on a personal, escrow or trust account representing or containing the contributor's personal funds; a money order; any similar negotiable instrument; or, for contributions by credit or debit card, a paper record, or an electronic record that can be reproduced on paper, of the transaction. For purposes of this section, the term *written instrument* also means, in the case of a contribution by a credit card or debit card, either a transaction slip or other writing signed by the cardholder, or in the case of such a contribution made over the Internet, an electronic record of the transaction created and transmitted by the cardholder, and including the name of the cardholder and the card number, which can be maintained electronically and reproduced in a written form by the recipient candidate or candidate's committee.

(c) The written instrument shall be: Payable on demand; and to the order of, or specifically endorsed without qualification to, the Presidential candidate, or his or her authorized committee. The written instrument shall contain: The full name and signature of the contributor(s); the amount and date of the contribution; and the mailing address of the contributor(s). For purposes of this section, the term *signature* means, in the case of a contribution by a credit card or debit card, either an actual signature by the cardholder who is the donor on a transaction slip or other writing, or in the case of such a contribution made over the Internet, the full name and card number of the cardholder who is the donor, entered and transmitted by the cardholder.

(1) In cases of a check drawn on a joint checking account, the contributor is considered to be the owner whose signature appears on the check.

(i) To be attributed equally to other joint tenants of the account, the check or other accompanying written document shall contain the signature(s) of the joint tenant(s). If a contribution on a joint account is to be attributed other than equally to the joint tenants, the check or other written documentation shall also indicate the amount to be attributed to each joint tenant.

(ii) In the case of a check for a contribution attributed to more than one person, where it is not apparent from the face of the check that each contributor is a joint tenant of the account, a written statement shall accompany the check stating that the contribution was made from each individual's personal funds in the amount so attributed and shall be signed by each contributor.

(iii) In the case of a contribution reattributed to a joint tenant of the account, the reattribution shall comply with the requirements of 11 CFR 110.1(k) and the documentation described in 11 CFR 110.1(l)(3), (5), and (6) shall accompany the reattributed contribution.

(2) Contributions in the form of checks drawn on an escrow or trust account are matchable contributions, provided that:

(i) The contributor has equitable ownership of the account; and

(ii) The check is accompanied by a statement, signed by each contributor to whom all or a portion of the contribution is being attributed, together with the check number, amount and date of contribution. This statement shall specify that the contributor has equitable ownership of the account and the account represents the personal funds of the contributor.

(3) Contributions in the form of checks written on partnership accounts or accounts of unincorporated associations or businesses are matchable contributions, so long as:

(i) The check is accompanied by a statement, signed by each contributor to whom all or a portion of the contribution is being attributed, together with the check number, amount and date of contribution. This statement shall specify that the contribution is made with the contributor's personal funds and that the account on which the contribution is drawn is not maintained or controlled by an incorporated entity; and

(ii) The aggregate amount of the contributions drawn on a partnership or unincorporated association or business does not exceed $1,000 to any one Presidential candidate seeking nomination.

(4) Contributions in the form of money orders, cashier's checks, or other similar negotiable instruments are matchable contributions, provided that:

(i) At the time it is initially submitted for matching, such instrument is signed by each contributor and is accompanied by a statement which specifies that the contribution was made in the form of a money order, cashier's check, traveler's check, or other similar negotiable instrument, with the contributor's personal funds;

(ii) Such statement identifies the date and amount of the contribution made by money order, cashier's check, traveler's check, or other similar negotiable instrument, the check or serial number, and the name of the issuer of the negotiable instrument; and

(iii) Such statement is signed by each contributor.

(5) Contributions in the form of the purchase price paid for the admission to any activity that primarily confers private benefits in the form of entertainment to the contributor (*i.e.*, concerts, motion pictures) are matchable. The promotional material and tickets for the event shall clearly indicate that the ticket purchase price represents a contribution to the Presidential candidate.

(6) Contributions in the form of a purchase price paid for admission to an activity that is essentially political are matchable. An "essentially political" activity is one the principal purpose of which is political speech or discussion, such as the traditional political dinner or reception.

(7) Contributions received from a joint fundraising activity conducted in accordance with 11 CFR 9034.8 are matchable, provided that such contributions are accompanied by a copy of the joint fundraising agreement when they are submitted for matching.

(8) Contributions by credit or debit card are matchable contributions, provided that:

(i) The requirements of paragraph (b) of this section concerning a written instrument and of paragraph (c) of this section concerning a signature are satisfied. Contributions by credit card or debit card where the cardholder's name and card number are given to the recipient candidate or candidate's committee only orally are not matchable.

(ii) Evidence is submitted by the committee that the contributor has affirmed that the contribution is from personal funds and not from funds otherwise prohibited by law.

[56 FR 34132, July 25, 1991, as amended at 56 FR 35934, July 29, 1991; 64 FR 32397, June 17, 1999; 67 FR 78683, Dec. 26, 2002; 81 FR 34864, June 1, 2016]

§ 9034.3 Non-matchable contributions.

A contribution to a candidate other than one which meets the requirements of 11 CFR 9034.2 is not matchable. Contributions which are not matchable include, for example:

(a) In-kind contributions of real or personal property;

(b) A subscription, loan, advance, or deposit of money, or anything of value;

(c) A contract, promise, or agreement, whether or not legally enforceable, such as a pledge card to make a contribution for any such purposes (but a gift of money by written instrument is not rendered unmatchable solely because the contribution was preceded by a promise or pledge);

(d) Funds from a corporation, labor organization, government contractor, political committee as defined in 11 CFR 100.5 or any group of persons other than those under 11 CFR 9034.2(c)(3);

(e) Contributions which are made or accepted in violation of 52 U.S.C. 30116, 30118, 30119, 30121, 30122, or 30123;

(f) Contributions in the form of a check drawn on the account of a committee, corporation, union or government contractor even though the funds represent personal funds earmarked by a contributing individual to a Presidential candidate;

(g) Contributions in the form of the purchase price paid for an item with significant intrinsic and enduring value, such as a watch;

(h) Contributions in the form of the purchase price paid for or other otherwise induced by a chance to participate in a raffle, lottery, or a similar drawing for valuable prizes;

(i) Contributions which are made by persons without the necessary donative intent to make a gift or made for any purpose other than to influence the result of a primary election;

(j) Contributions of currency of the United States or currency of any foreign country; and

(k) Contributions redesignated for a different election or redesignated for a legal and accounting compliance fund pursuant to 11 CFR 9003.3.

[56 FR 34132, July 5, 1991; 56 FR 35934, July 29, 1991, as amended at 64 FR 32397, June 17, 1999; 79 FR 77851, Dec. 29, 2014]

§ 9034.4 Use of contributions and matching payments; examples of qualified campaign expenses and non-qualified campaign expenses.

(a) *Qualified campaign expenses*—(1) *General.* Except as provided in paragraph (b)(3) of this section, all contributions received by an individual from the date he or she becomes a candidate and all matching payments received by the candidate shall be used only to defray qualified campaign expenses or to repay loans or otherwise restore funds (other than contributions which were received and expended to defray qualified campaign expenses), which were used to defray qualified campaign expenses.

(2) *Testing the waters.* Even though incurred prior to the date an individual becomes a candidate, payments made in accordance with the 11 CFR 100.131(a) for the purpose of determining whether an individual should become a candidate shall be considered qualified campaign expenses if the individual subsequently becomes a candidate and shall count against that candidate's limits under 52 U.S.C. 30116(b).

(3) *Winding down costs and continuing to campaign.* (i) Winding down costs subject to the restrictions in 11 CFR 9034.11 shall be considered qualified campaign expenses.

(ii) If the candidate continues to campaign after becoming ineligible due to the operation of 11 CFR 9033.5(b), the candidate may only receive matching funds based on net outstanding campaign obligations as of the candidate's date of ineligibility. The statement of net outstanding campaign obligations shall only include costs incurred before the candidate's date of ineligibility for goods and services to be received before the date of ineligibility and for which written arrangement or commitment was made on or before the candidate's date of ineligibility, and shall not include winding down costs until the date on which the candidate qualifies to receive winding down costs under 11 CFR 9034.11. Each contribution that is dated after the candidate's date of ineligibility may be used to continue to campaign, and may be submitted for matching fund payments. Payments from the matching payment account that are received after the candidate's date of ineligibility may be used to defray the candidate's net outstanding campaign obligations, but shall not be used to defray any costs associated with continuing to campaign unless the candidate reestablishes eligibility under 11 CFR 9033.8.

(4) *Taxes.* Federal income taxes paid by the committee on non-exempt function income, such as interest, dividends and sale of property, shall be considered qualified campaign expenses. These expenses shall not, however, count against the state or overall expenditure limits of 11 CFR 9035.1(a).

(5) *Monetary bonuses paid after the date of ineligibility and gifts.* Monetary bonuses paid after the date of ineligibility and gifts shall be considered qualified campaign expenses, provided that:

(i) All monetary bonuses paid after the date of ineligibility for committee employees and consultants in recognition of campaign-related activities or services:

(A) Are provided for pursuant to a written contract made prior to the date of ineligibility; and

(B) Are paid no later than thirty days after the date of ineligibility; and

(ii) Gifts for committee employees, consultants and volunteers in recognition of campaign-related activities or services do not exceed $150 total per individual and the total of all gifts does not exceed $20,000.

(6) *Expenses incurred by ineligible candidates attending national nominating conventions.* Expenses incurred by an ineligible candidate to attend, participate in, or conduct activities at a national nominating convention may be treated as qualified campaign expenses, but such convention-related expenses shall not exceed a total of $50,000.

(b) *Non-qualified campaign expenses—* (1) *General.* The following are examples of disbursements that are not qualified campaign expenses.

(2) *Excessive expenditures.* An expenditure which is in excess of any of the limitations under 11 CFR part 9035 shall not be considered a qualified campaign expense. The Commission will calculate the amount of expenditures attributable to the limitations in accordance with 11 CFR 9035.1(a)(2).

(3) *General election and post-ineligibility expenditures.* Except for winding down costs pursuant to paragraph (a)(3) of this section and certain convention expenses described in paragraph (a)(6) of this section, any expenses incurred after a candidate's date of ineligibility, as determined under 11 CFR 9033.5, are not qualified campaign expenses. In addition, any expenses incurred before the candidate's date of ineligibility for goods and services to be received after the candidate's date of ineligibility, or for property, services, or facilities used to benefit the candidate's general election campaign, are not qualified campaign expenses.

(4) *Civil or criminal penalties.* Civil or criminal penalties paid pursuant to the Federal Campaign Act are not qualified campaign expenses and cannot be defrayed from contributions or matching payments. Any amounts received or expended to pay such penalties shall not be considered contributions or expenditures but all amounts so received shall be subject to the prohibitions of the Act. Amounts received and expended under this section shall be reported in accordance with 11 CFR part 104.

(5) *Payments to candidate.* Payments made to the candidate by his or her committee, other than to reimburse funds advanced by the candidate for qualified campaign expenses, are not qualified campaign expenses.

(6) *Payments to other authorized committees.* Payments, including transfers and loans, to other committees authorized by the same candidate for a different election are not qualified campaign expenses.

(7) *Allocable expenses.* Payments for expenses subject to state allocation under 11 CFR 106.2 are not qualified

campaign expenses if the records retained are not sufficient to permit allocation to any state, such as the failure to keep records of the date on which the expense is incurred.

(8) *Lost, misplaced, or stolen items.* The cost of lost, misplaced, or stolen items may be considered a nonqualified campaign expense. Factors considered by the Commission in making this determination shall include, but not be limited to, whether the committee demonstrates that it made conscientious efforts to safeguard the missing equipment; whether the committee sought or obtained insurance on the items; whether the committee filed a police report; the type of equipment involved; and the number and value of items that were lost.

(c) [Reserved]

(d) *Transfers to other campaigns*—(1) *Other Federal offices.* If a candidate has received matching funds and is simultaneously seeking nomination or election to another Federal office, no transfer of funds between his or her principal campaign committees or authorized committees may be made. See 52 U.S.C. 30116(a)(5)(C) and 11 CFR 110.3(c)(5) and 110.8(d). A candidate will be considered to be simultaneously seeking nomination or election to another Federal office if he or she is seeking nomination or election to such Federal office under 11 CFR 110.3(c)(5).

(2) *General election.* If a candidate has received matching funds, all transfers from the candidate's primary election account to a legal and accounting compliance fund established for the general election must be made in accordance with 11 CFR 9003.3(a)(1).

(e) *Attribution of expenditures between the primary and the general election spending limits.* The following rules apply to candidates who receive public funding in either the primary or the general election, or both.

(1) *General rule.* Any expenditure for goods or services that are used for the primary election campaign, other than those listed in paragraphs (e)(2) through (e)(7) of this section, shall be attributed to the limits set forth at 11 CFR 9035.1. Any expenditure for goods or services that are used for the general election campaign, other than those listed in paragraphs (e)(2)

through (e)(7) of this section, shall be attributed to the limits set forth at 11 CFR 110.8(a)(2), as adjusted under 11 CFR 110.17(a).

(2) *Polling expenses.* Polling expenses shall be attributed according to when the results of the poll are received. If the results are received on or before the date of the candidate's nomination, the expenses shall be considered primary election expenses. If results are received from a single poll both before and after the date of the candidate's nomination, the costs shall be allocated between the primary and the general election limits based on the percentage of results received during each period.

(3) *State or national campaign offices.* Prior to the date of the last primary election in a Presidential election year, overhead and salary costs incurred in connection with state or national campaign offices shall be attributed to the primary election. With regard to overhead and salary costs incurred on or after June 1 of the Presidential election year, but before or on the date of nomination, the committee may attribute to the general election an amount not to exceed 15% of the limitation on primary-election expenditures set forth at 11 CFR 110.8(a)(1). Overhead and payroll costs associated with winding down the campaign and compliance activities shall be governed by paragraph (a)(3) of this section.

(4) *Campaign materials.* Expenditures for campaign materials, including bumper stickers, campaign brochures, buttons, pens and similar items, that are purchased by the primary election campaign committee and later transferred to and used by the general election committee shall be attributed to the general election limits. Materials transferred to but not used by the general election committee shall be attributed to the primary election limits.

(5) *Media production costs.* For media communications that are broadcast or published both before and after the date of the candidate's nomination, 50% of the media production costs shall be attributed to the primary election limits, and 50% to the general election limits. Distribution costs, including such costs as air time and advertising space in newspapers, shall be paid for

100% by the primary or general election campaign depending on when the communication is broadcast or distributed.

(6) *Campaign communications.* (i) *Solicitations and fundraising costs.* The costs of fundraising, including that of events and solicitation costs, shall be attributed to the primary election or to the GELAC, depending on the purposes of the fundraising. If a candidate raises funds for both the primary election and for the GELAC in a single communication or through a single fundraising event, the allocation of fundraising costs and the distribution of net proceeds will be made in the same manner as described in 11 CFR 9034.8(c)(8)(i) and (ii).

(ii) *Other communications.* Except as provided in paragraph (e)(5) of this section, the costs of a campaign communication that does not include a solicitation shall be attributed to the primary or general election limits based on the date on which the communication is broadcast, published or mailed. The cost of a communication that is broadcast, published or mailed before the date of the candidate's nomination shall be attributed to the primary election limits.

(7) *Travel costs.* Expenditures for campaign-related transportation, food, and lodging by any individual, including a candidate, shall be attributed according to when the travel occurs. If the travel occurs on or before the date of the candidate's nomination, the cost is a primary election expense. Travel to and from the convention shall be attributed to the primary election. Travel by a person who is working exclusively on general election campaign preparations shall be considered a general election expense even if the travel occurs before the candidate's nomination.

[56 FR 35934, July 29, 1991, as amended at 60 FR 31881, June 16, 1995; 60 FR 57537, 57538, Nov. 16, 1995; 64 FR 49364, Sept. 13, 1999; 64 FR 61781, Nov. 15, 1999; 67 FR 78683, Dec. 26, 2002; 68 FR 47418, Aug. 8, 2003; 79 FR 77851, Dec. 29, 2014]

§9034.5 Net outstanding campaign obligations.

(a) Within 15 calendar days after the candidate's date of ineligibility, as determined under 11 CFR 9033.5, the candidate shall submit a statement of net outstanding campaign obligations. The candidate's net outstanding campaign obligations under this section equal the difference between paragraphs (a)(1) and (2) of this section:

(1) The total of all outstanding obligations for qualified campaign expenses as of the candidate's date of ineligibility as determined under 11 CFR 9033.5, plus estimated necessary winding down costs as defined under 11 CFR 9034.4(a)(3), less

(2) The total of:

(i) Cash on hand as of the close of business on the last day of eligibility (including all contributions dated on or before that date whether or not submitted for matching; currency; balances on deposit in banks; savings and loan institutions; and other depository institutions; traveler's checks; certificates of deposit; treasury bills; and any other committee investments valued at fair market value);

(ii) The fair market value of capital assets and other assets on hand; and

(iii) Amounts owed to the committee in the form of credits, refunds of deposits, returns, receivables, or rebates of qualified campaign expenses; or a commercially reasonable amount based on the collectibility of those credits, returns, receivables or rebates.

(b) *Liabilities.* (1) The amount submitted as the total of outstanding campaign obligations under paragraph (a)(1) of this section shall not include any accounts payable for non-qualified campaign expenses nor any amounts determined or anticipated to be required as repayment under 11 CFR part 9038 or any amounts paid to secure a surety bond under 11 CFR 9038.5.

(2) The amount submitted as estimated necessary winding down costs under paragraph (a)(1) of this section shall be broken down by expense category and quarterly or monthly time period. This breakdown shall include estimated costs for office space rental, staff salaries, legal expenses, accounting expenses, office supplies, equipment rental, telephone expenses, postage and other mailing costs, printing and storage. The breakdown shall estimate the costs that will be incurred in

each category from the time the statement is submitted until the expected termination of the committee's political activity.

(c) (1) *Capital assets.* For purposes of this section, the term *capital assets* means any property used in the operation of the campaign whose purchase price exceeded $2000 when received by the committee. Property that must be valued as capital assets under this section includes, but is not limited to, office equipment, furniture, vehicles and fixtures acquired for use in the operation of the candidate's campaign, but does not include property defined as "other assets" under paragraph (c)(2) of this section. Capital assets include items such as computer systems and telecommunications systems, if the equipment is used together and if the total cost of all components that are used together exceeds $2000. A list of all capital assets shall be maintained by the committee in accordance with 11 CFR 9033.11(d). The fair market value of capital assets shall be considered to be 60% of the total original cost of such items when acquired, except that items received after the date of ineligibility must be valued at their fair market value on the date received. A candidate may claim a lower fair market value for a capital asset by listing that capital asset on the statement separately and demonstrating, through documentation, the lower fair market value. If the candidate receives public funding for the general election, a lower fair market value shall not be claimed under this section for any capital assets transferred or sold to the candidate's general election committee.

(2) *Other assets.* The term *other assets* means any property acquired by the committee for use in raising funds or as collateral for campaign loans. "Other assets" must be included on the candidate's statement of net outstanding campaign obligations if the aggregate value of such assets exceeds $5000. The value of "other assets" shall be determined by the fair market value of each item on the candidate's date of ineligibility or on the date the item is acquired if acquired after the date of ineligibility. A list of other assets shall

be maintained by the committee in accordance with 11 CFR 9033.11(d)(2).

(d) *Collectibility of accounts receivable.* If the committee determines that an account receivable of $500 or more, including any credit, refund, return or rebate, is not collectible in whole or in part, the committee shall demonstrate through documentation that the determination was commercially reasonable. The documentation shall include records showing the original amount of the account receivable, copies of correspondence and memoranda of communications with the debtor showing attempts to collect the amount due, and an explanation of how the lesser amount or full writeoff was determined.

(e) Contributions received from joint fundraising activities conducted under 11 CFR 9034.8 may be used to pay a candidate's outstanding campaign obligations.

(1) Such contributions shall be deemed monies available to pay outstanding campaign obligations as of the date these funds are received by the fundraising representative committee and shall be included in the candidate's statement of net outstanding campaign obligations.

(2) The amount of money deemed available to pay a candidate's net outstanding campaign obligations will equal either—

(i) An amount calculated on the basis of the predetermined allocation formula, as adjusted for 52 U.S.C. 30116 limitations; or

(ii) If a candidate receives an amount greater than that calculated under 11 CFR 9034.5(e)(2)(i), the amount actually received.

(f)(1) With each submission for matching fund payments filed after the candidate's date of ineligibility, the candidate shall certify that, as of the close of business on the last business day preceding the date of submission for matching funds, his or her remaining net outstanding campaign obligations equal or exceed the amount submitted for matching.

(2) A candidate who makes a submission for matching fund payments after his or her date of ineligibility shall also submit a revised statement of net outstanding campaign obligations.

This revised statement shall be due before the next regularly scheduled payment date, on a date to be determined and published by the Commission. This statement shall reflect the financial status of the campaign as of the close of business three business days before the due date of the statement. The revised statement shall also contain a brief explanation of each change in the committee's assets and obligations from the previous statement.

(3) After a candidate's date of ineligibility, if the candidate does not receive the entire amount of matching funds on a regularly scheduled payment date due to a shortfall in the matching payment account, the candidate shall also submit a revised statement of net outstanding campaign obligations. The revised statement shall be filed on a date to be determined and published by the commission, which will be before the next regularly scheduled payment date.

(g)(1) If the Commission receives information indicating that substantial assets of the candidate's authorized committee(s) have been undervalued or not included in the statement or that the amount of outstanding campaign obligations has been otherwise overstated in relation to committee assets, the Commission may decide to temporarily suspend further matching payments pending a final determination whether the candidate is entitled to receive all or a portion of the matching funds requested.

(2) In making a determination under 11 CFR 9034.5(g)(1), the Commission will follow the procedures for initial and final determinations under 11 CFR 9033.10 (b) and (c). The Commission will notify the candidate of its initial determination within 15 business days after receipt of the candidate's statement of net outstanding campaign obligations. Within 15 business days after service of the Commission's notice, the candidate may submit written legal or factual materials to demonstrate that he or she has net outstanding campaign obligations that entitle the campaign to further matching payments.

(3) If the candidate demonstrates that the amount of outstanding campaign obligations still exceeds committee assets, he or she may continue to receive matching payments.

(4) Following a final determination under this section, the candidate may file a petition for rehearing in accordance with 11 CFR 9038.5(a).

[56 FR 34132, July 25, 1991 and 56 FR 35934, July 29, 1991; 56 FR 42380, Aug. 27, 1991; 60 FR 31883, June 16, 1995; 64 FR 49364, Sept. 13, 1999; 79 FR 77851, Dec. 29, 2014]

§9034.6 Expenditures for transportation and services made available to media personnel; reimbursements.

(a) *General.* (1) Expenditures by an authorized committee for transportation, ground services or facilities (including air travel, ground transportation, housing, meals, telephone service, typewriters, and computers) provided to media personnel, Secret Service personnel or national security staff will be considered qualified campaign expenses, and, except for costs relating to Secret Service personnel or national security staff, will be subject to the overall expenditure limitations of 11 CFR 9035.1(a).

(2) Subject to the limitations in paragraphs (b) and (c) of this section, committees may seek reimbursement from the media for the expenses described in paragraph (a)(3) of this section, and may deduct reimbursements received from media representatives from the amount of expenditures subject to the overall expenditure limitation of 11 CFR 9035.1(a). Expenses for which the committee receives no reimbursement will be considered qualified campaign expenses, and, with the exception of those expenses relating to Secret Service personnel and national security staff, will be subject to the overall expenditure limitation.

(3) Committees may seek reimbursement from the media only for the billable items specified in the White House Press Corps Travel Policies and Procedures issued by the White House Travel Office.

(b) *Reimbursement limits; billing.* (1) The amount of reimbursement sought from a media representative under paragraph (a)(2) of this section shall not exceed 110% of the media representative's pro rata share (or a reasonable estimate of the media representative's pro rata share) of the actual cost of the transportation and services made available. Any reimbursement received in excess of this amount shall be disposed of in accordance with paragraph (d)(1) of this section.

(2) For the purposes of this section, a media representative's pro rata share shall be calculated by dividing the total actual cost of the transportation and services provided by the total number of individuals to whom such transportation and services are made available. For purposes of this calculation, the total number of individuals shall include committee staff, media personnel, Secret Service personnel, national security staff and any other individuals to whom such transportation and services are made available, except that, when seeking reimbursement for transportation costs paid by the committee under 11 CFR 100.93 and 9034.7(b)(5)(i), the total number of individuals shall not include national security staff.

(3) No later than sixty (60) days of the campaign trip or event, the committee shall provide each media representative attending the event with an itemized bill that specifies the amounts charged for air and ground transportation for each segment of the trip, housing, meals, telephone service, and other billable items specified in the White House Press Corps Travel Policies and Procedures issued by the White House Travel Office. Payments shall be due sixty (60) days from the date of the bill, unless the media representative disputes the charges.

(c) *Deduction of reimbursements from expenditures subject to the overall expenditure limitation.* (1) The Committee may deduct from the amount of expenditures subject to the overall expenditure limitation:

(i) The amount of reimbursements received from media representatives in payment for the transportation and services described in paragraph (a) of this section, up to the actual cost of the transportation and services provided to media representatives; and

(ii) An additional amount of the reimbursements received from media representatives, representing the administrative costs incurred by the committee in providing these services to

the media representatives and seeking reimbursement for them, equal to:

(A) Three percent of the actual cost of transportation and services provided to the media representatives under this section; or

(B) An amount in excess of 3% representing the administrative costs actually incurred by the committee in providing services to the media representatives, provided that the committee is able to document the total amount of administrative costs actually incurred.

(2) For the purposes of this paragraph, "administrative costs" includes all costs incurred by the committee in making travel arrangements and seeking reimbursement, whether these services are performed by committee staff or by independent contractors.

(d) *Disposal of excess reimbursements.* If the committee receives reimbursements in excess of the amount deductible under paragraph (c) of this section, it shall dispose of the excess amount in the following manner:

(1) Any reimbursement received in excess of 110% of the actual pro rata cost of the transportation and services made available to a media representative shall be returned to the media representative.

(2) Any amount in excess of the amount deductible under paragraph (c) of this section that is not required to be returned to the media representative under paragraph (d)(1) of this section shall be paid to the Treasury.

(e) *Reporting.* The total amount paid by an authorized committee for the services and facilities described in paragraph (a)(1) of this section, plus the administrative costs incurred by the committee in providing these services and facilities and seeking reimbursement for them, shall be reported as an expenditure in accordance with 11 CFR 104.3(b)(2)(i). Any reimbursement received by such committee under paragraph (b)(1) of this section shall be reported in accordance with 11 CFR 104.3(a)(3)(ix).

[60 FR 31883, June 16, 1995; 60 FR 57537, Nov. 16, 1995; 64 FR 42583, Aug. 5, 1999; 68 FR 69595, Dec. 15, 2003]

§9034.7 Allocation of travel expenditures.

(a) Notwithstanding the provisions of 11 CFR 106.3, expenditures for travel relating to the campaign of a candidate seeking nomination for election to the office of President by any individual, including a candidate, shall, pursuant to the provisions of paragraph (b) of this section, be qualified campaign expenses and be reported by the candidate's authorized committee(s) as expenditures.

(b)(1) For a trip which is entirely campaign-related, the total cost of the trip shall be a qualified campaign expense and a reportable expenditure.

(2) For a trip which includes campaign-related and non-campaign related stops, that portion of the cost of the trip allocable to campaign activity shall be a qualified campaign expense and a reportable expenditure. Such portion shall be determined by calculating what the trip would have cost from the point of origin of the trip to the first campaign-related stop and from that stop through each subsequent campaign-related stop, back to the point of origin. If any campaign activity, other than incidental contacts, is conducted at a stop, that stop shall be considered campaign-related. Campaign activity includes soliciting, making, or accepting contributions, and expressly advocating the election or defeat of the candidate. Other factors, including the setting, timing and statements or expressions of the purpose of an event and the substance of the remarks or speech made, will also be considered in determining whether a stop is campaign-related.

(3) For each trip, an itinerary shall be prepared and such itinerary shall be made available by the committee for Commission inspection. The itinerary shall show the time of arrival and departure and the type of event held.

(4) For trips by government conveyance or by charter, a list of all passengers on such trip, along with a designation of which passengers are and which are not campaign-related, shall be made available for Commission inspection. When required to be created, a copy of the government's or the charter company's official manifest shall also be maintained and made available by the committee.

(5)(i) If any individual, including a candidate, uses a government aircraft for campaign-related travel, the candidate's authorized committee shall pay the appropriate government entity an amount not less than the applicable rate set forth in 11 CFR 100.93(e).

(ii) [Reserved]

(iii) If any individual, including a candidate, uses a government conveyance, other than an aircraft, for campaign-related travel, the candidate's authorized committee shall pay the appropriate government entity an amount equal to the amount required under 11 CFR 100.93(d).

(iv) If any individual, including a candidate, uses accommodations, including lodging and meeting rooms, during campaign-related travel, and the accommodations are paid for by a government entity, the candidate's authorized committee shall pay the appropriate government entity an amount equal to the usual and normal charge for the accommodations, and shall maintain documentation supporting the amount paid.

(v) For travel by aircraft, the committee shall maintain documentation as required by 11 CFR 100.93(j)(1) in addition to any other documentation required in this section. For travel by other conveyances, the committee shall maintain documentation of the commercial rental rate as required by 11 CFR 100.93(j)(3) in addition to any other documentation required in this section.

(6) Travel expenses of a candidate's spouse and family when accompanying the candidate on campaign-related travel may be treated as qualified campaign expenses and reportable expenditures. If the spouse or family members conduct campaign-related activities, their travel expenses will be treated as qualified campaign expenses and reportable expenditures.

(7) If any individual, including a candidate, incurs expenses for campaign-related travel, other than by use of government conveyance or accommodations, an amount equal to that portion of the actual cost of the conveyance or accommodations which is allocable to all passengers, including

the candidate, who are traveling for campaign purposes will be a qualified campaign expense and shall be reported by the committee as an expenditure.

(i) If the trip is by charter, the actual cost for each passenger shall be determined by dividing the total operating cost for the charter by the total number of passengers transported. The amount which is a qualified campaign expense and a reportable expenditure shall be calculated in accordance with the formula set forth at 11 CFR 9034.7(b)(2) on the basis of the actual cost per passenger multiplied by the number of passengers traveling for campaign purposes.

(ii) If the trips is by non-charter commercial transportation, the actual cost shall be calculated in accordance with the formula set forth at 11 CFR 9034.7(b)(2) on the basis of the commercial fare. Such actual cost shall be a qualified campaign expense and a reportable expenditure.

(8) Non-commercial travel on aircraft, and travel on other means of transportation not operated for commercial passenger service is governed by 11 CFR 100.93.

[60 FR 31884, June 16, 1995, as amended at 68 FR 69596, Dec. 15, 2003; 74 FR 63968, Dec. 7, 2009]

§ 9034.8   Joint fundraising.

(a) *General.* Nothing in this section shall supersede 11 CFR part 300, which prohibits any person from soliciting, receiving, directing, transferring, or spending any non-Federal funds, or from transferring Federal funds for Federal election activities.

(1) *Permissible participants.* Presidential primary candidates who receive matching funds under this subchapter may engage in joint fundraising with other candidates, political committees or unregistered committees or organizations.

(2) *Use of funds.* Contributions received as a result of a candidate's participation in a joint fundraising activity under this section may be—

(i) Submitted for matching purposes in accordance with the requirements of 11 CFR 9034.2 and the Federal Election Commission's Guideline for Presentation in Good Order;

(ii) Used to pay a candidate's net outstanding campaign obligations as provided in 11 CFR 9034.5;

(iii) Used to defray qualified campaign expenses;

(iv) Used to defray exempt legal and accounting costs; or

(v) If in excess of a candidate's net outstanding campaign obligations or expenditure limit, used in any manner consistent with 11 CFR 113.2, including repayment of funds under 11 CFR part 9038.

(b) *Fundraising representatives*—(1) *Establishment or selection of fundraising representative.* The participants in a joint fundraising effort under this section shall either establish a separate committee or select a participating committee, to act as fundraising representative for all participants. The fundraising representative shall be a reporting political committee and an authorized committee of each candidate. If the participants establish a separate committee to act as the fundraising representative, the separate committee shall not be a participant in any other joint fundraising effort, but the separate committee may conduct more than one joint fundraising effort for the participants.

(2) *Separate fundraising committee as fundraising representative.* A separate fundraising committee established by the participants to act as fundraising representative for all participants shall—

(i) Be established as a reporting political committee under 11 CFR 100.5;

(ii) Collect contributions;

(iii) Pay fundraising costs from gross proceeds and funds advanced by participants; and

(iv) Disburse net proceeds to each participant.

(3) *Participating committee as fundraising representative.* A participant selected to act as fundraising representative for all participants shall—

(i) Be a political committee as defined in 11 CFR 100.5;

(ii) Collect contributions; however, other participants may also collect contributions and then forward them to the fundraising representative as required by 11 CFR 102.8;

(iii) Pay fundraising costs from gross proceeds and funds advanced by participants; and

(iv) Disburse net proceeds to each participant.

(4) *Independent fundraising agent.* The participants or the fundraising representative may hire a commercial fundraising firm or other agent to assist in conducting the joint fundraising activity. In that case, however, the fundraising representative shall still be responsible for ensuring that the recordkeeping, reporting and documentation requirements set forth in this subchapter are met.

(c) *Joint fundraising procedures.* Any joint fundraising activity under this section shall be conducted in accordance with the following requirements:

(1) *Written agreement.* The participants in a joint fundraising activity shall enter into a written agreement, whether or not all participants are political committees under 11 CFR 100.5. The written agreement shall identify the fundraising representative and shall state a formula for the allocation of fundraising proceeds. The formula shall be stated as the amount or percentage of each contribution received to be allocated to each participant. The fundraising representative shall retain the written agreement for a period of three years and shall make it available to the Commission on request.

(2) *Funds advanced for fundraising costs.* (i) Except as provided in 11 CFR 9034.8(c)(2)(ii), the amount of funds advanced by each participant for fundraising costs shall be in proportion to the allocation formula agreed upon under 11 CFR 9034.8(c)(1).

(ii) A participant may advance more than its proportionate share of the fundraising costs; however, the amount advanced which is in excess of the participant's proportionate share shall not exceed the amount that participant could legally contribute to the remaining participants. See 11 CFR 102.12(c)(2), part 110, and 9034.4(b)(6).

(3) *Fundraising notice.* In addition to any notice required under 11 CFR 110.11, a joint fundraising notice shall be included with every solicitation for contributions.

(i) This notice shall include the following information:

(A) The names of all committees participating in the joint fundraising activity whether or not such committees are political committees under 11 CFR 100.5;

(B) The allocation formula to be used for distributing joint fundraising proceeds;

(C) A statement informing contributors that, notwithstanding the stated allocation formula, they may designate their contributions for a particular participant or participants; and

(D) A statement informing contributors that the allocation formula may change if a contributor makes a contribution which would exceed the amount that contributor may give to any participant.

(ii) If one or more participants engage in the joint fundraising activity solely to satisfy outstanding debts, the notice shall also contain a statement informing contributors that the allocation formula may change if a participant receives sufficient funds to pay its outstanding debts.

(4) *Separate depository account.* (i) The participants or the fundraising representative shall establish a separate depository account to be used solely for the receipt and disbursement of the joint fundraising proceeds. All contributions deposited into the separate depository account must be permissible under Title 52, United States Code. Each political committee shall amend its Statement of Organization to reflect the account as an additional depository.

(ii) The fundraising representative shall deposit all joint fundraising proceeds in the separate depository account within ten days of receipt as required by 11 CFR 103.3. The fundraising representative may delay distribution of the fundraising proceeds to the participants until all contributions are received and all expenses are paid.

(iii) For contribution reporting and limitation purposes, the date of receipt of a contribution by a participating political committee is the date that the contribution is received by the fundraising representative. The fundraising representative shall report contributions in the reporting period in which they are received. Participating political committees shall report joint fundraising proceeds in accordance with 11 CFR 9034.8(c)(9) when such funds are received from the fundraising representative.

(5) *Recordkeeping requirements.* (i) The fundraising representative and participating committees shall screen all contributions received to insure that the prohibitions and limitations of 11 CFR parts 110 and 114 are observed. Participating political committees shall make their contributor records available to the fundraising representative to enable the fundraising representative to carry out its duty to screen contributions.

(ii) The fundraising representative shall collect and retain contributor information with regard to gross proceeds as required under 11 CFR 102.8 and shall also forward such information to participating political committees.

(iii) The fundraising representative shall retain the records required under 11 CFR 9033.11 regarding fundraising disbursements for a period of three years. Commercial fundraising firms or agents shall forward such information to the fundraising representative.

(6) *Contribution limitations.* Except to the extent that the contributor has previously contributed to any of the participants, a contributor may make a contribution to the joint fundraising effort which contribution represents the total amount that the contributor could contribute to all of the participants under the applicable limits of 11 CFR 110.1 and 110.2.

(7) *Allocation of gross proceeds.* (i) The fundraising representative shall allocate proceeds according to the formula stated in the fundraising agreement. Each contribution received shall be allocated among the participants in accordance with the allocation formula, unless the circumstances described in paragraphs (c)(7) (ii), (iii) or (iv) of this section apply. Funds may not be distributed or reallocated so as to maximize the matchability of the contributions.

(ii) If distribution according to the allocation formula extinguishes the debts of one or more participants or if distribution under the formula results in a violation of the contribution limits of 11 CFR 110.1(b), the fundraising representative may reallocate the surplus funds. The fundraising representative shall not reallocate funds so as to allow candidates seeking to extinguish outstanding debts to rely on the receipt of matching funds to pay the remainder of their debts; rather, all funds to which a participant is entitled under the allocation formula shall be deemed funds available to pay the candidate's outstanding campaign obligations as provided in 11 CFR 9034.5(c).

(iii) Reallocation shall be based upon the remaining participant's proportionate shares under the allocation formula. If reallocation results in a violation of a contributor's limit under 11 CFR 110.1, the fundraising representative shall return to the contributor the amount of the contribution that exceeds the limit.

(iv) Earmarked contributions which exceed the contributor's limit to the designated participant under 11 CFR part 110 may not be reallocated by the fundraising representative without the prior written permission of the contributor. A written instrument made payable to one of the participants shall be considered an earmarked contribution unless a written statement by the contributor indicates that it is intended for inclusion in the general proceeds of the fundraising activity.

(8) *Allocation of expenses and distribution of net proceeds.* (i) If participating committees are not affiliated as defined in 11 CFR 110.3 prior to the joint fundraising activity and are not committees of the same political party:

(A) After gross contributions are allocated among the participants under 11 CFR 9034.8(c)(7), the fundraising representative shall calculate each participant's share of expenses based on the percentage of the total receipts each participant had been allocated. To calculate each participant's net proceeds, the fundraising representative shall subtract the participant's share of expenses from the amount that participant has been allocated from gross proceeds.

(B) A participant may only pay expenses on behalf of another participant subject to the contribution limits of 11 CFR part 110. See also 11 CFR 9034.4(b)(6).

(C) The expenses from a series of fundraising events or activities shall be allocated among the participants on a per-event basis regardless of whether the participants change or remain the same throughout the series.

(ii) If participating committees are affiliated as defined in 11 CFR 110.3 prior to the joint fundraising activity or if participants are party committees of the same political party, expenses need not be allocated among those participants. Payment of such expenses by an unregistered committee or organization on behalf of an affiliated political committee may cause the unregistered organization to become a political committee.

(iii) Payment of expenses may be made from gross proceeds by the fundraising representative.

(9) *Reporting of receipts and disbursements*—(i) *Reporting receipts.* (A) The fundraising representative shall report all funds received in the reporting period in which they are received. Each Schedule A filed by the fundraising representative under this section shall clearly indicate that the contributions reported on that schedule represent joint fundraising proceeds.

(B) After distribution of net proceeds, each participating political committee shall report its share of net proceeds received as a transfer-in from the fundraising representative. Each participating political committee shall also file a memo Schedule A itemizing its share of gross receipts as contributions from original contributors to the extent required under 11 CFR 104.3(a).

(ii) *Reporting disbursements.* The fundraising representative shall report all disbursements in the reporting period in which they are made. Each participant shall report in a memo Schedule B his or her total allocated share of these disbursements in the same reporting period in which net proceeds are distributed and reported and include the amount on page 4 of Form 3–P, under "Expenditures Subject to Limit."

[56 FR 35934, July 29, 1991; 56 FR 42380, Aug. 27, 1991, as amended at 67 FR 49132, July 29, 2002; 79 FR 77851, Dec. 29, 2014]

§9034.9 **Sale of assets acquired for fundraising purposes.**

(a) *General.* A candidate may sell assets donated to the candidate's authorized committee(s) or otherwise acquired for fundraising purposes (See 11 CFR 9034.5(c)(2)), subject to the limitations and prohibitions of Title 52, United States Code and 11 CFR parts 110 and 114.

(b) *Sale after end of matching payment period.* A candidate whose outstanding debts exceed his or her cash on hand after the end of the matching payment period as determined under 11 CFR 9032.6 may dispose of assets acquired for fundraising purposes in a sale to a wholesaler or other intermediary who will in turn sell such assets to the public, provided that the sale to the wholesaler or intermediary is an arms-length transaction. Sales made under this subsection will not be subject to the limitations and prohibitions of Title 52, United States Code and 11 CFR parts 110 and 114.

[56 FR 34132, July 25, 1991 and 56 FR 35934, July 29, 1991, as amended at 79 FR 77851, Dec. 29, 2014]

§9034.10 **Pre-candidacy payments by multicandidate political committees deemed in-kind contributions and qualified campaign expenses; effect of reimbursement.**

(a) A payment by a multicandidate political committee is an in-kind contribution to, and qualified campaign expense by, a Presidential candidate, even though made before the individual becomes a candidate under 11 CFR 100.3 and 9032.2, if—

(1) The expenditure is made on or after January 1 of the year immediately following the last Presidential election year;

(2) With respect to the goods or services involved, the candidate accepted or received them, requested or suggested their provision, was materially involved in the decision to provide them, or was involved in substantial discussions about their provision; and

(3) The goods or services are—

(i) Polling expenses for determining the favorability, name recognition, or relative support level of the candidate involved;

(ii) Compensation paid to employees, consultants, or vendors for services rendered in connection with establishing and staffing offices in States where Presidential primaries, caucuses, or preference polls are to be held, other than offices in the candidate's home state and in or near the District of Columbia;

(iii) Administrative expenses, including rent, utilities, office supplies and equipment, in connection with establishing and staffing offices in States where Presidential primaries, caucuses, or preference polls are to be held, other than offices in the candidate's home state and in or near the District of Columbia; or

(iv) Expenses of individuals seeking to become delegates in the Presidential nomination process.

(b) Notwithstanding paragraph (a) of this section, if the candidate, through an authorized committee, reimburses the multicandidate political committee within 30 days of becoming a candidate, the payment shall not be deemed an in-kind contribution for either entity, and the reimbursement shall be an expenditure and a qualified campaign expense of the candidate.

[68 FR 47419, Aug. 8, 2003]

§ 9034.11   Winding down costs.

(a) *Winding down costs.* Winding down costs are costs associated with the termination of political activity related to a candidate's seeking his or her nomination for election, such as the costs of complying with the post election requirements of the Federal Election Campaign Act and the Presidential Primary Matching Payment Account Act, and other necessary administrative costs associated with winding down the campaign, including office space rental, staff salaries, and office supplies. Winding down costs are qualified campaign expenses.

(b) *Winding down limitation.* The total amount of winding down costs that may be paid for, in whole or part, with matching funds shall not exceed the lesser of:

(1) 10% of the overall expenditure limitation pursuant to 11 CFR 9035.1; or

(2) 10% of the total of:

(i) The candidate's expenditures subject to the overall expenditure limita-

tion as of the candidate's date of ineligibility; plus

(ii) The candidate's expenses exempt from the expenditure limitations as of the candidate's date of ineligibility; except that

(iii) The winding down limitation shall be no less than $100,000.

(c) *Allocation of primary and general election winding down costs.* A candidate who runs in both the primary and general election may divide winding down expenses between his or her primary and general election committees using any reasonable allocation method. An allocation method is reasonable if it divides the total winding down costs between the primary and general election committees and results in no less than one third of total winding down costs allocated to each committee. A candidate may demonstrate than an allocation method is reasonable even if either the primary or the general election committee is allocated less than one third of total winding down costs.

(d) *Primary winding down costs during the general election period.* A primary election candidate who does not run in the general election may receive and use matching funds for these purposes either after he or she has notified the Commission in writing of his or her withdrawal from the campaign for nomination or after the date of the party's nominating convention, if he or she has not withdrawn before the convention. A primary election candidate who runs in the general election, regardless of whether the candidate receives public funds for the general election, must wait until 31 days after the general election before using any matching funds for winding down costs related to the primary election. No expenses incurred by a primary election candidate who runs in the general election prior to 31 days after the general election shall be considered primary winding down costs.

[68 FR 47419, Aug. 8, 2003]

PART 9035—EXPENDITURE LIMITATIONS

Sec.

9035.2 Limitation on expenditures from personal or family funds.
9035.3 Contributions to and expenditures by Vice Presidential candidates.

AUTHORITY: 26 U.S.C. 9035 and 9039(b).

SOURCE: 56 FR 35491, July 29, 1991, unless otherwise noted.

§9035.1 Campaign expenditure limitation; compliance and fundraising exemptions.

(a) *Spending limit.* (1) No candidate or his or her authorized committee(s) shall knowingly incur expenditures in connection with the candidate's campaign for nomination, which expenditures, in the aggregate, exceed $10,000,000 (as adjusted under 52 U.S.C. 30116(c)), except that the aggregate expenditures by a candidate in any one State shall not exceed the greater of: 16 cents (as adjusted under 52 U.S.C. 30116(c)) multiplied by the voting age population of the State (as certified under 52 U.S.C. 30116(e)); or $200,000 (as adjusted under 52 U.S.C. 30116(c)).

(2) The Commission will calculate the amount of expenditures attributable to the overall expenditure limit or to a particular state using the full amounts originally charged for goods and services rendered to the committee and not the amounts for which such obligations were settled and paid, unless the committee can demonstrate that the lower amount paid reflects a reasonable settlement of a bona fide dispute with the creditor.

(3) In addition to expenditures made by a candidate or the candidate's authorized committee(s) using campaign funds, the Commission will attribute to the candidate's overall expenditure limitation and to the expenditure limitations of particular states under 11 CFR 110.8 the total amount of all:

(i) Coordinated expenditures under 11 CFR 109.20;

(ii) Coordinated communications under 11 CFR 109.21 that are in-kind contributions received or accepted by the candidate, the candidate's authorized committee(s), or agents, under 11 CFR 109.21(b);

(iii) Coordinated party expenditures, including party coordinated communications pursuant to 11 CFR 109.37 that are in-kind contributions received or accepted by the candidate, the candidate's authorized committee(s), or agents under 11 CFR 109.37(a)(3), and that exceed the coordinated party expenditure limitation for the Presidential general election at 11 CFR 109.32(a); and

(iv) Other in-kind contributions received or accepted by the candidate or the candidate's authorized committee(s) or agents.

(4) The amount of each in-kind contribution attributed to the expenditure limitations under this section is the usual and normal charge for the goods or services provided to the candidate or the candidate's authorized committee(s) as an in-kind contribution.

(b) *Allocation of expenditures.* Each candidate receiving or expecting to receive matching funds under this subchapter shall also allocate his or her expenditures in accordance with the provisions of 11 CFR 106.2.

(c) *Compliance, fundraising and shortfall bridge loan exemptions.* (1) A candidate may exclude from the overall expenditure limitation set forth in paragraph (a) of this section an amount equal to 15% of the overall expenditure limitation as exempt legal and accounting compliance costs under 11 CFR 100.146. In the case of a candidate who does not run in the general election, for purposes of the expenditure limitations set forth in this section, 100% of salary, overhead and computer expenses incurred after a candidate's date of ineligibility may be treated as exempt legal and accounting compliance expenses beginning with the first full reporting period after the candidate's date of ineligibility. Candidates who continue to campaign or re-establish eligibility may not treat 100% of salary, overhead and computer expenses incurred during the period between the date of ineligibility and the date on which the candidate either re-establishes eligibility or ceases to continue to campaign as exempt legal and accounting compliance expenses. For purposes of the expenditure limitations set forth in this section, candidates who run in the general election, regardless of whether they receive public funds, must wait until 31 days after the general election before they may treat 100% of salary, overhead and computer expenses as exempt legal and accounting compliance expenses.

(2) A candidate may exclude from the overall expenditure limitation of 11 CFR 9035.1 the amount of exempt fundraising costs specified in 11 CFR 100.152(c).

(3) If any matching funds to which the candidate is entitled are not paid to the candidate, or are paid after the date on which payment is due, the candidate may exclude from the overall expenditure limitation in paragraph (a) of this section the amount of all interest charges that accrued during the shortfall period on all loans obtained by the candidate or authorized committee that are guaranteed or secured with matching funds, provided the candidate submits documentation as to the amount of all interest charges on such loans. The shortfall period begins on the first regularly scheduled payment date on which the candidate does not receive the entire amount of matching funds and ends on the payment date when the candidate receives the previously certified matching funds or the date on which the Commission revises the amount previously certified to eliminate the entitlement to the previously certified matching funds.

(d) *Candidates not receiving matching funds.* The expenditure limitations of 11 CFR 9035.1 shall not apply to a candidate who does not receive matching funds at any time during the matching payment period.

[64 FR 49364, Sept. 13, 1999, as amended at 67 FR 78683, Dec. 26, 2002; 68 FR 47420, Aug. 8, 2003; 79 FR 77851, Dec. 29, 2014]

§ 9035.2 Limitation on expenditures from personal or family funds.

(a)(1) No candidate who has accepted matching funds shall knowingly make expenditures from his or her personal funds, or funds of his or her immediate family, in connection with his or her campaign for nomination for election to the office of President which exceed $50,000, in the aggregate. This section shall not operate to prohibit any member of the candidate's immediate family from contributing his or her personal funds to the candidate, subject to the limitations of 11 CFR part 110. The provisions of this section also shall not limit the candidate's liability for, nor

the candidate's ability to pay, any repayments required under 11 CFR part 9038. If the candidate or his or her committee knowingly incurs expenditures in excess of the limitations of 11 CFR 110.8(a), the Commission may seek civil penalties under 11 CFR part 111 in addition to any repayment determinations made on the basis of such excessive expenditures.

(2) Expenditures made using a credit card for which the candidate is jointly or solely liable will count against the limits of this section to the extent that the full amount due, including any finance charge, is not paid by the committee within 60 days after the closing date of the billing statement on which the charges first appear. For purposes of this section, the *closing date* shall be the date indicated on the billing statement which serves as the cutoff date for determining which charges are included on that billing statement.

(b) For purposes of this section, the term *immediate family* means a candidate, spouse, and any child, parent, grandparent, brother, half-brother, sister, or half-sister of the candidate, and the spouses of such persons.

(c) For purposes of this section, *personal funds* has the same meaning as specified in 11 CFR 9003.2.

[56 FR 35491, July 29, 1991, as amended at 68 FR 4002, Jan. 27, 2003]

§ 9035.3 Contributions to and expenditures by Vice Presidential candidates.

(a) *Aggregation of contributions and expenditures.* For purposes of the limitations on contributions and expenditures of this part and part 110, contributions to, and expenditures by, the authorized committee of a candidate who becomes the nominee of a political party for the office of Vice President of the United States shall be aggregated with contributions to and expenditures by the publicly funded primary candidate who obtains that political party's nomination for the office of President of the United States, provided that the contributions to or expenditures by the authorized committee of the Vice Presidential candidate were made on or after the date on which—

(1) The Presidential or Vice Presidential candidate publicly indicates

that the two candidates intend to run on the same ticket;

(2) The candidate for the office of Vice President accepts an offer by the publicly funded primary candidate for the office of President, or by the Presidential candidate's agent(s), to run on the same ticket; or

(3) The Presidential and Vice Presidential committees become affiliated pursuant to 11 CFR 100.5(g)(4)(i) or (ii).

(b) *Exceptions.* The following expenditures, if incurred by the authorized committee of a candidate who subsequently becomes the nominee of a political party for the office of Vice President of the United States, will not be aggregated under paragraph (a) of this section:

(1) The cost of attendance by the candidate, the candidate's family, and the candidate's authorized committee's staff at a political party's national nominating convention, including the cost of transportation, lodging, and subsistence;

(2) The cost of legal and accounting services associated with background checks during the Vice Presidential selection process; and

(3) The cost of raising funds for the expenses listed in paragraphs (b)(1) and (b)(2) of this section.

[64 FR 61781, Nov. 15, 1999]

PART 9036—REVIEW OF MATCHING FUND SUBMISSIONS AND CERTIFICATION OF PAYMENTS BY COMMISSION

Sec.
9036.1   Threshold submission.
9036.2   Additional submissions for matching fund payments.
9036.3   Submission errors and insufficient documentation.
9036.4   Commission review of submissions.
9036.5   Resubmissions.
9036.6   Continuation of certification.

AUTHORITY: 26 U.S.C. 9036 and 9039(b).

SOURCE: 56 FR 34132, July 25, 1991; 56 FR 35941, July 29, 1991, unless otherwise noted.

§9036.1   Threshold submission.

(a) *Time for submission of threshold submission.* At any time after January 1 of the year immediately preceding the Presidential election year, the candidate may submit a threshold submission for matching fund payments in accordance with the format for such submissions set forth in 11 CFR 9036.1(b). The candidate may submit the threshold submission simultaneously with or subsequent to his or her submission of the candidate agreement and certifications required by 11 CFR 9033.1 and 9033.2.

(b) *Format for threshold submission.* (1) For each State in which the candidate certifies that he or she has met the requirements of the certifications in 11 CFR 9033.2(b), the candidate shall submit an alphabetical list of contributors showing:

(i) Each contributor's full name and residential address;

(ii) The occupation and name of employer for individuals whose aggregate contributions exceed $200 in an election cycle;

(iii) The date of deposit of each contribution into the designated campaign depository;

(iv) The full dollar amount of each contribution submitted for matching purposes;

(v) The matchable portion of each contribution submitted for matching purposes;

(vi) The aggregate amount of all matchable contributions from that contributor submitted for matching purposes;

(vii) A notation indicating which contributions were received as a result of joint fundraising activities.

(2) For each list of contributors generated directly or indirectly from computerized files or computerized records, the candidate shall submit computerized magnetic media, such as magnetic tapes or magnetic diskettes, containing the information required by 11 CFR 9036.1(b)(1) in accordance with 11 CFR 9033.12.

(3) The candidate shall submit a full-size photocopy of each check or written instrument and of supporting documentation in accordance with 11 CFR 9034.2 for each contribution that the candidate submits to establish eligibility for matching funds. For purposes of the threshold submission, the photocopies shall be segregated alphabetically by contributor within each State,

and shall be accompanied by and referenced to copies of the relevant deposit slips. In lieu of submitting photocopies, the candidate may submit digital images of checks and other materials in accordance with the procedures specified in 11 CFR 9036.2(b)(1)(vi). Digital images of contributions do not need to be segregated alphabetically by contributor within each State.

(4) The candidate shall submit bank documentation, such as bank-validated deposit slips or unvalidated deposit slips accompanied by the relevant bank statements, which indicate that the contributions submitted were deposited into a designated campaign depository.

(5) For each State in which the candidate certifies that he or she has met the requirements to establish eligibility, the candidate shall submit a listing, alphabetically by contributor, of all checks returned by the bank to date as unpaid (e.g., stop payments, non-sufficient funds) regardless of whether the contribution was submitted for matching. This listing shall be accompanied by a full-size photocopy of each unpaid check, and copies of the associated debit memo and bank statement.

(6) For each State in which the candidate certifies that he or she has met the requirements to establish eligibility, the candidate shall submit a listing, in alphabetical order by contributor, of all contributions that were refunded to the contributor, regardless of whether the contributions were submitted for matching. For each refunded contribution, the listing shall state the contributor's full name and address, the deposit date and batch number, an indication of which matching fund submission the contribution was included in, if any, and the amount and date of the refund. The listing shall be accompanied by a full-sized photocopy of each refunded contributor check.

(7) In the case of a contribution made by a credit or debit card, including one made over the Internet, the candidate shall provide sufficient documentation to the Commission to insure that each such contribution was made by a lawful contributor who manifested an intention to make the contribution to the candidate or authorized committee that submits it for matching fund payments. Additional information on the documentation required to accompany such contributions is found in the Commission's Guideline for Presentation in Good Order. See 11 CFR 9033.1(b)(9).

(8) The candidate shall submit all contributions in accordance with the Federal Election Commission's Guideline for Presentation in Good Order.

(9) Contributions that are not submitted in compliance with this section shall not count toward the threshold amount.

(c) *Threshold certification by Commission.* (1) After the Commission has determined under 11 CFR 9033.4 that the candidate has satisfied the eligibility and certification requirements of 11 CFR 9033.1 and 9033.2, the Commission will notify the candidate in writing that the candidate is eligible to receive primary matching fund payments as provided in 11 CFR part 9034.

(2) If the Commission makes a determination of a candidate's eligibility under 11 CFR 9036.1(a) in a Presidential election year, the Commission shall certify to the Secretary, within 10 calendar days after the Commission has made its determination, the amount to which the candidate is entitled.

(3) If the Commission makes a determination of a candidate's eligibility under 11 CFR 9036.1(a) in the year preceding the Presidential election year, the Commission will notify the candidate that he or she is eligible to receive matching fund payments; however, the Commission's determination will not result in a payment of funds to the candidate until after January 1 of the Presidential election year.

[56 FR 34132, July 25, 1991, as amended at 56 FR 35941, July 29, 1991; 64 FR 42585, Aug. 5, 1999; 64 FR 49365, Sept. 13, 1999; 68 FR 47420, Aug. 8, 2003]

§ 9036.2 Additional submissions for matching fund payments.

(a) *Time for submission of additional submissions.* The candidate may submit additional submissions for payments to the Commission on dates to be determined and published by the Commission. On the last two submission dates in the year prior to the election year and on each submission date after the beginning of the matching payment period, the candidate may not make more than one additional submission, and either one resubmission under 11 CFR 9036.5 or one corrected submission under 11 CFR 9036.2(c) or (d)(2), as appropriate.

(b) *Format for additional submissions.* The candidate may obtain additional matching fund payments subsequent to the Commission's threshold certification and payment of primary matching funds to the candidate by filing an additional submission for payment. All additional submissions for payments filed by the candidate shall be made in accordance with the Federal Election Commission's Guideline for Presentation in Good Order.

(1) The first submission for matching funds following the candidate's threshold submission shall contain all the matchable contributions included in the threshold submission and any additional contributions to be submitted for matching in that submission. This submission shall contain all the information required for the threshold submission except that:

(i) The candidate is not required to resubmit the candidate agreement and certifications of 11 CFR 9033.1 and 9033.2;

(ii) The candidate is required to submit an alphabetical list of contributors (either solely in magnetic media from or in both printed and magnetic media forms), but not segregated by State as required in the threshold submission;

(iii) The candidate is required to submit a listing, alphabetical by contributor, of all checks returned unpaid, but not segregated by State as required in the threshold submission;

(iv) The candidate is required to submit a listing, in alphabetical order by contributor, of all contributions refunded to the contributor but not segregated by State as required in the threshold submission.

(v) The occupation and employer's name need not be disclosed on the contributor list for individuals whose aggregate contributions exceed $200 in the election cycle, but such information is subject to the recordkeeping and reporting requirements of 52 U.S.C. 30102(c)(3), 30104(b)(3)(A) and 11 CFR 102.9(a)(2), 104.3(a)(4)(i); and

(vi) The photocopies of each check or written instrument and of supporting documentation shall either be alphabetized and referenced to copies of the relevant deposit slip, but not segregated by State as required in the threshold submission; or such photocopies may be batched in deposits of 50 contributions or less and cross-referenced by deposit number and sequence number within each deposit on the contributor list. In lieu of submitting photocopies, the candidate may submit digital images of checks, written instruments and deposit slips as specified in the Computerized Magnetic Media Requirements. The candidate may also submit digital images of contributor redesignations, reattributions and supporting statements and materials needed to verify the matchability of contributions. The candidate shall provide the computer equipment and software needed to retrieve and read the digital images, if necessary, at no cost to the Commission, and shall include digital images of every contribution received and imaged on or after the date of the previous matching fund request. Contributions and other documentation not imaged shall be submitted in photocopy form. The candidate shall maintain the originals of all contributor redesignations, reattributions and supporting statements and materials that are submitted for matching as digital images.

(vii) In the case of a contribution made by a credit or debit card, including one made over the Internet, the candidate shall provide sufficient documentation to the Commission to insure that each such contribution was made by a lawful contributor who manifested an intention to make the contribution to the candidate or authorized committee that submits it for matching fund payments. Additional information on the documentation required to accompany such contributions is found in the Commission's Guideline for Presentation in Good Order. *See* 11 CFR 9033.1(b)(9).

(2) Following the first submission under 11 CFR 9036.2(b)(1), candidates may request additional matching funds on dates prescribed by the Commission by making a full submission as required under 11 CFR 9036.2(b)(1). The amount requested for matching may include contributions received up to

347

the last business day preceding the date of the request.

(c) *Additional submissions submitted in non-Presidential election year.* The candidate may submit additional contributions for review during the year preceding the presidential election year; however, the amount of each submission made during this period must exceed $50,000. Additional submissions filed by a candidate in a non-Presidential election year will not result in payment of matching funds to the candidate until after January 1 of the Presidential election year. If the projected dollar value of the nonmatchable contributions exceeds 15% of the amount requested, the procedures described in 11 CFR 9036.2(d)(2) shall apply, unless the submission was made on the last submission date in December of the year before the Presidential election year.

(d) *Certification of additional payments by Commission.* (1) When a candidate who is eligible under 11 CFR 9033.4 submits an additional submission for payment in the Presidential election year, and before the candidate's date of ineligibility, the Commission will review the additional submission and will certify to the Secretary at least once a month on dates to be determined and published by the Commission, an amount to which the candidate is entitled in accordance with 11 CFR 9034.1(b). See 11 CFR 9036.4 for Commission procedures for certification of additional payments.

(2) After a candidate's date of ineligibility, the Commission will review each additional submission and resubmission, and will certify to the Secretary, at least once a month on dates to be determined and published by the Commission, an amount to which the ineligible candidate is entitled in accordance with 11 CFR 9034.1(b), unless the projected dollar value of the nonmatchable contributions contained in the submission or resubmission exceeds 15% of the amount requested. In the latter case, the Commission will return the additional submission or resubmission to the candidate and request that it be corrected, unless the resubmission was made on the last date for resubmissions in September of the year following the Presidential election

year. Corrected submissions and resubmissions will be reviewed by the Commission in accordance with 11 CFR 9036.4 and 9036.5. Submissions and resubmissions will not be considered to be corrected unless the projected dollar value of nonmatchable contributions has been reduced to no more than 15% of the amount requested.

[56 FR 34132, July 25, 1991; 56 FR 41891, Aug. 23, 1991; 60 FR 31885, June 16, 1995; 64 FR 42585, Aug. 5, 1999; 64 FR 49365, Sept. 13, 1999; 68 FR 47420, Aug. 8, 2003; 79 FR 77852, Dec. 29, 2014]

§ 9036.3 Submission errors and insufficient documentation.

Contributions which are otherwise matchable may be rejected for matching purposes because of submission errors or insufficient supporting documentation. Contributions, other than those defined in 11 CFR 9034.3 or in the form of money orders, cashier's checks, or similar negotiable instruments, may become matchable if there is a proper resubmission in accordance with 11 CFR 9036.5 and 9036.6. Insufficient documentation or submission errors include but are not limited to:

(a) Discrepancies in the written instrument, such as:

(1) Instruments drawn on other than personal accounts of contributors and not signed by the contributing individual;

(2) Signature discrepancies; and

(3) Lack of the contributor's signature, the amount or date of the contribution, or the listing of the committee or candidate as payee.

(b) Discrepancies between listed contributions and the written instrument or supporting documentation, such as:

(1) The listed amount requested for matching exceeds the amount contained on the written instrument;

(2) A written instrument has not been submitted to support a listed contribution;

(3) The submitted written instrument cannot be associated either by accountholder identification or signature with the listed contributor; or

(4) A discrepancy between the listed contribution and the supporting bank documentation or the bank documentation is omitted.

(c) Discrepancies within or between contributor lists submitted, such as:

(1) The address of the contributor is omitted or incomplete or the contributor's name is alphabetized incorrectly, or more than one contributor is listed per item;

(2) A discrepancy in aggregation within or between submissions which results in a request that more than $250 be matched for that contributor, or a listing of a contributor more than once within the same submission; or

(3) A written instrument has been previously submitted and matched in full or is listed twice in the same submission.

(d) The omission of information, supporting statements, or documentation required by 11 CFR 9034.2.

§9036.4 Commission review of submissions.

(a) *Non-acceptance of submission for review of matchability.* (1) The Commission will make an initial review of each submission made under 11 CFR part 9036 to determine if it substantially meets the format requirements of 11 CFR 9036.1(b) and 9036.2(b) and the Federal Election Commission's Guideline for Presentation in Good Order. If the Commission determines that a submission does not substantially meet these requirements, it will not review the matchability of the contributions contained therein.

(2) For submissions made in the year before the Presidential election year (other than submissions made on the last submission date in that year), and submissions made after the candidate's date of ineligibility, the Commission will stop reviewing the submission once the projected dollar value of nonmatchable contributions exceeds 15% of the amount requested, as provided in 11 CFR 9036.2 (c) or (d), as applicable.

(3) Under either paragraphs (a)(1) or (a)(2) of this section, the Commission will return the submission to the candidate and request that it be corrected in accordance with the applicable requirements. If the candidate makes a corrected submission within 5 business days after the Commission's return of the original, the Commission will review the corrected submission prior to the next regularly scheduled submission date, and will certify to the Secretary the amount to which the candidate is entitled on the regularly scheduled certification date for the original submission. Corrected submissions made after this five-day period will be reviewed subsequent to the next regularly scheduled submission date, and the Commission will certify to the Secretary the amount to which the candidate is entitled on the next regularly scheduled certification date. Each corrected submission shall only contain contributions previously submitted for matching in the returned submission and no new or additional contributions.

(b) *Acceptance of submission for review of matchability.* If the Commission determines that a submission made under 11 CFR part 9036 satisfies the requirements of 11 CFR 9036.1(b) and 9036.2 (b), (c) and (d), and the Federal Election Commission's Guideline for Presentation in Good Order, it will review the matchability of the contributions contained therein. The Commission, in conducting its review, may utilize statistical sampling techniques. Based on the results of its review, the Commission may calculate a matchable amount for the submission which is less than the amount requested by the candidate. If the Commission certifies for payment to the Secretary an amount that is less than the amount requested by the candidate in a particular submission, or reduces the amount of a subsequent certification to the Secretary by adjusting a previous certification made under 11 CFR 9036.2(c)(1), the Commission will notify the candidate in writing of the following:

(1) The amount of the difference between the amount requested and the amount to be certified by the Commission;

(2) The amount of each contribution and the corresponding contributor's name for each contribution that the Commission has rejected as nonmatchable and the reason that it is not matchable; or if statistical sampling is used, the estimated amount of contributions by type and the reason for rejection;

(3) The amount of contributions that have been determined to be matchable

and that the Commission will certify to the Secretary for payment; and

(4) A statement that the candidate may supply the Commission with additional documentation or other information in the resubmission of any rejected contribution under 11 CFR 9036.5 in order to show that a rejected contribution is matchable under 11 CFR 9034.2.

(c) *Adjustment of amount to be certified by Commission.* (1) The candidate shall notify the Commission as soon as possible if the candidate or the candidate's authorized committee(s) has knowledge that a contribution submitted for matching does not qualify under 11 CFR 9034.2 as a matchable contribution, such as a check returned to the committee for insufficient funds or a contribution that has been refunded, so that the Commission may properly adjust the amount to be certified for payment.

(2) After the candidate's date of ineligibility, if the candidate does not receive the entire amount of matching funds on a regularly scheduled payment date due to a shortfall in the matching payment account, prior to each subsequent payment date on which the candidate receives payments from any previous certification, the Commission may revise the amount previously certified for payment pursuant to 11 CFR 9034.5(f). The Commission will promptly notify the Secretary and the candidate of any revision to the amount certified.

(d) *Commission audit of submissions.* The Commission may determine, for the reasons stated in 11 CFR part 9039, that an audit and examination of contributions submitted for matching payment is warranted. The audit and examination shall be conducted in accordance with the procedures of 11 CFR part 9039.

[56 FR 34133, July 25, 1991]

§ 9036.5   Resubmissions.

(a) *Alternative resubmission methods.* Upon receipt of the Commission's notice of the results of the submission review pursuant to 11 CFR 9036.4(b), or of an inquiry pursuant to 11 CFR 9039.3 that results in a downward adjustment to the amount of certified matching funds, a candidate may choose to:

(1) Resubmit the entire submission; or

(2) Make a written request for the identification of the specific contributions that were rejected for matching, and resubmit those specific contributions.

(b) *Time for presentation of resubmissions.* If the candidate chooses to resubmit any contributions under 11 CFR 9036.5(a), the contributions shall be resubmitted on dates to be determined and published by the Commission. The candidate may not make any resubmissions later than the first Tuesday in September of the year following the Presidential election year.

(c) *Format for resubmissions.* All resubmissions filed by the candidate shall be made in accordance with the Federal Election Commission's Guideline for Presentation in Good Order. In making a presentation of resubmitted contributions, the candidate shall follow the format requirements as specified in 11 CFR 9036.2(b)(1), except that:

(1) The candidate need not provide photocopies of written instruments, supporting documentation and bank documentation unless it is necessary to supplement the original documentation.

(2) Each resubmitted contribution shall be referenced to the submission in which it was first presented.

(3) Each list of resubmitted contributions shall reflect the aggregate amount of contributions submitted for matching from each contributor as of the date of the original submission.

(4) Each list of resubmitted contributions shall reflect the aggregate amount of contributions submitted for matching from each contributor as of the date of the resubmission.

(5) Each list of resubmitted contributions shall only contain contributions previously submitted for matching and no new or additional contributions.

(6) Each resubmission shall be accompanied by a statement that the candidate has corrected his or her contributor records (including the data base for those candidates maintaining their contributor list on computer).

(d) *Certification of resubmitted contributions.* Contributions that the Commission determines to be matchable will be certified to the Secretary at least once a month on dates to be determined and published by the Commission. If the candidate chooses to request the specific contributions rejected for matching pursuant to 11 CFR 9036.5(a)(2), the amount certified shall equal only the matchable amount of the particular contribution that meets the standards on resubmission, rather than the amount projected as being nonmatchable based on that contribution due to the sampling techniques used in reviewing the original submission.

(e) *Initial determinations.* If the candidate resubmits a contribution for matching and the Commission determines that the rejected contribution is still non-matchable, the Commission will notify the candidate in writing of its determination. The Commission will advise the candidate of the legal and factual reasons for its determination and of the evidence on which that determination is based. The candidate may submit written legal or factual materials to demonstrate that the contribution is matchable within 30 calendar days after service of the Commission's notice. Such materials may be submitted by counsel if the candidate so desires.

(f) *Final determinations.* The Commission will consider any written legal or factual materials timely submitted by the candidate in making its final determination. A final determination by the Commission that a contribution is not matchable will be accompanied by a written statement of reasons for the Commission's action. This statement will explain the reasons underlying the Commission's determination and will summarize the results of any investigation upon which the determination is based.

[56 FR 34134, July 25, 1991 and 56 FR 35941, July 29, 1991; 60 FR 31885, June 16, 1995]

§9036.6 Continuation of certification.

Candidates who have received matching funds and who are eligible to continue to receive such funds may continue to submit additional submissions for payment to the Commission on dates specified in the Federal Election Commission's Guideline for Presentation in Good Order. The last date for first-time submissions will be the first Monday in March of the year following the election. No contribution will be matched if it is submitted after the last submission date, regardless of the date the contribution was deposited.

[56 FR 34134, July 25, 1991]

PART 9037—PAYMENTS AND REPORTING

Sec.
9037.1 Payments of Presidential primary matching funds.
9037.2 Equitable distribution of funds.
9037.3 Deposits of Presidential primary matching funds.
9037.4 Alphabetized schedules.

AUTHORITY: 26 U.S.C. 9037 and 9039(b).

§9037.1 Payments of Presidential primary matching funds.

Upon receipt of a written certification from the Commission, but not before the beginning of the matching payment period, the Secretary will promptly transfer the amount certified from the matching payment account to the candidate. A matching fund certification may not result in full payment by the Secretary in the case of a shortfall in the matching payment account. See 26 CFR 702.9037–1 and 702.9037–2.

[56 FR 34134, July 25, 1991]

§9037.2 Equitable distribution of funds.

In making such transfers to candidates of the same political party, the Secretary will seek to achieve an equitable distribution of funds available in the matching payment account, and the Secretary will take into account, in seeking to achieve an equitable distribution of funds available in the matching payment account, the sequence in which such certifications are received. See 26 CFR 702.9037–2(c) regarding partial payments to candidates in the case of a shortfall in the matching payment account.

[56 FR 34134, July 25, 1991]

§9037.3 Deposits of Presidential primary matching funds.

Upon receipt of any matching funds, the candidate shall deposit the full amount received into a checking account maintained by the candidate's principal campaign committee in the depository designated by the candidate. The account(s) shall be maintained at a State bank, federally chartered depository institution or other depository institution, the deposits of which are insured by the Federal Deposit Insurance Corporation.

[56 FR 35944, July 29, 1991]

§ 9037.4 Alphabetized schedules.

If the authorized committee(s) of a candidate file a schedule of itemized receipts, disbursements, or debts and obligations pursuant to 11 CFR 104.3 that was generated directly or indirectly from computerized files or records, the schedule shall list in alphabetical order the sources of the receipts, the payees or the creditors, as appropriate. In the case of individuals, such schedule shall list all contributors, payees, and creditors in alphabetical order by surname.

[60 FR 31885, June 16, 1995]

PART 9038—EXAMINATIONS AND AUDITS

Sec.
9038.1 Audit.
9038.2 Repayments.
9038.3 Liquidation of obligations; repayment.
9038.4 Extensions of time.
9038.5 Petitions for rehearing; stays of repayment determinations.
9038.6 Stale-dated committee checks.
9038.7 Administrative record.

AUTHORITY: 26 U.S.C. 9038 and 9039(b).

SOURCE: 56 FR 35945, July 29, 1991, unless otherwise noted.

§ 9038.1 Audit.

(a) *General.* (1) The Commission will conduct an audit of the qualified campaign expenses of every candidate and his or her authorized committee(s) who received Presidential primary matching funds. The audit may be conducted at any time after the date of the candidate's ineligibility.

(2) In addition, the Commission may conduct other examinations and audits from time to time as it deems necessary to carry out the provisions of this subchapter.

(3) Information obtained pursuant to any audit and examination conducted under 11 CFR 9038.1(a) (1) and (2) may be used by the Commission as the basis, or partial basis, for its repayment determinations under 11 CFR 9038.2.

(b) *Conduct of fieldwork.* (1) If the candidate or the candidate's authorized committee does not maintain or use any computerized information containing the data listed in 11 CFR 9033.12, the Commission will give the candidate's authorized committee at least two weeks' notice of the Commission's intention to commence fieldwork on the audit and examination. The fieldwork shall be conducted at a site provided by the committee. If the candidate or the candidate's authorized committee maintains or uses computerized information containing any of the data listed in 11 CFR 9033.12, the Commission generally will request such information prior to commencement of audit fieldwork. Such request will be made in writing. The committee shall produce the computerized information no later than 15 calendar days after service of such request. Upon receipt of the computerized information requested and compliance with the technical specifications of 11 CFR 9033.12(b), the Commission will give the candidate's authorized committee at least two weeks' notice of the Commission's intention to commence fieldwork on the audit and examination. The fieldwork shall be conducted at a site provided by the committee. During or after audit fieldwork, the Commission may request additional or updated computerized information which expands the coverage dates of computerized information previously provided, and which may be used for purposes including, but not limited to, updating a statement of net outstanding campaign obligations, or updating the amount chargeable to a state expenditure limit. During or after audit fieldwork, the Commission may also request additional computerized information which was created by or becomes available to the committee and that is of assistance in the Commission's audit. The committee shall produce the additional or updated computerized information no later than 15 calendar days after service of the Commission's request.

(i) *Office space and records.* On the date scheduled for the commencement of fieldwork, the candidate or his or her authorized committee(s) shall provide Commission staff with office space and committee records in accordance with the candidate and committee agreement under 11 CFR 9033.1(b)(6).

(ii) *Availability of committee personnel.* On the date scheduled for the commencement of fieldwork, the candidate or his or her authorized committee(s) shall have committee personnel present at the site of the fieldwork. Such personnel shall be familiar with the committee's records and operation and shall be available to Commission staff to answer questions and to aid in locating records.

(iii) *Failure to provide staff, records or office space.* If the candidate or his or her authorized committee(s) fail to provide adequate office space, personnel or committee records, the Commission may seek judicial intervention under 52 U.S.C. 30107 or 26 U.S.C. 9040(c) to enforce the candidate and committee agreement made under 11 CFR 9033.1(b). Before seeking judicial intervention, the Commission will notify the candidate of his or her failure to comply with the agreement and will recommend corrective action to bring the candidate into compliance. Upon receipt of the Commission's notification, the candidate will have 10 calendar days in which to take the corrective action indicated or to otherwise demonstrate to the Commission in writing that he or she is complying with the candidate and committee agreement.

(iv) If, in the course of the audit process, a dispute arises over the documentation sought or other requirements of the candidate agreement, the candidate may seek review by the Commission of the issues raised. To seek review, the candidate shall submit a written statement, within 10 calendar days after the disputed Commission staff request is made, describing the dispute and indicating the candidate's proposed alternative(s).

(v) If the candidate or his or her authorized committee fails to produce particular records, materials, evidence or other information requested by the Commission, the Commission may issue an order pursuant to 52 U.S.C. 30107(a)(1) or a subpoena or subpoena duces tecum pursuant to 52 U.S.C. 30107(a)(3). The procedures set forth in 11 CFR 111.11 through 111.15, as appropriate, shall apply to the production of such records, materials, evidence or other information as specified in the order, subpoena or subpoena duces tecum.

(2) Fieldwork will include the following steps designed to keep the candidate and committee informed as to the progress of the audit and to expedite the process:

(i) *Entrance conference.* At the outset of the fieldwork, Commission staff will hold an entrance conference, at which the candidate's representatives will be advised of the purpose of the audit and the general procedures to be followed. Future requirements of the candidate and his or her authorized committee, such as possible repayments to the United States Treasury, will also be discussed. Committee representatives shall provide information and records necessary to conduct the audit, and Commission staff will be available to answer committee questions.

(ii) *Review of records.* During the fieldwork, Commission staff will review committee records and may conduct interviews of committee personnel. Commission staff will be available to explain aspects of the audit and examination as it progresses. Additional meetings between Commission staff and committee personnel may be held from time to time during the fieldwork to discuss possible audit findings and to resolve issues arising during the course of the audit.

(iii) *Exit conference.* At the conclusion of the fieldwork, Commission staff will hold an exit conference to discuss with committee representatives the staff's preliminary findings and recommendations that the staff anticipates it will present to the Commission for approval. Commission staff will advise committee representatives at this conference of the committee's opportunity to respond to these preliminary findings; the projected timetables regarding the issuance of the Preliminary Audit Report, the Audit Report, and any repayment determination; the committee's opportunity for an administrative review of any repayment determination; and the procedures involved in Commission repayment determinations under 11 CFR 9038.2.

(3) Commission staff may conduct additional fieldwork after the completion of the fieldwork conducted pursuant to 11 CFR 9038.1(b) (1) and (2). Factors that may necessitate such follow-up fieldwork include, but are not limited to, the following:

(i) Committee responses to audit findings;

(ii) Financial activity of the committee subsequent to the fieldwork conducted pursuant to 11 CFR 9038.1(b)(1);

(iii) Committee responses to Commission repayment determinations made under 11 CFR 9038.2.

(4) The Commission will notify the candidate and his or her authorized committee if follow-up fieldwork is necessary. The provisions of 11 CFR 9038.1(b) (1) and (2) shall apply to any additional fieldwork conducted.

(c) *Preliminary Audit Report: Issuance by Commission and committee response.* (1) Commission staff will prepare a written Preliminary Audit Report, which will be provided to the committee after it is approved by an affirmative vote of four (4) members of the Commission. The Preliminary Audit Report may include—

(i) An evaluation of procedures and systems employed by the candidate and committee to comply with applicable provisions of the Federal Election Campaign Act, the Presidential Election Campaign Fund Act and Commission regulations;

(ii) The accuracy of statements and reports filed with the Commission by the candidate and committee; and

(iii) Preliminary calculations regarding future repayments to the United States Treasury.

(2) The candidate and his or her authorized committee may submit in writing within 60 calendar days after receipt of the Preliminary Audit Report, legal and factual materials disputing or commenting on the proposed findings contained in the Preliminary Audit Report. In addition, the committee shall submit any additional documentation requested by the Commission. Such materials may be submitted by counsel if the candidate so desires.

(d) *Approval and issuance of audit report.* (1) Before voting on whether to issue and approve an audit report, the Commission will consider any written legal and factual materials timely submitted by the candidate or his or her authorized committee in accordance with paragraph (c) of this section. The Commission-approved audit report may address issues other than those contained in the Preliminary Audit Report. In addition, this report will contain a repayment determination made by the Commission pursuant to 11 CFR 9038.2(c)(1).

(2) The audit report may contain issues that warrant referral to the Office of General Counsel for possible enforcement proceedings under 52 U.S.C. 30109 and 11 CFR part 111.

(3) Addenda to the audit report may be approved and issued by the Commission from time to time as circumstances warrant and as additional information becomes available. Such addenda may be based on follow-up fieldwork conducted under paragraph (b)(3) of this section, and/or information ascertained by the Commission in the normal course of carrying out its supervisory responsibilities. The procedures set forth in paragraphs (c) and (d) (1) and (2) of this section will be followed in preparing such addenda. The addenda will be placed on the public record as set forth in paragraph (e) of this section. Such addenda may also include additional repayment determination(s).

(e) *Public release of audit report.* (1) The Commission will consider the audit report in an open session agenda document. The Commission will provide the candidate and the committee with copies of any agenda document to be considered in an open session 24 hours prior to releasing the agenda document to the public.

(2) Following Commission approval of the audit report, the report will be forwarded to the committee and released to the public. The Commission will provide the candidate and committee

with copies of the audit report approved by the Commission 24 hours before releasing the report to the public.

(f)(1) *Sampling.* In conducting an audit of contributions pursuant to this section, the Commission may utilize generally accepted statistical sampling techniques to quantify, in whole or in part, the dollar value of related audit findings. A projection of the total amount of violations based on apparent violations identified in such a sample may become the basis, in whole or in part, of any audit finding.

(2) A committee in responding to a sample-based finding concerning excessive or prohibited contributions shall respond only to the specific sample items used to make the projection. If the committee demonstrates that any apparent errors found among the sample items were not errors, the Commission shall make a new projection based on the reduced number of errors in the sample.

(3) Within 30 days of service of the Final Audit Report, the committee shall submit a check to the United States Treasury for the total amount of any excessive or prohibited contributions not refunded, reattributed or redesignated in a timely manner in accordance with 11 CFR 103.3(b) (1), (2) or (3); or take any other action required by the Commission with respect to sample-based findings.

[56 FR 35945, July 29, 1991; 56 FR 42380, Aug. 27, 1991; 60 FR 31885, June 16, 1995; 64 FR 61781, Nov. 15, 1999; 79 FR 77852, Dec. 29, 2014]

§9038.2 **Repayments.**

(a) *General.* (1) A candidate who has received payments from the matching payment account shall pay the United States Treasury any amounts which the Commission determines to be repayable under this section. In making repayment determinations under this section, the Commission may utilize information obtained from audits and examinations conducted pursuant to 11 CFR 9038.1 and part 9039 or otherwise obtained by the Commission in carrying out its responsibilities under this subchapter.

(2) The Commission will notify the candidate of any repayment determinations made under this section as soon as possible, but not later than 3 years after the close of the matching payment period. The Commission's issuance of the audit report to the candidate under 11 CFR 9038.1(d) will constitute notification for purposes of this section.

(3) Once the candidate receives notice of the Commission's repayment determination under this section, the candidate should give preference to the repayment over all other outstanding obligations of his or her committee, except for any federal taxes owned by the committee.

(4) Repayments may be made only from the following sources: personal funds of the candidate (without regard to the limitations of 11 CFR 9035.2), contributions and federal funds in the committee's account(s), and any additional funds raised subject to the limitations and prohibitions of the Federal Election Campaign Act of 1971, as amended.

(b) *Bases for repayment*—(1) *Payments in excess of candidate's entitlement.* The Commission may determine that certain portions of the payments made to a candidate from the matching payment account were in excess of the aggregate amount of payments to which such candidate was entitled. Examples of such excessive payments include, but are not limited to, the following:

(i) Payments made to the candidate after the candidate's date of ineligibility where it is later determined that the candidate had no net outstanding campaign obligations as defined in 11 CFR 9034.5;

(ii) Payments or portions of payments made to the candidate which are later determined to have been excessive due to the operation of the Commission's expedited payment procedures as set forth in the Federal Election Commission's Guideline for Presentation in Good Order;

(iii) Payments or portions of payments made on the basis of matched contributions later determined to have been non-matchable;

(iv) Payments or portions of payments made to the candidate which are later determined to have been excessive due to the candidate's failure to include funds received by a fundraising representative committee under 11

CFR 9034.8 on the candidate's statement of net outstanding campaign obligations under 11 CFR 9034.5; and

(v) Payments or portions of payments made to the candidate on the basis of the debts reflected in the candidate's statement of net outstanding campaign obligations, which debts are later settled for an amount less than that stated in the statement of net outstanding campaign obligations.

(2) *Use of funds for non-qualified campaign expenses.* (i) The Commission may determine that amount(s) of any payments made to a candidate from the matching payment account were used for purposes other than those set forth in paragraphs (b)(2)(i) (A)–(C) of this section:

(A) Defrayal of qualified campaign expenses;

(B) Repayment of loans which were used to defray qualified campaign expenses; and

(C) Restoration of funds (other than contributions which were received and expended to defray qualified campaign expenses) which were used to defray qualified campaign expenses.

(ii) Examples of Commission repayment determinations under 11 CFR 9038.2(b)(2) include, but are not limited to, the following:

(A) Determinations that a candidate, a candidate's authorized committee(s) or agents have made expenditures in excess of the limitations set forth in 11 CFR part 9035;

(B) Determinations that funds described in 11 CFR 9038.2(b)(2)(i) were expended in violation of State or Federal law;

(C) Determinations that funds described in 11 CFR 9038.2(b)(2)(i) were expended for expenses resulting from a violation of State or Federal law, such as the payment of fines or penalties; and

(D) Determinations that funds described in 11 CFR 9038.2(b)(2)(i) were expended for costs associated with continuing to campaign after the candidate's date of ineligibility.

(iii) The amount of any repayment sought under this section shall bear the same ratio to the total amount determined to have been used for non-qualified campaign expenses as the amount of matching funds certified to

the candidate bears to the candidate's total deposits, as of 90 days after the candidate's date of ineligibility. For the purposes of this paragraph (b)(2)(iii)—

(A) Total deposits is defined in accordance with 11 CFR 9038.3(c)(2); and

(B) In seeking repayment for non-qualified campaign expenses from committees that have received matching fund payments after the candidate's date of ineligibility, the Commission will review committee expenditures to determine at what point committee accounts no longer contain matching funds. In doing this, the Commission will review committee expenditures from the date of the last matching fund payment to which the candidate was entitled, using the assumption that the last payment has been expended on a last-in, first-out basis.

(iv) Repayment determinations under 11 CFR 9038.2(b)(2) will include all non-qualified campaign expenses paid before the point when committee accounts no longer contain matching funds, including non-qualified campaign expenses listed on the candidate's statement of net outstanding campaign obligations that may result in a separate repayment determination under 11 CFR 9038.2(b)(1).

(v) If a candidate or a candidate's authorized committee(s) exceeds both the overall expenditure limitation and one or more State expenditure limitations, as set forth at 11 CFR 9035.1(a), the repayment determination under 11 CFR 9038.2(b)(2)(ii)(A) shall be based on only the larger of either the amount exceeding the State expenditure limitation(s) or the amount exceeding the overall expenditure limitation.

(3) *Failure to provide adequate documentation.* The Commission may determine that amount(s) spent by the candidate, the candidate's authorized committee(s), or agents were not documented in accordance with 11 CFR 9033.11. The amount of any repayment sought under this section shall be determined by using the formula set forth in 11 CFR 9038.2(b)(2)(iii).

(4) The Commission may determine that the candidate's net outstanding campaign obligations, as defined in 11

CFR 9034.5, reflect a surplus. The Commission may determine that the net income derived from an investment or other use of surplus public funds after the candidate's date of ineligibility, less Federal, State and local taxes paid on such income, shall be paid to the Treasury.

(c) *Repayment determination procedures.* The Commission's repayment determination will be made in accordance with the procedures set forth at paragraphs (c)(1) through (c)(4) of this section.

(1) *Repayment determination.* The Commission will provide the candidate with a written notice of its repayment determination(s). This notice will be included in the Commission's audit report prepared pursuant to 11 CFR 9038.1(d), or inquiry report pursuant to 11 CFR 9039.3, and will set forth the legal and factual reasons for such determination(s), as well as the evidence upon which any such determination is based. The candidate shall repay to the United States Treasury in accordance with paragraph (d) of this section, the amount which the Commission has determined to be repayable.

(2) *Administrative review of repayment determination.* If a candidate disputes the Commission's repayment determination(s), he or she may request an administrative review of the determination(s) as set forth in paragraph (c)(2)(i) of this section.

(i) *Submission of written materials.* A candidate who disputes the Commission's repayment determination(s) shall submit in writing, within 60 calendar days after service of the Commission's notice, legal and factual materials demonstrating that no repayment, or a lesser repayment, is required. Such materials may be submitted by counsel if the candidate so desires. The candidate's failure to timely raise an issue in written materials presented pursuant to this paragraph will be deemed a waiver of the candidate's right to raise the issue at any future stage of proceedings including any petition for review filed under 26 U.S.C. 9041(a).

(ii) *Oral hearing.* A candidate who submits written materials pursuant to paragraph (c)(2)(i) of this section may at the same time request in writing that the Commission provide such candidate with an opportunity to address the Commission in open session to demonstrate that no repayment, or a lesser repayment, is required. The candidate should identify in this request the repayment issues he or she wants to address at the oral hearing. If the Commission decides by an affirmative vote of four (4) of its members to grant the candidate's request, it will inform the candidate of the date and time set for the oral hearing. At the date and time set by the Commission, the candidate or candidate's designated representative will be allotted an amount of time in which to make an oral presentation to the Commission based upon the legal and factual materials submitted under paragraph (c)(2)(ii) of this section. The candidate or representative will also have the opportunity to answer any questions from individual members of the Commission.

(3) *Repayment determination upon review.* In deciding whether to revise any repayment determination(s) following an administrative review pursuant to paragraph (c)(2) of this section, the Commission will consider any submission made under paragraph (c)(2)(i) and any oral hearing conducted under paragraph (c)(2)(ii), and may also consider any new or additional information from other sources. A determination following an administrative review that a candidate must repay a certain amount will be accompanied by a written statement of reasons supporting the Commission's determination(s). This statement will explain the legal and factual reasons underlying the Commission's determination(s) and will summarize the results of any investigation(s) upon which the determination(s) are based.

(d) *Repayment period.* (1) Within 90 calendar days of service of the notice of the Commission's repayment determination(s), the candidate shall repay to the United States Treasury the amounts which the Commission has determined to be repayable. Upon application by the candidate, the Commission may grant an extension of up to 90 calendar days in which to make repayment.

(2) If the candidate requests an administrative review of the Commission's repayment determination(s) under paragraph (c)(2) of this section, the time for repayment will be suspended until the Commission has concluded its administrative review of the repayment determination(s). Within 30 calendar days after service of the notice of the Commission's post-administrative review repayment determination(s), the candidate shall repay to the United States Treasury the amounts which the Commission has determined to be repayable. Upon application by the candidate, the Commission may grant an extension of up to 90 calendar days in which to make repayment.

(3) Interest shall be assessed on all repayments made after the initial 90-day repayment period established at paragraph (d)(1) of this section or the 30-day repayment period established at paragraph (d)(2) of this section. The amount of interest due shall be the greater of:

(i) An amount calculated in accordance with 28 U.S.C. 1961 (a) and (b); or

(ii) The amount actually earned on the funds set aside under this section.

(e) *Computation of time.* The time periods established by this section shall be computed in accordance with 11 CFR 111.2.

(f) *Additional repayments.* Nothing in this section will prevent the Commission from making additional repayment determinations on one or more of the bases set forth at 11 CFR 9038.2(b) after it has made a repayment determination on any such basis. The Commission may make additional repayment determinations where there exist facts not used as the basis for any previous determination. Any such additional repayment determination will be made in accordance with the provisions of this section.

(g) *Newly-discovered assets.* If, after any repayment determination made under this section, a candidate or his or her authorized committee(s) receives or becomes aware of assets not previously included in any statement of net outstanding campaign obligations submitted pursuant to 11 CFR 9034.5, the candidate or his or her authorized committee(s) shall promptly notify the Commission of such newly-discovered assets. Newly-discovered assets may include refunds, rebates, late-arriving receivables, and actual receipts for capital assets in excess of the value specified in any previously-submitted statement of net outstanding campaign obligations. Newly-discovered assets may serve as a basis for additional repayment determinations under 11 CFR 9038.2(f).

(h) *Petitions for rehearing; stays pending appeal.* The candidate may file a petition for rehearing of a repayment determination in accordance with 11 CFR 9038.5(a). The candidate may request a stay of a repayment determination in accordance with 11 CFR 9038.5(c) pending the candidate's appeal of that repayment determination.

[56 FR 35945, July 29, 1991, as amended at 60 FR 31886, June 16, 1995; 60 FR 57538, 57539, Nov. 16, 1995; 61 FR 69020, Dec. 31, 1996; 68 FR 47421, Aug. 8, 2003]

§ 9038.3 Liquidation of obligations; repayment.

(a) The candidate may retain amounts received from the matching payment account for a period not exceeding 6 months after the matching payment period to pay qualified campaign expenses incurred by the candidate.

(b) After all obligations have been liquidated, the candidate shall so inform the Commission in writing.

(c)(1) If on the last day of candidate eligibility the candidate's net outstanding campaign obligations, as defined in 11 CFR 9034.5, reflect a surplus, the candidate shall within 30 calendar days of the ineligibility date repay to the Secretary an amount which represents the amount of matching funds contained in the candidate's surplus. The amount shall be an amount equal to that portion of the surplus which bears the same ratio to the total surplus that the total amount received by the candidate from the matching payment account bears to the total deposits made to the candidate's accounts.

(2) For purposes of this subsection, total deposits means all deposits to all

candidate accounts minus transfers between accounts, refunds, rebates, reimbursements, checks returned for insufficient funds, proceeds of loans and other similar amounts.

(3) Notwithstanding the payment of any amounts to the United States Treasury under this section, the Commission may make surplus repayment determination(s) which require repayment in accordance with 11 CFR 9038.2.

§9038.4 Extensions of time.

(a) It is the policy of the Commission that extensions of time under 11 CFR part 9038 shall not be routinely granted.

(b) Whenever a candidate has a right or is required to take action within a period of time prescribed by 11 CFR part 9038 or by notice given thereunder, the candidate may apply in writing to the Commission for an extension of time in which to exercise such right or take such action. The candidate shall demonstrate in the application for extension that good cause exists for his or her request.

(c) An application for extension of time shall be made at least 7 calendar days prior to the expiration of the time period for which the extension is sought. The Commission may, upon a showing of good cause, grant an extension of time to a candidate who has applied for such extension in a timely manner. The length of time of any extension granted hereunder will be decided by the Commission and may be less than the amount of time sought by the candidate in his or her application. If a candidate seeks an extension of any 60-day response period under 11 CFR part 9038, the Commission may grant no more than one extension to that candidate, which extension shall not exceed 15 days.

(d) If a candidate fails to seek an extension of time, exercise a right or take a required action prior to the expiration of a time period prescribed by 11 CFR part 9038 the Commission may, on the candidate's showing of excusable neglect:

(1) Permit such candidate to exercise his or her right(s), or take such required action(s) after the expiration of the prescribed time period; and

(2) Take into consideration any information obtained in connection with the exercise of any such right or taking of any such action before making decisions or determinations under 11 CFR part 9038.

[56 FR 35945, July 29, 1991, as amended at 60 FR 31887, June 16, 1995]

§9038.5 Petitions for rehearing; stays of repayment determinations.

(a) *Petitions for rehearing.* (1) Following the Commission's final determination under 11 CFR 9033.10 or 9034.5(g) or the Commission's repayment determination under 11 CFR 9038.2(c), the candidate may file a petition for rehearing setting forth the relief desired and the legal and factual basis in support. To be considered by the Commission, petitions for rehearing must:

(i) Be filed within 20 calendar days after service of the Commission's final determination or repayment determination;

(ii) Raise new questions of law or fact that would materially alter the Commission's final determination or repayment determination; and

(iii) Set forth clear and convincing grounds why such questions were not and could not have been presented during the original determination process.

(2) If a candidate files a timely petition under this section challenging a Commission repayment determination, the time for repayment of the amount at issue will be suspended until the Commission serves notice on the candidate of its determination on the petition. The time periods for making repayment under 11 CFR 9038.2(d) shall apply to any amounts determined to be repayable following the Commission's consideration of a petition for rehearing under this section.

(b) *Effect of failure to raise issues.* The candidate's failure to raise an argument in a timely fashion during the original determination process or in a petition for rehearing under this section, as appropriate, shall be deemed a waiver of the candidate's right to present such arguments in any future stage of proceedings including any petition for review filed under 26 U.S.C. 9041(a). An issue is not timely raised in a petition for rehearing if it could have been raised earlier in response to the Commission's original determination.

(c) *Stay of repayment determination pending appeal.* (1)(i) The candidate may apply to the Commission for a stay of all or a portion of the amount determined to be repayable under this section or under 11 CFR 9038.2 pending the candidate's appeal of that repayment determination pursuant to 26 U.S.C. 9041(a). The repayment amount requested to be stayed shall not exceed the amount at issue on appeal.

(ii) A request for a stay shall be made in writing and shall be filed within 30 calendar days after service of the Commission's decision on a petition for rehearing under paragraph (a) of this section, or, if no petition for rehearing is filed, within 30 calendar days after service of the Commission's repayment determination under 11 CFR 9038.2(c).

(2) The Commission's approval of a stay request will be conditioned upon the candidate's presentation of evidence in the stay request that he or she:

(i) Has placed the entire amount at issue in a separate interest-bearing account pending the outcome of the appeal and that withdrawals from the account may only be made with the joint signatures of the candidate or his or her agent and a Commission representative; or

(ii) Has posted a surety bond guaranteeing payment of the entire amount at issue plus interest; or

(iii) Has met the following criteria:

(A) He or she will suffer irreparable injury in the absence of a stay; and, if so, that

(B) He or she has made a strong showing of the likelihood of success on the merits of the judicial action.

(C) Such relief is consistent with the public interest; and

(D) No other party interested in the proceedings would be substantially harmed by the stay.

(3) In determining whether the candidate has made a strong showing of the likelihood of success on the merits under paragraph (c)(2)(iii)(B) of this section, the Commission may consider whether the issue on appeal presents a novel or admittedly difficult legal question and whether the equities of

the case suggest that the status quo should be maintained.

(4) All stays shall require the payment of interest on the amount at issue. The amount of interest due shall be calculated from the date 30 days after service of the Commission's repayment determination under 11 CFR 9038.2(c) and shall be the greater of:

(i) An amount calculated in accordance with 28 U.S.C. 1961 (a) and (b); or

(ii) The amount actually earned on the funds set aside under this section.

[56 FR 35945, July 29, 1991, as amended at 60 FR 31887, June 16, 1995]

§ 9038.6 Stale-dated committee checks.

If the committee has checks outstanding to creditors or contributors that have not been cashed, the committee shall notify the Commission. The committee shall inform the Commission of its efforts to locate the payees, if such efforts have been necessary, and its efforts to encourage the payees to cash the outstanding checks. The committee shall also submit a check for the total amount of such outstanding checks, payable to the United States Treasury.

§ 9038.7 Administrative record.

(a) The Commission's administrative record for final determinations under 11 CFR part 9033, sections 9034.5, 9036.5 and part 9039, and for repayment determinations under 11 CFR 9038.2, consists of all documents or materials submitted to the Commission for its consideration in making those determinations. The administrative record will include the certification of the Commission's vote(s), the audit report that is sent to the committee (for repayment determinations), the statement(s) of reasons, and the candidate agreement. The committee may include documents or materials in the administrative record by submitting them within the time periods set forth at 11 CFR 9033.3(b), 9033.4(a)(2), 9033.6(c), 9033.7(b), 9033.9(b), 9034.5(g)(2), 9036.5(e), 9038.1(c) and 9038.2(c)(2), as appropriate.

(b) The Commission's administrative record for determinations under 11 CFR part 9033, sections 9034.5, 9036.5 and 9038.2 and part 9039 does not include:

(1) Documents and materials in the files of individual Commissioners or employees of the Commission that do not constitute a basis for the Commission's decisions because they were not circulated to the Commission and were not referenced in documents that were circulated to the Commission;

(2) Transcripts or audio tapes of Commission discussions other than transcripts or audio tapes of oral hearings pursuant to 11 CFR 9038.2(c)(2), although such transcripts or tapes may be made available under 11 CFR parts 4 or 5; or

(3) Documents properly subject to privileges such as an attorney-client privilege, or items constituting attorney work product.

(c) The administrative record identified in paragraph (a) of this section is the exclusive record for the Commission's determinations under 11 CFR part 9033, §§ 9034.5, 9036.5 and 9038.2 and part 9039.

[60 FR 31888, June 16, 1995]

PART 9039—REVIEW AND INVESTIGATION AUTHORITY

Sec.
9039.1 Retention of books and records.
9039.2 Continuing review.
9039.3 Examinations and audits; investigations.

AUTHORITY: 26 U.S.C. 9039.

SOURCE: 56 FR 35949, July 29, 1991, unless otherwise noted.

§ 9039.1 Retention of books and records.

The candidate and his or her authorized committee(s) shall keep all books, records and other information required under 11 CFR 9033.11, 9034.2 and part 9036 for a period of three years pursuant to 11 CFR 102.9(c) and shall furnish such books, records and information to the Commission on request.

§ 9039.2 Continuing review.

(a) In reviewing candidate submissions made under 11 CFR part 9036 and in otherwise carrying out its responsibilities under this subchapter, the Commission may routinely consider information from the following sources:

(1) Any and all materials and communications which the candidate and his or her authorized committee(s) submit or provide under 11 CFR part 9036 and in response to inquiries or requests of the Commission and its staff;

(2) Disclosure reports on file with the Commission; and

(3) Other publicly available documents.

(b) In carrying out the Commission's responsibilities under this subchapter, Commission staff may contact representatives of the candidate and his or her authorized committee(s) to discuss questions and to request documentation concerning committee activities and any submission made under 11 CFR part 9036.

§ 9039.3 Examination and audits; investigations.

(a) *General.* (1) The Commission will consider information obtained in its continuing review under 11 CFR 9039.2 in making any certification, determination or finding under this subchapter. If the Commission decides by an affirmative vote of four of its members that additional information must be obtained in connection with any such certification, determination or finding, it will conduct a further inquiry. A decision to conduct an inquiry under this section may be based on information that is obtained under 11 CFR 9039.2, received by the Commission from outside sources, or otherwise ascertained by the Commission in carrying out its supervisory responsibilities under the Presidential Primary Matching Payment Account Act and the Federal Election Campaign Act.

(2) An inquiry conducted under this section may be used to obtain information relevant to candidate eligibility, matchability of contributions and repayments to the United States Treasury. Information obtained during such an inquiry may be used as the basis, or partial basis, for Commission certifications, determinations and findings under 11 CFR parts 9033, 9034, 9036 and 9038. Information thus obtained may also be the basis of, or be considered in connection with, an investigation under 52 U.S.C. 30109 and 11 CFR part 111.

(3) Before conducting an inquiry under this section, the Commission will attempt to obtain relevant information under the continuing review provisions of 11 CFR 9039.2. Matching payments will not be withheld pending the results of an inquiry under this section unless the Commission finds patent irregularities suggesting the possibility of fraud in materials submitted by, or in the activities of, the candidate or his or her authorized committee(s).

(b) *Procedures.* (1) The Commission will notify the candidate of its decision to conduct an inquiry under this section. The notice will summarize the legal and factual basis for the Commission's decision.

(2) The Commission's inquiry may include, but is not limited to, the following:

(i) A field audit of the candidate's books and records;

(ii) Field interviews of agents and representatives of the candidate and his or her authorized committee(s);

(iii) Verification of reported contributions by contacting reported contributors;

(iv) Verification of disbursement information by contacting reported vendors;

(v) Written questions under order;

(vi) Production of documents under subpoena;

(vii) Depositions.

(3) The provisions of 52 U.S.C. 30109 and 11 CFR part 111 will not apply to inquiries conducted under this section except that the provisions of 11 CFR 111.12 through 111.15 shall apply to any orders or subpoenas issued by the Commission.

(4) If, at the close of the inquiry, the Commission determines that no action or no further action is warranted, the Commission shall so notify the candidate. If the inquiry results in an adjustment to the amount of certified matching funds, the procedures set forth at 11 CFR 9036.5 or 9038.1 shall be followed, as appropriate. If the inquiry coincides with an audit undertaken pursuant to 11 CFR 9038.1, the information obtained in the inquiry will be utilized in making the repayment determination. If the inquiry results in an initial or additional repayment determination, the procedures set forth at 11 CFR 9038.2, 9038.4, and 9038.5 shall be followed.

[56 FR 35949, July 29, 1991; 56 FR 42380, Aug. 27, 1991; 60 FR 31888, June 16, 1995; 79 FR 77852, Dec. 29, 2014]

PARTS 9040–9099 [RESERVED]

CHAPTER II—ELECTION ASSISTANCE COMMISSION

PARTS 9400–9404 [RESERVED]

PART 9405—PROCEDURES FOR DIS-CLOSURE OF RECORDS UNDER THE FREEDOM OF INFORMATION ACT

AUTHORITY: 5 U.S.C. 552, as amended.

SOURCE: 73 FR 54257, Sept. 18, 2008, unless otherwise noted.

§ 9405.1 Purpose and scope.

The regulations in this part implement the provisions of the Freedom of Information Act (FOIA), 5 U.S.C. 552, as amended, with respect to the availability of records for inspection and copying.

§ 9405.2 Definitions.

As used in this part, the term—

Chief FOIA Officer means the person designated under § 9405.3(d) who has Commission-wide responsibility for the efficient and appropriate compliance with the FOIA.

Commercial use request means a FOIA request from or on behalf of a person who seeks information for a use or purpose that furthers his/her commercial, trade, or profit interests, which can include furthering those interests through litigation. The FOIA Officer will determine, whenever reasonably possible, the use to which a requester will put the requested documents. Where the FOIA Officer has reasonable cause to doubt the use for which the requester claims to have made the FOIA request or where that use is not clear from the FOIA request itself, the FOIA Officer will seek additional clarifica-

tion before assigning the request to a specific category.

Commission means the U.S. Election Assistance Commission, established by the Help America Vote Act of 2002, 42 U.S.C. 15301 *et seq.*

Commissioner means an individual appointed to the Commission by the President and confirmed by the Senate under section 203 of the Help America Vote Act of 2002, 42 U.S.C. 15323.

Direct costs means those expenditures which the Commission actually incurs in searching for, duplicating, and, in the case of commercial use requesters, reviewing documents to respond to a FOIA request. Direct costs include, but are not limited to, the salary of the employee performing the work (the basic rate of pay for the employee plus 16 percent of that basic rate to cover benefits) and the cost of operating duplicating equipment. Direct costs do not include overhead expenses, such as the cost of space and heating or lighting the facility in which the records are stored.

Duplication means the process of making a copy of a document necessary to respond to a FOIA request. Examples of the form such copies can take include, but are not limited to, paper copy, microform, audio-visual materials, or machine readable documentation (e.g., magnetic tape, DVD, or CD). The Commission will honor a requester's specified preference of form or format of disclosure if the records requested are reasonably reproducible with reasonable efforts in the requested form or format.

Educational institution means a preschool, a public or private elementary or secondary school, an institution of undergraduate higher education, an institute of graduate higher education, an institution of professional education, and an institution of vocational education, which operates a program or programs of scholarly research.

Executive Director means the Executive Director of the Commission or his or her designee.

FOIA means Freedom of Information Act, 5 U.S.C. 552, as amended.

FOIA Officer means a person designated by the Chief FOIA Officer under § 9405.3(d) to carry out day-to-day implementation of the FOIA activities of the Commission.

FOIA Public Liaison means a person designated by the Chief FOIA Officer under § 9405.3(d) to assist in the resolution of any disputes between the requester and the Commission.

FOIA request means to seek the release of records under 5 U.S.C. 552, as amended.

General Counsel means the General Counsel of the Commission or his or her designee.

Non-commercial scientific institution means an organization that is not operated on a commercial basis and which is operated solely for the purpose of conducting scientific research, the results of which are not intended to promote any particular product or industry.

Record means any information that would be a Commission record subject to the requirements of this part when maintained by the Commission in any format, including, but not limited to, an electronic format. Record includes information that is maintained for the Commission by an entity under Government contract for the purposes of records management.

Representative of the news media means any person or entity that gathers information of potential interest to a segment of the public, uses editorial skills to turn the raw materials into a distinct work, and distributes that work to an audience. As used in this paragraph, "news" means information that is about current events or that would be of current interest to the public. Examples of news media entities include, but are not limited to, television or radio stations broadcasting to the public at large, web logs, and publishers of periodicals (but only in those instances in which these entities can qualify as disseminators of news, as defined in this paragraph) who make their products available for purchase or subscription by the general public. As used in this paragraph, a "web log" means a publicly available Web site, usually maintained by an individual, with regular entries of commentary, descriptions of events, or other material. A freelance journalist may be regarded as working for a news media entity and therefore, considered a rep-

resentative of the news media if that person can demonstrate a solid basis for expecting publication by a news organization (whether or not the journalist is actually employed by the entity). A publication contract would present a solid basis for such an expectation. The Commission may also consider the past publication record of the requester in making this determination.

Requester is any person who submits a FOIA request to the Commission for release of a record under 5 U.S.C. 552, as amended.

Review means the process of examining a document located in response to a commercial use request to determine whether any portion of the document located is exempt from disclosure. Review also refers to processing any document for disclosure, *i.e.,* doing all that is necessary to excise exempt portions of the document or otherwise prepare the document for release. Review time includes time spent considering any formal objection to disclosure made by a business submitter requesting confidential treatment but does not include time spent resolving general legal or policy issues regarding the application of exemptions.

Search means all time spent reviewing, manually or by automated means, Commission records for the purpose of locating those records that are responsive to a FOIA request, including, but not limited to, page-by-page or line-by-line identification of material within documents and also includes reasonable efforts to locate and retrieve information from records maintained in electronic form or format. Search time does not include review of material to determine whether the material is exempt from disclosure.

§ 9405.3 Policy on disclosure of records.

(a) The Commission will make the fullest possible disclosure of records to the public, consistent with the rights of individuals to privacy, the rights of individuals and other entities with respect to trade secrets and commercial or financial information entitled to privileged and confidential treatment, and the need for the Commission to promote free internal policy deliberations and to pursue its official activities without undue disruption.

(b) All Commission records shall be available to the public unless they are specifically exempt under this part.

(c) In the interest of efficiency and economy, the Commission's preference is to furnish records to requesters in electronic format, when possible.

(d) To carry out this policy, the Commission shall designate a Chief Freedom of Information Act Officer (Chief FOIA Officer). The Chief FOIA Officer shall designate one or more Commission officials, as appropriate, as FOIA Public Liaison and/or as FOIA Officers. A FOIA Public Liaison shall serve as a supervisory official to whom a FOIA requester can raise questions about the service the FOIA requester has received. A FOIA Officer shall have the authority, subject to the direction and supervision of the Chief FOIA Officer, the requirements of this part, and the FOIA, to make decisions concerning disclosure of records to the public.

§9405.4 Availability of records.

(a) The FOIA and its provisions apply only to existing Commission records; the FOIA does not require the creation of new records.

(b) In accordance with 5 U.S.C. 552(a)(2), the Commission shall make the following materials available for public inspection and copying:

(1) Statements of policy and interpretation that have been adopted by the Commission but have not been published in the FEDERAL REGISTER;

(2) Administrative staff manuals and instructions to staff that affect a member of the public;

(3) Copies of all records, regardless of form or format, that have been released to any person under this paragraph and that, because of their nature or subject matter, the Commission determines have become or are likely to become the subject of subsequent requests for substantially the same records; and

(4) A general index of the records referred to in paragraph (b)(3) of this section.

(c) In accordance with 5 U.S.C. 552(a)(3), the Commission shall make available, upon proper request, all non-exempt Commission records, or portions of records, not previously made public under 5 U.S.C. 552(a)(1) and (a)(2).

(d) The Commission shall maintain and make available current indexes and supplements providing identifying information regarding any matter issued, adopted, or promulgated after July 4, 1967. These indexes and supplements shall be published and made available on at least a quarterly basis for public distribution unless the Commission determines by Notice in the FEDERAL REGISTER that publication would be unnecessary, impracticable, or not feasible due to budgetary considerations. Nevertheless, copies of any index or supplement shall be made available upon request at a cost not to exceed the direct cost of duplication.

(e) If documents or files contain both disclosable and non-disclosable information, the non-disclosable information will be deleted and the disclosable information released, unless the disclosable portions cannot be reasonably segregated from the other portions in a manner which will allow meaningful information to be disclosed.

(f) All records created in the process of implementing provisions of 5 U.S.C. 552 will be maintained by the Commission in accordance with the authority granted by the National Archives and Records Service of the General Services Administration.

(g) The Commission encourages the public to explore the information available on the Commission's Web site, located at *http://www.eac.gov*.

§9405.5 Categories of exemptions.

(a) No FOIA requests under 5 U.S.C. 552 shall be denied release unless the record contains, or its disclosure would reveal, matters that are:

(1) Specifically authorized under criteria established by an Executive Order to be kept secret in the interest of national defense or foreign policy and are, in fact, properly classified under such Executive Order;

(2) Related solely to the internal personnel rules and practices of the Commission;

(3) Specifically exempted from disclosure by statute, provided that such statute:

(i) Requires that the matters be withheld from the public in such a manner as to leave no discretion on the issue, or

(ii) Establishes particular criteria for withholding or refers to particular types of matters to be withheld;

(4) Trade secrets and commercial or financial information obtained from a person that are privileged or confidential. Such information includes confidential business information which concerns or relates to the trade secrets, processes, operations, style of works, or apparatus, or to the production, sales, shipments, purchases, transfers, identification of customers, inventories, or amount of source of income, profits, losses, or expenditures of any person, firm, partnership, corporation, or other organization, if the disclosure is likely to have the effect of either impairing the Commission's ability to obtain such information as is necessary to perform its statutory functions or causing substantial harm to the competitive position of the person, firm, partnership, corporation, or other organization from which the information was obtained, unless the Commission is required by law to disclose such information. For purposes of this section, trade secret means a secret, commercially valuable plan, formula, process, or device that is used for the making, preparing, compounding, or processing of trade commodities and that can be said to be the end product of either innovation or substantial effort. Examples of trade secrets may include, but are not limited to, plans, schematics, specifications of materials used in production, source code used to develop software, technical descriptions of manufacturing process, quality control methodology, and test results. The following procedures shall be used for submitting business information in confidence:

(i) Clearly mark any portion of any data or information being submitted that in the submitter's opinion is a trade secret or commercial and financial information that the submitter is claiming should be treated as privileged and confidential and submit such data or information separately from other material being submitted to the Commission;

(ii) A request for confidential treatment shall be addressed to the Chief FOIA Officer, U.S. Election Assistance Commission, 1201 New York Avenue, NW., Suite 300, Washington, DC 20005 and shall indicate clearly on the envelope that it is a request for confidential treatment.

(iii) With each submission of, or offer to submit, business information which a submitter desires to be treated as confidential under paragraph (a)(4) of this section, the submitter shall provide the following, which may be disclosed to the public:

(A) A written description of the nature of the subject information and a justification for the request for its confidential treatment, and

(B) A certification in writing under oath that substantially identical information is not available to the public.

(iv) Approval or denial of requests shall be made only by the Chief FOIA Officer or his or her designees. A denial shall be in writing, shall specify the reason for the denial, and shall advise the submitter of the right to appeal to the Commission.

(v) For good cause shown, the Commission may grant an appeal from a denial by the Chief FOIA Officer or his or her designee if the appeal is filed within 15 days after receipt of the denial. An appeal shall be addressed to the Chief FOIA Officer, U.S. Election Assistance Commission, 1201 New York Avenue, NW., Suite 300, Washington, DC 20005 and shall clearly indicate that it is a confidential submission appeal. An appeal will be decided within 20 days after its receipt (excluding Saturdays, Sundays, and legal holidays) unless an extension, stated in writing with the reasons therefore, has been provided to the person making the appeal.

(vi) Any business information submitted in confidence and determined to be entitled to confidential treatment shall be maintained in confidence by the Commission and not disclosed except as required by law. In the event that any business information submitted to the Commission is not entitled to confidential treatment, the submitter will be permitted to withdraw the tender unless it is the subject of a request under the FOIA or of judicial discovery proceedings.

(5) Interagency or intra-agency memoranda or letters that would not be available by law to a party in litigation with the Commission;

(6) Personnel and medical files and similar files, the disclosure of which would constitute a clearly unwarranted invasion of personal privacy;

(7) Records or information compiled for law enforcement purposes, but only to the extent that the production of such law enforcement records or information:

(i) Could reasonably be expected to interfere with enforcement proceedings;

(ii) Would deprive a person of a right to a fair trial or an impartial adjudication;

(iii) Could reasonably be expected to constitute an unwarranted invasion of personal privacy;

(iv) Could reasonably be expected to disclose the identity of a confidential source, including a State, local, or foreign agency or authority or any private institution that furnished information on a confidential basis, and, in the case of a record or information compiled by a criminal law enforcement authority in the course of a criminal investigation, or by an agency conducting a lawful national security intelligence investigation, information furnished by a confidential source;

(v) Would disclose techniques and procedures for law enforcement investigations or prosecutions or would disclose guidelines for law enforcement investigations or prosecutions if such disclosure could reasonably be expected to risk circumvention of the law; or

(vi) Could reasonably be expected to endanger the life or physical safety of any individual.

(b) Any portion of a record that reasonably can be segregated from the balance of the record shall be provided to any individual requesting such record after deletion of the portions which are exempt. The amount of information deleted and the exemption under which the deletion is made shall be indicated on the released portion of the record, unless including that indication would harm an interest protected by an exemption in paragraph (a) of this section under which the deletion is made. If technically feasible, the amount of the information deleted shall be indicated at the place in the record where such deletion is made.

(c) If a requested record is one of another government agency or deals with subject matter to which a government agency other than the Commission has exclusive or primary responsibility, the request for such a record shall be promptly referred by the Commission to that agency for disposition or guidance as to disposition.

(d) Nothing in this part authorizes withholding of information or limiting the availability of records to the public, except as specifically provided; nor is this part authority to withhold information from Congress.

[73 FR 54257, Sept. 18, 2008, as amended at 75 FR 49814, Aug. 16, 2010]

§9405.6 Discretionary release of exempt records.

The Commission may, in its discretion, release requested records despite the applicability of the exemptions in §9405.5, if it determines that it is in the public interest and that the rights of third parties would not be prejudiced. The Executive Director will have the authority to determine that requested records may be released despite otherwise applicable exemptions.

§9405.7 Requests for records.

(a) Requests for copies of Commission records under the FOIA shall be made in writing and addressed to the Chief FOIA Officer, U.S. Election Assistance Commission, 1201 New York Avenue, NW., Suite 300, Washington, DC 20005. The request shall reasonably describe the records sought with sufficient specificity with respect to names, dates, and subject matter to permit the records to be located. A requester will be promptly advised if the records cannot be located on the basis of the description given and that further identifying information must be provided before the request can be satisfied.

(b) Requests for Commission records and copies thereof shall specify the preferred form or format (including electronic formats) of the response. The Commission shall accommodate requesters as to form or format if the record is readily available in that form or format. When requesters do not specify the form or format of the response, the Commission shall respond in the form or format in which the document is most accessible to the Commission. In the interest of efficiency and economy, the Commission's preference is to furnish records to requesters in electronic format, whenever possible.

(c) The Commission shall determine within 20 working days after receipt of a request, or 20 working days after an appeal is granted, whether to comply with such request, unless in unusual circumstances the time is extended. The 20-day period shall commence on the date on which the request was first received by the appropriate component of the Commission, but in any event, not later than 10 days after the request is first received by the component of the Commission designated to receive requests under this part. The 20-day period shall not be tolled by the Commission except—

(1) The Commission may make one request of the requester for information and toll the 20-day period while it is awaiting such information that it has reasonably requested from the requester.

(2) If it is necessary to clarify with the requester issues regarding fee assessment.

(3) Under paragraphs (c)(1) or (2) of this section, the Commission's receipt of the requester's response to the Commission's request for information or clarification ends the tolling period.

(d) In the event the time is extended under paragraph (c) of this section, the requester shall be notified of the reasons for the extension and the date on which a determination is expected to be made. An extension may be made if it is—

(1) Necessary to locate records or transfer them from physically separate facilities; or

(2) Necessary to search for, collect, and appropriately examine a large quantity of separate and distinct records that are the subject of a single request; or

(3) Necessary for consultation with another agency that has a substantial interest in the determination of the request.

(e) If the Commission determines that an extension of time is necessary to respond to a request satisfying the unusual circumstances specified in paragraph (c) of this section, the Commission shall so notify the requester and give the requester an opportunity to limit the scope of the request so that it may be processed within the time limit prescribed in paragraph (c) of this section or arrange with the Commission an alternative time frame for processing the request or a modified request.

(f) The Commission may aggregate and process as a single request requests by the same requester, or a group of requesters acting in concert, if the Commission reasonably believes that the requests actually constitute a single request that would otherwise satisfy the unusual circumstances specified in paragraph (c) of this section, and the requests involve clearly related matters.

(g) The Commission will process requests under the FOIA based on the order they are received.

(h) The Commission shall consider requests for the expedited processing of requests in cases where the requester demonstrates a compelling need for such processing.

(1) The term "compelling need" means, with respect to a request made by a person primarily engaged in disseminating information, urgency to inform the public concerning actual or alleged Federal government activity.

(2) Requesters for expedited processing must include in their requests a statement setting forth the basis for the claim that a "compelling need" exists for the requested information, certified by the requester to be true and correct to the best of his or her knowledge and belief.

(3) The Commission shall determine whether to grant a request for expedited processing and notify the requester of such determination within

10 days of receipt of the request. Denials of requests for expedited processing may be appealed as set forth in §9405.8. The Commission shall expeditiously determine any such appeal. As soon as practicable, the Commission shall process the documents responsive to a request for which expedited processing is granted.

(i) Any person denied access to records by the Commission shall be notified immediately of the denial, including the reasons for the decision and notified of his or her right to appeal the adverse determination to the Commission.

(j) The date of receipt of a request under this part shall be the date on which the Chief FOIA Officer actually receives the request.

(k) Each request received by the Chief FOIA Officer will be assigned an individualized tracking number. Requesters may call (866) 747–1471 and, using the tracking number, obtain information about the request, including the date on which the Commission originally received the request and an estimated date on which the Commission will complete action on the request.

[73 FR 54257, Sept. 18, 2008, as amended at 75 FR 49814, Aug. 16, 2010]

§9405.8 Appeals of denials of requests for records.

(a) Any person who has been notified under §9405.7(i) that his/her request for inspection of a record or for a copy of a record has been denied, or who has received no response within 20 working days (or within such extended period as is permitted under §9405.7(d)) after the request has been received by the Commission, or who has received no response within 20 days after a request for expedited processing has been received by the Commission, may appeal the adverse determination or the failure to respond by requesting the Commission to direct that the record be made available or that the expedited processing shall occur.

(b) The appeal request shall be in writing, shall clearly and prominently state on the envelope or other cover and at the top of the first page "FOIA Appeal," and shall identify the record

in the form in which it was originally requested.

(c) The appeal request should be delivered or addressed to the Chief FOIA Officer, U.S. Election Assistance Commission, 1225 New York Avenue, NW., Suite 1100, Washington, DC 20005.

(d) The requester may state facts and cite legal or other authorities as he or she deems appropriate in support of the appeal request.

(e) The Commission will make a determination with respect to any appeal within 20 working days after receipt of the appeal (or within such extended period as is permitted under §9405.7). If, on appeal, the denial of the request for a record or a copy is in whole or in part upheld, the Commission shall advise the requester of the denial and shall notify him or her of the provisions for judicial review of that determination as set forth in 5 U.S.C. 552(a)(4).

(f) Because of the risk of misunderstanding inherent in oral communications, the Commission will not entertain any appeal from an alleged denial or failure to comply with an oral request. Any person who has orally requested a copy of a record that he or she believes to have been improperly denied should resubmit the request in writing as set forth in §9405.7.

§9405.9 Fees in general.

(a) *Generally.* The Commission will charge fees that recoup the full allowable direct costs it incurs. The Commission will use the most efficient and least costly means to comply with requests for documentation.

(b) *Manual searches for records.* The Commission will charge fees at the salary rate(s) (basic pay plus 16 percent) of the employee(s) making the search.

(c) *Computer searches for records.* The Commission will charge the actual direct cost of operating the central processing unit (CPU) for that portion of operating time that is directly attributable to searching for records responsive to a FOIA request and operator/programmer salary apportionable to the search.

(d) *Review of records.* Only requesters who are seeking documents for commercial use may be charged for time spent reviewing records to determine whether they are exempt from mandatory disclosure. Charges may be assessed only for the initial review (*i.e.*, the review undertaken the first time the Commission analyzes the applicability of a specific exemption to a particular record or portion of a record). Records or portions of records withheld in full under an exemption that is subsequently determined not to apply may be reviewed again to determine the applicability of other exemptions not previously considered. The costs for such a subsequent review are assessable. The Commission will charge at the salary rate(s) (basic pay plus 16 percent) of the employee(s) reviewing records.

(e) *Duplication of records.* Records will be duplicated at a rate of fifteen (15) cents per page. For copies prepared by computers, such as tapes, CDs, DVDs, or printouts, the Commission shall charge the actual cost, including operator time, of production. For other methods of reproduction or duplication, the Commission will charge the actual direct costs of producing the document(s). If the Commission estimates that duplication charges are likely to exceed $25, it shall notify the requester of the estimated amount of fees, unless the requester has indicated in advance a willingness to pay fees as high as those anticipated. Such a notice shall offer a requester the opportunity to confer with agency personnel with the object of reformulating the request to meet his or her needs at a lower cost.

(f) *Other charges.* The Commission will recover the full costs of providing services such as those enumerated below when it provides them in response to a direct request for such services:

(1) Certifying that records are true copies; or

(2) Sending records by special methods such as express mail.

(g) *Payment of fees.* Remittance shall be in the form either of a personal check or bank draft drawn on a bank in the United States or a postal money order. Remittance shall be made payable to the order of the Treasury of the United States and mailed to the Chief FOIA Officer, U.S. Election Assistance Commission, 1225 New York Avenue, NW., Suite 1100, Washington, DC 20005.

(h) *Receipt of fees.* A receipt for fees paid will be given upon request. Refund of fees paid for services actually rendered will not be made.

(i) *Restrictions on assessing fees.* The Commission shall not assess search fees or duplication fees under this paragraph if the Commission fails to comply with any time limit in these regulations. The Commission will not charge fees to any requester, including commercial use requesters, if the cost of collecting a fee would be equal to or greater than the fee itself. With the exception of requesters seeking documents for a commercial use, the Commission will not charge fees for the first 100 pages of duplication and the first two hours of search time.

(1) The elements to be considered in determining the "cost of collecting a fee" are the administrative costs of receiving and recording a requester's remittance and processing the fee for deposit in the Treasury Department's special account.

(2) For purposes of these restrictions on assessment of fees, the word "pages" means paper copies of 8.5″ × 11″ or 11″ × 14″. Thus, requesters are not entitled to 100 computer disks, for example.

(3) For purposes of these restrictions on assessment of fees, the term "search time" means manual search. To apply this term to searches made by computer, the Commission will determine the hourly cost of operating the CPU and the operator's hourly salary plus 16 percent. When the cost of such search (including operator time and the cost of operating the computer to process a request) equals the equivalent dollar amount of two hours of salary of the person performing the search (*i.e.*, the operator), the Commission will begin assessing charges for computer search.

§ 9405.10 Fees to be charged—categories of requesters.

There are four categories of FOIA requesters: Commercial use requesters; educational and non-commercial scientific institutions; representatives of the news media; and all other requesters.

(a) *Commercial use requesters.* When the Commission receives a request for documents for commercial use, it will assess charges that recover the full direct costs of searching for, reviewing for release, and duplicating the record sought. Commercial use requesters are neither entitled to two hours of free search time nor 100 free pages of duplication. The Commission may recover the cost of searching for and reviewing records even if there is ultimately no disclosure of records (see §9405.11(b)).

(b) *Educational and non-commercial scientific institution requesters.* The Commission shall provide documents to requesters in this category for the cost of reproduction alone, excluding charges for the first 100 pages. To be eligible for inclusion in this category, requesters must show that the record is being made as authorized by and under the auspices of a qualifying institution and that the records are not sought for a commercial use but are sought in the furtherance of scholarly (if the request is from an educational institution) or scientific (if the request is from a non-commercial scientific institution) research.

(c) *Representatives of the news media.* The Commission shall provide documents to requesters in this category for the cost of reproduction alone, excluding charges for the first 100 pages. To be eligible for inclusion in this category, the requester must fit the definition of a representative of the news media as stated in §9405.2, and the request must not be made for commercial use. For purposes of this paragraph, a request for records supporting the news dissemination function of the requester shall not be considered to be a request that is for commercial use.

(d) *All other requesters.* The Commission shall charge requesters who do not fit into any of the categories above fees that recover the full reasonable direct cost of searching for and reproducing records that are responsive to the request, except that the first 100 pages of reproduction and the first two hours of search time shall be furnished without charge.

§9405.11 Miscellaneous fee provisions.

(a) *Charging Interest—notice and rate.* The Commission may begin assessing interest charges on an unpaid bill starting on the 31st day following the day on which the billing was sent. The

fact that the fee has been received by the Commission within the 30-day grace period, even if it is not processed, will suffice to stay the accrual of interest. Interest will be at the rate prescribed in section 3717 of title 31 of the United States Code and will accrue from the date of the billing.

(b) *Charges for unsuccessful search.* The Commission may assess charges for time spent searching, even if it fails to locate the records or if the records located are determined to be exempt from disclosure. If the Commission estimates that search charges are likely to exceed $25, it shall notify the requester of the estimated amount of fees, unless the requester has indicated in advance his willingness to pay fees as high as those anticipated. Such a notice shall offer the requester the opportunity to confer with agency personnel with the object of reformulating the request to meet his or her needs at a lower cost.

(c) *Aggregating requests.* A requester may not file multiple requests at the same time, each seeking portions of a document or documents, solely in order to avoid payment of fees. When the Commission reasonably believes that a requester or a group of requestors acting in concert has submitted requests that constitute a single request involving clearly related matters, the Commission may aggregate those requests and charge accordingly. One element to be considered in determining whether a belief would be reasonable is the time period over which the requests have occurred.

(d) *Advance payments.* The Commission may not require a requester to make an advance payment (*i.e.*, payment before work is commenced or continued on a request) unless:

(1) The Commission estimates or determines that allowable charges that a requester may be required to pay are likely to exceed $250. Then, the Commission will notify the requester of the likely cost and obtain satisfactory assurance of full payment where the requester has a history of prompt payment of FOIA fees or require an advance payment of an amount up to the full estimated charges in the case of requesters with no history of payment; or

(2) A requester has previously failed to pay a fee charged in a timely fashion (*i.e.*, within 30 days of the date of the billing). Then, the Commission may require the requester to:

(i) Pay the full amount owed plus any applicable interest as provided above or demonstrate that he or she has, in fact, paid the fee, and

(ii) Make an advance payment of the full amount of the estimated fee before the agency begins to process a new request or a pending request from that requester.

(3) When the Commission acts under paragraphs (d)(1) or (2) of this section, the administrative time limits prescribed in 5 U.S.C. 552(a)(6) will begin only after the Commission has received payments described in paragraphs (d)(1) and (2) of this section.

(e) *Effect of Debt Collection Act of 1982.* The Commission shall comply with the provisions of the Debt Collection Act, including disclosure to consumer reporting agencies and use of collection agencies, where appropriate, to encourage repayment.

§ 9405.12 Waiver or reduction of charges.

Records responsive to a request will be furnished without charge when the Chief FOIA Officer determines, based on all available information, that disclosure of the requested information is in the public interest because it is likely to contribute significantly to public understanding of the operations or activities of the government and is not primarily in the commercial interest of the requester.

PART 9407—IMPLEMENTATION OF THE GOVERNMENT IN THE SUNSHINE ACT

Sec.
9407.1 Purpose and scope.
9407.2 Definitions.
9407.3 Open meetings.
9407.4 Notice of meetings.
9407.5 Closed meetings.
9407.6 Procedures for closing meetings.
9407.7 Recordkeeping requirements.
9407.8 Public availability of records.

AUTHORITY: 5 U.S.C. 552b.

SOURCE: 73 FR 54257, Sept. 18, 2008, unless otherwise noted.

§ 9407.1 Purpose and scope.

This part contains the regulations of the U.S. Election Assistance Commission implementing the Government in the Sunshine Act (5 U.S.C. 552b). Consistent with the Act, it is the policy of the Commission that the public is entitled to the fullest practicable information regarding its decision making processes. This part sets forth the basic responsibilities of the Commission with regard to this policy and offers guidance to members of the public who wish to exercise the rights established by the Act. These regulations also fulfill the requirement of 5 U.S.C. 552b(g) that each agency subject to the Act promulgates regulations to implement the open meeting requirements of paragraphs (b) through (f) of section 552b.

§ 9407.2 Definitions.

As used in this part, the term—

Commission means the U.S. Election Assistance Commission, established by the Help America Vote Act of 2002, 42 U.S.C. 15301 *et seq.*

Commissioner means an individual appointed to the Commission by the President and confirmed by the Senate under section 203 of the Help America Vote Act of 2002, 42 U.S.C. 15323.

Executive Director means the Executive Director of the Commission or his or her designee.

General Counsel means the General Counsel of the Commission or his or her designee.

Meeting means the deliberations of at least three Commissioners where such deliberations determine or result in the joint conduct or disposition of official Commission business. A deliberation conducted through telephone or similar communications equipment in which all persons participating can hear each other shall be considered a meeting. For the purposes of this section, "joint conduct" does not include situations where the requisite number of members is physically present in one place but not conducting agency business as a body. In addition, the term "meeting" does not include a process of notation voting by circulated memorandum for the purpose of expediting consideration of official Commission business. The term "meeting" also does not include deliberations on whether to:

(1) Schedule a meeting;

(2) Hold a meeting with less than seven days notice, as provided in §9407.4(e);

(3) Change the subject matter of a publicly announced meeting or the determination of the Commission to open or close a meeting or portions of a meeting to public observation, as provided in §9407.4(f);

(4) Change the time or place of an announced meeting, as provided in §9407.4(g);

(5) Close a meeting or portions of a meeting, as provided in §9407.5; or

(6) Withhold from disclosure information pertaining to a meeting or portions of a meeting, as provided in §9407.5.

Public observation means attendance by one or more members of the public at a meeting of the Commission but does not include participation in the meeting.

Public participation means the presentation or discussion of information, raising of questions, or other manner of involvement in a meeting of the Commission by one or more members of the public in a manner that contributes to the disposition of Commission business.

§9407.3 Open meetings.

(a) The Commissioners shall not jointly conduct, determine, or dispose of agency business other than in accordance with this section.

(b) Except as otherwise provided in this part, every portion of every Commission meeting shall be open to public observation.

(c) No additional right to participate in Commission meetings is granted to any person by this part. Meetings of the Commission, or portions of a meeting, shall be open to public participation only when an announcement to that effect is issued under §9407.4(b)(4). Public participation shall be conducted in an orderly, non-disruptive manner and in accordance with any procedures as the chairperson of the meeting may establish. Public participation may be terminated at any time for any reason.

(d) When holding open meetings, the Commission shall make a diligent effort to provide appropriate space, sufficient visibility, and adequate acoustics to accommodate the public attendance anticipated for the meeting. When open meetings are conducted through telephone or similar communications equipment, the Commission shall make an effort to provide sufficient access to the public in a manner which allows the public to clearly hear, see, or otherwise follow the proceedings. The meeting room or other forum selected shall be sufficient to accommodate a reasonable number of interested members of the public. The Commission shall ensure that public meetings are held at a reasonable time and are readily accessible to individuals with disabilities.

(e) Members of the public attending open Commission meetings may use small electronic audio recording devices to record the proceedings. The use of any other recording equipment and cameras requires advance coordination with and notice to the Commission's Communications Office. The chair or acting chair of the Commission may prohibit, at any time, the use of any recording equipment during a public meeting if he or she determines that such recording would disrupt the orderly conduct of the meeting.

§9407.4 Notice of meetings.

(a) Except as otherwise provided in this section, the Commission shall make a public announcement at least seven days prior to a meeting.

(b) The public announcement shall include:

(1) The time and place of the meeting;

(2) The subject matter of the meeting;

(3) Whether the meeting is to be open, closed, or portions of a meeting will be closed;

(4) Whether public participation will be allowed; and

(5) The name and telephone number of the person who will respond to requests for information about the meeting.

(c) The public announcement requirement shall be implemented by:

(1) Publishing the announcement on the Commission's Web site; and

(2) Distributing the announcement to affected government entities and persons and organizations that the Executive Director determines may have an interest in the subject matter of the meeting.

(d) The announcement will be submitted for publication in the FEDERAL REGISTER immediately following the public posting and distribution noted in paragraph (c) of this section.

(e) A meeting may be held with less than seven days notice if a majority of the Commission determines by recorded vote that the business of the Commission so requires. The Commission shall make a public announcement to this effect at the earliest practicable time. The announcement shall include the information required by paragraph (b) of this section and shall be issued in accordance with those procedures set forth in paragraphs (c) and (d) of this section that are practicable given the available period of time.

(f) The subject matter of an announced meeting or the determination of the Commission to open or close a meeting or portions of a meeting to public observation may be changed only if:

(1) A majority of the Commissioners determine by a recorded vote that agency business so requires and that no earlier announcement of the change was possible,

(2) The Commission publicly announces the change and the vote of each Commissioner upon such change at the earliest practicable time.

(3) The announcement of the change noted in paragraph (f)(2) of this section is issued in accordance with those procedures set forth in paragraphs (c) and (d) of this section that are practicable given the available period of time.

(g) The time or place of an announced meeting may be changed only if a public announcement of the change is made at the earliest practicable time. The announcement shall be issued in accordance with those procedures set forth in paragraphs (c) and (d) of this section that are practicable given the available period of time.

§ 9407.5 Closed meetings.

(a) A meeting or portions of a meeting may be closed and information pertaining to such meeting or portions of a meeting may be withheld from the public only if the Commission determines that such meeting or portions of a meeting or the disclosure of such information is likely to:

(1) Disclose matters that are:

(i) Specifically authorized under criteria established by an Executive Order to be kept secret in the interest of national defense or foreign policy, and

(ii) To be properly classified under that Executive Order;

(2) Relate solely to the internal personnel rules and practices of the Commission;

(3) Disclose matters specifically exempted from disclosure by statute (other than the Freedom of Information Act, 5 U.S.C. 552) provided that the statute:

(i) Requires that the matters be withheld from the public in such a manner as to leave no discretion on the issue, or

(ii) Establishes particular criteria for withholding or refers to particular types of matters to be withheld;

(4) Disclose the trade secrets and commercial or financial information obtained from a person and privileged or confidential;

(5) Involve either accusing any person of a crime or formally censuring any person;

(6) Disclose information of a personal nature, if disclosure would constitute a clearly unwarranted invasion of personal privacy;

(7) Disclose either investigatory records compiled for law enforcement purposes or information which, if written, would be contained in such records but only to the extent that the production of the records or information would:

(i) Interfere with enforcement proceedings,

(ii) Deprive a person of a right to either a fair trial or an impartial adjudication,

(iii) Constitute an unwarranted invasion of personal privacy,

(iv) Disclose the identity of a confidential source or sources and, in the case of a record compiled either by a criminal law enforcement authority in the course of a criminal investigation or by an agency conducting a lawful national security intelligence investigation, confidential information furnished only by the confidential source or sources,

(v) Disclose investigative techniques and procedures, or

(vi) Endanger the life or physical safety of law enforcement personnel;

(8) Disclose information contained in or related to examination, operating, or condition reports prepared by, on behalf of, or for the use of an agency responsible for the regulation or supervision of financial institutions;

(9) Disclose information the premature disclosure of which would be likely to significantly frustrate implementation of a proposed action of the Commission. This exception shall not apply in any instance where the Commission has already disclosed to the public the content or nature of the proposed action or where the Commission is required by law to make such disclosure on its own initiative prior to taking final action on the proposal; or

(10) Specifically concern the issuance of a subpoena by the Commission; or the participation of the Commission in a civil action or proceeding, an action in a foreign court or international tribunal, or an arbitration; or the initiation, conduct, or disposition by the Commission of a particular case of formal adjudication under the procedures in 5 U.S.C. 554 or otherwise involving a determination on the record after opportunity for a hearing.

(b) Before a meeting or portions of a meeting may be closed to public observation, the Commission shall determine, notwithstanding the exemptions set forth in paragraph (a) of this section, whether the public interest requires that the meeting or portions of a meeting be open consistent with Federal law. The Commission may open a meeting or portions of a meeting that could be closed under paragraph (a) of this section if the Commission finds it to be in the public interest to do so and the disclosure is not otherwise prohibited by Federal law.

§9407.6 Procedures for closing meetings.

(a) A meeting or portions of a meeting may be closed and information pertaining to a meeting or portions of a

meeting may be withheld under §9407.5(a) only when a majority of the members of the Commission vote to take the action.

(b) A separate vote of the Commissioners shall be taken with respect to each meeting or portion of a meeting proposed to be closed and with respect to information which is proposed to be withheld. A single vote may be taken with respect to a series of meetings or portions of a meeting that are proposed to be closed, so long as each meeting or portion of a meeting in the series involves the same particular matter and is scheduled to be held no more than 30 days after the initial meeting in the series. The vote of each participating Commission member shall be recorded, and no proxies shall be allowed.

(c) A person whose interests may be directly affected by a portion of a meeting may request in writing that the Commission close that portion of the meeting for any of the reasons referred to in §9407.5(a)(5), (6), or (7) . Upon the request of a Commissioner, a recorded vote shall be taken whether to close such meeting or a portion of a meeting.

(d) Before the Commission may hold a meeting that is closed, in whole or part, a certification shall be obtained from the General Counsel that, in his or her opinion, the meeting may properly be closed. The certification shall be in writing and shall state each applicable exemption provision from §9407.5(a).

(e) Within one day of a vote taken under this section, the Commission shall make publicly available a written copy of such vote reflecting the vote of each Commissioner.

(f) In the case of the closure of a meeting or portions thereof, the Commission shall make publicly available within one day of the vote on such action a full written explanation of the reasons for the closing with a list of all persons expected to attend the meeting and their affiliation.

§9407.7 Recordkeeping requirements.

(a) The Commission shall maintain either a complete transcript or electronic recording of the proceedings of each meeting.

(b) In the case of either a meeting or portions of a meeting closed to the public under § 9407.5(a)(8) or (10), the Commission shall maintain a complete transcript, an electronic recording, or a set of minutes of the proceedings. If minutes are maintained, they shall fully and clearly describe all matters discussed and shall provide a full and accurate summary of any actions taken and the reasons for which such actions were taken, including a description of the views expressed on any item and a record reflecting the vote of each Commissioner. All documents considered in connection with any action shall be identified in the minutes.

(c) The transcript, electronic recording, or copy of the minutes of a meeting shall disclose the identity of each speaker.

(d) The Commission shall maintain a complete verbatim copy of the transcript, a complete electronic recording, or a complete copy of the minutes of the proceedings of each meeting for at least two years, or for one year after the conclusion of any Commission proceeding with respect to which the meeting was held, whichever occurs later.

§ 9407.8 Public availability of records.

The Commission shall make available to the public the transcript, electronic recording, or minutes of a meeting, except for items of discussion or testimony that relate to matters the Commission has determined to contain information that may be withheld under § 9407.5(a). This information shall be made available as soon as practicable after each meeting on the Commission's Web site. Otherwise, requests to receive or review transcripts, electronic recordings, or minutes of a meeting should be addressed to the Communications Director, U.S. Election Assistance Commission, 1201 New York Avenue, NW., Suite 300, Washington, DC 20005. Copies of a transcript, a transcription of the electronic recording, or the minutes of a meeting (except for items of discussion or testimony that relate to matters withheld under § 9407.5) shall be furnished at cost to any person upon written request

pursuant to the requirements of 11 CFR part 9405.

[73 FR 54257, Sept. 18, 2008, as amended at 75 FR 49814, Aug. 16, 2010]

PART 9409—TESTIMONY BY COMMISSION EMPLOYEES RELATING TO OFFICIAL INFORMATION AND PRODUCTION OF OFFICIAL RECORDS IN LEGAL PROCEEDINGS

AUTHORITY: 44 U.S.C. 3102.

SOURCE: 73 FR 54271, Sept. 18, 2008, unless otherwise noted.

§ 9409.1 Purpose and scope.

(a) This part sets forth policies and procedures you must follow when you submit a demand or request to an employee of the United States Election Assistance Commission to produce official records and information, or provide testimony relating to official information, in connection with a legal proceeding. You must comply with these requirements when you request the release or disclosure of official records and information.

(b) The Commission intends these provisions to:

(1) Promote economy and efficiency in its programs and operations;

(2) Minimize the possibility of involving the Commission in controversial issues not related to its functions;

(3) Maintain the Commission's impartiality among private litigants where the Commission is not a named party; and

(4) Protect sensitive, confidential information and the deliberative processes of the Commission.

(c) In providing for these requirements, the Commission does not waive the sovereign immunity of the United States.

(d) This part is intended only to provide guidance for the internal operations of the Commission and to inform the public about Commission procedures concerning the service of process and responses to demands or requests. The procedures specified in this part, or the failure of any Commission employee to follow the procedures specified in this part, are not intended to create, do not create, and may not be relied upon to create a right or benefit, substantive or procedural, enforceable at law by a party against the United States.

§ 9409.2 Applicability.

(a) This part applies to demands and requests to employees for factual or expert testimony relating to official information, or for production of official records or information, in legal proceedings in which the Commission is not a named party. However, it does not apply to:

(1) Demands upon or requests for a Commission employee to testify as to facts or events that are unrelated to his or her official duties or that are unrelated to the functions of the Commission;

(2) Demands upon or requests for a former Commission employee to testify as to matters in which the former employee was not directly or materially involved while at the Commission;

(3) Requests for the release of records under the Freedom of Information Act, 5 U.S.C. 552, or the Privacy Act, 5 U.S.C. 552a; and

(4) Congressional demands and requests for testimony or records.

(b) [Reserved]

§ 9409.3 Definitions.

As used in this part, the term—

Commission means the U.S. Election Assistance Commission, established by the Help America Vote Act of 2002, 42 U.S.C. 15301 *et seq.*

Commission employee or employee means:

(a) Any current or former officer or employee of the Commission;

(b) Any other individual hired through contractual agreement by or on behalf of the Commission or who has performed or is performing services under an agreement for the Commission; and

(c) Any individual who served or is serving in any consulting or advisory capacity to the Commission, whether formal or informal.

(d) This definition does not include persons who are no longer employed by the Commission and who are retained or hired as expert witnesses or who agree to testify about general matters, matters available to the public, or matters with which they had no specific involvement or responsibility during their employment with the Commission.

Demand means a subpoena, or an order or other command of a court or other competent authority, for the production, disclosure, or release of records or for the appearance and testimony of a Commission employee that is issued in a legal proceeding.

General Counsel means the General Counsel of the Commission or a person to whom the General Counsel has delegated authority under this part.

Legal proceeding means any matter before a court of law, administrative board or tribunal, commission, administrative law judge, hearing officer, or other body that conducts a legal or administrative proceeding. Legal proceeding includes all phases of litigation.

Records or official records and information means:

(a) All documents and materials that are Commission records under the Freedom of Information Act (5 U.S.C. 552);

(b) All other documents and materials contained in files of the Commission; and

(c) All other information or materials acquired by a Commission employee in the performance of his or her official duties or because of his or her official status.

Request means any informal request, by whatever method, for the production of records and information or for testimony that has not been ordered by a court or other competent authority.

Testimony means any written or oral statements, including depositions, answers to interrogatories, affidavits, declarations, interviews, and statements made by an individual in connection with a legal proceeding.

§ 9409.4 Production or disclosure prohibited unless approved by appropriate Commission official.

(a) No employee or former employee of the Commission shall, in response to a demand of a court or other authority, produce a record or disclose any information relating to any record of the Commission, or disclose any information or produce any material acquired as part of the performance of his official duties or because of his official status without the prior, written approval of the General Counsel of the Commission.

(b) Any expert or opinion testimony by a former employee of the Commission shall be excepted from the requirements of this part where the testimony involves only general expertise gained while employed at the Commission.

§ 9409.5 Procedures for demand for testimony or production of documents.

(a) A demand directed to the Commission for the testimony of a Commission employee or for the production of documents shall be served in accordance with the Federal Rules of Civil Procedure, Federal Rules of Criminal Procedure, or applicable State procedures and shall be directed to the General Counsel, U.S. Election Assistance Commission, 1201 New York Avenue, NW., Suite 300, Washington, DC 20005. Acceptance of a demand shall not constitute an admission or waiver with respect to jurisdiction, propriety of service, improper venue, or any other defense in law or equity available under the applicable laws or rules.

(b) If a subpoena is served on the Commission or a Commission employee before submitting a written request and receiving a final determination, the Commission will oppose the subpoena on grounds that the request was not submitted in accordance with this part.

(c) A written request must contain the following information:

(1) The caption of the legal proceeding, docket number, name and address of the court or other authority involved; and the procedural posture of the legal proceeding.

(2) A copy of the complaint or equivalent document setting forth the assertions in the case and any other pleading or document necessary to show relevance;

(3) A list of categories of records sought, a detailed description of how the information sought is relevant to the issues in the legal proceeding, and a specific description of the substance of the testimony or records sought;

(4) A statement as to how the need for the information outweighs the need to maintain any confidentiality of the information and outweighs the burden on the Commission to produce the records or provide testimony;

(5) A statement indicating that the information sought is not available from another source, from other persons or entities, or from the testimony of someone other than a Commission employee, such as a retained expert;

(6) If testimony is requested, the intended use of the testimony, a general summary of the desired testimony, and a showing that no document could be provided and used in lieu of testimony;

(7) A description of all prior decisions, orders, or pending motions in the case that bear upon the relevance of the requested records or testimony;

(8) The name, address, and telephone number of counsel to each party in the case;

(9) An estimate of the amount of time that the requester and other parties will require of each Commission employee for time spent by the employee to prepare for testimony, in travel, and for attendance in the legal proceeding; and

(10) Whether travel by the Commission employee is required to provide

the testimony; or, in lieu of in-person testimony, whether a deposition may be taken at the employee's duty station.

(d) The Commission reserves the right to require additional information to complete a request where appropriate.

(e) A request should be submitted at least 45 days before the date that records or testimony is required. Requests submitted in less than 45 days before records or testimony is required must be accompanied by a written explanation stating the reasons for the late request and the reasons for expedited processing.

(f) Failure to cooperate in good faith to enable the General Counsel to make an informed decision may serve as the basis for a determination not to comply with a request.

(g) Notification to the General Counsel:

(1) Employees shall immediately refer all inquiries and demands made on the Commission to the General Counsel.

(2) An employee who receives a subpoena shall immediately forward the subpoena to the General Counsel. The General Counsel will determine the manner in which to respond to the subpoena.

[73 FR 54271, Sept. 18, 2008, as amended at 75 FR 49814, Aug. 16, 2010]

§9409.6 Service of subpoenas or requests.

Subpoenas or requests for official records or information or testimony must be served on the General Counsel, U.S. Election Assistance Commission, 1201 New York Avenue, NW., Suite 300, Washington, DC 20005.

[73 FR 54271, Sept. 18, 2008, as amended at 75 FR 49814, Aug. 16, 2010]

§9409.7 Factors to be considered by the General Counsel.

The General Counsel, in his or her sole discretion, may grant an employee permission to testify on matters relating to official information, or produce official records and information, in response to a demand or request. Among the relevant factors that the General Counsel may consider in making this decision are whether:

(a) The purposes of this part are met;

(b) Allowing such testimony or production of records would be necessary to prevent a miscarriage of justice;

(c) The Commission has an interest in the decision that may be rendered in the legal proceeding;

(d) Allowing such testimony or production of records would assist or hinder the Commission in performing its statutory duties or use Commission resources where responding to the demand or request will interfere with the ability of Commission employees to do their work;

(e) Allowing such testimony or production of records would be in the best interest of the Commission or the United States;

(f) The records or testimony can be obtained from other sources;

(g) The demand or request is unduly burdensome or otherwise inappropriate under the applicable rules of discovery or the rules of procedure governing the case or matter in which the demand or request arose;

(h) Disclosure would violate a statute, Executive order or regulation;

(i) Disclosure would reveal confidential, sensitive, or privileged information, trade secrets or similar, confidential commercial or financial information, otherwise protected information, or information which would otherwise be inappropriate for release;

(j) Disclosure would impede or interfere with an ongoing law enforcement investigation or proceedings, or compromise constitutional rights;

(k) Disclosure would result in the Commission appearing to favor one litigant over another;

(l) Disclosure relates to documents that were produced by another agency;

(m) A substantial Government interest is implicated;

(n) The demand or request is within the authority of the party making it; and

(o) The demand or request is sufficiently specific to be answered.

§9409.8 Processing demands or requests.

(a) After service of a demand or request to testify, the General Counsel will review the demand or request and, in accordance with the provisions of this part, determine whether, or under what conditions, to authorize the employee to testify on matters relating to official information and/or produce official records and information.

(b) The Commission will process requests in the order in which they are received. Absent exigent or unusual circumstances, the Commission will respond within 45 days from the date a request is received. The time for response will depend upon the scope of the request.

(c) The General Counsel may grant a waiver of any procedure described by this part where a waiver is considered necessary to promote a significant interest of the Commission or the United States or for other good cause.

§ 9409.9 Final determination.

The General Counsel will make the final determination on demands and requests to employees for production of official records and information or testimony. All final determinations are within the sole discretion of the General Counsel. The General Counsel will notify the requester and the court or other authority of the final determination, the reasons for the grant or denial of the demand or request, and any conditions that the General Counsel may impose on the release of records or information, or on the testimony of a Commission employee.

§ 9409.10 Restrictions that apply to testimony.

(a) The General Counsel may impose conditions or restrictions on the testimony of Commission employees including, for example, limiting the areas of testimony or requiring the requester and other parties to the legal proceeding to agree that the transcript of the testimony will be kept under seal or will only be used or made available in the particular legal proceeding for which testimony was requested. The General Counsel may also require a copy of the transcript of testimony at the requester's expense.

(b) The Commission may offer the employee's written declaration in lieu of testimony.

(c) If authorized to testify under this part, an employee may testify as to facts within his or her personal knowl-edge, but, unless specifically authorized to do so by the General Counsel, the employee shall not:

(1) Disclose confidential or privileged information; or

(2) For a current Commission employee, testify as an expert or opinion witness with regard to any matter arising out of the employee's official duties or the functions of the Commission unless testimony is being given on behalf of the United States.

§ 9409.11 Restrictions that apply to released records.

(a) The General Counsel may impose conditions or restrictions on the release of official records and information, including the requirement that parties to the proceeding obtain a protective order or execute a confidentiality agreement to limit access and any further disclosure. The terms of the protective order or confidentiality agreement must be acceptable to the General Counsel. In cases where protective orders or confidentiality agreements have already been executed, the Commission may condition the release of official records and information on an amendment to the existing protective order or confidentiality agreement.

(b) If the General Counsel so determines, original Commission records may be presented for examination in response to a demand or request, but they are not to be presented as evidence or otherwise used in a manner by which they could lose their identity as official Commission records, nor are they to be marked or altered. In lieu of the original records, certified copies will be presented for evidentiary purposes (see 28 U.S.C. 1733).

§ 9409.12 Procedure when a decision is not made prior to the time a response is required.

If a response to a demand or request is required before the General Counsel's decision is received, a U.S. attorney or a Commission attorney designated for the purpose shall appear with the employee or former employee of the Commission upon whom the demand has been made and shall furnish the court or other authority with a copy of the regulations contained in this part and inform the court or other authority that the demand has been, or is being, as the case may be, referred for the prompt consideration of the appropriate Commission official and shall respectfully request the court or authority to stay the demand pending receipt of the requested instructions.

§9409.13 Procedures when the General Counsel directs an employee not to testify or provide documents.

(a) If the General Counsel determines that an employee or former employee should not comply with a subpoena or other request for testimony or the production of documents, the General Counsel will so inform the employee and the party who submitted the subpoena or made the request.

(b) If, despite the determination of the General Counsel that testimony should not be given and/or documents not be produced, a court of competent jurisdiction or other appropriate authority orders the employee or former employee to testify and/or produce documents; the employee shall notify the General Counsel of such order.

(1) If the General Counsel determines that no further legal review of, or challenge to, the order will be sought, the employee or former employee shall comply with the order.

(2) If the General Counsel determines to challenge the order, or that further legal review is necessary, the employee or former employee should not comply with the order. Where necessary, the employee should appear at the time and place set forth in the subpoena. If legal counsel cannot appear on behalf of the employee, the employee should produce a copy of this part and respectfully inform the legal tribunal that he/she has been advised by counsel not to provide the requested testimony and/or produce documents. If the legal tribunal rules that the subpoena must be complied with, the employee shall respectfully decline to comply, citing this section and *United States ex rel. Touhy* v. *Ragen*, 340 U.S. 462 (1951).

§9409.14 Fees.

(a) *Generally.* The General Counsel may condition the production of records or appearance for testimony upon advance payment of a reasonable estimate of the costs to the Commission.

(b) *Fees for records.* Requesters will reimburse the Commission for the actual costs of time and resources spent searching, reviewing and duplicating records. Fees for producing records will include fees for searching, reviewing, and duplicating records, costs of attorney time spent in reviewing the demand or request, and expenses generated by materials and equipment used to search for, produce, and copy the responsive information. The Commission will charge fees at the salary rate(s) (basic pay plus 16 percent) of employee time spent searching, reviewing, and duplicating records. Fees for duplication will be the same as those charged by the Commission for records disclosed under the Freedom of Information Act (11 CFR 9405), except that the Commission will charge for the actual costs for each page of duplication and will not provide the first 100 pages for free.

(c) *Witness fees.* Fees for attendance by a witness will include fees, expenses, and allowances prescribed by the court's rules. If no such fees are prescribed, witness fees will be determined based upon the rule of the Federal district court closest to the location where the witness will appear. The fees will include cost of time spent by the witness to prepare for testimony, in travel, and for attendance in the legal proceeding.

(d) *Payment of fees.* Witness fees shall be paid for current Commission employees and any records certification fees by submitting to the General Counsel a check or money order for the appropriate amount made payable to the Treasury of the United States. In the case of testimony by former Commission employees, applicable fees shall be paid directly to the former employee in accordance with 28 U.S.C. 1821 or other applicable statutes.

(e) *Certification (authentication) of copies of records.* The Commission may certify that records are true copies to facilitate their use as evidence. To obtain certification a request for certified copies shall be made to the Commission at least 45 days before the date the copies will be needed. The request should be sent to the General Counsel,

U.S. Election Assistance Commission, 1201 New York Avenue, NW., Suite 300, Washington, DC 20005.

(f) *Waiver or reduction of fees.* The General Counsel, in his or her sole discretion, may, upon a showing of reasonable cause, waive or reduce any fees in connection with the testimony, production, or certification of records.

[73 FR 54271, Sept. 18, 2008, as amended at 75 FR 49814, Aug. 16, 2010]

§ 9409.15 Penalties.

(a) An employee who discloses official records or information or gives testimony relating to official information, except as expressly authorized by the Commission or as ordered by a Federal court after the Commission has had the opportunity to be heard, may face the penalties provided in 18 U.S.C. 641 and other applicable laws. Former Commission employees are subject to the restrictions and penalties of 18 U.S.C. 207 and 216.

(b) A current Commission employee who testifies or produces official records and information in violation of this part shall be subject to disciplinary action in addition to any penalties assessed under paragraph (a) of this section.

PART 9410—IMPLEMENTATION OF THE PRIVACY ACT OF 1974

AUTHORITY: 5 U.S.C. 552a.

SOURCE: 73 FR 54257, Sept. 18, 2008, unless otherwise noted.

§ 9410.1 Purpose and scope.

(a) This part sets forth rules that inform the public as to what information is maintained by the U.S. Election Assistance Commission about identifiable individuals and that inform those identifiable individuals how they may gain access to and correct or amend information about them.

(b) The regulations in this part carry out the requirements of the Privacy Act of 1974 (Pub. L. 93–579) and in particular 5 U.S.C. 552a as added by that Act.

(c) The regulations in this part apply only to records disclosed or requested under the Privacy Act of 1974 and not to requests for information made under 5 U.S.C. 552, the Freedom of Information Act, or requests for reports or statements filed with the Election Assistance Commission which are public records and available for inspection and copying.

§ 9410.2 Definitions.

As used in this part, the term—

Commission means the U.S. Election Assistance Commission, established by the Help America Vote Act of 2002, 42 U.S.C. 15301 *et seq.*

Commissioner means an individual appointed to the Commission by the President and confirmed by the Senate under section 203 of the Help America Vote Act of 2002, 42 U.S.C. 15323.

Individual means a citizen of the United States or an alien lawfully admitted for permanent residence.

Maintain includes maintain, collect, use, or disseminate.

Record means any item, collection, or grouping of information about an individual that is maintained by the Commission including, but not limited to, his or her education, financial transactions, medical history, and criminal or employment history and that contains his or her name or the identifying number, symbol, or other identifying information particularly assigned to the individual, such as finger or voice print or a photograph.

Systems of records means a group of any records under the control of the Commission from which information is retrieved by the name of the individual or by some identifying number, symbol, or other identifying information particularly assigned to the individual.

§9410.3 Procedures for requests pertaining to individual records in a record system.

(a) Any individual may request the Commission to inform him or her whether a particular record system named by the individual contains a record pertaining to him or her. The request may be made in person or in writing at the location of the record system and to the person specified in the notice describing that record system.

(b) An individual, who believes that the Commission maintains records pertaining to him or her but cannot determine which record system contains those records, may request assistance by mail or in person from the Executive Director, U.S. Election Assistance Commission, 1201 New York Avenue, NW., Suite 300, Washington, DC 20005 during the hours of 9 a.m. to 5:30 p.m.

(c) Requests under paragraphs (a) or (b) of this section shall be acknowledged by the Commission within 15 working days from the date of receipt of the request. If the Commission is unable to locate the information requested under paragraphs (a) or (b) of this section, it shall so notify the individual within 15 working days after receipt of the request. The notification may request additional information to assist the Commission in locating the record, or it may advise the individual that no record or document exists about that individual.

[73 FR 54257, Sept. 18, 2008, as amended at 75 FR 49814, Aug. 16, 2010]

§9410.4 Times, places, and requirements for identification of individuals making requests.

(a) After being informed by the Commission that a record system contains a record pertaining to him or her, an individual may request that the Commission disclose that record in the manner described in this section. Each request for the disclosure of a record or a copy of a record it shall be made in person or by written correspondence to the U.S. Election Assistance Commission, 1201 New York Avenue, NW., Suite 300, Washington, DC 20005 and to the person identified in the notice describing the systems of records. Requests can also be made by specifically authorized agents or by parents or guardians of individuals.

(b) Each individual requesting the disclosure of a record or copy of a record shall furnish the following information with his or her request:

(1) The name of the record system containing the record;

(2) Proof as described in paragraph (c) of this section that he or she is the individual to whom the requested record relates; and

(3) Any other information required by the notice describing the record system.

(c) Proof of identity as required by paragraph (b)(2) of this section shall be provided as described in paragraphs (c)(1) and (c)(2) of this section. Requests made by an agent, parent, or guardian shall be in accordance with the procedures described in §9410.9.

(1) Requests made in writing shall include a statement affirming the individual's identity, signed by the individual and either notarized or witnessed by two persons (including witnesses' addresses). If the individual appears before a notary, he or she shall submit adequate proof of identification in the form of a driver's license, birth certificate, passport, or other identification acceptable to the notary. If the statement is witnessed, it shall include a sentence above the witnesses' signatures that they personally know the individual or that the individual has submitted proof of his or her identification to their satisfaction. In cases involving records of extreme sensitivity, the Commission may determine that the identification is not adequate and may request the individual to submit additional proof of identification.

(2) If the request is made in person, the requester shall submit proof of identification similar to that described in paragraph (c)(1) of this section, acceptable to the Commission.

[73 FR 54257, Sept. 18, 2008, as amended at 75 FR 49814, Aug. 16, 2010]

§ 9410.5 Disclosure of requested information to individuals.

(a) Upon submission of proof of identification as required by § 9410.4, the Commission shall allow the individual to see and/or obtain a copy of the requested record or shall send a copy of the record to the individual by registered mail. If the individual requests to see the record, the Commission may make the record available either at the location where the record is maintained or at a place more suitable to the requestor, if possible. The record shall be made available as soon as possible, but in no event later than 15 working days after proof of identification. The individual may have a person or persons of his or her own choosing accompany him or her when the record is disclosed.

(b) The Commission must furnish each record requested by an individual under this part in a form intelligible to that individual.

(c) If the Commission denies access to a record to an individual, he or she shall be advised of the reason for the denial and advised of the right to judicial review.

(d) Upon request, an individual will be provided access to the accounting of disclosures from his or her record under the same procedures as provided above and in § 9410.4.

§ 9410.6 Request for correction or amendment to record.

(a) Any individual who has reviewed a record pertaining to him or her that was furnished under this part may request that the Commission correct or amend all or any part of that record.

(b) Each individual requesting a correction or amendment shall send or provide in person the written request to the Commission through the person who furnished the record.

(c) Each request for a correction or amendment of a record shall contain the following information:

(1) The name of the individual requesting the correction or amendment;

(2) The name of the system of records in which the record sought to be amended is maintained;

(3) The location of the system of records from which the individual record was obtained;

(4) A copy of the record sought to be amended or corrected or a sufficiently detailed description of that record;

(5) A statement of the material in the record that the individual desires to correct or amend; and

(6) A statement of the basis for the requested correction or amendment including any material that the individual can furnish to substantiate the reasons for the correction or amendment sought.

§ 9410.7 Commission review of request for correction or amendment of record.

(a) The Commission shall, not later than 10 working days after the receipt of the request for a correction or amendment of a record under § 9410.6, acknowledge receipt of the request and inform the individual whether additional information is required before the correction or amendment can be considered.

(b) If no additional information is required, within 10 working days from receipt of the request, the Commission shall either make the requested correction or amendment or notify the individual of its refusal to do so, including in the notification the reasons for the refusal and the appeal procedures provided in § 9410.8.

(c) The Commission shall make each requested correction or amendment to a record if that correction or amendment will negate inaccurate, irrelevant, untimely, or incomplete information in the record.

(d) The Commission shall inform prior recipients of a record of any amendment or correction or notation of dispute of the individual's record if an accounting of the disclosure was made. The individual may request a list of prior recipients if an accounting of the disclosure was made.

§ 9410.8 Appeal of initial adverse determination on amendment or correction.

(a) Any individual whose request for a correction or amendment has been denied in whole or in part may appeal that decision to the Commissioners no later than 180 days after the adverse decision is rendered.

(b) The appeal shall be in writing and shall contain the following information:

(1) The name of the individual making the appeal;

(2) Identification of the record sought to be amended;

(3) The record system in which that record is contained;

(4) A short statement describing the amendment sought; and

(5) The name and location of the Commission official who initially denied the correction or amendment.

(c) Not later than 30 working days after the date on which the Commission receives the appeal, the Commissioners shall complete their review of the appeal and make a final decision thereon. However, for good cause shown, the Commissioners may extend that 30-day period. If the Commissioners extend the period, the individual requesting the review shall be promptly notified of the extension and the anticipated date of a decision.

(d) After review of an appeal, the Commission shall send a written notice to the requestor containing the following information:

(1) The decision and, if the denial is upheld, the reasons for the decision;

(2) The right of the requestor to institute a civil action in a Federal District Court for judicial review of the decision; and

(3) The right of the requestor to file with the Commission a concise statement setting forth the reasons for his or her disagreement with the Commission's denial of the correction or amendment. The Commission shall make this statement available to any person to whom the record is later disclosed, together with a brief statement, if appropriate, of the Commission's reasons for denying the requested correction or amendment. The Commission shall also send a copy of the statement to prior recipients of the individual's record if an accounting of the disclosures was made.

§ 9410.9 Disclosure of record to person other than the individual to whom it pertains.

(a) Any individual who desires to have a record covered by this part disclosed to or mailed to another person may designate such person and authorize the person to act as his or her agent for that specific purpose. The authorization shall be in writing, signed by the individual, and notarized or witnessed as provided in §9410.4(c).

(b) The parent of any minor individual or the legal guardian of any individual who has been declared by a court of competent jurisdiction to be incompetent due to physical or mental incapacity or age may act on behalf of that individual in any matter covered by this part. A parent or guardian who desires to act on behalf of such an individual shall present suitable evidence of parentage or guardianship, by birth certificate, certified copy of a court order, or similar documents, and proof of the individual's identity in a form that complies with §9410.4(c).

(c) An individual to whom a record is to be disclosed in person under this part may have a person or persons of his or her own choosing accompany him or her when the record is disclosed.

§ 9410.10 Fees.

(a) The Commission shall not charge an individual for the cost of making a search for a record or the cost of reviewing the record. When the Commission makes a copy of a record as a necessary part of the process of disclosing the record to an individual, the Commission shall not charge the individual for the cost of making that copy. When the Commission makes a copy of a record in response to a request from an individual, the Commission may charge the individual for the reasonable cost of making the copy.

(b) If an individual requests that the Commission furnish a copy of the record, the Commission shall charge the individual for the cost of making the copy. The fee that the Commission has established for making a copy is fifteen (15) cents per page.

§ 9410.11 Penalties.

Any person who makes a false statement in connection with any request for a record or an amendment or correction thereto under this part is subject to the penalties prescribed in 18 U.S.C. 494 and 495 and 5 U.S.C. 552a (i)(3).

PART 9411—STANDARDS OF CONDUCT

AUTHORITY: 5 CFR parts 2634 through 2638; 5 CFR part 2641; 5 CFR parts 734 and 735.

SOURCE: 73 FR 54275, Sept. 18, 2008, unless otherwise noted.

§ 9411.1   Cross-reference to executive branch-wide regulations.

(a) Employees of the U.S. Election Assistance Commission are subject to the following standards of conduct and ethical requirements:

(1) Executive Branch Financial Disclosure, Qualified Trusts, and Certificates of Divestiture as provided in 5 CFR part 2634;

(2) Standards of Ethical Conduct for Employees of the Executive Branch as provided in 5 CFR part 2635;

(3) Limitations on Outside Earned Income, Employment and Affiliations for Certain Noncareer Employees as provided in 5 CFR part 2636;

(4) Regulations Concerning Post-Employment Conflict of Interest as provided in 5 CFR part 2637;

(5) Interpretation, Exemptions and Waiver Guidance Concerning 18 U.S.C. 208 (Acts Affecting a Personal Financial Interest) as provided in 5 CFR part 2638;

(6) Post-Employment Conflict of Interest Restrictions as provided in 5 CFR part 2641;

(7) Political Activities of Federal Employees as provided in 5 CFR part 734; and

(8) Employee Responsibilities and Conduct as provided in 5 CFR part 735.

(b) For purposes of this part, employee shall have the definition given to it by each standard of conduct or ethical requirement in paragraph (a) of this section.

PART 9420—NONDISCRIMINATION ON THE BASIS OF HANDICAP IN PROGRAMS OR ACTIVITIES CONDUCTED BY THE U.S. ELECTION ASSISTANCE COMMISSION

AUTHORITY: 29 U.S.C. 794.

SOURCE: 73 FR 54275, Sept. 18, 2008, unless otherwise noted.

§ 9420.1   Purpose and scope.

This part sets forth the nondiscrimination policy of the U.S. Election Assistance Commission to prohibit discrimination on the basis of handicap in programs or activities conducted by the Commission.

§ 9420.2   Definitions.

As used in this part, the term—

Auxiliary aids means services, including attendant services, or devices that enable handicapped persons, including those with impaired sensory, manual, or speaking skills to have an equal opportunity to participate in, and enjoy the benefits of, programs or activities conducted by the Commission. For example, auxiliary aids useful for disabled persons with impaired vision include readers, brailled materials, audio recordings, telecommunications devices and other similar services and devices. Auxiliary aids useful for disabled persons with impaired hearing include telephone handset amplifiers, telephones compatible with hearing aids, telecommunication devices for deaf persons (TDDs), interpreters, notetakers, written materials, and other similar services and devices.

Commission means the U.S. Election Assistance Commission, established by the Help America Vote Act of 2002, 42 U.S.C. 15301 *et seq.*

Complete complaint means a written statement that contains the complainant's name and address and describes the complainant's name and address and describes the Commission's actions in sufficient detail to inform the Commission of the nature and date of the alleged violation of section 504, as defined in this part. It shall be signed by the complainant or by someone authorized to do so on his or her behalf. Complaints filed on behalf of classes or third parties shall describe or identify (by name if possible) the alleged victims of discrimination.

Facility means all or any portion of buildings, structures, equipment, roads, walks, parking lots, rolling stock or other conveyances, or other real or personal property whether owned, leased or used on some other basis by the Commission.

Handicapped person means any person who has a physical or mental impairment that substantially limits one or more major life activities, has a record of such impairment, or is regarded as having such impairment. As used in this definition, the phrase:

(1) *Physical or mental impairment* includes:

(i) Any physiological disorder or condition, cosmetic disfigurement, or anatomical loss affecting one of more of the following body systems: Neurological; musculoskeletal; special sense organs; respiratory, including speech organs; cardiovascular; reproductive; digestive; genitourinary; hemic and lymphatic; skin; and endocrine; or

(ii) Any mental or psychological disorder, such as mental retardation, organic brain syndrome, emotional or mental illness, and specific learning disabilities. The term "physical or mental impairment" includes, but is not limited to, such diseases and conditions as orthopedic; visual, speech, and hearing impairments; cerebral palsy; epilepsy; muscular dystrophy; multiple sclerosis; cancer; heart disease; diabetes; mental retardation; emotional illness; and drug addition and alcoholism.

(2) *Major life activities* include functions such as caring for one's self, performing manual tasks, walking, seeing, hearing, speaking, breathing, learning, and working.

(3) *Has a record of such an impairment* means has a history of or has been misclassified as having a mental or physical impairment that substantially limits one or more major life activities.

(4) *Is regarded as having an impairment* means:

(i) Has a physical or mental impairment that does not substantially limit major life activities, but is treated by the Commission as constituting such a limitation;

(ii) Has a physical or mental impairment that substantially limits major life activities only as a result of the attitudes of others toward the impairment; or

(iii) Has none of the impairments defined in paragraph (1) of this definition, but is treated by the Commission as having an impairment.

Qualified handicapped person means (1) with respect to any Commission program or activity under which a person is required to perform services or to achieve a level of accomplishment, a handicapped person who, with reasonable accommodation, meets the essential eligibility requirements and who can achieve the purpose of the program or activity; and

(2) With respect to any other program or activity, a handicapped person who meets essential eligibility requirements for participation in, or receipt of benefits from, that program or activity.

Section 504 means section 504 of the Rehabilitation Act of 1973 (Pub. L. 93–112, 87 Stat. 394), as amended by the Rehabilitation Act Amendments of 1974 (Pub. L. 93–516, 88 Stat. 1617) and the Rehabilitation, Comprehensive Services, and Developmental Disabilities Act of 1978 (Pub. L. 95–602, 92 Stat. 2955). As used in this part, section 504 applies only to programs or activities conducted by the Commission and not to any federally assisted programs or activities that it administers.

§9420.3 General prohibitions against discrimination.

(a) No qualified handicapped person shall, on the basis of handicap, be excluded from participation in, be denied the benefits of, or otherwise be subjected to discrimination under any program or activity conducted by the Commission.

(b)(1) The Commission, in providing any aid, benefit, or service, may not, directly or through contractual, licensing, or other arrangement, on the basis of handicap—

(i) Deny a qualified handicapped person the opportunity to participate in or benefit from the aid, benefit, or service;

(ii) Afford a qualified handicapped person an opportunity to participate in or benefit from the aid, benefit, or service that is not equal to that afforded others;

(iii) Provide a qualified handicapped person with an aid, benefit, or service that is not as effective in affording equal opportunity to obtain the same result, to gain the same benefit, or to reach the same level of achievement as that provided to others;

(iv) Provide different or separate aids, benefits, or services to handicapped persons or to any class of handicapped persons than is provided to others unless such action is necessary to provide qualified handicapped persons with aids, benefits, or services that are as effective as those provided to others;

(v) Deny a qualified handicapped person the opportunity to participate as a member of planning or advisory boards; or

(vi) Otherwise limit a qualified handicapped person in the enjoyment of any right, privilege, advantage, or opportunity enjoyed by others receiving aid, benefit, or service.

(2) The Commission may not deny a qualified handicapped person the opportunity to participate in programs or activities that are not separate or different, despite the existence of permissibly separate or different programs or activities.

(3) The Commission may not, directly or through contractual or other arrangements, utilize criteria or methods of administration the purpose or effect of which would—

(i) Subject qualified handicapped persons to discrimination on the basis of handicap; or

(ii) Defeat or substantially impair accomplishment of the objectives of a program or activity with respect to handicapped persons.

(4) The Commission may not, in determining the site or location of a facility, make selections the purpose or effect of which would—

(i) Exclude handicapped persons from, deny them the benefits of, or otherwise subject them to discrimination under any program or activity conducted by the Commission; or

(ii) Defeat or substantially impair the accomplishment of objectives of a program or activity with respect to handicapped persons.

(5) The Commission, in selection of procurement contractors, may not use criteria that subject qualified handicapped persons to discrimination on the basis of handicap.

(6) The Commission may not administer a certification program in a manner that subjects qualified handicapped persons to discrimination on the basis of handicap, nor may the Commission establish requirements for the programs or activities of certified entities that subject qualified handicapped persons to discrimination on the basis of handicap. The programs or activities of entities that are certified by the Commission are not, themselves, covered by this part.

(c) The exclusion of non-handicapped persons from the benefits of a program limited by Federal statute or Executive Order to handicapped persons or the exclusion of a specific class of handicapped persons from a program limited by Federal statute or Executive Order to a different class of handicapped persons is not prohibited by this part.

(d) The Commission will administer programs and activities in the most integrated setting appropriate to the needs of qualified handicapped persons.

§ 9420.4 Program accessibility: Discrimination prohibited.

Except as otherwise provided in 11 CFR 9420.6 and 11 CFR 9420.7, no qualified handicapped person shall be denied the benefits of, be excluded from participation in, or otherwise be subjected to discrimination under any program or activity conducted by the Commission because its facilities are inaccessible to or unusable by handicapped persons.

§ 9420.5 Program accessibility: Existing facilities.

(a) *General.* The Commission will operate each program or activity so that the program or activity, when viewed in its entirety, is readily accessible to and usable by handicapped persons. This paragraph does not—

(1) Necessarily require the Commission to make each of its existing facilities accessible to and usable by handicapped persons;

(2) Require the Commission to take any action that it can demonstrate would result in a fundamental alteration in the nature of a program or activity or in undue financial and administrative burdens. The Commission has the burden of proving that compliance with 11 CFR 9420.6(a) would result in such alterations or burdens. The decision that compliance would result in such alteration or burdens must be made by the Commission after considering all agency resources available for use in the funding and operation of the conducted program or activity, and must be accompanied by a written statement of the reasons for reaching that conclusion. If an action would result in such an alteration or such burdens, the Commission will take any other action that would not result in such an alteration or such a burden but would nevertheless ensure that handicapped person receive the benefits and services of the program or activity.

(b) *Methods.* The Commission may comply with the requirements of this section through such means as redesign of equipment, reassignment of services to accessible buildings, assignment of aides to beneficiaries, home visits, delivery of services at alternate accessible sites, alteration of existing facilities and construction of new facilities, use of accessible rolling stock, or any other methods that result in making its programs or activities readily accessible to and usable by handicapped persons. The Commission is not required to make structural changes in existing facilities where other methods are effective in achieving compliance with this section. The Commission, in making alterations to existing buildings will meet accessibility requirements to the extent compelled by the Architectural Barriers Act of 1968, as amended, 42 U.S.C. 4151–4157, and any regulations implementing it. In choosing among available methods for meeting the requirements of this section, the Commission will give priority to those methods that offer programs and activities to qualified handicapped persons in the most integrated setting appropriate.

(c) *Time period for compliance.* The Commission shall comply with the obligations established under this section within sixty days of the effective date of this part except that where structural changes in facilities are undertaken, such changes will be made within three years of the effective date of this part, but in any event as expeditiously as possible.

(d) *Transition plan.* In the event that structural changes to facilities will be undertaken to achieve program accessibility, the Commission will develop, within six months of the effective date of this part, a transition plan setting forth the steps necessary to complete such changes. The plan will be developed with the assistance of interested persons, including handicapped persons and organizations representing handicapped persons. A copy of the transition plan will be made available for public inspection. The plan will, at a minimum—

(1) Identify physical obstacles in the Commission's facilities that limit the accessibility of its programs or activities to handicapped persons;

(2) Describe in detail the methods that will be used to make the facilities accessible;

(3) Specify the schedule for taking the steps necessary to achieve compliance with this section and, if the time period of the transition plan is longer than one year, identify steps that will be taken during each year of the transition period;

(4) Indicate the official responsible for implementation of the plan; and

(5) Identify the person or groups with whose assistance the plan was prepared.

§9420.6 Program accessibility: New construction and alterations.

Each building or part of a building that is constructed or altered by, on behalf of, or for the use of the Commission shall be designed, constructed, or altered so as to be readily accessible to and usable by handicapped persons. The definitions, requirements, and standards of the Architectural Barriers Act, 42 U.S.C. 4151–4157 apply to buildings covered by this section.

§9420.7 Communications.

(a) The Commission will take appropriate steps to ensure effective communication with applicants, participants, personnel of other Federal entities, and members of the public.

(1) The commission will furnish appropriate auxiliary aids when necessary to afford a handicapped person an equal opportunity to participate in, and enjoy the benefits of, a program or activity conducted by the Commission.

(i) In determining what type of auxiliary aid is necessary, the Commission will give primary consideration to the requests of the handicapped person.

(ii) Where the Commission communicates with applicants and beneficiaries by telephone, telecommunication devices for deaf persons (TDDs) or equally effective telecommunication systems will be used.

(b) The Commission will ensure that interested persons, including persons with impaired vision or hearing can obtain information as to the existence and location of accessible services, activities, and facilities.

(c) To the extent that the Commission controls signage at its facilities, the Commission will provide signage at a primary entrance to each of its inaccessible facilities, directing users to a location at which they can obtain information about accessible facilities. To the extent practicable, the international symbol for accessibility shall be used at each primary entrance of an accessible facility.

(d) The Commission will take appropriate steps to provide handicapped persons with information regarding their section 504 rights under the Commission's programs or activities.

(e) This section does not require the Commission to take any action that it can demonstrate would result in a fundamental alteration in the nature of a program or activity or in undue financial and administrative burdens. The Commission has the burden of proving that compliance with this section would result in such alterations or burdens. The decision that compliance would result in such alteration or burdens must be made by the Commission after considering all agency resources available for use in the funding and operation of the conducted program or activity, and must be accompanied by a written statement of the reasons for reaching that conclusion. If an action required to comply with this section would result in such an alteration or such burdens, the Commission will take any other action that would not result in such an alteration or such a burden but would nevertheless ensure that, to the maximum extent possible, handicapped persons receive the benefits and services of the program or activity.

§ 9420.8 Compliance procedures.

(a) Except as provided in paragraph (b) of this section, this section applies to all allegations of discrimination on the basis of handicap in programs or activities conducted by the Commission.

(b) The Commission will process complaints alleging violations of section 504 with respect to employment according to the procedures established in 29 CFR 1614.101 et seq. pursuant to section 501 of the Rehabilitation Act of 1973 (29 U.S.C. 791).

(c) Responsibility for implementation and operation of this section shall be vested in the Rehabilitation Act Officer.

(d)(1) Requirement to file complaint with the Rehabilitation Act Officer.

(i) Any person who believes that he or she or any specific class of persons of which he or she is a member has been subjected to discrimination prohibited by this part may file a complaint with the Rehabilitation Act Officer.

(ii) Any person who believes that a denial of his or her services will result or has resulted in discrimination prohibited by this part may file a complaint with the Rehabilitation Act Officer.

(2) Timing of filing of complaint. All complete complaints must be filed within 180 days of the alleged act of discrimination. The Commission may extend this period for good cause.

(3) Complaints filed under this part shall be addressed to the Rehabilitation Act Officer, U.S. Election Assistance Commission, 1201 New York Avenue, NW., Suite 300, Washington, DC 20005.

(e) The Commission will notify the Architectural and Transportation Barriers Compliance Board upon receipt of any complaint alleging that a building or facility that is subject to the Architectural Barriers Act of 1968, as amended (42 U.S.C. 4151–4157), or section 502 of the Rehabilitation Act of 1973, as amended (29 U.S.C. 792), are not readily accessible and usable to handicapped persons.

(f) *Review of complaints*—(1) The Commission will accept and investigate a complete complaint that is filed in accordance with paragraph (d) of this section and over which it has jurisdiction. The Rehabilitation Act Officer will notify the complainant and the respondent of receipt and acceptance of the complaint.

(2) If the Rehabilitation Act Officer receives a complaint that is not complete, he or she will notify the complainant within 30 days of receipt of the incomplete complaint, that additional information is needed. If the complainant fails to complete the complaint within 30 days of receipt of this notice, the Rehabilitation Act Officer will dismiss the complaint without prejudice.

(3) If the Rehabilitation Act Officer receives a complaint over which the Commission does not have jurisdiction, the Commission will promptly notify the complainant and will make reasonable efforts to refer the complaint to the appropriate government entity.

(g) Within 180 days of receipt of a complete complaint for which it has jurisdiction, the Commission will notify the complainant of the results of the investigation in a letter containing—

(1) Findings of fact and conclusions of law.

(2) A description of a remedy for each violation found; and

(3) A notice of the right to appeal.

(h) Appeals of the findings of fact and conclusions of law or remedies must be filed by the complainant within 90 days of receipt from the Commission of a letter required by §9420.9(g). The Commission may extend this time for good cause.

(i) Timely appeals to the Commission shall be addressed to the Rehabilitation Act Officer, U.S. Election Assistance Commission, 1201 New York Avenue, NW., Suite 300, Washington, DC 20005.

(j) The Commission will notify the complainant of the results of the appeal within 60 days of the receipt of the request. If the Commission determines it needs additional information from the complainant, it shall have 60 days from the date it receives the additional information to make its determination on the appeal.

(k) The Commission may extend the time limits in paragraphs (g) and (j) of this section for good cause.

(l) The Commission may delegate its authority for conducting complaint investigations to other Federal agencies, except that the authority for making the final determination may not be delegated.

[73 FR 54275, Sept. 18, 2008, as amended at 75 FR 49815, Aug. 16, 2010]

PART 9428—NATIONAL VOTER REGISTRATION ACT (42 U.S.C. 1973gg–1 *et seq.*)

Subpart A—General Provisions

Sec.
9428.1 Purpose & scope.
9428.2 Definitions.

Subpart B—National Mail Voter Registration Form

9428.3 General Information.
9428.4 Contents.
9428.5 Format.
9428.6 Chief state election official.

Subpart C—Recordkeeping and Reporting

9428.7 Contents of reports from the states.

AUTHORITY: 42 U.S.C. 1973gg–1 *et seq.*, 15532

SOURCE: 59 FR 32323, June 23, 1994, unless otherwise noted. Redesignated at 74 FR 37520, July 29, 2009.

Subpart A—General Provisions

§9428.1 Purpose & scope.

The regulations in this part implement the responsibilities delegated to the Commission under Section 9 of the National Voter Registration Act of 1993, Public Law 103–31, 97 Stat. 77, 42 U.S.C. 1973gg–1 *et seq.* ("NVRA"). They describe the format and contents of the national mail voter registration form and the information that will be required from the states for inclusion in the Commission's biennial report to Congress.

§ 9428.2 Definitions.

As used in this part:

(a) *Form* means the national mail voter registration application form, which includes the registration application, accompanying general instructions for completing the application, and state-specific instructions.

(b) *Chief state election official* means the designated state officer or employee responsible for the coordination of state responsibilities under 42 U.S.C. 1973gg-8.

(c) *Active voters* means all registered voters except those who have been sent but have not responded to a confirmation mailing sent in accordance with 42 U.S.C. 1973gg-6(d) and have not since offered to vote.

(d) *Inactive voters* means registrants who have been sent but have not responded to a confirmation mailing sent in accordance with 42 U.S.C. 1973gg-6(d) and have not since offered to vote.

(e) *Duplicate registration application* means an offer to register by a person already registered to vote at the same address, under the same name, and (where applicable) in the same political party.

(f) *State* means a state of the United States and the District of Columbia not exempt from coverage under 42 U.S.C. 1973gg-2(b).

(g) *Closed primary state* means a state that requires party registration as a precondition to vote for partisan races in primary elections or for other nominating procedures.

Subpart B—National Mail Voter Registration Form

§ 9428.3 General information.

(a) The national mail voter registration form shall consist of three components: An application, which shall contain appropriate fields for the applicant to provide all of the information required or requested under 11 CFR 9428.4; general instructions for completing the application; and accompanying state-specific instructions.

(b) The state-specific instructions shall contain the following information for each state, arranged by state: the address where the application should be mailed and information regarding the state's specific voter eligibility and registration requirements.

(c) States shall accept, use, and make available the form described in this section.

[59 FR 32323, June 23, 1994. Redesignated and amended at 74 FR 37520, July 29, 2009]

§ 9428.4 Contents.

(a) *Information about the applicant.* The application shall provide appropriate fields for the applicant's:

(1) Last, first, and middle name, any suffix, and (optional) any prefix;

(2) Address where the applicant lives including: street number and street name, or rural route with a box number; apartment or unit number; city, town, or village name; state; and zip code; with instructions to draw a locational map if the applicant lives in a rural district or has a non-traditional residence, and directions not to use a post office box or rural route without a box number;

(3) Mailing address if different from the address where the applicant lives, such as a post office box, rural route without a box number, or other street address; city, town, or village name; state; and zip code;

(4) Month, day, and year of birth;

(5) Telephone number (optional); and

(6) Voter identification number as required or requested by the applicant's state of residence for election administration purposes.

(i) The application shall direct the applicant to consult the accompanying state-specific instructions to determine what type of voter identification number, if any, is required or requested by the applicant's state.

(ii) For each state that requires the applicant's full social security number as its voter identification number, the state's Privacy Act notice required at 11 CFR 9428.6(c) shall be reprinted with the instructions for that state.

(7) Political party preference, for an applicant in a closed primary state.

(i) The application shall direct the applicant to consult the accompanying state-specific instructions to determine if the applicant's state is a closed primary state.

(ii) The accompanying instructions shall state that if the applicant is registering in a state that requires the declaration of party affiliation, then failure to indicate a political party preference, indicating "none", or selecting a party that is not recognized under state law may prevent the applicant from voting in partisan races in primary elections and participating in political party caucuses or conventions, but will not bar an applicant from voting in other elections.

(8) Race/ethnicity, if applicable for the applicant's state of residence. The application shall direct the applicant to consult the state-specific instructions to determine whether race/ethnicity is required or requested by the applicant's state.

(b) *Additional information required by the Act.* (42 U.S.C. 1973gg–7(b) (2) and (4)). The form shall also:

(1) Specify each eligibility requirement (including citizenship). The application shall list U.S. Citizenship as a universal eligibility requirement and include a statement that incorporates by reference each state's specific additional eligibility requirements (including any special pledges) as set forth in the accompany state instructions;

(2) Contain an attestation on the application that the applicant, to the best of his or her knowledge and belief, meets each of his or her state's specific eligibility requirements;

(3) Provide a field on the application for the signature of the applicant, under penalty of perjury, and the date of the applicant's signature;

(4) Inform an applicant on the application of the penalties provided by law for submitting a false voter registration application;

(5) Provide a field on the application for the name, address, and (optional) telephone number of the person who assisted the applicant in completing the form if the applicant is unable to sign the application without assistance;

(6) State that if an applicant declines to register to vote, the fact that the applicant has declined to register will remain confidential and will be used only for voter registration purposes; and

(7) State that if an applicant does register to vote, the office at which the applicant submits a voter registration application will remain confidential and will be used only for voter registration purposes.

(c) *Other information.* The form will, if appropriate, require an applicant's former address or former name or request a drawing of the area where the applicant lives in relation to local landmarks.

[59 FR 32323, June 23, 1994; 59 FR 40639, Aug. 9, 1994. Redesignated and amended at 74 FR 35720, July 29, 2009]

§9428.5 Format.

(a) The application shall conform to the technical specifications described in the Commission's National Mail Voter Registration Form Technical Specifications.

(b) *Size.* The application shall consist of a 5″ by 8″ application card of sufficient stock and weight to satisfy postal regulations. The application card shall be attached by a perforated fold to another 5″ by 8″ card that contains space for the information set forth at 11 CFR 9428.4(c).

(c) *Layout.* (1) The application shall be sealable.

(2) The outside of the application shall contain an appropriate number of address lines to be completed by the applicant using the state information provided.

(3) Both sides of the application card shall contain space designated "For Official Use Only."

(d) *Color.* The application shall be of ink and paper colors of sufficient contrast to permit for optical scanning capabilities.

(e) *Signature field.* The application shall contain a signature field in lieu of a signature line.

(f) *Type size.* (1) All print on the form shall be of the largest practicable type size.

(2) The requirements on the form specified in 11 CFR 9428.4(b)(1), (6), and (7) shall be in print identical to that used in the attestation portion of the application required by 11 CFR 9428.4(b)(2).

[59 FR 32323, June 23, 1994. Redesignated and amended at 74 FR 37520, July 29, 2009]

§9428.6 Chief state election official.

(a) Each chief state election official shall certify to the Commission within 30 days after July 25, 1994:

(1) All voter registration eligibility requirements of that state and their corresponding state constitution or statutory citations, including but not limited to the specific state requirements, if any, relating to minimum age, length of residence, reasons to disenfranchise such as criminal conviction or mental incompetence, and whether the state is a closed primary state.

(2) Any voter identification number that the state requires or requests; and

(3) Whether the state requires or requests a declaration of race/ethnicity;

(4) The state's deadline for accepting voter registration applications; and

(5) The state election office address where the application shall be mailed.

(b) If a state, in accordance with 11 CFR 9428.4(a)(2), requires the applicant's full social security number, the chief state election official shall provide the Commission with the text of the state's privacy statement required under the Privacy Act of 1974 (5 U.S.C. 552a note).

(c) Each chief state election official shall notify the Commission, in writing, within 30 days of any change to the state's voter eligibility requirements or other information reported under this section.

[59 FR 32323, June 23, 1994. Redesignated and amended at 74 FR 35720, July 29, 2009]

Subpart C—Recordkeeping and Reporting

§ 9428.7 Contents of reports from the states.

(a) The chief state election official shall provide the information required under this section with the Commission by March 31 of each odd-numbered year beginning March 31, 1995 on a form to be provided by the Commission. Reports shall be mailed to: National Clearinghouse on Election Administration, Election Assistance Commission, 1201 New York Avenue, NW., Suite 300, Washington, DC 20005. The data to be reported in accordance with this section shall consist of applications or responses received up to and including the date of the preceding federal general election.

(b) Except as provided in paragraph (c) of this section, the report required under this section shall include:

(1) The total number of registered voters statewide, including both "active" and "inactive" voters if such a distinction is made by the state, in the federal general election two years prior to the most recent federal general election;

(2) The total number of registered voters statewide, including both "active" and "inactive" voters if such a distinction is made by the state, in the most recent federal general election;

(3) The total number of new valid registrations accepted statewide between the past two federal general elections, including all registrations that are new to the local jurisdiction and re-registrations across jurisdictional lines, but excluding all applications that are duplicates, rejected, or report only a change of name, address, or (where applicable) party preference within the local jurisdiction;

(4) If the state distinguishes between "active" and "inactive" voters, the total number of registrants statewide that were considered "inactive" at the close of the most recent federal general election;

(5) The total number of registrations statewide that were, for whatever reason, deleted from the registration list, including both "active" and "inactive" voters if such a distinction is made by the state, between the past two federal general elections;

(6) The statewide number of registration applications received statewide (regardless of whether they were valid, rejected, duplicative, or address, name or party changes) that were received from or generated by each of the following categories:

(i) All motor vehicle offices statewide;

(ii) Mail;

(iii) All public assistance agencies that are mandated as registration sites under the Act;

(iv) All state-funded agencies primarily serving persons with disabilities;

(v) All Armed Forces recruitment offices;

(vi) All other agencies designated by the state;

(vii) All other means, including but not limited to, in person, deputy registrars, and organized voter registration drives delivering forms directly to registrars;

(7) The total number of duplicate registration applications statewide that, between the past two federal general elections were received in the appropriate election office and generated by each of the categories described in paragraphs (b)(6) (i) through (vii) of this section;

(8) The statewide number of confirmation notices mailed out between the past two federal general elections and the statewide number of responses received to these notices during the same period;

(9) Answers to a series of questions with categorical responses for the state to indicate which options or procedures the state has selected in implementing the NVRA or any significant changes to the state's voter registration program; and

(10) Any additional information that would be helpful to the Commission for meeting the reporting requirement under 42 U.S.C. 1973gg–7(a)(3).

(c) For the State report due March 31, 1995, the chief state election official need only provide the information described in paragraph (b)(2) of this section and a brief narrative or general description of the state's implementation of the NVRA.

[59 FR 32323, June 23, 1994, as amended at 59 FR 64560, Dec. 15, 1994. Redesignated and amended at 74 FR 37520, July 29, 2009; 75 FR 49815, Aug. 16, 2010]

PART 9430—DEBT COLLECTION

Sec.
9430.1 Cross-reference to executive branch-wide debt collection regulations.
9430.2–9430.5 [Reserved]

AUTHORITY: 31 U.S.C. 3716(b); 31 U.S.C. 3711(d)(2); 31 CFR parts 900–904,

SOURCE: 74 FR 27906, June 12, 2009, unless otherwise noted.

§ 9430.1 Cross-reference to executive branch-wide debt collection regulations.

The U.S. Election Assistance Commission adopts the regulations at 31 CFR parts 900–904, governing administrative collection, offset, compromise, and the suspension or termination of collection activity for civil claims for money, funds, or property, as defined by 31 U.S.C. 3701(b).

§§ 9430.2–9430.5 [Reserved]

PARTS 9431–9499 [RESERVED]

FINDING AIDS

A list of CFR titles, subtitles, chapters, subchapters and parts, and an alphabetical list of agencies publishing in the CFR are included in the CFR Index and Finding Aids volume to the Code of Federal Regulations which is published separately and revised annually.

INDEXES TO REGULATIONS

EDITORIAL NOTE: These listings are provided for information purposes only. They are compiled and kept up to date by the Federal Election Commission. The indexes are updated as of January 1, 2018.

ADMINISTRATIVE REGULATIONS, PARTS 1-8; 200-201

A

Index, Administrative Regulations

S

GENERAL, PARTS 100-116

A

ACCEPTANCE OF CONTRIBUTIONS
See: CONTRIBUTIONS
ACCOUNT
Allocation between federal and Levin, *See:* ALLOCATION OF EXPENSES
Allocation between federal and nonfederal, *See:* ALLOCATION OF EXPENSES
Credit union, disbursements from, § 102.9(b)(2)(iii)
Established by collecting agent, § 102.6(c)(4)
Federal, separate from nonfederal, § 102.5(a)(1)(i) and (b)(1)(i)
Levin, *See:* "LEVIN" FUNDS
Office, *See:* OFFICE ACCOUNT
Transmittal, for joint fundraising, § 102.17(c)(4)
See also: CAMPAIGN DEPOSITORY
ACCOUNTANTS' SERVICES
See: LEGAL AND ACCOUNTING SERVICES
ACT
Definition, § 100.18
ADMINISTRATIVE EXPENSES
Allocation of, § 106.1(e)
— by nonconnected committee, § 106.6(b)(1)(i)
— by publicly funded presidential candidate, § 106.2(b)(2)(iii)
— by separate segregated fund, § 106.6(b)(1)(i)
— by State, district or local party committees, 106.7(c)(2) and (d)(2)
— not attributable to specific candidate, § 106.1(c)
— reporting by party committee, § 104.17(b)(1)
— reporting by separate segregated fund or nonconnected committee, § 104.10(b)(1)
Corporate/labor expenses for separate segregated fund, § 114.1(b); § 114.5(b)
Delegate selection, § 110.14(c)(1)(ii)
Polling results purchased by unauthorized committee, § 106.4(d)
Rent, salary, other recurring expenses not reported as debts, § 104.11(b)
ADMINISTRATIVE FINES
See: COMPLIANCE
ADMINISTRATIVE PERSONNEL
Definition, § 100.134(d); § 114.1(c)
See also: CORPORATION/LABOR ORGANIZATION/NATIONAL BANK
ADVERTISING
See: COMMUNICATIONS/ADVERTISING
ADVISORY OPINIONS
Issuance of, § 112.4
Reconsideration of, § 112.6
Reliance on, § 112.5
Requests for, § 112.1
— made public, § 112.2
— public comments on, § 112.3
Standing to receive, § 112.1(a)
AFFILIATED COMMITTEE
Assignment of debts to, § 116.2(c)(3)
Circumstantial factors determining affiliation, § 100.5(g)(4)(ii); § 110.3(a)(3)(ii)
Committees automatically considered as, § 110.3(a)(2)

407

CANDIDATE—Continued
Loans—Continued
— restriction on repayment of loans made by candidate to authorized committee, §116.11
Name included in
— authorized committee's name, §102.14(a)
— communication or special project opposing, §102.14(b)(3)
— unauthorized committee's name, §102.14(a) and (b)
Nonfederal campaign of federal candidate
— facilities and personnel, shared with federal campaign, §110.8(d)(3)
— separate organization from candidate's federal campaign required, §110.8(d)(1)
— solicitation of donors to, §110.3(d); §300.63
— transfers to federal campaign, prohibited, §110.3(d); §110.8(d)(2)
Personal funds, *See:* PERSONAL FUNDS
Personal use of campaign funds, §113.1(g); §113.2(f)(5)
Pre-1975, §110.2(g)
Presidential, *See:* CANDIDATE FOR PRESIDENT
Referred to in party solicitation, §102.5(a)(3)
State and local candidates
— contributions by, to federal campaign of another candidate, §102.5(b)(1); §110.1(a) and (b); §300.61
— contributions to, by a federal candidate, §113.2(d)
— endorsement of, by federal candidate, §109.21(g)
— federal funds not required for certain communications, §300.72
— federal funds required for certain communications, §300.71
— fundraising for, by federal candidate, §109.21(g); §300.62
— party activity for, when not considered federal election activity, §100.24(c)
— registration threshold for federal political activity, §100.5(a)
— solicitation of donors to, §109.21(g); §110.3(d); §300.62; §300.63
— transfers to federal campaign of same candidate, prohibited, §110.3(d); §110.8(d)(2)
See also: STATE OFFICEHOLDER
Support of, definition, §102.12(c)(2); §102.13(c)(2)
Testing-the-waters activity, §100.72(a) and (b); §100.131(a) and (b); §101.3; §106.4(a)
See also: TESTING THE WATERS EXPENSES
Transfers between
— federal/nonfederal campaigns, prohibited, §110.3(d); §110.8(d)(2)
— previous and current federal campaigns, §110.3(c)(4)
— two federal campaigns of same candidate, §110.3(c)(5); §110.8(d)(2)
See also: TRANSFER OF FUNDS
Travel by, *See:* TRAVEL
Unopposed, §100.2(c)(5); §110.1(j)(2) and (3); §110.2(k)
Vice presidential candidate, *See:* CANDIDATE FOR PRESIDENT
Voter guide, responses included in, §114.4(c)(5)
Voting record of, distributed by corporation or labor organization, §114.4(c)(4)
CANDIDATE FOR PRESIDENT
Appearances by
— at corporation/labor organization, §114.3(c)(2); §114.4(b)(1) and (2)
— at educational institution, §110.12; §114.4(c)(7)
— at fundraising event for State, district or local party committee, §300.64
— at fundraising event for tax-exempt organization, §300.65
— election year, §110.8(e)(2)(ii)
— party-building, §110.8(e)
See also: COMMUNICATIONS/ADVERTISING
Clearly identified, *See:* CLEARLY IDENTIFIED CANDIDATE
Contributions to, *See:* CONTRIBUTIONS
Debates, *See:* DEBATES
Delegate communications referring to, §110.14(f) and (i)

419

Index, General

CORPORATION/LABOR ORGANIZATION/NATIONAL BANK—Continued
  Separate segregated fund solicitations—Continued
    — corporate methods available to labor organizations, §114.5(k) and (l); §114.6(e)(3)
    — member of trade association, §114.8(c), (d), (e) and (f)
    — notice not required, §110.11(f)(2)
    — payroll deduction/check-off plan, §104.8(b) and (e)(4); §114.5(k)(1); §114.6(e)(1)
    — restrictions on who may be solicited, §114.5(g); §114.7(a)
    — twice yearly solicitations, §114.6
    — voluntary contribution only, §114.1(i); §114.5(a)
    See also: SEPARATE SEGREGATED FUND
  Stockholder, definition, §100.134(c); §114.1(h)
  Treasury funds, use of, §114.5(b)
  See also: MEMBERSHIP ORGANIZATION; TRADE ASSOCIATION; VOTER DRIVES
CREDIT CARDS
  Candidate advance from, §100.83
  Recordkeeping requirements, §102.9(b)(2)(ii)
  Use of individual's, §116.5(b)
CREDIT, EXTENSION OF
  By
    — any person, §100.55
    — brokerage loan or line of credit to candidate, §100.83
    — commercial vendor, §116.3
    — federally regulated industry, §116.3(d)
    — incorporated vendor, §116.3(b)
    — lending institution, §100.82(e); §100.142(e)
    — unincorporated vendor, §116.3(a)
  Defined, §116.1(e)
  In ordinary course of business, §100.55; §116.3(c)
  See also: COMMERCIAL VENDOR; CREDITOR; DEBTS; LOANS
CREDITOR
  Commercial vendor, See: COMMERCIAL VENDOR
  Defined, §116.1(f)
  Extension of credit, See: CREDIT, EXTENSION OF
  Lending institution, See: BANK; LOANS
  Out-of-business or with no known address, §116.9
  Remedies taken to collect on debts, §100.55; §116.4(d)(3)
  Settlement/forgiveness of debts, §100.55; §116.4; §116.8
  See also: DEBTS
CURRENCY
  See: CASH

D

DEBATES
  Candidate selection, criteria for, §110.13(c); §114.4(f)
  Funds used for
    — donated by corporation/labor organization, §114.4(f)
    — exemption, §100.29(c)(4); §100.92; §100.154
  Staging organizations, §110.13(a); §114.4(f)(1) and (2)
  Structure of, §110.13(b)
DEBTS
  Advances of goods/services from individuals, treatment as, §116.5(c)
  Assignment of, to another authorized committee, §116.2(c)(3)
  Bankruptcy, debts discharged in, §116.7(g)
  Collection of, by vendor, §100.55; §116.4(d)(3)
  Contributions to retire
    — calculation of net debts outstanding by campaign, §110.1(b)(3)(ii) and (iii); §110.2(b)(3)(ii)

Index, General

DEFINITIONS—Continued

Best efforts, to file reports in a timely manner, §111.35(b)(3)
Best efforts, to obtain, maintain and submit contributor information, §104.7
Bundled contribution, §104.22(a)(6)
Campaign traveler, §100.93(a)(3)(i)
Candidate, §100.3(a)
Cash on hand, §110.1(b)(3)(ii); §110.2(b)(3)(ii)
Caucus, §100.2(e)
Clearly identified candidate, §100.17; §106.1(d)
Collecting agent, §102.6(b)(1)
Commercial travel, §100.93(a)(3)(iv)
Commercial vendor, §116.1(c)
Commission, §100.9
Comparable aircraft, §100.93(a)(3)(vi)
Conduit, §110.6(b)(2)
Connected organization, §100.6
Consumer price index, §110.9(c)(2)
Contribution, §100.51-100.56; §114.1(a)(1)
Contribution exemptions, §100.71-100.92; §114.1(a)(2)
Contribution made, date of, §110.1(b)(6); §110.1(b)(4); §110.2(b)(6)
Convention, §100.2(e)
Coordinated, §109.20
Coordinated communication, §109.21
Corporation, §100.134(l)
Covered period, §104.22(a)(5)
Creditor, §116.1(f)
Current federal campaign committee, §110.3(c)(4)(ii)
Delegate, §110.14(b)(1)
Delegate committee, §100.5(e)(5); §110.14(b)(2)
Designated contribution, §110.1(b)(3) and (4); §110.1(j); §110.2(b)(3) and (4)
Direct, when raising/spending federal or nonfederal funds, §300.2(n)
Direct costs of producing or airing electioneering communications, §104.20(a)(2)
Direct mailing, §100.78; §100.87(a); §100.147(a); §100.149(a); §110.11(a); §110.14(f)(4)
Directly or indirectly establish, maintain, finance or control, §300.2(c)
Disbursement, §300.2(d)
Disclaimer notice, §110.11(a)
Disclosure date for electioneering communications, §104.20(a)(1)
Disputed debt, §116.1(d)
District or local committee, §100.14(b)
Donation, §300.2(e)
Donation to inaugural committee, §104.21(a)
Dual candidacy, §110.3(c)(5)
Earmarked contribution, §110.6(b)
Election, §100.2(a); §100.134(k); §104.6(a)(1) and (2)
Election cycle, §100.3(b)
Electioneering communication, §100.29
Employee participation plan, §114.11(a)
Employer, §100.21
Equipment and services used in internet activity, §100.94(c); §100.155(c)
Established or controls, §104.22(a)(4)
Executive or administrative personnel, §100.134(d); §114.1(c)
Expenditure, §100.110(a); §114.1(a)(1)
Expenditure exemptions, §100.130(a); §114.1(a)(2)
Expressly advocating, §100.22
Extension of credit, §116.1(e)
Facilitating the making of contributions, §114.2(f)
Family of candidate, §113.1(g)(7)
Federal account, §300.2(f)

Index, General

Index, General

DISCLAIMER NOTICE—Continued
Required for—Continued
— public communication by anyone that contains express advocacy, § 110.11(a)(2)
— public communication by anyone that contains solicitation, § 110.11(a)(3)
— public communication by political committee, § 110.11(a)(1)
— solicitation in public communication, § 102.16; § 102.17(c)(2); § 110.11(a)(3)
— television and radio communications, additional requirements for, § 110.11(c)(1), (3) and (4)
— website of political committee, § 110.11(a)(1)
See also: CAMPAIGN MATERIALS; COMMUNICATIONS/ADVERTISING; COORDINATED COMMUNICATIONS; DIRECT MAIL; ELECTIONEERING COMMUNICATIONS; EXPRESS ADVOCACY; INDEPENDENT EXPENDITURES; PUBLIC COMMUNICATION; PUBLIC POLITICAL ADVERTISING
DISCLOSURE
Access to FEC information
— Freedom of Information Act, Part 4
— Privacy Act, Part 1
See also: PUBLIC INSPECTION OF DOCUMENTS
Best efforts to obtain and submit information, *See:* BEST EFFORTS
By corporations and labor organizations
— for electioneering communications, § 104.5(j); § 104.20; § 114.10(b)(2)
— for express advocacy communications to restricted class, § 100.134(a); § 104.6; § 105.4; § 114.3(b); § 114.5(e)(2)(i)
— for independent expenditures, § 104.4(a); § 109.10; § 114.10(b)(1)
See also: COMMUNICATIONS; ELECTIONEERING COMMUNICATIONS; INDEPENDENT XPENDITURES
By independent spenders, *See:* INDEPENDENT EXPENDITURES/Reporting
Change in filing frequency, § 104.5(c)
Of fundraising activity
— bundled contributions, *See:* BUNDLING
— joint, § 102.6(c)(7); § 102.17(c)(3)(iii) and (8)
— using collecting agents, § 102.6(c)(7)
— using payroll deduction plan, *See:* PAYROLL DEDUCTION PLAN
Preemption of state laws governing, by Federal Election Campaign Act, § 108.7(b)(2)
Reporting deadlines, *See:* FILING
Reporting forms, *See:* FORMS
Reporting liability, *See:* TREASURER OF POLITICAL COMMITTEE
Reporting requirements/procedures, *See:* PAYROLL DEDUCTION PLAN; REPORTING
DISTRICT OF COLUMBIA
Filing exemption, § 108.8
DOCUMENT FILING
See: FILING
DRAFT COMMITTEE
Name of, restrictions, § 102.14(b)(2)
DUAL CANDIDACY
Contributions to, § 110.1(f); § 110.2(f)
Separate campaign organizations required, § 110.8(d)
Transfers between
— federal/nonfederal campaign committees, prohibited, § 110.3(d)
— federal principal campaign committees, § 110.3(c)(5); § 110.8(d)(2)

E

EARMARKED CONTRIBUTION
Collection of, § 110.6; § 114.2(f)
— by separate segregated fund, § 110.6; § 114.2(f)(2)(iii) and (4)(iii)

432

Index, General

EARMARKED CONTRIBUTION—Continued
  Collection of, § 110.6; § 114.2(f)—Continued
    — corporate/labor resources and facilities used for, § 114.2(f); § 114.3(c)(1); § 114.9
    See also: BUNDLING
  Conduit or intermediary, § 110.6(b)(2); § 114.2(f)(2)(iii), (3)(ii) and (4)(iii)
    See also: CONDUIT/INTERMEDIARY
  Contribution limits affected, § 110.6(a); § 114.2(f)(2)(iii) and (4)(iii)
  Definition, § 110.6(b)(1)
  Direction or control exercised, § 110.6(d)
    — reporting of, by conduit and recipient, § 110.6(d)(2)
  Facilitating the making of contributions, § 114.2(f)
    — by corporation/labor organization, prohibited, § 114.2(f)(1)
    — examples of, § 114.2(f)(2); § 114.3(c)(2)(iii)
    — separate segregated fund activity, exempt, § 114.2(f)(3) and (4)
  In joint fundraising, § 102.17(c)(2)(i)(C)
  Procedures for forwarding, § 102.8(c); § 110.6(b)(2)(iii)
  Reporting by
    — conduit, § 110.6(c)(1)
    — recipient, § 110.6(c)(2)
  Return required, § 110.6(b)(2)(iii)(B)
ELECTION
  Ballot access payments, § 100.90; § 100.150
  Contributions, per election
    — accounting for primary/general election contributions, § 102.9(e)
    — designated/undesignated, § 110.1(b); § 110.2(b)
    — for unopposed candidate, § 110.1(j)(2) and (3); § 110.2(k)
    — limits, § 110.1(b) and (j); § 110.2(b), (d), (e) and (i)
    — presidential primary, § 110.1(j)(1); § 110.2(i)
    — primary, § 110.1(j)(3) and (4); § 110.2(i)
  Definitions, § 100.2(a); § 100.134(k); § 104.6(a)(1) and (2); § 110.1(b)(2)
    — caucus or convention, § 100.2(e)
    — cycle, § 100.3(b)
    — general, § 100.2(b)
    — in connection with, in which federal candidate appears on ballot, § 100.24(a)
    — primary, § 100.2(c)
    — runoff, § 100.2(d)
    — special, § 100.2(f)
  Federal
    — candidate on ballot, in connection with, § 100.24(a)
    — referred to in party solicitation, § 102.5(a)(3)
  Recount expenses, § 100.91; § 100.151
  Reporting, election-year, § 104.5(a)(1), (b)(1) and (c)(1)
ELECTION INFLUENCING
  Communications advocating election/defeat of candidate, *See:* CLEARLY
    IDENTIFIED CANDIDATE; EXPRESS ADVOCACY; INDEPENDENT
    EXPENDITURES
  Contributions made for, *See:* CONTRIBUTIONS
  Corporate/labor activity, part 114
  Exempt activities for, *See:* CONTRIBUTION/EXPENDITURE EXEMPTIONS;
    PARTY COMMITTEE
  Expenditures made for, *See:* EXPENDITURES; INDEPENDENT
    EXPENDITURES
ELECTIONEERING COMMUNICATIONS
  By individuals, reporting, § 104.5(j); § 104.20
  By corporations, § 104.5(j); § 104.20; § 114.10
  By foreign national, prohibited, § 110.20(e)
  By labor organizations, § 104.5(j); § 104.20; § 114.10
  Coordination with campaign or party
    — content standard for coordinated communication, § 109.21(c)(1)
    — contribution in-kind results if coordinated, § 109.21(b)

433

EXPENDITURES—Continued

Advances of goods or services paid from individual's funds, §100.111(a); §116.5(b)

Allocation of, *See:* ALLOCATION OF EXPENDITURES

By authorized committee, *See:* CAMPAIGN FUNDS, USE OF

By candidate, *See:* CAMPAIGN FUNDS, USE OF; CANDIDATE

By cash, §102.11; §103.3(a)

By check, §102.10; §103.3(a)

By corporation/labor organization/national bank
— defined, §114.1
— when prohibited, §114.2(a)

By delegate, §110.14(e) and (f)

By delegate committee, §110.14(h) and (i)

By Federal contractor, §115.2

By foreign national, prohibited, §110.20(f)

By party committee, §100.24; §102.13(b); §104.17; §106.7; §106.8; §109.23(b)(5); §109.30-109.37; §300.10; §300.30(b)(3)(iii); §300.32

By spouse, §100.110(b); §100.130(b)

By State, district or local party committee, for federal election activity, §300.32(b) and (c)

By vice presidential candidate, §110.8(f) and (g)

Communications, made for, *See:* COMMUNICATIONS/ADVERTISING; DIRECT MAIL; INDEPENDENT EXPENDITURES; PUBLIC POLITICAL ADVERTISING

Contract or agreement to make, §100.112; §104.11(b)

Coordinated party, §102.13(b); §109.23(b)(5); §109.30-109.34

Delegate selection, §110.14(c)(1)

Definition, §100.110(a); §114.1(a)(1)

Exemptions, §100.130(a); §114.1(a)(2)
See also: CONTRIBUTION/EXPENDITURE EXEMPTIONS

Electioneering communications not considered as, §100.29(c)(3)
See also: ELECTIONEERING COMMUNICATIONS

Expressly advocating, definition, §100.22
See also: EXPRESS ADVOCACY; COMMUNICATIONS/ADVERTISING; INDEPENDENT EXPENDITURES

Illegal, §110.9(a); §110.14(c)(2); §110.20(f); §114.2(a) and (b); §115.2

Independent, *See:* INDEPENDENT EXPENDITURES

In joint fundraising, §102.17(b)(3)

In-kind contribution, considered expenditure, §104.13(a)(2); §106.1(b); §109.20; §109.21(b); §110.14(f)(2)(i)
See also: COORDINATION; COMMUNICATIONS/ADVERTISING; IN-KIND CONTRIBUTION

Limitations
— based on voting age population, §109.32(a)(2) and (b)(2)(i)(A); §110.8(a)(3); §110.18
— increases, based on price index, §110.9(c)
— party committees' coordinated expenditures, §109.32
— presidential candidates receiving public funding, §110.8

Loans, *See:* LOANS

"Made on behalf of," defined, §110.8(g)

Overhead, of state offices, §106.2(b)(2)(iv)

Payee, identification of, §104.9

Personal funds, §100.153; §106.3(b)(1); §110.8(f)(2); §110.10

Political committee status, criterion for, §100.5(a), (c) and (f)

Polling, §106.2(b)(2)(vi) and (c)(1)(iii); §106.4

Prohibited, §110.9(a); §110.14(c)(2); §114.2(a) and (b); §115.2

Promise to make, §100.112

Purpose of, definition, §104.3(b)(3)(i)(A) and (B); §104.9(a)

Recordkeeping, *See:* RECORDKEEPING

Reporting, *See:* REPORTING

Specific expenditures by campaign, *See:* CAMPAIGN FUNDS, USE OF

EXPENDITURES—Continued
  Testing-the-waters expenses, §100.72(a) and (b); §100.131(a) and (b); §106.4(a);
    §101.3
  Transfers, *See:* TRANSFER OF FUNDS
  Travel expenses, *See:* TRAVEL
  Treasurer's authorization, §102.7(c)
  Violations, §110.9(a)
EXPRESS ADVOCACY
  Allocation of expenditures for, §106.1
  Functional equivalent of, definition, §109.21(c)(5)
  Communications containing
    — by corporation or labor organization, §114.2; §114.3
    — content standard for coordinated communication, §109.21(c)(3);
      §109.37(a)(2)(ii)
    — coordination of, with candidate or party, §109.20; §109.21; §114.2(c);
      §114.10(a)
    — functional equivalent of, content standard for coordinated communication,
      §109.21(c)(5)
    — not coordinated with any candidate or party, *See:* INDEPENDENT
      EXPENDITURE
    See also: COMMUNICATIONS/ADVERTISING; COORDINATION; DIRECT
      MAIL; INDEPENDENT EXPENDITURES; PUBLIC COMMUNICATION;
      PUBLIC POLITICAL ADVERTISING
  Corporate/labor communications containing, §104.6; §114.2(a)(1) and (c); §114.3;
    §114.4(c)(1) and (6); §114.10
    — endorsement, public announcement of, §114.4(c)(6)
    — reporting costs of, §100.134(a); §104.6; §105.4; §114.3(b); §114.5(e)(2)(i)
    — to restricted class only, §114.1(j); §114.3(a)
  Definition of, §100.22
  Disclaimer notice required, §109.11; §110.11(a)(2); §114.10(c)
    See also: DISCLAIMER NOTICE
  Electioneering communications do not contain, §100.29(c)(3)
  Independent expenditure contains, *See:* INDEPENDENT EXPENDITURES
  Newspaper stories/editorials/commentaries, exempted as expenditures for,
    §100.73; §100.132
  Reporting requirements, *See:* COORDINATION; FILING; COMMUNICATIONS/
    ADVERTISING; INDEPENDENT EXPENDITURES/Reporting; REPORTING
  Used by
    — corporations and labor organizations, §100.134(a); §104.6; §105.4; §110.11(a)(2);
      §114.2(a) and (c); §114.3; §114.5(e)(2)(i); §114.7(h) and (k)(2); §114.8(h); §114.10
    — delegates, for federal candidates, §110.14(f)(2)(ii)
    — party committees, §100.87; §100.147; §110.11(a)
  Used in
    — campaign materials, *See:* CAMPAIGN MATERIALS
    — independent expenditures, §100.16; §114.10
    — political ads, §110.11
    — volunteer activity, *See:* VOLUNTEER ACTIVITY
    — voter drives, *See:* VOTER DRIVES
    See also: CLEARLY IDENTIFIED CANDIDATE; COMMUNICATIONS/
      ADVERTISING; INDEPENDENT EXPENDITURES

F

FEDERAL COMMUNICATIONS COMMISSION
  Database for electioneering communications, §100.29(b)(6)(i)
FEDERAL CONTRACTOR
  Acting as conduit, prohibited, §110.6(b)(2)(ii)
  Contributions/expenditures by, prohibited, §115.2
  Definition, §115.1(a)
  Earmarked contribution received by, §110.6(b)(2)(iii)(B)

Index, General

FORMS—Continued
  Computer-produced, § 104.2(d); § 104.18
  Consolidated reports (FEC Form 3Z), § 104.3(f)
  Debts and obligations, § 104.3(d); § 104.18(h)
  Electioneering communications (FEC Form 9), § 104.20(b)
  Electronically filed, § 104.18
  Inaugural committee reports (FEC Form 13), § 104.21(c)
  Independent expenditure reports, § 104.4(a); § 109.10(b) and (c)
  Loans, § 104.3
    — from lending institutions, § 104.3(d)(1)
  Notification of Multicandidate Status (FEC Form 1M), § 102.2(a)(3)
  Obtainable from the Commission, § 102.2(a); § 104.2(b)
  Receipts/disbursements, reports of
    — by congressional committees, § 104.2(e)(2)
    — by presidential committees, § 104.2(e)(1); § 106.2(d) and (e)
    — by unauthorized committees, § 104.2(e)(3); § 300.36
  Reproducing FEC forms, § 104.2(c)
  Statement of Candidacy (FEC Form 2), § 101.1
  Statement of Organization (FEC Form 1), § 102.1(a); § 102.2(a)(1)
  Termination reports, § 102.3(a)
  See also: FILING; REPORTING
FREEDOM OF INFORMATION ACT, See: Index for ADMINISTRATIVE
    REGULATIONS/Freedom of Information Act
FUNDRAISING
  Allocation of expenses for, See: ALLOCATION OF EXPENSES
  By candidate/federal officeholder
    — direct, definition of, § 300.2(n)
    — for State, district or local committee of political party, § 300.64
    — for State party candidates, § 300.63
    — for tax-exempt organization, § 300.52; § 300.65
    — prohibitions, § 300.60-300.62
    — solicit, definition of, § 300.2(m)
  Bundled, See: BUNDLING
  By collecting agent, § 102.6(b) and (c)
  By commercial firm, § 102.6(b)(3); § 110.6(b)(2)(i)(D)
  By corporation/labor organization
    — for candidates and political committees, § 114.2(f); § 114.3(c)(2)(iii)
    — for segregated account used for electioneering communications, § 114.10(d)
    — for separate segregated fund, § 114.5(b)
  By presidential candidates receiving public funds
    — before state primary, § 110.8(c)(2)
    — exemption, § 100.152; § 106.2(b)
  By unauthorized committee
    — use of candidate's name for, § 102.14(a)
    — use of corporate/labor facilities and resources for, § 114.2(f); § 114.9; § 114.13
  Combined dues/contributions, § 102.6(c)(3)
  Coordinated with nonfederal campaign, § 110.3(d)
  Corporate/labor facilities and resources used for, § 114.2(f); § 114.9; § 114.13
  Disclaimer requirements
    — for best efforts notice, § 104.7(b)(1)
    — for public communication soliciting funds, § 110.11(a)(2) and (b)
    — for separate segregated fund, § 110.11(f)(2); § 114.5(a)(2);-(5)
    — when soliciting both federal/nonfederal funds, § 102.5(a)(2)
    See also: DISCLAIMER NOTICE
  Exemption for publicly funded candidate
    — national, § 100.152
    — state, § 110.8(c)(2)
  For "Levin" funds, § 300.31
  For separate segregated fund, See: SEPARATED SEGREGATED FUND
  Joint, See: JOINT FUNDRAISING

FUNDRAISING—Continued
  Limitation, § 100.152
  Name of candidate used in, § 102.14(a) and (b)(3)
  Notices required when, *See:* DISCLAIMER NOTICE
  Payment to attend event, § 100.53
  Prohibitions for
    — federal candidates and officeholders, § 300.31(e); § 300.52; § 300.61-300.65
    — national party committee, § 300.10; § 300.11; § 300.50
    — State, district or local party committee, § 300.37; § 300.51
  Project using candidate's name, § 102.14(a) and (b)(3)
  Representative, § 102.17(b)(1) and (2)
  Sale of fundraising items, § 100.53
  See also: COMMUNICATIONS/ADVERTISING; CONTRIBUTIONS; DISCLAIMER
    NOTICE

G

GENERAL ELECTION
  Contributions for, separated from primary contributions, § 102.9(e)
  Definition, § 100.2(b)
  See also: ELECTION; PRIMARY ELECTION
GET-OUT-THE-VOTE DRIVE
  See: VOTER DRIVES
GIFT
  Campaign funds used to purchase, § 113.1(g)(4)
  Made to influence election, § 100.52(a); § 100.111(a)
GOVERNMENT CONTRACTOR
  See: FEDERAL CONTRACTOR
GOVERNMENT CONVEYANCE
  See: TRAVEL

H

HANDICAPPED PERSONS
  See: Index for ADMINISTRATIVE REGULATIONS/Handicapped Persons
HOST COMMITTEE (CONVENTION)
  Registration and reporting, § 107.2
HOUSE CAMPAIGN COMMITTEE
  Contributions by, § 110.2(b)(1); § 110.3(b)(1) and (2)(i)
  Contributions to, § 110.1(c)(2); § 110.2(c)(2); § 110.3(b)(1) and (2)(i)
  Prohibition on fundraising for and donating to certain tax-exempt
    organizations, § 300.11
  Prohibition on raising and spending nonfederal funds, § 300.10; § 300.50
  See also: NATIONAL PARTY COMMITTEE; PARTY COMMITTEE

I

IDENTIFICATION
  Definition, § 100.12
  Requesting, § 104.7(b)
  See also: BEST EFFORTS; RECORDKEEPING; REPORTING
INAUGURAL COMMITTEE
  Definition, § 104.21(a)(1)
  Donations to
    — by foreign nationals, prohibited, § 110.20(j)
    — definition, § 104.21(a)(2)
  Initial filing by, § 104.21(b)
  Recordkeeping by, § 104.21(d)
  Reporting requirements for, § 104.21(c)
INCORPORATION
  Of political committee, § 114.12(a)

INCUMBENT
Federal officeholder defined, § 113.1(c)
Government transportation used by, for presidential campaign, *See:* Index for GENERAL ELECTION FINANCING/Travel; Index for PRIMARY ELECTION FINANCING/Qualified Campaign Expenses
Office account of, *See:* OFFICE ACCOUNT
Personal use of campaign funds by, § 113.1(g); § 113.2(f)
See also: CAMPAIGN FUNDS, USE OF; CANDIDATE
Qualified Member, definition, § 113.1(f)
*See also:*CANDIDATE; CONGRESS, MEMBER OF
INDEPENDENT EXPENDITURES
Agent of candidate or party, definition, § 109.3
Attribution of, among candidates, § 106.1(a)
Authorized committee, involvement of
— agent of, definition, § 109.3(b)
— campaign materials produced by candidate, precluded, § 109.21(c)(2); § 109.23(a)(1); § 109.37(a)(2)(i); § 110.14(f)(3)
— contribution in-kind, if coordinated, § 100.16(c); § 109.20(b); § 109.21(a) and (b); § 109.37(b)
— coordination with candidate or party precludes, § 109.20(b); § 109.21(a) and (b); § 109.37(b); § 114.2(c); § 114.10(a)
See also: COORDINATION; COMMUNICATIONS/ADVERTISING
By corporations and labor organizations
— disclaimer required, § 110.11; § 114.10(c)
— permitted, § 114.10(a)
— reporting of, § 104.4(a); § 109.10; § 114.10(b)(1)
By party committees
— by national party committee, when prohibited, § 109.36
— can be made before or after nomination, § 109.34
— permissible, § 109.30
See also: COORDINATION; COMMUNICATIONS/ADVERTISING; PARTY COMMITTEE
Certification of independence, § 109.10(e)(2)
Clearly identified candidate, definition, § 100.17; § 106.1)(d)
Contribution in-kind, if coordinated, § 109.20(b); § 109.21(a) and (b); § 109.37(b); § 114.2(c); § 114.10(a)
See also: COORDINATION; COMMUNICATIONS/ADVERTISING
Contributions made to political committees making, § 110.1(n)
Coordination of
— contribution in-kind, § 109.20(b); § 109.21(a) and (b); § 109.37(b)
— corporate/labor communication, § 114.2(c); § 114.10(a)
See also: COORDINATION; COMMUNICATIONS/ADVERTISING; PARTY COMMITTEE
Defined as expenditure, § 100.113
Definition, § 100.16
Delegate/delegate committee expenditures for federal candidate, § 110.14(f)(2) and (i)(2)
Electioneering communication, exempt from definition, § 100.29(c)(3)
Express advocacy required, § 100.16(a)
See also: EXPRESS ADVOCACY
Notice of nonauthorization required, § 109.11; § 110.11(b)(3) and (c)(1) and (4); § 114.10(c)
See also: DISCLAIMER NOTICE
Opposing candidate, use of candidate's name in title, § 102.14(b)(3)
Reporting, § 104.4; § 109.10
— 24 hour reports, § 100.19(d); § 104.4(c); § 104.5(g)(2); § 105.2(b); § 109.10(d)
— 48 hour reports, § 100.19(d); § 104.4(b)(2); § 104.5(g)(1); § 105.2(b); § 109.10(c)
— aggregating, § 104.4(f)
— by corporations and labor organizations, § 104.4(a); § 109.10; § 114.10(b)(1)
— by persons other than political committees, § 104.4(a); § 105.4; § 109.10

Index, General

Index, General

LOANS—Continued

Reporting—Continued

— repayment of loan from brokerage account or advances from lines of credit to candidate by third party, § 100.83(c)(3)

Standards for loans from lending institutions

— basis that assures repayment, § 100.82(e); § 100.142(e)

— ordinary course of business, § 100.82; § 100.83(a); § 100.142(a)-(d)

See also: DEBTS

LOCAL PARTY COMMITTEE

Definition, § 100.14(b)

Contributions

— from committee, § 110.1; § 110.2; § 110.3(b)

— limits shared with state party committee, § 110.3(b)(3)

— to committee, § 110.1(c); § 110.3(b)

Coordinated party expenditures by, *See:* COORDINATION; PARTY COMMITTEE/Coordinated Party Expenditures

Exempt activities conducted by

— campaign materials, § 100.87; § 100.147

— disclaimer notice for, § 110.11(e)

— federal election activity, may be considered, § 100.24(b)(3); § 100.26; § 300.33(c)

— slate cards and sample ballots, § 100.80; § 100.140

— voter registration and get-out-the-vote for presidential candidates, § 100.89; § 100.149

See also: CAMPAIGN MATERIALS; FEDERAL ELECTION ACTIVITY; PARTY COMMITTEE; PUBLIC COMMUNICATION; SLATE CARD/SAMPLE BALLOT; VOTER DRIVES

Federal election activity, *See:* FEDERAL ELECTION ACTIVITY

Independent expenditures by, *See:* COORDINATION; INDEPENDENT EXPENDITURES; PARTY COMMITTEE

"Levin" funds, use of, *See:* FEDERAL ELECTION ACTIVITY; "LEVIN" FUNDS

Prohibition on fundraising for and donating to certain tax-exempt organizations, § 300.37; § 300.51

Registration

— requirements, § 102.1(d)

— threshold, § 100.5(c)

Salaries, benefits and wages paid by, § 100.24(b)(3); § 106.7(c)(1) and (d)(1); § 300.33(d)

Subordinate committee, definition, § 100.14(c)

See also: PARTY COMMITTEE

M

MAILING LIST

Electronic mailing address list purchased for or transferred to political committee, § 100.94(e)(2) and (3); § 100.155(e)(2) and (3)

Federal election activity, use for, § 100.24(a)(4) and (b)(2); § 300.32(b)(1)(ii); § 300.33(a)(2)

In-kind contribution, donation results in, § 100.52(d)(1); § 100.94(e)(2) and (3); § 100.155(e)(2) and (3)

Information from FEC reports used for, prohibited, § 104.15(a)

See also: DIRECT MAIL

MEDIA

See: COMMUNICATIONS/ADVERTISING

MEMBER OF CONGRESS

See: CONGRESS, MEMBERS OF; FEDERAL OFFICEHOLDER

MEMBERS

Definition, § 100.134(f); § 114.1(e)(2); § 114.7(i)

Financial obligations/voting rights, criteria for membership in membership organization, § 100.134(f); § 114.1(e)(2)

447

MEMBERSHIP ORGANIZATION
  Affiliation, § 100.134(h) and (i); § 114.1(e)(4)
  Communications by, § 100.134(a); § 110.11(f)(2); § 114.7(h); § 114.10
    — beyond restricted class, § 114.4; § 114.10
    — containing express advocacy, to restricted class, § 114.1(j); § 114.3; § 114.7(h)
       and (k)(2)
    — disclaimer notice not required, § 110.11(f)(2)
    — electioneering, § 114.10
    — reporting, § 100.134(a); § 104.6
    — restricted class for, § 114.1(j)
    — to general public, § 114.4(a) and (c); § 114.10
  Definition of, § 100.134(e); § 114.1(e)(1)
  Electioneering communications by, § 104.20; § 114.10
    — disclaimer requirements, § 110.11; § 114.10(c)
    — reporting required, § 104.5(j); § 114.10(b)(2)
    — segregated bank account may be established for, § 114.10(d)
    See also: ELECTIONEERING COMMUNICATIONS
  Fundraising by
    — combined dues/contribution payments, § 102.6(c)(3)
    — disclaimer notice not required, § 110.11(f)(2)
    — using affiliates as collecting agents, § 102.6(b) and (c)
    See also: COLLECTING AGENT; STATE ASSOCIATION
  Independent expenditure by, § 114.10
    — disclaimer requirements, § 110.11; § 114.10(c)
    — reporting required, § 109.10(b)-(e); § 114.10(b)(1)
    See also:COORDINATION; INDEPENDENT EXPENDITURES
  Member of, defined, § 100.134(f); § 114.1(e)(2); § 114.7(i)
  Multitiered, § 100.134(i) and § 114.1(e)(5)
  Separate segregated fund established by, § 114.1(a)(2)(iii) and (b); § 114.7(a) and
     (e)
    See also: SEPARATE SEGREGATED FUND
  Student members of, § 100.134(g); § 114.1(e)(3)
  See also: COMMUNICATIONS/ADVERTISING; COOPERATIVE; CORPORATION/
    LABOR ORGANIZATION/NATIONAL BANK/Labor Organization;
    CORPORATION WITHOUT CAPITAL STOCK; MEMBERSHIP
    ORGANIZATION, INCORPORATED; TRADE ASSOCIATION
MINORS
  Contributions made
    — must be made knowingly and voluntarily, § 110.19(a)
    — funds, goods, or services contributed are owned or controlled by minor,
       § 110.19(b)
    — not made from the proceeds of a gift that is controlled by another
       individual, § 110.19(c)
MULTICANDIDATE COMMITTEE
  Contributions by, limitations, § 110.2
  Definition, § 100.5(e)(3)
  Notification of status as
    — to candidates receiving contributions, § 110.2(a)(2)
    — to Commission, § 102.2(a)(3)
  See also: POLITICAL COMMITTEE; UNAUTHORIZED COMMITTEE

N

NAME
  Acronym, use of, § 102.14(c)
  Candidate's, use of
    — by party committee, § 102.5(a)(3)
    — by unauthorized committee, § 102.14(a) and (b)(3)
    — clearly identifying candidate, § 100.17; § 106.1(d)
  Contributor's, request for, § 104.7(b)

452

POLITICAL COMMITTEE—Continued
Audits of, § 104.16
See also: AUDITS
Authorized, *See:* AUTHORIZED COMMITTEE
Campaign depository, *See:* CAMPAIGN DEPOSITORY
Collecting agent for, § 102.6(b) and (c)
Communications/advertising by, § 110.11(a)
See also: COMMUNICATIONS/ADVERTISING; PUBLIC COMMUNICATION
Contributions to, § 110.1(d)
Definition, § 100.5
Debts owed by, *See:* DEBTS
Delegate committee, *See:* DELEGATE/Committee
Federal/nonfederal, § 100.24(c); § 102.5; § 106.1(e); § 106.6; § 106.7; § 300.10; § 300.30
Filing reports, *See:* FILING; FORMS; REPORTING
Forwarding contributions to, § 102.8
Fundraising by, § 110.11(a)
See also: FUNDRAISING
Funds, separate from personal, § 102.15
Host committee (convention), registration and reporting, § 107.1
Identification number, § 102.2(c)
Incorporation of, § 114.12(a)
Independent expenditures by, *See:* COORDINATION; COMMUNICATIONS/
ADVERTISING; DISCLAIMER NOTICE; EXPRESS ADVOCACY;
INDEPENDENT EXPENDITURES
Internet activities by, *See:* COMMUNICATIONS/ADVERTISING; DISCLAIMER
NOTICE; INTERNET ACTIVITIES
Joint fundraising, committee established for, § 102.17(b)(1) and (2)
Leadership PAC, *See:* LEADERSHIP PAC
Multicandidate, *See:* MULTICANDIDATE COMMITTEE
Municipal Fund (convention), registration and reporting, § 107.1
Name of, restrictions, § 102.14
Nonconnected, *See:* NONCONNECTED COMMITTEE
Ongoing, *See:* ONGOING COMMITTEE
Organization of, § 102.7
Party, *See:* LOCAL PARTY COMMITTEE; NATIONAL PARTY COMMITTEE;
PARTY COMMITTEE; STATE PARTY COMMITTEE
Petty cash fund, § 102.11; § 103.3(a)
Principal campaign, *See:* PRINCIPAL CAMPAIGN COMMITTEE
Recordkeeping requirements, *See:* RECORDKEEPING
Registration, § 102.1; § 102.2; § 102.6(a)(2); § 102.17(a)(1)
Reporting requirements, *See:* REPORTING
Separate segregated fund, *See:* SEPARATE SEGREGATED FUND
Single candidate, *See:* SINGLE CANDIDATE COMMITTEE
Statement of Organization, § 102.1; § 102.2
Termination of, *See:* TERMINATION OF COMMITTEE
Transfers among, *See:* TRANSFER OF FUNDS
Treasurer, *See:* TREASURER OF POLITICAL COMMITTEE
Unauthorized, *See:* UNAUTHORIZED COMMITTEE
POLITICAL PARTY
See: LOCAL PARTY COMMITTEE; NATIONAL PARTY COMMITTEE; PARTY
COMMITTEE; STATE PARTY COMMITTEE
POLLING
Acceptance of results, § 106.4(b) and (c)
Allocation of expenditure
— by candidate, § 106.4(e)
— by candidate, presidential, § 106.2(b)(2)(v)
— by unauthorized committee, § 106.4(d)
— methods for, § 106.4(e)
— reporting of, § 106.4(f), (g) and (h)
Contribution in-kind, § 106.4

PUBLIC FINANCING
  See: Indexes for GENERAL ELECTION FINANCING; FEDERAL FINANCING
    OF PRESIDENTIAL NOMINATING CONVENTIONS; PRESIDENTIAL
    PRIMARY MATCHING FUND
PUBLIC INSPECTION OF DOCUMENTS
  Advisory opinions and requests for, § 112.2
  Compliance proceedings
    — confidentiality, § 111.21
    — public disclosure, § 111.20
  Reports
    — filed with State officials, § 108.6(c)
    — sale/use restriction, § 104.15
  See also: Index for ADMINISTRATIVE REGULATIONS/Public Disclosure
PUBLIC POLITICAL ADVERTISING
  Allocation of expenditures for
    — among several candidates, § 100.52(d); § 106.1(b)
    — on behalf of presidential candidate, § 106.2(b)(2)(i)
  Coordinated with campaign or party, *See:* COORDINATION
  Defined, § 100.26; § 110.11(a)
  Electioneering communication, *See:* ELECTIONEERING COMMUNICATION
  Expressly advocating, definition, § 100.22; § 109.2(b)(2)
  Independent expenditures made for, *See:* COORDINATION; INDEPENDENT
    EXPENDITURES
  Media used for, § 100.26; § 110.11(a)
  Notice required for, § 102.16; § 109.11; § 110.11(a)
    See also: DISCLAIMER NOTICE
  Public communication, *See:* PUBLIC COMMUNICATION
  Rates charged for space, § 110.11(g)
  Television and radio ads, additional requirements for, § 110.11(c)(3) and (4)
  Uses
    — campaign materials mentioning other candidates, § 100.88(a) and (b);
      § 100.148; § 109.21(g)
    — exempted party activities, prohibited, § 100.80; § 100.87(a); § 100.89(a); § 100.140;
      § 100.147(a); § 100.149(a)
    — testing-the-waters activities, indicator of candidacy, § 100.72(a) and (b);
      § 100.131(a) and (b)
  See: COMMUNICATIONS/ADVERTISING

R

RECEIPTS
  Deposit of, § 103.3(a)
  Reporting, *See:* REPORTING
  See also: CONTRIBUTIONS
RECORDKEEPING
  Allocation, documentation of
    — for party committee, § 104.17(a)(4) and (b)(4)
    — for presidential campaigns, § 106.2(b) and (d)
    — for separate segregated fund and nonconnected committee, § 104.10(a)(4) and
      (b)(5)
  Collecting agent, duties of, § 102.6(c)(5) and (6)
  Contributions
    — aggregate of individual's, § 104.8(b)
    — best efforts, *See:* BEST EFFORTS
    — bundled, § 104.22(a)(6) and (j)
    — by check, § 104.8(c) and (d)
    — by payroll deduction, § 104.8(b)
    — contributor identification, § 100.12; § 104.7(b); § 104.8(a) and (b)
    — designations/redesignations, § 102.9(e); § 110.1(l)
    — earmarked, § 102.8(c); § 110.6(b)(2)(iii)

REPORTING—Continued

Pseudonyms, § 104.3(e)

Public inspection of reports, *See:* PUBLIC INSPECTION OF DOCUMENTS

Quarterly report
— by congressional committee, § 104.5(a)(1)
— by presidential committee, § 104.5(b)(1)(ii) and (2)(ii)
— by unauthorized committee, § 104.5(c)(1)(i)
— waivers, § 104.5(a)(1)(iii) and (c)(1)(i)(C)

Receipts
— cash-on-hand, § 104.3(a)(1); § 104.12
— categories of, § 104.3(a)(2) and (3)
— itemization of, § 104.3(a)(4)
— uniform reporting of, § 104.8

Requirements, formal, § 104.14; § 104.18

Sale/use restriction on filed reports, § 104.15

Semiannual report by unauthorized committee, § 104.5(c)(2)(i)

Separate segregated fund reports, § 114.5(e)

Special election reports, § 104.5(h)

State filing, *See:* FILING

State officers' duties, § 108.6

Stocks, bonds, art objects, § 104.13(b)

Termination report, § 102.3(a)

Testing-the-waters activity, § 101.3

Transfers
— assigned debts, § 116.2(c)(3)(ii)
— between federal and nonfederal accounts, by party committee, § 104.17(a)(2) and (b)(2)
— between federal and nonfederal accounts, by separate segregated fund or nonconnected committee, § 104.10(a)(2) and (b)(3)
— from political committee, § 104.3(b)(3)(ii) and (4)(ii)
— of Levin funds, § 300.36(b)(2)(ii)
— to committee, § 104.3(a)(4)(iii)

Transmittal of reports to Commission by Secretary of the Senate, § 105.5

Treasurer of committee, duties of, § 104.1(a); § 104.14

Vice presidential committee reports, § 104.5(d)

Voluntary, § 104.1(b)

Waivers
— for special election, § 104.5(h)(2)
— monthly, § 104.5(b)(1)(i)(C) and (c)(3)(ii)
— quarterly, § 104.5(a)(1)(iii) and (c)(1)(i)(C)

Year-end report
— by presidential committee, § 104.5(b)(1)(i)(C)
— by unauthorized committee, § 104.5(c)(1)(i)(A) and (2)(i)(B)

See also: FILING; FORMS; RECORDKEEPING

RESTRICTED CLASS

Communications directed to, by corporations, membership organizations and labor organizations, § 100.134(a); § 114.1(a)(2)(i) and (j); § 114.2(a) and (c); § 114.3; § 114.7(g) and (k)(2); § 114.8(h)

Defined
— for communications, § 114.1(j); § 114.7(g) and (k)(2); § 114.8(h)
— for cooperatives, § 100.134(f); § 114.1(e)(2) and (j); § 114.5(g)(1); § 114.7(a), (h) and (k)
— for corporations, § 100.134(c) and (d); § 114.1(c), (h) and (j); § 114.5(g)(1)
— for labor organizations, § 100.134(f); § 114.1(e)(2); § 114.5(g)(2)
— for membership organization, § 100.134(f); § 114.1(e)(2) and (j); § 114.5(g)(1); § 114.7(a) and (h)
— for national banks, § 100.134(c) and (d); § 114.1(c), (h) and (j); § 114.5(g)(1)
— for trade associations, § 100.134(f); § 114.1(e)(2); § 114.5(g)(1); § 114.7(c); § 114.8(c), (f), (h) and (i)
— for unincorporated association, § 100.134(f)

461

Index, General

GENERAL ELECTION FINANCING, PARTS 9001-9007 AND 9012*

A

ACCOUNTS
  See: CAMPAIGN DEPOSITORY
ADJUSTMENT OF ENTITLEMENT
  See: ENTITLEMENT; PAYMENTS
AGREEMENT
  Candidate agrees to
    — accept burden of proof, §9003.1(b)(1)
    — comply with Act and regulations, §9003.1(b)(8)
    — comply with documentation requirements, §9003.1(b)(2)
    — file reports electronically, §9003.1(b)(11)
    — furnish computerized records, if kept, §9003.1(b)(4)
    — identify depositories, §9003.1(b)(7)
    — identify treasurer, §9003.1(b)(7)
    — keep books and records, §9003.1(b)(4)
    — make repayments, §9003.1(b)(6)
    — pay civil penalty, if required, §9003.1(b)(9)
    — permit/facilitate audit and examination, §9003.1(b)(6)
    — provide explanation/additional information, §9003.1(b)(3), (4) and (5); §9012.4
    — use closed captioning in television ads, §9003.1(b)(10)
  Eligibility for payments requires, §9003.1(a)(1)
  Submission dates for, §9003.1(a)(2)
  See also: ELIGIBILITY
ALLOCATION
  Alternative methods of determining compliance-related costs,
      §9003.3(a)(2)(ii)(F) and (b)(7)
  Of expenditures among states, §106.2
  Of travel expenditures, §9004.7
  Recordkeeping, §9003.3(a)(2)(ii)(A) and (3)
AUDIT AND EXAMINATION
  Additional, §9007.1(a)(2); §9007.4
  Agreement to permit, §9003.1(b)(6)
  Committee response to, §9007.1(c)
    — extension of time for, §9007.3
    — repayment determination, §9007.2(a)(2)
  Computerized records provided for, §9003.1(b)(4); §9003.6; §9007.1(b)(1)
  Exit Conference, §9007.1(b)(2)(iii)
  Fieldwork, §9007.1(b)
    — conduct of, §9007.1(b)(1)
    — exit conference, §9007.1(b)(2)(iii)
    — information provided to committee, §9007.1(b)(2), (3) and (4)
    — records, office and staff provided for, §9007.1(b)(1)
    — settlement of dispute arising during, §9007.1(b)(1)(iv)
  Investigative procedures, §9007.1(b)(1)(v)
  Preliminary audit report, §9007.1(c)
  Report, prepared by FEC, §9007.1(d)-(f)
    — copy to committee, §9007.1(e)(3)
    — copy to public, §9007.1(d)(2) and (e) (1) and (2)

---

*This index makes occasional reference to parts 100-116 of 11 CFR, governing Federal election financing.

D

F

FILING
Dates, § 104.5; § 9006.2
Electronic, required, § 9003.1(b)(11)
See also: REPORTING
FUNDRAISING
See: CONTRIBUTIONS; LEGAL AND ACCOUNTING COMPLIANCE FUND
FUNDS
See: ENTITLEMENT; PAYMENTS; USE OF FUNDS

G

GELAC FUND
See: LEGAL AND ACCOUNTING COMPLIANCE FUND (GELAC FUND)
GENERAL ELECTION
See: ELECTION
GOVERNMENT CONTRACTOR
Contributions from, prohibited, § 9003.3(a)(1)(i)(B), (b)(4) and (c)(2)

I

INVESTMENT OF PUBLIC FUNDS
Permissible, § 9004.5
Repayment of income/loss resulting from, § 9004.5; § 9007.2(b)(4)

L

LABOR ORGANIZATION
Contributions from, prohibited, § 9003.3(a)(1)(i)(B), (b)(4) and (c)(2)
LEGAL AND ACCOUNTING COMPLIANCE FUND (GELAC FUND)
Contributions to, § 9003.3(a)(1)
— designation of contributions for, § 9003.3(a)(1)(i)(C) and (vi)
— redesignation of contributions to, § 9003.3(a)(1)(ii)-(v)
— subject to limitations and prohibitions, § 9003.3(a)(1)(i)(B)
Establishment of, prior to nomination, § 9003.3(a)(1)(i)
Expenditures from, exempt from limitations, § 9003.3(a)(2)(iii)
Recordkeeping, § 9003.3(a)(3)(ii)
Reporting, § 9003.3(a)(3)(ii); § 9006.1(b)(2)
Separate account required for, § 9003.3(a)(3)(i)
Solicitations for, § 9003.3(a)(1)(i)(A) and (2)(i)(E)
Transfers into GELAC fund, § 9003.3(a)(1)(ii)-(v)
Uses of funds in
— administrative expenses, § 9003.3(a)(2)(i)(B) and (ii)
— civil and criminal penalties, payment of, § 9003.3(b)(2)(i)(C)
— computer costs, § 9003.3(a)(2)(ii)(D) and (E)
— defraying expenses incurred prior to expenditure report period, § 9003.4(a)(2)
— legal and accounting services, § 9003.3(a)(2)(i)(A) and (B)
— repayments, § 9003.3(a)(2)(i)(D)
— transfers to other accounts, § 9003.3(a)(2)(iv)
— transportation and services for Secret Service, § 9003.3(a)(2)(i)(H)
LOANS
Incurred for qualified campaign expenses, § 9003.4(b)
Public funds used to repay, § 9004.4(a)(2)
Repayment of, § 9003.4(b)
Source of
— banks, § 9003.4(b)(1)
— excess primary campaign funds, § 9003.4(b)(4)(i)
— legal and accounting compliance fund, § 9003.3(a)(2)(i)(G) and (iii)
— personal funds, § 9003.4(a)(5)

NOTIFICATIONS—Continued
  By FEC to candidate concerning—Continued
    — final audit report, § 9007.1(e)(3)
    — repayment, § 9007.2(a)(2), (b) and (c)(1)
  See also: REPORTING

P

PARTY
  See: MAJOR PARTY; MINOR PARTY; NATIONAL PARTY COMMITTEE; NEW PARTY
PAYMENTS
  Audit may affect, § 9007.1
  Campaign depository for
    — major party candidate, must be separate, § 9005.2(c)
    — minor party candidate, § 9003.3(c)(3)
  Deficiency in, *See:* DEFICIENCY IN FUND
  Eligibility for, certification by FEC of, § 9003.1(a)(1)
    — major party candidate, § 9003.2(a)
    — minor/new party candidate, § 9003.2(b)
  Entitlement to funds
    — major party candidate, § 9004.1
    — minor/new party candidate, § 9004.2; § 9004.3
  See also: ENTITLEMENT
  FEC certification to Secretary of Treasury, § 9005.2(a)
  Future, used as loan collateral, § 100.82(e)(2); § 100.142(e)(2)
  Investment of, § 9004.5; § 9007.2(b)(4)
  Secretary of Treasury makes, § 9005.2(a) and (b)
  Unlawful use of, § 9012.3
  Use of, examples of qualified campaign expenses and non-qualified campaign expenses, § 9004.4(a)
  Withheld, if deficiency in fund, § 9005.2(b)
  See also: QUALIFIED CAMPAIGN EXPENSES; REPAYMENTS
PERSONAL FUNDS
  Definition, § 9003.2(c)(3)
  Expended prior to expenditure report period, § 9003.4(b)(5)
  Expenditures from, by vice presidential candidate, § 9003.2(c)(4)
  Liability for repayments, § 9003.2(c)(7)
  Limitations on, § 9003.2(c)
  Reporting of, § 9006.1(b)(1)(iv)
  Source of repayment, § 9007.2(a)(4)
POLITICAL COMMITTEE
  Definition, § 9002.9
  See also: AUTHORIZED COMMITTEE
POST-ELECTION PAYMENTS
  See: ENTITLEMENT; PAYMENTS
PRESIDENTIAL ELECTION CAMPAIGN FUND
  See: PAYMENTS; SECRETARY OF THE TREASURY
PRINCIPAL CAMPAIGN COMMITTEE
  See: AUTHORIZED COMMITTEE
PUBLIC FUNDS
  See: ENTITLEMENT; PAYMENTS; REPAYMENTS; USE OF FUNDS

Q

QUALIFIED CAMPAIGN EXPENSES
  Authorized committees incur, § 9002.1; § 9002.11(b)
  Burden of proof on candidate, § 9003.1(b)(1); § 9003.5(a)
  Certification not to exceed limitations on
    — major party candidate, § 9003.2(a)
    — minor party candidate, § 9003.2(b)

Index, General Election Financing

QUALIFIED CAMPAIGN EXPENSES—Continued
Contributions solicited to defray, by minor/new party candidate
- — administrative costs, §9003.3(c)(6), (7) and (8)
- — campaign depository for, §9003.3(c)(3)
- — legal and accounting compliance costs, §9003.3(c)(6), (7) and (8)
- — limitations and prohibitions, §9012.2
- — reporting of, §9003.3(c)(4) and (9); §9006.1(b)(1)(ii)
- — solicitation costs, §9003.3(c)(5)
- — to supplement public funds, §9003.3(c)(1)

Definition, §9002.11(a)
Defrayal of, if candidate withdraws, §9004.8(b)(1)
Documentation required for, §9003.1(b)
Expenditures in excess of limitations, §9007.2(b)(2)(ii)(A); §9012.1
Furthering election of other candidates, §9002.11(b)(3)
Gifts and bonuses, §9004.4(a)(6)
Incurred before expenditure report period, §9002.11(c); §9003.4(a)
Incurred on behalf of vice presidential candidate, §9002.11(b)(1)
Legal and accounting compliance costs, *See:* LEGAL AND ACCOUNTING
  COMPLIANCE FUND
Loans incurred for, §9003.4(b)
Media personnel, transportation and services provided to, §9004.6
Net outstanding, statement of, §9004.9
Nonqualified, *See:* EXPENDITURES
Polling costs, §9003.4(a)(1)
Recordkeeping, §9003.1(b)(1); §9003.5
Reporting, §9006.1
Secret Service personnel, §9004.6
Solicitation of contributions by major party candidate, *See:* DEFICIENCY IN
  FUND
Travel, §9004.7
  See also: TRAVEL
Unauthorized expenditures, limitations for, §9012.6
Use of personal funds for, §9003.4(c)
Use of public funds for, §9004.4(a)
Use of public funds for other than, §9007.2(b)(2)
Winding down costs, §9004.4(a)(4); §9004.11

R

RECORDKEEPING
Candidate agreement, §9003.1(b)(4)
Capital and other assets, §9003.5(d)
Computerized records, production of, §9003.1(b)(4); §9003.6
Documentation requirements
- — candidate and committee agreements, §9003.1(b)
- — collectability of accounts receivable, §9004.9(e)
- — computer tapes, §9003.1(b)(4)
- — disbursements, §9003.5
- — other organizations related to candidate, §9003.1(b)(5)

Falsification in, §9012.4
Legal/accounting compliance fund, §9003.3(a)(3) and (c)(4)
Production of computer tapes and software, §9003.1(b)(4)
Qualified campaign expenses, §9003.1(b); §9003.3(b)(2); §9003.5
Retention of records, §9003.5(c)

REIMBURSEMENTS
For travel by media personnel, §9004.6
In computing qualified campaign expenses, §9002.11(b)(4)
May be deposited with public funds, §9005.3(d)

REPAYMENTS
Additional, §9007.2(f)

Index, General Election Financing

SOLICITATION OF CONTRIBUTIONS
  See: CONTRIBUTIONS
STATE
  Qualification for State ballots defines candidates, § 9002.2(a)(2)
  Support of candidates for State office, § 9002.11(b)(3)
STATE PARTY
  Expenditure limitations, § 109.32(a)

T

TRANSFERS
  From GELAC fund to primary election account, § 9003.3(a)(2)(iv)
  From primary election account to GELAC fund, § 9003.3(a)(1)(ii)-(v)
  Loans to general election account
    — from GELAC fund, § 9003.3(a)(2)(i)(G), (a)(2)(iii) and (b)(3); § 9003.4(b)(2)
    — from primary election account, § 9003.3(b)(3); § 9003.4(b)(4)
  To campaign for different election, § 110.3(c)(4) and (5); § 9004.4(b)(7)
TRAVEL
  Allocation of expenditures for, § 9004.7
  Commercial transportation used for, § 9004.7
  Computing campaign- and noncampaign-related costs, § 9004.7(b)(1) and (2)
  Corporate conveyance used, § 9004.7(b)(8)
  Government conveyance used, § 9004.7(b)(4) and (5)
  Itinerary required, § 9004.7(b)(3)
  Media personnel, transportation and services provided to, § 9004.6
  Passenger list required, § 9004.7(b)(4)
  Qualified campaign expense for campaign-related, § 9004.7(a)
  Reimbursement to government, § 9004.7(b)(5)
  Reporting of, § 9004.6(c); § 9004.7
  Secret Service, costs of, § 9003.3(a)(2)(i)(H); § 9004.6
  Spouse or family, costs for, § 9004.7(b)(6)
  Staff's costs, § 9004.7(a)

U

UNAUTHORIZED COMMITTEE
  Contributions and expenditures by, § 9012.6
USE OF FUNDS
  Contributions from individuals, uses for
    — make up deficiency in payments, § 9003.3(b)(1)
    — may not pay primary debt, § 9003.3(a)(2)(iv)
    — must be segregated from public funds, § 9003.3(a)(3)
    — legal and accounting compliance costs, § 9003.3(a)
  Legal and accounting compliance fund, uses of, § 9003.3(a)(2)
    — *See also:* LEGAL AND ACCOUNTING COMPLIANCE FUND (GELAC FUND)
  Public funds used by candidate
    — control over, § 9005.3(a)
    — defray qualified campaign expenses, § 9004.4(a)(1)
    — gifts and bonuses, § 9004.4(a)(6)
    — investment, § 9004.5; § 9007.2(a)(6)
    — loan repayment, § 9004.4(a)(2)
    — support other candidates, § 9002.11(b)(3)
    — transfer to previous campaign, § 9004.4(b)(7)
    — winding down costs, § 9004.4(a)(4)
  See also: QUALIFIED CAMPAIGN EXPENSES

V

VICE PRESIDENTIAL CANDIDATE
  See: CANDIDATE

W

FEDERAL FINANCING OF PRESIDENTIAL NOMINATING CONVENTIONS, PART 9008

A

ACCOUNTS
Maintained by convention committee
— for deposit of private and public funds, § 9008.3(a)(4)(iii); § 9008.6(a)(3)
— limitation on payments from, § 9008.4(c)
— records for, furnished when requested by FEC, § 9008.10(f)
ADMINISTRATIVE EXPENSES
Host committee's, defrayed by contributions, § 9008.52(b)(4)(iv)
National committee's, defrayed by public funds, § 9008.7(a)(4)(x)
AGREEMENTS
By convention committee, letter of agreement, § 9008.3(a)(1) and
(4)
— binding also for national committee, § 9008.3(a)(4)
— date for filing, § 9008.3(a)(5)
— to comply with expenditure limitations, § 9008.3(a)(4)(i)
— to comply with Federal Election Campaign Act and FEC regulations,
§ 9008.3(a)(4)(vii)
— to establish accounts, § 9008.3(a)(4)(iii)
— to file convention reports, § 9008.3(a)(4)(ii)
— to furnish books, records and computerized information, § 9008.3(a)(4)(v)
— to make repayments, § 9008.3(a)(4)(vi)
— to pay civil penalties, § 9008.3(a)(4)(viii)
— to permit audits and examinations, § 9008.3(a)(4)(vi)
By national committee, application statement, § 9008.3(a)(1) and (3)
AUDITS AND EXAMINATIONS
Additional, § 9008.13
Agreement to permit, § 9008.3(a)(4)(vi)
Computerized information required, § 9008.10(h)
Conducted by FEC, § 9008.11; § 9008.13; § 9008.54
Documentation of disbursements, § 9008.10
See also: DOCUMENTATION
Of
— convention committee, § 9008.11; § 9008.13
— host committee, § 9008.13; § 9008.54
Repayments based on findings of, § 9008.12(a)(1)

B

BANKS
May not donate to municipal funds, § 9008.53(a)
May not donate to host committee, § 9008.52(a)
May provide items of de minimis value, § 9008.9(c)
See also: ACCOUNTS

C

CANDIDATE
Expenditure by, to attend convention, excepted from expenditure
limitation, § 9008.8(b)(3)
Expenses of, may not be defrayed by convention funds, § 9008.7(b)(1)

ENTITLEMENT—Continued
Adjustment of
— by amount of private contributions received, § 9008.5(b)
— by Consumer Price Index, § 9008.5(a)
Eligibility requirements, § 9008.3(a)
See also: ELIGIBILITY
New parties, not entitled to receive payments, § 9008.1(a)
Of major parties, § 9008.1(a); § 9008.4(a)
Of minor parties, § 9008.1(a); § 9008.4(b)
Private contributions, effect on, § 9008.5(b); § 9008.6(a)(2)
To payments from fund, § 9008.4
See also: PAYMENTS
EXAMINATIONS
See: AUDITS AND EXAMINATIONS
EXPENDITURES
By
— convention committee, § 9008.7
— delegates, § 9008.8(b)(3)
— municipal funds, § 9008.53
— host committee, § 9008.52
Documentation of, § 9008.3(a)(4)(iv); § 9008.10
See also: DOCUMENTATION
Limitation on, § 9008.8(a)
— agreement to adhere to, § 9008.3(a)(4)(i)
— authorization to exceed, § 9008.8(a)(3)
— exceeded, repayment required, § 9008.12(b)(2)
— major parties, § 9008.8(a)(1)
— minor parties, § 9008.8(a)(2)
Limitation on, exceptions to, § 9008.8(b)
— computerized information, § 9008.8(b)(5)
— discounts by commercial vendor, § 9008.9(d)
— expenditures by municipal funds, § 9008.8(b)(2)
— expenditures to participate in or attend convention, § 9008.8(b)(3)
— legal and accounting fees, § 9008.8(b)(4)
Prohibited, § 9008.7(b)
— civil/criminal penalties, § 9008.7(b)(3)
— defraying expenses of candidate or delegate, § 9008.7(b)(1)
— expenses violating state and federal law, § 9008.7(b)(2)
Use of public funds
See: USE OF FUNDS

F

FEDERAL ELECTION COMMISSION
Authorization by, to exceed expenditure limitation, § 9008.8(a)(3)
Certification by, to Secretary of Treasury, § 9008.6(d)
Definition, § 9008.2(a)
Examinations and audits conducted by, § 9008.11; § 9008.13; § 9008.54
See also: AUDITS AND EXAMINATIONS
Repayments
— notification by, to national committee, § 9008.12(a)(2)
— petitions for rehearing, § 9008.14
See also: REPAYMENTS
FUNDS
See: ENTITLEMENT; PAYMENTS; USE OF FUNDS

G

GOVERNMENT AGENCY
Expenditures by, not considered expenditure subject to limit, § 9008.8(b)(2)
Federal Election Commission, *See:* FEDERAL ELECTION COMMISSION

MUNICIPAL FUND—Continued
  Funding for, §9008.55
  Funds, use of, §9008.53(b)
  Registration of, §9008.50; §9008.51(a)
  Reporting by, §9008.50; §9008.51(b)

N

NATIONAL COMMITTEE
  Convention committee established by, §9008.3(a)(2)
    See also: CONVENTION COMMITTEE
  Definition, §9008.2(e)
  Eligibility for public funds, §9008.3(a)
    See also: ELIGIBILITY
  Entitlement to public funds, §9008.1(a); §9008.4(a)
    See also: ENTITLEMENT
  Expenditures by, *See:* EXPENDITURES
  Payments to, §9008.6(a)(1)
    See also: PAYMENTS
  Repayments by, §9008.12(a)(1) and (5)
    See also: REPAYMENTS
  Use of public funds by
    — permissible uses, §9008.7(a)
    — prohibited uses, §9008.7(b)
  See also: USE OF FUNDS
NET OUTSTANDING CONVENTION EXPENSES
  Capital asset, defined, §9008.10(g)(4)
  Determination that debt is not collectible, §9008.10(g)(6)
  Other assets, defined, §9008.10(g)(5)
  Statement of
    — certain debts not included in, §9008.10(g)(3)
    — filed by convention committee, §9008.10(g)
    — review of, §9008.10(g)(8)
    — when filed, §9008.10(g)
  Winding down costs, defined, §9008.10(g)(7)
NEW PARTY
  Definition, §9008.2(f)
  Not entitled to public funds, §9008.1(a)
NOMINATING CONVENTION
  Committee established for, §9008.3(a)(2)
    See also: CONVENTION COMMITTEE
  Definition, §9008.2(g)
  Expenditure limitations, *See:* EXPENDITURES
  Use of funds for, §9008.7
    See also: USE OF FUNDS

P

PARTY
  See: MAJOR PARTY; MINOR PARTY; NATIONAL COMMITTEE; NEW PARTY
PAYMENTS
  Acceptance of, §9008.6(a)(1) and (2)
  Application for, §9008.3(a)(1) and (3)
  Bank depository for, §9008.3(a)(4)(iii); §9008.6(a)(3)
  Certification by Commission to Secretary of Treasury, §9008.6(d)
  Convention committee receives, §9008.3(a)(2); §9008.6(a)(3)
  Date for receiving, §9008.6(c)
  Eligibility for, §9008.3(a)
    See also: ELIGIBILITY
  Entitlement of national committee to, §9008.1(a); §9008.4; §9008.5
    See also: ENTITLEMENT

REPORTING—Continued
  Civil or criminal penalties paid, §9008.7(b)(3)
  Exceptions
    — State or local party committees, §9008.3(b)(1)(iii)
    — unsuccessful efforts to attract convention, §9008.50
  Legal and accounting fees, §9008.8(b)(4)(iii)
  Private contributions received, §9008.6(a)(3)

S

SECRETARY OF TREASURY
  Definition, §9008.2(h)
  FEC certifications to, for payment of entitlement, §9008.6(d)
  Repayments made to, §9008.12(a)(1)

U

USE OF FUNDS
  By
    — convention committee, §9008.7
    — host committee, §9008.52(b)
    — national committee, §9008.7
  Investment of funds, §9008.7(a)(5)
  Permissible uses of public funds
    — biographical film about presidential candidate, §9008.7(a)(4)(xiii)
    — convention-related expenses, §9008.7(a)(4)(i)-(x)
    — gifts and bonuses, §9008.7(a)(4)(xii)
    — investment of funds, §9008.7(a)(5)
    — repayment of loans and interest, §9008.7(a)(4)(xi)
  Private contributions used by national committee, §9008.6(a)(2)
      and (3)
  Prohibited uses of public funds
    — candidate's convention expenses, §9008.7(b)(1)
    — civil or criminal penalties, §9008.7(b)(3)
    — delegate's convention expenses, §9008.7(b)(1)
    — expenses violating State or federal law, §9008.7(b)(2)
    — lost, misplaced or stolen items, §9008.7(c)

PRESIDENTIAL PRIMARY MATCHING FUND, PARTS 9031-9039 *

A

ACCOUNTS
Matching payment account maintained by U.S. Treasury
— definition of, § 9032.5
— equal distribution of funds from, § 9037.2
— repayment of funds from, § 9038.2
— transfer of funds from, § 9037.1
Special account maintained by principal campaign committee
— deposit of matching funds into, § 9037.3
— designation of, § 9033.1(b)(8)
— matching funds no longer contained, § 9038.2(b)(2)(iv)
— source of repayment, § 9034.4(c)
AGREEMENTS
Candidate must agree to
— adhere to campaign expenditure limitation, § 9035.1(a)
— adhere to personal funds limitation, § 9035.2
— comply with agreements, § 9033.1(a)
— comply with documentation requirements, § 9033.1(b)
— comply with law and regulations governing, § 9033.1(b)(10)
— file reports electronically, § 9033.1(b)(13)
— furnish information on other candidate organizations, § 9033.1(b)(6)
— gather books and records in centralized location, § 9033.1(b)(7)
— keep and furnish books, computer tapes and records, § 9033.1(b)(5);
    § 9033.11(c)
— make repayments, § 9033.1(b)(7)
— obtain and furnish evidence of qualified expenses, § 9033.1(b)(1)
— pay civil penalties, § 9033.1(b)(11)
— permit audits and examinations, § 9033.1(b)(7)
— prepare submissions in good order, § 9033.1(b)(9)
— use closed captioning in television ads, § 9033.1(b)(12)
Date for submitting, § 9033.2(a)(1)
Eligibility contingent upon, § 9033.1(a)
Failure to comply with disclosure requirements, § 9033.9
Joint fundraising, § 9034.8(c)(1)
ALLOCATION
Among states, § 106.2; § 110.8(c)
Categories of, § 106.2(b)
— administrative costs, § 106.2(b)(2)(iii)
— mass mailings, § 106.2(b)(2)(ii)
— media, § 106.2(b)(2)(i)
— methods for, § 106.2(b)
— overhead expenditures of state/regional offices, § 106.2(b)(2)(iii)(A) and (B)
— polling, § 106.2(b)(2)(v)
— recordkeeping, § 106.2(d)
— reporting, § 106.2(c)
— telephone programs targeted to State, § 106.2(b)(2)(iv)
— testing-the-waters, § 106.2(a)(2)
Disputed by Commission, § 106.2(a)(1)

---

*This index makes occasional reference to parts 100-116 of 11 CFR, governing Federal election financing.

491

CANDIDATES—Continued
  Nonparticipation in primary, § 9033.5(b)
  Personal funds of, § 9035.2(a)
  Repayments, *See:* REPAYMENTS
  Use of credit card, § 9035.2(a)(2)
  Use of funds, *See:* USE OF FUNDS
CAPITAL ASSETS
  See: ASSETS
CERTIFICATIONS
  Administrative record for, § 9038.7
  By candidates to FEC
    — date for submitting, § 9033.2(a)
    — for threshold amount, § 9033.2; § 9036.1
    — of active candidacy, § 9033.7(a)
    — of inactive candidacy, § 9033.5(a)
    — of satisfying requiring for each State, § 9033.2(b)(3)
    — to comply with expenditure limitations, § 9033.2
  By FEC concerning expenditure limitations, § 9033.3
  By FEC to Secretary of Treasury
    — additional, § 9036.2
    — continued, § 9036.6
    — initial, § 9036.1
    — payments of less than requested amount, § 9036.4(b) and (c)(2)
    — required for payments to candidate, § 9037.1
    — requirements for, § 9036.1; § 9036.2
    — resubmissions, § 9036.5(d)
    — revised amount, § 9036.4(c)(2)
    — schedule for, § 9036.2(d); § 9036.5(d)
    — withheld if expenditure limit exceeded, § 9033.3(a)
    See also: PAYMENTS; SUBMISSIONS
COMPLIANCE COSTS
  See: EXPENDITURES
CONTRIBUTIONS
  Aggregation of, to presidential and vice presidential candidates, § 9035.3
  Allocation of, in joint fundraising, § 9034.8(c)(7)
  By credit or debit card, § 9034.2(b) and (c)(8)
  By internet *See:* INTERNET
  By money order, § 9034.2(c)(4)
  By written instrument, § 9034.2(a)(4)
  Certification of threshold amount of, § 9036.1
  Costs of soliciting, § 9035.1(c)(2)
  Deposit on receipt of, § 9034.2(a)(3)
  Documentation of excess over purchase price, § 9034.2(c)(5)
  Earmarked, § 9034.8(c)(7)(iv)
  From escrow/trust account, § 9034.2(c)(2)
  From immediate family, § 9035.2
  From joint account, § 9034.2(c)(1)
  From partnership, unincorporated business, § 9034.2(c)(3)
  Fundraising, *See:* FUNDRAISING; JOINT FUNDRAISING
  Matchable, *See:* MATCHABLE CAMPAIGN CONTRIBUTIONS
  Name of issuer, identified, § 9034.2(c)(4)(ii)
  Nonmatchable
    — check drawn on account of committee, corporation, labor organization, government contractor, § 9034.3(f)
    — contract, promise, § 9034.3(c)
    — currency, § 9034.3(j)
    — definition of, § 9034.3
    — from corporation, labor organization, government contractor, political committee, § 9034.3(d)
    — illegally made or accepted, § 9034.3(e)

EXPENDITURES—Continued

  Limitations, § 110.8; § 9035.1—Continued

  — full debt charged against, § 9035.1(a)(2)

  — made using a credit card, § 9035.2(a)(2)

  — voting age population used to determine, § 110.8(a)(3)

  Made by ineligible candidate, § 9033.8(c)

  Made by party, § 110.8(e)

  Made on behalf of a candidate, § 9032.1; § 9032.9(b)

  Made on behalf of vice presidential candidate, § 110.8(f)(1) and (g)

  Media, transportation and services, expenses for, § 9034.6

    See also: MEDIA

  Nonqualified expenses

  — civil or criminal penalty, § 9034.4(b)(4)

  — continuing campaign after ineligibility, § 9034.4(a)(3) and (b)(3)

  — excess of limitations, § 9034.4(b)(2)

  — expenses incurred after date of ineligibility, § 9034.4(b)(3)

  — expenses incurred for goods and services received after ineligibility, § 9034.4(b)(3)

  — expenses insufficiently documented, § 9034.4(b)(7)

  — general election expenses, § 9034.4(b)(3) and (e)

  — lost, misplaced or stolen items, § 9034.4(b)(8)

  — payments to candidate, § 9034.4(b)(5)

  — seeking of repayment for, § 9038.2(b)(2)(iii)

  Polling, allocation of, § 106.4; § 9034.4(e)(2)

  Pre-candidacy payments by multicandidate committees, § 9034.10

  Qualified campaign expenses, *See:* QUALIFIED CAMPAIGN EXPENSES

  Starting date of review of expenditures, § 9038.2(b)(2)(iii)(B)

  Transfers to other campaigns, § 9034.4(d)

F

FILING

  Dates, § 104.5(b)

  Electronic, required, § 104.18

  Places of, § 105.3; § 108.2

FUNDRAISING

  Allocation of expenditures made for, § 106.2(b); § 110.8(c)

  By candidates in both primary and general, § 9034.4(e)(6)

  "Donative intent" required for matching contributions, § 9034.3(i)

  Entertainment, purchase price of, § 9034.2(c)(5)

  "Essentially political" activity, admission price for, § 9034.2(c)(6)

  Expenditures exempted from State allocation, § 110.8(c)(2); § 9035.1(c)

  Joint, *See:* JOINT FUNDRAISING

  Sale of assets for, § 9034.9

  Sale of lottery/raffle tickets, § 9034.3(h)

G

GOVERNMENT CONTRACTORS

  Contributions from, nonmatchable, § 9034.3(d) and (f)

  Contributions from, prohibited, § 115.2(a)

H

HEARINGS

  See: APPEALS

I

INACTIVE CANDIDACY

  Candidate shall notify FEC, § 9033.5(a)

496

Index, Primary Election Financing

INACTIVE CANDIDACY—Continued
  Criteria determination, §9033.6(a) and (b)
    See also: CANDIDATE
INELIGIBILITY
  Appeal of FEC determination, §9033.3(b)
  Date of, §9033.5
  Expenses
    — incurred during, §9033.8(c)
    — post-ineligibility, §9034.4(a)(3) and (b)(3)
  For exceeding expenditure limitations, §9033.3
  Inactive candidacy, §9033.6
  Net outstanding campaign obligation after, §9034.1(a) and (b); §9034.5
    See also: ELIGIBILITY
INTERNET
  Contributions made over, §9034.2(b) and (c); §9036.1(b)(7); 9036.2(b)(1)(vii)
INVESTIGATIONS
  See: AUDITS

J

JOINT FUNDRAISING
  Aggregate contribution to, §9034.8(c)(6) and (7)
  Agreement required, §9034.8(c)(1)
  Allocation of contributions, §9034.8(c)(7)
  Committee/representative/agent for, §9034.8(b)
  Contribution limitations, §9034.8(c)(6) and (7)
  Depository for receipts from, separate, §9034.8(c)(4)
  Disbursements, reporting of, §9034.8(c)(9)(ii)
  Exemptions from allocation, §9034.8(c)(7)
  Expenditure exemption for, §9035.1(c)
  Expenses, allocation of, §9034.8(c)(8)
  Expenses from series, allocation of, §9034.8(c)(8)(i)(C)
  Formula for allocation, §9034.8(c)(1)
  Funds advanced for start-up costs, §9034.8(c)(2)
  Notice required for solicitations, §9034.8(c)(3)
  Procedures for, §9034.8(c)
  Proceeds, allocation of, §9034.8(c)(7)
  Receipts from, submitted for matching payments, §9034.2(c)(7); §9034.8(a)(2)(i)
      and (c)(7)
  Recordkeeping requirements, §9034.8(c)(5) and (9)
  Representative
    — duties, §9034.8(c)(5)
    — participant as, §9034.8(b)(3)
    — selection of, §9034.8(b)
    — separate committee as, §9034.8(b)(1) and (2)
  Sale of assets acquired for, §9034.9
  Use of contributions received from, §9034.8(a)(2)

L

LABOR ORGANIZATION
  Contributions from union account, nonmatchable, §9034.3(d) and (f)
  Contributions from union account, prohibited, §114.2(a)
LOANS
  Future matching payments as collateral, §100.82(e)(2); §100.142(e)(2)
  Not matchable, §9034.3(b)
  Public funds may be used to repay, §9034.4(a)(1)

M

MATCHABLE CAMPAIGN CONTRIBUTIONS
  Additional submissions for, §9036.2

497

Index, Primary Election Financing

USE OF FUNDS—Continued
 Expenses incurred during period of ineligibility, §9034.1(c)
 Net outstanding campaign obligations, §9034.1(b)
 Qualified campaign expenses, §9034.4
  — *See also:* QUALIFIED CAMPAIGN EXPENSES
 State or national campaign offices, §9034.4(e)(3)
 Terminating political activity, §9034.4(a)(3)(i)
 Transfers to other campaigns, §110.3(c)(5); §110.8(d); §9034.4(d)
 Winding down costs, §9034.4(a)(3); §9034.11

V

VICE PRESIDENTIAL CANDIDATES
 Contributions to and expenditures by, §9035.3
VOTING AGE POPULATION
 Definition, §110.18
 Used in determining expenditure limitations, §110.8(a)(3)

W

WINDING DOWN COSTS
 Allocation of primary and general elections, §9034.11(c)
 Definition, §9034.11(a)
 For primary paid during the general election, §9034.11(d)
 Limitation of amount paid for with matching funds, §9034.11(b)

Table of CFR Titles and Chapters

(Revised as of January 1, 2018)

Title 1—General Provisions

Title 2—Grants and Agreements

Title 2—Grants and Agreements—Continued

Title 3—The President

Title 4—Accounts

Title 5—Administrative Personnel

509

Title 5—Administrative Personnel—Continued

Title 6—Domestic Security

Title 7—Agriculture

Title 12—Banks and Banking—Continued

Title 13—Business Credit and Assistance

Title 14—Aeronautics and Space

Title 15—Commerce and Foreign Trade

Title 15—Commerce and Foreign Trade—Continued

Title 16—Commercial Practices

Title 17—Commodity and Securities Exchanges

Title 18—Conservation of Power and Water Resources

Title 19—Customs Duties

Title 20—Employees' Benefits

Title 23—Highways—Continued

Title 24—Housing and Urban Development

Title 24—Housing and Urban Development—Continued
Chap.

XXIV Board of Directors of the HOPE for Homeowners Program (Parts 4000—4099) [Reserved]

XXV Neighborhood Reinvestment Corporation (Parts 4100—4199)

Title 25—Indians

I Bureau of Indian Affairs, Department of the Interior (Parts 1—299)

II Indian Arts and Crafts Board, Department of the Interior (Parts 300—399)

III National Indian Gaming Commission, Department of the Interior (Parts 500—599)

IV Office of Navajo and Hopi Indian Relocation (Parts 700—899)

V Bureau of Indian Affairs, Department of the Interior, and Indian Health Service, Department of Health and Human Services (Part 900)

VI Office of the Assistant Secretary, Indian Affairs, Department of the Interior (Parts 1000—1199)

VII Office of the Special Trustee for American Indians, Department of the Interior (Parts 1200—1299)

Title 26—Internal Revenue

I Internal Revenue Service, Department of the Treasury (Parts 1—End)

Title 27—Alcohol, Tobacco Products and Firearms

I Alcohol and Tobacco Tax and Trade Bureau, Department of the Treasury (Parts 1—399)

II Bureau of Alcohol, Tobacco, Firearms, and Explosives, Department of Justice (Parts 400—699)

Title 28—Judicial Administration

I Department of Justice (Parts 0—299)

III Federal Prison Industries, Inc., Department of Justice (Parts 300—399)

V Bureau of Prisons, Department of Justice (Parts 500—599)

VI Offices of Independent Counsel, Department of Justice (Parts 600—699)

VII Office of Independent Counsel (Parts 700—799)

VIII Court Services and Offender Supervision Agency for the District of Columbia (Parts 800—899)

IX National Crime Prevention and Privacy Compact Council (Parts 900—999)

XI Department of Justice and Department of State (Parts 1100—1199)

517

Title 29—Labor

Title 30—Mineral Resources

Title 31—Money and Finance: Treasury

Title 31—Money and Finance: Treasury—Continued

Title 32—National Defense

Title 33—Navigation and Navigable Waters

Title 34—Education

519

Title 34—Education—Continued

Title 35 [Reserved]

Title 36—Parks, Forests, and Public Property

Title 37—Patents, Trademarks, and Copyrights

Title 38—Pensions, Bonuses, and Veterans' Relief

Title 39—Postal Service

Title 40—Protection of Environment

Title 41—Public Contracts and Property Management

Title 41—Public Contracts and Property Management—Continued

Title 42—Public Health

Title 43—Public Lands: Interior

Title 44—Emergency Management and Assistance

Title 45—Public Welfare

Title 45—Public Welfare—Continued

Title 47—Telecommunication—Continued

Title 48—Federal Acquisition Regulations System

Title 49—Transportation

Title 50—Wildlife and Fisheries

Title 50—Wildlife and Fisheries—Continued

Alphabetical List of Agencies Appearing in the CFR

(Revised as of January 1, 2018)

Agency	CFR Title, Subtitle or Chapter
Administrative Committee of the Federal Register	1, I
Administrative Conference of the United States	1, III
Advisory Council on Historic Preservation	36, VIII
Advocacy and Outreach, Office of	7, XXV
Afghanistan Reconstruction, Special Inspector General for	5, LXXXIII
African Development Foundation	22, XV
Federal Acquisition Regulation	48, 57
Agency for International Development	2, VII; 22, II
Federal Acquisition Regulation	48, 7
Agricultural Marketing Service	7, I, IX, X, XI
Agricultural Research Service	7, V
Agriculture Department	2, IV; 5, LXXIII
Advocacy and Outreach, Office of	7, XXV
Agricultural Marketing Service	7, I, IX, X, XI
Agricultural Research Service	7, V
Animal and Plant Health Inspection Service	7, III; 9, I
Chief Financial Officer, Office of	7, XXX
Commodity Credit Corporation	7, XIV
Economic Research Service	7, XXXVII
Energy Policy and New Uses, Office of	2, IX; 7, XXIX
Environmental Quality, Office of	7, XXXI
Farm Service Agency	7, VII, XVIII
Federal Acquisition Regulation	48, 4
Federal Crop Insurance Corporation	7, IV
Food and Nutrition Service	7, II
Food Safety and Inspection Service	9, III
Foreign Agricultural Service	7, XV
Forest Service	36, II
Grain Inspection, Packers and Stockyards Administration	7, VIII; 9, II
Information Resources Management, Office of	7, XXVII
Inspector General, Office of	7, XXVI
National Agricultural Library	7, XLI
National Agricultural Statistics Service	7, XXXVI
National Institute of Food and Agriculture	7, XXXIV
Natural Resources Conservation Service	7, VI
Operations, Office of	7, XXVIII
Procurement and Property Management, Office of	7, XXXII
Rural Business-Cooperative Service	7, XVIII, XLII
Rural Development Administration	7, XLII
Rural Housing Service	7, XVIII, XXXV
Rural Telephone Bank	7, XVI
Rural Utilities Service	7, XVII, XVIII, XLII
Secretary of Agriculture, Office of	7, Subtitle A
Transportation, Office of	7, XXXIII
World Agricultural Outlook Board	7, XXXVIII
Air Force Department	32, VII
Federal Acquisition Regulation Supplement	48, 53
Air Transportation Stabilization Board	14, VI
Alcohol and Tobacco Tax and Trade Bureau	27, I
Alcohol, Tobacco, Firearms, and Explosives, Bureau of	27, II
AMTRAK	49, VII
American Battle Monuments Commission	36, IV
American Indians, Office of the Special Trustee	25, VII

527

528

529

Agency	CFR Title, Subtitle or Chapter
Workers' Compensation Programs, Office of	20, I, VII
World Agricultural Outlook Board	7, XXXVIII

Redesignation Table

At 67 FR 50584, Aug. 5, 2002, a document was published restructuring part 100. For the convenience of the user, the following Redesignation Table shows the relationship of the old regulations to the new regulations.

100.7 AND 100.8 DISTRIBUTION TABLE

Old section	New section
100.7	100.51(a)
100.7(a)(1)	100.52(a)
100.7(a)(1)(i)	100.52(b)
100.7(a)(1)(i)(A)	100.52(b)(1)
100.7(a)(1)(i)(B)	100.52(b)(2)
100.7(a)(1)(i)(C)	100.52(b)(3)
100.7(a)(1)(i)(D)	100.52(b)(4)
100.7(a)(1)(i)(E)	100.52(b)(5)
100.7(a)(1)(ii)	100.52(c)
100.7(a)(1)(iii)(A)	100.52(d)(1)
100.7(a(1)(iii)(B)	100.52(d)(2)
100.7(a)(2)	100.53
100.7(a)(3)	100.54
100.7(a)(3)(i)	100.54(a)
100.7(a)(3)(ii)	100.54(b)
100.7(a)(3)(iii)	100.54(c)
100.7(a)(4)	100.55
100.7(b)	100.71(a)
100.7(b)(1)(i)	100.72(a)
100.7(b)(1)(ii)	100.72(b)
100.7(b)(1)(ii)(A)	100.72(b)(1)
100.7(b)(1)(ii)(B)	100.72(b)(2)
100.7(b)(1)(ii)(C)	100.72(b)(3)
100.7(b)(1)(ii)(D)	100.72(b)(4)
100.7(b)(1)(ii)(E)	100.72(b)(5)
100.7(b)(2)	100.73
100.7(b)(3)	100.74
100.7(b)(4)	100.75
100.7(b)(5)	100.76
100.7(b)(6)	100.77
100.7(b)(7)	100.78
100.7(b)(8)	100.79
100.7(b)(9)	100.80
100.7(b)(10)	100.81
100.7(b)(11)	100.82(a) through (d)
100.7(b)(11)(i)	100.82(e)
100.7(b)(11)(ii)(A)(1)	100.82(e)(1)(i)
100.7(b)(11)(ii)(A)(2)	100.82(e)(1)(ii)
100.7(b)(11)(i)(B)	100.82(e)(2)
100.7(b)(11)(i)(B)(1)	100.82(e)(2)(i)
100.7(b)(11)(i)(B)(2)	100.82(e)(2)(ii)
100.7(b)(11)(i)(B)(3)	100.82(e)(2)(iii)
100.7(b)(11)(i)(B)(4)	100.82(e)(2)(iv)
100.7(b)(11)(i)(B)(5)	100.82(e)(2)(v)
100.7(b)(11)(ii)	100.82(e)(3)
100.7(b)(12)	100.84
100.7(b)(13)	100.85
100.7(b)(14)	100.86
100.7(b)(15)	100.87
100.7(b)(15)(i)	100.87(a)
100.7(b)(15)(ii)	100.87(b)
100.7(b)(15)(iii)	100.87(c)
100.7(b)(15)(iv)	100.87(d)
100.7(b)(15)(v)	100.87(e)
100.7(b)(15)(vi)	100.87(f)
100.7(b)(15)(vii)	100.87(g)
100.7(b)(16)	100.88(a) and (b)

100.7 AND 100.8 DISTRIBUTION TABLE—CONTINUED

Old section	New section
100.7(b)(17)	100.89
100.7(b)(17)(i)	100.89(a)
100.7(b)(17)(ii)	100.89(b)
100.7(b)(17)(iii)	100.89(c)
100.7(b)(17)(iv)	100.89(d)
100.7(b)(17)(v)	100.89(e)
100.7(b)(17)(vi)	100.89(f)
100.7(b)(17)(vii)	100.89(g)
100.7(b)(18)	100.90
100.7(b)(19) reserved	Removed
100.7(b)(20)	100.91
100.7(b)(21)	100.92
100.7(b)(22)	100.83
100.7(c)	100.51(b) and 100.71(b)
100.8(a)	100.110(a)
100.8(a)(1)	100.111(a)
100.8(a)(1)(i)	100.111(b)
100.8(a)(1)(ii)	100.111(c)
100.8(a)(1)(iii)	100.111(d)
100.8(a)(1)(iv)(A)	100.111(e)(1)
100.8(a)(1)(iv)(B)	100.111(e)(2)
100.8(a)(2)	100.112
100.8(a)(3)	100.113
100.8(b)	100.130(a)
100.8(b)(1)(i)	100.131(a)
100.8(b)(1)(ii)	100.131(b)
100.8(b)(1)(ii)(A)	100.131(b)(1)
100.8(b)(1)(ii)(B)	100.131(b)(2)
100.8(b)(1)(ii)(C)	100.131(b)(3)
100.8(b)(1)(ii)(D)	100.131(b)(4)
100.8(b)(1)(ii)(E)	100.131(b)(5)
100.8(b)(2)	100.132
100.8(b)(2)(i) and (ii)	100.132(a) and (b)
100.8(b)(3)	100.133
100.8(b)(4)	100.134(a)
100.8(b)(4)(i)	100.134(b)
100.8(b)(4)(ii)	100.134(c)
100.8(b)(4)(iii)	100.134(d)
100.8(b)(4)(iii)(A)(1)	100.134(d)(1)(i)
100.8(b)(4)(iii)(A)(2)	100.134(d)(1)(ii)
100.8(b)(4)(iii)(B)(1)	100.134(d)(2)(i)
100.8(b)(4)(iii)(B)(2)	100.134(d)(2)(ii)
100.8(b)(4)(iii)(B)(3)	100.134(d)(2)(iii)
100.8(b)(4)(iii)(B)(4)	100.134(d)(2)(iv)
100.8(b)(4)(iii)(C)	100.134(d)(3)
100.8(b)(4)(iii)(D)	100.134(d)(4)
100.8(b)(4)(iv)(A)	100.134(e)
100.8(b)(4)(iv)(A)(1)	100.134(e)(1)
100.8(b)(4)(iv)(A)(2)	100.134(e)(2)
100.8(b)(4)(iv)(A)(3)	100.134(e)(3)
100.8(b)(4)(iv)(A)(4)	100.134(e)(4)
100.8(b)(4)(iv)(A)(5)	100.134(e)(5)
100.8(b)(4)(iv)(A)(6)	100.134(e)(6)
100.8(b)(4)(iv)(B)	100.134(f)
100.8(b)(4)(iv)(B)(1)	100.134(f)(1)

100.7 AND 100.8 DISTRIBUTION TABLE—
CONTINUED

Old section	New section
100.8(b)(4)(iv)(B)(2)	100.134(f)(2)
100.8(b)(4)(iv)(B)(3)	100.134(f)(3)
100.8(b)(4)(iv)(C)	100.134(g)
100.8(b)(4)(iv)(D)	100.134(h)
100.8(b)(4)(iv)(E)	100.134(i)
100.8(b)(4)(iv)(F)	100.134(j)
100.8(b)(4)(v)	100.134(k)
100.8(b)(4)(vi)	100.134(l)
100.8(b)(4)(vii)	100.134(m)
100.8(b)(5)	100.135
100.8(b)(6)	100.136
100.8(b)(7)	100.137
100.8(b)(8)	100.138
100.8(b)(9)	100.139
100.8(b)(10)	100.140
100.8(b)(11)	100.141
100.8(b)(12)	100.142(a) through (d)
100.8(b)(12)(i)	100.142(e)
100.8(b)(12)(i)(A)(1)	100.142(e)(1)(i)
100.8(b)(12)(i)(A)(2)	100.142(e)(1)(ii)
100.8(b)(12)(i)(B)	100.142(e)(2)
100.8(b)(12)(i)(B)(1)	100.142(e)(2)(i)
100.8(b)(12)(i)(B)(2)	100.142(e)(2)(ii)
100.8(b)(12)(i)(B)(3)	100.142(e)(2)(iii)
100.8(b)(12)(i)(B)(4)	100.142(e)(2)(iv)
100.8(b)(12)(i)(B)(5)	100.142(e)(2)(v)
100.8(b)(12)(ii)	100.142(e)(3)
100.8(b)(13)	100.144
100.8(b)(14)	100.145
100.8(b)(15)	100.146

100.7 AND 100.8 DISTRIBUTION TABLE—
CONTINUED

Old section	New section
100.8(b)(16)	100.147
100.8(b)(16)(i)	100.147(a)
100.8(b)(16)(ii)	100.147(b)
100.8(b)(16)(iii)	100.147(c)
100.8(b)(16)(iv)	100.147(d)
100.8(b)(16)(v)	100.147(e)
100.8(b)(16)(vi)	100.147(f)
100.8(b)(16)(vii)	100.147(g)
100.8(b)(17)	100.148
100.8(b)(18)	100.149
100.8(b)(18)(i)	100.149(a)
100.8(b)(18)(ii)	100.149(b)
100.8(b)(18)(iii)	100.149(c)
100.8(b)(18)(iv)	100.149(d)
100.8(b)(18)(v)	100.149(e)
100.8(b)(18)(vi)	100.149(f)
100.8(b)(18)(vii)	100.149(g)
100.8(b)(19)	100.150
100.8(b)(20)	100.151
100.8(b)(21)(i)	100.152(a)
100.8(b)(21)(ii)	100.152(b)
100.8(b)(21)(iii)	100.152(c)
100.8(b)(21)(iii)(A)	100.152(c)(1)
100.8(b)(21)(iii)(B)	100.152(c)(2)
100.8(b)(22)	100.153
100.8(b)(23)	100.154
100.8(b)(24)	100.143
100.8(c)	100.110(b) and 100.130(b)

List of CFR Sections Affected

All changes in this volume of the Code of Federal Regulations (CFR) that were made by documents published in the FEDERAL REGISTER since January 1, 2013 are enumerated in the following list. Entries indicate the nature of the changes effected. Page numbers refer to FEDERAL REGISTER pages. The user should consult the entries for chapters, parts and subparts as well as sections for revisions.

For changes to this volume of the CFR prior to this listing, consult the annual edition of the monthly List of CFR Sections Affected (LSA). The LSA is available at *www.fdsys.gov.* For changes to this volume of the CFR prior to 2001, see the "List of CFR Sections Affected, 1949–1963, 1964–1972, 1973–1985, and 1986–2000" published in 11 separate volumes. The "List of CFR Sections Affected 1986–2000" is available at *www.fdsys.gov.*

11 CFR—Continued

11 CFR—Continued

2015

11 CFR

2016

11 CFR

81 FR
Page

11 CFR—Continued

81 FR
Page

2017

11 CFR

82 FR
Page

○

* 9 7 8 1 6 4 0 2 4 2 7 4 6 *